This modern text is designed to prepare you for your future professional career. While theories, ideas, techniques, and data are dynamic, the information contained in this volume will provide you a quick and useful reference as well as a guide for future learning for many years to come. Your familiarity with the contents of this book will make it an important volume in your professional library.

EX LIBRIS

Auditing

Auditing

Jack C. Robertson, Ph.D., CPA
C. T. Zlatkovich Centennial Professor
The University of Texas at Austin

Frederick G. Davis, Ph.D., CPA
Associate Professor of Accounting
North Texas State University

1985   Fourth Edition

BUSINESS PUBLICATIONS, INC.
Plano, Texas   75075

ISBN 0-256-03274-2

Library of Congress Catalog Card No. 84–71559

Printed in the United States of America

1 2 3 4 5 6 7 8 9 0 K 2 1 0 9 8 7 6 5

Dedicated to
Jim Tom Barton
and
Albert L. Wade

Preface

The fourth edition of *AUDITING* is an introduction to auditing for students who have not had extensive work experience. The book is designed to provide structures for organizing students' thought processes about audit problems and practices. The emphasis is on the analysis of evidence and information, for the purpose of resolving different kinds of decision problems dealing with such diverse topics as audit objectives, audit theory, professional ethics, legal liability, audit evidence, internal control evaluation, audit programs, statistical applications, computer auditing and audit reports.

As authors, instructors and occasional practitioners, we believe the most significant audit activity is *decision-making*. We bring this belief to the text in the form of *decision-making methodology* involving: (1) problem recognition, (2) hypothesis formulation, (3) audit program development, (4) evidence-gathering, (5) evidence evaluation and (6) decision-making. This kind of methodology is generalized for students in the early chapters (Chapters 1–12) because they need to be able to have a general framework in mind for application to the hundreds of diverse circumstances that arise in field work. The general framework is made more specific in later chapters (Chapters 13–22) to contribute some realistic example circumstances and to make the generalities come alive.

The book contains numerous cross-references to authoritative statements on auditing standards and to standards governing other areas of practice. Even so, the text tries to avoid mere repetition of passages from the standards, concentrating instead on explaining their substance and operational meaning in the context of a decision-making methodology.

Instructors and students may wish to supplement the text with current editions of pronouncements published by the American Institute of Certified Public Accountants (AICPA) and by Commerce Clearing House (CCH).

The following abbreviations used by the AICPA and by CCH in their compendiums of standards are used throughout the book:

AU   Auditing Standards
MS   Management Advisory Services Standards
TX   Responsibilities in Tax Practice
AR   Accounting and Review Services Standards
ET   Ethics Rules, Interpretations and Rulings
BL   AICPA Bylaws
QC   Quality Control Standards
AC   Accounting Standards

CHANGES IN THE FOURTH EDITION

The writing style has been thoroughly edited to enhance readability. We do not claim that all the difficult topics are thereby made easy, but at least they are clearly explained. Also, we have made a conscious effort to remove the ambiguous use of the word "test" from the text. In auditing literature, "test" is used to mean; (1) perform an audit procedure, hence *audit,* (2) take a sample and (3) recalculate the client's calculations. We have replaced "test" with words and phrases designed to express clearly the activity intended.

The book incorporates references to statements on auditing standards through No. 48. Throughout the book, terminology is aligned with the terms and jargon of the standards.

Completely new material consists of the following:

☐ Each chapter begins with a set of *learning objectives* for students. These objectives are expressed in terms of what the students should be able to *do* after studying the chapter.

☐ End-of-chapter review questions, problems and discussion cases carry topical titles for easy identification and are associated with one or more of the learning objectives. (A matrix of objectives, review questions, problems and cases is in the instructors' manual.)

☐ Chapter 4—Legal Relationships and Fraud Detection—contains new material on the formal and informal operations of the U.S. Securities and Exchange Commission.

☐ Chapter 5—Governmental and Internal Auditing—is a new chapter. It pulls together the material that was previously in other chapters and appendixes and adds some organization to governmental/internal auditors' objectives, procedures and reports.

- □ *Audit risk* definitions and concepts (SAS 47) are introduced and integrated in Chapter 7—Internal Control Theory and Review Techniques.

- □ Chapter 8—Audit Sampling and Program Planning—integrates the concepts of audit risk and materiality (SAS 47) and explains sampling in the same terms as found in official pronouncements (SAS 39). The mathematics and technical details of statistical sampling are treated separately in Chapters 11 and 12, which serve as technical extensions of Chapter 8. Instructors can thus choose the level and extent of their coverage of the sampling topics.

- □ The *computer auditing* chapters (Chapters 9 and 10) are updated to include the most recent technology, with explanation of how SAS 48 can be implemented.

- □ The *reporting* chapters (Chapters 20–22) are updated with new example reports. Chapter 22 contains a more extensive coverage of auditors' association with, and reports on, forecasts.

- □ Most chapters now have one or more discussion cases. Many new review questions (tracking the sequence of topics in the chapters) and problems have been added. The new problem material is mostly original, but a few problems have been adapted from recent Uniform CPA Examinations.

ORGANIZATION   Each chapter of this text contains a conceptual introduction to technical standards and procedures. Through this organization of the content, a student may obtain not only an introductory familiarity with "how it is done" but also a thorough understanding of "why it is done." In the sequence of chapters the following content is developed:

- □ Auditing is defined in terms of the objectives of independent auditors. A general scientific method for making audit decisions is introduced. (Governmental and internal auditing are covered in a separate chapter.)

- □ Auditing theory is given a full chapter with emphasis on the basic foundation of generally accepted auditing standards. Practice standards of management advisory services and tax practice are integrated.

- □ Professional ethics is given a full chapter, beginning with an introduction to self-regulation and quality control and including a comprehensive discussion of the AICPA Rules of Conduct.

- □ Legal liability also is given a full chapter including duties under both common law and statute. Coverage of the SEC and the

Securities Acts is in this chapter. Significant court cases are briefed in two appendixes.

☐ The general theory of evidence, audit program planning and documentation are introduced in a single chapter to provide an overview of the audit process.

☐ Internal control theory is covered in three chapters. The material is organized systematically along these lines:

1. Audit risk, general control characteristics, use of questionnaires and flowchart techniques.

2. Compliance auditing using sampling, placing the statistical and nonstatistical sampling methods in the context of the internal control evaluation.

3. Internal control in a computer environment, dealing with the special problems of computer auditing in connection with computer system reviews and compliance auditing.

☐ The uses of advanced computer auditing technology and generalized computer-audit software are covered immediately following the chapter on internal control in a computer environment in order to place computer-related subjects in logical order. The chapter has been revised to include material on advanced computer-auditing tools.

☐ Statistical decisions and statistical estimates receive thorough, up-to-date coverage with considerations of materiality, risk evaluation, and decision analysis. Coverage is based on a straightforward approach to analysis of evidence. Appendixes cover auxiliary estimators, stratified sampling and dollar-unit sampling.

☐ The technical application chapters lend ease and organization for instructional purposes. Four of the chapters emphasize internal control study and evaluation with relation to important *cycles:*

1. Auditing Internal Control in the Revenue Cycle.

2. Auditing Internal Control in the Acquisition and Expenditure Cycle.

3. Auditing Internal Control in the Personnel and Payroll Cycle.

4. Auditing Internal Control in the Conversion Cycle.

☐ The technical coverage of auditing procedures is condensed into three chapters on substantive procedural applications.

1. Auditing Current Assets and Liabilities.

2. Auditing Long-Term Assets and Equities.

3. Completion of Audit Field Work.

□ Two chapters give thorough coverage to various report forms used by independent auditors. Many examples of real opinions are used as illustrations.

□ The final chapter covers other important practice areas—required and voluntary supplementary information, special reports, association with forecasts, and compilation and review services.

ACKNOWLEDG- MENTS

The American Institute of Certified Public Accountants has generously given permission for liberal quotations from official pronouncements and other AICPA publications, all of which lend authoritative sources to the text. In addition, several publishing houses, professional associations and accounting firms have granted permission to quote from their copyrighted material. Since a great amount of significant auditing thought exists in a wide variety of sources, we are especially grateful for the cooperation of all those interested in auditing education.

We appreciate receiving permission from the Institute of Management Accounting of the National Association of Accountants and the Institute of Internal Auditors, Inc. to use problem materials from past CMA and CIA examinations.

We gratefully acknowledge also the reviews and suggestions offered by professors Ron Abraham of the University of Northern Iowa, Bob Hamilton of the University of Minnesota, Ira Solomon of the University of Illinois, Shere Strickland of the University of Houston at Clear Lake, Glenn Summers of Louisiana State University, Clinton White of Pennsylvania State University and other anonymous reviewers, all of whom contributed many worthwhile recommendations. Their attention to reviews greatly enhanced several portions of the text, but as is traditional, for all errors of commission and omission, we remain responsible.

We owe a great debt of gratitude to two accountants who are truly professional in every meaning of the word: To an author of Texana literature, Jim Tom Barton, and to Albert L. Wade, the fourth edition of AUDITING is rededicated in trust that it conveys to others the sense of professional values these two men have exhibited freely in their personal and professional lives. We also gratefully acknowledge Susan and Laura. Their encouraging support was exceeded only by their practical skills of editing, word processing and general management, in which they excel.

Jack C. Robertson
Frederick G. Davis

Contents

PART 4   Reporting Responsibilities

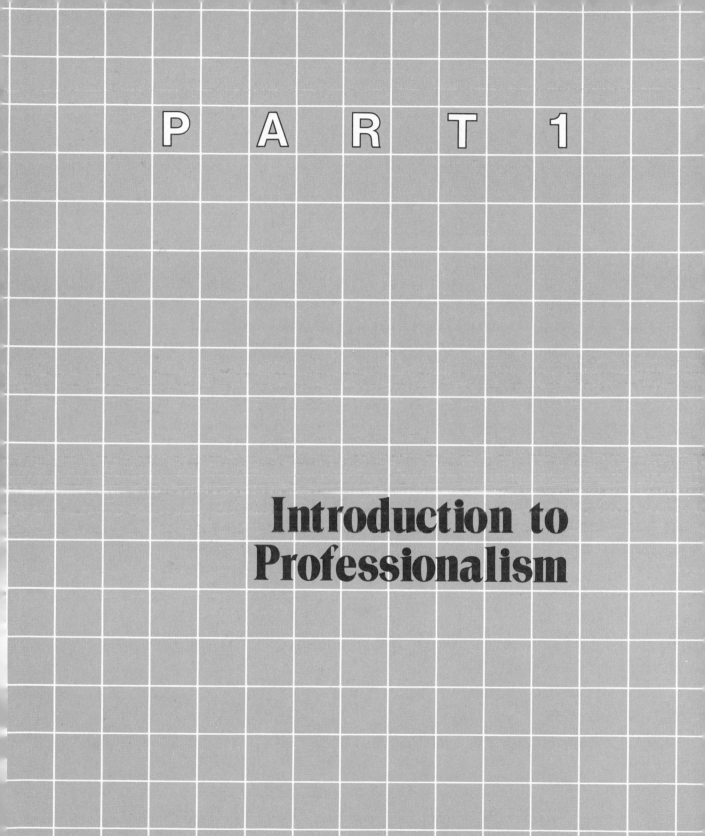

P A R T 1

Introduction to Professionalism

C H A P T E R 1

PROFESSIONAL STANDARDS SOURCES

Compendium Section	Document Reference	Topic
AU 110	SAS 1	Responsibilities and Functions of the Independent Auditor
AU 411	SAS 5	The Meaning of "Present Fairly in Conformity with GAAP" in the Independent Auditor's Report
AU 509	SAS 2	Reports on Audited Financial Statements
AU 530	SAS 1	Dating of the Independent Auditor's Report
AU 642	SAS 30	Reporting on Internal Accounting Control
AU 722	SAS 36	Review of Interim Financial Information
AU 8001	IAG 1	Objective and Scope of the Audit of Financial Statements
AR 100	SSARS 1	Compilation and Review of Financial Statements

Professional Practice

LEARNING OBJECTIVES Learning objectives are statements of what you should be able to do after you have studied each chapter of this textbook, examined related professional standards, answered the review questions at the end of the chapters and completed assigned homework problems. For example, in an auto mechanic school one learning objective would be: "Be able to take a carburetor apart and put it back together in 15 minutes."

Learning objectives for auditing, however, are not this task-specific. The learning objectives given at the beginning of each chapter are general, and your instructor may give you more specific ones.

Chapter 1 gives you an introduction to professional accounting practice. Other accounting courses helped you learn the principles and methods of accounting. Now you are starting a study of the ways and means of practicing accounting outside the classroom. Your objectives are to be able to:

☐ Define and explain auditing.

☐ Explain the content of basic types of independent auditors' standard reports.

☐ Use a scientific decision-making approach in a simple decision problem.

☐ Explain why accountants and auditors are professionals.

☐ Describe the accounting and auditing activities of the American Institute of Certified Public Accountants.

☐ Explain several basic sequential steps in a public accounting audit engagement.

As an accountant, you will work to satisfy society's demand for accounting services. Three underlying conditions generate this demand by creating investors' and lenders' needs for meaningful financial information. Decisions to purchase or sell securities, lend money, extend commercial credit, enter into employment agreements, and other kinds of economic decisions depend in large part on financial information. Investors, bankers, suppliers, labor unions and other business people—the users of financial statements—need your accounting services because of these conditions:

1. *Complexity.* A company's transactions can be numerous and complicated. Users of financial information are not trained to collect and compile it themselves. They need the services of professional accountants.

2. *Remoteness.* Users of financial information are usually separated from a company's accounting records by distance and time, as well as by lack of expertise. They need to employ full-time professional accountants to do the work they cannot do for themselves.

3. *Consequences.* Financial decisions are important to the state of investors' and other users' wealth. Decisions can involve large dollar amounts and massive efforts. The consequences are so important that good information, obtained through accountants, is an absolute necessity.

Financial decision makers (users of financial information) usually obtain their accounting information from accountants and managers employed by the organization for which an investment or loan is contemplated. This circumstance creates a ***potential conflict of interest,*** which is a condition that creates society's demand for your services as an ***auditor.*** Users not only need information, they need reliable information. Preparers and issuers (directors, managers, accountants, and others employed in a business) might benefit by giving false, misleading or just overly optimistic information. The potential conflict has become real often enough to create a natural skepticism on the part of users. Thus, they depend upon you as a professional auditor to serve as an objective intermediary who will lend some credibility to financial information. This "lending of credibility" is also known as ***attestation,*** and independent auditing of financial statements is described as an ***attest function.***

Reliable financial information helps make capital markets efficient and helps people know the consequences of a wide variety of economic decisions. However, independent auditors practicing the attest function are not the only auditors at work in the economy. Bank examiners, IRS auditors, state regulatory agency auditors (for example, auditors in a state's insurance department), internal auditors employed by a company and federal government agency auditors all practice auditing in one form or another.

Your study of auditing is best begun by learning definitions. The most general definition is from a committee of the American Accounting Association—an organization of accounting professors. The viewpoints of practicing auditors are reflected in the two statements of independent audit objectives. Definitions by governmental and internal auditors are presented in Chapter 5.

AMERICAN ACCOUNTING ASSOCIATION DEFINITION

The AAA Committee on Basic Auditing Concepts (1971) has prepared the most comprehensive definition of auditing.

> Auditing is a systematic process of objectively obtaining and evaluating evidence regarding assertions about economic actions and events to ascertain the degree of correspondence between those assertions and established criteria and communicating the results to interested users.

This definition contains several concepts relevant to auditing theory and practice. Each of the concepts is explained in order.

"Auditing is a systematic process . . ."

This definition refers to auditing as a *process,* which implies a dynamic activity. The important connotation in this concept is that auditing is a *systematic* process. It is purposeful and logical and is based on the discipline of a structured, scientific approach to decision making. It is not haphazard, unplanned, or unstructured.

". . . of objectively obtaining and evaluating evidence . . ."

This second phrase contains one of the more important concepts in auditing—*evidence.* Evidence consists of all those influences on auditors which ultimately guide their decisions. This definition points out that auditing involves *objective methods* for gathering and evaluating evidence.

". . . regarding assertions about economic actions and events . . ."

This phrase identifies the general subject matter of the audit process— *assertions* about economic matters and the *information* (particularly accounting information) that is contained in the assertions. The word *assertion* is important. When beginning an audit engagement, an independent auditor of financial statements is given financial statements and other disclosures by management and thus obtains management's explicit assertions about economic actions and events.

Independent auditors generally begin work with explicit representations from management—the subject matter under audit. Other auditors, however, are typically not so well provided with definite and explicit assertions. An internal auditor may be assigned to "evaluate the economy of the company's policy to lease rather than purchase heavy equipment."

A governmental auditor may be assigned to "determine whether goals of providing equal educational opportunity" have been achieved with federal grant funds. Oftentimes, these latter two types of auditors must develop the explicit statements of performance for themselves.

However, no matter what the form of the assertions, all auditors should be open-minded enough to view accounting information broadly to include economic information needed by users for their informed judgments and decisions. A broad view of accounting information takes an auditor beyond transaction information captured in debit-credit entries. Accounting-economic information subject to audit or review includes many disclosures found only in footnotes to the financial statement schedules.

". . . to ascertain the degree of correspondence between those assertions and established criteria . . ."

This phrase specifies why auditors are interested in assertions and related evidence. Auditors will ultimately communicate their findings to users. In order to communicate in an efficient and understandable manner, a commonly accepted and understood basis for measuring and describing financial information must exist. Such a basis constitutes the *established criteria* essential for effective communication.

Established criteria may be found in a variety of sources. For independent auditors, governmental auditors, and Internal Revenue Service agents, the criteria largely consist of the generally accepted accounting principles. IRS agents also rely heavily on criteria specified in the Internal Revenue Code. Governmental auditors may rely on criteria established in legislation or regulatory agency rules. Bank examiners and state insurance board auditors look to definitions and rules of law. Internal auditors and governmental auditors rely a great deal on financial and managerial models of efficiency and economy as well as upon generally accepted accounting principles. All auditors rely to some extent on elusive criteria of general truth and fairness.

". . . and communicating the results to interested users."

The final activity, essential to the social usefulness of auditing, is the communication of findings and results to decision makers. With respect to the activities of independent auditors, this communication output is called *attestation.* The essence of attestation is the act of *lending credibility* to information transmitted by management to users of financial information.

The attestation communication is *one* possible output of an audit, and independent auditors' opinions on financial statements are the most familiar examples. However, internal audits, governmental audits, and other types of audits are characterized by a variety of report forms.

OBJECTIVES OF INDEPENDENT AUDITING

The American Accounting Association definition just discussed is broad and general enough to encompass independent, internal, and governmental auditing. Presented next are two statements of independent auditing objectives.

American Institute of Certified Public Accountants

In its first paragraph, *Statement on Auditing Standards No. 1* (AU 110.01) describes the principal objective of a financial audit.

> The objective of the ordinary examination of financial statements by the independent auditor is the expression of an opinion on the fairness with which they present financial position, results of operations and changes in financial position in conformity with generally accepted accounting principles. The auditor's report is the medium through which he expresses his opinion or, if circumstances require, disclaims an opinion. In either case, he states whether his examination has been made in accordance with generally accepted auditing standards.[1]

The AICPA statement of objective restricts auditing interest to independent CPAs' audit of the three traditional financial statements and their footnotes. However, as the needs of users change, new audit objectives and reports are created to meet new needs. Thus, the Statements on Auditing Standards also contain guides relating to reports on internal accounting control, letters to underwriters, and special reports on financial statements that do not conform to generally accepted accounting principles. These aspects of auditors' practices are discussed in Chapters 7 and 20–22.

International Federation of Accountants (IFA)

The first International Auditing Guideline (IAG) issued by the International Auditing Practices Committee of the IFA contains a statement of objective very similar to that of the AICPA. IAG 1 (AU 8001.02–.03), quoted below, uses terms and phrases broad enough to cover practices in many nations. You should note the phrase "prepared within a framework of recognized accounting policies" in contrast to the AICPA reference to "generally accepted accounting principles." Also, note the warnings about an entity's viability, efficiency and effectiveness.

> The objective of an audit of financial statements, prepared within a framework of recognized accounting policies, is to enable an auditor to express an opinion on such financial statements.
>
> The auditor's opinion helps establish the credibility of the financial statements. The user, however, should not assume that the auditor's opinion is an assurance as to the future viability of the entity nor an opinion as to the efficiency or effectiveness with which management has conducted the affairs of the entity.

Observation on Definitions

The AICPA and IFA definitions cover only the *audit* practice of American and international auditors. In contrast, Chapter 5 explains the auditing

---

[1] The Statements on Auditing Standards are authoritative AICPA pronouncements on auditing theory and practice. Statements on Auditing Procedure numbers 1–54 were codified into SAS 1 in 1973; and Statements on Auditing Standards numbers 2–48 had been issued by July, 1984. Throughout this text, SAS references are followed by parenthetical section numbers which refer to the SAS volumes published by AICPA and by Commerce Clearing House. The section numbers preceded by AU, MS, TX, AR, and QC refer to the auditing standards, management advisory standards, tax practice standards, accounting and review standards, and quality control standards, respectively.

definitions and practices of governmental and internal auditors, and these fields appear at first glance to be broader than public accountants' auditing practice. Careful comparison, however, shows that the governmental and internal audit definitions are broad because they are intended to cover all facets of governmental and internal audit work. Similarly, the American Accounting Association definition is stated broadly to cover a wide range of audit practice—independent, governmental and internal.

Most public accounting firms perform the kind of work done routinely by governmental and internal auditors, but public accountants call it "management advisory services (MAS)." Public accountants are reluctant to call work an "audit" unless its end product is an opinion on financial statements, regardless of the nature of the work performed. The principal reasons for this reluctance have to do with legal liability and the lack of rule-book standards.

This variety of audit work and mixture of auditors causes some problems with terminology. Hereafter in this textbook, "independent auditor" or "CPA" are used to refer to people doing *audit* work with public accounting firms. The terms "accountant," "public accountant," "MAS practitioner," "tax practitioner" and "consultant" are used to refer to people doing *nonaudit* work (for example, bookkeeping, tax planning, management consulting) when employed by public accounting firms. In the governmental and internal context, auditors are identified as "governmental auditors" or "internal auditors." While many governmental and internal auditors are certified public accountants, the term "CPA" is reserved for reference to auditors in public practice. This textbook deals mainly with independent audits of financial statements, although public practice in other service areas is also discussed. Governmental and internal audit work is covered in Chapter 5.

ACCOUNTANTS' AND AUDITORS' SERVICES AND REPORTS

The following descriptions of selected standard reports are a very brief introduction to accountants' and auditors' products.[2] However, basic knowledge of the reporting framework is useful for grasping the purpose and context of auditing ethics, standards, and procedures explained in subsequent chapters. Matters of reporting variations are considered in more detail in the last three chapters of this book.

Accountants in public practice provide services in three main areas: (1) accounting and auditing, (2) taxation, and (3) management advisory services. Included in the category of accounting and auditing services are the following types of engagements.

> Audit of financial statements conforming to generally accepted accounting principles (GAAP).

---

[2] For the sake of brevity, this part of the text does not cover Reports on Forecasts and Projections, Special Reports (AU 621), or Letters for Underwriters (AU 631).

Review of unaudited financial statements.

Compilation of unaudited financial statements.

Review of interim financial information.

Study and evaluation of internal accounting control.

Review or compilation of financial forecasts and projections.

Engagements to give a special report on partial or non-GAAP financial information.

Engagements to submit a letter to underwriters.

Standard Reports   All independent audit engagements result in a report submitted to the *client*. A company's management is considered the party with primary responsibility for the financial statements or other information presented. Accountants and auditors are responsible for their own reports. In general, the ***client*** is the person (company, board of directors, agency, or some other person or group) who retains the auditor and usually pays the fee. Reports can take a wide variety of forms and content. The reports shown in Exhibit 1–1 have three things in common. They are all addressed to the person or organization that engaged the auditors. Occasionally, the addressee-client may differ from the ***auditee***—the entity audited. For example, Conglomerate Corporation may engage and pay auditors to audit Newtek Company in connection with a proposed merger. Newtek is the auditee, but the report will be addressed to the directors of Conglomerate Corporation—the client. All the reports are signed with the name of the audit firm and dated. The appropriate date is the day on which substantially all "field work" is completed. The date of the report may be one to six weeks or more after the balance sheet date, depending on the time needed to complete the field work. (Field work is defined and explained in Chapter 2.)

The standard report for audited financial statements should carry a title containing the word *independent*. This title is supposed to distinguish the independent auditor's report from reports by management, by the audit committee of the board or by the internal auditors when these other reports appear in a document containing audited financial statements, such as the corporate annual report. The title also carries the message of auditor independence. None of the reports are *required* to have a title, but they should be titled in some way in an enterprise's financial statements or other presentation.

"Scope" Paragraphs   All the reports in Exhibit 1–1 contain a *scope paragraph* that briefly explains the character of the engagement. The scope paragraph is the audit team's report on its own work on the engagement. This paragraph identifies the objects of the engagement (financial statements, interim information, system of internal accounting control) and states the standards observed in performing the engagement. These standards include

EXHIBIT 1–1
Selected Standard Reports

Description	Audited Financial Statements Conforming to GAAP (SAS 2, AU 509.04)	Reviewed Financial Statements (SSARS 1, AR 100.35)
Title	Report of Independent Auditor	(None specified)
Address	To the Board of Directors and Stockholders of Anycompany	To the Owners or Directors or Stockholders of Anycompany
Explanatory scope paragraph	We have examined the balance sheet of Anycompany as of December 31, 1985, and the related statements of income, retained earnings, and changes in financial position for the year then ended. Our examination was made in accordance with generally accepted auditing standards and, accordingly, included such tests of the accounting records and such other auditing procedures as we considered necessary in the circumstances.	We have reviewed the accompanying balance sheet of Anycompany as of December 31, 1985, and the related statements of income, retained earnings, and changes in financial position for the year then ended, in accordance with standards established by the American Institute of Certified Public Accountants. All information included in these financial statements is the representation of the management (owners) of Anycompany.
Other explanatory paragraph(s)		A review consists principally of inquiries of company personnel and analytical procedures applied to financial data. It is substantially less in scope than an examination in accordance with generally accepted auditing standards, the objective of which is the expression of an opinion regarding the financial statements taken as a whole. Accordingly, we do not express such an opinion.
Opinion, negative assurance, or disclaimer paragraph	In our opinion, the financial statements referred to above present fairly the financial position of Anycompany as of December 31, 1985, and the results of its operations and the changes in its financial position for the year then ended, in conformity with generally accepted accounting principles applied on a basis consistent with that of the preceding year.	Based on our review, we are not aware of any material modifications that should be made to the accompanying financial statements in order for them to be in conformity with generally accepted accounting principles.
Signature, date	_____, CPA February 29, 1986	_____, CPA February 29, 1986

EXHIBIT 1–1 (*concluded*)

Compiled Financial Statements (SSARS 1, AR 100.17)	Reviewed Interim Information (SAS 36, AU 722.18)	Internal Accounting Control (SAS 30, AU 642.39)
(None specified)	(None specified)	(None specified)
To the Owners or Directors or Stockholders of Anycompany	To the Company, or Directors or Stockholders of Anycompany	To the Company, Directors, Stockholders, Management, a Regulatory Agency, or Specified Others
We have compiled the accompanying balance sheet of Anycompany as of December 31, 1985, and the related statements of income, retained earnings, and changes in financial position for the year then ended, in accordance with standards established by the American Institute of Certified Public Accountants.	We have made a review of the balance sheet and statement of income of Anycompany and consolidated subsidiaries as of September 30, 1986, and for the three-month and nine-month periods then ended, in accordance with standards established by the American Institute of Certified Public Accountants.	We have made a study and evaluation of the system of internal accounting control of Anycompany and subsidiaries in effect at December 31, 1985. Our study and evaluation was conducted in accordance with standards established by the American Institute of Certified Public Accountants.
A compilation is limited to presenting in the form of financial statements information that is the representation of management (owners).	A review of interim financial information consists principally of obtaining an understanding of the system for the preparation of interim financial information, applying analytical review procedures to financial data, and making inquiries of persons responsible for financial and accounting matters. It is substantially less in scope than an examination in accordance with generally accepted auditing standards, the objective of which is the expression of an opinion regarding the financial statements taken as a whole. Accordingly, we do not express such an opinion.	The management of Anycompany is responsible for establishing and maintaining a system of internal accounting control. In fulfilling this responsibility . . . . The objectives of a system are to provide management with reasonable, but not absolute, assurance that assets are safeguarded . . . and that transactions are executed in accordance with management's authorization and recorded properly to permit the preparation of financial statements in accordance with generally accepted accounting principles. Because of inherent limitations in any system of internal accounting control, errors or irregularities may occur and not be detected . . .
We have not audited or reviewed the accompanying financial statements and, accordingly, do not express an opinion or any other form of assurance on them.	Based on our review, we are not aware of any material modifications that should be made to the accompanying financial statements for them to be in conformity with generally accepted accounting principles.	In our opinion, the system of internal accounting control of Anycompany and subsidiaries in effect at December 31, 1985, taken as a whole, was sufficient to meet the objectives stated above insofar as those objectives pertain to the prevention or detection of errors or irregularities in amounts that would be material in relation to the consolidated financial statements.
_____, CPA February 29, 1986	_____, CPA October 10, 1986	_____, CPA February 29, 1986

generally accepted auditing standards (GAAS), accounting and review services standards (SSARS standards) and internal accounting control study and evaluation standards.

Also, the scope paragraphs and other explanatory paragraphs are used to convey additional information. The reports on reviewed and compiled financial statements and on internal control emphasize the facts that the statements and the control system are management's representation and responsibility. The reports contain information explaining the nature and limitations of the work done and of the subject matter of the engagement.

"Opinion" (Conclusions) Paragraph

In each report, the last paragraph contains the conclusion(s). The reports on audited financial statements and internal accounting control contain *expressions of opinion*—the former regarding presentation of the financial statements in conformity with GAAP and the latter regarding sufficiency of the system for meeting internal accounting control objectives. In both cases, the auditor's professional opinion is an informed judgment based on evidence. In contrast, the reports on reviewed (unaudited) financial statements and on reviewed interim information contain an expression known as *negative assurance.* Negative assurance is not permitted in reports on audited financial statements presented in conformity with GAAP because it is considered a weak conclusion not suitable for an audit. However, it is permitted as a form of limited assurance in connection with reviewed financial information. The middle paragraphs of the review reports and the conclusion paragraph on compiled (unaudited) financial statements contain *disclaimers*—statements of "no opinion." In a disclaimer, auditors report that they have so little evidence, they can only conclude not to lend any positive degree of credibility.

Meaning of "Present Fairly . . ."

In the opinion on audited financial statements, the phrase "present fairly the financial position . . . and the results of its operations and the changes in its financial position . . . in conformity with generally accepted accounting principles" means that auditors have decided: (*a*) the accounting principles selected and applied have general acceptance,[3] (*b*) the accounting principles are appropriate in the circumstances,[4] (*c*) the financial statements, including the related notes, are adequately informa-

---

[3] According to SAS 5 and SAS 43 (AU 411.04–.08), the sources of *general acceptance* and *authoritative support* are: (*a*) FASB standards, FASB interpretations, APB opinions (1959–1972) and AICPA accounting research bulletins (prior to 1959); (*b*) AICPA industry audit and accounting guides (listed in an AU Appendix) and AICPA statements of position (issued by the AICPA accounting standards executive committee); (*c*) FASB technical bulletins and AICPA accounting interpretations; and (*d*) other accounting literature, including APB statements, AICPA issues papers, FASB statements on financial accounting concepts, Cost Accounting Standards Board pronouncements, SEC rules and regulations, and accounting textbooks and journal articles. Students should note that *official pronouncements* are considered the highest order of authoritative support and textbooks the lowest.

[4] SAS 5 (AU 411.09) points out that this decision requires auditors to consider the substance as well as the form of transactions.

tive for users, (*d*) the financial statement information is classified and summarized in a manner that is neither too detailed nor too condensed for users, and (*e*) the financial statements are accurate within practical materiality limits.

Departures from the standard (unqualified) wording of the reports shown in Exhibit 1–1 are necessary when the conclusions are nonstandard. In general, the departures (qualified reports) in reports on audited financial statements follow along these lines:

Scope Paragraph Qualification. When GAAS have not been observed (in whole or in part), the scope paragraph contains a description and explanation of the failure. Most cases involve a client- or auditor-imposed restriction on auditors' access to information or an unusual circumstance like late appointment of the audit firm. A scope paragraph qualification is always followed by some form of conclusions paragraph qualification.

Middle or Extra Paragraph(s). Many scope qualifications will require an extra paragraph for full explanation. In some cases, auditors may need to use more words to explain a departure from GAAP or a business uncertainty. In other cases, auditors may simply wish to draw attention to and emphasize some important facet of the financial or control information. Such "emphasis of a matter" paragraphs usually have no implications for changing any standard wording elsewhere in a report.

Conclusions Paragraph Modified. Sometimes auditors cannot give the conclusions indicated by the standard (unmodified or unqualified) wording.

In reports on audited financial statements, the opinion may be:

Adverse. An adverse opinion is the opposite of the standard unqualified opinion. With an explanation of reasons (middle paragraph), the conclusion is that the financial statements do *not* present financial position, results of operations and changes in financial position in conformity with GAAP.

Qualified Opinion. The conclusion can be an overall positive one regarding conformity with GAAP but also mention *exceptions* taken for such things as: (1) information not audited because of a scope limitation, (2) information not presented in conformity with GAAP, yet an adverse opinion is not required, and (3) information "subject to" the uncertain outcome of future events.

Disclaimer of Opinion. A disclaimer is an expression of no opinion. Auditors explain the reasons and explicitly state that no opinion is rendered. The disclaimer in an audit engagement is most often given when not enough evidence was gathered upon which to base an opinion on the financial statements taken as a whole. A disclaimer can also be given when one or more pervasive uncertainties exist and give the auditors doubts about whether the business will continue to operate or will fail.

In other reports, departures from the standard language may arise from the following circumstances:

Review Reports and Interim Information Reports. The standard negative assurance may not be appropriate. If some material modification is needed to make the information conform to GAAP, the conclusions paragraph should contain an explanation of it.

Compilation Report Disclaimer. Even though no opinion is given, if an accountant knows that substantially all disclosures required by GAAP are omitted or knows of a departure from GAAP, the conclusion paragraph should be modified to explain the omission or the departure.

Internal Accounting Control Report. If the study and evaluation revealed one or more material weaknesses, the report should describe it (them) and the potential errors or irregularities that might occur as a result.

SCIENTIFIC METHOD FOR AUDITING DECISIONS

Inherent in the definitions and objectives of auditing is a central emphasis on making decisions. The important aspect of audit decision making is the *method* of approaching and solving an audit problem. An inquiring "audit attitude" is very important. A structured (scientific) approach to problems can help you develop such an attitude.

The scientific method is both an attitude and an organized procedure for reaching logical and supportable conclusions. Auditors must possess the inquiring mentality of a problem solver. For the auditor, the ever-present question is: "What economic action or event is being asserted?" Following closely is the next question: "Is it so?"

Use of the scientific method in auditing involves a five-step process:

1. *Recognize* the assertion(s), problems, and preliminary data required to formulate a testable hypothesis.
2. *Formulate* the hypothesis so that either acceptance or rejection yields a useful auditing decision.
3. *Collect* competent evidence that contributes to the decision. Collection of evidence involves the following two aspects of audit program planning:
   a. *Selection* of applicable evidence-gathering techniques and procedures.
   b. *Performance* of techniques to obtain evidence.

4. *Evaluate* the evidence related to the decision problem and assess its sufficiency for an accept or reject decision about the hypothesis.

5. *Make the decision* to accept or reject the problem-related hypothesis.

How Auditors Use the Five Steps

The most important step is the first one—to recognize the problem. Audit problems requiring decisions are numerous, ranging from questions of the actual existence of things (assets, liabilities) and the actual occurrence of events (sales, cash receipts) to the proper accounting treatment for reporting purposes (classification, disclosure).

In ordinary audit engagements, problem hypotheses are first formulated as positive propositions. For example: "The recorded value of accounts receivable is materially accurate," or "The contract terms are being met satisfactorily." However, auditors must also be aware of alternative conditions (negative propositions)—that the recorded value of accounts receivable is materially misstated or that the contract terms have been violated. In general, the decision process is started by stating a proposition (a hypothesis) that expresses tentative beliefs in the truth of records and amounts. If this initial belief is not supported by the evidence, an auditor should be prepared to decide otherwise.

The third and fourth steps in the decision method are the technical-procedural aspects of hypothesis testing in auditing. By collecting evidence, auditors attempt to answer the ever-present question: "Is it so?".

The last step forces the choice of one of the decision alternatives. An auditor must decide whether, for example, the recorded value of accounts receivable is materially accurate or if contract terms are being met satisfactorily. These assertions must be assessed in light of available evidence.

Consequently, the scientific method applied in auditing decisions is completed with this step: *Formulate a judgment on the conformity of the assertion with reality as the auditor perceives reality at the time the evidence is evaluated.* This final statement of the decision-making method incorporates the concept of the careful, prudent practitioner—one who is not omniscient but who is professionally competent, careful, and knowledgeable.

Example of Scientific Method

As an example of this method, consider the line item on a balance sheet entitled "Trade Accounts Receivable . . . $100,000." This single line contains several assertions, including the following:

All the accounts are due from trade customers.

None are due from officers, directors, or affiliates.

All are collectible within the next year (current assets).

None are due after one year.

The collectible amount is $100,000.

Allowance has been made for doubtful accounts.

Accounts are not pledged or otherwise restricted.

To keep this example brief, consider only the first two assertions. With the assertions made explicit, the first two steps of the scientific method have been accomplished—the problem has been recognized and the hypotheses have been formulated. Now the auditor needs to identify customers, officers, and directors and relate their identities to the names of the debtors. Evidence is gathered by comparing these names to the subsidiary accounts. The result of the comparison is evaluated to yield the facts about the actual identities and affiliations of the debtors. With the evidence and evaluation in hand, the auditor is now prepared to decide whether the first two assertions conform to reality as that reality is presently determinable.

This example is a preview of more complex assertions, procedures, and evidence-gathering techniques covered in more detail in the technical chapters of this textbook. Throughout these subsequent chapters, the scientific methodology for auditing decisions is considered the essence of a practical, inquiring audit attitude.

AICPA ORGANIZATION

The general public recognizes CPAs as *professionals* largely because they must pass the Uniform CPA Examination, obtain experience, and hold a license from a state regulatory agency. Public recognition is enhanced by the existence of a professional organization—the American Institute of Certified Public Accountants (AICPA). In general, central professional organizations continually update and refine the body of professional knowledge, regulate membership admission, innovate new social responsibilities in emerging areas of practice, and police the conduct of members.

The AICPA limits its membership to CPAs. You can be a member as an individual. Also, an accounting firm can elect to become a member of the AICPA Division for Firms.

The AICPA is organized into several divisions and committees. Some *senior committees* of the AICPA are authorized to issue public statements on practice standards by a committee vote. The entire AICPA membership does not vote on these standards. The following divisions and committees are most closely connected with public practice in general and auditing practice in particular.

Auditing Standards Division.   This division has primary responsibility in the area of auditing practice. Its senior committee is the Auditing Standards Board (ASB). The ASB issues Statements on Auditing Standards (SASs) and interpretations of the standards. SASs provide the basis for a large part of the theory and practice presented in this textbook. Auditing standards apply to all audits of public and nonpublic companies and to all work done by CPAs on unaudited financial statements of public companies.

Professional Ethics Executive Committee. This committee has authority to issue interpretations of and rulings on the AICPA Code of Ethics. However, the ethics committee cannot issue or amend rules of conduct in the Code of Ethics. Amendments and new rules must be voted by the entire AICPA membership.

Federal Taxation Executive Committee. This committee has issued a series of Statements on Responsibilities in Tax Practice. The committee can amend these statements and issue new ones.

Accounting Standards Executive Committee (AcSEC). AcSec has several modes of operations. The committee cooperates with the U.S. Securities and Exchange Commission to study accounting problems. It prepares issues papers on accounting matters for presentation to FASB. It writes comment letters on FASB proposals. It also writes accounting guides on narrow accounting issues when FASB will not issue a detailed procedural pronouncement on the matter. The committee's public statements on accounting are considered GAAP, but they do not have the high level of authority reserved for FASB Statements on Financial Accounting Standards.

Accounting and Review Services Committee (ARSC). The ARSC issues Statements on Standards for Accounting and Review Services (SSARS), which are the standards that govern accountants' practice with the unaudited financial statements of nonpublic companies. Basically, ARSC fills the role related to "unaudit practice" that ASB fills for "audit practice."

Management Advisory Services Executive Committee (MASEC). The MAS committee issues Statements of Standards for MAS Practice (SSMAS). These standards govern accountants' consulting practice work.

Division for CPA Firms. The division consists of two sections—the Private Companies Practice Section (PCPS) and the SEC Practice Section (SECPS). Accounting firms can volunteer to join one or both of the sections. The division and its sections are the backbone of the profession's design for "self-regulation." Rules for membership include requirements for an average of 40 hours of continuing professional education (CPE) each year for professional employees and a *peer review* every three years. The peer review is a study of a firm's quality-control policies and procedures and an "audit" of a firm's quality of audit practice. Both sections have peer review committees that review the work and reports of the peer reviewers. In addition, the SECPS has a Public Oversight Board (POB) which is like a board of outside directors. The POB consists of prominent people who serve as representatives of the public at large—overseeing the self-regulation of firms that audit companies registered with the U.S. Securities and Exchange Commission.

The AICPA also had a Quality Control Standards Committee from 1977 until 1982. This senior committee was dissolved after it issued its *Statement on Quality Control Standards No. 1* (QCS 1). The AICPA believed the work of quality control and self-regulation was being handled well by the Division for Firms, and a separate committee was no longer needed. Nevertheless, QCS 1 remains as an authoritative practice standard.

OTHER PROFESSIONAL ORGANIZATIONS

Several other nation-wide accountants' organizations serve the interests of segments of the profession. Each one listed below conducts research and makes various publications available upon request:

Organization	Accountants	Journal Publication
National Association of Accountants (NAA)	Accountants in industry, banking, insurance, not-for-profit, and other fields	*Management Accounting*
Institute of Internal Auditors (IIA)	Practicing internal auditors	*The Internal Auditor*
Financial Executives Institute (FEI)	Corporate accounting and financial officers	*The Financial Executive*
Association of Government Accountants (AGA)	Accountants in federal offices and agencies	*The Federal Accountant*
American Accounting Association (AAA)	Accounting educators	*The Accounting Review*
U.S. General Accounting Office (GAO)	Accountants and experts employed by GAO	*The GAO Review*
EDP Auditors Association	Internal and external computer audit specialists	*The EDP Auditing Journal*

ORIENTATION TO AUDIT THEORY AND PRACTICE

When you begin a study of auditing, you may be eager to attack the "nitty-gritty" problems of *doing* audit work. This textbook covers the professional practice standards, ethics and legal responsibilities of auditors in Chapters 2–5 before getting into technical subjects. Instructors may elect to cover some of these chapters at the end of a course however.

The technical material starts in Chapter 6 and continues through Chapter 19. The textbook will enable you to learn *about* auditing, but instructors are seldom able to duplicate a practice environment in a classroom setting. You may feel frustrated about knowing "how to do it." This frustration is natural because auditing is done in the field under the pres-

sure of time limits and in the surroundings of client personnel, paperwork
and accounting information systems. The textbook can provide a foundation and framework for understanding auditing, but nothing can substitute
for the first few months of work when the classroom study comes alive in
the field.

Exhibit 1–2 contains a broad overview of a public accounting audit
engagement. Before beginning the "nitty-gritty" audit work, auditors do
(1) pre-engagement activities and (2) planning activities. The six activities
shown in Exhibit 1–2 are all necessary for beginning the audit field work.
The next phases of (3) internal control evaluation activities and (4) account balance audit activities are the evidence-gathering and evaluation/

EXHIBIT 1–2
Overview of a Public
Accounting Audit
Engagement

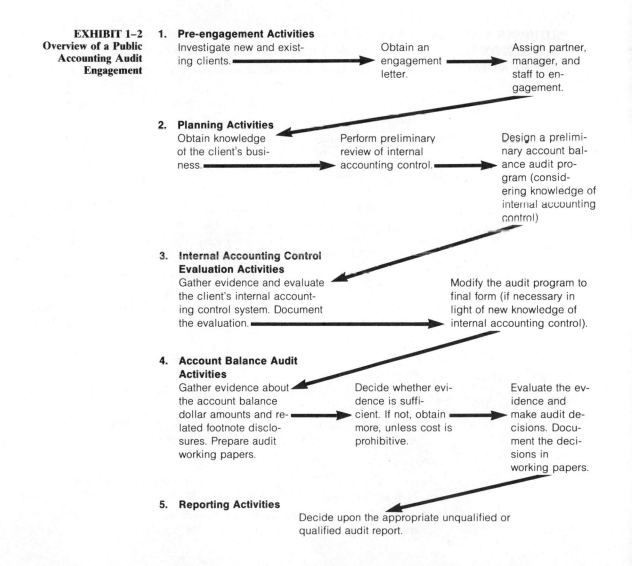

1. **Pre-engagement Activities**
Investigate new and existing clients.

Obtain an
engagement
letter.

Assign partner,
manager, and
staff to en-
gagement.

2. **Planning Activities**
Obtain knowledge
of the client's busi-
ness.

Perform preliminary
review of internal
accounting control.

Design a prelimi-
nary account bal-
ance audit pro-
gram (consid-
ering knowledge of
internal accounting
control)

3. **Internal Accounting Control**
   Evaluation Activities
Gather evidence and evaluate
the client's internal accounting control system. Document
the evaluation.

Modify the audit program to
final form (if necessary in
light of new knowledge of
internal accounting control).

4. **Account Balance Audit**
   Activities
Gather evidence about
the account balance
dollar amounts and re-
lated footnote disclo-
sures. Prepare audit
working papers.

Decide whether evi-
dence is suffi-
cient. If not, obtain
more, unless cost is
prohibitive.

Evaluate the ev-
idence and
make audit de-
cisions. Docu-
ment the deci-
sions in
working papers.

5. **Reporting Activities**
Decide upon the appropriate unqualified or
qualified audit report.

decision phases of the scientific decision process in action. Most people think of these activities when they think of auditing, overlooking the pre-engagement and planning work. The final activity is (5) writing the audit report. Details about reports have been previewed in this chapter and are explained more fully in Chapters 20, 21 and 22 of this text.

The first part of Chapter 6 adds to Exhibit 1–2 and discusses the stages of an audit engagement in more detail. Chapters hereafter explain the technical terms used in Exhibit 1–2. To assist with further study of auditing, each chapter begins with a list of professional standards sources and ends with a bibliography of sources and references for additional reading.

SOURCES AND ADDITIONAL READING REFERENCES

Burns, D. C., and W. J. Haga. "Much Ado about Professionalism: A Second Look at Accounting." *Accounting Review,* July 1977, pp. 705–15.

Burton, John C. "The Profession's Institutional Structure in the 1980's." *Journal of Accountancy,* April 1978, pp. 63–69.

Carey, John L. *The CPA Plans for the Future.* New York: American Institute of Certified Public Accountants, 1965.

Commission on Auditors' Responsibilities. *Report, Conclusions, and Recommendations.* New York: CAR, 1978.

Commission on Auditors' Responsibilities. "Summary of Conclusions." *Journal of Accountancy,* April 1978, pp. 92–102.

Committee on Basic Auditing Concepts. "A Statement of Basic Auditing Concepts." *Accounting Review,* supplement to vol. 47, 1972.

Commission on Professional Accounting Education. "A Postbaccalaureate Education Requirement for the CPA Profession," July 1983.

————. "Implementation of a Postbaccalaureate Education Requirement for the CPA Profession," July 1983.

Mautz, R. K., and Hussein A. Sharaf. *The Philosophy of Auditing.* American Accounting Association Monograph No. 6, American Accounting Association, 1961.

Rappaport, Alfred. "The Strategic Audit." *Journal of Accountancy,* June 1980, pp. 71–77.

Rehmet, R., and A.E. Mackay "The Division for Firms." *CPA Journal,* February 1981, pp. 15–21.

Roy, Robert H., and James H. MacNeil. *Horizons for a Profession.* American Institute of Certified Public Accountants, 1967.

Scope and Structure Committee. "Final Report." AICPA, 1975.

Sommer, A. A., Jr. "The Lion and the Lamb: Can the Profession Live with 'Cooperative Regulation'?" *Journal of Accountancy,* April 1978, pp. 70–75.

Stamp, E., and M. Moonitz. *International Auditing Standards.* England: Prentice-Hall Intl., 1978, p. 159.

Subcommittee on Reports, Accounting, and Management of the U.S. Senate Committee on Governmental Affairs. "Improving the Accountability of Publicly Owned Corporations and Their Auditors," reprinted in *Journal of Accountancy,* January 1978, pp. 88–96.

REVIEW QUESTIONS

1.1. Define and explain auditing. What would be your answer if asked by an anthropology major: "What do auditors do?"

1.2. What is the meaning of the terms *attest* and *attest function?*

1.3. What is the difference between a *client* and an *auditee?*

1.4. Why are users of financial statements likely to insist that the statements carry the opinion of an independent CPA?

1.5. Refer to the five reports shown in Exhibit 1–1. What distinguishes the report on audited financial statements from the other reports in the *scope paragraph?* For each report, describe the nature of the assurance given in the *conclusions paragraph.*

1.6. Who is charged with primary responsibility for the form and content of published financial statements?

1.7. Present a useful framework of a scientific, orderly approach to making an audit decision.

1.8. What *assertions* are made in the line entitled "Sales . . . $5,000,000" in an income statement?

EXERCISES AND PROBLEMS

1.9. **Comptroller as Auditor**
The chairman of the board of Hughes Corporation proposed that the board hire as comptroller a CPA who had been the manager on the corporation's audit performed by a firm of independent accountants. The chairman thought that hiring this person would make the annual audit unnecessary and would consequently result in saving the professional fee paid to the auditors. The chairman proposed to give this new comptroller a full staff to conduct such investigations of accounting and operating data as necessary. Evaluate this proposal.

1.10. **Comptroller as Auditor**
Put yourself in the position of the person hired as comptroller in the above situation. Suppose that the chairman of the board makes a motion to discontinue the annual audit because Hughes Corporation now has your services on a full-time basis. You are invited to express your views to the board. Explain how you would discuss the nature of your job as comptroller and your views on the discontinuance of the annual audit.

1.11. **Opinion or Fact?**
When an auditor conducts a professionally competent audit examination, why is the attest communication considered an expression of opinion rather than a statement of fact?

1.12. **Definition of Financial Position**
Every independent auditor's attest opinion refers to the presentation of financial position in conformity with generally accepted accounting principles. Search the authoritative accounting and economics literature (or conduct interviews with practicing auditors) and find the official definition of *financial position.* Determine whether the definition(s) is adequate for you and defend your support or criticism of the definition.

1.13. **Auditor as Guarantor**
Your neighbor invited you to lunch yesterday. Sure enough, it was no "free lunch"

because he wanted to discuss the annual report of Dodge Corporation. He owns Dodge stock and just received the annual report. He says, "Price Waterhouse prepared the audited financial statements and gave an unqualified opinion, so my investment must be safe."

Required:
What misconception does your neighbor seem to have about the auditor's role with respect to Dodge Corporation?

1.14. **Audit Report Language**
The independent auditor's standard unqualified report contains several important sentences and phrases. Give an explanation of why each of the following phrases is used instead of the alternative language indicated.

1. Address: "To the Board of Directors and Stockholders" instead of "To Whom It May Concern."

2. "We have examined the balance sheet of Anycompany as of December 31, 1985, and the related statements of income, retained earnings, and changes in financial position for the year then ended" instead of, "We have audited the attached financial statements."

3. "Our examination was made in accordance with generally accepted auditing standards" instead of, "Our audit was conducted with due audit care appropriate in the circumstances."

4. "In our opinion, the financial statements referred to above present fairly . . . in conformity with generally accepted accounting principles" instead of, "The financial statements are true and correct."

1.15. **Deficiencies and Omissions in an Audit Report**
Upon completion of all field work on September 23, 1985, the following report was rendered by Timothy Ross to the directors of the Rancho Corporation.

To the Directors of the Rancho Corporation. The accompanying balance sheet of Rancho Corporation and the related statements of income and retained earnings as of July 31, 1985, are management's representations. In accordance with your instructions, we have conducted a complete audit.

In many respects, this was an unusual year for the Rancho Corporation. The weakening of the economy in the early part of the year and the strike of plant employees in the summer of 1985 led to a decline in sales and net income. After making several tests of sales records, nothing came to our attention that would indicate sales have not been properly recorded.

In our opinion, with the explanation given above and with the exception of some minor errors that are considered immaterial, the aforementioned financial statements present the financial position of the Rancho Corporation at July 31, 1985, and the results of its operations for the year then ended, in conformity with pronouncements of the Accounting Principles Board and the Financial Accounting Standards Board applied consistently throughout the period.

Timothy Ross, CPA
September 23, 1985

Required:
List and explain deficiencies and omissions in the auditor's report.

Organize your answer by paragraph (scope, explanatory, and opinion) of the auditor's report.

(*AICPA* adapted)

1.16. **Authoritative Support**
Auditors' reports on audited financial statements contain an opinion on the conformity of the statements with generally accepted accounting principles (GAAP). An audit decision on GAAP includes the determination of whether an accounting treatment is "generally accepted," and this determination is made by finding the *authoritative support* for the accounting treatment.

Required:
List in order of priority the sources of *authoritative support* an auditor can consult when faced with a decision about GAAP.

1.17. **Logic and Method**

You have 12 solid spherical objects, 11 of which have an identical weight and volume, but the other sphere has a *different* weight. All 12 spheres look exactly alike.

You have been given a balance scale (a weighing instrument), and you have three (and only three) weighing trials in which to determine (*a*) which sphere has the different weight and (*b*) whether it is heavier or lighter than the other 11.

1.18. **Characteristics of Professionals**

A CPA in public practice and another person who is president of a large drug company are both engaged in providing services and goods that are important to society as a whole. May both persons claim membership in a profession—the CPA as a professional accountant and the president as a professional manager?

1.19. **CPA Examination Requirements**

Call or write your state board of accountancy and learn the requirements for (*a*) sitting for all or part of the CPA examination, (*b*) grade scores required to pass and to retake exam parts if not passed the first time, (*c*) experience, (*d*) reciprocity, and (*e*) fees.

1.20. **AICPA Organization**

The organizational hierarchy of the AICPA consists of its board of directors, council, and president. The AICPA Council is a representative legislative type of body consisting of elected members representing the state societies of CPAs and certain appointed members. Council plays a part in high-level AICPA policy. The AICPA also has some important *senior committees* empowered to pronounce practice standards by a committee vote without ratification by council and without a referendum of the AICPA membership.

Required:

a. Identify and describe the senior committees and the areas of practice in which they have authority.

b. What body is empowered to pronounce accounting standards that must be followed by CPAs? What reasons can you give to explain why AcSEC's accounting statements are lower in authority than FASB statements?

1.21. **Report Writing Case—Harper Hoe Company**

You have been assigned to the Harper Hoe Company audit. Harper is a nonpublic company that manufactures garden tools. The board of directors must submit financial statements for 1985 to the Merchants National Bank (a local bank) in connection with an application for a large loan.

Harper sells its products to over 100 small hardware outlets, most of them within a 500-mile radius of the city plant. The hardware stores are mostly locally owned, small retail businesses, and they sell the wares in their own rural areas. Josh Harper, president of Harper Hoe, is personally acquainted with almost all of these hardware store owners.

You have begun to prepare confirmations on the accounts owed Harper by the hardware store customers. Josh Harper asked about the procedure, and when you explained it to him he exclaimed, "You can't send those! They'll never understand why an 'outsider' should know how much they owe me! Anyway, you don't have time, the report must be finished by January 10." The receivables are 40 percent of current assets and 20 percent of total assets.

While auditing the inventory valuation, you discovered that Harper's policy is to value inventory at direct cost, expensing all overhead currently. Direct costing is not in conformity with GAAP, and the method affects many accounts in the financial statements. Overhead in the amount of $1 million has been expensed currently (50 percent of total expenses) of which you estimate about $200,000 should go in the inventory balance as of December 31. The $200,000 is about 25 percent of the direct cost inventory value and about 10 percent of total assets. Net income, as calculated by Harper, is $500,000 before income taxes.

On January 8, 1986, you completed all your field work at Harper's offices. You took the working papers to your office and the typed financial statements (balance sheet, statements of income, retained earnings, and changes in financial position and all footnote disclosures) and your report was ready for delivery on January 10. You finished the Harper tax return on January 11 and delivered everything to Josh Harper on January 12.

Required:

a. Write an appropriate scope paragraph for this report (including title and addressee).

b. Write any explanatory middle paragraph(s) you believe necessary.

c. Write an appropriate conclusions paragraph (including signature and report date), assuming:

(1) Proper absorption cost accounting had been used to value the inventory.

(2) Direct costing was used as stated in the case.

d. Out of curiosity, Josh Harper asks you what kind of review report on unaudited financial statements you would have written if the board had engaged your firm to perform a review. What would you tell him?

C H A P T E R   2

PROFESSIONAL STANDARDS SOURCES		
Compendium Section	**Document Reference**	**Topic**
AU 150	SAS 1	Generally Accepted Auditing Standards (GAAS)
AU 161	SAS 25	Relationship of GAAS to Quality Control Standards
AU 201	SAS 1	Nature of the General Standards
AU 210	SAS 1	Training and Proficiency of the Independent Auditor
AU 220	SAS 1	Independence
AU 230	SAS 1	Due Care in the Performance of Work
AU 310	SAS 1	Adequacy of Planning and the Timing of Field Work
AU 410	SAS 1	Adherence to Generally Accepted Accounting Principles (GAAP)
AU 420	SAS 1	Consistency of Application of GAAP
AU 431	SAS 32	Adequacy of Disclosure in Financial Statements
MS		Management Advisory Services Practice Standards
TX		Statements on Responsibilities in Tax Practice

Auditing Theory and Practice Standards

LEARNING OBJECTIVES

Chapter 1 gave you a general introduction to professional accounting practice. Chapter 2 examines the theory of auditing and the professional practice standards for auditing, management advisory services and taxation services offered by CPAs. Your objectives are to be able to:

☐ Write and explain the 10 AICPA generally accepted auditing standards (GAAS), categorizing them as general, field work or reporting standards.

☐ Associate the concepts and postulates of auditing theory with GAAS, explaining the meaning of the postulates.

☐ Explain how GAAS was or was not followed in specific fact situations.

☐ Interpret GAAS in the context of a computer environment.

☐ Write and explain the MAS general standards related to Rule 201 of the AICPA Rules of Conduct and the MAS technical standards related to Rule 204.

☐ Choose actions consistent with CPAs' responsibilities in tax practice in specific fact situations.

You can understand the practice of auditing only if you understand the theories and professional practice standards that govern it. Theory and practice go together. Theories exist to guide practice, and developments in practice provide bases for refining theories.

Current auditing theory, as explained in this chapter, is mostly derived from observed practices. Thus, you will find many theory ideas to be *descriptive*—describing actual practice. You will also find some theory ideas to be *normative*—indicating what good practice should be. The theory ideas and practice standards are useful for describing, explaining and predicting various aspects of auditing practice.

With a strong understanding of theoretical propositions, you will be well prepared to reach meaningful solutions to difficult problems. Without this understanding, you may reach some good solutions by chance, but chance is an unreliable basis for professional decisions.

The AICPA Generally Accepted Auditing Standards (GAAS) were first written as a short statement of 10 standards. Since 1939, these 10 have been augmented by additional explanations and requirements in Statements on Auditing Procedures (1939–1972) and in Statements on Auditing Standards (1972–present). The 10 basic standards are:

General Standards
1. The examination is to be performed by a person or persons having adequate technical training and proficiency as an auditor.
2. In all matters relating to the assignment, an independence in mental attitude is to be maintained by the auditor or auditors.
3. Due professional care is to be exercised in the performance of the examination and the preparation of the report.

Field Work Standards
1. The work is to be adequately planned, and assistants, if any, are to be properly supervised.
2. There is to be a proper study and evaluation of the existing internal control as a basis for reliance thereon and for the determination of the resultant extent of the tests to which auditing procedures are to be restricted.
3. Sufficient competent evidential matter is to be obtained through inspection, observation, inquiries and confirmations to afford a reasonable basis for an opinion regarding the financial statements under examination.

Reporting Standards
1. The report shall state whether the financial statements are presented in accordance with generally accepted accounting principles.
2. The report shall state whether such principles have been consistently observed in the current period in relation to the preceding period.
3. Informative disclosures in the financial statements are to be regarded as reasonably adequate unless otherwise stated in the report.
4. The report shall contain either an expression of opinion regarding the financial statements, taken as a whole, or an assertion to the effect that an opinion cannot be expressed. When an overall opinion cannot be expressed, the reasons therefore should be stated. In all cases where an auditor's name is associated with financial statements, the report should contain a clear-cut indication of the character of the auditor's examination, if any, and the degree of responsibility he is taking.

THEORY FRAMEWORK

Almost all auditing problems can be approached by relating them to one or more theoretical propositions and practice standards. So you will need a *framework* for organizing your knowledge of theory. Recall from Chapter 1 your study of another general framework—the scientific method for solving decision problems. This scientific method can be applied in combination with your knowledge of theory.

Three main elements constitute the theory framework explained in this chapter—concepts, postulates and standards. *Concepts* are organizing ideas that will help you classify the more specific parts of theory. *Postulates* are fundamental beliefs which provide a basis for defining guides to action. The discussion of postulates in this chapter shows them to be beliefs that help explain the meaning of the auditing standards. Auditing *standards* (GAAS) are the most specific elements of theory. They are the practical guides to action. The 10 generally accepted auditing standards issued by the AICPA are the guiding criteria for the quality of independent CPAs' audit practice.[1]

Auditing *standards* are quite different from auditing *procedures,* which are the particular and specialized things auditors do on a specific audit engagement. Standards are quality guides. They remain the same through time and for all audits, including audits of computerized systems. Procedures, on the other hand, may vary depending upon the complexity of an accounting system (whether manual or computerized), the type of company, and other factors unique to a particular job. This difference is the reason the audit report refers to an audit "conducted in accordance with generally accepted auditing standards" rather than in accordance with auditing procedures. Considerable judgment is required to apply audit procedures in specific situations.

GENERAL STANDARDS

The AICPA generally accepted auditing standards (GAAS) are divided into three groups—general standards, field standards, and reporting standards. The three general standards of GAAS relate to the personal integrity and professional qualifications of auditors.[2] The meanings of the three general standards are captured very well in the theoretical concepts and postulates related to them.

Conceptual Basis for General Standards

Three of the five concepts of auditing theory provide the primary framework for the general standards. They are (1) ethical conduct, (2) independence, and (3) due audit care. The other two—(4) evidence and (5) fair presentation—are related to other standards.

---

[1] The 10 AICPA standards are found in SAS 1 (AU 150.02). They are incorporated to a significant extent in auditing standards that guide governmental and internal audit practice, as explained in Chapter 5.

[2] *Statements on Auditing Standards* deal briefly with the three general standards in SAS 1 (AU 201, 210, 220, and 230).

Ethical Conduct.   The concept of ethical conduct belongs equally to all professional accounting practice, not just to auditing. In addition to general notions of ethics applicable to all persons, accountants have a code of conduct to guide their behavior. Important rules in this code deal with matters of general standards, independence and due care. When you study the Code of Ethics (Chapter 3), you will see the rules related to the general standards of GAAS.

Independence.   In auditing theory and practice, independence is a matter of intellectual honesty. Auditors are expected to be unbiased and impartial with respect to financial statements and other information they audit. They are expected to be fair to both the companies and executives who issue financial information and to the outside persons who use it. Independence is important enough to stand alone as a concept. The general public will grant social recognition of professional status to auditors only so long as they are perceived to be independent.

Some critics of the public accounting profession say the fact that auditors are paid by their clients is an undesirable arrangement. They argue that it is impossible to be independent from the party paying the fee. Accountants have generally not taken such criticism very seriously because the alternative would be some form of public-government control of accounting fees, and very few people want government involvement.

The notion of individual independence is more specific in the conduct of each audit engagement. In essence, an individual auditor must not subordinate his or her judgment to others and must stay away from influences that might bias judgment. In more specific terms, auditors must preserve their independence in the following practical ways:

Programming independence. Auditors must remain free from interference by managers who try to restrict, specify or modify the procedures auditors want to perform, including any attempts to assign personnel or otherwise control the audit work.

Investigative independence. Auditors must have free access to books, records, correspondence and other evidence. They must have the cooperation of management without any attempts to interpret or screen evidence.

Reporting independence. Auditors must not let any feelings of loyalty to the client or auditee interfere with their obligation to report fully and fairly. Neither should management be allowed to overrule auditors' judgments on the appropriate content of an audit report.

Due Audit Care.   All general standards are closely related to the concept of due audit care. Auditors must be competent, trained and independent if they expect to be properly careful. Their training includes knowledge of computer systems and computer auditing techniques.

Due audit care is best understood in the context of the *prudent auditor*. The idea of a prudent professional practitioner is present in other social science theories, for example, the "economic man" of economic theory and the "reasonable man" in law. In law, the prudent man is one who exercises judgment characteristic of his community, who is not expected to be omniscient, who is presumed to have knowledge specific to his profession and who is expected to be aware of his own ignorance. Additionally, the prudent man is expected to possess the skills of his profession whether he is a beginner or a veteran.

Adapting these dimensions from law, Mautz and Sharaf have summarized the qualities of the prudent auditor:

> A prudent practitioner is assumed to have a knowledge of the philosophy and practice of auditing, to have the degree of training, experience, and skill common to the average independent auditor, to have the ability to recognize indications of irregularities, and to keep abreast of developments in the perpetration and detection of irregularities. Due audit care requires the auditor to acquaint himself with the company under examination . . . to review the method of internal control operating in the company . . . to obtain any knowledge readily available which is pertinent to the accounting and financial problems of the company . . . to be responsive to unusual events and unfamiliar circumstances, to persist until he has eliminated from his own mind any reasonable doubts he may have about the existence of material irregularities, and to exercise caution in instructing his assistants and reviewing their work.[3]

Due audit care is a matter of what auditors do and how well they do it. A determination of proper care must be reached on the basis of all facts and circumstances in a particular case. When an audit firm's work becomes the subject of a lawsuit, the question of due audit care is usually at issue, as you will see in the law cases in Chapter 4.

Postulates Underlying the General Standards

Postulates in auditing theory are basic beliefs that help explain the auditing standards. However, the postulates should not be accepted blindly and without critical thought given to the circumstances of a particular audit engagement.

When considering the postulates, you can ask this question: "What would auditing practice be like if this belief were not accepted?" However, you should also recognize that a postulated condition might be false in a particular audit engagement, and to act as if it were true (thus ignoring any evidence to the contrary) could result in negligent performance in the audit.

The postulates most closely related to the three general standards are: (1) potential conflicts of interest, (2) exclusively an auditor, and (3) professional obligations.

---

[3] R. K. Mautz and H. A. Sharaf, *The Philosophy of Auditing* (American Accounting Association, 1961), p. 140.

Potential Conflicts of Interest.   The current social environment dictates this postulate: *A potential conflict of interest always exists between the auditor and the management of the enterprise under audit*. Auditors have not always held this view. For a long time, auditors preferred to believe no necessary conflict of interest existed between themselves and management. In the 1970s, however, widespread disclosures of corporate bribes, kickbacks, and payoffs, and the resulting public clamor for auditors to "do something" caused changes.

Holding a belief that a potential conflict of interests always exists causes auditors to perform procedures to search for errors or irregularities that would have a material effect on financial statements. This requirement tends to make audits more extensive and more expensive. The extra work is not needed in the vast majority of audits where no errors or irregularities exist. Nevertheless, auditors have responded in all audits to "do something" because of misdeeds perpetrated by a few people.

Even though auditing theory contains a postulate about ever-existing potential conflict, auditors must be careful about this belief. Once an audit examination is under way and procedures designed to search for errors and irregularities have been performed and none have been found, the audit team must be willing to accept the apparent fact that there is no evidence that the *potential* conflict is a *real* one. Overtones of suspicion can be dispelled by evidence.

Still, due audit care requires a healthy skepticism on the part of auditors—a disposition to question and test all material assertions made by management whether oral, written or incorporated in the accounting records. However, this attitude of skepticism must be balanced with an open mind about the integrity of management. Auditors should not blindly assume that every management is dishonest nor should management be assumed perfectly honest without a thought. The key lies in auditors' objectivity and in the audit attitude toward gathering the evidence necessary to reach reasonable, supportable audit decisions.

Exclusively an Auditor.   The next postulate is: *When examining financial data for the purpose of expressing an independent opinion thereon, the auditor acts exclusively in the capacity of an auditor*. The essence of this postulate is auditors' independence. Although auditors may act in other capacities to serve client management—as consultants or tax advisors—these additional services should be perceived as secondary to the duties and responsibilities expected in an audit engagement. If management advisory services or tax advice become so important that they interfere with the primary objective, they can damage the professional standing of the audit firm. These considerations are also important in the postulate on professional obligations discussed below.

The idea of acting exclusively in the capacity of an auditor, while phrased in terms of independent audits by CPAs, is not strictly limited to independent audits of financial statements. The postulate may also be applied to internal auditors' assignments to assess performance efficiency and especially to government auditors when assigned to evaluate programs having sociopolitical implications.

Professional Obligations. A close relative of the preceding postulate is: *The professional status of the independent auditor imposes commensurate professional obligations.* One important facet of this idea is that auditors' primary responsibility is both to *users* of their work and to *readers* of their reports. Users include management, directors and outsiders who receive audit reports. This postulate is as much a basic belief for all areas of accounting practice as it is for auditing practice. Chapters 3 and 4 on professional ethics and legal relationships draw their importance from this postulate.

FIELD WORK STANDARDS   The AICPA field work standards set forth general quality criteria for conducting an audit.[4] Auditors cannot effectively satisfy the general standard requiring due audit care if they have not also satisfied the standards of field work. Likewise, auditors' proficiency and independence are also necessary prerequisites for proper conformity with the field work standards. The meanings of the three field work standards are captured very well in the theoretical concepts and postulates related to them.

Conceptual Basis for Field Work Standards   The concept of due audit care is particularly evident in the first of the field standards. Adequate planning and proper supervision are indications of care, and their absence is an indication of careless work.

Due Audit Care—Timing Aspects. In order to have time to plan an audit, auditors should be engaged before the client's fiscal year-end. The more advance notice auditors can have, the better they are able to provide enough time for planning. An early appointment benefits both auditor and client. The audit team may be able to perform part of the audit at an *interim date*—a time some weeks or months before the fiscal year-end—and thereby make the rest of the audit work more efficient.

At an interim date, auditors can do a preliminary evaluation of internal control, audit some account balances, and possibly discover problem areas. Advance knowledge of problems can enable auditors to alter the audit program as necessary so year-end work (performed on and after the

---

[4] Several *Statements of Auditing Standards* elaborate at length on criteria for observing these three field standards. SAS 22 (AU 311) is entitled *Planning and Supervision*. SAS 1 (AU 320) is *The Auditor's Study and Evaluation of Internal Control*. SAS 31 (AU 326) entitled *Evidential Matter*, SAS 39 (AU 350) entitled *Audit Sampling*, and several other *Statements on Auditing Standards* deal with matters of obtaining sufficient competence evidence.

fiscal year-end date) can be more efficient. Advance planning for the observation of physical inventory counts and for the confirmation of accounts receivable is particularly important.

Evidence.   The fourth of the auditing concepts is *evidence*. Evidence was defined earlier as consisting of "all those influences upon the minds of auditors which ultimately guide their decisions." The second and third field work standards are specifically concerned with the process of gathering evidence.

Relevant evidence may be quantitative or qualitative; it may be objective or it may have subjective qualities; it may be absolutely compelling to a decision or it may be only mildly persuasive. The audit team's task is to collect and evaluate sufficient competent evidence to afford a reasonable and logical basis for decisions. Evidence has several important dimensions and features, and the process of gathering evidence is a principle feature of audit field work. Chapter 6 goes into the matter of evidence in more depth, along with an explanation of general procedures for gathering it.

First, however, you need to know some other matters of basic beliefs underlying the field standards.

Postulates Underlying the Field Standards

Three postulates are closely related to the field standards. They help explain the purposes for requiring a proper study and evaluation of internal control and for obtaining sufficient competent evidential matter. As before, these basic beliefs should be received on their merits in a particular engagement, not merely accepted without a second thought.

Verifiability.   The first necessary belief about auditing is: *Financial statements and financial data are verifiable*. If auditors had to assume that financial statements and financial data were not verifiable, then auditing would be presumed impossible at the outset.

The word *verifiable* is used in this postulate (and throughout auditing literature) with some qualification. "Verification" in auditing does not mean that fundamental truths are known as a result of gathering and evaluating evidence. The word refers merely to the ability to gather evidence about something.

Audit verification is the means by which auditors make the scientific approach to decisions operational, especially the steps involving collection and evaluation of evidence. Since absolute proof is not obtainable, the audit decision maker must accept some risks of wrong decisions. These risks can be measured in some circumstances. Thus, the third field work standard refers to "sufficient" rather than "absolute" evidence. Auditors do not audit *all* of a company's transactions and events. They audit data samples and make audit decisions by inference in most cases.

The verifiability postulate also sets some bounds on the scope of auditing practice, although different bounds may exist for independent auditors, internal auditors, IRS agents, government auditors and others. Independent auditors accept tasks with a great potential for verifiability. Internal auditors may accept assignments requiring more innovative judgment than hard evidence. Government auditors may receive assignments to report on performance efficiency in situations where standards are not fully developed. All types of auditors, in their own sphere of interest, nevertheless assume some degree of verifiability consistent with their social role and the type of report expected. The verifiability postulate is of prime importance when considering the extension of auditors' reporting responsibility to new kinds of information, such as internal control systems and forecasts.

Internal Control and Reliability. The companion to the preceding postulate is: *The existence of a satisfactory system of internal control reduces the probability of errors and irregularities.* This basic belief provides the foundation for a major portion of present-day audit practice. Auditors always assess the state of control over the information processing system that produces the financial and nonfinancial records for the purpose of relying upon the system.

Internal control may be defined simply as a system's capability to prevent or detect material data processing errors and provide for their correction on a timely basis. In *Statement on Auditing Standards No. 1,* accounting controls are defined as methods and procedures concerned mainly with safeguarding assets from loss through errors and irregularities and with providing reliable financial records for external reporting purposes.[5] These definitions and other technical aspects of the proper study and evaluation of internal control are covered in depth in Chapters 7, 8, and 9.

The primary objective contemplated in the second field work standard is that auditors use the decision about an internal control system for planning subsequent audit procedures. Thus, a connection exists between the reliance on a system and the criterion of *sufficient* evidence mentioned in the third field work standard.

The postulate provides two necessary relationships: First, (*a*) the better a system of controls over data processing accuracy, the more reliable the output, and an auditor thus has a reasonable basis for minimizing the extent of subsequent verification procedures. Conversely, (*b*) the poorer a system of controls over data processing accuracy, the less reliable the output, and an auditor must tend to increase the extent of subsequent verification procedures. If auditors were to assume no relationship between the quality of accounting controls and the accuracy of output, then proper study and evaluation of internal control would be pointless. Expe-

---

[5] *Statement on Auditing Standards No. 1* (AU 320.10, 320.15, 320.17, 320.19, 320.28).

rience has shown that audits are usually more efficient when auditors can rely on the existing system of internal control.

The Past Holds True for the Future. This controversial postulate holds a rather subtle meaning for auditing practice: *In the absence of clear evidence to the contrary, what has held true in the past for the enterprise under examination will hold true in the future.* The opening phrase "In the absence of clear evidence to the contrary . . ." could be an appropriate preface to all the other postulates but is particularly relevant to auditors' concern with future events.

Even in the audit of historical cost-basis financial statements, auditors make many inferences about the future. Examples of these inferences are most evident in: (*a*) evaluating the collectibility of accounts receivable on the basis of previous collection experience, (*b*) evaluating inventory obsolescence on the basis of past usage patterns, (*c*) assessing the economic usefulness and useful lives of fixed assets on the basis of experience with similar assets, and (*d*) in a negative sense, expecting to encounter classification and valuation problems when management has been known to have made such accounting errors in the past.

With this postulate about the future, you can infer that auditors' responsibility for predicting the future is limited. Auditors are responsible for decisions based upon knowledge available at the time their decisions were made. They are relatively protected from having decisions judged on the basis of hindsight. The sufficiency and competency of evidence is judged in this perspective. If this assumption were released, massive uncertainty about current decisions vis-a-vis future developments would be imposed. Audit decisions and reports would have to be phrased explicitly to recognize reservations based on undefined and undefinable uncertainties. In a utilitarian sense, the belief that the past predicts the near future (in the absence of contrary evidence) has served the needs of both auditors and society reasonably well.

REPORTING STANDARDS
The ultimate objective of independent auditors—the report on the audit—is guided by the AICPA reporting standards.[6] The importance of these four standards cannot be overemphasized.

The first standard is a straightforward directive. Exhibit 1–1 (Chapter 1) quotes the standard reporting language: *"In our opinion,* the financial statements . . . present fairly the financial position . . . and the results of operations and the changes in financial position . . . *in conformity with generally accepted accounting principles."*

---

[6] Numerous *Statements on Auditing Standards* deal with various aspects of observing and using the reporting standards. Report construction is probably the most complicated auditing topical area.

In this opinion paragraph, auditors make a statement of fact about their belief (opinion). Since the auditor is the professional expert in attestation, his or her belief is considered reliable. Users of financial statements do in fact rely upon the audit opinion. The standard wording carries the required references to conformity with generally accepted accounting principles (GAAP) and to consistency of application.

Generally accepted accounting principles include not only financial reporting standards found in official pronouncements and other sources of authoritative support, but also the methods of applying the principles. In addition, certain practices may have general acceptance yet not be covered in any official pronouncement. When auditors find such accounting used, they must use judgment to determine whether the accounting reflects the substance of transactions.

The consistency phrase required by the second standard has the objectives of: (*a*) giving assurance that the comparability of financial statements has not been materially affected by accounting changes and (*b*) requiring full disclosure if accounting changes have been made. Nevertheless, consistency does not absolutely assure *comparability* of financial statements. Changes in accounting estimates or substantially different transactions may have occurred in one year that do not require consistency-related disclosure under the second reporting standard.[7]

The third reporting standard requires auditors to use professional judgment to decide whether the financial statements and related disclosures contain all the important financial information users need for their decisions. Disclosure of information not specified completely by written rules in official pronouncements of accounting principles may be necessary. Auditors might need to deal with a rare and unusual fact situation nobody has encountered before. In this standard, auditors have latitude for determining what is important and what is not. Likewise, users of financial statements also have the right to claim that certain information is necessary for adequate disclosure. In fact, many lawsuits are brought on this issue: Investors may claim that certain necessary information was not disclosed, and auditors must show reasons for lack of disclosure.

The third reporting standard is *implicit* in the standard report, while the other three are *explicit*. The standard report must contain explicit statements about GAAP conformity and consistency and statements of audit scope and opinion or disclaimer. However, when the standard report *says nothing about the adequacy of disclosure,* users are entitled to believe the auditors considered it adequate.

The fourth reporting standard is the most complex. It contains three important elements:

---

[7] Further details on consistency matters are found in *Statement of Auditing Standards No. 1* (AU 420 and 546).

1. The report shall either contain an expression of opinion on the financial statements taken as a whole or an assertion to the effect that an opinion cannot be expressed.

This first sentence divides opinion statements into two classes: (*a*) opinions on statements *taken as a whole* (i.e., unqualified, adverse, and qualified opinions) and (*b*) the disclaimer of opinion. The reference to *statements taken as a whole* applies equally to a set of financial statements and footnotes and to each individual financial statement and footnote. The second sentence adds to the idea of "statements taken as a whole" as follows:

2. When an overall opinion cannot be expressed, the reasons therefor should be stated.

An "overall opinion" here refers to the unqualified opinion. Thus, when the adverse opinion, qualified opinions or disclaimer of opinion is rendered, all the substantive reasons for doing so must be explained. A middle paragraph is generally used for such an explanation.

The last sentence refers both to the scope paragraph and the opinion paragraph.

3. In all cases where an auditor's name is associated with financial statements, the report should contain a clear-cut indication of:
    a. the character of the auditor's examination, if any.
    b. the degree of responsibility he is taking.

This last sentence means precisely what it says when referring to "in all cases." Every time CPAs (even when acting as accountants associated with unaudited financial statements) are associated by name or by action with financial statements, they must report on their examination and responsibility. The character of the examination is usually described by the standard short-form reference to an audit in accordance with "generally accepted auditing standards." But if an audit has been restricted in some way or if the statements are simply unaudited, the auditor must say so in the scope paragraph.

The "degree of responsibility" is indicated by the form of the opinion. Auditors take full responsibility for their opinion about conformity with GAAP when they give either an unqualified or an adverse opinion. They take no responsibility whatsoever when they give a disclaimer of opinion. They take responsibility when they give the qualified opinions for all matters except those stated as the reasons for the qualification.

The Concept of Fair Presentation

The fifth concept in auditing theory is that of *fair presentation*. The quality of the report is a critical test for the usefulness of auditing services rendered by independent auditors. For independent auditors, this report is the opinion on the fair presentation of financial statements and related disclosures in conformity with GAAP.

Decisions about fair presentation may produce conflicts. In the first place, GAAP is usually presented as means of finding "answers" to disclosure and presentation problems. GAAP is usually presented as a fairly complete and unambiguous set of rules. Yet auditing theory accepts the accounting principles only on the grounds that nothing better is available for a standard. With regard to problems associated with reporting decisions related to "fair presentation," no quick and easy solutions are available. Issues of accounting "fairness" inherent in the accounting rules are always difficult. Auditors tend to be limited to using existing GAAP, and so they inherit the problems of accounting.

The first phrase in the standard opinion paragraph is: "In our opinion, the . . . financial statements *present fairly* . . . ." For auditors, these two italicized words have the traditional meaning that the financial statements are free from material errors. These words are supposed to express the art of accounting—putting readers on notice that "exact" statements are not what are intended. Over the years, however, users of financial statements have forgotten (or never learned) this meaning and have become accustomed to reading these words literally in the context of general "fairness." Consequently, auditors sometimes find themselves embroiled in controversies over what is fair and what is misleading.

The Postulate of Fairness

The seventh postulate was proposed with reservation in 1961 and is subject to interpretation today: *Consistent application of generally accepted accounting principles (GAAP) results in the fair presentation of financial position and the results of operations.* This assumption explicitly merges accounting and auditing for the process of financial communication. Nevertheless, the reliance on generally accepted accounting principles is expressed solely for the purpose of providing auditors with *some* standard. (The general argument is that if this postulate were not accepted, *no* statement of standards would exist for auditors to use to judge fairness.)

Events since 1961 have revealed that accountants and others have contrary views on the relationship between "fair presentation" and GAAP. One study showed that each of the following opinions was held by an approximately equal proportion of CPAs: (*a*) Financial statements are fair *because* of conformity with GAAP (the postulated condition); (*b*) Financial statements are fairly presented *and* in conformity with GAAP and (*c*) Financial statements are fair *despite* conformity with GAAP. The last opinion is held by critics of accountants and auditors.

The issue, however, has been resolved about as well as possible by SAS 5.[8] Financial accounting standards are constantly undergoing change and revision. What may have been an acceptable practice in one year may be prohibited the next. For example, deferral of research and develop-

---

[8] *Statement on Auditing Standards No. 5* (AU 411), "The Meaning of 'Present Fairly in Conformity with Generally Accepted Accounting Principles' in the Independent Auditor's Report," July 1975, as amended by SAS 43, August 1982.

ment costs was generally accepted until late 1974 when FASB Statement No. 2 required most types of internal research and development costs to be expensed.

The importance of the reporting standards cannot be overemphasized, and the problems of reporting cannot be swept away. They will appear again and again throughout the remaining chapters of this textbook.

AUDITING STANDARDS IN A COMPUTER ENVIRONMENT

The AICPA auditing standards were formulated in the early 1940s before computers were used in accounting. Nevertheless, the general and field work standards guide audit quality in a computer environment as well as in a manual accounting system environment. Some interpretation, however, will help you put the standards in context.

General Standards

To be considered adequately trained and proficient, auditors must have a working knowledge of the functions of computerized accounting and control systems. Levels of required knowledge include a minimum competency expected of new staff accountants, a supervisory capability expected of senior accountants, managers and partners, and a technical expertise expected of computer audit specialists. New staff accountants should be familiar with computer terminology, be able to comprehend the flow of data in clients' computerized systems, be able to read and understand system and logic flowcharts, and know the nature of common organizational arrangements in computer departments. Supervising accountants must have knowledge beyond these fundamentals so they can decide what level of technical support is needed and can review the audit plans of technical computer specialists and the results of their work in relation to the audit engagement as a whole. Computer audit specialists, usually trained in special technical courses and given extensive job experience, are the people who need to know how to work directly with the computers.

Sufficient training and proficiency in computer auditing are necessary to enable auditors to make their own evaluations and decisions about the computer operations in a client's accounting system. Without knowledge of computers, independence is threatened. An auditor might be inappropriately influenced by experts' technical explanations and terminology. At the very least, supervisory auditors should know enough about computers to be able to recognize situations calling for the technical assistance of computer audit specialists. With specialists at work, the engagement can be completed as a team effort.

Field Work Standards

The exercise of due audit care in an engagement depends upon observance of the three standards of field work. Special care is required when assigning personnel to the job and planning the audit. Among other things, the audit planner needs to know: the computer systems in use, so compatible audit tools can be provided; the extent of internal auditor involvement in reviewing and controlling computer operations, so the extent of audit effort can be estimated; the computer department schedule, so auditor access to the client's files and systems can be arranged. Above all, the partner in charge of the audit needs to plan ahead to arrange for the appropriate level of expertise needed for supervision of computer audit specialists and for the level of expertise needed for review of their work.

Probably the most complex task is performing a proper study and evaluation of internal accounting control. Computer audit specialists are required for all but the simplest computer systems. The ability to evaluate manual control over input data and over output distribution is usually not sufficient. Computerized accounting applications typically have control features built into both the systems and program software. Some members of the audit team must be able to evaluate the operations of such controls using the computer. Clients spend a great deal of money developing systems and controls, and they expect auditors to be able to understand them.

Computerized accounting systems lend themselves to computer-assisted methods of gathering sufficient competent evidence. Auditors can program a computer with a limit test to scan a client's files and identify unusual items (loans receivable with credit balances, debits in revenue accounts and credits in expense accounts), to recalculate accounting calculations (depreciation) calculated by the client to make accounting entries, and to select accounts receivable for confirmation and print the confirmation information. These are examples of computer-assisted methods for obtaining sufficient competent evidential matter.

Reporting Standards The technical problems and opportunities presented by the computer environment add complications to the general standards and field work standards. However, the reporting standards are not affected by the technology of the accounting system. It matters not whether the financial statements were produced by chiseling them on a stone or by engraving them on paper with a laser beam. Reporting requirements regarding conformity with generally accepted accounting principles, consistency, adequate disclosure and auditor responsibility remain the same. When a standard audit report is written, the *output* of the system, not its *process,* is the subject of the report.

SUMMARY:
AUDITING
THEORY

The general framework for auditing theory is:

Concepts → Postulates → Standards

Practicing auditors are most concerned with the standards because GAAS are the direct guides for the quality of everyday audit practice. As you will learn in Chapter 3 (Professional Ethics), the AICPA auditing standards are enforced through certain rules of conduct in the AICPA Code of Ethics.

This chapter has expanded the bare-bones AICPA list of 10 auditing standards by presenting the five organizing concepts and seven basic postulates of auditing theory. The concepts and postulates will help you understand the standards. Exhibit 2–1 summarizes the interrelationships of the three elements of the theory.

EXHIBIT 2–1
Auditing Theory
Interrelationships

Concepts	Postulates	Auditing Standards (AICPA)
1. Ethical conduct 2. Independence 3. Due audit care	1. Potential conflicts of interest 2. Exclusively an auditor 3. Professional obligation	Proficiency as an auditor Independent attitude Due professional care
4. Evidence	4. Verifiability 5. Internal control and reliability 6. Past holds true for the future	Planning and supervision Study and evaluation of internal control Sufficient, competent evidential matter
5. Fair presentation	7. Application of generally accepted accounting principles results in fair presentation	Generally accepted accounting principles Consistency Adequate informative disclosures Expression of opinion or a disclaimer

Auditing standards apply in all independent audits, no matter what kind of manual or computerized accounting systems are used. You must have an entry-level knowledge of computers to progress beyond the first year of audit work. Supervisory and technical levels of computer knowledge can be obtained through a combination of college study, professional courses and on-the-job experience. Your facility with computer auditing will eventually become an integrated feature of your basic knowledge of auditing theory and practice standards.

MANAGEMENT ADVISORY SERVICES PRACTICE STANDARDS

CPAs in public practice perform services in three main areas—accounting and auditing, taxation, and management advisory services. Work in the first two areas is fairly easy to define in terms of bookkeeping and write-up work, auditing, and tax return preparation. MAS is harder to describe. Essentially, MAS practice is any and all work (other than bookkeeping auditing and tax services) directed toward helping a client improve the use of its capabilities and resources to achieve its objectives. Thus, MAS includes, but is not limited to, systems design and installation, financial and economic analysis, managerial planning, cost accounting studies, personnel administration, operations research, electronic data processing and actuarial services. Many of these services are practiced in the same way the nonaccounting management consulting firms practice them. In fact, a 1983 study showed a ''Big Eight'' accounting firm as the largest management consulting firm and listed six of the other ''Big Eight'' accounting firms among the top 20 along with such consulting firms as Booz, Allen & Hamilton, Inc., McKinsey & Co., Inc., and Arthur D. Little, Inc.

Consulting is big business in public accounting firms. The public accounting profession does not want to inhibit the development of service opportunities. However, it is still sensitive to public perceptions of the proper scope of services offered by *audit* firms. Acknowledging some criticism of firms' scope of services, the SEC Practice Section of the AICPA Division for Firms prohibited members' performance of the following for audit clients: (1) psychological testing, (2) public opinion polls, (3) merger and acquisition assistance for a finder's fee, (4) direct recruitment of managers, executives and directors, (5) primary actuarial services other than in an advisory or audit capacity and (6) any other services for an audit client inconsistent with the firm's responsibilities to the public. These prohibitions are related to potential conflicts of MAS and audit independence. Further discussion is found in the Chapter 3 discussion of professional ethics. MAS practice standards are issued in *Statements on Standards for Management Advisory Services* (SSMAS) by the Management Advisory Services Executive Committee of the AICPA.

MAS Engagements SSMAS 1 defines MAS *engagements* as analytical work typically involving more than incidental effort. MAS engagements can include one or more of these tasks: gathering and analyzing data about the client's problem, evaluating alternative actions, reporting the findings, implementing management's action choice and following up on results. SSMAS 2 explains MAS engagements in terms of a significant amount of knowledge, planning, supervision and on-the-job effort.

MAS Consultations SSMAS 1 defines MAS *consultations* as advice given by practitioners in a short time frame, usually based on existing knowledge of the client's business problem. In comparison to MAS engagements, SSMAS 3 describes consultations as work involving less planning, fewer personnel and usually little or no new data-gathering. Consultations may be quite casual, taking place on the telephone or in nonbusiness settings. Much of the time, the information base for a consultation is provided by the client and not verified, corroborated or reviewed by the consultant. Consultations frequently occur along with accounting and auditing, taxation, and MAS engagement services. The fee for such work is thus included in the fee for the larger job.

General Standards   The MAS Executive Committee of AICPA has been authorized by the
AICPA Council to interpret the general standards contained in one of the
AICPA Rules of Conduct. These standards resemble some of the general
and field work standards for audits. (See Rule 201 explained in Chapter 3.)

Professional Competence.   A practitioner should undertake only
those engagements and consultations which he or his firm can reasonably
expect to complete with professional competence. Competence involves
consultants' ability to identify and define a client's problem, to select and
supervise appropriate staff, to determine and evaluate possible solutions,
to communicate recommendations effectively, and to assist in implementing recommendations when requested.

Due Professional Care.   A practitioner should exercise due professional care in the performance of MAS engagements and consultations.
The standard of due professional care has the same meaning as the auditing standard of due care explained earlier in this chapter. When management advisory services are complex and require expertise beyond that
normally held by accountants, the due professional care standard suggests that other experts ought to be added to the consulting team.

Planning and Supervision.   A practitioner shall adequately plan and
supervise engagements and consultations. Since management advisory
services tend to be very diverse, more so than audit engagements, practitioners should continually monitor the work in terms of accomplishment,
time schedule and quality.

Sufficient Relevant Data.   A practitioner should obtain sufficient relevant data to afford a reasonable basis for conclusions or recommendations in relation to engagements and consultations. The phrase "sufficient
relevant data" carries the same meaning as does "sufficient competent
evidence" in the audit field work standard. The point is that consultants
must gather and document support for their conclusions and recommendations.

These general standards differ from generally accepted auditing standards in two significant respects. First, they contain no explicit standard
about independence. However, the integrity, objectivity and independence required of management consultants are very similar to the qualities required of auditors. Consultants should ensure that their work and
results are free of distortions and misstatements and free of any bias
unrelated to the engagement. A client generally expects consultants to
maintain an impartial attitude in MAS engagements and consultations.[9]

---

[9] Concepts of Professional Ethics discussion of "Independence, Integrity and Objectivity." (especially ET 52.11)

The second difference is that the MAS standards say nothing about always conducting a proper study and evaluation of internal accounting control. The reason is simple. In general, internal accounting control may not be relevant in an engagement or consultation assignment.

Technical Standards The MAS Executive Committee has also been authorized by the AICPA Council to establish "other technical standards" under the AICPA Rules of Conduct. (See the discussion of Rule 204 in Chapter 3.) These standards purport to be unique to MAS engagements and consultations.

Role of MAS Practitioners.   MAS practitioners should not assume the role of management or take any position that impairs objectivity. If a consultant actually serves as a member of management, he or she no longer is a consultant, and the MAS standards no longer apply.

Understanding with Client.   An oral or written understanding should be reached with the client concerning the nature, scope and limitations of MAS engagements and consultations. The *nature, scope and limitations* are items that should go into an engagement letter or contract. Typically they include: (*a*) engagement objectives and nature of services, (*b*) engagement scope and limitations, (*c*) the roles and responsibilities of client personnel or other consultants involved in the study but not as members of the practitioner's staff, (*d*) the engagement approach and methods, (*e*) the manner and timing of reporting and (*f*) the work schedule and fee arrangement. All these matters should be agreed in advance, preferably in writing, so that later misunderstandings might be avoided. Standards for consultations acknowledge that such matters in many cases are communicated orally. Circumstances, however, might call for written understandings even in a consultation.

Client Benefit.   An MAS practitioner should notify the client of reservations regarding potential benefits expected to be derived by the client from MAS engagements and consultations. Results should not be explicitly or implicitly guaranteed. Estimates should be clearly identified, and their support disclosed.

Communication of Results.   Significant information about the results of MAS engagements and consultations, together with any limitations, qualifications or reservations needed to assist the client in making its decision, should be communicated orally or in writing. The final report should include descriptions of significant alternatives considered by the practitioner, the rationale supporting his or her recommendations, any assumptions made and the bases for them, plus any limitations, qualifications, or reservations. When an oral report is given, the practitioner should write a memorandum of the report for his or her own records.

RESPONSIBILITIES IN TAX PRACTICE

The *Statements on Responsibilities in Tax Practice* have been issued by AICPA taxation committees. The U.S. Treasury Department has also published regulations on income tax preparers. The AICPA statements draw their authority from the general acceptance of the standards they express. The Treasury regulations, meanwhile, have the force and effect of law.[10]

Signatures

The AICPA guidelines about signatures were rescinded in 1981. Income tax regulations govern, and persons who prepare tax returns for compensation are required to sign them. Preparers can be liable for a $100 penalty for negligent or intentional disregard of rules and regulations and a $500 penalty for willful understatement of tax liability. So, as a matter of common sense, you should not as a tax practitioner ''prepare'' a tax return and accept compensation if you know something is wrong with it.

According to tax regulations, a preparer is *not* considered to have negligently or intentionally disregarded a rule or regulation if he or she exercises *due diligence* to apply rules and regulations to the information supplied by the taxpayer. A rule or regulation can be disregarded if a preparer takes the position in good faith and with reasonable basis that it does not accurately reflect the Income Tax Code. However, the preparer has the burden of proof.

A *willful* understatement of liability arises if the preparer intentionally disregards facts supplied by the taxpayer, for example, preparing a return showing six personal exemptions when the taxpayer supplied information on only three. The regulations say a preparer may rely in good faith on taxpayer-supplied information, *unless the facts imply that additional verification and documentation would be required.* Independent verification by preparers without cause is not required, but when cause exists, preparers should seek more information.

Answers to Questions

A CPA should sign the preparer's declaration on a federal tax return only if he is satisfied that reasonable effort has been made to provide appropriate answers. Otherwise, a CPA should not sign an incomplete return that does not explain the reason for omitting answers to questions.

Administrative Proceedings of a Prior Year

A CPA may sign the preparer's declaration on a federal tax return when the client has selected a current tax treatment of an item that was the subject of an earlier administrative proceeding concluded by a taxpayer waiver. When the taxpayer is not bound to a particular treatment in closing an administrative proceeding, a different tax treatment can be selected in subsequent tax returns.

---

[10] U.S. Treasury Department regulations on income tax preparers differ in some respects from the AICPA Statements on Responsibilities in Tax Practice.

Estimates and Errors in Tax Returns A CPA may prepare federal tax returns involving the use of estimates, especially when it is impracticable to obtain exact data. However, a CPA should be satisfied that estimated amounts are not unreasonable.

When a CPA learns of an error in a client's previously filed federal tax return (or learns of the failure to file a required return), the client should be advised promptly with a recommendation to file an amended return (or file the return in the first place). If the client requests a CPA to prepare subsequent returns, the CPA should consider the client's willingness (or lack of it) to correct previous errors before proceeding with preparation of current tax returns.

When a CPA is representing a client in an administrative proceeding and knows of an error in a federal tax return, the CPA should request the client's agreement to disclose the error to IRS. The problem is a serious one if the IRS questions the item. The CPA cannot lie about it, but to speak openly without the client's agreement might amount to a breach of the confidentiality relationship with the client. The best thing to do is obtain the client's agreement. Lacking that, the guidelines suggest that the CPA may be under a duty to withdraw from the engagement.

Advice to Clients Keeping up with federal taxation changes is difficult at best. CPAs may carry on continuous communication with clients about changes. However, a CPA is not required to initiate such communication and keep a tax client informed unless there is a specific agreement with the client to do so.

Procedural Aspects of Return Preparation When preparing a federal tax return, a CPA is not required to examine or review documents or other evidence supporting the tax information submitted by a client. However, a CPA should encourage clients to provide supporting data where appropriate. If a CPA recognizes information to be incorrect or incomplete, he or she is required to make inquiries, one of which would probably be for supporting data. When a CPA signs the preparer's declaration, it should not be modified with any penned changes to suit the CPA's taste.

Contrary Positions In a federal tax return, a CPA may take positions contrary to Treasury Department or IRS interpretations of the code without disclosure if there is reasonable support for the position. However, rare positions contrary to the Internal Revenue Code itself, even when there is reasonable support (e.g., a constitutional question or conflicts between two code sections), cannot be taken without disclosure. In light of possible penalties for negligence and fraud, it is prudent to disclose any type of contrary position.

SUMMARY   To help you put the contents of this chapter together, here is a list of the variety of practice standards covered:

AICPA Generally Accepted Auditing Standards (GAAS).

Concepts of GAAS.

Postulates underlying GAAS.

GAAS in a computer environment.

Management Advisory Services Practice Standards.

Responsibilities in Tax Practice.

You ought to be aware that professional standards exist in other areas of practice. The AICPA Code of Ethics and its Rules of Conduct are discussed in Chapter 3. The AICPA also has one Quality Control Statement (QCS) that deals with CPA firms' internal policies and procedures. The QCS is mentioned in this textbook but not explained in detail.

You will also find that governmental auditors and internal auditors have statements of practice standards. Both of these sets of standards are discussed in Chapter 5. You will be able to see that the governmental standards incorporate all of GAAS, and the internal auditors' standards have many elements in common with GAAS.

PUTTING THEORY TO WORK   As an auditor, you must have a thorough understanding of auditing theory and practice standards. It helps, too, to know the practice standards in tax work, MAS, quality control, governmental auditing and internal auditing. The topics discussed throughout the remainder of this textbook all have one or more connections to the concepts, postulates and practice standards. All practical problems can be approached beginning with a consideration of the practice standards in question. Auditing theory does not exist in a vacuum: It is put to work in numerous practical applications. Practical applications of theoretical standards will be shown in subsequent chapters on audit program planning, execution of auditing procedures, gathering evidence and making auditing decisions.

SOURCES AND ADDITIONAL READING REFERENCES   AICPA Committee on Scope and Structure. "Final Report." AICPA, 1975.

American Accounting Association Committee on Auditing Concepts. "A Statement of Basic Auditing Concepts." *Accounting Review,* supplement to vol. 47, 1972, pp. 15–76.

Anderson, H. M., J. W. Giese, and Jon Booker. "Some Propositions about Auditing." *Accounting Review,* July 1970, pp. 524–31.

Carey, J. L., and W. O. Doherty. "The Concept of Independence— Review and Restatement." *Journal of Accountancy,* January 1966.

Dominiak, G. F., and J. G. Louderback. "Present Fairly and Generally Accepted Accounting Principles." *CPA Journal,* January 1972, pp. 45–49.

Hicks, E. L. "Standards for the Attest Function." *Journal of Accountancy,* August 1974, pp. 39–45.

Kramer, John L. "Disclosure of Positions Contrary to the IRC." *CPA Journal,* January 1978, pp. 41–45.

Mautz, R. K., and Hussein A. Sharaf. *The Philosophy of Auditing.* American Accounting Association Monograph No. 6, especially chap. 3, "The Postulates of Auditing," and chap. 10, "Auditing in Perspective." American Accounting Association, 1961.

Robertson, J. C., and C. W. Alderman. "Comparative Auditing Standards." *Journal of Accounting, Auditing, and Finance,* Winter 1981, pp. 144–61.

Schneidman, Arnold. "Need for Auditor's Computer Education." *CPA Journal,* June 1979, pp. 29–36.

Thorne, Jack F. "Tough Regulations for Tax Return Preparers." *CPA Journal,* May 1978, pp. 21–25.

Wood, Thomas D. "Auditors' Concern for Compliance with Laws." *CPA Journal,* January 1978, pp. 17–21.

REVIEW QUESTIONS

2.1. Is theory useful in auditing? Does "theory" exist only in college textbooks?

2.2. What are the seven underlying *postulates* of auditing theory?

2.3. What are the five major *concepts* in auditing theory?

2.4. Distinguish between auditing *standards* and auditing *procedures.*

2.5. By what standard would a judge determine the quality of *due audit care?* Explain.

2.6. Why should auditors act as though there is always a potential conflict of interest between the auditor and the management of the enterprise under audit?

2.7. What are the three specific aspects of independence that an auditor should carefully guard in the course of an engagement?

2.8. For what reasons does an auditor conduct a proper study and evaluation of internal controls? Must such an evaluation *always* be made of every data processing subsystem?

2.9. Explain the term *verification* as it is commonly used by auditors.

2.10. Give examples of how an auditor might assume that "what has held true in the past for the enterprise under examination will hold true in the future."

2.11. Define audit evidence.

2.12. Do the general and field work standards of generally accepted auditing standards apply when the client uses a computerized accounting system? Explain.

2.13. Are CPAs *required* to sign all federal tax returns they help prepare? Explain.

EXERCISES AND PROBLEMS

2.14. **Audit Independence and Planning**
You are meeting with executives of Cooper Cosmetics Corporation to arrange your firm's engagement to examine the corporation's financial statements for the year ending December 31. One executive suggests

the audit work be divided among three audit staff members. One person would examine asset accounts, a second would examine liability accounts, and the third would examine income and expense accounts to minimize audit time, avoid duplication of staff effort, and curtail interference with company operations.

Advertising is the corporation's largest expense, and the advertising manager suggests a staff member of your firm, whose uncle owns the advertising agency which handles the corporation's advertising, be assigned to examine the Advertising Expense account. The staff member has a thorough knowledge of the rather complex contract between Cooper Cosmetics and the advertising agency on which Cooper's advertising costs are based.

Required:

a. To what extent should a CPA follow his client's suggestions for the conduct of an audit? Discuss.

b. List and discuss the reasons why audit work should not be assigned solely according to asset, liability, and income and expense categories.

c. Should the staff member of your CPA firm whose uncle owns the advertising agency be assigned to examine advertising costs? Discuss.

2.15. Field Work Standards

You have accepted the engagement of auditing the financial statements of the Thorne Company, a small manufacturing firm that has been your client for several years. Because you were busy writing the report for another engagement, you sent an assistant accountant to begin the audit with the suggestion that she start with the accounts receivable. Using the prior year's working papers as a guide, the assistant prepared a trial balance of the accounts, aged them, prepared and mailed positive confirmation requests, examined underlying support for charges and credits, and performed such other work as she deemed necessary to obtain evidence about the validity and collecti-

bility of the receivables. At the conclusion of her work you reviewed the working papers she prepared and found she had carefully followed the prior year working papers.

Required:

The opinion rendered by a CPA states that the audit was made in accordance with generally accepted auditing standards.

List the three generally accepted standards of field work. Relate them to the above illustration by indicating how they were fulfilled or, if appropriate, how they were not fulfilled.

(*AICPA* adapted)

2.16. Time of Appointment and Planning

Your public accounting practice is located in a city of 15,000 population. Your work, conducted by you and two assistants, consists of compiling clients' monthly statements and preparing income tax returns for individuals from cash data and partnership returns from books and records. You have a few corporate clients; however, service to them is limited to preparation of income tax returns and assistance in year-end closings where bookkeeping is deficient.

One of your corporate clients is a retail hardware store. Your work for this client has been limited to preparing the corporation income tax return from a trial balance submitted by the bookkeeper.

On December 26 you receive from the president of the corporation a letter containing the following request:

"We have made arrangements with the First National Bank to borrow $50,000 to finance the purchase of a complete line of appliances. The bank has asked us to furnish our auditor's certified statement as of December 31, which is the closing date of our accounting year. The trial balance of the general ledger should be ready by January 10, which should allow ample time to prepare your report for submission to the bank by January 20. In view of the importance of this certified report to our financing program, we trust you will arrange to comply with the foregoing schedule.''

Required:
From a theoretical viewpoint, discuss the difficulties that are caused by such short notice an audit request.

(*AICPA* adapted)

2.17. Reporting Standards

CPA Davis and his assistants audited the financial statements of North Company, a computer equipment retailer. Davis conducted the audit in accordance with the general and field work standards of generally accepted auditing standards and therefore wrote a standard scope paragraph in his audit report. Then he received an emergency call to fill in as a substitute tenor in his barbershop quartet.

No one else was in the office that Saturday afternoon, so he handed you the completed financial statements and footnotes and said: ''Make sure it's OK to write an unqualified opinion on these statements. The working papers are on the table. I'll check with you on Monday morning.''

Required:
In general terms, what must you determine in order to write an unqualified opinion paragraph for Davis' signature?

2.18. GAAS in a Computer Environment

The Lovett Corporation uses an IBM mainframe computer system with peripheral optical reader and high-speed printer equipment. Transaction information is initially recorded on paper documents (e.g., sales invoices) and then read by optical equipment which produces a magnetic disk containing the data. These data file disks are processed by a computer program and printed listings, journals and general ledger balances are produced on the high-speed printer equipment.

Required:
Explain how the audit standard requiring ''adequate technical training and proficiency'' is important for satisfying the general and field work standards in the audit of Lovett Corporation's financial statements.

2.19. MAS Standards

Savage, CPA, has been requested by a public company audit client to perform a nonrecurring engagement involving the implementation of an EDP information and control system. The client requests that in setting up the new system and prior to conversion to the new system Savage:

1. Counsel on potential expansion of business activity plans.
2. Search for and interview new personnel.
3. Hire new personnel.
4. Train personnel.

In addition, the client requests that during the three months subsequent to the conversion Savage:

1. Supervise the operation of the new system.
2. Monitor client-prepared source documents and make changes in basic computer generated data as Savage may deem necessary without concurrence of the client.

Savage responds that he may perform some of the services requested, but not all of them.

A good response to CPA Savage's problems depend upon knowledge of the MAS Practice Standards covered in MS 11—Definitions and Standards for MAS Practice and MS 21—MAS Engagements.

Required:
a. Which of these services may Savage perform and which may Savage not perform? Explain.
b. Before undertaking this engagement, Savage should inform the client of all significant matters related to the engagement. What are these significant matters?
c. If Savage adds to his staff an individual who specializes in developing computer systems, what degree of knowledge

must Savage possess in order to supervise the specialist's activities?

(*AICPA* adapted)

2.20. Tax Practice Standards

In the short cases below, indicate whether the CPA's conduct was or was not in accordance with the AICPA Statements on Responsibilities in Tax Practice. Also, discuss whether the CPA's conduct is subject to criticism on any other grounds.

a. Rupert Rose, CPA, prepared, signed, and delivered his widowed mother's individual federal income tax return based on information she supplied. She claimed a $2,000 itemized deduction for charitable contributions, figuring her 200 hours of volunteer hospital work at $10 per hour. Rupert thought the item was a cash contribution but did not ask to see her receipt or canceled checks.

b. Susan Bugg, CPA, was engaged by a new corporate client to prepare the federal business income tax return. The client gave her unaudited financial statements and other relevant tax information. Being somewhat uncertain since she did not audit or verify the information, although nothing seemed to be wrong, Bugg changed the declaration to read as follows:

Declaration of preparer (other than taxpayer) is based on

unaudited financial statements supplied by taxpayers.

~~all information of which preparer has any knowledge.~~

c. Lois Hughes, CPA, obtained a new tax client, Gordon Printing Company. While preparing the current year federal tax return, she discovered an error in the previous year's return. The previous year's depreciation deduction had been calculated in error, resulting in a $10,000 overstatement of the deduction.

But the year had been a good business period, and taxable income was $47,000, about the same as in earlier years. Hughes pointed out the error to Gordon's controller and suggested the company file an amended return. The controller stated that he would be happy to pay any additional tax due if a revenue agent found the error but would not file an amended return. He said, "Just reduce this year's deduction by $10,000. This year is not too good anyway. Taxable income will then be about $25,000." Hughes thought this position was reasonable, prepared the return, and signed it.

d. Daniel Carroll, CPA, prepared, signed, and delivered A. Capone's individual federal income tax return after discussing Mr. Capone's reluctance to supply information on the question about taxpayer's having authority over a bank account in Bermuda. Mr. Capone believed that his inactive accounts were of no concern to IRS, and anyway, something in the constitution probably made it unlawful for IRS to ask taxpayers the question. Carroll transmitted the return without attaching any explanations to it.

2.21. Auditing Standards Case Study

Ray, the owner of a small company, asked Holmes, CPA, to conduct an audit of the company's records. Ray told Holmes that an audit is to be completed in time to submit audited financial statements to a bank as part of a loan application. Holmes immediately accepted the engagement and agreed to provide an auditor's report within three weeks. Ray agreed to pay Holmes a fixed fee plus a bonus if the loan was granted.

Holmes hired two accounting students to conduct the audit and spent several hours telling them exactly what to do. Holmes told the students not to spend time reviewing the controls but instead to concentrate on proving the mathematical accuracy of the ledger accounts and summarizing the data in the accounting records that support Ray's financial statements. The students followed Holmes' instructions and after two weeks gave Holmes the financial statements which did not include footnotes. Holmes reviewed the statements and prepared an unqualified auditor's report. The report, however, did not refer to generally accepted accounting principles or to the fact that Ray had adopted the new accounting standard for capitalizing interest.

Required:

Briefly describe each of the generally accepted auditing standards and indicate how the action(s) of Holmes resulted in a failure to comply with each standard.

(AICPA adapted)

CHAPTER 3

PROFESSIONAL STANDARDS SOURCES		
Compendium Section	**Document Reference**	**Topic**
AU 161	SAS 25	The Relationship of Generally Accepted Auditing Standards to Quality Control Standards
AU 220	SAS 1	Independence
QC 10	QCS 1	System of Quality Control for a CPA Firm
QC 90	Guide*	Quality Control Policies and Procedures for CPA Firms
QC 100	Guide	Voluntary Quality Control Review Program for CPA Firms
QC 110	*	Scope of the Quality Control Document Review
QC 200	**	Quality Control Policies and Procedures for Participating CPA Firms
QC 300	**	Performing and Reporting on Quality Control Compliance Reviews
ET 50		Five Essays on Concepts of Professional Ethics
ET 100		Rules of Conduct, Interpretations and Rulings on Independence, Integrity and Objectivity
ET 200		Rules of Conduct, Interpretations and Rulings on General and Technical Standards
ET 300		Rules of Conduct, Interpretations and Rulings of Confidentiality and Contingent Fees

* Issued by the AICPA Quality Control Standards Committee.

** Developed by the Special Committee on Proposed Standards for Quality Control Policies and Procedures for guidance to firms participating in the AICPA Voluntary Quality Control Review Program.

Professional Ethics

LEARNING OBJECTIVES Previous chapters have focused on the theory and practice of auditing. This chapter tells you about the regulation of accountants and accounting practice. Regulation and discipline depend on published codes of ethics and upon effective enforcement practices. Your objectives in this chapter on professional ethics are:

☐ Name and explain the various professional associations and government agencies that enforce rules of conduct and explain the types of penalties they can impose on accountants.

☐ Tell about the sequence of events in the recent history of criticism of the accounting profession and how the criticism led to the AICPA self-regulation structure.

☐ Reason through an ethical decision problem using the imperative, utilitarian and generalization principles of moral philosophy.

☐ Analyze fact situations and decide whether an accountant's conduct does or does not conform to the AICPA rules of conduct.

☐ Identify and explain the major differences between AICPA and SEC views on auditors' independence.

☐ Identify and discuss specific potential pitfalls in MAS and tax practice that could impair independence as an auditor.

As a CPA, you will be expected to observe rules of conduct published in several codes of ethics. If you join the AICPA and a state society of CPAs and practice before the U.S. Securities and Exchange Commission (SEC), you will be subject to the following:

Source of Rules of Conduct	Applicable to
State Board of Accountancy	Persons licensed by the state to practice accounting
American Institute of CPAs	Members of AICPA
State Society of CPAs	Members of state society of CPAs
U.S. Securities and Exchange Commission	Persons who practice before the SEC as accountants and auditors for SEC-registered companies.

If you are an internal auditor, you will be expected to observe the rules of conduct of The Institute of Internal Auditors. If you are a Certified Internal Auditor (CIA), you will also be expected to observe the CIA Code of Ethics. As a management accountant, you will be expected to observe the National Association of Accountants' standards of ethical conduct for management accountants.

This chapter concentrates on the AICPA Code of Professional Ethics and CPAs' regulatory structures. Most state board and state society rules are very similar to the AICPA rules, so you can learn most of your local rules by studying the AICPA Code. The concise SEC rules are applied differently and are discussed later in the chapter.

REGULATION AND QUALITY CONTROL

Regulation and *professional ethics* go hand-in-hand. Codes of ethics provide the underlying authority for regulation. Quality control practices and disciplinary proceedings provide the mechanisms of self-regulation. *Self-regulation* refers to quality control reviews and disciplinary actions conducted by fellow CPAs—professional peers. (Quality control matters are discussed later in this chapter.)

Self-Regulatory Discipline

Individual persons (not accounting firms) are subject to the rules of conduct of state CPA societies and the AICPA only if they choose to join these organizations. The AICPA and many state societies have entered into a Joint Ethics Enforcement Program (JEEP), wherein complaints against CPAs can be referred by the AICPA to the state societies or by the state societies to AICPA. Both organizations have ethics committees and trial boards to hear complaints. Both can act independently on a case, or they can agree to take the matter to an AICPA regional trial board.

The trial board has the power to: (1) acquit the CPA, (2) admonish the CPA, (3) suspend the CPA's membership in the state society and AICPA for up to two years or (4) expel the CPA from the state society and AICPA. The AICPA bylaws (not the code of ethics) provide for automatic expulsion of CPAs judged to have committed a felony, failed to file their tax returns or aided in the preparation of a false and fraudulent income tax return. The trial boards are required to publish the names of CPAs disciplined in their proceedings. However, CPAs can appeal regional trial board decisions to an AICPA national review board, whose decision is final.

The penalties listed above cover a range of severity. In many cases, trial boards admonish or suspend a CPA and require a number of hours of continuing professional education (CPE) to be undertaken. The goal is to help the CPA attain an appropriate level of professional competence and awareness. Although intended as a constructive resolution, the CPE requirement is similar to "serving time." Persons who fail to satisfy CPE conditions will find themselves charged with "acts discreditable to the profession" (AICPA Rule 501 or a similar state rule) and expelled as "second offenders."

The expulsion penalty, while severe, does not prevent a CPA from continuing to practice accounting. Membership in AICPA and state societies, while beneficial, is not required. However, a CPA must have a valid state license in order to practice.

Public Regulation Discipline

State boards of accountancy are government agencies consisting of CPA and non-CPA officeholders. They issue licenses to practice accounting in their jurisdictions. Most state laws require a license to use the designation "CPA" or "Certified Public Accountant" and limit the attest (audit) function to license holders. Most state laws do not regulate work in areas of management consulting, tax practice or bookkeeping services.

State boards have rules of conduct and trial boards. They can admonish a license holder, but more importantly, they can suspend or revoke the license to practice. Suspension and revocation are severe penalties because a person no longer can use the "CPA" title and cannot sign audit reports.

The SEC also conducts public regulation disciplinary actions. Its authority comes from its rules of practice, of which Rule 2(e) provides that the SEC can deny, temporarily or permanently, the privilege of practice before the SEC to any person found: (1) not to possess the requisite qualifications to represent others, or (2) to be lacking in character or integrity or to have engaged in unethical or improper professional conduct, or (3) to have willfully violated any provision of the federal securities laws or their rules and regulations. When conducting a "Rule 2(e) proceeding," the SEC acts in a quasi-judicial role as an administrative agency.

The SEC penalty bars an accountant from signing any documents filed by a SEC-registered company. The penalty effectively stops the accountant's SEC practice. In a few severe cases, Rule 2(*e*) proceedings have resulted in settlements barring not only the individual accountant but also the accounting firm or certain of its practice offices from accepting new SEC clients for a period of time.

The Internal Revenue Service (IRS) can also discipline accountants as a matter of public regulation. IRS can suspend or disbar from practice before the IRS any CPA shown to be incompetent or disreputable or who refuses to comply with tax rules and regulations.

Criticism of the Public Accounting Profession

Beginning in the mid-1970s, congressional attention turned toward the public accounting profession. Several well-publicized corporate bankruptcies had created an impression that auditors had failed. In time-honored tradition, certain congressmen began to investigate ways and means to "do something about it." First, former U.S. Congressman Moss's (D-California) subcommittee on oversight and investigations, in a 1976 report, ranked the U.S. Securities and Exchange Commission first in effectiveness among nine agencies. However, the report also was very critical of perceived shortcomings in the SEC's diligence in overseeing the accounting profession.

Soon afterward (1976) under the direction of the late Senator Metcalf (D-Montana), the staff of the U.S. Senate Subcommittee on Reports, Accounting and Management issued a stinging report entitled "The Accounting Establishment." This report essentially called for federal government takeover of many accounting and auditing functions performed by the independent Financial Accounting Standards Board and by the AICPA Auditing Standards Board. Later (1977), the subcommittee issued a final report entitled "Improving the Accountability of Publicly Owned Corporations and their Auditors." This report adopted a position of waiting to see whether the accounting profession could make the changes necessary to satisfy the critics.

Congressman Moss did not wait. In 1978, he introduced legislation to establish a "National Organization of SEC Accountancy," which would operate like the existing National Association of Security Dealers (95th Congress, 2d Session, H.R. 13175). Firms in SEC practice would have to register and have periodic quality reviews. The SEC role in oversight and standards setting would be expanded. Congress did not act on this proposal, and Moss was not reelected. However, the potential for federal legislation still lurks in the background.

AICPA Responses to Criticism

During this period of criticism from Washington, D.C., the AICPA was not inactive.

Commission on Auditor's Responsibilities (CAR).   The CAR issued its tentative report only months after the Metcalf staff published "The Accounting Establishment." The CAR report was not intended as a response to Congress, but the timing was fortuitous. The final report entitled, "Report, Conclusion, and Recommendations," was issued in 1978 and served for several years as a compendium of over 100 suggestions for change. Many of the CAR recommendations dealt with regulation, maintenance of independence and the structure of the auditing standards-setting body. (The Auditing Standards Board, much like it exists today, was recommended by the CAR.)

While the CAR final report was in production, the AICPA annual business meeting was held in October 1977. At this meeting, the Quality Control Standards Committee and the Division for Firms were created.

Quality control.   The Quality Control Standards Committee was created late in 1977 at the same time the AICPA Division for Firms was authorized. These changes were stimulated by congressional criticisms and by the report of the independent Commission on Auditor's Responsibilities, which the AICPA appointed in 1975.

Earlier (1974), SAS 4, entitled "Quality Control Considerations for a Firm of Independent Auditors," was issued. This SAS dealt with nine areas where policies and procedures could affect the quality of work on audit engagements. The nine elements of quality control were:

- ☑ Independence of personnel.
- ☑ Assigning qualified personnel to engagements.
- ☑ Consultation with experts.
- ☑ Supervision of work at all organizational levels.
- ☑ Hiring of personnel.
- ☑ Professional development and continuing education.
- ☑ Advancement of personnel in the firm.
- ☑ Acceptance and continuance of clients.
- ☑ Inspection—"internal audit" or review of the effectiveness of the other quality control considerations.

As subsequent events unfolded, SAS 4 was superceded by SAS 25 in 1979[1]. The essential content of SAS 4, however, was reissued in *Statement on Quality Control Standards No. 1* (1979), entitled "System of Quality Control for a CPA Firm." The AICPA Quality Control Standards Committee had a short life, issuing only the one official pronouncement and a nonauthoritative guide (entitled "Establishing Quality Control Policies and Procedures") before it was disbanded in 1983. The AICPA believed a sufficient body of standards was in place and wanted to avoid any further "standards overload" that could result from continuation of the committee. After all, the AICPA Division for Firms by then had become fully operational, and peer review and quality control standards were

---

[1] *SAS 25* (AU 161), "The Relationship of Generally Accepted Auditing Standards to Quality Control Standards."

being written in both the SEC Practice Section (SECPS) and the Private Companies Practice Section (PCPS) of the division.

Accounting firms which are not members of the AICPA Division for Firms can participate in a voluntary quality control review program. The guidance materials, which were not issued by the Quality Control Standards Committee as authoritative pronouncements, are listed below. You can get a good idea of the content of the SECPS and PCPS standards by reading these materials. However, as you might expect, most accounting firms interested in quality control reviews are members of the Division for Firms.

Voluntary Quality Control Review Program for CPA Firms (AICPA, 1976). This pamphlet describes a voluntary program whereby CPA firms can request review by the AICPA staff and a selected panel of experts.

Quality Control Policies and Procedures for Participating CPA Firms (AICPA, 1978). This booklet gives examples of specific policies and procedures for firms to use as a guide for preparing their own quality control documents.

Performing and Reporting on Quality Control Compliance Reviews (AICPA, 1978). This document provides guidance for firms intending to participate in the voluntary review and the nature and extent of procedures that would be performed by a review team conducting and reporting on a compliance review.

A quality control review is very similar to an audit. Of course, in an audit a business's financial statements are the representations taken under examination. In a quality control review, an auditing firm's quality control document contains the "representations" about the policies and procedures which will be reviewed. These documents range from 30 to over 100 pages in length (depending on the firm's size) and contain a wealth of information about a firm's professional activities. Students—prospective employees of the firms—should obtain and read the document. Policies include specific firm procedures concerning ownership of stock in clients, pay, rotation of duties, promotion, continuing education and other matters of special interest to new employees.

AICPA Division for Firms.   The division is essentially an organizational structure for quality control and self-regulation of *accounting firms*. In all other respects, AICPA influence is exerted on members who are individuals. Until the division was created, the AICPA had no jurisdiction over accounting firms.

The division contains two sections: the SEC Practice Section (SECPS) for firms who practice before the SEC, and the Private Companies Practice Section (PCPS) for all other firms. About 20,000 firms or "practice units'' are represented in the AICPA, and all of them are potential members of the two sections.

Both sections impose membership requirements, the most important of which are:

☐ *Peer reviews every three years.* Peer reviews are quality control reviews. The SECPS and PCPS both have peer review committees that monitor the conduct of the peer reviews. Both sections follow the broad outlines of the Quality Control Standards.

☐ *Continuing professional education (CPE).* The SECPS and PCPS both require 120 CPE hours every three years for professionals employed by member firms. Therefore, even persons who do not work in states with mandatory CPE licensing requirements may be subject to a CPE requirement.

Both sections are governed by their respective executive committees, and the SECPS is subject to review by a Public Oversight Board (POB). The POB members are prominent persons not directly connected with public accounting practice (lawyers, former SEC officials, corporate executives). The POB is obligated to report to the SEC on SECPS activities.

One such SECPS activity is the work of the Special Investigations Committee (SIC). SECPS member firms are required to report to SIC any litigation involving the firm and its SEC clients. The SIC studies the case to try to decide whether the firm has a quality control problem. The firm may have had a recent peer review, but the peer review work concentrates on the *system* of quality control policies and procedures. Peer reviews are not designed to search for audit failures. When an alleged audit failure surfaces in the form of litigation involving an accounting firm, the SIC investigates. Through late 1983, the SIC has revealed no conclusions or actions based on its investigations. The SECPS considers these cases quite sensitive since litigation is underway and believes that self-regulation is best served by confidentiality.

Corporate Audit Committees

Corporate audit committees have aided auditors' independence and have influenced the regulation of corporate activities. Criticisms from the same congressional sources discussed earlier had also been aimed at corporate boards of directors for lack of diligence in performing directorship duties related to oversight and audit. Some observers believed directors generally did not pay enough attention to auditing functions—both internal and external—performed within their companies.

Audit committees consisting of board members have been encouraged since 1939, and the AICPA has joined others in expressing such encouragement from time to time. In the late 1970s, pressures were exerted on the AICPA to require a corporation to establish an audit committee as a condition for obtaining an audit by independent CPAs. The AICPA studied the proposition and decided that accountants had no right or authority to intrude in corporate governance matters and impose such a requirement. Many practical matters influenced this decision, including such considerations as cost and benefit, the impact on small companies, the distinction (or lack thereof) between an audit of an entity having an audit committee and one of an entity without such a committee (for example, a partnership) and the power and role of the AICPA. The conclusion was that if audit committees were to be required, the SEC and stock exchanges should establish the requirement.

Many auditors, however, welcome the existence of an audit committee of the board. The committee operates within the boardroom (apart from management) and bears the first responsibility for overseeing independent audits, internal audits, and other exploratory and investigative matters dealing with financial accounting and internal controls. This committee stands as auditors' direct pipeline to the board, opening up communications channels to the top of the corporate organization.

The SEC, in a number of investigations and disciplinary hearings, has forced corporations to form audit committees composed of outside (non-management) directors. Court decisions have also required formation of audit committees, and judges have specified their duties and responsibilities.

After many years of encouraging voluntary formation, the New York Stock Exchange required all listed domestic companies to establish audit committees by June 30, 1978. The committee members must be outside directors free from relationships (other than board membership) which might interfere with their exercise of independent judgment. The emphasis on outside directors is meant to ensure that the interests of shareholders are not subordinated to any conflicting responsibilities an officer-director might have.

Summary: Discipline, Regulation, and Quality Control

Public accounting practice is not really a regulated industry. It is a self-regulated profession, with the exception of disciplinary procedures performed by government-appointed state boards of accountancy and the SEC and IRS. Discipline of the members of a professional association is carried out by peers. The sections of the AICPA Division for Firms are operated by accountants for accountants, acting with respect for the public interest. Everyone keeps an eye on Congress and on state legislatures as more states subject their accountancy boards to "sunset legislation review." The future of the regulatory environment depends a great deal on how well these self-regulatory activities are executed.

GENERAL ETHICS

A sense of proper ethical conduct must underlie all human activity. A pervasive sense of ethics is particularly important for professional persons. Two aspects of ethics operate in the professional environment—general ethics (the spirit) and professional ethics (the rules). Mautz and

Sharaf have contributed the following thoughts to the association of general ethics and professional ethics:

> The theory of ethics has been a subject of interest to philosophers since the beginnings of recorded thought. Because philosophers are concerned with the good of all mankind, their discussions have been concerned with what we may call general ethics rather than the ethics of small groups such as the members of a given profession. We cannot look, therefore, to their philosophical theories for direct solutions to our special problems. Nevertheless, their work with general ethics is of primary importance to the development of an appropriate concept in any special field. *Ethical behavior in auditing or in any other activity is no more than a special application of the general notion of ethical conduct devised by philosophers for men generally. Ethical conduct in auditing draws its justification and basic nature from the general theory of ethics. Thus, we are well advised to give some attention to the ideas and reasoning of some of the great philosophers on this subject.* (Emphasis added.)

Overview   What is ethics? Wheelwright defined ethics as: "that branch of philosophy which is the systematic study of reflective choice, of the standards of right and wrong by which it is to be guided, and of the goods toward which it may ultimately be directed."[2] In this definition, you can detect three key elements: (1) ethics involves questions requiring reflective choice (decision problems), (2) ethics involves guides of right and wrong (moral principles) and (3) ethics is concerned with the consequences *(goods)* of decisions.

What is an ethical problem? A *problem situation* exists when you have to make a choice among alternatives, and the right choice is not absolutely clear. An *ethical problem situation* may be described as one in which the choice of alternative actions affects the well-being of other persons.

What is ethical behavior? You can find two standard philosophical answers to this question: (1) ethical behavior is that which produces the greatest good and (2) ethical behavior is that which conforms to moral rules and moral principles. The most difficult problem situations arise when two or more rules conflict or when a rule and the criterion of "greatest good" conflict. Some cases are given later in this chapter to illustrate these difficulties.

Why does an individual or group need a code of ethical conduct? While it has been said that a person should *be* upright and not be *kept* upright, a code serves a useful purpose as a reference and a benchmark for individuals. A code makes explicit some of the criteria for conduct peculiar to the profession, and in this way codes of professional ethics are able to provide some direct solutions that may not be available in general ethics

---

[2] Philip Wheelwright, *A Critical Introduction to Ethics,* 3rd ed. (Indianapolis, Ind.: Odyssey Press, 1959), p. 4.

theories. Furthermore, an individual is better able to know what the profession expects. From the viewpoint of the organized profession, a code is a public declaration of principled conduct, and it is a means of facilitating *enforcement* of standards of conduct. Practical enforcement and profession-wide internal discipline would be impossible if members were not first put on notice of the standards.

A Variety of Roles   While one of the main purposes of ethics is to guide the actions of decision makers, the role of decision maker does not fully describe the professional person's entire obligation. Each person acts not only as an individual but also as a member of a profession and as a member of society. Hence, accountants and auditors are also *spectators* (observing the decisions of colleagues), *advisors* (counselling with co-workers), *instructors* (teaching accounting students or new employees on the job), *judges* (serving on disciplinary committees of a state society, a state board of accountancy or the AICPA) and *critics* (commenting on the ethical decisions of others). All of these roles are important in the practice of professional ethics.

AN ETHICAL   In considering general ethics, your primary goal is to arrive at a set of
DECISION   acceptable methods for making ethical decisions. Consequently, an un-
PROCESS   derstanding of some of the general principles of ethics can contribute background for a detailed consideration of the behavior directed by the AICPA *Code of Professional Ethics*.

In the earlier definition of ethics, one of the key elements was *reflective choice*. This element bears a great similarity to the process described in Chapter 1 as scientific decision-making methodology. Both of these methodologies involve an important sequence of events beginning with the recognition of a decision problem, the identification of alternative actions, the assessment of evidence, and ending with a decision and appropriate action. The process of moral deliberation, or reflective choice, is characterized by these beginning steps:

> *First*. Examine and clarify the alternative actions. Ask what the relevant possibilities for action in the circumstances are. Search for all the action alternatives available.
>
> *Second*. Think through the consequences of each possible action. Try to predict a hypothetical future state of affairs that would follow action on each alternative.
>
> *Third*. Use imagination to project yourself into these hypothetical future states of affairs. Think about what it will be like to live with your decision.
>
> *Fourth*. Identify yourself with the points of view of other people who will be affected by your decision. Put yourself in *their* shoes in these hypothetical futures.

These steps bring you to the point of choice. A review is given next of some of the principles of ethics that may help your choice.

PRINCIPLES IN ETHICS

Theory, whether ethical theory or technical theory, has practical value in its ability as a guide to decisions and actions. We could dispense with the following discussion of ethical theories if we were willing to accept a simple rule: "Let conscience be your guide." Such a rule is appealing because it is a call on an individual's own judgment which may be based on wisdom, insight, adherence to custom, or an authoritative code. However, it might also be based on caprice, immaturity, ignorance, stubbornness, or misunderstanding. Consciences, individually and collectively, sometimes fail to show the consistency, clarity, practicability, impartiality and adequacy essential for maintaining ethical standards and behavior.

In a similar manner, reliance on the opinions of others or on the weight of opinion of a particular social group is not always enough. Another person or a group of persons may perpetuate a custom or habit that is wrong. To adhere blindly to custom or to group habits is to abdicate individual responsibility. Titus and Keeton summarized this point succinctly: "Each person capable of making moral decisions is responsible for making his own decisions. The ultimate locus of moral responsibility is in the individual."[3] Thus, the function of ethical *principles* is not to provide a simple and sure rule but to provide some insights into guides for decisions and actions.

Two illustrations are given below to show some problem situations that for most persons would present difficult choices. Consider them in light of the method of reflective choice and in terms of the *imperative,* the *utilitarian,* and the *generalization* theories explained afterward.

Illustration.   As a result of your fine reputation as a public accountant, you were invited to become a director of a local bank and were pleased to accept the position. While serving on the board for a year, you learned that a bank director is under a duty to use care and prudence in administering the affairs of a bank, and failure to do so in such a way that the bank suffers a financial loss means that the director(s) may be held liable for damages. This month, in the course of an audit, you discover a seriously weakened financial position in a client who has a large loan from your bank. Prompt disclosure to the other bank directors would minimize the bank's loss, but since the audit report cannot be completed for another three weeks such disclosure would amount to divulging confidential information gained in the course of an audit engagement (prohibited by AICPA Rule 301). You can remain silent and honor Rule 301 (and fail to honor your duty as a bank director), or you can speak up to the other directors (thus violating Rule 301). Which shall it be?

---

[3] Harold H. Titus and Morris Keeton, *Ethics for Today,* 4th ed. (Saddle Brook, N.J.: American Book-Stratford Press, Inc., 1966), p. 131.

Illustration.   In your work as an auditor, you discover that the cashier, who has custody over the petty cash fund, has forged several vouchers in order to cover innocent mistakes and make the fund balance each month when it is replenished. Your investigation reveals that the amount involved during the year is $240. The cashier is a woman, age 55, and the president of the company is a man who can tolerate no mistakes, intentional or otherwise, in the accounting records. In fact, he is unyielding in this respect. He asks you about the results of your audit. Not doubting that the cashier would be fired if the forgeries were known, should you remain silent and thus not tell the truth?

The Imperative Principle

An imperative theory directs a decision maker to act according to the requirements of an ethical rule. Strict versions of imperative theories maintain that the decision should be made without looking to see which alternatives will probably create the greatest balance of good over evil. Ethics in this sense is a function of moral rules and principles and not a situation-specific calculation of the consequences.[4]

The philosopher Immanuel Kant (1724–1804) is perhaps the foremost advocate of the imperative school. Kant was unwilling to rely solely upon decision makers' inclinations and value preferences for choice in various circumstances. He strongly preferred rules without exceptions to the varied and frequently inconsistent choices of individuals. He maintained that *reason* and the strict *duty to be consistent* governed the formulation of his first law of conduct: "Act only on that maxim whereby you can at the same time will that it should become a universal law." This law of conduct is Kant's first formulation of his *categorical imperative,* meaning that it specifies an *unconditional obligation*. One such maxim (rule), for example, is: "Lying is wrong."

Suppose you believed it proper to lie by remaining silent about the cashier's attempts to cover mistakes (or any other specific kind of lie). The Kantian test of the morality of such a lie is: Can this maxim be a moral rule which should be followed without exception by all persons when asked about the results of audit work? In order for all persons to follow a rule, all persons must know of it, and when everyone knows that the rule is to lie about the results of some audit work, then no one is fooled by the auditor's silence (or false response).

A lie succeeds only when the hearer of it does not know it is a lie. The nature of the universal rule is universal knowledge of it. Therefore, any manner of lying is bound to fail the test because no one would believe the speaker of the lie. Thus, lying is wrong because, when made universal, no one could be believed and virtually all common communication would become impossible.

A decision maker who followed the imperative principle would be on

---

[4] I. Kant, *Foundations of the Metaphysics of Morals* (originally published in 1785), trans. Lewis W. Beck (Indianapolis, Ind.: Bobbs-Merrill, 1959).

the horns of a dilemma in the case of conflicting duties as bank director and auditor. To remain silent to the other directors could be construed as a lie, since a director's duty is to speak up. Yet, to speak up would mean that the auditor's implicit promise to the client not to divulge confidential information would be a lie. However, following the imperative, the auditor in the other illustration would tell the employer about the forged vouchers. By this principle, it does not matter that the circumstances might be different (for example, the cashier was a 22-year-old man and the amount was $24,000). Kant maintained that motive and duty alone define a moral act, not the consequences of the act.

The general objection to the imperative principle is the belief that no universal rule can be made that does not admit exceptions. The general response to this objection is that if the rule is stated properly to include the exceptional cases, then the principle is still valid. The problem with this response, however, is that human experience is sufficiently complicated, and extremely complex universal rules would have to be constructed in order to encompass all possible cases.[5]

One value of the Kantian categorical imperative with its emphasis on universal, unconditional obligations is that it lets you know when you are faced with an ethical decision problem. When only one rule derived from the categorical imperative is applicable, you may have no trouble following it. When two rules or two duties are in conflict, a serious problem exists. Assume for the sake of illustration, another rule is "Live up to all your professional duties." In the illustrative case, these two rules ("Lying is wrong" and "Live up to all your professional duties") may be in conflict. Such conflicts of rules and duties create difficult problems of ethical choice because adherence to one of the rules means breaking the other.

The Kantian imperative theory, however, does not provide an easy way to make the decision. Someone who is rule bound may find himself or herself in a dilemma. Just this kind of dilemma is what prompts people to look for ways to weigh the consequences of actions, and one way is described by the theory of utilitarianism discussed in the section below.

Most professional codes of ethics have characteristics of the imperative type of theory. As a general matter, professionals are expected to act in a manner in conformity with the rules. However, society frequently questions not only conduct itself but the rules on which conduct is based. Thus, a dogmatic imperative approach to ethical decisions may not necessarily be completely sufficient for the maintenance of professional standards. Society may question the rules, and conflicts among them are always possible. A means of estimating the consequences of alternative actions may be useful.

---

[5] Several rules in the AICPA Rules of Conduct are explicitly phrased in such a way as to provide for exceptions to the general rules, notably Rules 203 and 301. Imperative rules also seem to generate borderline cases, so the AICPA ethics division issues *interpretations* and *rulings* to explain the applicability of the rules.

The Principle of Utilitarianism

The principle of utilitarianism maintains that the ultimate criterion of an ethical decision is the balance of good over evil consequences produced by the action.[6] The emphasis in utilitarianism is on the consequences of action rather than on the following of rules. The criterion of producing the greater good is made an explicit part of the decision process.

In *act-utilitarianism,* the center of attention is the individual act as it is affected by the specific circumstances of a situation. An act-utilitarian's ethical problem may be framed in this way: "What effect will my doing this act in this situation have on the general balance of good over evil?" This theory admits general guides such as, "Telling the truth is probably always for the greatest good." However, the emphasis is always on the specific situation, and decision makers must determine whether they have independent grounds for thinking that it would be for the greatest general good not to tell the truth in a particular case.

The general difficulty with act-utilitarianism is that it seems to permit too many exceptions to well-established rules. By focusing attention on individual acts, the long-run effect of setting examples for other people appears to be ignored. If an act-utilitarian decision is to break a moral rule, then the decision's success usually depends on everyone else's adherence to the rule. For example, to benefit from tax evasion for a good reason depends on everyone else not having an equally good reason for not paying their taxes.

Rule-utilitarianism, on the other hand, emphasizes the centrality of rules for ethical behavior while still maintaining the criterion of the greatest universal good. This kind of utilitarianism means that decision makers must first determine the rules which will promote the greatest general good for everyone. The initial question is not which *action* has the greatest utility, but which *rule.* Thus, the rule-utilitarian's ethical decision problem can be framed as follows: "What effect will everyone's doing this kind of act in this kind of situation have on the general balance of good over evil?" The principle of utility becomes operative not only in determining what particular action to take in a specific decision situation in which rules conflict but also in determining what the rules should be in the first place.

The statement of the rule-utilitarian's problem may be given a very commonsense expression: "What would happen if everybody acted this way?" In this form the question is known as *generalization.*

The Generalization Argument

For all practical purposes, the *generalization argument* may be considered a judicious combination of the imperative and utilitarian principles. Stated succinctly, the argument is: "If all relevantly similar persons acting under relevantly similar circumstances were to act in a certain way

---

[6] J. S. Mill, *Utilitarianism* (originally published in 1861), ed. Oskar Piest (Indianapolis, Ind.: Bobbs-Merril, 1957).

and the consequences would be undesirable, then no one ought to act in that way without a reason."[7] A more everyday-expression of the argument is the question: "What would happen if everyone acted in that certain way?" If the answer to the question is that the consequences would be undesirable, then your conclusion according to the generalization test is that that way of acting is unethical and ought not be done.

The key ideas implicit in the generalization test are "similar persons" and "similar circumstances." These features provide the needed flexibility for you to consider the many variations that may arise in real problem situations. They also demand you exercise considerable judgment in determining whether persons and circumstances are genuinely different or are just arbitrarily rationalized as different so that a preconceived preference can be "explained" as right.

The problem over conflict of duties as a bank director and public accountant can arise only when accounting clients are customers of the bank. As long as circumstances of conflict do not exist, the question of, "What if every CPA served as a bank director of a bank with whom no accounting client did business?" is easily answerable. There is no problem because no conflict can arise. But when the *potential* for conflict exists, the question becomes, "What if every CPA were exposed to conflict-of-duty situations like this one?" In this case, the results would be undesirable, and the conclusion would be that no CPAs should serve as bank directors unless none of their accounting clients did business with the bank.

Assume in the other illustration that the custodian of the petty cash fund had forged vouchers involving $24,000 instead of $240. Now one feature of the circumstances is different. When posing the generalization question, you must judge whether the money amount tips the balance. Would it make a difference if it were $1, $241 or $23,999? The money amount characteristics helps determine whether the case is insignificant or important, and accountants and auditors are called upon constantly to make judgments about the importance of money amounts in a variety of decisions.

This brief review of principles in ethics should have provided some guide to the ways that many people may think about and approach difficult decision problems. The greatest task is to take general notions of ethics—the imperative, utilitarianism or generalization—and apply them to a real decision. Their application through codes of professional ethics is a challenge.

CODE OF ETHICS   Various codes of professional ethics can usually be distinguished from each other in one important respect—they tend to either be general state-

---

[7] Marcus G. Singer, *Generalization in Ethics* (New York: Atheneum Publishers, 1961, 1971), especially pp. 5, 10–11, 61, 63, 73, 81, 105–22.

ments of ideals and purposes or specific about prohibited acts. General codes are subject to wide interpretation and, consequently, are very difficult to enforce. Specific codes are more amenable to enforcement, but the professional group must take care to review the rules for periodic revision lest they become outdated and inappropriate to the changing social environment.

The AICPA *Code of Professional Ethics* consists of four parts. (1) The "Concepts of Professional Ethics" contains five essays that are statements of general ideals and purposes. These essays are found in the AICPA booklet entitled *Restatement of the Code of Professional Ethics* and in the annual *AICPA Professional Standards* published for the AICPA by Commerce Clearing House, Inc. The Concepts section does not contain enforceable rules of ethics. (2) The "Rules of Conduct" section contains definitions and rules that are the enforceable ethical standards applicable to members of the AICPA. (3) The "Interpretations of Rules of Conduct" are detailed explanations issued by the AICPA Division of Professional Ethics that serve as guidelines as to the scope and applicability of the Rules of Conduct. The interpretations are not themselves enforceable, but anyone who departs from their guidelines has the burden of justifying the departure in any disciplinary hearing. (4) The ethics division also publishes "rulings" on the applicability of rules in specific situations. Like the interpretations, members must be able to justify departures from the rulings.

AICPA Rules of Conduct   The AICPA *Code of Professional Ethics* derives its authority from the bylaws of the AICPA. The Rules of Conduct apply to all services performed in the practice of public accounting in the United States, including tax and management advisory services, except where the wording of a rule limits its applicability to audits.

Members of the AICPA are held responsible for compliance with the rules by all persons associated with them in their public practice, including employees, partners, and shareholders. In addition, members may not permit other people to carry out on their behalf acts which are prohibited by the rules. Most of the rules relate specifically to the practice of public accounting. However, members of the AICPA who are not in public practice must observe Rules 102 and 501. All of the other rules relate to the practice of public accounting.

INDEPENDENCE, INTEGRITY, AND OBJECTIVITY

A certified public accountant should maintain his integrity and objectivity and, when engaged in the practice of public accounting, be independent of those he serves.

Rule 101—Independence.   A member or a firm of which he is a partner or shareholder shall not express an opinion on financial statements of an enterprise unless he and his firm are independent with respect to such enterprise. Independence will be considered to be impaired if, for example:

A. During the period of his professional engagement, or at the time of expressing his opinion, he or his firm

1. *a.* Had or was committed to acquire any direct or material indirect financial interest in the enterprise; or

   b. Was a trustee of any trust or executor or administrator of any estate if such trust or estate had or was committed to acquire any direct or material indirect financial interest in the enterprise, or

2. Had any joint closely held business investment with the enterprise or any officer, director, or principal stockholder thereof which was material in relation to his or his firm's net worth, or

3. Had any loan to or from the enterprise or any officer, director, or principal stockholder thereof. This latter proscription does not apply to the following loans from a financial institution when made under normal lending procedures, terms, and requirements:

   a. Loans obtained by a member or his firm which are material in relation to the net worth of such borrower.

   b. Home mortgages.

   c. Other secured loans, except loans guaranteed by a member's firm which are otherwise unsecured.

B. During the period covered by the financial statements, during the period of the professional engagement, or at the time of expressing an opinion, he or his firm

1. Was connected with the enterprise as a promoter, underwriter or voting trustee, a director or officer, or in any capacity equivalent to that of a member of management or of an employee, or

2. Was a trustee for any pension or profit-sharing trust of the enterprise.

The above examples are not intended to be all-inclusive.

Rule 102—Integrity and Objectivity. A member shall not knowingly misrepresent facts and, when engaged in the practice of public accounting, including the rendering of tax and management advisory services, shall not subordinate his judgment to others. In tax practice, a member may resolve doubt in favor of his client as long as there is reasonable support for his position.

ANALYSIS

The concept of independence is the cornerstone of the accounting profession. Since the principle purpose of independent financial auditing is to lend credibility to financial assertions and representations made by management, auditors must in fact be impartial and unbiased with respect to both the client management and the client entity itself.

Not only must auditors be independent *in fact,* they must also *appear* independent to outside decision makers who rely on their attestation. Independence *in fact* is truly a mental condition and is thus difficult to demonstrate by physical or visual means. Thus, some appearances of lacking independence are the relationships prohibited specifically in sections A and B of Rule 101.

Rule 101 applies to "members," but you should not confuse being a member of AICPA with the use of the word "member" in the rule. For purposes of Rule 101, the terms "member" and "he and his firm" include CPAs performing audit services for a client, all partners or shareholders in the accounting firm, and all other managerial-level employees (e.g., audit managers) located in the CPA firm office that does all or a significant part of the audit. Financial interests of spouses and dependent persons (whether or not related) are attributed to the member. Managerial relations of such persons are also attributed to the member, except for cases where such persons' employment with a client is not connected with the audit work. The AICPA also attributes to "members" some, but not all, associations of nondependent close relatives (children, brothers, sisters, grandparents, parents-in-law and their respective spouses). The details of these rules can be found in AICPA Ethics Interpretation 101–9.

Therefore, according to the AICPA, nonmanagerial employees who do not participate in the audit of a particular client and managerial employees (but not partners) located in offices that do not participate in the audit of a particular client can have the financial interests and managerial relationships (directly or through relatives) that are prohibited to members by Rule 101.

Section 101(A) deals with the financial interests in an audit client. Note that the "period covered by the financial statements" is not relevant to this section as it is in Section B. A member may divest of a prohibited financial interest before the first audit of a new client begins, after which it is improper to reinvest when the engagement will continue for future years' audits. *Any direct* financial interest (e.g., common stock, preferred stock, convertible debt) is prohibited, even the beneficial ownership of a single share, no matter how acquired. This rule is the strictest one in the code. There are no exceptions in the rule's wording. *Indirect* financial interests, on the other hand, are allowed up to the point of materiality (with reference to the member's wealth). This provision permits members to hold mutual fund shares and have some limited business transactions with audit clients so long as they do not reach material proportions. Items 2 and 3 of 101(A) define certain specific types of prohibited and allowed indirect financial interests.

Section 101(B) prohibits activities that amount to the abilities to make decisions for the audit client—to act as management broadly defined. The appearance of independence is impaired if such a connection existed at any time during the period covered by the financial statements, regardless of whether the association was terminated prior to the beginning of the audit work. The presumption is that members cannot be independent and objective when auditing decisions in which they took part or with which they appeared to be connected.

Rule 102 essentially reaffirms the general concept of independence and extends the requirement of maintaining integrity and objectivity to tax and management advisory services. This rule specifically allows the CPA to act in the client's best interests—to act as an advocate—in tax practice. Neither Rule 101 nor Rule 102 prohibits direct or material indirect financial interests or other business relationships with nonaudit clients (tax and management advisory services clients). However, such relations are not recommended, and some public accounting firms extend the rule to these other areas of practice.

In terms of ethics principles, these rules may be justified on a *rule-utilitarian* basis as far as direct financial interests are concerned. The logic is something like this: The greatest good is created by making a situation free of any suspicious circumstances, no matter how innocent they may be in truth. The goodwill of public reliance and respect is greater than the CPA's sacrifice of the opportunity to invest in securities of audit clients.

COMPETENCE AND TECHNICAL STANDARDS

A certified public accountant should observe the profession's technical standards and strive continually to improve his competence and the quality of his services.

Rule 201—General Standards. A member shall comply with the following general standards as interpreted by bodies designated by Council and must justify any departures therefrom.

a. *Professional competence.* A member shall undertake only those engagements which he or his firm can reasonably expect to complete with professional competence.

b. *Due professional care.* A member shall exercise due professional care in the performance of an engagement.

c. *Planning and supervision.* A member shall adequately plan and supervise an engagement.

d. *Sufficient relevant data.* A member shall obtain sufficient relevant data to afford a reasonable basis for conclusions or recommendations in relation to an engagement.

e. *Forecasts.* A member shall not permit his name to be used in conjunction with any forecast of future transactions in a manner which may lead to the belief that the member vouches for the achievability of the forecast.

Rule 202—Auditing Standards. A member shall not permit his name to be associated with financial statements in such a manner as to imply that he is acting as an independent public accountant unless he has complied with the applicable generally accepted auditing standards promulgated by the Institute. Statements on Auditing Standards issued by the Institute's Auditing Standards Executive Committee (Board) are, for purposes of this rule, considered to be interpretations of the generally accepted auditing standards, and departures from such statements must be justified by those who do not follow them.

Rule 203—Accounting Principles.   A member shall not express an opinion that financial statements are presented in conformity with generally accepted accounting principles if such statements contain any departure from an accounting principle promulgated by the body designated by Council to establish such principles which has a material effect on the statements taken as a whole, unless the member can demonstrate that due to unusual circumstances the financial statements would otherwise have been misleading. In such cases his report must describe the departure, the approximate effect thereof, if practicable, and the reasons why compliance with the principle would result in a misleading statement.

Rule 204—Other Technical Standards.   A member shall comply with other technical standards promulgated by bodies designated by Council to establish such standards, and departures therefrom must be justified by those who do not follow them.

ANALYSIS

Rule 201 is a comprehensive statement of general standards that accountants are expected to observe in all areas of practice. Upon analysis, you can see in Rule 201 elements of the generally accepted auditing standards and MAS practice standards that were discussed in Chapter 2. Rule 201 covers the *general standards* published by the AICPA for auditing and MAS practice and can be considered an expression of such standards for CPAs' tax practice. In the future, interpretation of the Rule 201 general standards can be expected from the Accounting and Review Services Committee, the Auditing Standards Board, and the MAS Executive Committee.

Rule 201 effectively prohibits the acceptance of any engagement that the CPA knows he or she cannot handle. Such engagements may involve audits that require extensive capability with computers—knowledge that the auditor may lack—or tax and management advisory services in areas unknown to the practitioner. This rule covers all areas of public accounting practice. Of course, a CPA may have to do some research to learn more about a unique problem or technique and may engage a colleague as a consultant.

Rule 201(*e*) reflects auditors' reluctance to be associated with future uncertainties. However, the rule limits association only to the extent of predictions about achievability. Several other varieties of associations short of asserting achievability are possible, and some CPA firms are moving into work related to published forecasts. Accountants in Great Britain currently offer reports on certain types of forecasts, and some aspects of this service are beginning to emerge in the United States.

Rule 202 simply requires adherence to applicable GAAS when issuing a report on financial statements. This rule does not prohibit association with unaudited financial statements of public companies. The rule refers to *applicable* GAAS, and the auditing standards pronouncements contain provisions governing association with unaudited financial statements. The practical effect of Rule 202 is merely to make noncompliance with auditing standards (in addition to the Rule 201 general standards) subject to disciplinary proceedings.

Changing times have complicated Rule 203. The rule was written when the FASB statements on accounting standards contained only standards for information required to be presented in conformity with GAAP. Now the FASB also issues statements that require supplementary information to be presented *outside* the basic financial statements (information about changing prices and certain oil and gas and other mineral reserve information). Rule 203 has been interpreted officially to apply only to FASB statements establishing accounting standards with respect to basic financial statements and *not* to FASB standards that require supplementary information to be presented outside the basic financial statements.

However, Rule 204 requires general compliance with other technical standards, and the AICPA has ruled that such standards regarding disclosure of information outside financial statements are made by the FASB. Furthermore, the Auditing Standards Board has authority under Rule 204 to establish standards for the responsibilities of members regarding this required supplementary information. Thus, Rule 203 and 204 in combination yield the following results:

☐ Audit opinions on conformity with GAAP can be given without qualification about departure from FASB statements requiring supplementary information outside the basic financial statements.

☐ Auditors must expand the audit report to call attention to the omission of supplementary information required by the FASB or material departures from FASB guidelines.

Otherwise, Rule 203 requires adherence to Accounting Research Bulletins of the Committee on Accounting Procedures (to 1959), Opinions of the Accounting Principles Board (1959–1973), and statements and interpretations of financial accounting standards adopted by the Financial Accounting Standards Board (1973 to present), with the important exception in unusual circumstances where adherence would create misleading statements. The rule itself admits that unusual circumstances may exist, permits auditors to decide for themselves the applicability of official pronouncements, and places on them the burden of an ethical decision. The rule is not strictly imperative because it allows auditors to exercise a utilitarian calculation for special circumstances. Rule 203 requires adherence to official pronouncements *unless* such adherence would be misleading. The consequences of misleading statements to outside decision makers would be financial harm, so presumably the greater good would be realized by explaining a departure and thereby "breaking the rule of officially promulgated accounting principles."

Rule 204 is a catch-all rule for enforcing standards other than the general auditing and accounting ones covered in Rules 201, 202 and 203. In addition to designating the Auditing Standards Board and the FASB as discussed above, Council of the AICPA has also designated the MAS Executive Committee and the Accounting and Review Services Committee as bodies having authority to promulgate standards enforceable under Rule 204 of the Code of Ethics.

RESPONSIBILITIES TO CLIENTS

A certified public accountant should be fair and candid with his clients and serve them to the best of his ability with professional concern for their best interests, consistent with his responsibilities to the public.

Rule 301—Confidential Client Information.   A member shall not disclose any confidential information obtained in the course of a professional engagement except with the consent of the client.

This rule shall not be construed (*a*) to relieve a member of his obligation under Rules 202 and 203, (*b*) to affect in any way his compliance with a validly issued subpoena or summons enforceable by order of a court, (*c*) to prohibit review of a member's professional practices as a part of voluntary quality review under Institute authorization, or (*d*) to preclude a member from responding to any inquiry made by the ethics division or Trial Board of the Institute, by a duly constituted investigative or disciplinary body of a state CPA society, or under state statutes.

Members of the ethics division and Trial Board of the Institute and professional practice reviewers under Institute authorization shall not disclose any confidential client information which comes to their attention from members in disciplinary proceedings or otherwise in carrying out their official responsibilities. However, this prohibition shall not restrict the exchange of information with an aforementioned duly constituted investigative or disciplinary body.

Rule 302-Contingent Fees.   Professional services shall not be offered or rendered under an arrangement whereby no fee will be charged unless a specified finding or result is attained, or where the fee is otherwise contingent upon the findings or results of such services. However, a member's fees may vary depending, for example, on the complexity of the service rendered.

Fees are not regarded as being contingent if fixed by courts or other public authorities or, in tax matters, if determined based on the results of judicial proceedings or the findings of governmental agencies.

ANALYSIS

Confidential information, according to Rule 301, is information that should not be disclosed to outside parties unless demanded by a court or an administrative body having subpoena or summons power. Privileged information, on the other hand, is information that cannot even be demanded by a court. Common-law privilege exists for husband-wife and attorney-client relationships, and physician-patient and priest-penitent relationships have obtained the privilege through state statutes. No confidential accountant-client privilege exists under federal law, and no state-created privilege has been recognized in federal courts. In all the recognized privilege relationships, the professional person is obligated to observe the privilege, which can be waived only by the client, patient, or penitent. (These persons are said to be the holders of the privilege.)

Accountants and clients, however, have attempted to establish accountants' work-product immunity for tax accrual workpapers from the reach of Internal Revenue Service summons demands. (Tax accrual workpapers contain accountants' analyses of "soft spots" and potential tax liability for questionable tax positions.) The IRS summoned such workpapers prepared by Arthur Young & Co. in its audit of Amerada Hess Corporation. The summons was challenged, and, after a Federal District Court ordered compliance, the Court of Appeals refused to enforce the summons on the grounds of public policy: The Court decided it better to deny IRS access to auditors' tax accrual workpapers than run the risk of "chilling" the communications about taxes between auditors and clients. (*U.S.* v. *Arthur Young,* 677 F.2d 211, 1982.) The U.S. Supreme Court disagreed, holding that auditors have a *public responsibility* transcending any employment relationship with the client, and their tax accrual workpapers are not protected by any form of work-product immunity from disclosure in response to IRS summons. (*U.S.* v. *Arthur Young,* SC 82–687, 1984.)

Rule 301 does not assume accountant-client relations to be privileged, although several states have statutes granting modified privilege. Few states extend the privilege to information gained during an audit engagement, and the AICPA *Code of Professional Ethics* specifically provides that the confidential relationship must not infringe upon auditors' independence and obligation to report fully and fairly on audited financial statements. Indeed, in the *U.S.* v. *Arthur Young* case mentioned above, the U.S. Supreme Court had this to say:

> The independent public accountant performing this [audit] function owes ultimate allegiance to the corporation's creditors and stockholders, as well as to [the] investing public. This "public watchdog" function demands that the accountant maintain total independence from the client at all times and requires complete fidelity to the public trust. To insulate from disclosure a certified public accountant's interpretations of the client's financial statements would be to ignore the significance of the accountant's role as a disinterested analyst charged with public obligations.
>
> . . . [The] independent certified public accountant cannot be content with the corporation's representations that its tax accrual reserves are adequate; the auditor is ethically and professionally obligated to ascertain for

himself as far as possible whether the corporation's contingent tax liabilities have been accurately stated. If the auditor were convinced that the scope of the examination had been limited by management's reluctance to disclose matters relating to the tax accrual reserves, the auditor would be unable to issue an unqualified opinion [on] the corporation's financial statements.

The rules of privileged and confidential communication are based on the premise that they facilitate a free flow of information between parties to the relationship. The nature of accounting services makes it necessary for the accountant to have access to information about salaries, products, contracts, merger or divestment plans, tax matters and other data required for the best possible professional work. Managers would be less likely to reveal such information if they could not trust the accountant to keep it confidential. If accountants were to reveal such information, the resultant reduction of the information flow might be undesirable, so no accountants should break the confidentiality rule without a good reason. According to the U.S. Supreme Court, the public policy implications of responding to an IRS summons is a good reason.

Of course, conflicts can arise. Information about past or near-future adverse financial events might be considered confidential by management. For example, management might not want to disclose the failure of a major investment which, if written off, would give signals to industry competitors. Auditors have no choice but to insist upon proper accounting or appropriate disclosure in their reports in keeping with the reporting requirements of generally accepted auditing standards.

Difficult problems arise over auditors' obligations to "blow the whistle" about clients' shady or illegal practices. Auditing standards deal with this problem: If a client refuses to accept an audit report that has been modified because of inability to obtain sufficient competent evidence about a suspected illegal act, failure to account for or disclose properly a material amount connected with an illegal act, or inability to estimate amounts involved in an illegal act, the audit firm should withdraw from the engagement and give the reasons in writing to the board of directors (AU 328.17). In such an extreme case, the withdrawal amounts to "whistle blowing," but the action results from the client's decision not to disclose the information. For all practical purposes, such information is not considered confidential because disclosure of it is necessary to make financial statements not misleading.

The Securities and Exchange Commission requires registered companies to explain reasons for changing auditors related to accounting measurement, disclosure and auditing disagreement. Conflicts over information thought to be confidential and auditors' whistle-blowing responsibility come to light through these means. Successor auditors ought to be well aware that the board of directors may have received written reasons for the previous auditor's withdrawal and should be sure to ask about the reasons.

Auditors are not, in general, legally *obligated* to blow the whistle on clients. However, circumstances may exist where auditors are legally *justified* in making disclosures to a regulatory agency or a third party. Such circumstances include: (1) when a client has intentionally and without authorization associated or involved a CPA in its misleading conduct, (2) when a client has distributed misleading draft financial statements prepared by a CPA for internal use only or (3) when a client prepares and distributes in an annual report or prospectus misleading information for which the CPA has not assumed any responsibility.[8]

CPAs should not view Rule 301 on confidential information as a license or excuse for inaction where action may be appropriate to right a wrongful act committed or about to be committed by a client. In some cases, auditors' inaction may be viewed as part of a conspiracy or willingness to be an accessory to a wrong. Such situations are dangerous and potentially damaging. A useful initial course of action is to consult with an attorney about possible legal pitfalls of both whistle blowing and silence.

Rule 302 prohibits fees contingent upon findings that are the product of an audit engagement. For example, a fee of $10,000 for each 1-cent-per-share income increase over last year's per share income, or a fee dependent upon approval of a bank loan based on audited financial statements, or a fee that cannot be paid unless an unqualified opinion is rendered are all considered contingent fees. The pressures on independence and the probable erosion of public confidence in such arrangements are reasons for this prohibition. However, a contingent fee based upon the ruling of a tax court or a renegotiation claim ruling is permitted because the basis for the contingency is not within the accountant's power and because in such cases the accountant is acting in the role of advocate. Fees that depend upon the number of hours or days worked or on technical qualifications of accountants are not considered contingent on the findings or results of audit services.

RESPONSIBILITIES TO COLLEAGUES

A certified public accountant should conduct himself in a manner which will promote cooperation and good relations among members of the profession.

In light of a numbering system for the Rules of Conduct and the existence of an essay about responsibilities to colleagues, you might wonder why no rule is numbered in the 400 series and why no rules deal directly with such responsibilities. The last rule in this section (Rule 401, which basically prohibited encroachment by one member on the clients and practice of another) was repealed by vote of the AICPA membership in

---

[8] The context of this analysis is more fully explained in: Chazen, Miller, and Solomon, "When the Rules Say: 'See Your Lawyer,'" *Journal of Accountancy,* January 1981, p. 70.

1979. The rule was then being challenged by the U.S. Department of Justice as an unwarranted restraint on competition.

The former rule was a rule of etiquette, dictating some desirable behavior. Now the only thing left in its place is an interpretation of Rule 201 ("Shopping for Accounting and Auditing Standards") which states that if a client of another public accounting firm requests a member to provide professional advice on accounting or auditing matters, the member must consult with the other accountant in order to ascertain that he (the member) is aware of all the relevant facts, keeping in mind that the client and the other accountant may have disagreed about some matter of accounting or auditing standards.

OTHER RESPONSIBILITIES AND PRACTICES

A certified public accountant should conduct himself in a manner which will enhance the stature of the profession and its ability to serve the public.

Rule 501—Acts Discreditable.   A member shall not commit an act discreditable to the profession.

Rule 502—Advertising and Other Forms of Solicitation.   A member shall not seek to obtain clients by advertising or other forms of solicitation in a manner that is false, misleading, or deceptive. Solicitation by the use of coercion, overreaching or harassing conduct is prohibited.

Rule 503—Commissions.   A member shall not pay a commission to obtain a client, nor shall he accept a commission for a referral to a client of products or services of others. This rule shall not prohibit payments for the purchase of an accounting practice or retirement payments to individuals engaged in the practice of public accounting or payments to their heirs or estates.

Rule 504—Incompatible Occupations.   A member who is engaged in the practice of public accounting shall not concurrently engage in any business or occupation which would create a conflict of interest in rendering professional services.

Rule 505—Form of Practice and Name.   A member may practice public accounting, whether as an owner or employee, only in the form of a proprietorship, a partnership or a professional corporation whose characteristics conform to resolutions of Council.

A member shall not practice under a firm name which includes any fictitious name, indicates specialization, or is misleading as to the type of organization (proprietorship, partnership, or corporation). However, names of one or more past partners or shareholders may be included in the firm name of a successor partnership or corporation. Also, a partner surviving the death or withdrawal of all other partners may continue practice under the partnership for up to two years after becoming a sole practitioner.

A firm may not designate itself as "Member of the American Institute of Certified Public Accountants" unless all of its partners or shareholders are members of the Institute.

ANALYSIS

Rule 501 may be called the *morals clause* of the code. It is seldom the basis for disciplinary action. Penalties normally are invoked under the AICPA Bylaws, which provide penalties for members found by a court to have committed any fraud, who have been convicted of any criminal offense, or who are found by the Trial Board (AICPA) to have been guilty of an act discreditable to the profession. Discreditable acts also include: (*a*) gross negligence in making, permitting others to make, or directing others to make false and misleading entries in financial statements and (*b*) employment discrimination on the basis of race, color, religion, sex, or national origin.

Rule 502 permits advertising with only a few limitations. Basic guidelines about advertising include:

1. Advertising should be informative and objective.
2. Advertising should be in good taste and professionally dignified.
3. No restrictions are placed on media, frequency, size, art or type style.
4. False, misleading or deceptive advertising is not in the public interest and is prohibited.

Rule 503 prohibits the payment or acceptance of commissions or referral fees for obtaining a client or sending a client to another professional. The intent of this rule is to eliminate payments that would not produce professional accounting services of direct benefit to clients. In 1984, the Ethics Division proposed to interpret the rule to permit acceptance of commissions for referring products or services to *nonclients*; for example, permitting commissions for referring a nonclient who invests in a tax shelter. (A *nonclient* was to be defined as someone who has not specifically engaged the CPA to perform audit, accounting, tax or MAS work.) However, the AICPA Council viewed this proposal as a move toward permitting accountants to mix commercial and brokerage business with accounting practice and ordered the Ethics Division not to issue the interpretation. The lesson of this episode is that the AICPA leaders think it best for accountants to avoid commercialism and limit their practices to public accounting for clients.

Rule 504 complements the rules on independence, integrity and objectivity by prohibiting concurrent work in another business or occupation that might damage auditors' objectivity. The AICPA has not produced extensive examples of other businesses or occupations that would or would not violate the rule. However, three rulings have identified certain conflict-of-interest occupations, namely: (1) serving as the state controller, (2) serving as a member of a municipal board of tax appeals and (3) serving as a bank director whose accounting clients have loans with the bank. Otherwise, each CPA must decide about incompatible occupation circumstances on a case-by-case basis.

Rule 505 allows members to practice in any form of organization but with severe limitations on the characteristics of the corporate form. These limitations preserve the *substance* of a partnership within the *form* of an incorporated practice. In brief, the rules provide: (*a*) Impersonal or fictitious company names cannot be used; (*b*) Services incompatible with public accounting practice cannot be provided; (*c*) Shareholders must be engaged in the practice of public accounting; (*d*) Shares can only be held by, or transferred to, persons engaged in the practice of public accounting; (*e*) The principal executive shall be a stockholder and director, and non-CPAs shall not exercise any authority over professional matters; (*f*) The AICPA Rules of Conduct are applicable and (g) Stockholders shall be individually and jointly liable for the acts of the corporation. (See ET Appendix C for details.)

The last paragraph of Rule 505 effectively blocks persons who are not CPAs from being designated as general partners or shareholders. (A person cannot be a member of the AICPA unless he or she is a CPA.) This rule section creates problems for tax and management advisory services personnel who are not CPAs. They cannot be admitted to full partnerships or become shareholders without causing the other partners who are CPAs to be in violation of the rule. Thus, a firm may employ non-CPAs who are high on the organization chart, but these persons may not be unrestricted partners under current rules.

Summary: AICPA Rules and Ethical Principles

Specific rules in the AICPA Rules of Conduct may not necessarily be classified under one of the ethics principles. Decisions based on a rule may involve imperative, utilitarian, or generalization considerations, or elements of all three. The rules have the form of imperative because that is the nature of the code. However, elements of utilitarianism and generalization seem to be apparent in the underlying rationale for most of the rules. If this perception is accurate, then these two principles may be utilized by auditors in difficult decision problems where adherence to a rule would produce an undesirable result.

THE SEC ON INDEPENDENCE

The Securities and Exchange Commission was established in 1934 to administer the Securities Act of 1933, the Securities Exchange Act of 1934, and several other regulatory acts. In addition to administrative powers, the SEC also has rule-making and judicial powers. The SEC relies heavily on the accounting profession and has a great interest in auditing standards and standards of professional conduct.

The SEC rule on independence is contained in Rule 2-01(*b*) of *Regulation S-X*. Except for differences in the choice of words, the content of the SEC rule appears to be very similar to Rule 101 of the AICPA rules of conduct. The SEC and AICPA define "member" (auditor) essentially the same with reference to independence matters. However, these surface similarities mask some substantive differences in the way the two agencies interpret their rules. The main differences are in the areas of bookkeeping, family relations, financial interests and retired partners.

Bookkeeping The SEC prohibits the combination of bookkeeping (accounting)and auditing services. The AICPA does not consider independence impaired if an accountant first prepares the client's books and then audits the financial statements prepared from them. However, the client must be able to accept responsibility for accounting decisions and for the financial statements. The SEC views the two services as incompatible, believing that an auditor cannot appear to be independent when auditing the bookkeeping work he or she has done. Even CPA's keeping clients' books by offering computerized accounting services impairs independence in SEC eyes. However, exceptions can be made in the case of emergency, in other unusual situations, and when computer services are merely routine, mechanical and of short duration—all situations where the auditor does not take over management's accounting responsibilities.

Family Relations The SEC tends to go further than the AICPA in attributing family relations to a "member." The SEC considers independence impaired in most cases when a spouse, dependent person or nondependent close relative (children, brothers, sisters, grandparents, parents, parents-in-law, and their respective spouses) has direct or material indirect financial interests or managerial relationships in an audit client. The AICPA makes allowance for the "audit sensitivity" of a relative's employment, letting independence be considered intact if the position is not sensitive. However, the AICPA interpretations warn members to be aware of the appearances no matter what the specific facts may be. Overall, the AICPA position appears to be flexible and permits assessment of the circumstances in each case. In contrast, the SEC position tends to prohibit most relationships involving relatives, especially when the relative holds an executive position or is in a position to mold the shape of the financial statements.

Financial Interest The SEC tends to be stricter than AICPA on matters of prohibited indirect financial interests. The tendency is to be conservative and to consider that most financial relationships, investments in concert with client's officers and directors, and other joint business ventures as impairments of independence.

Retired Partners The SEC is stricter than AICPA about the effect of a retired or resigned partner's association with his or her former firm's appearance of independence. Broadly, the SEC considers the firm's independence impaired if: (*a*) A retired partner who was closely associated with an audit becomes a director of the auditee within two years after retirement; (*b*) A retired partner who was "prominent in his former firm" becomes a director of a client of his former firm within five years; or (*c*) A retired or resigned partner becomes an executive of a client of his former firm without a total separation, including settlement of retirement benefits, from his former firm. But retired partners can become directors of auditees and still receive retirement benefits from the accounting firm so long as the benefits were fixed at the time of retirement. The AICPA requires only that retired partners involved with clients must not be active in, or associated with, his former firm, and that fees the accounting firm receives from such a client must not have a material effect on the partner's retirement benefits.

SEC Views The SEC has emphasized an important facet of factual independence saying: "Perhaps the most critical test of the actuality of an accountant's independence is the strength of his insistence upon full disclosure of transactions between the company and members of its management as individuals; accession to the wishes of management in such cases must inevitably raise a serious question [of] whether the accountant is, in fact, independent." The AICPA rules do not contain emphasis on this point.

SEC interpretations on independence are made by staff members in the Office of the Chief Accountant. In the past, accountants presented fact situations and requested decisions about their independence in a particular situation. The staff prepared letters expressing case-specific conclusions. Periodically, some of these conclusions were compiled and published. At present, they can be found in *Financial Reporting Release No. 1*, section 602, published by the SEC. These case decisions are used by accountants as analogies to new fact situations and as guides to figuring out the SEC position.

Accountants are always welcome to submit their independence questions to the chief accountant for a decision. It is much better to settle a question before an audit is conducted than to have an issue of independence raised later. Accountants' letters describing fact situations and letters containing SEC conclusions are available to the public on request.

INDEPENDENCE MAS in public accounting practice defies definition because the field is so
ISSUES diverse. MAS includes information systems design, financial analysis, cost accounting studies and operations research to name a few. Many of
Independence and the largest CPA firms offer as varied a range of services as the financial
Management and operations research departments of large corporations and the non-
Advisory Services CPA management consulting firms themselves. Accountants are justifiably proud of being able to serve business on such a wide scale.

However, some critics have suggested that accounting firms may get so involved in the business of giving managerial advice that they loose their independent perspective in the audit function. Often, this criticism is raised as a question of the "compatibility of MAS and independence." All accountants and critics agree that when an accounting firm becomes too closely identified with managerial decisions and interests, the appearance of independence for audit purposes can be impaired.

The Standards for MAS Practice deal with matters of independence by warning MAS practitioners not to assume the role of management. Services should be limited to objective research, analysis, advice or technical assistance. MAS practitioners must not make decisions for management, act in a capacity equivalent to a member of management or otherwise employ or take any positions that might impair the MAS practitioner's objectivity.

To analyze the independence issues involved when MAS work is performed by the same firm that does the audit, you need to understand the process of managerial decision making. This method is much the same as the scientific method described in Chapter 1.

1. A manager must recognize a problem situation or a potential problem that demands a solution.
2. A manager must define the problem and seek out alternative courses of action.
3. A manager must assess the costs and benefits of each of the alternative solutions.
4. A manager must estimate the subjective probabilities of success of each alternative, thus allowing calculation of expected costs and benefits.
5. A manager must then choose one alternative solution.
6. Finally, a manager must implement, supervise and control the operation of the alternative.

All management consulting activities involve some of the above managerial functions. The important question relative to audit independence is how far auditors can go and still not be too closely identified with management. No accountant who wants to maintain independence would perform steps 5 and 6. Choice and implementation are clearly the responsibilities of management. On the other hand, a large number of accountants (and critics) would go as far as step 3—allowing problem identification, definition of alternatives, and assessment of costs and benefits. Steps 3 and 4 are the gray areas. Once the probabilities of success are estimated, the cost-benefit data then generally point to the most profitable alternative. Exercise of step 4 effectively makes the choice, according to some. According to others, too many "nonquantifiables" still exist to say that the estimation of probabilities amounts to the same thing as choice.

In response to public and congressional pressure, however, the AICPA has taken steps to prohibit certain management advisory services. A firm that is a member of the SEC Practice Section commits itself not to perform advisory services that:

□ Would create a loss of the firm's independence for the purpose of expressing opinions on financial statements of such clients.

□ Are predominantly commercial in character and inconsistent with the firm's professional status as CPAs.

□ Consist of the following types of services:
    Psychological testing.
    Public opinion polls.
    Merger and acquisition assistance for a finder's fee.

The controversy came to a head in 1978–79, and the Public Oversight Board of the SEC Practice Section conducted public hearings to investigate. The POB decided that no evidence indicated the need for further proscriptions of MAS services provided to audit clients. The SEC (still sensitive to the issue) has suggested that the board of directors or the audit committee ought to take responsibility for deciding whether MAS services provided by the auditing firm impairs their auditor's independence and approve the rendering of such services.

Independence and Tax Advisory Services

Rule 102 effectively defines tax advisors as *advocates* of reasonably supportable positions taken by taxpayer-clients. All other ethics rules that do not refer specifically to the audit function, however, are equally applicable to the accountant in the role of tax practitioner. In addition, the AICPA series entitled "Statements on Responsibilities in Tax Practice" defines specific behavior criteria for tax practice. Generally, these statements set forth the dimensions of accountants' responsibilities for fair dealing in the complex area of tax practice.

Perhaps the most relevant observation for an auditing textbook is that the preparer's signature at the bottom of a tax return does not represent an audit opinion. The declaration on the tax return reads as follows:

> Under penalties of perjury, I declare that I have examined this return, including accompanying schedules and statements, and to the best of my knowledge and belief it is true, correct, and complete. Declaration of preparer (other than taxpayer) is based on all information of which he has any knowledge.

Accountants are not obligated to perform an audit in order to sign a tax return as preparer. However, they cannot close their eyes to unreasonable or contradictory data that place taxpayer-provided information in doubt. Sufficient inquiries to resolve reasonable doubts are expected of a careful tax accountant.

Audits of tax returns are performed by Internal Revenue Service auditors. The IRS may select returns with certain signal characteristics (for example, large charitable deductions relative to income) and ask the taxpayer to show evidence to support the deduction. IRS agents epitomize independence from their "clients." Their methods of gathering evidence in the normal investigation do not differ from the methods of other auditors, but IRS agents may be armed with special investigative powers to pursue cases of suspected fraud and concealment. In this respect, they are quite different from other auditors.

Public accountants who perform both tax and audit services for the same client have a dual role as advocate and independent auditor. In some engagements, auditors prepare the client's tax return, thus establishing amounts for tax expenses and tax liability in the financial statements under audit. Clearly, this dual service can result in auditors auditing their own tax work. If accountants are acting as advocates for allowance of a controversial deduction (thus a lower tax liability), they must somehow take into account as auditors the probability that some part of the deduction may be disallowed by IRS. It is not easy (some would say impossible) to serve two masters—the taxpayer-client and the users of published financial statements. Some writers have suggested auditors should exercise considerable care to reflect the possibility of a deficiency assessment in the tax liability account while at the same time advocating the validity of the tax item in question in the tax return.

SUMMARY

Professional ethics for accountants is not simply a matter covered by a few rules in a formal *Code of Ethics*. Concepts of proper professional conduct permeate all areas of practice. Ethics, and its accompanying disciplinary potential, are the foundation for public accountants' self-regulatory efforts. Criticism of the profession—the quality of practice and manner of conduct—has led to an elaborate system of AICPA Division for Firms membership, peer review and a heightened concentration on high-quality performance.

Your knowledge of principles in ethics—the imperative, the utilitarian and generalization—will help you when making decisions about conduct and its relation to the AICPA rules of conduct. This structured approach to thoughtful decisions is important not only when you are employed in public accounting but also when you work in government, industry and education. The ethics rules may appear to be restrictive, but they are intended for the benefit of the public as well as for the discipline of CPAs.

Public accountants must be careful in all areas of practice. The SEC views on ethics rules differ in several respects from the AICPA views. Also, auditors need to be especially careful when performing tax advocacy and management advisory services for audit clients. These areas of practice offer pitfalls for auditors' independence.

As an accountant, you must not lose sight of the nonaccountants' perspective. No matter how complex or technical a decision may be, a simplified view of it always tends to cut away the details of special technical issues to get directly to the heart of the matter. A sense of professionalism coupled with a sensitivity to the impact of decisions on other people are invaluable in the practice of accounting and auditing.

SOURCES AND ADDITIONAL READING REFERENCES

Bolton, S. E., and J. H. Crockett, Jr. "Are Auditors Independent?" *Financial Analysts Journal,* November/December 1979, pp. 76–78.

Brenner, S. N., and E. A. Molander. "Is the Ethics of Business Changing?" *Harvard Business Review,* January/February 1977, pp. 57–71.

Burton, John C. "A Critical Look at Professionalism and Scope of Services." *Journal of Accountancy,* April 1980, pp. 48–57.

Burton, John C., ed. *Corporate Financial Reporting: Ethical and Other Problems.* New York: American Institute of Certified Public Accountants, 1972.

Carmichael, D. R., and R. J. Sweiringa. "Compatibility of Auditing Independence and Management Services—An Identification of Issues." *Accounting Review,* October 1968, pp. 697–706.

Cook, J. M., and H. G. Robinson. "Peer Review—The Accounting Profession's Program." *CPA Journal,* March 1979, pp. 11–16.

Cowen, Scott S. "Nonaudit Services: How Much is Too Much?" *Journal of Accountancy,* December 1980, pp. 51–56.

Fletcher, Joseph. *Situation Ethics.* Philadelphia: Westminster Press, 1966.

Goldman, A., and B. Barlev. "The Auditor-Firm Conflict of Interests: Its Implications for Independence." *Accounting Review,* October 1974, pp. 707–18.

Hanson, R. E. and W. J. Brown. "CPA's Workpapers: The IRS Zeros In." *Journal of Accountancy,* July 1981, pp. 68–77.

Hartley, R. V. and T. L. Ross. "MAS and Audit Independence: An Image Problem." *Journal of Accountancy,* November 1972, pp. 42–52.

Hoyle, Joe. "Mandatory Auditor Rotation: The Arguments and the Alternative." *Journal of Accountancy,* May 1978, pp. 69–78.

Larson, Rholan E. "Self-Regulation: A Professional Step Forward." *Journal of Accountancy,* September 1983, pp. 58–67.

Lavin, David. "Perceptions of the Independence of the Auditor." *Accounting Review,* January 1976, pp. 41–50.

Mautz, R. K., and Hussein A. Sharaf. *The Philosophy of Auditing.* American Accounting Association monograph no. 6, especially chap. 8, "Independence" and chap. 9, "Ethical Conduct," American Accounting Assn., 1961.

Mautz, Robert K. "Self-Regulation: Perils and Problems" *Journal of Accountancy,* May 1983, pp. 76–85.

Mead, George. "Auditing, Management Advisory Services, Social Service, and the Profit Motive." *Accounting Review,* October 1960, pp. 659–66.

Raby, William L. "Ethics in Tax Practice." *Accounting Review,* October 1966, pp. 714–20.

————. "Advocacy versus Independence in Tax Liability Accrual." *Journal of Accountancy,* March 1972, pp. 40–47.

Reports, Accounting and Management Subcommittee of the U.S. Senate Committee on Government Operations, 95th Congress, 1st session, Document no. 95–34. *The Accounting Establishment.* Washington, D.C.: U.S. Government Printing Office, March 31, 1977.

Shockley, Randolph A. "Perceptions of Audit Independence: A Conceptual Model." *Journal of Accounting, Auditing and Finance,* Winter 1982, pp. 126–143.

Singer, Marcus G. *Generalization in Ethics.* New York: Antheneum Publishers, 1961, 1971.

Thomas, Barbara S. "SEC Oversight Role in Self-Regulation." *CPA Journal,* May 1983, pp. 10–15.

Weygandt, Jerry J. "The CPA and His Duty to Silence." *Accounting Review,* January 1970, pp. 60–75.

Wheelwright, Philip. *A Critical Introduction to Ethics.* Indianapolis, Ind.: Odyssey Press, 1959.

Wilcox, Edward B. "Ethics: The Profession on Trial." *Journal of Accountancy,* November 1955, pp. 72–79.

Windal, F. W., and R. N. Corley. *The Accounting Profession: Ethics, Responsibility and Liability.* Englewood Cliffs, N.J.: Prentice-Hall, 1980, 456 pages.

REVIEW QUESTIONS

3.1. What organizations and agencies have rules of conduct you must observe when practicing public accounting? Internal auditing? Management accounting?

3.2. What penalties can be imposed by AICPA and the state societies on CPAs in their "self-regulation" of ethics code violators?

3.3. What penalties can be imposed by public regulatory agencies on CPAs who violate rules of conduct?

3.4. During 1976–1978, a series of events occurred involving criticism of the accounting profession and the AICPA's responses. What was the chronology of these events and responses?

3.5. What benefit does an independent auditor gain when a client corporation has an audit committee of the board of directors?

3.6. What *roles* must a professional accountant be prepared to occupy in regard to ethical decision problems?

3.7. What are the steps of the decision process called *reflective choice?*

3.8. Why might the rule "Let conscience be your guide" not be sufficient basis for your personal ethics decisions? For your professional ethics decisions?

3.9. Assume that you accept the following ethical rule: "Failure to tell the whole truth is wrong." In the textbook illustrations about (*a*) your position as a bank director and (*b*) your knowledge of the cashier's forgeries, what would this rule require you to do? Why is an unalterable rule like this classed as an element of *imperative* ethical theory?

3.10. How does *utilitarian* ethics differ from *imperative* ethics theory?

3.11. Which of the AICPA Rules of Conduct apply to a member: (*a*) in tax practice, (*b*) in management advisory services practice, (*c*) in practice exclusively outside the United States, and (*d*) who is not engaged in the practice of public accounting (for example, an internal auditor, GAO auditor, IRS agent)?

3.12. What ethical responsibilities do members of the AICPA have for acts of nonmembers who are under their supervision (for example, recent college graduates who are not yet CPAs)?

3.13. Is an incorporated accounting practice substantially different from an accounting practice organized in the form of a partnership?

3.14. Compare the AICPA and SEC views on independence. How are they similar? How do they differ?

3.15. What are the six phases of the managerial decision process? Why should accountants in public practice be concerned with this kind of decision process?

EXERCISES AND PROBLEMS

3.16. **General Ethics**
Is there any moral difference between a disapproved action in which you are caught and the same action that never becomes known to anyone else? Do many persons in business and professional society make a distinction between these two circumstances? If you respond that *you* do (or do not) perceive a difference while *persons in business and professional society* do not (or do), then how do you explain the differences in attitudes?

3.17. **Ethics Decision Problem**
You are treasurer of a church. A member approaches you with the following proposition: "I will donate stock to the church on October 15 if, on October 16, you will sell it back to me. All you will have to do is convey the certificate with your signature to me in return for my check, which will be for the asking price of the stock quoted that day without reduction for commissions."

The member's objective, of course, is to obtain the income tax deduction for the value of the stock on October 15, but he wants to maintain his ownership interest. The policy of the church board is not to hold any stock but to sell shares within a reasonably short time.

Consider:

1. Should the treasurer accommodate the member? Would you if you were treasurer?

2. Would your considerations and conclusions be any different if:

   a. The church were financially secure and the gift were small in amount?

   b. The church were financially secure and the gift were large?

   c. The church would be in a deficit position for the year were it not for this gift?

3.18. **Ethics Relating to Financial Forecasts**
Is the AICPA prohibition (Rule 201(*e*)) of vouching for the achievability of a forecast a complete prohibition of an accountant's association with forecasts of financial results? What are the ethical theory reasons underlying the existence of Rule 201(*e*)? (Hint: Try the steps of reflective choice using a utilitarian theory as a guide.)

3.19. **Ethics Relating to MAS Practice**
Your client, Newsell Corporation, requested that you conduct a feasibility study to advise management of the best way the corporation can utilize electronic data processing equipment and which computer, if any, best meets the corporation's requirements. You are technically competent in this area and accept the engagement. Upon completion of your study, the corporation accepts your suggestions and installs the computer and related equipment that you recommended.

Required:
Discuss the effect acceptance of this management advisory services engagement would have upon your independence in expressing an opinion on the financial statements of Newsell Corporation.

(*AICPA* adapted)

3.20. **Independence, Integrity and Objectivity Cases**
Knowledge of the rules of conduct and interpretations thereof on independence, in-

tegrity and objectivity is necessary for adequate responses to the following cases. For each case, state whether the action or situation shows violation of the AICPA Code of Ethics, explain why, and cite the relevant rule, interpretation or ruling.

a. CPA Eldora Schwartz performs the audit of the local symphony society. Because of her good work, she was elected an honorary member of the board of directors.

b. Alex Pratt, a retired partner of your CPA firm, has just been appointed to the board of directors of Palmer Corporation, your firm's client. Pratt is also an ex officio member of your firm's income tax advisory committee which meets monthly to discuss income tax problems of the partnership's clients, some of which are competitors of Palmer Corporation. The partnership pays Pratt $100 for each committee meeting attended and a monthly retirement benefit, fixed by a retirement plan policy, of $1,000.

(*AICPA* adapted)

c. CPA K. Boney performs significant day-to-day bookkeeping services for Harper Corporation and supervises the work of the one part-time bookkeeper employed by Marvin Harper. This year Marvin wants to engage CPA Boney to perform an audit.

d. CPA Jacque's wife owns 20 percent of the common stock of Botacel Co., which wants Jacque to perform the audit for 1985.

e. Jacque's wife gave her stock to their 10-year-old daughter on July 1, 1985.

f. Jacque's daughter, acting through an appropriate custodian, sold the stock to her grandfather on August 1, 1985. His purchase, as an accommodation, took one half of his retirement savings.

g. Jacque's father managed to sell the stock on August 15 to his brother who lives in Brazil. The brother fled there 20 years ago and has not returned since.

h. Clyde Kaye is a manager in the Boston office of a large national CPA firm. His wife Bonnie is assistant controller in ATC Corp., a client of the firm whose audit is performed by the New York office. Bonnie and Clyde live in Rhode Island and commute to their respective workplaces.

i. Clyde Kaye just received word that he has been admitted to the partnership.

j. The Rockhard Savings Association, a client of your firm, privately told your local managing partner that a block of funds would be set aside for home loans for qualified new employees. Rockhard's president is well aware that your firm experiences some difficulty hiring good people in the midsize but growing community and is willing to do what he can to help while mortgage money is so tight. Several new assistant accountants obtained home loans under this arrangement.

3.21. **Independence, Integrity and Objectivity Cases**

Knowledge of the rules of conduct, interpretations thereof, and related rulings on independence, integrity and objectivity is necessary for adequate responses to the following cases. For each case, state whether the action or situation shows violation of the AICPA Code of Ethics, explain why, and cite the relevant rule, interpretation, or ruling.

a. Your client, Contrary Corporation, is very upset over the fact that your audit last year failed to detect an $800,000 inventory overstatement caused by employee theft and falsification of the records. The board discussed the matter and authorized its attorneys to explore the possibility of a lawsuit for damages.

b. Contrary Corporation filed a lawsuit alleging negligent audit work seeking $1 million in damages.

c. In response to the lawsuit by Contrary, you decided to start litigation against certain officers of the company alleging management fraud and deceit. You are asking for a damage judgment of $500,000.

d. The Allright Insurance Company paid Contrary Corporation $700,000 under fidelity bonds covering the employees involved in the inventory theft. Both you and Contrary Corporation have dropped your lawsuits. However, under subrogation rights, Allright has sued your audit firm for damages on the grounds of negligent performance of the audit.

e. Your audit client, Science Tech, Inc., installed a cost accounting system devised by the management advisory services department of your firm. The system failed to account properly for certain product costs (according to management), and the system had to be discontinued. Science Tech management was very dissatisfied and filed a lawsuit demanding return of the $10,000 MAS fee. The audit fee is normally about $50,000, and $10,000 is not an especially large amount for your firm. However, you believe that Science Tech management operated the system improperly. While you are willing to do further MAS work at a reduced rate to make the system operate, you are unwilling to return the entire $10,000 fee.

f. A group of dissident shareholders filed a class-action lawsuit against both you and your client, Amalgamated, Inc., for $30 million. They allege there was a conspiracy to present misleading financial statements in connection with a recent merger.

g. CPA Anderson, a shareholder in the firm of Anderson, Olds and Watershed, P.C. (a professional accounting corporation) owns 25 percent of the common stock of Dove Corporation (not a client of AO&W). This year Dove purchased a 32 percent interest in Tale Co. and is accounting for the investment using the equity method of accounting. The investment amounts to 11 percent of Tale's consolidated net assets. Tale Co. has been an audit client of AO&W for 12 years.

h. Ready and Able, CPAs, regularly perform the audit of the First National Bank, and the firm is preparing for the audit of the financial statements for the year ended December 31, 1985.

    1. Two directors of the First National Bank became partners in Ready and Able, CPAs, on July 1, 1985, resigning their directorships on that date. They will not participate in the audit.

    2. During 1985, the former controller of the First National Bank, now a partner of Ready and Able, was frequently called upon for assistance regarding loan approvals and the bank's minimum checking account policy. In addition, he conducted computer feasibility study for First National.

    (AICPA adapted)

i. The Moore Corporation is indebted to a CPA for unpaid fees and has offered to give the CPA unsecured interest-bearing notes. Alternatively, Moore Corporation offered to give two shares of its common stock, after which 10,002 shares would be outstanding.

    (AICPA adapted)

j. Robert Binkheart is not yet a CPA but is doing quite well in his first employment with a large CPA firm. He's been on the job two years and has become a "heavy junior." If he passes the CPA exam in November, he'll be promoted to senior accountant. This month, during the audit of Row Lumber Co., Robert told the controller about how he is remodeling an old house. The controller likes Robert and had a load of needed materials delivered to the house, billing Robert at a 70 percent discount—a savings over the normal cash discount of about $300. Robert paid the bill and was happy to have the materials that he otherwise could not afford on his meager salary.

k. CPA Bonnie Roberts inherited $1 million from her grandfather, $100,000 of which was the value of stock in the Madison National Bank. Bonnie practices accounting in Madison, and several of her audit clients have loans from the bank.

l. Groaner Corp. is in financial difficulty. You are about to sign the report on the 1985 audit when your firm's office manager informs you the audit fee for 1984 has not yet been paid.

m. Your audit client, Glow Co., is opening a plant in a distant city. Glow's president asks that your firm's office in that city recruit and hire a new plant controller and a cost accountant.

3.22. **General and Technical Rule Cases**

Knowledge of the rules of conduct, interpretations thereof, and related rulings and resolutions of Council related to general and technical standards is necessary for adequate responses to the following cases. For each case, state whether the action or situation shows violation of the AICPA Code of Ethics, explain why, and cite the relevant rule, interpretation or ruling.

a. CPA I. May helped Price Corporation prepare a cash flow forecast of hospital operations. The forecast was presented by May at a city council hearing for approval under the city's health services ordinance. May's report, which accompanied the forecast, consisted entirely of a full description of the sources of information used and the major assumptions made.

b. Durwood Short of Short & Sharp, CPAs, received a telephone call from his friend Dan, who is financial vice president of Langhorn Auto Parts. Langhorn distributes parts over a wide area and does about $40 million in business a year. Langhorn is not a client but is audited by Olds & Watershed, CPAs, a venerable firm in the city. "Dur" has been hoping Dan would switch auditors. Today Dan wants to get Dur's opinion about accounting for lease capitalizations of a particularly complicated agreement with franchise dealers. Dur makes notes and promises to call Dan tomorrow.

c. CPA Summers gave a clean opinion on the financial statements of Kathy Korp. The annual report document did not contain the supplementary changing prices disclosures required by SFAS 33.

d. "Razor" Tabor is a former university football player. Razor is a CPA who works for Aggregate Corp., which owns controlling interests in 42 other corporations. Anna Fowl, president of Aggregate, has assigned Razor the task of performing audits of these corporations and submitting audit opinions directly to her for later presentation to the board of directors.

e. CPA Kellog audits the Huber Hope Co. Huber's controller, also a CPA, has conducted his own audit of Little Hope, Inc., Huber's single subsidiary which amounts to one tenth of the total assets, revenue, and income of the consolidated entity. Kellog has written an audit report which carefully explains reliance on "part of examination made by other independent auditors" (SAS 1, AU 543), with added language to explain the controller's role.

f. The Lowell Corporation, a public company, issued quarterly financial statements which were unaudited. On the back page of the small brochure containing these statements was a list of the board of directors and the names of the company's underwriters and auditors, Dietrich and Deitrick. No statement or report by D & D appeared in the brochure.

g. CPA Welch and K. D. Larnof are part-
    ners in an accounting-MAS practice.
    Larnof is not a CPA. Their work for the
    Deeken Company included both a pen-
    sion plan analysis (performed by
    Larnof) and an audit (performed by
    Welch and several assistants). Welch
    prepared an unqualified audit report,
    signing it first with the partnership
    name—Welch & Larnof—and below
    with her own name—Irma Welch,
    CPA.

3.23. **Confidentiality and Contingent Fee Cases**
    Knowledge of the rules of conduct, interpre-
    tations thereof, and related rulings on confi-
    dential client information and contingent
    fees is necessary for adequate responses to
    the following cases. For each case, state
    whether the action or situation shows viola-
    tion or potential for violation of the AICPA
    Code of Ethics, explain why, and cite the
    relevant rule, interpretation or ruling.

    a. CPA Sally Black has discovered a way
        to eliminate most of the boring work of
        processing routine accounts receivable
        confirmations by contracting with the
        Jones Mail Service. After the auditor
        has prepared the confirmations, Jones
        will stuff them in envelopes, mail them,
        receive the return replies, open the re-
        plies, and return them to Sally.

    b. Cadentoe Corporation, without consult-
        ing its CPA, has changed its accounting
        so that it is not in conformity with gen-
        erally accepted accounting principles.
        During the regular audit engagement,
        the CPA discovers that the statements
        based on the accounts are so grossly
        misleading that they might be consid-
        ered fraudulent. CPA Kellner resigns
        the engagement after a heated argu-
        ment. Kellner knows that the state-
        ments will be given to Gary Richard, his
        friend at the Last National Bank, and
        knows that Gary is not a very astute
        reader of complicated financial state-
        ments. Two days later, Richard calls
        Kellner and asks some general ques-

tions about Cadentoe's statements and
remarks favorably on the very thing
that is misrepresented. Kellner corrects
the erroneous analysis, and Gary is
very much surprised.

c. A CPA who had reached retirement age
    arranged for the sale of his practice to
    another certified public accountant.
    Their agreement called for the transfer
    of all working papers and business cor-
    respondence to the accountant purchas-
    ing the practice.

d. Martha Jacoby, CPA, withdrew from
    the audit of Harvard Company after dis-
    covering irregularities in Harvard's in-
    come tax returns. One week later, Ms.
    Jacoby was telephoned by Jake Henry,
    CPA, who explained that he had just
    been retained by Harvard Company to
    replace Ms. Jacoby. Mr. Henry asked
    Ms. Jacoby why she withdrew from the
    Harvard engagement. She told him.

e. Caroline Daniel, CPA, is approached by
    a prospective tax client who promises
    to pay a fee of "4 percent of whatever
    amount you save me in taxes." She ac-
    cepted the arrangement.

f. David Moore, CPA, offers a consulting
    service to clients in which he reviews
    their needs for computer-related sup-
    plies (magnetic tapes, disks, cards, pa-
    per, and so on) and places their orders
    with Computographics, Inc. This sup-
    plier offers a special discount price be-
    cause of the volume of business gener-
    ated by Moore. David is considering
    two alternative billing arrangements:

    (1) Charge the clients no fee and in-
         stead accept a 3 percent commis-
         sion from Computographics, Inc.

    (2) Charge his regular consulting rate
         of $60 per hour.

3.24. **Other Responsibilities and Practices Cases**
    Knowledge of the rules of conduct, interpre-
    tations thereof, and related rulings on vari-
    ous other responsibilities and practices is
    necessary for adequate responses to the fol-

lowing cases. For each case, state whether the action or situation shows violation or potential for violation of the AICPA Code of Ethics, explain why and cite the relevant rule, interpretation or ruling.

a. CPA Whitney completed a review of the unaudited financial statements of Kay Gifts. Ms. Kay was very displeased with the report. An argument ensued, and she told Whitney never to darken her door again. Two days later, she telephoned Whitney and demanded he return: (1) Kay's cash disbursement journal, (2) Whitney's working paper schedule of adjusting journal entries, (3) Whitney's inventory analysis working papers, and (4) all other working papers prepared by Whitney. Since Kay had not yet paid her bill, Whitney replied that state law gave him a lien on all the records and he would return them as soon as she paid his fee.

b. The CPA firm of Foot & Counts had received promissory notes in payment of the Henshaw Hacksaw Co. tax return preparation fee. Six months after the notes were due, CPA Counts notified Dave Henshaw that the notes had been turned over to the National Bank for collection.

c. CPA Whitman has been invited to conduct a course in effective tax planning for the City Chamber of Commerce. The C. of C. president said a brochure would be mailed to members giving the name of Whitman's firm, his educational background and degrees held, professional society affiliations, and testimonials from participants in the course held last year comparing his excellent performance with other CPAs who have offered competing courses in the city.

d. CPA Gillen is a member of the State Bar. Her practice is a combination of law and accounting, and she is heavily involved in estate planning engagements. Her letterhead gives the affiliations: Member, State Bar of _____, and Member, AICPA.

e. The CPA firm of Baker & Baker has made a deal with White & Co., a firm of management consulting specialists, for mutual business advantage. B & B agreed to recommend White to clients who need management consulting services. White agreed to recommend B & B to clients who need improvements in their accounting systems. During the year, both firms would keep records of fees obtained by these mutual referrals. At the end of the year, White and B & B would settle the net difference based on a referral rate of 5 percent of fees.

f. Sturm & Drang, CPAs, conduct an aggressive, growing practice in Middle City. The firm pays 20 percent of first-year fees to any staff member (below partner) who brings in a new client.

g. Sarah Ehlan and Elizabeth Hughes, both CPAs, have engaged in the practice of public accounting in Big City since 1974. Their practice consisted of 50 percent audit work, 10 percent tax work, and 40 percent consulting, mainly in the area of pension and employee benefit plans. Their staff has grown to a complement of 40 professionals.

The consulting business is quite profitable, and in a move to expand, Sarah and Elizabeth plan to buy the computer programs, library, and other assets and assume the employment contracts of 15 persons, all of which constitute the actuarial and compensation services of an insurance brokerage firm. They plan to merge these services into their existing consulting practice. None of the new employees will be partners of the firm.

Before this investment is completed, they wish to have an authoritative opinion on whether their plan would put them in the position of engaging in an occupation incompatible with the practice of public accounting.

h. Jack Robinson and Archie Robertson

(both CPAs) are not partners, but they have the same office, the same employees, a joint bank account, and they work together on audits. A letterhead they use shows both their names and the description "Members, AICPA."

i. CPA Dewey retired from the firm of Dewey & Cheatham. One year later, D & C merged practices with Howe & Co., to form a regional firm under the name of Dewey, Cheatham & Howe, Co.

j. CPA Krock is the sole stockholder in a properly organized professional corporation. She employs 20 staff persons in her practice of public accounting, five of whom are CPAs. The name of the corporation is Krock & Associates.

k. CPA Krock recently sold 20 percent of her stock to CPA Stock, a long-time and trusted staff member.

3.25. SEC Independence Rule Case
J. R. Reed, CPA, retired on July 30, 1984, from the accounting firm of Reed, Landis & Douglas, which he had founded in 1955. Landis and Douglas continued to practice under this firm name, but their new letterhead lists Landis and Douglas as the only partners. J. R. Reed became the president and a director of Marvel Investment Company on September 30, 1984. He received a fixed retirement payment from the Reed, Landis and Douglas firm, but otherwise is completely disassociated from any activity or influence with his former firm.

Required:
Al Landis, inquiring on behalf of Reed, Landis & Douglas, wants to know whether the SEC would consider the firm's independence impaired if the firm were engaged to perform the audit of Marvel Securities for the year ended December 31, 1984.

3.26. SEC on Independence Cases
The accounting firms involved in these cases want to know if their independence will be questioned by the SEC. You have been asked to submit an analysis and conclusion in each case taken separately.

a. Pecora & Co. loaned a senior accountant to its audit client, United Furniture, Inc. for a six-week period ended June 15, 1984. United had converted its accounting system from manual to computerized processing as of January 1, 1984, and had experienced great difficulty. The senior accountant reviewed and analyzed the records and helped the new controller correct the accounts as of March 31, 1984, and get the computer processing straightened out. The work involved collecting and summarizing data into machine-usable form and did not involve any managerial decisions about the manner of classifying or recording transactions. No one from Pecora & Co. was involved in the company's accounting and bookkeeping after June 15, and the firm does not intend to provide such services to United in the future. The question of independence relates to the audit for the year ended December 31, 1984.

b. On March 1, 1984, Spectra Corporation bought the Laser Division of Omnitech, Inc. Benson & Co. has been the auditor of Spectra for six years. Since March 1, Benson & Co. has performed controllership accounting work on the Laser Division books because the records were in terrible shape. The next SEC filing, due March 30, 1985, is supposed to contain three years of audited financial statements of the Laser Division. Benson & Co. had no connection with Omnitech prior to March 1, 1984. Floyd Benson is worried about any independence question relating to the calendar years 1982, 1983, and 1984 concerning his client relationship with Spectra since his firm has been performing bookkeeping for the Laser Division. The division will amount to 27 percent of the total assets and 32 percent of the revenue and net income of Spectra for the year ended December 31, 1984.

c. Kris Kroger is an audit partner in the one-office accounting firm of Gilead-Balm & Co. The firm has a total of seven partners and 26 other professional accountants. G-B & Co. audits the Valley Bank, and Kris' sister, Annabelle, has just taken a job as financial vice president in charge of preparing the bank's financial statements. Eli Gilead is concerned about independence since the bank plans to become a holding company and file statements with the SEC.

d. Tom Jones is an audit manager in the White & Dorsett accounting firm. He has just been assigned to the audit of the Ordinary Money Market Fund. Tom has maintained a money market account with OMMF since it opened in 1982. All his savings, amounting to 75 percent of his total assets, are in this account, which pays the highest interest available in money market funds. However, his account constitutes only .00001 percent of the fund's assets.

DISCUSSION CASES

3.27. **Form of Practice, Technical Standards, Confidentiality and Compatibility of Occupations**

Knowledge of the rules of conduct, interpretations therof, and resolutions of Council is necessary for an adequate response to this case problem.

Gilbert and Bradley formed a corporation called Financial Services, Inc. Each man took 50 percent of the authorized common stock. Gilbert is a CPA and a member of the American Institute of CPAs. Bradley is a CPCU (Chartered Property Casualty Underwriter). The corporation performs auditing and tax services under Gilbert's direction and insurance services under Bradley's supervision. The opening of the corporation's office was announced by a three-inch, two-column "card" in the local newspaper.

One of the corporation's first audit clients was the Grandtime Company. Grandtime had total assets of $600,000 and total liabilities of $270,000. In the course of his examination, Gilbert found that Grandtime's building with a book value of $240,000 was pledged as security for a 10-year-term note in the amount of $200,000. The client's statements did not mention that the building was pledged as security for the 10-year-term note. However, as the failure to disclose the lien did not affect either the value of the assets or the amount of the lia-

bilities and his examination was satisfactory in all other respects, Gilbert rendered an unqualified opinion on Grandtime's financial statements. About two months after the date of his opinion, Gilbert learned that an insurance company was planning to loan Grandtime $150,000 in the form of a first-mortgage note on the building. Realizing that the insurance company was unaware of the existing lien on the building, Gilbert had Bradley notify the insurance company of the fact that Grandtime's building was pledged as security for the term note.

Shortly after the events described above, Gilbert was charged with a violation of professional ethics.

Required:

Identify and discuss the rules of the AICPA Code of Professional Ethics violated by Gilbert and the nature of the violations.

(*AICPA* adapted)

3.28. **Technical Standards, Tax Practice and Confidentiality**

With the approval of its board of directors, the Thames Corporation made a sizable payment for advertising during the year being audited. The corporation deducted the full amount in its federal income tax return. The controller acknowledges that this deduction will probably be disallowed because it relates to political matters. He has not provided for this disallowance in his federal income tax provision and refuses to do so because he fears that this will cause the revenue agent to believe the deduction is not valid. What is the CPA's responsibility in this situation? Explain with regard to ethical responsibilities, audit responsibilities, and tax practice responsibilities.

(AICPA adapted)

3.29. **Disclosure Dilemma**

The Roberts-On Ringer Corporation, a conglomerate, acquired the Granof Grain Storage Company in 1983. Unbeknown to Roberts-On's management, Granof Grain executives had engaged in illegal price-fixing activities during the period 1966–1982. In 1984, one of those executives died and curiously included in his last will and testament a full account of the illegal activities. The president of Roberts-On, in a moment of indiscretion, allowed the auditor (you) to see a copy of this document. Thus, you have full knowledge of the situation.

With regard to matters of timing, you are auditing the financial statements for the year ended December 31, 1984, and plan to complete the fieldwork and write the report on February 15, 1985. It is now January 28,

1985. The will and testament will be read in open probate court on February 28. Assume that the statute of limitations, which will bar lawsuit action, runs out on February 20. In other words, after February 20 no prosecution can take place.

As you begin to complete the field work and write your report, you realize that you and the president know the facts. Fourteen other Granof executives also know, but they have remained silent. The customers of Granof are apparently unaware of the price-fixing situation in 1966–1982. Roberts' total assets amount to $1 billion, stockholders' equity is $300 million, and net current assets amount to $100 million. Treble damages that could arise from this kind of violation are conservatively estimable at $150 million. The president of Roberts-On has implored you to forget having seen the documents.

Required:
a. Discuss the ethical and technical decision problems the auditor faces in this situation.
b. What should the auditor do? Why?
c. What may be the consequences of the auditor's decision(s)? Explain.

CHAPTER 4

PROFESSIONAL STANDARDS SOURCES		
Compendium Section	**Document Reference**	**Topic**
AU 311	SAS 22	Planning and Supervision
AU 320	SAS 1	Auditor's Study and Evaluation of Internal Control
AU 323	SAS 20	Required Communication of Material Weaknesses in Internal Accounting Control
AU 327	SAS 16	Independent Auditors' Responsibility for Detection of Errors or Irregularities
AU 328	SAS 17	Illegal Acts by Clients
AU 333	SAS 19	Client Representations
AU 1020	SAS 45	Related Parties
AU 711	SAS 37	Filings under Federal Securities Statutes

Legal Relationships
and Fraud Detection

LEARNING OBJECTIVES The previous chapter on professional ethics dealt mainly with accountants' *self-regulation*. This chapter focuses on *public regulation* enforced by the SEC and the state and federal court systems. The discussion will give you perspectives on auditors' responsibilities for fraud detection and help you understand accountants' legal liability for professional work. Your learning objectives are to be able to:

☐ Write an essay explaining the theoretical extent and limits of auditors' responsibilities to detect errors, irregularities and illegal acts.

☐ Specify the similarities and differences between accountants' liability situations under common law and under the securities acts, including plaintiffs' and defendants' burdens of affirmative proof.

☐ Explain the applicability of the 1933 Securities Act and the general exemptions related to it, including a few qualifying criteria for using the S-1, S-2, S-3 and S-18 registration forms.

☐ Explain the applicability of the Securities Exchange Act of 1934, including the nature of periodic reporting in forms 10-K, 10-Q and 8-K and independent accountants' association with each.

☐ Identify the legal liability theories and precedents (common law and statute) tested or established in particular court decisions and case situations.

Common law and statutory law are formal expressions of ethics rules you must observe as a professional accountant. The law is an extension of general ethics and the AICPA *Code of Professional Ethics*.

Accountants are potentially liable for monetary damages and even subject to criminal penalties, including fines and jail terms, for failure to perform professional services properly. They can be sued by clients, clients' creditors, investors and by the government. Exposure to large lawsuit claims are possible through *class actions* permitted under federal rules of court procedure in the United States. In a class action suit, a relatively small number of aggrieved plaintiffs with small individual claims can bring suit for large damages in the name of an extended class. After a bankruptcy, for example, 40 bondholders who lost $40,000 might decide to sue, and they can sue on behalf of the entire class of bondholders for *all* their alleged losses (say, $40 million). Lawyers will take such suits on a contingency fee basis (a percentage of the judgment, if any). The size of the claim and zeal of the lawyers makes the class action suit a serious matter.

A study of law cases decided between 1960 and 1976 showed that accountants' and auditors' legal troubles arose from five major types of errors. One hundred twenty-nine cases were analyzed. In these cases, 334 errors were found, classified as follows: 33 percent involved misinterpretation of accounting principles, 15 percent involved the misinterpretation of auditing standards, 29 percent involved faulty implementation of auditing procedures, 13 percent involved client fraud, and 7 percent involved fraud by the auditor.[1] These data suggest how accountants and auditors are exposed to liability for failure to report known departures from accounting principles, for failure to conduct audits properly, for failure to detect management fraud and for actually being parties to frauds. Threat of lawsuits has also affected the way public accountants conduct their work in management advisory services and tax practice.

RESPONSIBILITIES FOR FRAUD DETECTION

Fraud is a term accountants prefer to avoid because it covers a variety of sources for material misstatements in financial statements. Auditing standards deal with auditors' responsibilities regarding *related parties* (SAS 45, AU 1020) *errors and irregularities* (SAS 16, AU 327), and *illegal acts* (SAS 17, AU 328). When reading about these subjects, you should keep in mind the fact that auditors are subject to liability for failure to detect material *management fraud*. A useful definition of **management fraud** is: Deliberate fraud (an intentional act designed to deceive or mislead someone else) committed by management that injures investors or creditors through materially misleading financial statements.

---

[1] K. St. Pierre, and J. Anderson, "An Analysis of Audit Failures Based on Documented Legal Cases," *Journal of Accounting, Auditing and Finance,* Spring 1982, pp. 236–7.

Foreign Corrupt Practices Act of 1977

In 1976, under a program of voluntary disclosure, some 250 American companies notified the Securities and Exchange Commission that they had made illegal or questionable payments in the United States and abroad. Millions of dollars were involved in some cases, as were high officials in the United States, Europe, and Japan. These disclosures were begun with discovery of some illegal corporate political contributions and with a dramatic story of political payoffs in a Central American country. The pattern of payments involved contributions to U.S. and foreign politicians, bribes to win overseas contracts, and under-the-table payments to expedite performance of services. Some payments were made with the apparent consent of chief executive officers, while others were authorized at lower management levels without the knowledge of top executives. Some disbursements came from general corporate funds and others from secret "slush funds" maintained off the books.

A rising tide of public indignation and impatience with wrongdoing prompted enactment of the Foreign Corrupt Practices Act of 1977(FCPA). This law—an amendment of the Securities Exchange Act of 1934—makes it a criminal offense for U.S. companies to give anything of value (for example, a bribe) to a foreign official, a foreign political party, or a candidate for foreign political office for the purpose of influencing acts or decisions in favor of the business interests of the company. Companies may be fined up to $1 million and individuals up to $10,000 and imprisoned up to five years for violations.

The law also amended the Securities Exchange Act of 1934 to include some accounting and internal control standards. These provisions require companies registered with the Securities and Exchange Commission (SEC) to keep books, records and accounts which, in reasonable detail, accurately and fairly reflect the transactions and dispositions of the company's assets. Companies must also devise and maintain a system of internal accounting controls sufficient to provide reasonable assurance that the following four objectives are met:

☐ Transactions are executed in accordance with management's general or specific authorization.

☐ Transactions are recorded as necessary (*a*) to permit preparation of financial statements in conformity with generally accepted accounting principles or any other criteria applicable to such statements and (*b*) to maintain accountability for assets.

☐ Access to assets is permitted only in accordance with management's general or specific authorization.

☐ The recorded accountability for assets is compared with the existing assets at reasonable intervals, and appropriate action is taken with respect to any differences.

These four objectives are quoted directly from *Statement on Auditing Standards No. 1* (AU 320.28). The effect of the Foreign Corrupt Practices

Act of 1977 was to make a company's failure to satisfy the objectives a violation of federal law in addition to being mere matters of poor business practice. However, the monetary fines and prison terms that apply to bribes do not apply to violations of the accounting and internal control requirements.

The law gives the Securities and Exchange Commission another way to bring action against companies and accountants. Only three months after the law was passed, the SEC charged a company's officers with making false entries in the books and records and failing to maintain an adequate accounting control system. The case was settled with an *injunction*—the SEC's most frequent settlement method—in which the company, without admitting or denying a violation of law, agreed not to violate the law in the future. Accountants' disciplinary proceedings are also settled frequently with an injunction. You might think this kind of agreement is not a harsh penalty. However, the public notoriety of the proceedings singles out the defendants, and an injunction has some teeth. If a company or an accountant later breaks the law, the persons can be charged with criminal contempt of court. Penalties for contempt can be severe.

When companies or accountants are taken to court with FCPA or other charges of securities acts violations, the case is *litigated* (decided by a judge). The SEC got its first litigated decision under FCPA in 1983 and won. However, the SEC is not interested in harassment or in unnecessarily expensive responses to internal control needs. In the first five years, the SEC brought only 26 FCPA cases against U.S. companies, and the U.S. Justice Department brought only eight cases. The principal purpose of FCPA is to reach knowing and reckless managerial misconduct and managers' efforts to "cook the books." As one judge put it: FCPA was enacted on the principle that reasonably accurate recordkeeping is essential to promote management responsibility and thwart management misfeasance, misuse of corporate assets, and other conduct reflecting adversely on management's integrity.

AICPA: Statements on Auditing Standards

Several Statements on Auditing Standards (SAS) were designed to establish standards of auditor responsibility for various sources of material misstatement in financial reports. Collectively, the SASs explained below form the basis of professional responsibility in this sensitive area.

SAS 45 (AU 1020)—Related Parties.   Several cases involving materially misleading financial statements resulted from corporate officers' dealings among themselves, with affiliated companies, with family members, and with shell companies. Transactions included borrowing or lending funds at interest rates below the current market, selling real estate at prices significantly different from its appraised value, exchanging property and making loans with no repayment schedule. SAS 45 specifies procedures for determining the existence of related parties, identifying transactions with related parties and auditing the identified transactions. Accounting standards for such transactions are in SFAS 57—*Related Party Disclosures*.

SAS 16 (AU 327)—The Independent Auditor's Responsibility for the Detection of Errors or Irregularities. *Errors* are basically defined as unintentional mistakes, and *irregularities* refer to intentional distortions of financial statements. Auditors' concerns with these arise from the fact that persons who rely on financial statements look to entities' controls and independent audits to provide reasonable assurance that financial statements are not materially misstated as a result of errors or irregularities.

Under generally accepted auditing standards, independent auditors have the responsibility, within the inherent limitations of the auditing process, to: (1) plan the audit to search for errors or irregularities that would have a material effect on the financial statements and (2) exercise due skill and care in the conduct of the audit. In addition to the procedures judged appropriate for forming an opinion on financial statements, extended procedures are required if evidence indicates that material errors or irregularities might exist. SAS 16 also states that the standard audit report implicitly indicates a belief that the financial statements are not materially misstated as a result of errors or irregularities.

Two terms used above deserve some closer scrutiny and definition. *Reasonable assurance* is a concept that recognizes relative costs and benefits. In terms of internal control (SAS 1, AU 320.32), the concept of reasonable assurance recognizes that the cost of internal control should not exceed the benefits expected. The concept, however, is hard to use because it is hard to measure the costs and benefits involved. In the context of SAS 16, obtaining reasonable assurance that financial statements are not materially misstated as a result of errors or irregularities means that diligent effort should be made to obtain evidence. Auditors are not expected to disregard *all* costs and *all* time constraints and make audits so minutely detailed that they are completed only at great cost and delay.

The second term is *inherent limitations of the auditing process.* Like *reasonable assurance,* the concept of *inherent limitation* is based on time and cost considerations. Audit *procedures* are often applied to samples of transactions. When the audit is anything less than a census examination, material errors or irregularities might not be detected. Another source of inherent limitation is the fact that other persons might lie to auditors and actively conceal evidence.

The subsequent discovery that errors or irregularities existed during the period of an audit does not necessarily indicate inadequate performance on the part of the audit team. If the matter goes before outside reviewers (judge, jury), the determination will be one of deciding whether the substance of SAS 16 standards was observed. Much depends on the reviewers' attitude toward what constitutes due skill and care in the circumstances. Hopefully, reviewers realize auditors should not be expected to serve as absolute insurers or guarantors. However, when undiscovered errors and irregularities are material and appear to have been discoverable, reviewers can decide properly that the audit work was inadequate and not in accordance with standards.

SAS 17 (AU 328)—Illegal Acts by Clients.   Many of the corporate disclosures of the mid-1970s involved illegal and ''questionable'' payments. SAS 17 explains auditors' responsibilities for being alert to the possibility that illegal acts may have occurred and for reporting them.

An auditor is neither a legal expert nor an administrative enforcement agent. However, auditors should have enough acquaintance with law in general to recognize a questionable act or transaction and seek expert legal advice. This is true especially for financially related transactions that enter into the accounting system (income tax transactions, selling prices controlled by legislation or administrative rules). Actions that exist outside the accounting system such as violation of health and safety laws and pollution control laws, are much less likely to come to an auditor's attention. One court has held that auditors should be expected to detect illegal acts that could be uncovered with the exercise of normal professional skill and care.

SAS 17 explains some procedures to help identify illegal acts by clients. If one is discovered, auditors are directed to assess its materiality with regard to possible ramifications. For example, outside knowledge of a relatively small bribe (say $100,000 in a $1 billion company) may endanger a large contract, a business license, or the right to operate in a foreign country. Findings should be reported to a high level in the client organization, up to and including the audit committee, for appropriate action and decision about financial statement disclosure. However, SAS 17 does not require auditors to search for illegal acts (as SAS 16 requires planning to search for material errors and irregularities). SAS 17 only warns auditors to be alert and follow the guidance for taking action when illegal acts happen to be discovered.

Depending upon management's decisions on disclosure in the financial statements, auditors may have to qualify the opinion or give an adverse opinion if an unqualified opinion is not warranted. In cases where management and directors fail to give the matter proper consideration, the audit firm may consider withdrawing from the engagement because withdrawal may be better than continuing the association with such a client. Auditing standards do not require auditors to report unresolved questions of illegal acts to persons outside the company (for example, law enforcement agencies). Nevertheless, auditors must be careful to be sure that silence does not make them co-conspirators or accessories to a criminal act.

SAS 19 (AU 333)—Client Representations. One of the most useful auditing procedures for obtaining evidence is to ask client personnel about a matter under investigation. For example, subjects of inquiries may include questions about related party transactions, collectibility of receivables, obsolescence of inventory, possible litigation and loss contingencies, and plans to discontinue a line of business. Ordinarily, auditors can corroborate clients' responses by obtaining evidence from other sources, but in some cases (for example, plans to discontinue a line of business) no other source exists, and in others the corroborating evidence may be very difficult to find (for example, some kinds of related party transactions). Thus, auditors may have to rely on client cooperation in important areas. SAS 19 contains an illustrative list of 20 items about which representations should be obtained.

Important client representations must be in writing. If management refuses to furnish a written representation the audit team believes is essential, the scope of the audit is considered limited and a qualified opinion may be appropriate.

The SEC has put some teeth in the law concerning such representations. Rules adopted in 1979 include: No officer or director shall make a materially false or misleading statement to an accountant (either independent or internal) in connection with audits or preparation of reports required to be filed with the SEC under the Securities and Exchange Act of 1934. Penalties for violation can be imposed, and officers and directors must be careful and truthful.

SAS 20 (AU 323)—Required Communication of Material Weaknesses in Internal Accounting Control. Most auditors report internal control weaknesses to management in a *management letter*. This letter is a private communication between auditor and management and is viewed as an additional service to management as a result of the audit. SAS 20 established a *requirement* that auditors report material weaknesses in internal accounting control to senior management and the board of directors or its audit committee.

A *material weakness in internal accounting control* is defined in SAS 1, AU 320.77 as follows: ". . . a condition in which the specific control procedures or the degree of compliance with them do not reduce to a relatively low level the risk that errors or irregularities in amounts that would be material in relation to the financial statements being audited may occur and not be detected within a timely period by employees in the normal course of performing their assigned functions."

A report of a material weakness may indicate a violation of the accounting and internal control standards section of the Foreign Corrupt Practices Act of 1977. However, SAS 20 does not require public reports. Standards for voluntary, public internal control reports exist in SAS 30 (AU 642). Generally accepted auditing standards as set forth in SAS 20 do not require auditors to evaluate each and every control feature for the purpose of rendering a report to management. The audit team can evaluate those controls on which reliance is to be placed (in accordance with the second AICPA standard of field work) and is not required to go further.

The purpose of this required communication is to assist management in discharging its primary responsibility for establishing and maintaining a system of internal accounting control. Since internal control is the first line of defense against errors and irregularities, this kind of information is very important to managers and directors. If the audit team does not become aware of any material weaknesses during the audit, this fact may be reported to management, but a formal report is not required.

Corporate Policy and Internal Audit

The internal audit department can perform an important role in preventing and detecting fraud, especially when it is functionally independent. Internal auditors can be assigned to tasks such as the following: Review the company's policies regarding questionable payments; investigate compliance with policies; audit large, abnormal or unexplained expenditures, especially where higher than normal levels of authority are involved in overriding regular approval controls; audit sensitive expenses such as legal fees, consultants' fees, advertising and foreign sales commissions; and audit company contributions that appear to be unusual.

Many corporate managements and boards of directors have formulated company policy statements on proper business behavior and ethics. They have become aware of sensitive areas and are trying to institute controls that will prevent errors, irregularities and illegal acts. This task is not easy; sometimes it is hard to imagine what kinds of problems might arise. Accounting firms and other organizations, however, have developed checklists of conditions or events that might signal the possible existence of a fraud situation.

LIABILITY UNDER COMMON LAW

Legal liabilities of professional accountants may arise from lawsuits brought on the basis of the law of contracts or as a tort action for negligence. Breach of contract is a claim that accounting or auditing services were not performed in the manner agreed upon. This basis is most characteristic of lawsuits involving a public accountant and his or her client. Tort actions cover civil complaints other than breach of contract, including fraud, deceit, and injury.

Suits for civil damages under common law usually result when someone suffers a financial loss after relying upon financial statements later found to be materially misleading. However, legal liability may also arise between accountants and their clients for breach of contract and tort in connection with tax practice and management advisory services practice. However, clients also have duties and responsibilities in the accountant-client relationship, and the dimensions of liability do not run entirely in the accountant's direction.

Characteristics of Common Law Actions

When an injured party considers himself damaged by an accountant and brings a lawsuit, he generally asserts all possible causes of action, including breach of contract, tort, deceit, fraud and whatever else may be relevant to the claim. Actions brought under common law place most of the burdens of affirmative proof on the plaintiff, who must prove: (1) he was damaged or suffered a loss, (2) the financial statements were materially misleading or the accountant's advice was faulty, (3) he relied upon the statements or advice, (4) they were the direct cause of his loss and (5) the accountant was negligent, grossly negligent, deceitful or otherwise responsible for unlawful behavior. The defendant accountant, on the other hand, must offer evidence to mitigate or refute the plaintiff's claims and evidence. In a subsequent section dealing with the securities acts, you will see how the statutes shift some of these burdens of affirmative proof to the professional accountant.

Clients may bring a lawsuit for breach of contract. The relationship of direct involvement between parties to a contract is known as ***privity***. When privity exists, a plaintiff usually need only show that the defendant accountant was negligent. (***Ordinary negligence***—a lack of reasonable care in the performance of professional accounting tasks—is usually meant when the word *negligence* stands alone.) If negligence is proved, the accountant may be liable, provided the client has not been involved in some sort of contributory negligence in the dispute. (See Appendix 4–A, *Smith* v. *London Assur. Corp.*)

Fifty years ago, it was very difficult for parties other than contracting clients to succeed in lawsuits against auditors. Other parties not in privity had no cause of action for breach of contract. However, the court opinion in the case known as *Ultramares* (Appendix 4–A) expressed the view that if negligence were so great as to constitute ***gross negligence***—lack of even minimum care in performing professional duties, indicating reckless disregard for duty and responsibility—grounds might exist for concluding that the accountant had engaged in ***constructive fraud***. Actual fraud is characterized as an intentional act designed to deceive, mislead or injure the rights of another person. *Constructive fraud,* however, may not have the same element of intent, but the result is the same—to deprive or injure another unsuspecting party. Fraud is a basis for liability in tort, so parties not in privity with the accountant may have causes of action when negligence is gross enough to amount to constructive fraud. (See Appendix 4–A, *State Street Trust Co.* v. *Ernst.*) These other parties include primary beneficiaries, actual foreseen and limited classes of persons, and all other injured parties.

Primary beneficiaries are third parties for whose primary benefit the audit or other accounting service is performed. Such a beneficiary will be identified to, or reasonably foreseeable by, the accountant prior to or during the engagement, and the accountant will know that his or her work will influence the primary beneficiary's decisions. For example, an audit firm may be informed that the report is needed for a bank loan application at the First National Bank. Recent cases indicate that proof of ordinary negligence may be sufficient to make accountants liable for damages to primary beneficiaries. (See Appendix 4–A, *CIT Financial* v. *Glover*.)

Accountants may also be liable to creditors, investors or potential investors who rely on accountants' work. If the accountant is reasonably able to *foresee* a limited class of potential users of his work (for example, local banks, regular suppliers), liability may be imposed for ordinary negligence. This, however, is an uncertain area, and liability in a particular case depends entirely on the unique facts and circumstances. (See Appendix 4–A, *Rusch Factors, Inc.* v. *Levin* and *Rhode Island Hospital Trust National Bank* v. *Swartz*.) Beneficiaries of the types mentioned above and all other injured parties may recover damages if they are able to show an accountant was grossly negligent and perpetrated a constructive fraud.

Liability in Compilation and Review Services
You may find it easy to think about common law liability in connection with *audited* financial statements. Do not forget, however, that accountants also render compilation and review services and are associated with *unaudited* financial information. People expect public accountants to perform these services in accordance with professional standards, and courts can impose liability for accounting work found to be substandard. Accountants have been assessed damages for work on such statements, as shown in the *1136 Tenants' Corp.* v. *Max Rothenberg & Co.* case (Appendix 4–A).

One significant risk is that the client may fail to understand the nature of the service being given. Accountants should use a conference and an engagement letter to explain clearly that a compilation service ("write-up") involves little or no investigative work, and it is lesser in scope than a review service. Similarly, a review service should be explained in terms of being less extensive than a full audit service. Clear understandings at the outset can enable accountants and clients to avoid later disagreements.

Yet, even with these understandings, public accountants cannot merely accept client-supplied information that appears to be unusual or misleading. A court has held that a public accountant's preparation of some erroneous and misleading journal entries without sufficient support was enough to trigger common law liability for negligence, even though the accountant was not associated with any final financial statements. AICPA standards for compilations require accountants to obtain additional information if client-supplied accounting data is incorrect, incomplete or otherwise unsatisfactory. Courts might hold accountants liable for failure to obtain additional information in such circumstances.

When financial statements are reviewed, accountants' reports declare: "Based on our review, we are not aware of any material modifications that should be made to the accompanying financial statements in order for them to be in conformity with generally accepted accounting principles."

Courts can look to the facts of a case and rule on whether the review was performed properly. Some courts might decide an accountant's review was substandard if necessary adjustments or "material modifications" should have been made. These risks tend to induce more work by accountants beyond superficial looking-it-over and inquiry procedures.

RELATIONSHIPS UNDER STATUTORY LAW

Several federal statutes provide sources of potential liability for accountants, including: Federal False Statements Statute, Federal Mail Fraud Statute, Federal Conspiracy Statute, Racketeer Influenced and Corrupt Organizations Act, Securities Act of 1933, and Securities and Exchange Act of 1934. The securities acts contain provisions defining certain civil and criminal liabilities of accountants. Because a significant segment of accounting practice is under the jurisdiction of the securities acts, the following discussion will concentrate on duties and liabilities under these laws. First, however, you should become familiar with the scope and function of the securities acts and the Securities and Exchange Commission (SEC).

Federal securities regulation in the United States was enacted in 1933 not only as a reaction to the events of the early years of the Great Depression, but in the spirit of the New Deal era and as a culmination of attempts at "blue-sky" regulation by the states. The *Securities Act of 1933* and the *Securities and Exchange Act of 1934* require disclosure of all information required for an informed investment decision. The securities acts and the SEC operate for the protection of investors and for the facilitation of orderly capital markets. Even so, no government agency, including the SEC, rules on the quality of investments. The securities acts have been characterized as "truth-in-securities" law. Their spirit favors the otherwise uninformed investing public, while *caveat vendor* is applied to the issuer—let the *seller* beware of violations.

Regulation of Accountants and Accounting

The SEC has made rules governing the conduct of persons practicing before it. Rule 2(*e*) of its Rules of Practice provides a means of public regulation discipline. The rules relating to auditor independence were discussed in Chapter 3. Through these rules, the SEC can apply direct regulatory authority to individual accountants and accounting firms.

Section 19 of the Securities Act (1933) and Section 13 of the Exchange Act (1934) give the SEC power to establish accounting rules and regulations. *Regulation S-X* contains accounting requirements for audited annual and unaudited interim financial statements filed under both the Securities Act and the Exchange Act. Equally important, *Regulation S-K* contains requirements relating to all other business, analytical, and supplementary financial disclosures. In general, Regulation S-X governs the content of the financial statements themselves, and Regulation S-K governs *all other disclosures* in financial statement footnotes and other places in reports required to be filed.

For more than 50 years, the SEC has followed a general policy of relying on the organized accounting profession to establish generally accepted accounting principles (GAAP). However, the SEC makes its influence and power known in the standard-setting process. Its chief accountant monitors the development of FASB standards, meets with FASB staff and decides whether a proposed pronouncement is reasonable. The SEC view is communicated to FASB, and the two organizations try to work out major differences before a new Statement on Financial Accounting Standards (SFAS) is made final. Usually the two bodies reach agreement.

In the past, however, the SEC itself has made a few accounting rules because: (1) The SEC could act faster when an emerging problem needed quick attention and (2) The SEC thought GAAP was deficient and wanted to prod the FASB to act. Consequently, GAAP and Regulation S-X differ in a few respects, but not many. Examples where Regulation S-X requires more than GAAP include nonequity classification of redeemable preferred stock, separate presentation of some income tax details and additional disclosures about compensating balances, inventories and long-term debt maturities. Otherwise, "SEC accounting" is not fundamentally different from GAAP accounting. The spirit of the force and effect of accounting principles and the respective roles of FASB and SEC are explained by an early SEC policy statement as follows:

1. When financial statements filed with the commission are prepared according to principles that have no authoritative support, *they will be presumed to be misleading. Other disclosures or footnotes will not cure this presumption.*

2. When financial statements involve a principle on which the commission disagrees, but has promulgated no explicit rules or regulations, and the principle has substantial authoritative support, *then supplementary disclosures will be accepted in lieu of correction of the statements.*

3. When financial statements involve a principle that (1) has authoritative support in general, but (2) the commission has ruled against its use, then *the statements will be presumed misleading. Supplementary disclosures will not cure this presumption.*[2]

The biggest difference between SEC practice and other accounting practice involves the disclosures required by Regulation S-K. These requirements are detailed, and accountants must be well aware of them. In

[2] *Accounting Series Release No. 4* (1938). Also *Accounting Series Release No. 150* (1973) affirmed that pronouncements of the FASB will be considered to constitute substantial authoritative support of accounting principles, standards and practices (FRR No. 1, Section 101). Other sources of authoritative support are enumerated in SAS 5.

many respects, Regulation S-K goes beyond GAAP because FASB pronouncements usually do not specify much detail about footnote disclosures. Also, accountants must keep up-to-date on the SEC's *Financial Reporting Releases* (FRRs, a new name for the Accounting Series Releases issued through 1982), which express new rules and policies about accounting and disclosure. Finally, accountants must keep up-to-date on the SEC's *Staff Accounting Bulletins* (SABs), which are unofficial but important interpretations of Regulation S-X and Regulation S-K.

Integrated Disclosure System

Prior to 1982, the SEC required different kinds of reports for filings under the Securities Act and filings under the Exchange Act. The SEC also had requirements for an annual report sent to shareholders in connection with solicitation of proxies (votes) for corporate resolutions. This situation created a complicated set of reporting requirements. In 1982, the system was simplified by adoption of *integrated disclosure.*

Under the integrated disclosure system, companies still must give annual reports to shareholders, file annual reports on Form 10-K (discussed later in this chapter), and file registration statements (also discussed later in this chapter) when securities are offered to the public. However, companies can now prepare the annual report to shareholders in conformity with Regulation S-X and Regulation S-K. Then the shareholders' report can be used to provide most of the other information required for the Form 10-K annual report. Some companies can also use these reports as the basic reports required in a Securities Act registration statement because the integrated disclosure system basically has made the 10-K requirements the same as the registration statement disclosure requirements.

The integrated disclosure system is intended to simplify and coordinate various reporting requirements. It also has had the not-too-subtle effect of making most of Regulation S-X and Regulation S-K required in annual reports to shareholders, making them GAAP for companies that want to obtain the benefits of integration.

Regulation of Auditing Standards

In contrast to its concern for the quality of accounting principles, the SEC's involvement in auditing standards and procedural matters has been minimal since the developments of the McKesson and Robbins affair (see Appendix 4–A). Following an investigation of the McKesson case, the SEC ruled that auditors' reports must state that an audit was performed in accordance with "generally accepted auditing standards." At that time (1938), the 10 standards had not yet been issued by the AICPA. They were written and adopted soon afterwards.

The SEC's chief accountant also monitors the development of auditing standards by the AICPA Auditing Standards Board (ASB). His staff attends ASB meetings, analyzes new proposals and decides whether an issue of relevance to SEC-registered public companies is involved. The chief accountant discusses differences of opinion with the ASB, and the two try to work them out. Ordinarily, the SEC does not get as involved with technical auditing standards and ASB proceedings as it does with accounting standards and FASB proceedings. The SEC has rules about audit reports that correspond with generally accepted auditing standards (GAAS), but the SEC has no technical body of rules similar to the *Statements on Auditing Standards*.

Regulation of Securities Sales

For the most part, the Securities Act (1933) regulates the issue of securities, and the Exchange Act (1934) regulates trading in securities. You need to understand, however, that neither these securities laws nor the SEC approves or guarantees investments. The laws and the SEC's regulation concentrate on *disclosure of information* to investors, who have the responsibility for judging investment risk and reward potential. Section 5 of the Securities Act provides that no person may lawfully buy, sell, offer to buy, or offer to sell any security by the means of interstate commerce unless a registration statement meeting requirements of Sections 7 and 10 is in effect. This prohibition should be interpreted literally: *No person can buy or sell any security* by means of *interstate commerce* (for example, telephone, mail, highway, national bank), unless a registration statement is in effect.

Section 5 is all-encompassing, but Sections 3 and 4 offer exemptions. In general, Section 3 exempts from registration (but not from antifraud provisions): government securities, short-term obligations maturing within nine months, charitable and educational institutions, securities of business subject to regulation by the Interstate Commerce Commission, and intrastate issues sold by local companies to state residents. SEC rules also exempt small issues on the grounds that a sufficiently broad public interest is not involved. Section 4 exempts from registration (but not from antifraud provisions) certain specified *transactions,* principally any transaction *not* involving a "public offering,"[3] and transactions by any person who is *not* an issuer, underwriter, or dealer (for example, a small investor).

Since 1981, in a spirit of deregulation, the SEC has made it easier for companies to offer securities to the public. *Regulation D,* adopted in 1982, provides for offerings without registration of: (1) Up to $500,000 in a 12-month period by nonpublic companies, with no limit on the number of purchasers[4]; (2) Up to $5 million in a 12-month period to fewer than 35

---

[3] In general, a nonpublic offering ("private placement") is a sale of securities to a small number of persons or institutional investors (usually not more than 35), who can demand and obtain sufficient information without the formality of SEC registration.

[4] Generally, a "nonpublic company" ("non-reporting" company) is one that has less than $3 million assets and fewer than 500 shareholders and is not required to register or is not required to file reports under the Exchange Act.

nonaccredited investors or an unlimited number of accredited investors[5] and (3) An unlimited amount to an unlimited number of accredited investors. In essence, Regulation D expanded the concept of ''nonpublic offering'' to include deals involving accredited investors, who are presumed to have the financial knowledge and ability to take care of themselves. However, the regulation requires certain kinds of minimum disclosures, even though formal filing of a registration statement is not required.

The general point relevant to most auditors concerning the 1933 act is that *all* sales must be registered, except those exempted by Sections 3 and 4 or by other regulations (including Regulation D). One fine point of the law is that *offerings* are registered, but specific securities are not. This means that a corporation holding treasury stock, or a large shareholder (10 percent or more), must consult the law before selling. Even if the shares held were acquired pursuant to an earlier registration, subsequent sales may have to be registered anew.

A registration statement must be filed and must be *effective* before a sale is lawful. On the basis of Sections 7 and 10 of the Securities Act, the SEC adopted a series of forms for use in registrations. The forms most commonly used for general public offerings are Forms S-1, S-2, and S-3. These forms are related to the integrated disclosure system discussed earlier. They are not sets of ''forms'' as in an income tax return, however. A registration ''form'' is a list of financial statement and disclosure requirements cross-referenced to Regulation S-X and Regulation S-K.

Form S-1 is the general registration form. It is available to all issuers but must be used by issuers who do not qualify to use Forms S-2 or S-3. A certain set of financial statements and disclosures (Part I) in an S-1 is known as the ***prospectus,*** which must be distributed to all purchasers. The complete S-1, containing all the required information, can be obtained from the SEC.

Form S-3 represents the SEC's acknowledgment of ''efficient markets'' for widely distributed information about well-known companies. Part I (the prospectus) can be concise—containing information about the terms of the securities being offered, the purpose and use of proceeds, the risk factors and some other information about the offerings. The remainder of the financial information is ''incorporated by reference.'' It is not enclosed with the prospectus, but reference is merely made to reports filed earlier (10-K, 10-Q and 8-K reports, which will be discussed later). The information in these reports is presumed to have been obtained and used by securities analysts and already impounded in current securities prices. Form S-3 can be used by companies which have made timely

---

[5] In general, ''accredited investors'' are financial institutions, investment companies, large tax-exempt organizations, directors and executives of the issuer, and individuals with net worth of $1 million or more or income of $200,000 or more.

reports under the Exchange Act for 36 months, which have not recently defaulted on obligations and which have $150 million of stock trading or $100 million of stock trading with annual trading volume of 3 million shares.[6] These requirements describe reasonably large, "seasoned" companies.

Form S-2 is for seasoned companies that do not meet the size criteria for Form S-3. However, these companies must have made timely reports under the Exchange Act for 36 months and must not have defaulted recently on obligations. Part I (the prospectus) of Form S-2 is similar to Form S-3, but all the financial information cannot be merely "incorporated by reference." The issuer must include and deliver to prospective purchasers its latest annual report to shareholders and up-to-date quarterly financial information. In other words, the "efficient market" for information incorporated by reference in Form S-3 is not relied upon as heavily for smaller companies using Form S-2.

Another often-used registration is Form S-18. It can be used in lieu of Form S-1 for *initial public offerings* up to $7.5 million. Form S-18 is not as complicated or as extensive as Form S-1. It is a short form designed to facilitate access to public securities markets by smaller companies.

Regulation of Periodic Reporting

The Exchange Act primarily regulates daily trading in securities and requires registration of most companies whose securities are traded in interstate commerce. Companies having total assets of $3 million or more and 500 or more stockholders are required to register under the Exchange Act. The purpose of these size and share criteria is to define securities in which there is a significant public interest. (From time to time these criteria may be changed.)

For auditors and accountants, the most significant aspect of the Exchange Act is the requirement for annual reports, quarterly reports and periodic special reports. These reports are referred to by the form numbers 10-K, 10-Q, and 8-K, respectively. Under the integrated disclosure system, a company's regular annual report to shareholders may be filed as a part of the 10-K to provide part or all of the information required by law. The 10-Q quarterly report is filed after each of the first three fiscal-year quarters, and its contents are largely financial statement information. Form 8-K, the "current events report," is required whenever certain significant events occur, such as changes in control, legal proceedings, and changes in accounting principles. These reports are "filed" with the SEC but are not usually sent to all shareholders and creditors. They can be obtained from the SEC and therefore are considered publicly available information. Indeed, commercial information services obtain the filings

---

[6] The actual technical requirements are more extensive than this brief list, but these major requirements are sufficient for understanding the general purpose.

and disseminate the information to clients and newsletter subscribers. Anyone can obtain the filings by requesting them and paying a fee.

One of the events considered significant for an 8-K report is a change of auditors. When a company changes auditors, the company must report the fact and state whether in the past 18 months there has been any disagreement with the auditors concerning matters of accounting principles, financial statement disclosure or auditing procedure. At the same time, the former auditor must submit a letter stating whether he agrees with the explanation and, if he disagrees, giving particulars. These documents are available to the public on request and their purpose is to make information available about client-auditor conflicts that might have a bearing on financial presentations and consequent investment decisions. Reported disagreements have included disputes over recoverability of asset cost, revenue-recognition timing, expense-recognition timing, amounts to be reported as liabilities, and necessity for certain auditing procedures.

LIABILITY PROVISIONS: SECURITIES ACT OF 1933

Section 11 of the Securities Act is of great interest to auditors because it alters significantly the duties and responsibilities otherwise required by common law. This section contains the principal criteria defining civil liabilities under the statute. Portions of Section 11 pertinent to auditors' liability are:

Section 11—General Liability

Sec. 11(a) . . . any person acquiring such security [in a registered offering] . . . may sue:

Every person who signed the registration statement.

Every person who was a director of . . . or partner in, the issuer.

Every accountant, engineer, or appraiser.

Every underwriter with respect to such security.

If such person acquired the security after the issuer has made generally available to its security holders an earning statement covering a period of at least 12 months beginning after the effective date of the registration statement, then the right of recovery . . . shall be conditioned on proof that such person acquired the security relying upon . . . the registration statement . . . .

Sec. 11(b) Notwithstanding the provisions of subsection (a) no person, other than the issuer, shall be liable as provided therein who shall sustain the burden of proof . . .

that (A) as regards any part of the registration statement *not purporting to be made on the authority of an expert,* . . . he had, after reasonable investigation, reasonable ground to believe . . . that the statements therein were true and that there was no omission to state a material fact . . .

and (B) as regards any part of the registration statement *purporting to be made upon his authority as an expert* . . . he had, after reasonable investigation, reasonable ground to believe . . . that the statements therein were true and that there was no omission to state a material fact . . .

and (C) as regards any part of the registration statement *purporting to be made on the authority of an expert (other than himself)* . . . he had no reasonable ground to believe . . . that the statements therein were untrue or that there was an omission to state a material fact . . . .

Section 11(*c*) In determining, for the purpose of . . . subsection (*b*) of this section, what constitutes reasonable investigation and reasonable ground for belief, the standard of reasonableness shall be that required of a prudent man in the management of his own property.

Section 11(*e*) . . . if the defendant proves that any portion or all of such damages [claimed in a lawsuit] represents other than the depreciation in value of such security resulting from such part of the registration statement, with respect to which his liability is asserted, not being true or omitting to state a material fact required to be stated therein . . . such portion of or all such damages shall not be recoverable.

The effect of Section 11 is to shift the major burdens of affirmative proof from the injured plaintiff to the expert accountant. Recall that under the common law, the *plaintiff* had to allege and prove damages, misleading statements, reliance, direct cause and negligence. Under Section 11, the plaintiff still has to show that he or she was damaged and has to allege and show proof that financial statements in the registration statement were materially misleading, but here the plaintiff's duties essentially are ended. Exhibit 4–1 summarizes these common law and statutory duties.

Privity Not Required   The plaintiff does not have to be in privity with the auditor. Section 11 provides that *any purchaser* may sue the accountant. The purchaser-plaintiff does not have to prove that he or she relied on the financial statements in the registration statement. In fact, the purchaser may not have even read them.[7] The purchaser is not required to show that the misleading statements caused him or her to make an unwise decision and thus suffer a loss.

Section 11 was written with the protection of the investing public in mind, not the protection of the expert auditor. The first significant court case under Section 11 was *Escott et al.* v. *BarChris Construction Corp. et al.* (Refer to Appendix 4–B.) The ruling in this case was that the auditors

---

[7] This matter of reliance is modified by Section 11(*a*) to the extent that when enough time had elapsed and the registrant has filed an income statement covering a 12-month period beginning after the effective date, then the plaintiff must prove that he or she purchased after that time in reliance on the registration statement. However, the plaintiff may prove reliance without proof of actually having read the registration statement.

EXHIBIT 4–1
Comparison of Common
Law and Statutory
Litigation

Under Common Law	Under 1933 Act Section 11	Under 1934 Act Section 18
Plaintiff proves damages or loss and necessary privity or beneficiary relationship.	Plaintiff proves damages or loss, but any purchaser may sue the accountant.	Plaintiff proves damages or loss, but any purchaser or seller may sue the accountant.
Plaintiff alleges, shows evidence, and the court decides whether financial statements were misleading.	Same.	Same.
Plaintiff proves he relied on the misleading statements, and they were the direct cause of his loss.	Proof of purchaser's reliance not required unless a 12-month earnings statement had been issued.	Same as common law.
Plaintiff proves the requisite degree of negligence by the accountant.	Accountant must prove he performed a reasonable investigation (due diligence).*	Accountant must prove he acted in good faith and did not know the statements were misleading.

* Upon failing to prove due diligence, the accountant may try to prove that the plaintiff's loss was caused by something other than the misleading financial statements (the *causation* defense).

did not conduct a reasonable investigation and thus did not satisfy Section 11(*b*)(B).

Section 11(*a*)
Exemption

Financial reporting has changed since 1933. The SEC now requires some larger companies to present interim financial information and encourages the presentation of forecasts. To remove the legal liability barrier to auditor association with such information, the SEC has exempted auditors from Section 11 liability related to interim information and has enacted a "safe harbor" with respect to forecasts. (A "safe harbor" means that plaintiffs in a lawsuit must show that the auditor did not act in good faith when reporting on a forecast, effectively placing the burden of proof on the plaintiff.) The FASB requires some kinds of supplementary information outside the basic financial statements (changing prices and oil and gas reserve information), and auditing standards require *implicit* or *exception-basis* reporting. (*Implicit* reporting means that auditors modify the standard audit report only when some *exception* is taken to the presentation of the supplementary information, otherwise the report is silent.) The SEC has not exempted auditors' implicit reports on supplementary information from Section 11 liability exposure.

Statute of
Limitations

Section 13 of the Securities Act defines the statute of limitations in such a way that suit is barred if not brought within one year after discovery of the misleading statement or omission, or in any event if not brought within three years after the public offering. These limitations and the reliance limitation related to a 12-month earnings statement restrict auditors' liability exposure to a determinable time span. Oftentimes, the statute of limitations is the best defense available to auditors.

Due Diligence Defense

Section 11 also states the means by which the auditor can prove himself or herself not liable. Section 11(*b*) enunciates what is known as the "due diligence" defense. If the auditor can prove that a *reasonable examination* was performed, then the auditor is not liable for damages. Section 11(*c*) states the standard of reasonableness to be that degree of care required of a prudent person in the management of his own property. In a context more specific to auditors, a reasonable investigation would be shown by the conduct of an audit in accordance with generally accepted auditing standards in both form and substance.

Section 11(*b*) also gives a diligence defense standard for portions of a registration statement made on the authority of an expert. Any person who relies upon an "expert" is not required to conduct a reasonable investigation of his own, but only to have no reasonable grounds for disbelief. Thus, the auditor who relies on the opinion of an actuary or engineer need not make a personal independent investigation of that expert's area. Similarly, any officer, director, attorney or underwriter connected with a registration has a far lesser diligence duty respecting any information that is covered by an auditor's expert opinion. In the *BarChris* judgment, officers, directors, attorneys and underwriters were found lacking in diligence *except* with respect to audited financial statements.

Causation Defense

Section 11(*e*) defines the last line of defense available to an auditor when lack of diligence has been proved. This defense is known as the "causation defense." Essentially, if auditors can prove the plaintiff's damages (all or part) resulted from something other than the misleading and negligently prepared registration statement, then all or part of the damages will not have to be paid. This defense may create some imaginative "other reasons." In the *BarChris* case, at least one plaintiff had purchased securities *after* the company had gone bankrupt. The presumption that the loss in this instance resulted from events other than the misleading registration statement is fair, but this claim was settled out of court, so there is no judicial determination for reference.

Section 17 Antifraud

Section 17 of the Securities Act is the antifraud section. The wording and intent of this section is practically identical to Section 10(*b*) and Rule 10(*b*)(5) under the Exchange Act. The difference between the two acts is the Securities Act reference to "offer or sale" and the Exchange Act reference to "use of securities exchanges." (See Appendix 4–B, *U.S.* v. *White.*) The pertinent portion of Section 17 is:

Section 17. (*a*) It shall be unlawful for any person in the offer or sale of any securities by the use of any means or instruments of transportation in interstate commerce or by the use of the mails, directly or indirectly—(1) to employ any device, scheme, or artifice to defraud, or (2) to obtain money or property by means of any untrue statement of a material fact or any omission to state a material fact . . . (3) to engage in any transaction, practice, or course of business which operates or would operate as a fraud or deceit upon the purchaser.

Section 24 Criminal Liability

Section 24 sets forth the criminal penalties imposed by the Securities Act. Criminal penalties are characterized by monetary fines and/or prison terms. The key words in Section 24 are *willful* violation and *willfully* causing misleading statements to be filed. (See Appendix 4–B, *U.S.* v. *Benjamin*.)

Section 24. Any person who willfully violates any of the provisions of this title, or the rules and regulations promulgated by the commission under authority thereof, or any person who willfully, in a registration statement filed under this title, makes any untrue statement of a material fact or omits to state any material fact required to be stated therein or necessary to make the statements therein not misleading, shall upon conviction be fined not more than $5,000 or imprisoned not more than five years, or both.

LIABILITY PROVISIONS: SECURITIES AND EXCHANGE ACT OF 1934

Section 10 of the Exchange Act is used against accountants quite frequently. Like Section 17 of the Securities Act, Section 10 is a general antifraud section. The law itself reveals Section 10(*b*) as follows:

Section 10. It shall be unlawful for any person, directly or indirectly, by use of any means or instrumentality of interstate commerce or of the mails, or of any facility of any national securities exchange . . . (*b*) to use or employ, in connection with the purchase or sale of any security registered on a national securities exchange or any security not so registered, any manipulative or deceptive device or contrivance in contravention of such rules and regulations as the commission may prescribe as necessary or appropriate in the public interest or for the protection of investors.

Rule 10b-5, Antifraud

Rule 10b-5, which is equally as actionable as the statute itself, is more explicit. The rule is:

Rule 10b-5. Employment of Manipulative and Deceptive Devices. It shall be unlawful for any person, directly or indirectly, by the use of any means of instrumentality of interstate commerce, or of the mails, or of any facility of any national securities exchange,

1. To employ any device, scheme, or artifice to defraud.
2. To make any untrue statement of material fact or to omit to state a material fact necessary in order to make the statements made, in the light of the circumstances under which they were made, not misleading.

3. To engage in any act, practice, or course of business which operates or would operate as a fraud or deceit upon any person in connection with the purchase or sale of any security.

The *Fischer* v. *Kletz* ruling and the *Hochfelder* decision briefed in Appendix 4–B explain Section 10 more fully. An important point about Rule 10b-5 liability is that plaintiffs must prove **scienter**—that an accountant acted with intent to deceive—in order to impose liability under the rule. Mere negligence is not enough cause for liability. (The U.S. Supreme Court ruled in 1980 that the SEC, when bringing a case must prove scienter under 10(*b*) of the Exchange Act and 17(*a*)(1) of the Securities Act, but need *not* prove scienter for 17(*a*)(2)(3) of the Securities Act.)

Section 18, Civil Liability

Section 18 sets forth the pertinent civil liability definition under the Exchange Act as follows:

> Section 18. (*a*) Any person who shall make or cause to be made any statement . . . which . . . was at the time and in the light of the circumstances under which it was made false or misleading with respect to any material fact shall be liable to any person (not knowing that such statement was false or misleading) who, in reliance upon such statement, shall have purchased or sold a security at a price which was affected by such statement, for damages caused by such reliance, unless the person sued shall prove that he acted in good faith and had no knowledge that such statement was false or misleading.

Good Faith Defense

Interestingly, under Rule 10b-5 and Section 18, a plaintiff has to prove reliance on misleading statements and damages caused thereby—the same requirement as under common law. As a defense, the auditor must then prove action in good faith and no knowledge of the misleading statement. This requirement appears to be the *Ultramares* rule written into statute, to the extent that proving good faith is equivalent to showing that any negligence was no greater than ordinary negligence. (The *Ultramares* decision is reviewed in Appendix 4–A.)

Section 32, Criminal Liability

Section 32 states the criminal penalties for violation of the Exchange Act. Like Section 24 of the Securities Act, the critical test is whether the violator acted "willfully and knowingly." The defendant accountants in the *Continental Vending* case (*U.S.* v. *Simon*) and in *U.S.* v. *Natelli* discussed in Appendix 4–B were charged with violation of Section 32.

> Section 32. (*a*) Any person who willfully violates any provision of this title, or any rule or regulation thereunder . . . or any person who willfully and knowingly makes, or causes to be made, any statement . . . which . . . was false or misleading with respect to any material fact, shall upon conviction be fined not more than $10,000, or imprisoned not more than two years, or both . . . but no person shall be subject to imprisonment under this section for the violation of any rule or regulation if he proves that he had no knowledge of such rule or regulation.

EXTENT OF LIABILITY You may be interested in knowing about *who* suffers exposure and penalties in lawsuits—the accounting firm, partners, managers, senior accountants, staff assistants or all of these? Most lawsuits center attention on the accounting firm and on the partners and managers involved in the audit or other accounting work. However, court opinions have cited the work of senior accountants, and there is no reason that the work of new staff assistant accountants should not come under review. All persons involved in professional accounting are exposed to potential liability.

Statement of Auditing Standards No. 22 (AU 311.12) entitled "Planning and Supervision" offers some important thoughts for accountants who question the validity of some of the work. Accountants can express their own positions and let the working paper records show the nature of the disagreement and the resolution of the question. SAS 22 expressed the appropriate action as follows:

> The auditor with final responsibility for the examination and assistants should be aware of the procedures to be followed when differences of opinion concerning accounting and auditing issues exist among firm personnel involved in the examination. Such procedures should enable an assistant to document his disagreement with the conclusions reached if, after appropriate consultation, he believes it necessary to disassociate himself from the resolution of the matter. In this situation, the basis for the final resolution should also be documented.

SUMMARY To the credit of the accounting profession, litigation under the securities acts has not been widespread when considered in light of the many thousands of documents filed with the SEC. Nevertheless, the suits that have gone to trial have resulted in judgments rich with implications for practice and laden with portents of the judicial atmosphere of the future. Exhibit 4–2 below summarizes the liability sections of the Securities Act and the Exchange Act.

EXHIBIT 4–2
Summary of Securities Acts Liability Sections

	Securities Act (1933)	Exchange Act (1934)
Financial statement liability	Section 11	Section 18
Fraud liability	Section 17	Section 10, Rule 10b-5
Criminal liability	Section 24	Section 32

SOURCES AND ADDITIONAL READING REFERENCES

"AICPA Brief in Natelli-Scansaroli." *Journal of Accountancy,* May 1975, pp. 69–76.

"AICPA—NYSSCPA Brief in 1136 Tenants' Corporation Case." *Journal of Accountancy,* March 1971, pp. 57–73.

AICPA Special Advisory Committee. "Reports by Management: Conclusions and Recommendations." AICPA, 1979, 36 pages.

American Bar Association Committee on Corporate Law and Accounting. "A Guide to the New Section 13(*b*)(2) Accounting Requirements of the Securities Exchange Act of 1934 (Section 102 of the Foreign Corrupt Practices Act of 1977)." *Journal of Accountancy,* April 1979, pp. 110–22.

Barnett, A. H. and F. F. Galer. "Scienter Since Hochfelder." *CPA Journal,* November 1982, pp. 40–45.

Causey, Denzil Y. *Duties and Liabilities of Public Accountants.* Homewood, Ill.: Dow Jones-Irwin, 1982.

————. "Foreseeability as a Determinant of Audit Responsibility." *Accounting Review,* April 1973, pp. 258–267.

————. "Newly Emerging Standards of Auditor Responsibility." *The Accounting Review,* January 1976, pp. 19–30.

Chazen, C.; R. L. Miller; and K. I. Solomon. "When the Rules Say: See Your Lawyer." *Journal of Accountancy,* January 1981, pp. 60–70.

Chira, Robert. "Deception of Auditors and False Records." *Journal of Accountancy,* July 1979, pp. 61–72.

Collin, F., and J. L. Porter. "Engagement Withdrawal: The Legal Perils." *Journal of Accountancy,* February 1979, pp. 66–71.

"The Continental Vending Case." *Journal of Accountancy,* November 1968, pp. 54–62.

"Continental Vending Decision Affirmed." *Journal of Accountancy,* February 1970, pp. 61–69.

Cook, J. M., and T. P. Kelley. "Internal Accounting Control: A Matter of Law." *Journal of Accountancy,* January 1979, pp. 56–64.

Dunfee, T. W., and I. N. Gleim. "Criminal Liability of Accountants: Sources and Policies." *American Business Law Journal,* Spring 1971, pp. 1–20.

"1136 Tenants' Corporation—Decision of the Appellate Division of the Supreme Court of the State of New York." *Journal of Accountancy,* November 1971, pp. 67–73.

Elliott, R. K., and J. J. Willingham. *Management Fraud: Detection and Deterrence,* Princeton, N.J.: Petrocelli Books, 1980, 300 pages.

Isbell, David B. "The Continental Vending Case: Lessons for the Profession." *Journal of Accountancy,* August 1970, pp. 33–40.

Isbell, David B., and D. R. Carmichael. "Disclaimers and Liability—The Rhode Island Trust Case." *Journal of Accountancy,* April 1973, pp. 37–42.

Johnson, Kenneth P. "The Auditor's Responsibility to Detect Fraud." Series of four articles. *CPA Journal,* December 1980, January, February, March 1981.

McKesson & Robbins, Inc. "Summary of Findings and Conclusions of the SEC." *Journal of Accountancy,* January 1941, pp. 90–95. Also *SEC Accounting Series Release No. 19,* December 1940.

Mautz, R. K., and R. D. Neary. "Corporate Audit Committee-Quo Vadis?" *Journal of Accountancy,* October 1979, pp. 83–88.

"Report of Special Committee on Audit Committees." AICPA, 1978, 16 pages.

"Report of the Special Committee on Equity Funding." New York: AICPA, 1975.

Schnepper, Jeff A. "The Accountant's Liability Under Rule 10b-5 and Section 10(*b*) of the Securities Exchange Act of 1934: The Hole in Hochfelder." *Accounting Review,* July 1977, pp. 653–57.

Schultz, J. J., and K. Pany. "The Independent Auditor's Civil Liability—An Overview." *Accounting Review,* April 1980, pp. 319–326.

Securities and Exchange Commission. "In the Matter of Peat, Marwick, Mitchell & Co." *Accounting Series Release No. 173,* July 2, 1975.

Slavin, Nathan S. "The Elimination of 'Scienter' in Determining Auditors' Statutory Liability." *The Accounting Review,* April 1977, pp. 360–68.

St. Pierre, K., and J. Anderson. "An Analysis of Audit Failures Based on Documented Legal Cases." *Journal of Accounting, Auditing & Finance,* Spring 1982, pp. 229–247.

Whalen, Richard J. "The Big Skid at Yale Express." *Fortune,* November 1965, pp. 144–49.

Williams, Harold M. "Audit Committees—The Public Sector's View." *Journal of Accountancy,* September 1977, pp. 71–75.

Winters, Alan J. "Avoiding Malpractice Liability Suits." *Journal of Accountancy,* August 1981, pp. 69–74.

REVIEW QUESTIONS

4.1. What similarities and differences are found between rules of ethics and rules of law? Consider scope, enforcement and penalty in your answer.

4.2. Give five general ways public accountants can get themselves into legal difficulty.

4.3. What does the Foreign Corrupt Practices Act prohibit? What does it require?

4.4. How are *errors and irregularities* and *clients' illegal acts* defined in auditing standards?

4.5. What difference, if any, exists between auditors' responsibilities concerning errors and irregularities and responsibilities concerning clients' illegal acts?

4.6. In what form of the law will one find provision for criminal penalties? Civil remedies?

4.7. What must be proved by the plaintiff in a common law action seeking recovery of damages from an independent auditor of financial statements? What must the defendant accountant do in such a court action?

4.8. What legal theory is derived from the *Ultramares* decision? Can auditors rely on the *Ultramares* rule today?

4.9. On what grounds were the auditors judged liable for damages in the *Rhode Island Hospital Trust* case? Explain.

4.10. Do any pronouncements of the AICPA, other than the rules of ethics, define duties and responsibilities of accountants in nonaudit engagements?

4.11. What is *Regulation S-X? Regulation S-K? Regulation D? Financial Reporting Releases? Staff Accounting Bulletins?*

4.12. How does the SEC's integrated disclosure system simplify and coordinate various SEC report filings?

4.13. What is a "nonpublic offering" (private

placement) of securities? What are "accredited investors," and how are they related to nonpublic offerings?

4.14. What are the 10-K, 10-Q, and 8-K reports? To which securities act do they relate? How has the 8-K report been used to strengthen the independent auditor's position?

4.15. How does Section 11 of the Securities Act (1933) change the legal environment that previously existed under common law?

4.16. What must be proved by the plaintiff in a suit under Section 11 of the Securities Act (1933) seeking recovery of damages from an independent auditor of financial statements? What must the defendant auditor do in such a court action?

4.17. Why should officers, directors and underwriters want auditors to include under the audit opinion such information as the plan for use of the proceeds of an offering, the description of the organization and busi-

ness, the description of physical properties and other quasi-financial information such as plant floor space and sales order backlog?

4.18. What liability exposure for accountants is found in Section 17 of the Securities Act (1933)? In Section 10(*b*) of the Exchange Act (1934)? In Section 18 of the Exchange Act (1934)?

4.19. What liability exposure for accountants is found in Section 24 of the Securities Act (1933)? In Section 32 of the Exchange Act (1934)?

4.20. With reference to the *BarChris* and *Continental Vending* decisions, what lessons might be learned about the force and effect of generally accepted accounting principles?

4.21. With reference to the *BarChris* decision, what lessons might be learned about the force and effect of generally accepted auditing standards?

DISCUSSION CASES AND PROBLEMS

4.22. **Responsibility for Errors and Irregularities**
Huffman & Whitman, a large regional CPA firm, was engaged by the Ritter Tire Wholesale Company to audit its financial statements for the year ended January 31. Huffman & Whitman had a busy audit engagement schedule from December 31 through April 1, and they decided to audit Ritter's purchase vouchers and related cash disbursements on a sample basis. They instructed staff accountants to select a random sample of 300 purchase transactions and gave directions about what to look for. Boyd, the assistant in charge, completed the working papers, properly documenting the fact that 30 of the purchases sampled had been recorded and paid without the receiving report (required by stated internal control procedures) being included in the file of supporting documents. Whitman, the partner in direct charge of the audit, showed the

findings to Lock, Ritter's chief accountant. Lock appeared surprised but promised that the missing receiving reports would be inserted into the files before the audit was over. Whitman was satisfied, noted in the workpapers that the problem was solved, and did not say anything to Huffman about it.

Unfortunately, Lock was involved in a fraudulent scheme in which he diverted shipments to a warehouse leased in his name and sent the invoices to Ritter for payment. He then sold the tires for his own profit. Internal auditors discovered the scheme during a study of slow-moving inventory items. Ritter's inventory was overstated by about $200,000—the amount Lock had diverted.

Required:

a. Did Lock's activity amount to an error or an irregularity?

b. Were any related party transactions involved?

c. With regard to the 30 missing receiving reports, does a material weakness in internal control exist? If so, does Huffman & Whitman have any reporting responsibility? Explain.

d. Was the audit conducted in a negligent manner?

4.23. Responsibility for Errors and Irregularities

Herbert McCoy is the chief executive officer of McCoy Forging Corporation, a small but rapidly growing manufacturing company. For the past several years, Donovan & Company, CPAs, had been engaged to do compilation work, a systems improvement study, and to prepare the company's federal and state income tax returns. In 1985, McCoy decided that due to the growth of the company and requests from bankers it would be desirable to have an audit. Moreover, McCoy had recently received a disturbing anonymous letter which stated: "Beware, you have a viper in your nest. The money is literally disappearing before your very eyes! Signed: A friend."

McCoy believed that the audit was entirely necessary and easily justifiable on the basis of the growth and credit factor mentioned above. He decided he would keep the anonymous letter to himself.

Therefore, McCoy, on behalf of McCoy Forging, engaged Donovan & Company, CPAs, to render an opinion on the financial statements for the year ended June 30, 1986. He told Donovan he wanted to verify that the financial statements were "accurate and proper." He did not mention the anonymous letter. The usual engagement letter providing for an audit in accordance with generally accepted auditing standards (GAAS) was drafted by Donovan & Company and signed by both parties.

The audit was performed in accordance with GAAS. The audit did not reveal a clever defalcation plan by which Harper, the assistant treasurer, was siphoning off substantial amounts of McCoy Forging's money. The defalcations occurred both before and after the audit. Harper's embezzlement was discovered by McCoy's new internal auditor in October, 1986, after Donovan had delivered the audit report. Although the scheme was fairly sophisticated, it could have been detected had additional checks and procedures been performed by Donovan & Company. McCoy Forging demands reimbursement from Donovan for the entire amount of the embezzlement, some $20,000 of which occurred before the audit and $25,000 after. Donovan has denied any liability and refuses to pay.

Required:

Discuss Donovan's responsibility in this situation. Do you think McCoy Forging would prevail in whole or in part in a lawsuit against Donovan under common law? Explain your conclusions.

(*AICPA* adapted)

4.24. Common Law Liability Exposure

A CPA firm was engaged to examine the financial statements of Martin Manufacturing Corporation for the year ending December 31, 1985. Martin needed cash to continue its operations and agreed to sell its common stock investment in a subsidiary through a private placement. The buyers insisted that the proceeds be placed in escrow because of the possibility of a major contingent tax liability that might result from a pending government claim against Martin's subsidiary. The payment in escrow was completed in late November 1982. The president of Martin told the audit partner that the proceeds from the sale of the subsidiary's common stock, held in escrow, should be shown on the balance sheet as an unrestricted current account receivable. The president was of the opinion that the government's claim was groundless and that Martin needed an "uncluttered" balance sheet and a "clean" auditor's opinion to obtain additional working capital from lenders. The audit partner agreed with the president and issued an unqualified opinion on the Martin financial statements which did not refer to the contingent liability and did not properly describe the escrow arrangement.

The government's claim proved to be valid, and pursuant to the agreement with the buyers, the purchase price of the subsidiary was reduced by $450,000. This adverse development forced Martin into bankruptcy. The CPA firm is being sued for deceit (fraud) by several of Martin's unpaid creditors who extended credit in reliance upon the CPA firm's unqualified opinion on Martin's financial statements.

Required:

a. What deceit (fraud) do you believe the creditors are claiming?

b. Is the lack of privity between the CPA firm and the creditors important in this case?

c. Do you believe the CPA firm is liable to the creditors? Explain.

(*AICPA* adapted)

4.25. **Common Law Liability Exposure**
Risk Capital Limited, a Delaware corporation, was considering the purchase of a substantial amount of treasury stock held by Florida Sunshine Corporation, a closely held corporation. Initial discussions with the Florida Sunshine Corporation began late in 1984.

Wilson and Wyatt, Florida Sunshine's accountants, regularly prepared quarterly and annual unaudited financial statements. The most recently prepared financial statements were for the year ended September 30, 1985.

On November 15, 1985, after protracted negotiations, Risk Capital agreed to purchase 100,000 shares of no par, Class A capital stock of Florida Sunshine at $12.50 per share. However, Risk Capital insisted upon audited statements for calendar year 1985. The contract which was made available to Wilson & Wyatt specifically provided:

Risk Capital shall have the right to rescind the purchase of said stock if the audited financial statements of Florida Sunshine for the calendar year 1985 show

a material adverse change in the financial condition of the corporation.

The audited financial statements furnished to Florida Sunshine by Wilson and Wyatt showed no such material adverse change. Risk Capital relied upon the audited statements and purchased the treasury stock of Florida Sunshine. It was subsequently discovered that, as of the balance sheet date, the audited statements were incorrect and that in fact there had been a material adverse change in the financial condition of the corporation. Florida Sunshine is insolvent, and Risk Capital will lose virtually its entire investment.

Risk Capital seeks recovery against Wilson and Wyatt.

Required:

Assuming that only ordinary negligence is proved, will Risk Capital prevail:

a. Under the *Ultramares* decision?

b. Under the *Rusch Factors* decision?

4.26. **Common Law Liability Exposure**
Meglow Corporation manufactured ladies' dresses and blouses. Because its cash position was deteriorating, Meglow sought a loan from Busch Factors. Busch had previously extended $25,000 credit to Meglow but refused to lend any additional money without obtaining copies of Meglow's audited financial statements.

Meglow contracted the CPA firm of Watkins, Winslow & Watkins to perform the audit. In arranging for the examination, Meglow clearly indicated that its purpose was to satisfy Busch Factors as to the corporation's sound financial condition and thus to obtain an additional loan of $50,000. Watkins, Winslow & Watkins accepted the engagement, performed the examination in a negligent manner, and rendered an unqualified auditor's opinion. If an adequate examination had been performed, the financial statements would have been found to be misleading.

Meglow submitted the audited financial statements to Busch Factors and obtained an additional loan of $35,000. Busch refused to lend more than that amount. After several other factors also refused, Meglow was finally able to persuade Maxwell Department Stores, one of its customers, to lend the additional $15,000. Maxwell relied upon the financial statements examined by Watkins, Winslow & Watkins.

Meglow is now in bankruptcy, and Busch seeks to collect from Watkins, Winslow & Watkins the $60,000 it loaned Meglow. Maxwell seeks to recover from Watkins, Winslow & Watkins the $15,000 it loaned Meglow.

Required:

Under common law:

a. Will Busch recover? Explain.

b. Will Maxwell recover? Explain.

(*AICPA* adapted)

4.27. Common Law Liability Exposure

Smith, CPA, is the auditor for Juniper Manufacturing Corporation, a privately owned company which has a June 30 fiscal year. Juniper arranged for a substantial bank loan which was dependent upon the bank receiving, by September 30, audited financial statements which showed a current ratio of at least 2 to 1. On September 25, just before the audit report was to be issued, Smith received an anonymous letter on Juniper's stationery indicating that a five-year lease by Juniper, as lessee, of a factory building which was accounted for in the financial statements as an operating lease was in fact a capital lease. The letter stated that there was a secret written agreement with the lessor modifying the lease and creating a capital lease.

Smith confronted the president of Juniper who admitted that a secret agreement existed but said it was necessary to treat the lease as an operating lease to meet the current ratio requirement of the pending loan and that nobody would ever discover the secret agreement with the lessor. The president said that if Smith did not issue his report by September 30, Juniper would sue Smith for substantial damages which would result from not getting the loan. Under this pressure and because the working papers contained a copy of the five-year lease agreement which supported the operating lease treatment, Smith issued his report with an unqualified opinion on September 29. In spite of the fact that the loan was received, Juniper went bankrupt. The bank is suing Smith to recover its losses on the loan and the lessor is suing Smith to recover uncollected rents.

Required:

Answer the following, setting forth reasons for any conclusions stated.

a. Is Smith liable to the bank?

b. Is Smith liable to the lessor?

c. Was Smith independent?

(*AICPA* adapted)

4.28. Common Law Liability Exposure

The Bigelow Corporation decided to liquidate. A board member suggested the possibility of electing a one calendar month liquidation pursuant to section 333 of the Internal Revenue Code. In order to determine whether this type of liquidation was desirable, Bigelow engaged Fanslow & Angelo, CPAs, to perform a tax analysis of the corporation's data to ascertain the amount of dividend income to the shareholders if this method of liquidation were elected. Such a determination is largely dependent on the amount of "earnings and profits," both current and historical.

In making the computation, Fanslow and Angelo treated retained earnings as stated in the financial statements as "earnings and profits" for tax purposes. However, on two prior occasions transfers were made from retained earnings to stated capital upon the issuance of stock dividends. The result of failure to adjust "earnings and profits" to reflect these transfers was to understate the amount of taxable dividend income per share by some $20 per share.

Required:

Do Fanslow & Angelo have any liability under the above-stated facts? Explain.

4.29. Common Law Liability Exposure

Farr & Madison, CPAs, audited Glamour, Inc. Their audit was deficient in several respects:

1. Farr and Madison failed to audit properly certain receivables which later proved to be fictitious.

2. With respect to other receivables, although they made a cursory check, they did not detect many accounts which were long overdue and obviously uncollectible.

3. No physical inventory was taken of the securities claimed to be in Glamour's possession, which in fact had been sold. Both the securities and cash received from the sales were listed on the balance sheet as assets.

There is no indication that Farr & Madison actually believed that the financial statements were false. Subsequent creditors, not known to Farr & Madison, are now suing based upon the deficiencies in the audit described above. Farr and Madison moved to dismiss the lawsuit against it on the basis that the firm did not have actual knowledge of falsity and therefore did not commit fraud.

Required:

May the creditors recover without demonstrating Farr & Madison had actual knowledge of falsity? Explain.

4.30. Securities Act (1933) Exemption/Registration

Your client, Lux Corporation, is a small food manufacturing company with a single plant located in its state of incorporation and has outstanding 200,000 shares of $100 par value common stock which is selling at about that price in infrequent sales. Lux desires to raise $10 million of additional working capital and is considering the following alternatives:

1. Sale of $10 million of a new issue of convertible debentures to Kelly, a rich investor who formerly had been an executive of the company. Kelly retired and now lives in a neighboring state.

2. Sale of $10 million of additional common stock to local business executives and other local investors.

Required:

Discuss the impact of the registration requirements of the Securities Act (1933) as it applies to each alternative.

4.31. Applicability of Securities Act and Exchange Act

1. The partnership of Zelsch & Co., CPAs, has been engaged to audit the financial statements of Snake Oil, Inc., in connection with filing an S-1 registration statement under the Securities Act (1933). Discuss the following two statements made by the senior partner of Zelsch & Co.

   a. "The partnership is assuming a much greater liability exposure in this engagement than exists under common law."

   b. "If our examination is not fraudulent, we can avoid any liability claims that might arise."

2. State whether the following are true or false. Explain each.

   Xavier, Francis & Paul is a growing, medium-sized partnership of CPAs located in the Midwest. One of the firm's major clients is considering offering its stock to the public. This will be the firm's first client to go public.

   a. The firm should thoroughly familiarize itself with the securities acts, Regulation S-X and Regulation S-K.

   b. If the client is unincorporated, the Securities Act (1933) will not apply.

   c. If the client is going to be listed on an organized exchange, the Exchange Act (1934) will not apply.

   d. The Securities Act (1933) imposes an additional potential liability on firms such as Xavier, Francis & Paul.

   e. So long as the company engages in exclusively intrastate business, the federal securities laws will not apply.

4.32. Subsequent Events and the Securities Act (1933)

You should study SAS 1 (AU 560) and SAS 37 (AU 711) to deal with the following questions.

A registration statement filed under the Securities Act (1933) is said to "speak as of its *effective date*," meaning that an auditor's responsibility for obtaining evidence about subsequent events extends beyond the normal date of the audit report. The effective date of a registration statement is always after the date of completion of the audit fieldwork.

a. What procedures should auditors perform relative to subsequent events between the date of the latest audited balance sheet and the date of the audit report?

b. What procedures should auditors perform relative to subsequent events between the date of the audit report and the effective date of a registration statement?

c. With reference to Section 11 of the Securities Act (1933), why does an auditor need to be so concerned with subsequent event auditing procedures?

4.33. Section 11 of Securities Act (1933) Liability Exposure

The Chriswell Corporation decided to raise additional long-term capital by issuing $10 million of 12-percent subordinated debentures to the public. May, Clark & Company, CPAs, the company's auditors, were engaged to examine the June 30, 1985, financial statements which were included in the bond registration statement.

May, Clark & Company completed its examination and submitted an unqualified auditor's report dated July 15, 1985. The registration statement was filed and later became effective on September 1, 1985. On August 15, one of the partners of May, Clark & Company called on Chriswell Corporation and had lunch with the financial vice president and the controller. He questioned both officials on the company's operations since June 30 and inquired whether there had been any material changes in the company's financial position since that date. Both officers assured him that everything had proceeded normally and that the financial condition of the company had not changed materially.

Unfortunately, the officers' representation was not true. On July 30, a substantial debtor of the company failed to pay the $400,000 due on its account receivable and indicated to Chriswell that it would probably be forced into bankruptcy. This receivable was shown as a collateralized loan on the June 30 financial statements. It was secured by stock of the debtor corporation which had a value in excess of the loan at the time the financial statements were prepared but was virtually worthless at the effective date of the registration statement. This $400,000 account receivable was material to the financial condition of Chriswell Corporation, and the market price of the subordinated debentures decreased by nearly 50 percent after the foregoing facts were disclosed.

The debenture holders of Chriswell are seeking recovery of their loss against all parties connected with the debenture registration.

Required:

Is May, Clark & Company liable to the Chriswell debenture holders under Section 11 of the Securities Act (1933)? Explain.

(*AICPA* adapted)

4.34. Rule 10b-5 Liability Exposure Under the Exchange Act (1934)

Gordon & Groton, CPAs, were the auditors of Bank & Company, a brokerage firm and member of a national stock exchange. Gordon & Groton examined and reported on the financial statements of Bank which were filed with the Securities and Exchange Commission.

Several of Bank's customers were swindled by a fraudulent scheme perpetrated by Bank's president who owned 90 percent of the voting stock of the company. The facts establish that Gordon & Groton were negligent in the conduct of the audit and neither participated in the fraudulent scheme nor knew of its existence.

The customers are suing Gordon & Groton under the antifraud provisions of Section 10(*b*) and Rule 10b-5 of the Exchange Act (1934) for aiding and abetting the fraudulent scheme of the president. The customers' suit for fraud is predicated exclusively on the nonfeasance of the auditors in failing to conduct a proper audit, thereby failing to discover the fraudulent scheme.

Required:

Answer the following, setting forth reasons for any conclusions stated.

a. What is the probable outcome of the lawsuit?

b. What might be the result if plaintiffs had sued under a common law theory of negligence? Explain.

(*AICPA* adapted)

4.35. **Corporate Audit Committees**

For many years, the financial and accounting community has recognized the importance of the use of audit committees and has endorsed their formation.

At this time, the use of audit committees has become widespread. Independent auditors have become increasingly involved with audit committees and consequently have become familiar with their nature and function.

Required:

a. What is a corporate audit committee? Describe one.

b. Identify the reasons why audit committees have been formed and are currently in operation.

c. What are the functions of an audit committee?

APPENDIX 4–A

Cases in Common Law

Smith v. **London Assur. Corp.**   (Appellate Division, New York, 1905, 109 App. Div. 882, 96 N.Y.S. 820.) This case gives an example of breach of contract liability.

This was the first American case involving an auditor. The auditor sued for an unpaid fee, and the company counterclaimed for a large sum that had been embezzled by one of its employees which they claimed would not have occurred except for the auditor's breach of contract. The evidence indicated that the auditors indeed failed to check cash accounts at one branch office as stipulated in an engagement contract. The court recognized the auditors as skilled professionals and held them liable for embezzlement losses which could have been prevented by nonnegligent performance under the contract.

Ultramares Corp. v. Touche   (Court of Appeals of New York, 1931, 255 N.Y. 170, 174 N.E. 441.) Ultramares is the most famous early case about auditor liability. It established the precedent of a strong privity doctrine and laid the basis for constructive fraud liability exposure.

Ultramares is considered an important landmark case for accountants because it dealt specifically with issues of contract, privity, tort, deceit, degrees of negligence, and third-party beneficiaries. Nevertheless, the gross negligence test for liability to third parties applied in *Ultramares* is beginning to be modified in more current decisions.

Ultramares Corp. relied upon financial statements audited by Touche and made loans to the Fred Stern & Co., Inc., an importer of rubber. Stern went bankrupt, and the evidence presented in court indicated that Touche had failed to investigate the significance of penciled sales-accounts receivable entries at the bottom of the last month's sales journal which turned out to be fictitious.

Ultramares suffered damages in the amount of the loans that could not be collected.

The *Ultramares* decision stated criteria for an auditor's liability to third parties for *deceit* (a tort action). In order to prove deceit: (1) a false representation must be shown, (2) the tort-feasor must possess **scienter**—either knowledge of falsity or insufficient basis of information, (3) an intent to induce action in reliance must be shown, (4) the damaged party must show justifiable reliance and (5) there must have been a resulting damage. The court held that an accountant could be liable when he did not have sufficient information (audit evidence) to lead to a sincere or genuine belief. In other words, an audit report is deceitful when the auditor purports to speak from knowledge when he has none.

However, the court also held that the auditor was not liable to unidentified third parties for negligence. The plaintiff was not known to Touche at the time the report was issued, although the auditor knew it would be shown to and used by third parties. Only this lack of identification caused the court to say:

> If liability for negligence exists, a thoughtless slip or blunder, the failure to detect a theft or forgery beneath the cover of deceptive entries, may expose accountants to a liability in an indeterminate amount for an indeterminate time to an indeterminate class.

The court also wrote that the degree of negligence might be so gross, however, as to amount to a constructive fraud. Then the auditor could be liable in tort to a third party beneficiary. Some modern court decisions currently are modifying the *Ultramares* rule by holding the auditor liable for negligence to third parties who can be foreseen by the auditor. (Refer to the discussion of *Rusch Factors* v. *Levin* below.)

McKesson & Robbins Inc.   This controversy was settled out of court. SEC investigations used the facts to prompt development of profession-wide standards.

In 1938, a receiver was appointed to oversee the affairs of McKesson & Robbins, Inc., and an introductory chapter in American auditing was begun. The company had, out of a total of $87 million in assets, an approximate $10 million inventory overstatement and $9 million in fictitious accounts receivable. The trustee's claim against the auditor was settled without litigation by refund of over $500,000 previously paid in audit fees since 1933.

At the time this audit was conducted, acceptable audit procedures did not include independent confirmation of accounts receivable or observation of inventories. Certain company officials had simply taken advantage of their knowledge of auditing to create false entries for purchases and sales, thereby creating a paper empire.

In a subsequent investigation by the SEC (*Accounting Series Release No. 19,* 1940), the following findings were made:

1. The auditors failed to employ that degree of vigilance, inquisitiveness, and analysis of the evidence available that is necessary in a professional undertaking and is recommended in all well-known and authoritative works on auditing. Meticulous verification of the inventory was not needed to discover the fraud.

2. Even though the auditors are not guarantors and should not be responsible for detecting all fraud, the discovery of gross overstatements in the accounts is a major purpose in an audit even though every minor defalcation might not be disclosed.

The response of accountants and auditors was the development of auditing standards and the beginning in 1939 of the series of Statements on Auditing Procedures.

State Street Trust Co. v. Ernst   (278 N.Y. 104, 15 N.E. 2d 416, 1938.) This case established precedent for auditor liability to parties not in privity on grounds of heedless, reckless work (gross negligence).

This case is very similar to *Ultramares* except that here the auditors *did examine* receivables but failed to detect an overstatement due to the uncollectibility of many accounts. The court found that auditors could be liable to third parties and expressed the criteria forthrightly as follows:

> Accountants, however, may be liable to third parties, even where there is lacking deliberate or active fraud. A representation certified as true to the knowledge of the accountants when knowledge there is none, a reckless misstatement, or an opinion based on grounds so flimsy as to lead to the conclusion that there was no genuine belief in its truth, are all sufficient upon which to base liability. A refusal to see the obvious, a failure to investigate the doubtful, if sufficiently gross, may furnish evidence leading to an inference of fraud so as to impose liability for losses suffered by those who rely on the balance sheet. In other words, heedlessness and reckless disregard of consequences may take the place of deliberate intention.
>
> In *Ultramares Corp.* v. *Touche* (255 N.Y. 170) we said with no uncertainty that negligence, if gross, or blindness, even though not equivalent to fraud, was sufficient to sustain an inference of fraud. Our exact words were:

"In this connection we are to bear in mind the principle already stated in the course of this opinion that negligence or blindness, even when not equivalent to fraud, is none the less evidence to sustain an inference of fraud. At least this is so if the negligence is gross."

CIT Financial Corp. v. Glover. (U.S. Court of Appeals for the Second Circuit, 1955, 224 F. 2d 44.) This case established a precedent related to auditor liability to primary beneficiaries for ordinary negligence.

In this case, plaintiff had suffered losses on loans and claimed that audited financial statements were materially misleading. The suit alleged negligence and gross negligence. The court interpreted *Ultramares* to mean that auditors are liable to third parties for ordinary negligence if their reports are for the primary benefit of the third party. Thus, the privity criterion may not serve as a defense when third party beneficiaries are known. However, the jury evaluated evidence presented in court and determined (1) that there was no negligence because the report adequately communicated the auditor's opinion and knowledge and (2) that the auditor's report was not for the primary benefit of the third party.

Rusch Factors, Inc. v. Levin. (U.S. District Court for the District of Rhode Island, 1968, 248 F. Supp. 85.) In Rusch Factors, privity was no defense in a fraud action. Accountants are liable to actual foreseen and limited classes of persons for ordinary negligence.

The plaintiff had relied upon audited financial statements to make loans to a company that soon after went bankrupt. These circumstances are not different from earlier cases, but the court in *Rusch Factors* did three things of note: (1) liberalized the liability exposure rule respecting the privity defense, (2) modified the *Ultramares* rule to shift more responsibility to the accountant, and (3) quoted and applied the Restatement (Second) of Torts (1966). These parts of the court opinion are of sufficient importance to quote them below in their entirety.

> Privity of contract is clearly no defense in a fraud action. An intentionally misrepresenting accountant is liable to all those persons whom he should reasonably have foreseen would be injured by his misrepresentation. (*Ultramares* v. *Touche & Co.*) . . . Neither actual knowledge by the accountant of the third person's reliance nor quantitative limitation of the class of reliant persons is requisite to recovery for fraud. . . . The same broad perimeter prevails if the misrepresenter's conduct is heedless enough to permit an inference of fraud. (*State St. Trust Co. v. Ernst*). . . . There are several reasons which support the broad rule of liability for fraudulent misrepresentation. First, liability should extend at least as far in fraud, an intentional tort, as it does in negligence cases resulting in personal injury or property damage. Second, the risk of loss for intentional wrongdoing should invariably be placed on the wrongdoer who caused the harm, rather than on the innocent victim of the harm. Finally, a broad rule of liability may deter

future misconduct. . . . The court determines, for the above stated reasons, that the plaintiff's complaint is sufficient in so far as it alleges fraud.

The wisdom of the decision in *Ultramares* had been doubted, . . . and this court shares the doubt. Why should an innocent reliant party be forced to carry the weighty burden of an accountant's professional malpractice? Isn't the risk of loss more easily distributed and fairly spread by imposing it on the accounting profession, which can pass the cost of insuring against the risk onto the entire consuming public? Finally, wouldn't a rule of foreseeability elevate the cautionary techniques of the accounting profession? For these reasons, it appears to this court that the decision in *Ultramares* constitutes an unwarranted inroad upon the principle that "the risk reasonably to be perceived defines the duty to be obeyed." . . .

This court need not, however, hold that the Rhode Island Supreme Court would overrule the *Ultramares* decision, if presented the opportunity, for the case at bar is qualitatively distinguishable from *Ultramares*. There, the plaintiff was a member of an undefined, unlimited class of remote lenders and potential equity holders not actually foreseen but only foreseeable. Here the plaintiff is a single party whose reliance was actually foreseen by the defendant. . . .

With respect, then, to the plaintiff's negligence theory, this court holds that an accountant should be liable in negligence for careless financial misrepresentations relied upon by actually foreseen and limited classes of persons. According to the plaintiff's complaint in the instant case, the defendant knew that his certification was to be used for, and had as its very aim and purpose, the reliance of potential financiers of the Rhode Island corporation. The defendant's motion is, therefore, denied. The court does not rule upon, but leaves open for reconsideration in the light of trial development, the question of whether an accountant's liability for negligent misrepresentation ought to extend to the full limits of foreseeability.

Rhode Island Hospital Trust National Bank **v.** *Swartz.*   (455 F. 2d, 847, 4th Cir., 1972.) The auditor was found liable to a bank that relied on his negligent and faulty audit report.

This case is similar to *Rusch Factors* in the court's citation and reliance on the Restatement of Torts. The client company represented in its financial statements that certain additions to fixed assets in the form of self-construction of warehouse improvements had been made at several locations. The auditors *disclaimed* an opinion and stated in their report, in part: "Additions to fixed assets in 1963 were found to include principally warehouse improvements and installation of machinery and equipment in (several locations named). . . . Unfortunately, fully complete detailed cost records were not kept of these improvements and no exact determination could be made as to the actual cost of said improvements."

In fact, *no* cost records were kept, and the asset additions did not exist at all. The court held that the auditor was negligent in failing to give a clear explanation of the reasons for the qualification (the disclaimer of opinion) and the effect on financial position and results of operations as required by AICPA auditing standards. Being ruled negligent, under the Restatement of Torts, the auditors were held liable for plaintiff's damage.

1136 Tenants' Corp. v. *Max Rothenberg & Co.*   (Appellate Division, New York, 1967, 27 A.D. 2d 830, 277 N.Y.S. 2d 996.) Liability was imposed for negligent work on unaudited financial statements.

This is one of the leading cases involving unaudited financial statements and the accountant's responsibilities to stockholder-users of the statements.

The accountant Rothenberg had been engaged to perform write-up work for a fee of $600 per year for Riker & Company—a managing agent that handled maintenance payments of several cooperative apartment houses, including the plaintiffs'. The accountant prepared statements of receipts and disbursements, and Riker sent these to the tenants. The statements showed that various taxes and expenses had been paid, but in fact these were not paid and Riker had embezzled the money. The statements carried the legend "unaudited," and a cover letter stated that "the statements were prepared from the books and records of the corporation and no independent verifications were undertaken thereon."

Despite claims to the contrary, the court found that defendant was engaged to audit and not merely write-up plaintiff's books and records. The accountant had, in fact, performed some limited auditing procedures including preparation of a worksheet entitled "Missing Invoices 1/1/63–12/31/63." These were items Riker claimed to have paid but did not. The court held that even if accountants were hired only for write-up work, they had a duty to inform plaintiffs of any circumstances that gave reason to believe that a fraud had occurred (e.g., the record of "missing invoices").

The plaintiffs recovered damages of about $237,000. This decision prompted the AICPA to issue a booklet entitled *Guide for Engagements to Prepare Unaudited Financial Statements* which has now been superseded by SAS 26 and by the SSARS pronouncements of the AICPA Accounting and Review Services Committee.

APPENDIX 4–B

Cases under the Securities Acts

Escott et al. v. *BarChris Construction Corporation et al.*   (U.S. District Court for the Southern District of New York, 1968, 283 F. Supp. 643.) BarChris is an example of diligence defense that failed, and auditors were judged liable under Section 11 of the Securities Act (1933). The judge's opinion includes decisions on appropriate accounting principles, the materiality of errors, and the diligence standard for persons who rely on auditor's work.

Suit was brought on October 25, 1962, under Section 11 of the Securities Act (1933) by purchasers of the company's 5½ percent convertible subordinated debentures. The company had filed a registration statement on March 30, 1961, which became effective May 16, 1961. Seventeen months later, on October 29, 1962, it filed under Chapter XI of the Bank-ruptcy Act. The auditors had given an unqualified opinion on the balance sheet as of December 31, 1960, in a report dated February 23, 1961.

BarChris was in the business of constructing bowling alleys. Usually, the completed structures were sold to an operator, who made a down payment and gave an installment note for the balance. BarChris would then discount the note with a factor and receive proceeds reduced by an amount withheld by the factor as a loss reserve. As the purchaser paid the note, the proportionate part of this loss reserve would be remitted to BarChris. On at least one occasion, a customer could not take possession, so BarChris sold the bowling alley at a gain to the factor, who then leased it to a wholly owned BarChris subsidiary for operation. BarChris ac-counted for construction operations on the percentage-of-completion method.

The important points of the court opinion were these:

1. Plaintiffs charged in general that the 1960 financial statements were materially misleading, that the percentage-of-completion method was erroneous and misleading, and that even if the method were appropri-ate, it was applied in error to cause the statements to be materially misleading.

    a. The court ruled that the percentage-of-completion method was a widely used, generally accepted accounting method and was thus appropriate and did not of itself cause financial statements to be misleading.

    b. The court ruled that errors had been made in applying the method but that the errors were not material. The auditor had treated two contracts as 100 percent complete, relying on management's oral representations, when they were in fact only partially completed.

    c. The court ruled that the sale and subsequent leaseback of a bowl-ing alley was not in fact a sale because the property did not leave the company's control. Thus sales and gross profits were over-stated. (This sale occurred in 1960, prior to issuance of *APB Opinion No. 5* in 1964. Before 1964, profits on sale and leaseback could be recognized currently with full disclosure, but only after APB 5 was this prohibited.)

    d. The court ruled that the income statement data was not materi-ally misstated. Sales were overstated by 8 percent, net operating income by 16 percent, and earnings per share by 15 percent. The apparent reasoning for ruling these overstatements not material was that sales and earnings were significantly greater in 1960 than in 1959 even with the overstatements removed. Sales were up 256 percent instead of the reported 276 percent, net operating income up $1,055,093 instead of $1,301,698, and earnings per share up 97 percent (to 65 cents) instead of up 128 percent (to 75 cents).

    e. The court ruled that the balance sheet data, especially the current assets and liabilities, were materially misstated. Noncurrent assets (a temporary cash advance from a nonconsolidated subsidiary and the factor's loss reserve retentions) were improperly classified as current, an allowance for uncollectibility was judged erroneous, and some current liabilities were omitted. Altogether, these errors caused the current ratio to be shown as 1.9:1 and the court decided that it should have been reported as 1.6:1.

In brief outline then, the *BarChris* court made judgments that both upheld and disregarded then-current generally accepted accounting principles and judgments that distinguish both material and immaterial error.

2. Defendant accountants, officers, directors, attorneys, and underwriters all asserted the defense of due diligence.

The court ruled that the auditors were the *only experts* under Section 11 and specifically ruled that the attorneys were not considered experts.

In individual findings against all defendants (except the auditors), the court generally ruled that they had not conducted reasonable investigations to form a basis for belief and that they had not satisfied the diligence requirement, *except to the extent that they had relied upon the portions of the prospectus expertised by the auditors.* (A lesser diligence requirement.) The court ruled that the auditors had also failed to perform a diligent and reasonable investigation. Particularly, the court specified the misclassification of the factor's loss reserve retentions, the exercise of bad judgment in evaluating collectibility of a receivable, and a "useless" S-1 review. This last point is of particular relevance to the responsibility for subsequent events running to the effective date. The S-1 review is a common term for the audit program for review of subsequent events, and the auditors had prepared a program in full accord with the then-current Chapter 11 of SAP 33. However, the court found that the auditor had spent "only" 20½ hours on this review, had read no important documents, and, "He asked questions, he got answers that he considered satisfactory, and he did nothing to verify them . . . He was too easily satisfied with glib answers to his inquiries." The court also said:

Accountants should not be held to a standard higher than that recognized in their profession. *I do not do so here.* [Accountant's name] *review did not come up to that standard. He did not take some of the steps which (the) written program prescribed. He did not spend an adequate amount of time on a task of this magnitude.* (Emphasis added.)

3. The defendant accountants asserted the causation defense, citing general economic conditions and particularly the decline in the bowling industry. The court did not rule on this defense because of the diverse circumstances of the plaintiffs and because some cross-claims among

the defendants had to be settled first. One plaintiff had purchased his debentures after the bankruptcy, so one may assume that the causation defense was complete as to his claim.

United States v. *White*   (124 F. 2d 181, 2d Cir., 1941.) An accountant was found liable for fraud and deceit as a result of grossly negligent work.

In this 1941 case, an accountant was convicted of using the mails to defraud in violation of Section 17 of the 1933 act. The auditor's defense was that he had extracted facts from the books and from what management had told him in apparent disregard of other factual circumstances and events. The prosecution maintained that anyone with the auditor's experience and intelligence would have been aware of the irregularity. The jury apparently decided guilt on the basis of the auditor's being "so credulous or so ill acquainted with his calling" that a finding of innocence was not undeniably demanded by the evidence.

Fischer v. *Kletz*   (Popularly styled the "*Yale Express* case," U.S. District Court for the Southern District of New York, 266 F. Supp. 180, 1967.) The judge ruled that "aiding and abetting" allegations were sufficient grounds for proceeding to trial on the merits of the lawsuit.

This decision is the court's ruling to deny the defendant's motion to dismiss the suit. No other public record exists because the suit was later settled without trial. Plaintiff's allegations were based on common law deceit, Section 18 of the 1934 act and Section 10(*b*), and Rule 10b-5 under the 1934 act. The case was complicated by the accounting firm's involvement in a management services engagement *following* the financial statement audit. Thus, there are many instructive dimensions to this ruling: Reading of the complete decision is recommended.

Stockholders and debenture holders of Yale Express System, Inc., sued the auditor, alleging their false certification of false financial statements and failure to disclose subsequently acquired information. The 1963 financial statements, with auditor's opinion, were released around April 9, 1964, showing net income of $1,140,000. Sometime around June 29, 1964, the company filed a 10-K report with the SEC reporting essentially the same information. Early in 1964 (the exact date was disputed), the accounting firm that did the 1963 audit was engaged to perform special studies of the company's past and current income and expenses. In the course of this nonaudit engagement, the accountants discovered that the 1963 financial statements were materially in error. The plaintiffs contended that the misstatement was known before the 10-K report was filed, and the defendants maintained that discovery was later. In any event, the misstatement was disclosed sometime between February and May 1965, when the 1964 audit was completed. At that time (which also was in dispute), the financial statements and auditor's report revealed that 1963 net income had been revised downward to a *loss* of $1,254,000 (not considering $629,000 in special charges to retained earnings).

In brief, the court's findings dealt with the following subjects: (1) The accounting firm's role of consultant and not that of statutory independent auditor on the management services engagement; (2) the aspect of silence and inaction rather than affirmative misrepresentations as criteria for deceit; (3) the dimensions of "aiding and abetting" in connection with Section 10(*b*) and Rule 10(*b*)-5 liability and (4) the responsibilities of an auditor in connection with unaudited interim financial statements.

The *Yale Express* case stimulated promulgation of SAP 41, (AU 561), *Subsequent Discovery of Facts Existing at the Date of the Auditor's Report* (1969). This SAP requires positive action by the CPA who later becomes aware of facts existing at the date of his report which might have affected his audit opinion had he then known those facts. The CPA is required to disclose his knowledge to client management and seek wider disclosure and, failing that, notify the SEC and stock exchanges as appropriate representatives of the public interest.

United States* v. *Benjamin   (328 F. 2d 854, 2d Cir., 1964.) Willful violation evidenced by recklessness is enough for criminal liability.

The judgment in this case resulted in conviction of an accountant for willingly conspiring by use of interstate commerce to sell unregistered securities and to defraud in the sale of securities, in violation of Section 24 of the 1933 act. The accountant had prepared "pro forma" balance sheets and claimed that use of the words "pro forma" absolved him of responsibility. He also claimed he did not know his reports would be used in connection with securities sales. The court found otherwise, showing that he did in fact know about the use of his reports and that certain statements about asset values and acquisitions were patently false and the accountant knew that they were false. The court made two significant findings: (1) that the willfulness requirements of Section 24 may be proved by showing that due diligence would have revealed the false statements and (2) that use of limiting words such as "pro forma" do not justify showing false ownership of assets in any kind of financial statements.

United States* v. *Simon   (United States Court of Appeals for the Second Circuit, 425 F. 2d, 796, 1969). The circumstances were judged to be evidence of willful violation of the Securities and Exchange Act of 1934. Generally accepted accounting principles were viewed by the judge as persuasive but not conclusive criteria for financial reporting.

The defendants (two partners and an audit manager) were prosecuted for filing false statements with a government agency, mail fraud, and violation of Section 32 of the 1934 Act. The first trial resulted in a jury hung in favor of acquittal, and a mistrial was declared. The second jury trial in 1968 resulted in conviction, which was confirmed by the appeals court in 1969. The U.S. Supreme Court denied certiorari in 1970. In 1973, the defendants received a full presidential pardon. In related civil suits, the accounting firm settled out of court for slightly less than $2 million. Coupled with the sensational nature of the case, many practical lessons can be learned from the various briefs and judgments. (Refer to the reading list at the end of Chapter 4.)

The auditors were engaged in the audit of Continental Vending Machine Corporation. Roth was president and owner of 22 percent of the stock of Continental, and he also owned about 25 percent of the stock of Valley Commercial Corporation and supervised that company's operations. Continental would issue notes to Valley which would discount them with banks and remit the proceeds to Continental. These transactions created the account known as the "Valley payable." In an unrelated series of transactions, Roth would have Continental "lend" cash to Valley, which then would lend to Roth for his personal use, thus creating the account known as the "Valley receivable." For the fiscal years 1960–62, the relative account balances were as follows:

September 30	Receivable from Valley	Payable to Valley
1960	$ 397,996	$ 949,852
1961	848,006	780,472
1962	3,543,335	1,029,475

In the financial statements, the receivable was classified among the assets and the payable among the liabilities, but in the footnote disclosure (the alleged false statement at issue in the trials), the two accounts were *netted together*. When asked why the offset of liability against an asset, clearly contrary to accounting principles, the auditors admitted error and explained that sometime in the past someone had netted the two amounts, and it just was not questioned. So lesson one is: Never rely only on the fact that "this is the way we did it last year."

Continental's auditors learned that Valley probably was not in any position to repay the receivable, so Roth and others put up collateral *to Valley*. (Knowledge was not certain because other auditors were engaged to audit Valley's statements, and their report was not delivered to Continental's auditors.) This collateral consisted largely of stock in Continental which the court characterized as singularly unsuitable to secure the receivable. The footnote disclosure revealed only (1) Roth's relation to Valley as "officer, director, and stockholder," (2) that the collateral, assigned to Valley by Continental, exceeded the *net* receivable and (3) that the collateral consisted of "equity in certain marketable securities."

The government contended that the disclosure should have included the following information: (1) that the Valley receivable was uncollectible since Valley had loaned approximately the same amount to Roth who was unable to pay; (2) that the Valley receivable and payable could not be offset; (3) that the Valley receivable was $3,900,000 (It had increased since the fiscal year-end to the February 15, 1963, date of the audit report.); (4) that the value of the collateral was \$2,978,000 and (5) that approximately 80 percent of the collateral was in securities of Continental. In fact, the unencumbered value of the collateral was only \$1,978,000 because of prior liens that the auditors had not discovered.

The audited financial statements were dismal anyway. When they were released, Continental stock plunged, the value of the collateral evaporated, and the accounting firm then withdrew its opinion of the financial statements.

The case, as it progressed, became a *cause celebre* over the role of generally accepted accounting principles as standards for fixing the responsibility of professional accountants. The defense brought an array of well-versed accountants to testify that standards did not require an auditor to inquire deeply into the affairs of an affiliated company that was not an audit client (Valley) to the extent of learning what practices it conducted (the loans to Roth) and that GAAP did not require disclosure of the *nature* of any collateral. Their problem was that no authoritative written source for GAAP spells out these positions, so the strength of their testimony rested entirely on "general acceptability" as it was perceived by the common sense of practicing accountants.

The jury was not convinced, and the trial judge instructed them that knowledge of generally accepted accounting principles could be highly persuasive, *but not necessarily conclusive*. Later, the appeals judge, in affirming the conviction stated that it should be the auditor's responsibility to report factually whenever corporate activities are carried out for the benefit of the president and when "looting" has occurred.

Thus, two other lessons may be inferred: (1) that generally accepted accounting principles to be forceful in a court of law will have to be written and (2) that auditors should be careful to be knowledgeable of the financial affairs of affiliated companies, even to the extent of insisting upon auditing them directly. The events connected with this case led in part to the issuance of standards for the audit of related party transactions.

United States* v. *Natelli.   (U.S. Ct. Appeals, 2nd Circuit, 1975, F. 2d.) Circumstances and actions on the part of accountants were construed to amount to willful violation of the Securities and Exchange Act of 1934.

This case is better known as the *National Student Marketing Corporation (NSMC)* case. Two auditors were charged with violation of Section 32(*e*) of the Securities Exchange Act of 1934 which provides criminal penalties for any person who willfully and knowingly makes, or causes to be made, any statement filed under the act which was false or misleading with respect to any material fact.

Natelli was in charge of the audit of NSMC, a company whose first issue of stock had risen from \$6 to \$80 per share in five months. The company sold marketing programs to companies for promotion on college campuses. Many of the programs had heavy front-end development costs before they were ready, and accounting decisions had been made to apply percentage-of-completion accounting for revenue recognition. This accounting resulted in recording of certain "unbilled receivables" representing commitments from customers. Some commitments totaling $1.7 million in fiscal 1968 were not in writing, but these were nonetheless included in the financial statements for that year.

As fiscal year 1969 proceeded, about $1 million of these commitments were written off, and indications were that they were not valid in the first place. Some decisions were made to adjust the 1968 figures. This is where the accountants got into trouble.

NSMC had acquired several companies in pooling transactions. A footnote in financial statements included in a proxy statement filed in 1969 showed 1968 sales and income figures exhibited below:

Net Sales	1968
Originally reported.	$ 4,989,446
Pooled companies reflected retroactively	6,552,449
Per statement of earnings.	11,541,895

Net Earnings	
Originally reported.	388,031
Pooled companies reflected retroactively	385,121
Per statement of earnings.	773,152

The footnote also explained that certain retroactive adjustments had a net effect of reducing net earnings for the year 1968 by $21,000.

The trouble arose out of the fact that about $350,000 of the write-offs were recorded in the year 1969 and about $678,000 was subtracted from the 1968 sales figures of the pooled companies and not from the "originally reported" net sales. Also, the net income effect was really a $210,000 *reduction,* but the firm's tax department had reported that a deferred tax item in the amount of $189,000 should be reversed. The accountant improperly netted these two items together to report in the footnote, a rather minor $21,000 income reduction.

The appeals court stated: "It is hard to probe the intent of a defendant. . . . When we deal with a defendant who is a professional accountant, it is even harder at times to distinguish between simple errors of judgment and errors made with sufficient criminal intent to support a conviction, especially when there is no financial gain to the accountant other than his legitimate fee." Nevertheless, the court affirmed one accountant's conviction by the lower trial court because of his apparent motive and action to conceal the effect of the accounting adjustments. The footnote in particular, as it was written, failed to reveal what it should have revealed—the write-off of $1 million of "sales" (about 20 percent of the amount previously reported) and the large operating income adjustment ($210,000 compared to $388,031 originally reported). The court concluded that the concealment of the retroactive adjustments to NSMC's 1968 revenues and earnings were properly found to have been intentional for the very purpose of hiding earlier errors.

Ernst & Ernst **v.** *Hochfelder* (U.S. Supreme Court, 1976.) The decision in this case established precedent for plaintiffs' needs to allege and prove *scienter*—intent to deceive—to impose Section 10(*b*) liability under the Securities and Exchange Act of 1934. Mere negligence is not enough. However, reckless professional work might yet be a sufficient basis for 10(*b*) liability even though scienter is not clearly established.

This decision is considered a landmark for accountants because it relieved them of liability for negligence under Section 10(*b*) of the Securities Exchange Act of 1934 and its companion SEC Rule 10b-5. The point of law at issue in the case was whether scienter is a necessary element for a cause of action under 10(*b*) or whether negligent conduct alone is sufficient. *Scienter* refers to a mental state embracing intent to deceive, manipulate, or defraud. Section 10(*b*) makes unlawful the use or employment of any manipulative or deceptive device or contrivance in contravention of Securities and Exchange Commission rules. The respondents (Hochfelder) specifically disclaimed any allegations of fraud or intentional misconduct on the part of Ernst & Ernst, but they wanted to see liability under 10(*b*) imposed for negligence. The court reasoned that Section 10(*b*) in its reference to "employment of any manipulative and deceptive device" meant that intention to deceive, manipulate, or defraud is necessary to support a private cause of action under Section 10(*b*), and negligent conduct is not sufficient.

Ernst & Ernst was retained by First Securities Company of Chicago, a small brokerage firm, to perform periodic audits and did so from 1946 until 1967. Respondents (Hochfelder) were customers of First Securities who invested in a fraudulent securities scheme perpetrated by Leston B. Nay, president of First Securities and owner of 92 percent of its stock. Nay induced some clients to invest funds in "escrow" accounts to earn high rates of return (12 percent at first and later 9 percent). They did so from 1942 through 1966. There were no such accounts because Nay converted the funds to his own use. Hence, there were never any accounts of this type available for Ernst & Ernst to audit.

Investors were instructed to make checks payable to Nay, and he instituted a "mail rule" at First Securities to ensure that he alone received them. The mail rule was that only he could open mail addressed to him at First Securities or addressed to First Securities to his attention, even if it arrived in his absence.

Ernst & Ernst was charged with having aided and abetted Nay's scheme by negligent failure to conduct a proper audit, specifically the failure to discover the mail rule. The premise was that, upon discovery, disclosure would have been made to the SEC of an irregular procedure that prevented an effective audit, and the whole scheme would have been exposed by a subsequent investigation. Ernst & Ernst did have a duty to perform an audit in accordance with generally accepted auditing standards, which under SEC rules includes a review of the accounting system, the internal accounting control, and procedures for safeguarding securities (held by a brokerage firm).

Ernst & Ernst advanced the view that Nay's mail rule was not relevant to the system of internal control and that First Securities did in fact maintain adequate internal accounting controls. The Hochfelder group countered with three expert witnesses who testified that the mail rule represented a material inadequacy in internal control. A "material inadequacy" in internal accounting control was defined in the AICPA audit guide *Audits of Brokers and Dealers in Securities* (1963) as:

> . . . a condition that would permit a person acting individually in the brokerage concern's organization to perpetrate errors or irregularities involving the accounting records, assets of the brokerage concern, and/or assets of customers that could not be detected through the internal control procedures in time to prevent material loss or misstatement of the concern's financial statements, or serious violation of rules of the regulatory agencies.

The trial court granted Ernst & Ernst's motion for summary judgment and dismissal on the grounds that there was no genuine issue of material fact with respect to whether Ernst & Ernst had conducted proper audits. In effect, the trial court decided that there was no negligence on the part of Ernst & Ernst. The appeals court later reversed the trial court and remanded the case for trial, saying there were genuine issues of material fact to be decided, namely (1) whether Nay's "mail rule" constituted a material inadequacy in First Securities' system of internal accounting control and (2) whether Ernst & Ernst failed to exercise due care in that it did not discover a material inadequacy. Before a new trial could decide these issues, Ernst & Ernst appealed to the Supreme Court, which rendered the decision explained at the beginning of this brief. So the substantive issues of material inadequacy and auditor's due care were never taken before a trial jury.

The Supreme Court did not, however, address the issue of whether reckless behavior and disregard for duty can be considered a form of intentional conduct (scienter) for purposes of imposing liability under Section 10(*b*) and Rule 10b-5. Thus, you might expect future cases of this type, lacking an allegation of scienter, to allege that accountants acted in such a reckless way as to constitute intent. Nevertheless, this standard is more forgiving than a standard of mere negligence.

Post-Hochfelder Developments.   Since the Hochfelder case was decided in 1976, the U.S. Courts of Appeal have apparently followed a strict construction of scienter. Several appellate decisions have included discussion of the point that reckless conduct, however, can be construed as scienter, and liability under Rule 10b-5 can be imposed. One court explained: "Recklessness is closer in meaning to 'intent' (the crucial element in scienter) than it is to 'negligence.'" (*Sanders* v. *Nureen,* 554 F2d 790, 7th Cir., 1977.) Another court held that knowledge of a false statement amounts to recklessness (hence, scienter), even absent an intent to deceive. (*First Virginia Bankshares* v. *Benson,* 559 F2d 1307, 5th Cir., 1977.)

All of the cases mentioned above bear on the matter of using Rule 10b-5 in a *private action,* that is, by a plaintiff other than the federal government. In 1980, the U.S. Supreme Court extended the Hochfelder theory to SEC injunctive actions *(public actions)* as well. (*Aaron* v. *SEC,* 100 SC 1945, 1980.)

CHAPTER 5

PROFESSIONAL STANDARDS SOURCES		
Compendium Section	Document Reference	Topic
AU 9642		Interpretation: Report Required by U.S. General Accounting Office
	SIAS 1	Control: Concepts and Responsibilities
	SIAS 2	Communicating Results

Governmental and Internal Auditing

This chapter introduces you to governmental and internal auditing. These two fields differ in important respects from financial statement auditing practiced by independent CPAs in public accounting. However, you will find all the fields of auditing share many similarities. The explanations and examples in this chapter will help you understand the working environment, objectives and procedures that characterize governmental and internal auditing. Your learning objectives are to be able to:

☐ Define governmental auditing and internal auditing and explain how they compare with independent auditing.

☐ Compare aspects of governmental, internal and external auditors' independence problems.

☐ Specify the elements of expanded scope auditing in both governmental and internal audit practice.

☐ List and explain several requirements for governmental and internal audit reports.

☐ Explain governmental and internal auditors' analytical approach in terms of the scientific method described in Chapter 1.

☐ Describe a sequence of work in governmental and internal audits in terms of preliminary survey, evaluation of administrative control, evidence-gathering field work and report preparation.

☐ Develop standards and measurements for simple cases of economy and efficiency and program results audits.

Governmental and internal auditors perform important tasks that could be explained completely only in large books on each area. This short chapter, however, will explain some of the main features of governmental and internal auditing. Even though points of similarity and differences in comparison to "external" auditing would be useful, space does not permit presentation of a detailed comparison. Many such similarities and differences will be apparent, however, when you study this chapter after having studied Chapters 1 and 2.

Perhaps you have already noticed the new reference to "external" auditing. Ordinarily, you can refer to government, internal and independent auditors—the latter referring to CPAs in public practice. Yet, labels are potentially confusing. Many governmental and internal auditors are CPAs, and they take pride in their independence in mental attitude. For purposes of this chapter, therefore, the name of "external" auditing will be used to refer to auditing performed by CPAs in public accounting firms and thereby distinguish public practice from governmental and internal practice.

Internal auditing is practiced by auditors employed by an organization, such as a bank, hospital, city government, or industrial company. The governmental auditors discussed in this chapter are persons employed by the U.S. General Accounting Office (GAO), which is an accounting, auditing and investigating agency of the U.S. Congress. The GAO is headed by the U.S. Comptroller General. In one sense, GAO auditors are the highest level of internal auditors for the federal government as a whole. Many states also have audit agencies similar to the GAO. They answer to state legislatures and perform the same types of work described herein as GAO auditing. In another sense, GAO and similar state agencies are really external auditors with respect to government agencies they audit because they are organizationally independent.

Many government agencies have their own internal auditors and inspectors general. Well-managed local governments also have internal audit departments. For example, most federal agencies (Department of Defense, Department of Human Resources, Department of the Interior), state agencies (education, welfare, controller) and local governments (cities, counties, tax districts) have audit staffs which function as internal auditors for the agency. In the private sector, some huge industrial companies have revenues and assets as large as some governments, and the corporate internal auditors are in a position relative to such a company as a whole as the GAO is to the federal government. Both in matters of scale and the positions they occupy, governmental and internal auditors have much in common. The discussion in this chapter combines and compares their activities.

DEFINITIONS AND OBJECTIVES   The Institute of Internal Auditors defined internal auditing and stated its objective as follows:

Internal auditing is an independent appraisal function established within an organization to examine and evaluate its activities as a service to the organization. The objective of internal auditing is to assist members of the organization in the effective discharge of their obligations. To this end, internal auditing furnishes them with analyses, appraisals, recommendations, counsel and information concerning the activities reviewed.

Operational Auditing

Internal auditors perform audits of financial reports for internal use, much as external auditors audit financial statements distributed to outside users. Thus, much internal auditing work is similar to the auditing described elsewhere in this textbook. However, some internal auditing activity is known as *operational auditing*. Operational auditing (also known as *performance auditing* and *management auditing*) refers to auditors' study of business operations for the purpose of making recommendations about economic and efficient use of resources, effective achievement of business objectives and compliance with company policies. The goal of operational auditing is to help managers discharge their management responsibilities and improve profitability. In this context, operational auditing is included in the modern definition of internal auditing given above. In a similar context, an AICPA committee defined operational auditing performed by independent CPA firms as a distinct type of management advisory service (MAS) having the goal of helping a client improve the use of its capabilities and resources to achieve its objectives. So, operational auditing is a type of internal auditing as well as a type of MAS offered by public accounting firms.

Independence

Internal auditors, like external auditors, hold independence as a goal. Although internal auditors cannot be disassociated from their employers in the eyes of the public, they seek operational and reporting independence. Operationally, internal auditors should be independent when obtaining evidence in the sense of being free from direction or constraint by the managers of the business unit under audit (program, division, subsidiary, for example). Independence is enhanced by having the authority and responsibility to report to a high executive level and to the audit committee of the board of directors. Their goal is a measure of practical independence from the control or direct influence of operating managers whose functions, operations and results they may be assigned to audit. Practical independence enables internal auditors to be objective in reporting findings without having to fear for their jobs.

Government auditors, like external and internal auditors, hold independence as a goal. GAO standards speak to substantive issues of integrity and objectivity as well as to the independence-damaging appearance of financial and managerial involvement. As a government auditor, one must be aware that personal factors such as preconceived ideas about programs, political or social convictions, and loyalty to a level of government may impair the integrity and objectivity that is the foundation of real independence. Like internal auditors, government auditors must be wary of external sources of independence impairment, such as interference by higher-level officials and threats to job security.

Organizational separation from such influences is essential for independence, so auditors can report directly to top management without fear of job or compensation retribution. Auditors of governmental units are presumed independent when they are: (1) free from sources of personal impairment; (2) free from sources of external impairment; (3) organizationally independent; (4) independent under AICPA Code of Professional Ethics Rules; (5) elected or appointed and reporting to a legislative body of government or (6) auditing in a level or branch of government other than the one to which they are normally assigned.

On any particular assignment, governmental auditors may perform services for the benefit of several interested parties—the management of the auditee, officials of the agency requiring the audit, officials of one or more agencies that fund the auditee's programs, members and committees of local governments, a state legislature or the U.S. Congress, and the public. GAO standards provide that all such parties should receive the audit report, unless laws or regulations restrict public distribution (e.g., for reasons of national security). In contrast, standard audit reports on financial statements given by independent auditors are addressed to the client and distributed only by the client to whomever the client wishes (except in the case of SEC-registered companies where the law requires the reports to be filed for public inspection).

Scope of Service   The stated objective of internal auditing is phrased in terms of service to "the organization," not just to management or some narrow internal interest group. Internal auditors, exercising their objectivity, function for the benefit of the whole organization—whether it is represented by the board of directors, the chief executive officer, the chief financial officer or other executives from time to time. The services provided by internal auditors include: (1) audits of financial reports and accounting control systems; (2) reviews of control systems that ensure compliance with company policies, plans and procedures and with laws and regulations; (3) appraisals of the economy and efficiency of operations and (4) reviews of effectiveness in achieving program results in comparison with pre-established objectives and goals.

The U.S. General Accounting Office shares with internal auditors these same elements of scope of services. The GAO standards, however, emphasize the accountability of public officials for the efficient, economical and effective use of public funds and other resources. Also, GAO pronouncements define and describe *expanded scope* governmental auditing as follows:

> The term "audit" is used to describe not only work done by accountants and auditors in examining financial statements but also work done in re-

viewing (*a*) compliance with applicable laws and regulations, (*b*) economy and efficiency of operations, and (*c*) effectiveness in achieving program results.

The GAO elaboration on the three elements of expanded scope auditing is instructive and can be considered consistent with internal auditors' views. GAO explains the three areas as follows:

1. *Financial and compliance*—determines (*a*) whether the financial statements of an audited entity present fairly the financial position and the results of financial operations in accordance with generally accepted accounting principles and (*b*) whether the entity has complied with laws and regulations that may have a material effect upon the financial statements.

2. *Economy and efficiency*—determines (*a*) whether the entity is managing and utilizing its resources (such as personnel, property, space), economically and efficiently, (*b*) the causes of inefficiencies or uneconomical practices, and (*c*) whether the entity has complied with laws and regulations concerning matters of economy and efficiency.

3. *Program results*—determines (*a*) whether the desired results or benefits established by the legislature or other authorizing body are being achieved and (*b*) whether the agency has considered alternatives that might yield desired results at a lower cost.

The audit of a governmental organization, program, activity or function may involve one, two or all three of the elements of expanded scope auditing. GAO standards do not require all engagements to include all three elements. The scope of the work is supposed to be determined according to the needs of the users of the audit results. However, the GAO recommends observance of its standards in audits of governmental units by external auditors as well as by governmental auditors at federal, state and local levels.

IIA Standards   The *Standards for the Professional Practice of Internal Auditing* were issued by The Institute of Internal Auditors (IIA) in 1978. (See Appendix 5A.) The IIA now issues *Statements on Internal Auditing Standards* (SIAS's) intended to provide authoritative interpretations of the 1978 standards. SIAS 1 was issued in 1983 on the subject of control concepts and responsibilities.

The 1978 standards are classified in five major categories. Altogether, 25 different guiding standards are included under these five headings:

1. Independence.
2. Professional Proficiency.
   a. The Internal Auditing Department.
   b. The Internal Auditor.

3. Scope of Work.
4. Performance of Audit Work.
5. Management of the Internal Auditing Department.

Students usually learn AICPA generally accepted auditing standards (GAAS) first, then study other auditing standards. The IIA standards include the spirit of all the general and field work standards of AICPA generally accepted auditing standards. On the assumption that GAAS, including the AICPA Statements on Auditing Standards, are familiar, we will look only at the IIA standards that are significantly different.[1]

Internal auditors are expected to comply with The Institute of Internal Auditors' (IIA) standards of professional conduct. (See Appendix 5B.) IIA *audit standards* are recommended and encouraged, but compliance with them depends on their acceptance, adoption and implementation by practicing internal auditors. The IIA standards require internal auditors to be skilled in dealing with people and in communicating effectively. Such a requirement may be considered implicit in GAAS related to training and proficiency, but little is said in GAAS about effective communication, perhaps because the reporting language is so standardized. External auditors tend to believe the public has the responsibility to learn how to understand their audit reports, while internal auditors believe it is their own responsibility to see that their reports are understood properly.

Three of the IIA standards call for: (1) review of compliance with policies, plans, procedures, laws and regulations; (2) review of economy and efficiency in the use of resources and (3) review of the results of programs. These standards closely resemble the three elements of GAO expanded scope auditing, all of which go considerably beyond requirements of the AICPA generally accepted auditing standards.

The IIA standards include a requirement for following up to ascertain that appropriate action is taken on reported audit findings or ascertaining that management or the board of directors has taken the risk of not taking action on reported findings. AICPA standards have no comparable follow-up requirement because external audit reports do not make recommendations related to financial statements.

Ten of the IIA standards deal with the organization and management of the internal audit department. CPAs in public practice have similar standards, but their standards are in the AICPA quality control standards rather than in GAAS. However, observance of quality control standards is considered essential for proper auditing practice in accordance with GAAS. The AICPA quality control standards are "incorporated by refer-

---

[1] Parallels in the respective standards are found in various *Statements on Auditing Standards*, as well as in the summary of 10 generally accepted auditing standards (AU 150.02). For a complete comparison, refer to the article by J. C. Robertson and C. W. Alderman, "Comparative Auditing Standards," *Journal of Accounting, Auditing & Finance*, (Winter 1981), pp. 144–61.

ence" in GAAS and enforced through the peer reviews of accounting firms.

The four AICPA reporting standards are comprehensive insofar as audit reports on financial statements are concerned, but the related IIA standard merely says, "Internal auditors should report the results of their audit work." Since the details under this standard are similar to the GAO reporting standards, further explanation will be given later in the discussion of the GAO standards.

GAO STANDARDS   The *Standards for Audit of Governmental Organizations, Programs, Activities, and Functions* (1981 Revision) incorporates the AICPA generally accepted auditing standards as well as a number of ideas from the AICPA Statements on Auditing Standards. However, GAO standards go beyond those of the AICPA in several respects.

The GAO standards explicitly require a review for compliance with applicable laws and regulations. Since most governmental programs are created by regulated grants and operate under laws and regulations, compliance review is very important. GAAS requires such a review only when noncompliance with laws and regulations would result in errors or irregularities that could be material to the financial statements taken as a whole.

The GAO standards have a more stringent requirement concerning working papers—requiring documentation that does not need additional supplementation with detailed oral explanations. GAAS requires working papers, but the general spirit of practice compliance is that such documentation need not be as complete as the GAO standard suggests

The GAO reporting standards, unlike the AICPA standards, contain a requirement for external reporting of instances or indication of fraud, abuse or illegal acts. External auditors maintain that notification within the auditee organization is normally sufficient. However, they believe in extreme cases an auditor should seek the advice of an attorney about what action to take. GAO auditors apparently are less concerned about client relations and legal liability matters than external auditors.

The GAO reporting standards require a report on the auditee's system of internal accounting control. Under GAAS, such a report is optional at the election of the client. GAAS interpretations have been written on such reports, however, and can be found in AU 9642.18–.25.

The GAO standards contain an elaborate set of guides for reports on economy, efficiency and program results audits. These audits cover such a wide range of subjects (from food programs to military contracts) that no "standard" report is possible. The GAO standards are reproduced below. All auditors—internal and external, and also CPAs reporting on management advisory services engagements—can find useful guidance in these standards. Indeed, the ones marked by an asterisk (*) are virtually identical to the detail reporting guides in the internal auditors' reporting standards.

GAO Reporting Standards For Economy and Efficiency and Program Results Audits

☐ Written audit reports are to be prepared giving the results of each government audit.*

☐ Written audit reports are to be submitted to the appropriate officials of the organization audited and to the appropriate officials of the organizations requiring or arranging for the audits unless legal restrictions or ethical considerations prevent it. Copies of the report should also be sent to other officials who may be responsible for taking action on audit findings and recommendations and to others authorized to receive such reports. Unless restricted by law or regulation, copies should be made available for public inspection.

☐ Reports are to be issued on or before the dates specified by law, regulation, or other special arrangement. Reports are to be issued promptly so as to make the information available for timely use by management and by legislative officials.

☐ The report shall include:
A description of the scope and objectives of the audit.*
A statement that the audit (economy and efficiency or program results) was made in accordance with generally accepted government auditing standards.
A description of material weaknesses found in the internal control system (administrative controls).
A statement of positive assurance on those items of compliance tested and negative assurance on those items not tested. This should include significant instances of noncompliance and instances of, or indications of, fraud, abuse, or illegal acts found during or in connection with the audit. However, fraud, abuse, or illegal acts normally should be covered in a separate report, thus permitting the overall report to be released to the public.
Recommendations for actions to improve problem areas noted in the audit and to improve operations.
Pertinent views of responsible officials of the organization, program, activity, or function audited, and the auditors' findings, conclusions, and recommendations.*
A description of noteworthy accomplishments, particularly when management improvements in one area may be applicable elsewhere.*
A listing of any issues and questions needing further study and consideration.
A statement as to whether any pertinent information has been omitted because it is deemed privileged or confidential. The nat-

ure of such information should be described, and the law or other basis under which it is withheld should be stated.

☐ The report shall:
Present factual data accurately and fairly.
Present findings and conclusions in a convincing manner.
Be objective.*
Be written in language as clear and simple as the subject matter permits.*
Be concise, but at the same time, clear enough to be understood by users.*
Present factual data completely to fully inform the users.
Place primary emphasis on improvement rather than on criticism of the past; critical comments should be presented in a balanced perspective considering any unusual difficulties or circumstances faced by the operating officials concerned.*

AUDIT ASSIGNMENTS

One question you might ask is: "How are GAO and internal auditors assigned to an audit job in the first place?" Herbert pointed out that government auditors are assigned as a result of:

☐ Specific statutory or policy requirements for audits.

☐ Legislative, audit committee or executive department requests.

☐ Auditors' own initiative resulting from recognition of the importance of a program, activity or organization because of the size of its revenues, expenditures or investment in assets.

☐ Auditors' own initiative resulting from recognition of the potential importance of a new program or activity.

☐ Auditors' response to a request for proposal to audit a specific organization, program, activity or function.[2]

Internal auditors undertake specific assignments for similar reasons. Corporate policy or the audit committee of the board of directors may require certain audits, or executives may request them. Also, a well-managed internal audit department will often take the initiative to recommend an agenda or schedule of certain audit assignments.

CPAs in public practice most often get involved in governmental audits as a result of responding to an agency's request for proposal (RFP). Well-prepared RFP's specify the audit work requested, making it clear what extent of expanded scope auditing is needed. When responding to a RFP, a public accountant is effectively bidding for the job in competition with other respondents. The response to a RFP will specify the engagement

---

[2] Adapted from: Leo Herbert, *Auditing the Performance of Management* (Belmont, Calif.: Lifetime Learning Publications, 1979), p. 24.

objectives and nature of services, the engagement scope and limitations, the roles and responsibilities of the auditee's personnel and other consultants, the engagement approach and methods, the manner and timing of reporting, the work schedule and the fee. A good RFP response contains the same points recommended for agreement in the AICPA's MAS standard related to *understanding with client* discussed in Chapter 2.

The process of getting the assignment is important because it includes an understanding and definition of the objectives of the audit. Auditors must know these objectives—whether they relate to financial reports, compliance review, internal control review, economy and efficiency studies, or program results studies—in order to plan and manage the evidence-gathering activities. Governmental and internal auditors do not need to reply to a RFP, but must take similar care in planning the assignment.

EVIDENCE GATHERING The evidence-gathering field work can best be described in general terms as an application of the ***analytical approach.*** The general steps of an analytical approach can be associated with the scientific method discussed in Chapter 1 as follows:

☐   *Problem recognition.* Ascertain the pertinent facts and circumstances.

☐   *Hypothesis formulation.* Identify specific objectives in more detail than the overall engagement objectives.
      Define problem areas or opportunities for improvement.
      Define program goals.

☐   *Evidence collection.* Select and perform procedures designed to produce information related to problem areas, opportunities for improvement or achievement of program goals.

☐   *Evidence evaluation.* Evaluate activities in terms of economy, efficiency and goal achievement.

☐   *Decision-making.* Report findings and recommendations.[3]

Preliminary Survey Most government and many internal audit engagements begin with a ***preliminary survey.*** A preliminary survey is an auditor's familiarization process of gathering information, without detailed investigation or verification procedures, on the organization, program or activity being audited. It is designed to identify problem areas needing additional review in order to plan and accomplish the audit.[4] Sawyer has pointed out that the prelimi-

---

[3] Adapted from: *Guidelines for CPA Participation in Government Audits to Evaluate Economy, Efficiency and Program Results.* MAS Guideline Series No. 6 (New York: AICPA, 1977), p. 19.

[4] Adapted from: *Standards for Audit of Governmental Organizations, Programs, Activities, and Functions* (GAO, 1981), p. 71.

nary survey is a logical means of salvaging order out of a complex chaos of information by answering these questions: What is the job? Who does it? Why is it done? How is it done?[5] These questions require auditors to have a business sense about the audit objectives, so they can get the big picture.

Using interview techniques, auditors can learn about the nature of the entity under audit and its program goals, the organizational structure of the entity, its policies and procedures, its administrative and internal accounting control systems, its financial data and its nonfinancial measurement system. In many respects, economy and efficiency audits and program results audits depend on the administrative controls of the entity and the nonfinancial measures of its program results. For example, efficiency, economy and program outputs may be measured not only in terms of monetary expenditure, but more importantly, in terms of employee productivity, student educational achievement, medical service delivered, research and development achievement or defense readiness.

As a part of the preliminary survey, or even before one is conducted, auditors must determine the specific standards for economy, efficiency and program results relevant in the circumstances. Some of these standards for government agencies can be found in laws, legislative committee reports, legislative or administrative orders and resolutions, local ordinances and resolutions, grant proposals and contracts made by a grantee or agency. Similarly, business units may be under orders from the board of directors or may be undertaking a project resulting from an internal proposal that sets forth budgets and objectives.

Standards for economy and efficiency are sometimes hard to determine. Auditors' challenges are to determine the appropriate standards as objectively as possible. Some reference books are available. An AICPA committee has identified the publications of the Urban Institute, the International City Management Association and the National Planning Association as sources of standards. These organizations have produced data about various city services and social services, transportation, energy and environmental protection programs. Auditors should not overlook available reference books but should also be able to apply good management principles to recognize under-utilized facilities, nonproductive work, costly procedures and overstaffing or understaffing in particular circumstances.

The preliminary survey should be an organized activity, with a written plan or program. It should not be a haphazard "get acquainted" activity conducted loosely. It should lead to a program for a study and evaluation of the administrative controls of the business unit, program, activity or function being audited.

---

[5] Lawrence B. Sawyer, *The Practice of Modern Internal Auditing* (The Institute of Internal Auditors, Inc., 1973), p. 126.

**Emphasis on
Administrative
Controls**

Auditors classify controls in two broad categories: administrative controls and internal accounting controls. ***Administrative control*** is defined by the AICPA as ". . . *the plan of organization and the procedures and records that are concerned with the decision processes leading to management's authorization of transactions.* This management function is directly associated with the responsibility for achieving the organization's objectives. It is the starting point for establishing accounting control of transactions" (emphasis added, SAS 1, AU 320.27). Administrative control sets the stage for detailed accounting control.

Another aspect of control is ***internal accounting control.*** It consists of the plan of organization and procedures designed to prevent, detect and correct accounting errors that may occur and get recorded in ledger accounts and financial statements. External auditors are primarily concerned with the accounting controls and are concerned with the administrative controls only insofar as they have a direct influence on accounting accuracy. The external auditors' study and evaluation of accounting control is a fairly complicated subject and is covered in detail in other chapters in this textbook.

In connection with governmental and internal audits, however, you should recognize that auditors have primary concern with the administrative controls because they directly affect economy, efficiency and program results. Administrative control is a broad concept involving all management activities, such as responsibilities for production, quality control, transportation, research and development, personnel relations and many other areas. The focus is not limited to accounting-related activities. This breadth makes it difficult to express specific standards and objectives for administrative control.

Chapter 7 explains specific standards and objectives of internal accounting control used by auditors of financial statements. For now, however, you should think of accounting controls as being very specific and accounting-related and administrative controls as being more general and management-related. Some examples illustrating the contrast are given below in Exhibit 5–1.

One key question is: Given the lack of specific standards, how can you cope with the need to study and evaluate administrative controls? Answer: It is not easy! You need to rely on knowledge of marketing, management, production, finance, statistics, business law, economics, taxation, operations research, political science, physical sciences and other subjects. These are some of the nonaccounting courses you can take in your college curriculum. Such studies are important because they serve as a foundation for organizing your early practical experiences and your development of a common sense of business management. Last, but far from least, you will also need to be able to exercise imagination to adapt your classroom and on-the-job experience knowledge of good management practice to specific audit engagement circumstances. You can ex-

EXHIBIT 5–1
Accounting and
Administrative Control
Techniques

Accounting Control Techniques	**Administrative Control Techniques**
Cash	
Establish a control total of cash receipts as soon as they are received, so subsequent deposits, journal entries and ledger entries can be compared to the total.	Prepare timely forecasts of cash flow and provide for temporary borrowing to cover needs or temporary investment to generate interest income.
Accounts Receivable	
Reconcile customer's subsidiary ledger accounts with the control account total to control bookkeeping accuracy.	Prepare an aged trial balance of customer receivables for the credit manager's collection efforts.
Inventory	
Assign physical control responsibility to a storekeeper to safeguard inventory from theft or other unauthorized removal.	Coordinate inventory purchases with sales and production forecasts so stockout losses and inventory carrying cost can be optimized.

pect very little to be routine or "canned" in a study and evaluation of administrative control, and that is what makes governmental and internal auditing assignments such exciting challenges.

Audit Procedures

No magic solutions are available for the problems of selecting and performing audit procedures. Actually, the general evidence-gathering procedures in governmental and internal audits are about the same as the ones used by external auditors in the audit of financial statements. These procedures are explained in general in Chapter 6 and in more specific terms in Chapters 13–19 of this textbook. However, the audit problems are usually different in audits of economy, efficiency and program results.

Governmental and internal auditors must be as objective as possible when developing conclusions about efficiency, economy and program results. This objectivity is achieved by: (1) finding *standards* for evaluation and (2) using *measurements* of actual results, so (3) the actual results can be *compared* to the standards. Finding standards and deciding upon relevant measurements takes imagination. Sawyer has presented two examples, one rather routine and the other very unusual, to illustrate the role of standards and measurements.[6]

> *Routine Problem.* Evaluate the promptness with which materials pass through a receiving inspection before being accepted and placed in inventory.
>
> ☐ *Source of a Standard.* Management policy about acceptable delay between date of receipt and date of inspection approval.

---

[6] Ibid, pp. 275–76.

□ *Measurement Unit*. Number of days between date of receipt and date of inspection approval.

□ *Audit Procedures*. Select a sample of inspection reports and record the two relevant dates and the number of elapsed days. Develop descriptive statistics of the sample data. Compare these measurements to the management policy standard. Report the findings and conclusions.

Unusual Problem. Determine whether the company's test pilots are reporting aircraft defects properly.

□ *Background Information*. Test pilots fill out check sheets as they fly, recording such things as pressure instrument readings under various flight conditions. If a reading is outside acceptable limits, the pilot is supposed to prepare a report, which will trigger an investigation of the reason for the unacceptable instrument reading.

□ *Source of a Standard*. Engineering specifications of acceptable limits for pressure readings under specific flight conditions. For example, the fuel pressure at 20,000 feet and a power setting of 85 percent should be between 90 and 110 pounds.

□ *Measurement Unit*. Number of times an instrument reading is reported improperly by a test pilot.

□ *Audit Procedures*. Select a sample of check sheets and related test pilot reports. Compare each instrument reading on the check sheet to the engineering specifications. Read the test pilot's reports and look for no unfavorable mention of acceptable readings and for appropriate mention of unacceptable readings. Tally and describe all report deficiencies. Summarize the findings and report the conclusions. (Notice that the procedure involves reading the test pilot's reports for *two* possible deficiencies—inappropriate reporting of acceptable readings as well as failure to report unacceptable readings.)

When dealing with standards, measurements and comparisons, auditors must keep *inputs* and *outputs* in perspective. Evidence about inputs—personnel hours and cost, materials quantities and cost, asset investment—are most important in connection with reaching economy and efficiency conclusions. For economy, efficiency and program results conclusions, however, output measurements are equally important. Management has the responsibility for devising information systems to measure output. Such measurements should correspond to program objectives set forth in laws, regulations, administrative policies, legislative reports or other such sources. Auditors must realize that output measurements are usually not expressed in financial terms—for example, water quality improvement, educational progress, weapons effectiveness, materials-inspection time delays, and test pilot reporting accuracy.

Many economy and efficiency audits and most program results audits are *output-oriented*. Auditors need to be careful not to equate program activity with program success, without measuring program results. These features are significantly different from auditors' roles with respect to financial statement audits where the primary concern is with reporting on the accounting for inputs.

REPORTING   Governmental and internal audit reports are not standardized as are external auditors' reports on financial statements. Each report is different because governmental and internal auditors need to communicate findings on a variety of assignments and audit objectives. The key criterion for such a report is its ability to communicate clearly and concisely. Relevant reporting guides were given earlier in this chapter under the heading of "GAO reporting standards for economy and efficiency and program results audits."

GAO Audit Report   Exhibit 5–2 contains an example of findings from a report by government auditors. This example is highly condensed from a more lengthy report but shows the nature and emphasis of typical governmental audit reports.

The emphasis is on economical and efficient resource utilization by Department of Agriculture managers of the Commodity Distribution Program (a program enacted by Congress). The general audit assignment was to assess how efficiently the program was being operated. One feature of efficiency is highlighted in the excerpts in Exhibit 5–2—the package sizes used in commodity distributions.

Administrative instructions from the Department of Agriculture directed agents to distribute the commodities to institutions such as schools, in the "most economical size packages," whatever that size might be, but presumably the large sizes suggested in the report. The auditors found, however, that small sizes were being used at a considerable cost that could be avoided. Judging strictly on a dollar-cost basis, the programs were found to be inefficient.

Internal Audit Report   The reporting stage is the internal auditor's opportunity to capture management's undivided attention. To be effective, a report cannot be unduly long, tedious, technical and laden with minutiae. It must be accurate, concise, clear and timely. There is no standard form for internal audit reports, and there will likely never be one, given the diversity of assignments and the diversity of managers' abilities and interests.

Exhibit 5–3 contains an example of an internal audit report on the study of a personnel department. The report begins with a summary or overall conclusion that conveys the essential findings and captures the reader's attention. The personnel department report may be characterized as a broad evaluation of a management function.

EXHIBIT 5–2
Governmental Audit
Report

In an audit of the Commodity Distribution Program of the Department of Agriculture, GAO reported that savings could be realized if larger package sizes of commodities are used when possible.

CRITERIA USED TO MEASURE EFFICIENCY AND ECONOMY

The Department of Agriculture's instructions to state distribution agencies require that, to the extent practicable, commodities be donated to schools and institutions in the most economical size packages. When commodities are available in packages of more than one size, the instructions require that state agencies requisition the commodities to the maximum extent practicable, in large-size packages—such as 50-pound containers—for schools and institutions.

CONDITIONS FOUND BY AUDITORS

In seven states covered by the review, distributing agencies were requisitioning foodstuffs for large users in small-size packages instead of large-size packages.

EFFECT OF THE CONDITIONS

A substantial part of the additional costs of providing flour, shortening, and nonfat dry milk in small containers to schools and institutions could be saved. GAO estimated that, nationwide, for fiscal year 1970 these additional costs totaled about $1.6 million.

CAUSE OF THE SITUATION

Agriculture regional officials said that, although they encouraged state distributing agencies to requisition commodities in the most economical size package practicable, they had not questioned the propriety of state agencies requesting commodities in small-size packages for schools and institutions and that they had not required the agencies to justify such requests because they believed the agencies were making the proper determinations as to package sizes.

AUDITORS' RECOMMENDATIONS

In view of the savings available by acquiring commodities in large-size packages, GAO recommended that Agriculture take appropriate action to have regional offices vigorously enforce the requirement that state agencies requisition commodities—particularly, flour, vegetable shortening, and nonfat dry milk—in the most economical size packages practicable. GAO also recommended that state agencies be required to justify, when necessary, the requisitioning of the commodities in small-size packages for schools and institutions.

Source: "Examples of Findings from Governmental Audits," *Audit Standards Supplement Series No. 4* (U.S. General Accounting Office, 1973), pp. 19–20.

MAS Engagement Reports by CPAs

In contrast to the well-defined areas of audit and tax practice, public accountants' practice in management advisory services (MAS) can be described only by cataloging a variety of such services. On a specific engagement basis, independent accountants, acting as management consultants, perform services in areas as diverse as those performed by governmental and internal auditors. Consultants may accept engagements to evaluate compliance, economy and efficiency, and program results. Consequently, MAS engagement reports exhibit the same characteristics as internal audit reports and GAO reports: The problem is identified, some

EXHIBIT 5–3
Internal Audit Report

Personnel Director
ABC Company

Dear Bob:

Our analysis of your Personnel Department is now completed. This report summarizes our findings and recommendations.

FOCUS

Personnel services 2,200 office and technical employees who are located in five different divisions or operating units within the metropolitan area. Approximately one half of these employees are in the XYZ Division.

The department has 36 people and operates on a budget of about $600,000 annually.

Our analysis was confined to the three major personnel functional responsibilities of Placement, Manpower Development/Training, and Compensation Practices.

XYZ Personnel provides service to operating management on an "as requested" basis; when provided, our review revealed this service to be generally adequate.

OVERALL ASSESSMENT

However, XYZ Personnel's role in the management of office and technical personnel is mainly passive. As such, most personnel practices are handled by the operating people, who are not technically trained in personnel administration.

Further, the personnel department is not knowledgeable in the extent, quality and consistency of personnel administration practices performed by the operating people.

Finally, we believe that Personnel concentrates too much of its efforts and resources on activities that are of low priority in the management of human resources.

The department's whole approach to the acquisition, development, and retention of people does not assure operating management of optimum use of their investment in manpower.

MAJOR RECOMMENDATIONS

1. Analyze and define the role of the residential personnel department.

    The personnel department does not play a major role in the administering of personnel practices upon employees. Personnel does not know either the extent, quality, or consistency (and inconsistency) of these practices among the many managers and departments.

    Many important personnel practices are the complete prerogative of individual operating managers. Examples of these practices are:
    a. Manpower requirement forecasting.
    b. Employee performance appraisals.
    c. Career counseling and career development.
    d. Determination of specific individual training needs and training received.
    e. Early identification of "marginal" and "failing" employees. Establishment of corrective action programs.
    f. Analysis of absenteeism levels and control.
    g. Information flow to employee's personnel jackets.

Personnel usually does not participate in, or monitor, these activities. We contribute this passive role to two factors:

The lack of a formally defined charter from top management.

EXHIBIT 5–3
(*concluded*)

A low level of expertise among department employees, below the managerial position, due to an aggressive job rotation policy. (Departmental management considers this necessary to keep employees challenged.)

Several steps are required before Personnel can undertake a more aggressive, employee-oriented service role.

Develop a formal written charter of operations, approved by top divisional management.

Describe areas of personnel administration where the personnel department has sole responsibility.

Delineate those areas where Personnel should play an advisory or monitoring role.

Discontinue the rapid rotation practice.

Develop greater vertical growth potential within the personnel department.

Gradually implement the above charter through assignments of specific action programs to individual department employees.

The major benefit of this effort will be to give assurance that the biggest investment—the investment in people—is always being well managed.

2. Improve the accuracy of the manpower forecast.

3. Implement a disciplined program for job description development and maintenance.

4. Assist and monitor operating management in the employee appraisal function. Utilize appraisal information.

5. Guide and monitor personnel training activities.

6. Compile and utilize statistical information to improve effectiveness and efficiency in personnel activities.

7. Improve the quality and completeness of employee personnel information.

8. Investigate the desirability of an organizational realignment.

We believe that implementation of our recommendations will substantially increase and improve the level of service now being offered by the Personnel function to operating management. Furthermore, the company will have greater assurance that their biggest investment—the investment in people—is being well managed.

The specific details supporting these and other recommendations are contained in the interim recommendation reports which have been furnished you.

_____
Manager

_____
Lead Analyst

explanation of the investigation is given and the findings and recommendations are expressed clearly and concisely.

The MAS report in Exhibit 5–4 is the full text of an actual report. The assignment was a relatively uncomplicated one—evaluation of the system for controlling inventory—and the resultant report is a good example of clarity and direct communication.

EXHIBIT 5–4
MAS Report by a Public
Accounting Firm

Mr. C. D. Derfin
Control Instruments, Inc.

Dear Mr. Derfin:

We have completed our review of the cost accounting system of Control Instruments, Inc., as outlined in our engagement letter to you. The primary objective of our review was to determine if your new system should be modified. Our conclusion is that the present system for controlling inventory is sound. It is simple, but it should provide for good control of inventory. The problem is one of improper utilization of the existing system.

We believe that control of inventory is vital to company operations. We understand there are numerous shortages of parts which delay the assembly process. However, we do not believe that this problem is primarily due to a systems weakness. We observed that additions to inventory are properly entered on the perpetual records when receiving reports are received by the inventory control clerk. Items are deducted from the records when they are pulled from the warehouse, and an adequate system exists for keeping track of material shortages. We believe that the warehouse operation is the primary source of inventory control problems. Our observations and recommendations in this area are summarized below.

WAREHOUSE OPERATIONS

Warehouse personnel are currently taking cycle counts of raw materials to locate differences between perpetual records and actual quantities on hand. We noted there were many such discrepancies. In an attempt to find a reason for these discrepancies, we unpacked three pulled orders in the warehouse and compared actual items packed with the amounts indicated as being packed on the bills of material. In each case we found discrepancies.

In order to identify the source of these errors, we recommend that the warehouse be required to initial the bills of material for the orders they pull. They have already been instructed to do this. The production supervisor currently unpacks all pulled orders and counts the contents before the orders go to the production line. We believe he should take the additional step of reporting the exact discrepancies daily to John Roberts. Additional recommendations to improve the warehouse operation are summarized below. Some of these recommendations are already being implemented.

1. Continue the cycle count procedure, but take time to resolve differences daily. Report reasons for differences to John Roberts.
2. Temporarily assign a man full-time to maintain inventory records.
3. Stock inventory in the correct locations or attach a note to the bin stating where additional items are located.
4. Adopt a "last bag" system for control of "C" items.

EXHIBIT 5–4
(continued)

5. When an order for several units on the small line requires more than one box, pack all of one-type of part in the same box.

6. When pulling an order for several units on the large line, pack as many complete units as possible and limit the shortages to the remaining units.

7. Require warehousemen to pack orders neatly, particularly general kits.

8. Adopt a daily routine in the warehouse as follows:
   a. Stock the items received.
   b. Fill short orders.
   c. Fill remaining orders.
   d. Work on special projects.

   We noted that physical control of inventory has been substantially improved by constructing a chain-link fence around the warehouse area. Since access to the warehouse is now very limited, it will be difficult for unauthorized personnel to remove parts.

GENERAL OBSERVATION

   While most of our time was spent in the warehouse, we also noted some opportunities to improve the general operation of the Control Instruments facility. Our recommendations are summarized below:

1. Revise the cost book to contain an accurate description and the current cost of each item.

2. Revise the Bills of Material to make them accurate and adopt a formal procedure for keeping them current.

3. Redesign the forms used for Bills of Material. They can be changed to indicate more clearly the number of items packed versus the number of items specified. They could also indicate which items are used in the electrical subassembly process, so these items could be packed together. These forms should be ordered as snap-out multiple part forms.

4. Redesign the "owe sheets" to make them consistent and easy to understand.

5. Assign part numbers to all purchased parts except common nuts and bolts.

6. Assign part numbers to sheet metal parts and include these parts in the cost book and Bills of Material.

7. Adopt a tag method for keeping track of labor hours spent on individual units and revise labor time standards as appropriate.

ACCOUNTING PROCEDURES

   There is some confusion over exactly what accounting procedures have been employed in the past. We recommend that the following procedures be used in the future to account for the costs of materials and labor. We believe most of these procedures are already understood by accounting personnel and are being used.

1. Record raw materials purchased at standard cost and maintain a purchase price variance account. For internal financial statements, the variance can be treated as part of cost of goods sold.

2. Charge labor to cost of goods sold at standard time. Charge the difference between standard and actual to labor efficiency variance, which is part of cost of goods sold.

3. At the end of each month, count the finished goods inventory and estimate work-in-process inventory.

EXHIBIT 5–4
(*concluded*)

> We would be pleased to discuss this letter further at your convenience.
> We appreciate this opportunity to be of service to you.
>
>
>   Very truly yours,
>   Alexander Grant & Co., CPAs

The MAS report, like the governmental and internal audit reports, gets to the main problem quickly, identifying the source of trouble as the warehouse operation. The consultants found and reported that the trouble was not the result of a basic system weakness. The report makes specific points and recommendations on inventory handling procedures as well as on recordkeeping procedures. This particular engagement required not only ordinary expertise as an accountant, but also an ability to perceive some elementary materials-handling problems and offer good managerial solutions.

SUMMARY Governmental and internal auditing standards include the essence of the AICPA generally accepted auditing standards (GAAS) and go much further by expressing standards for audits of economy, efficiency and program results. In addition, the internal auditing standards contain many guides for the management of an internal audit department within a company. GAO standards contain technical computer auditing guidance as well.

All auditors hold independence as a primary goal, but internal auditors must look to an internal organization independence from the managers and executives whose areas they audit. Governmental auditors must be concerned about factual independence with regard to social, political and level-of-government influences.

Audit engagements are, in concept, an application of a scientific analytical approach—essentially a fact-finding approach. Auditors start the work with an understanding of the audit objectives involved in the assignment and carry them out through the major blocks of work—preliminary survey, study and evaluation of administrative control, application of audit procedures, and reporting the audit conclusions and recommendations. Auditors try to achieve objectivity by determining appropriate standards for economy, efficiency and program results, by measuring their evidence and by comparing their measurements to the standards in order to reach objective conclusions.

Governmental and internal audit reports and similar reports on public accountants' management advisory services are not standardized like the

GAAS reports on audited financial statements. Auditors must be very careful that their reports communicate their conclusions and recommendations in a clear and concise manner. The variety of assignments and the challenge of reporting in such a free-form setting contribute to making governmental auditing, internal auditing and management advisory services exciting fields for career opportunities.

SOURCES AND ADDITIONAL READING REFERENCES

Abt, Clark C. "The State of the Art of Program Evaluation." *The GAO Review,* Spring 1979, pp. 21–25.

Broadus, W. A., Jr., and J. F. Moraglio. "Governmental Audit Standards: A New Perspective." *Journal of Accountancy,* May 1982, pp. 80–90.

Bromage, M. C. "Wording the Management Audit Report." *Journal of Accountancy,* February 1972, pp. 50–57.

Burton, John C. "Management Auditing." *Journal of Accountancy,* May 1968, pp. 41–46.

Campbell, James T. "Fraud Detection: What is the Auditor's Role?" *The GAO Review,* Winter 1979, pp. 25–27.

Committee on Relations with the General Accounting Office. "Auditing Standards Established by GAO: Their Meaning and Significance for CPAs." New York: AICPA, 1973.

Comptroller General of the United States. "Examples of Findings from Governmental Audits." *Audit Standards Supplement Series No. 4.* U.S. General Accounting Office, 1973.

Gobeil, Robert E. "The Common Body of Knowledge for Internal Auditors." *The Internal Auditor,* November/December 1972, pp. 20–29.

Granof, Michael H. "Operational Audit Standards for Audits of Government Services." *CPA Journal,* December 1973, pp. 1079–85.

Guidelines for CPA Participation in Government Audit Engagements to Evaluate Economy, Efficiency, and Program Results. MAS Guideline Series No. 6, AICPA, 1977.

Herbert, Leo. *Auditing the Performance of Management.* Belmont, Calif.: Lifetime Learning Publications, 1979.

Langenderfer, H. Q., and J. C. Robertson. "A Theoretical Structure for Independent Audits of Management." *Accounting Review,* October 1969, pp. 777–87.

Norgaard, C. T. "Extending the Boundaries of the Attest Function." *Accounting Review,* July 1972, pp. 433–42.

Operational and Management Auditing Special Committee, "Operational Audit Engagements." AICPA, 1983.

Pomeranz, Felix. "Public Sector Auditing: New Opportunities for CPAs." *Journal of Accountancy,* March 1978, pp. 48–55.

Robertson, J. C., and C. W. Alderman. "Comparative Auditing Standards." *Journal of Accounting, Auditing & Finance,* Winter 1981, pp. 144–61.

Robertson, J. C., and R. W. Clarke. "Verification of Management Representations: A First Step Toward Independent Audits of Management." *Accounting Review,* July 1971, pp. 562–71.

Sawyer, Lawrence B. *The Practice of Modern Internal Auditing.* The Institute of Internal Auditors, Inc., 1973.

Sawyer, L. B., A. A. Murphy, and M. Crossley. "Management Fraud: The Insidious Specter." *The Internal Auditor,* April 1979, pp. 11–25.

Scantlebury, D. L., and R. B. Raaum. *Operational Auditing.* AGA Monograph Series No. 1. The Association of Government Accountants, 1978.

Smith, William S. "Certification—A Giant Step." *The Internal Auditor,* November/December 1972, pp. 10–19.

Staats, Elmer B. "Governmental Auditing—Yesterday, Today and Tomorrow." *The GAO Review,* Spring 1979, pp. 1–9.

Staats, Elmer B. "Grant Audits: A New Vista for CPAs." *Journal of Accountancy,* April 1979, pp. 68–72.

Standards for Audit of Governmental Organizations, Programs, Activities, and Functions. U.S. General Accounting Office, 1981 Revision.

Standards for the Professional Practice of Internal Auditing. The Institute of Internal Auditors, Inc., 1978.

Statement of Responsibilities of Internal Auditing. The Institute of Internal Auditors, Inc., 1981.

Steinberg, H. I., J. R. Miller, and T. E. Menzel. "The Single Audit in Government." *Journal of Accountancy,* June 1981, pp. 56–67.

Ward, D. D. and J. C. Robertson. "Reliance on Internal Auditors." *Journal of Accountancy,* October 1980, pp. 62–73.

Wolbert, R. H. "The Two-Edged Sword of Internal Audit Professionalism." *The Internal Auditor,* February 1981, pp. 40–52.

Wood, Thomas D. "Auditors' Concern for Compliance with Laws." *The CPA Journal,* January 1978, pp. 17–21.

REVIEW QUESTIONS

5.1. What is operational auditing, and why can it be called a type of management advisory service (MAS)?

5.2. How can internal auditors achieve practical independence?

5.3. What general auditing services do internal auditors provide?

5.4. What general auditing services do governmental auditors provide?

5.5. What factors should governmental auditors consider in determining whether they are independent?

5.6. Why do GAO standards require a review for compliance with laws and regulations in conjunction with financial audits?

5.7. Why do you think the GAO reporting standards permit the report to include "pertinent views of responsible officials [of the auditee] concerning the auditor's findings, conclusions and recommendations"?

5.8. What is a request for proposal (RFP), and what significance does it have in a governmental audit engagement performed by an independent CPA in public practice?

5.9. Specify and describe a general analytical approach that can be used in audits of economy, efficiency and program results.

5.10. What four major blocks of work characterize governmental and internal audit engagements?

5.11. What information can an auditor expect to obtain in a preliminary survey?

5.12. Where can an auditor expect to find information about economy, efficiency, or program results standards for governmental agencies? For business units? For municipal services and social programs?

5.13. What is administrative control, and what does it accomplish?

5.14. How can governmental and internal auditors try to achieve objectivity when developing conclusions about economy, efficiency or program results?

PROBLEMS AND DISCUSSION CASES

5.15. **Identification of Audits and Auditors**
Audits may be characterized as: (*a*) financial statement audits, (*b*) compliance audits, (*c*) economy and efficiency audits and (*d*) program results audits. The work can be done by independent (external) auditors, internal auditors, or governmental auditors (including IRS auditors and federal bank examiners). Below is a list of the purpose or products of various audit engagements.

1. Determining the equity of interest rates charged on Farmers Home Administration (FHA) loans.

2. Determining the fair presentation in conformity with GAAP of an advertising agency's financial statements.

3. Study of the Department of the Interior policies and practices on grant-related income.

4. Determination of costs of municipal garbage pickup services compared to comparable service subcontracted to a private business.

5. Audit of tax-shelter partnership financing terms.

6. Study of a private aircraft manufacturer's test pilot performance in reporting on the results of test flights.

7. Periodic U.S. Comptroller of Currency examination of a national bank for solvency.

8. Evaluation of the promptness of materials inspection in a manufacturer's receiving department.

9. Report of how better care and disposal of vehicles confiscated by drug enforcement agents could save money and benefit law enforcement.

10. Rendering a public report on the assumptions and compilation of a revenue forecast by a sports stadium/racetrack complex.

Required:
Prepare a three-column schedule showing: (1) Each of the engagements listed above; (2) the type of audit (financial statement, compliance, economy and efficiency or program results); and (3) the kind of auditors you would expect to be involved.

5.16. **GAO Auditor Independence (Study of Chapter 3 on Professional Ethics is recommended for this problem.)**

The GAO reporting standards for economy, efficiency and program results audits state that each report should include "recommendations for action to improve problem areas noted in the audit and to improve operations." For example, a 1983 audit of the Washington Metropolitan Area Transit Authority found management decision deficiencies affecting some $230 million in federal funds. The GAO auditors recommended that the transit authority could improve its management control over railcar procurement through better enforcement of contract requirements and development of a master plan to test cars.

Suppose that the transit authority accepted and implemented specific recommendations made by the GAO auditors. Do you believe these events would be enough to impair the independence of the GAO auditors in a subsequent audit of the transit authority? Explain and tell if it makes any difference to you whether the same or different persons perform both the first and subsequent audits.

5.17. **Organizing a Preliminary Survey**

You are the director of internal auditing of a large municipal hospital. You receive monthly financial reports prepared by the accounting department, and your review of them has shown that total accounts receivable from patients have steadily and rapidly increased over the past eight months.

Other information in the reports show the following conditions:

The number of available hospital beds has not changed.

The bed occupancy rate has not changed.

Hospital billing rates have not changed significantly.

The hospitalization insurance contracts have not changed since the last modification 12 months ago.

Your internal audit department audited the accounts receivable 10 months ago. The working paper file for that assignment contains financial information, a record of the preliminary survey, documentation of the study and evaluation of administrative and internal accounting controls, documentation of the evidence-gathering procedures used to produce evidence about the validity and collectibility of the accounts, and a copy of your report which commented favorably on the controls and collectibility of the receivables.

However, the current increase in receivables has alerted you to a need for another audit, so things will not get out of hand. You remember news stories last year about the manager of the city water system who got into big trouble because his accounting department double-billed all the residential customers for three months.

Required:

You plan to perform a preliminary survey in order to get a handle on the problem, if indeed a problem exists. Write a memo to your senior auditor listing at least eight questions he should use to guide and direct the preliminary survey. (Hint: The questions used in the last preliminary survey were organized under these headings: (1) Who does the accounts receivable accounting; (2) What data processing procedures and policies are in effect; and (3) How is the accounts receivable accounting done? This time, you will add a fourth category: What financial or economic events have occurred in the last 10 months?).

(*CIA* Adapted)

5.18. **Study and Evaluation of Administrative Control**

The study and evaluation of administrative controls in a governmental or internal audit is not easy. First, auditors must determine the controls subject to audit. Then, they must find a standard by which performance of the control can be evaluated. Next, they must specify procedures to obtain the evidence upon which an evaluation can be based. Insofar as possible, the standards and related evidence must be quantified.

Students working on this case usually do not have the experience or theoretical background to figure out control standards and audit procedures, so the description below gives certain information *(in italics)* that internal auditors would know about or be able to figure out on their own. Fulfilling the requirement thus amounts to taking some information from the scenario below and figuring out other things by using accountants' and auditors' common sense.

The Scenario: Ace Corporation ships building materials to more than a thousand wholesale and retail customers in a five-state region. The company's normal credit terms are net/30 days, and no cash discounts are offered. Fred Clark is the chief financial officer, and he is concerned about maintaining control over customer credit. In particular, he has stated two administrative control principles for this purpose.

1. Sales are to be billed to customers accurately and promptly. *Fred knows that errors will occur but thinks company personnel ought to be able to hold quantity, unit price and arithmetic errors down to 3 percent of the sales invoices. He considers an invoice error of $1 or less not to matter.* He believes prompt billing is important since customers are expected to pay within 30 days. *Fred is very strict in thinking that a bill should be sent to the customer one day after shipment.* He believes he has staffed the billing department well enough to be able to handle this workload. The relevant company records consist of: an accounts receivable control account; a subsidiary ledger of customers' accounts in which charges are entered by billing (invoice) date and credits are entered by date of payment receipts; a sales journal that lists invoices in chronological order; and a file of shipping documents cross-referenced by number on the sales invoice copy, which is kept on file numerically.

2. Accounts receivable are to be aged and followed up to ensure prompt collection. *Fred has told the accounts receivable department to classify all the customer accounts in categories of: (a) current, (b) 31–59 days overdue, (c) 60–90 days overdue, and (d) more than 90 days overdue. He wants this trial balance to be complete and to be transmitted to the credit department within five days after each month-end. In the credit department, prompt follow-up means sending a different (stronger) collection letter to each category, cutting off credit to customers over 60 days past due (putting them on cash basis), and giving the over-90 days accounts to an outside collection agency. These actions are supposed to be taken within five days after receipt of the aged trial balance.* The relevant company records, in addition to the ones listed above, consist of the aged trial balance, copies of the letters sent to customers, copies of notices of credit cutoff, copies of correspondence with the outside collection agent, and reports of results—statistics of subsequent collections.

Required:

Take the role of a senior internal auditor. You are to write a memo to the "internal audit staff" to inform them about comparison standards for the study and evaluation of these two administrative control policies. You also need to specify two or three procedures for gathering evidence about performance of the controls. The body of your memo should be structured as follows:

1. Control: Sales are billed to customers accurately and promptly.
   a. Accuracy.
      (1) Policy standard . . .
      (2) Audit procedures . . .
   b. Promptness.
      (1) Policy standard . . .

(2) Audit procedures . . .
2. Control: Accounts receivable are aged and followed up to ensure prompt collection.
    a. Accounts receivable aging.
      (1) Policy standard . . .
      (2) Audit procedures . . .
    b. Follow-up for prompt collection.
      (1) Policy standard . . .
      (2) Audit procedures . . .

5.19. Analytical Review of Inventory

External auditors usually calculate inventory turnover (cost of goods sold for the year divided by average inventory) and use the ratio as a broad indication of inventory age, obsolescence or overstocking. External auditors are interested in evidence relating to the material accuracy of the financial statements taken as a whole. Internal auditors, on the other hand, calculate turnover by categories and classes of inventory in order to detect problem areas that might otherwise get overlooked. This kind of detailed analytical review might point to conditions of buying errors, obsolescence, overstocking and other matters that could be changed to save money.

The data shown below are turnover, cost of sales and inventory investment data for a series of four history years and the current year. In each of the history years, the external auditors did not recommend any adjustments to the inventory valuations.

	Inventory Turnover				Current Year Inventory (000)	
	19X1	**19X2**	**19X3**	**19X4**	**Beginning**	**Ending**
Total inventory	2.1	2.0	2.1	2.1	$3,000	$2,917
Materials and parts	4.0	4.1	4.3	4.5	1,365	620
Work in process	12.0	12.5	11.5	11.7	623	697
Finished products:						
Computer games	6.0	7.0	10.0	24.0	380	500
Floppy disk drives	8.0	7.2	7.7	8.5	64	300
Semiconductor parts	4.0	3.5	4.5	7.0	80	400
Electric typewriters	3.0	2.5	2.0	1.9	488	400

Additional information

Current Year (000)

	Transfers	Sales	Cost of Goods Sold	Gross Profit	Compared to 19X4
Materials and parts	$3,970(1)	NA	NA	NA	
Work in process	7,988(2)	NA	NA	NA	
Computer games	2,320(3)	$2,000	$2,200	$ (200)	Sales volume declined 60%(4)
Floppy disk drives	2,236(3)	3,000	2,000	1,000	Sales volume increased 35%
Semiconductor parts . . .	2,720(3)	4,000	2,400	1,600	Sales volume increased 40%
Electric typewriters	712(3)	1,000	800	200	Sales volume declined 3%

(1) Cost of materials transferred to Work in Process.
(2) Cost of materials, labor and overhead transferred to Finished Goods.
(3) Cost of goods transferred from Work in Process to Finished Product Inventories.
(4) Selling prices were also reduced and the gross margin declined.

Required:

Calculate the current-year inventory turnover ratios. Interpret the ratio trends and point out what conditions might exist and write a memo to the vice president for production explaining your findings and what further investigation might be conducted.

5.20. CPA Involvement in an Expanded-Scope Audit

A public accounting firm received an invitation to bid for the audit of a local food commodity distribution program funded by the U.S. Department of Agriculture. The audit is to be conducted in accordance with the audit standards published by the General Accounting Office (GAO). The accountants have become familiar with the GAO standards and recognize that the GAO standards incorporate the AICPA generally accepted auditing standards (GAAS).

The public accounting firm has been engaged to perform the audit of the program, and the audit is to encompass all three elements that constitute the expanded scope of a GAO audit.

Required:

a. The accountants should perform sufficient audit work to satisfy the financial and compliance element of the GAO standards. What is the objective of such audit work?

b. The accountants should be aware of general and specific kinds of uneconomical or inefficient practices in such a program. What are some examples?

c. What might be some standards and sources of standards for judging program results?

5.21. Auditing the Effectiveness of a Loan Program

The Office of Economic Opportunity (OEO) designed Special Impact programs to have a major impact on unemployment, dependency, and community tensions in urban areas with large concentrations of low-income residents or in rural areas having substantial migration to such urban areas. The purpose of these experimental programs—combining business, community, and manpower development—is to offer the poor an opportunity to become self-supporting through the free enterprise system. The pro-

grams are intended to create training and job opportunities, improve the living environment, and encourage development of local entrepreneurial skills.

One area chosen to participate in the Special Impact Program was Bedford-Stuyvesant. The Bedford-Stuyvesant program was the first and largest such program to be sponsored by the federal government. It has received more than $30 million in federal funds from its inception through the current year. Another $7.7 million was obtained from private sources, such as the Ford Foundation and the Astor Foundation.

Problems:

Bedford-Stuyvesant is a five-square mile area with a population of 350,000 to 400,000 in New York City's borough of Brooklyn. This area has serious problems of unemployment and underemployment and inadequate housing.

Bedford-Stuyvesant's problems are deep seated and have resisted rapid solution. They stem primarily from the fact that local residents, to a considerable degree, lack the education and training required for the jobs available elsewhere in the city and from the lack of jobs in the area. Unemployment and underemployment, in turn, reduce buying power, which has a depressing effect on the area's economy.

The magnitude of the Bedford-Stuyvesant problems in indicated by the following data disclosed by the U.S. census.

Of the total civilian labor force, 8.9 percent were unemployed, compared with unemployment rates of 7.1 percent for New York City and 6.8 percent for the New York Standard Metropolitan Statistical Area (SMSA).

Per capita income was $2,106, compared with $3,720 for New York City and $3,909 for the SMSA.

Families below the poverty level made up 24.8 percent of the population, compared with 11.4 percent in New York City and 9.2 percent in the SMSA.

Families receiving public assistance

made up 25.4 percent of the population, compared with 9.6 percent in New York City and 7.5 percent in the SMSA.

A number of factors serve to aggravate the area's economic problems and make them more difficult to solve. Some of these are:

A reluctance of industry to move into New York City.

A net outflow of industry from New York City. High city taxes and a high crime rate.

A dearth of local residents possessing business managerial experience.

The area's housing problems resulted from the widespread deterioration of existing housing and are, in part, a by-product of below-average income levels resulting from unemployment and underemployment. They were aggravated by a shortage of mortgage capital for residential housing associated with a lack of confidence in the area on the part of financial institutions, which, as discussed later, seems to have been somewhat overcome.

Bedford-Stuyvesant was the target of several "special impact" programs. Included were programs designed to stimulate private business, to improve housing, to establish community facilities and to train residents in marketable skills. There were two programs to stimulate private business: a program to loan funds to local businesses and a program to attract outside businesses to the area.

Under the business loan program begun five years ago, the sponsors proposed to create jobs and stimulate business ownership by local residents. At first, investments in local businesses were made only in the form of loans. Later, the sponsors adopted a policy of making equity investments in selected companies to obtain for the sponsors a voice in management. Equity investments totaling about $159,000 were made in four companies.

Loans were to be repaid in installments over periods of up to 10 years, usually with a moratorium on repayment for six months or longer. Repayment was to be made in cash or by applying subsidies allowed by the sponsors for providing on-the-job training to unskilled workers. Loans made during the first two years of the program were interest free. Later, the sponsors revised the policy to one of charging below-market interest rates. Rates charged were from 5 to 8.5 percent. This policy change was made to: (1) emphasize to borrowers their obligations to repay the loan and (2) help the sponsors monitor borrowers' progress toward profitability.

Prospective borrowers learned of the loan program through: (1) information disseminated at neighborhood centers; (2) advertisements on radio and television and in a local newspaper and (3) word of mouth. Those who wished to apply for loans were required to complete application forms providing information relating to their education and business and work experience, personal financial statements and references. The sponsors set up a management assistance division, which employed consultants to supplement its internal marketing assistance efforts and to provide management, accounting, marketing, legal, and other assistance to borrowers.

The sponsors proposed to create at least 1,700 jobs during the first four years of the loan program by making loans to some 73 new and existing businesses.

Required:

Put yourself in the position of the GAO manager in charge of all audits pertaining to Office of Economic Opportunity. The New York City field office has been assigned the job of conducting a detailed review of the Special Impact program described above. Prepare a memo to the New York City field office in which you indicate to them, in as great detail as is possible from the information provided, the specific steps they should perform in conducting an evaluation of the program effectiveness of the Special Impact Loan Program.

APPENDIX 5–A

Summary of General and Specific Standards for the Professional Practice of Internal Auditing.

100 *Independence*—**Internal auditors should be independent of the activities they audit.**

    110 *Organizational Status*—The organizational status of the internal auditing department should be sufficient to permit the accomplishment of its audit responsibilities.

    120 *Objectivity*—Internal auditors should be objective in performing audits.

200 *Professional Proficiency*—**Internal audits should be performed with proficiency and due professional care.**

THE INTERNAL AUDITING DEPARTMENT

    210 *Staffing*—The internal auditing department should provide assurance that the technical proficiency and educational background of internal auditors are appropriate for the audits to be performed.

    220 *Knowledge, Skills, and Disciplines*—The internal auditing department should possess or should obtain the knowledge, skills, and disciplines needed to carry out its audit responsibilities.

    230 *Supervision*—The internal auditing department should provide assurance that internal audits are properly supervised.

THE INTERNAL AUDITOR

    240 *Compliance with Standards of Conduct*—Internal auditors should comply with professional standards of conduct.

    250 *Knowledge, Skills, and Disciplines*—Internal auditors should possess the knowledge, skills, and disciplines essential to the performance of internal audits.

    260 *Human Relations and Communications*—Internal auditors should be skilled in dealing with people and in communicating effectively.

    270 *Continuing Education*—Internal auditors should maintain their technical competence through continuing education.

    280 *Due Professional Care*—Internal auditors should exercise due professional care in performing internal audits.

Source: *Summary of Standards for the Professional Practice of Internal Auditing,* by The Institute of Internal Auditors, Inc. Copyright 1978 by The Institute of Internal Auditors, Inc., 249 Maitland Avenue, Altamonte Springs, Florida, 32701. Reprinted with permission.

300 *Scope of Work*—**The scope of the internal audit should encompass the examination and evaluation of the adequacy and effectiveness of the organization's system of internal control and the quality of performance in carrying out assigned responsibilities.**

310 *Reliability and Integrity of Information*—Internal auditors should review the reliability and integrity of financial and operating information and the means used to identify, measure, classify, and report such information.

320 *Compliance with Policies, Plans, Procedures, Laws and Regulations*—Internal auditors should review the systems established to ensure compliance with those policies, plans, procedures, laws, and regulations which could have a significant impact on operations and reports and should determine whether the organization is in compliance.

330 *Safeguarding of Assets*—Internal auditors should review the means of safeguarding assets and, as appropriate, verify the existence of such assets.

340 *Economical and Efficient Use of Resources*—Internal auditors should appraise the economy and efficiency with which resources are employed.

350 *Accomplishment of Established Objectives and Goals for Operations or Programs*—Internal auditors should review operations or programs to ascertain whether results are consistent with established objectives and goals and whether the operations or programs are being carried out as planned.

400 *Performance of Audit Work*—**Audit work should include planning the audit, examining and evaluating information, communicating results, and following up.**

410 *Planning the Audit*—Internal auditors should plan each audit.

420 *Examining and Evaluating Information*—Internal auditors should collect, analyze, interpret, and document information to support audit results.

430 *Communicating Results*—Internal auditors should report the results of their audit work.

440 *Following Up*—Internal auditors should follow up to ascertain that appropriate action is taken on reported audit findings.

500 *Management of the Internal Auditing Department*—**The director of internal auditing should properly manage the internal auditing department.**

510 *Purpose, Authority and Responsibility*—The director of internal auditing should have a statement of purpose, authority, and responsibility for the internal auditing department.

520   *Planning*—The director of internal auditing should establish plans to carry out the responsibilities of the internal auditing department.

530   *Policies and Procedures*—The director of internal auditing should provide written policies and procedures to guide the audit staff.

540   *Personnel Management and Development*—The director of internal auditing should establish a program for selecting and developing the human resources of the internal auditing department.

550   *External Auditors*—The director of internal auditing should coordinate internal and external audit efforts.

560   *Quality Assurance*—The director of internal auditing should establish and maintain a quality assurance program to evaluate the operations of the internal auditing department.

APPENDIX 5–B

The Institute of Internal Auditors, Inc., Code of Ethics

INTRODUCTION: Recognizing that ethics are an important consideration in the practice of internal auditing and that the moral principles followed by members of The Institute of Internal Auditors, Inc., should be formalized, the Board of Directors at its regular meeting in New Orleans on December 13, 1968, received and adopted the following resolution:

Whereas the members of The Institute of Internal Auditors, Inc., represent the profession of internal auditing; and

Whereas managements rely on the profession of internal auditing to assist in the fulfillment of their management stewardship; and

Whereas said members must maintain high standards of conduct, honor and character in order to carry on proper and meaningful internal auditing practice;

Therefore be it resolved that a Code of Ethics be now set forth, outlining the standards of professional behavior for the guidance of each member of The Institute of Internal Auditors, Inc.

In accordance with this resolution, the Board of Directors further approved of the principles set forth.

INTERPRETATION OF PRINCIPLES: The provisions of this Code of Ethics cover basic principles in the various disciplines of internal auditing practice. Members shall realize that individual judgment is required in the application of these principles. They have a responsibility to conduct themselves so that their good faith and integrity should not be open to question. While having due regard for the limit of their technical skills, they will promote the highest possible internal auditing standards to the end of advancing the interest of their company or organization.

ARTICLES:

I. Members shall have an obligation to exercise honesty, objectivity, and diligence in the performance of their duties and responsibilities.

II. Members, in holding the trust of their employers, shall exhibit loyalty in all matters pertaining to the affairs of the employer or to whomever they may be rendering a service. However, members shall not knowingly be a party to any illegal or improper activity.

III. Members shall refrain from entering into any activity which may be in conflict with the interest of their employers or which would prejudice their ability to carry out objectively their duties and responsibilities.

IV. Members shall not accept a fee or a gift from an employee, a client, a customer, or a business associate of their employer without the knowledge and consent of their senior management.

V. Members shall be prudent in the use of information acquired in the course of their duties. They shall not use confidential information for any personal gain nor in a manner which would be detrimental to the welfare of their employer.

VI. Members, in expressing an opinion, shall use all reasonable care to obtain sufficient factual evidence to warrant such expression. In their reporting, members shall reveal such material facts known to them, which, if not revealed, could either distort the report of the results of operations under review or conceal unlawful practice.

VII. Members shall continually strive for improvement in the proficiency and effectiveness of their service.

VIII. Members shall abide by the bylaws and uphold the objectives of The Institute of Internal Auditors, Inc. In the practice of their profession, they shall be ever mindful of their obligation to maintain the high standard of competence, morality, and dignity which The Institute of Internal Auditors, Inc., and its members have established.

APPENDIX 5–C

Summary of GAO Standards for Audit of Governmental Organizations, Programs, Activities and Functions (1981 Revision)

SCOPE OF AUDIT WORK

The expanded scope of auditing a government organization, a program, an activity, or a function should include:

1. *Financial and compliance*—determines (*a*) whether the financial statements of an audited entity present fairly the financial position and the results of financial operations in accordance with generally accepted accounting principles and (*b*) whether the entity has complied with laws and regulations that may have a material effect upon the financial statements.

2. *Economy and efficiency*—determines (*a*) whether the entity is managing and utilizing its resources (such as personnel, property, space) economically and efficiently, (*b*) the causes of inefficiencies or uneconomical practices, and (*c*) whether the entity has complied with laws and regulations concerning matters of economy and efficiency.

3. *Program results*—determines (*a*) whether the desired results or benefits established by the legislature or other authorizing body are being achieved and (*b*) whether the agency has considered alternatives that might yield desired results at a lower cost.

In determining the scope for a particular audit, responsible audit and entity officials should consider the needs of potential users of audit findings.

GENERAL STANDARDS

1. Qualifications: The auditors assigned to perform the audit must collectively possess adequate professional proficiency for the tasks required.

2. Independence: In all matters relating to the audit work, the audit organization and the individual auditors, whether government or public, must be free from personal or external impairments to independence, must be organizationally independent, and shall maintain an independent attitude and appearance.

3. Due professional care: Due professional care is to be used in conducting the audit and in preparing related reports.

4. Scope impairments: When factors external to the audit organization and the auditor restrict the audit or interfere with the auditor's ability to form objective opinions and conclusions, the auditor should attempt to remove the limitation or, failing that, report the limitation.

EXAMINATION AND EVALUATION (FIELD WORK) AND REPORTING STANDARDS FOR FINANCIAL AND COMPLIANCE AUDITS

1. AICPA Statements on Auditing Standards for field work and reporting are adopted and incorporated in this statement for government financial and compliance audits. Future statements should be adopted and incorporated, unless GAO excludes them by formal announcement.

2. Additional standards and requirements for government financial and compliance audits.

   a. Standards on examination and evaluation:

   (1) Planning shall include consideration of the requirements of all levels of government.

   (2) A review is to be made of compliance with applicable laws and regulations.

   (3) A written record of the auditors' work shall be retained in the form of working papers.

   (4) Auditors shall be alert to situations or transactions that could be indicative of fraud, abuse, and illegal expenditures and acts and if such evidence exists, extend audit steps and procedures to identify the effect on the entity's financial statements.

   b. Standards on reporting:

   (1) Written audit reports are to be submitted to the appropriate officials of the organization audited and to the appropriate officials of the organizations requiring or arranging for the audits unless legal restrictions or ethical considerations prevent it. Copies of the reports should also be sent to other officials who may be responsible for taking action and to others authorized to receive such reports. Unless restricted by law or regulation, copies should be made available for public inspection.

   (2) A statement in the auditors' report that the examination was made in accordance with generally accepted government auditing standards for financial and compliance audits will be acceptable language to indicate that the audit was made in accordance with these standards.

   (3) Either the auditors' report on the entity's financial statements or a separate report shall contain a statement of positive assurance on those items of compliance tested and negative assurance on those items not tested. It shall also include material instances of noncompliance and instances or indications of fraud, abuse, or illegal acts found during or in connection with the audit.

   (4) The auditors shall report on their study and evaluation of internal accounting controls made as part of the financial and compliance audit. They shall identify as a minimum: (*a*)

the entity's significant internal accounting controls, (*b*) the controls identified that were evaluated, (*c*) the controls identified that were not evaluated (the auditor may satisfy this requirement by identifying any significant classes of transactions and related assets not included in the study and evaluation), and (*d*) the material weaknesses identified as a result of the evaluation.

(5)   Either the auditors' report on the entity's financial statements or a separate report shall contain any other material deficiency findings identified during the audit not covered in (3) above.

(6)   If certain information is prohibited from general disclosure, the report shall state the nature of the information omitted and the requirement that makes the omission necessary.

EXAMINATION AND EVALUATION STANDARDS FOR ECONOMY AND EFFICIENCY AUDITS AND PROGRAM RESULTS AUDITS

1.   Work is to be adequately planned.

2.   Assistants are to be properly supervised.

3.   A review is to be made of compliance with applicable laws and regulations.

4.   During the audit, a study and evaluation shall be made of the internal control system (administrative controls) applicable to the organization, program, activity, or function under audit.

5.   When audits involve computer-based systems, the auditors shall:

a.   Review general controls in data processing systems to determine whether (1) the controls have been designed according to management direction and known legal requirements and (2) the controls are operating effectively to provide reliability of, and security over, the data being processed.

b.   Review application controls of installed data processing applications upon which the auditor is relying to assess their reliability in processing data in a timely, accurate, and complete manner.

6.   Sufficient, competent and relevant evidence is to be obtained to afford a reasonable basis for the auditors' judgments and conclusions regarding the organization, program, activity, or function under audit. A written record of the auditors' work shall be retained in the form of working papers.

7.   The auditors shall:

a.   Be alert to situations or transactions that could be indicative of fraud, abuse, and illegal acts.

b.   If such evidence exists, extend audit steps and procedures to identify the effect on the entity's operations and programs.

REPORTING STANDARDS FOR ECONOMY AND EFFICIENCY AUDITS AND PROGRAM RESULTS AUDITS

1. Written audit reports are to be prepared giving the results of each government audit.

2. Written audit reports are to be submitted to the appropriate officials of the organization audited and to the appropriate officials of the organizations requiring or arranging for the audits unless legal restrictions or ethical considerations prevent it. Copies of the reports should also be sent to other officials who may be responsible for taking action on audit findings and recommendations and to others authorized to receive such reports. Unless restricted by law or regulation, copies should be made available for public inspection.

3. Reports are to be issued on or before the dates specified by law, regulation, or other special arrangement. Reports are to be issued promptly so as to make the information available for timely use by management and by legislative officials.

4. The report shall include:

   a. A description of the scope and objectives of the audit.

   b. A statement that the audit (economy and efficiency or program results) was made in accordance with generally accepted government auditing standards.

   c. A description of material weaknesses found in the internal control system (administrative controls).

   d. A statement of positive assurance on those items of compliance tested and negative assurance on those items not tested. This should include significant instances of noncompliance and instances of or indications of fraud, abuse, or illegal acts found during or in connection with the audit. However, fraud, abuse, or illegal acts normally should be covered in a separate report, thus permitting the overall report to be released to the public.

   e. Recommendations for actions to improve problem areas noted in the audit and to improve operations. The underlying causes of problems reported should be included to assist in implementing correction actions.

   f. Pertinent views of responsible officials of the organization, program, activity, or function audited concerning the auditors' findings, conclusions, and recommendations. When possible, their views should be obtained in writing.

   g. A description of noteworthy accomplishments, particularly when management improvements in one area may be applicable elsewhere.

   h. A listing of any issues and questions needing further study and consideration.

   i. A statement as to whether any pertinent information has been omitted because it is deemed privileged or confidential. The nature of such information should be described, and the law or other basis under which it is withheld should be stated. If a separate report was issued containing this information, it should be indicated in the report.

5. The report shall:
   a. Present factual data accurately and fairly. Include only information, findings, and conclusions that are adequately supported by sufficient evidence in the auditors' working papers to demonstrate or prove the bases for the matters reported and their correctness and reasonableness.
   b. Present findings and conclusions in a convincing manner.
   c. Be objective.
   d. Be written in language as clear and simple as the subject matter permits.
   e. Be concise, but at the same time, clear enough to be understood by users.
   f. Present factual data completely to fully inform the users.
   g. Place primary emphasis on improvement rather than on criticism of the past; critical comments should be presented in a balanced perspective considering any unusual difficulties or circumstances faced by the operating officials concerned.

PART 2

General Technology of Auditing

CHAPTER 6

		PROFESSIONAL STANDARDS SOURCES	

Compendium Section	Document Reference	Topic
AU 161	SAS 25	The Relationship of Generally Accepted Auditing Standards to Quality Control Standards
AU 230	SAS 1	Due Care in the Performance of Work
AU 310	SAS 1	Adequacy of Planning and the Timing of Field Work
AU 311	SAS 22	Planning and Supervision
AU 312	SAS 47	Audit Risk and Materiality in Conducting an Audit
AU 315	SAS 7	Communications between Predecessor and Successor Auditors
AU 318	SAS 23	Analytical Review Procedures
AU 322	SAS 9	The Effect of an Internal Audit Function on the Independent Auditor's Examination
AU 326	SAS 31	Evidential Matter
AU 331	SAS 1	Evidential Matter for Receivables and Inventories
AU 336	SAS 11	Using the Work of a Specialist
AU 339	SAS 41	Working Papers
AU 8002	IAG 2	Audit Engagement Letters

Beginning an Audit Engagement

LEARNING OBJECTIVES

This chapter begins a new section covering technical field work subjects. The topics in this and the next six chapters explain the general technology of auditing. This chapter focuses on how to begin an audit engagement. Considerations of planning, risk and materiality, evidence, objectives and procedures and working paper documentation are important in all audits. Your learning objectives are to be able to:

□ Specify and explain the importance of a series of pre-engagement and planning activities auditors undertake in the early stages of preparing to perform an audit.

□ Recite the general characteristics of analytical review procedures and give some examples of specific applications.

□ Describe a conceptual model of audit risk and explain the meaning and importance of its components in terms of professional judgments.

□ Analyze a financial statement materiality assessment case and explain how the materiality judgment would be used in planning and performing an audit.

□ Classify items of evidence according to their relative competence.

□ Express the explicit and implicit assertions contained in a specific financial presentation and list general procedures for obtaining evidence relevant to the assertions.

□ Review an audit working paper for proper form and content.

**AUDIT
PLANNING**

An audit engagement consists of several sequential elements or phases, beginning with decisions about client acceptance and retention and ending with reviews of the quality of the completed audit work. This chapter deals only with the first stages of conducting an audit—described in Exhibit 1–2 as the "pre-engagement activities" and the "planning activities."[1]

**Client Selection and
Retention**

An important element of an accounting firm's quality control policies and procedures is a system for deciding to accept a new client and, on a continuing basis, deciding whether to resign from audit engagements. Accounting firms are not obligated to accept undesirable clients, nor are they obligated to continue to audit clients when relationships deteriorate or when the management comes under a cloud of suspicion.[2]

Accounting firms have procedures for client acceptance and retention. Policies and procedures include: (1) obtaining and reviewing financial information about the prospective client—annual reports, interim statements, registration statements, Forms 10-K and reports to regulatory agencies; (2) inquiring of the prospective client's banker, legal counsel, underwriter or other persons who do business with the company for information about the company and its management; (3) communicating with the predecessor auditor, if any, for information on the integrity of management, on disagreements with management about accounting principles, auditing procedures or similar matters, and on the reasons for a change of auditors,[3] (4) considering whether the engagement would require special attention or involve unusual risks; (5) evaluating the accounting firm's independence with regard to the prospective client; and (6) considering the need for special skills (for example, computer auditing or specialized industry knowledge).

Decisions to continue auditing a client are similar to acceptance decisions, except that the accounting firm will have more firsthand experience with the company. Retention reviews may be done periodically (say, annually) or upon occurrence of major events, such as changes in management, directors, ownership, legal counsel, financial condition, litigation status, nature of the client's business or scope of the audit engagement. In general, conditions which would have caused an accounting firm to reject a prospective client may develop and lead to a decision to discontinue the engagement. For example, a client company may expand and

---

[1] *Statement on Auditing Standards No. 22* (AU 311), "Planning and Supervision," specifies numerous considerations involved in planning and conducting an audit.

[2] *Statement on Auditing Standards No. 25* (AU 161), "The Relationship of Generally Accepted Auditing Standards to Quality Control Standards," makes reference to the *Statement on Quality Control Standards,* which includes the matter of acceptance and continuance of clients.

[3] *Statement on Auditing Standards No. 7* (AU 315), "Communications Between Predecessor and Successor Auditors," describes the required procedures involved in making inquiries of a predecessor auditor.

diversify on an international scale to the extent that a small accounting firm may not have the competence to continue the audit. In an actual case, a firm discontinued the audit of seven companies under the managerial influence of one person after he admitted falsifying some financial statements and using corporate funds for his personal benefit.

Engagement Letters

Upon acceptance, an accounting firm should prepare an *engagement letter.* (The letter should be obtained each year from continuing clients.) This letter sets forth the terms of the engagement and the auditor-client understandings, including an agreement about the fee to be charged. In effect, it is the audit contract. It may contain special requests and assignments to be undertaken by the auditors, or it may be a rather standard letter stating that an audit of financial statements will be performed in accordance with generally accepted auditing standards. An engagement letter is highly recommended as a means of avoiding misunderstandings with the client and as a means of avoiding legal liability for claims that the auditors did not perform the work promised. A typical engagement letter is illustrated in Exhibit 6–1.[4]

Staff Assignment

Accounting firms engage in competition for audit clients. Usually, a company searches for an accounting firm by inviting several firms to submit proposals to the board of directors. Accounting firms prepare and present elaborate proposals explaining their audit approaches, special technical skills, experience in the client's industry or in similar companies, and the experience and reputation of their personnel. A company can also ask for a fee bid in a proposal. The board of directors selects an accounting firm or nominates one for shareholder ratification on the basis of a combination of price and quality considerations.

When a new client is obtained, most accounting firms assign a *full-service team* to the new client. This team usually consists of the audit engagement partner (the person with final responsibility for the audit), the audit manager, one or more senior audit staff members, statistics, computer and industry specialists (if needed), a tax partner, a MAS partner, and a second audit partner. The tax and MAS partners are consultants to the audit team if the engagement does not include other specific tax and MAS work contracted by the client. The *second audit partner* is one who reviews the work of the audit team. This partner is supposed to have a detached professional point of view because he or she is not directly responsible for "keeping the client happy." A second audit partner is required for audits of financial statements filed with the U.S. Securities and Exchange Commission.

---

[4] *International Auditing Guideline No. 2* (AU 8002), "Audit Engagement Letters," gives detail guidance. The IAGs are issued by the International Auditing Practice Committee of the International Federation of Accountants. IAGs are not enforceable under Rule 202 of the AICPA Code of Ethics.

EXHIBIT 6–1
Engagement Letter

Anderson, Olds and Watershed
Certified Public Accountants
Chicago, Illinois
July 15, 1985

Mr. Larry Lancaster, Chairman
Apple Blossom Cologne Company
Chicago, Illinois

Dear Mr. Lancaster:

This will confirm our understanding of the arrangements made with you covering the audit which you wish us to make of the financial statements of Apple Blossom Cologne Company for the year ending December 31, 1985.

We contemplate that, as in previous years, our work will consist of an audit of the balance sheet at December 31, 1985, and the related statements of income, retained earnings, and changes in financial position for the year ending that date. Our audit will be made in accordance with generally accepted auditing standards and will include such tests of the accounting records and such other auditing procedures as we consider necessary.

Our audit will be based on samples of recorded transactions. We will plan our procedures to search for material errors and irregularities that may affect your financial statements. We expect to obtain reasonable but not absolute assurance that major misstatements do not exist. Our findings regarding your system of internal accounting control, including information about material weaknesses, will be reported to you in a separate letter at the close of the audit.

At your request, we will perform the following other services: (1) timely preparation of all required federal tax returns and (2) a review and report on the company's methods for estimating current cost information in accordance with *FASB Statement No. 33*.

We will provide your staff with a package of schedule formats needed by our staff during the audit. The delivery dates have been discussed and mutually agreed upon. We understand that your staff will prepare all the schedules in the package, all the financial statements and notes thereto, and the Form 10-K for our review. The scope of our services does not include preparation of any of such financial statements.

Mr. Dalton Wardlaw will be the partner in charge of all work performed for you. He will inform you immediately if we encounter any circumstances which could significantly affect our fee estimate of $46,000 discussed with you on July 1, 1985. He is aware of the due date for the audit report, May 10, 1986. You should feel free to call on him at any time.

If the specifications above are in accordance with your understanding of the terms of our engagement, please sign below and return the duplicate copy to us. We look forward again to serving you as independent public accountants.

Sincerely yours,
Arnold Anderson, CPA

Accepted by _____   Date _____

Staff assignments change from year to year on continuing engagements. Assistant accountants are assigned to various audits at the request of senior accountants and managers, who usually compete internally for the best assistants. People get promoted and move on to other clients, thus the full-service team changes. On SEC engagements, the audit engagement partner is required to rotate to other clients, so that he or she does not remain in charge of a particular client for more than seven years.

Understanding the Client's Business

A working knowledge of the client's business is important. Auditors must understand the broad economic environment in which the client operates, including such things as the effects of national economic policies (for example, price regulation and import restriction), the geographic location and its economy (Northeastern states v. "Sunbelt" states), and developments in the taxation and regulatory areas (for example, the encouragement of more price competition in air transport and trucking). Next, the industry characteristics are important. Banking, insurance, and savings and loan companies operate in industry environments altogether different from auto manufacture and chemical processors. At the client level, the personnel, products, production methods, and financing methods utilized in the business are important. Sources of this information include general business and economic magazines, industry and trade journals, AICPA industry accounting and auditing guides, Moody's and Standard and Poor's records, and company histories contained in registration statements and in auditors' permanent file working papers. Auditors must be well read. In addition, a walking tour of the client's plant and offices can contribute a great deal toward firsthand acquaintance with the layout, physical facilities, accounting personnel and information systems.

PRELIMINARY ANALYTICAL REVIEW

In general, *analytical review procedures* are methods of obtaining new information by studying and comparing relationships among data. For example, you can infer that a company's production efficiency is improving if its gross profit has increased from year to year while prices remained stable. Various analytical procedures are useful throughout an audit, but the emphasis in the planning stage is to use analytical review to identify potential problem areas so the audit work can be planned to emphasize them.

SAS 23 (AU 318), entitled *Analytical Review Procedures,* lists five types of procedures:

1. Comparison of the financial information with information for comparable prior period(s). (The example above is of this type.)
2. Comparison of the financial information with anticipated results (for example, budgets and forecasts).
3. Study of the relationships of elements of financial information that

would be expected to conform to a predictable pattern based on the entity's experience.

4. Comparison of the financial information with similar information regarding the industry in which the entity operates.

5. Study of relationships of the financial information with relevant nonfinancial information.

Comparing a client's financial information with industry averages is a way to understand the business and see how it compares to other companies. For example, suppose you are auditing the Majestic Hotel, which advertises itself as ''an elegant high-price lodging experience with the best of service and cuisine.'' Simple observation of the location, decor and service might match this image. Further support could come from seeing that Majestic's average daily room rate is $160 while the hotel industry is $120, that Majestic's ratio of salaries and wages to room revenue is 18.9 percent while the industry is 15.7 percent, and that Majestic's cost of food and beverages sold is 42.1 percent of sales while the industry is at 37.0 percent. However, even though the financial comparisons match the hotel's image, the higher ratio of salaries and wages might be the result of padded payrolls. The higher cost of food might be a product of poor control, mismanagement, theft or cost misallocation.

Preliminary analytical reviews play a large role in the initial engagement planning phase. Industry statistics can be obtained from services such as Dun & Bradstreet and Robert Morris Associates. These statistics include industry averages for important financial yardsticks, such as gross profit margin, return on sales, current ratio, debt/net worth, and many others. A comparison with client data may reveal out-of-line statistics, indicating a relatively strong feature of the client, a weak financial position, or possibly an error or misstatement in the client's financial information. The client's own internal and interim financial statements should also be reviewed at this stage.[5]

A large number of analytical comparisons are possible, limited only by an auditor's imagination. You learned numerous financial ratios in accounting and finance courses. In audit planning, you put them to work by comparing period-to-period changes in a company. Ratio relationships that appear to be out of line raise questions, and the audit plan should deal with them. For example, if a company shows a gross profit much higher than prior years, and you know that industry price competition has cut unit sales prices significantly, the increase may be the result of cost of goods sold and inventory accounting errors. The inventory may be overstated because some costs of goods sold have not been entered in the records. The audit plan should provide time and perhaps specialized ex-

---

[5] These and other elements of analytical review are discussed in *Statement on Auditing Standards No. 23* (AU 318), ''Analytical Review Procedures.'' However, no specific analytical review procedures are required to be performed.

perts (if needed to analyze a special kind of product) to determine whether the accounting is appropriate.

Comparing reported financial results with internal budgets and forecasts can also be useful. If the budget or forecast represents management's estimate of probable future outcomes, planning questions can arise for items that fall short or exceed the budget. If a company expected to sell 10,000 units of a product but sold only 5,000 units, an auditor would want to plan a careful lower of cost-or-market study of the inventory of unsold units. If 15,000 were sold, an auditor would want to audit for sales validity. Budget comparisons can be tricky, however. Some companies use budgets and forecasts as goals rather than expressions of probable outcomes. Also, meeting the budget with little or no shortfall or excess can result from managers manipulating the numbers to "meet the budget." Auditors must be careful to know something about a company's business conditions from sources other than the internal records when analyzing comparisons with budgets and forecasts.

Other helpful review procedures may be carried out in the planning stage. The corporate charter and bylaws, articles of partnership, terms of a government grant (for grant-holding agencies), minutes of the meetings of directors, executive committee, audit committee and finance committee, and important new contracts and leases should all be reviewed with an eye to authorization of important accounting and auditing matters. Such reviews should be followed up by subsequent evidence-gathering procedures, and pertinent minutes should be extracted or copied for inclusion in the working papers.

All of these applications of analytical review procedures in the planning stage can be termed *attention directing*. The results provide little direct evidence about the amounts and disclosures in the financial statements. Nevertheless, the procedures are valuable tools for planning areas of emphasis in the remainder of the audit work. Planning then proceeds with considerations of audit risks and materiality.

PRELIMINARY ASSESSMENT OF AUDIT RISKS

In the engagement planning stage, auditors must make preliminary assessments of audit risks. Understanding the client's business and the results of the preliminary analytical review can help auditors make tentative risk assessments. However, estimates of risk always involve significant elements of professional judgment that cannot be fully defined. Risks include the concept of inherent risk, internal control risk, detection risk and audit risk. Since several terms are used to describe "risk," you should never speak of risk without a modifier (inherent, internal control, etc.) to specify which one you mean.

Inherent Risk

Inherent risk is the probability that material errors or irregularities have entered the data processing system used to develop financial statements. Inherent risk is purely and simply a professional judgment based on knowledge of the client's business, the major types of transactions and the effectiveness of its accountants. An assessment of inherent risk can be based on a variety of information. Auditors may know that material errors or irregularities were discovered during last year's audit, so inherent risk will be considered higher than it would be if last year's audit had shown no material errors or irregularities. Auditors might believe the client's accounting clerks tend to misunderstand GAAP and the company's own accounting policies, thus suggesting a significant inherent risk. The nature of the client's business may produce complicated transactions and calculations generally known to be subject to data processing and accounting treatment error. (Without casting aspersions on any business organizations, real estate, franchising, and oil and gas transactions are frequently complicated and subject to accounting error. Some kinds of inventories are harder than others to count, value and keep accurately in perpetual records.)

Auditors can express inherent risk in terms of the client's whole business. However, it is expressed much more commonly in relation to particular accounting areas, such as revenue recognition, real estate asset valuation, and oil and gas full-cost accounting valuation. Most audit decisions are made on particular components and accounts, and inherent risk judgments should be specifically related to them.

The concept of *relative risk* is closely related. In auditing practice, relative risk is a term used to mean that some accounts or areas (for example, cash and inventory) are more susceptible to embezzlement, theft or other loss than other accounts or areas (for example, land or prepaid expenses). The important relationship you should understand is that auditors' emphasis and attention should be greater where relative risk and inherent risk are considered higher.

Internal Control Risk *Internal control risk* is the probability that the client's system of internal accounting control policies and procedures will *fail* to detect material errors and irregularities, provided any enter the data processing system in the first place. An auditor's assessment of this risk is usually made after the study and evaluation of internal control is completed. You will study this process in more detail in Chapter 7. The assessment is largely a product of auditors' professional judgment, based in part on evidence.

This risk assessment may be made on a preliminary basis for planning purposes. Auditors often carry over preconceived notions about internal control risk when they perform the audit on a client year after year. This carry-over is known as *anchoring* the internal control judgment, and it represents: (1) a useful continuity of experience with a particular client and (2) a potential pitfall if conditions change for the worse and the auditor fails to acknowledge the deterioration of control.

Auditing standards do not permit internal control risk to be assessed so low that auditors place complete reliance on controls and do not perform any other audit work. You can see this relation more clearly in the summary at the end of this section.

Detection Risk   *Detection risk* is the probability that audit procedures will *fail* to produce evidence of material errors and irregularities, provided any have entered the data processing system in the first place *and* have not been detected and corrected by the client's internal control procedures. These audit procedures represent the last chance to detect material errors and irregularities that can cause financial statements to be misleading.

In subsequent chapters, you will study **substantive procedures.** These are the procedures used to obtain direct evidence about dollar amounts and disclosures presented in the financial statements and footnotes. Two categories of substantive procedures are recognized in auditing standards: (1) audit of the details of transactions and balances and (2) analytical review procedures performed at the planning stage, during the remainder of the audit or at the conclusion as a means of review and supervision. When you speak of detection risk, you speak of the failure of procedures in these two categories to detect material errors and irregularities.

Auditors normally do not make explicit assessments of detection risk in the audit planning stage. Assessments and calculations are made when the study and evaluation of internal accounting control is complete and the audit program is finalized. However, auditors take some aspects of detection risk under consideration when they plan the number of people and the amount of time for particular audit areas.

Audit Risk   In a global sense, **audit risk** is the probability that an auditor will give an inappropriate opinion on financial statements. For example, the worst manifestation of this risk is giving an unqualified opinion on financial statements that are misleading because of material errors and irregularities the auditors failed to discover. Such a risk *always* exists, even when audits are well planned and carefully performed. Of course, the risk is much greater in poorly planned and carelessly performed audits.

The concept of audit risk, however, also applies to particular account balances and disclosures. In this case, the risk is that material errors or irregularities are not discovered in an account (for example, the inventory total) or in a disclosure (for example, a pension-plan footnote explanation). Audit risk is most often utilized in practice with regard to particular balances and disclosures. You should keep this context in mind when you study the risk model summary presented next.

Risk Model—A Summary   The foregoing concepts of audit risks can be expressed in a model which assumes the elements of risk are **independent.** Thus, the risks are *multiplied* as follows:

Audit Risk (AuR) = Inherent Risk (IR) $\times$ Internal Control Risk (IC) $\times$ Detection Risk (DR)

Auditors want to perform an audit of a particular balance or disclosure well enough to hold the audit risk (AuR) to a relatively low level (for example, 0.05). As such, AuR is a quality criterion based on professional judgment. All the other risk assessments are estimates based on professional judgment and evidence.

For example, suppose an auditor thought a particular inventory balance was subject to great inherent risk of material error (say, IR = 0.90) and that the client's internal control was not very effective (say, IC = 0.70). If he or she wanted to control audit risk at a low level (say, AuR = 0.02), the other procedures would need to be designed so that detection risk (DR) did not exceed 0.03 (approximately). According to the model, this example would produce the following results:

$$\text{AuR} = \text{IR} \times \text{IC} \times \text{DR}$$
$$0.02 = 0.90 \times 0.70 \times \text{DR}$$
$$\text{Solving for DR: DR} = 0.032$$

The practical problem here is knowing whether the audit has been planned and performed well enough to hold the detection risk as low as 0.03. Despite the simplicity of the risk model, it is only a conceptual tool. Auditors have few ways to calculate detection risk, so the model represents more of a way to think about audit risks than a way to calculate them.

The model, however, produces some insights, including these:

1. Auditors cannot rely entirely on an estimate of zero inherent risk to the exclusion of other evidence-gathering procedures. Thus, you cannot have the condition:

$$\text{AuR} = \text{IR} (=0) \times \text{IC} \times \text{DR} = 0$$

2. Auditors cannot place complete reliance on internal accounting control to the exclusion of other audit procedures. Thus, you cannot have the condition:

$$\text{AuR} = \text{IR} \times \text{IC} (=0) \times \text{DR} = 0$$

3. Audits would not seem to exhibit due audit care if the risk of failure to detect material errors and irregularities were too high, for example:

$$\text{AuR} = \text{IR} (=0.80) \times \text{IC} (=0.80) \times \text{DR} (=0.50) = 0.32$$

4. Auditors *can* choose to rely almost exclusively on evidence produced by substantive procedures, even if they think inherent risk is high and internal control is not very good. For example, this combination is acceptable (provided AuR = 0.02 is acceptable):

$$\text{AuR} = \text{IR} (=1.00) \times \text{IC} (=1.00) \times \text{DR} (=0.02) = 0.02$$

Audit risk assessments and estimates ought to be a part of the audit planning stage. Likewise, considerations of materiality are also important.

PRELIMINARY ASSESSMENT OF MATERIALITY

When planning an audit, auditors should think about *materiality* in terms of the largest amount of uncorrected dollar error that could exist in published financial statements, yet they would still *not* be considered materially misleading. Accounting firms, however, differ greatly on how to carry out this idea. Some do not even mention it in their own audit guidance. Some believe in the "blunt instrument" approach to auditing—just beat the accounts to death for the evidence. Some of these auditors go to an engagement and start performing procedures without bothering with theoretical niceties of making preliminary materiality estimates. Some firms tell their staffs to "think about it, but don't try to put a number on it." Some firms guide their staffs with directions about how to use numbers to quantify a preliminary materiality amount.

When materiality is quantified, some accounting firms prefer a *bottoms-up approach*—judging amounts in each audit area separately, then combining them to see what the overall effect might be. Some firms prefer a *top-down approach*—judging an overall material amount for the financial statements, then allocating it to particular areas (for example, receivables, inventory) to help determine the amount of work in each area. For example, if $1 million were considered a maximum misstatement of total assets, $50,000 might be permitted in the cash account, $200,000 in the accounts receivable, $300,000 in the inventory and $450,000 in the fixed assets and other accounts.

A top-down approach may be considered theoretically preferable. It requires auditors to think first about the financial statements taken altogether. Then, it forces the planning for each area into the context of the financial statements taken as a whole. The top-down approach helps avoid the problems of "being surprised" when judgments about separate account areas (the bottoms-up approach), add up to more than a material amount appropriate for the income statement, balance sheet or statement of changes in financial position.

The major reason for thinking about materiality at the planning stage is to try to fine tune the audit for effectiveness and efficiency. Thinking about it in advance helps you avoid surprises. Suppose near the end of an audit, the partner decided that individual and aggregate errors over $500,000 would be considered material, but then realized that the nature, timing and extent of audit procedures resulted in an acceptable audit risk only at the $1-million level! More work should be done, and now it is very late to do it. Conversely, an audit team might *overaudit,* perform much more audit work than is necessary, thinking in terms of detecting $100,000 misstatements when accuracy to the nearest $500,000 is satisfactory.

Financial Statement Materiality

So what is materiality, and *how* can you deal with it? The concept of materiality pervades financial accounting and reporting in this context: Information is material and should be disclosed if it is likely to influence the economic decisions of financial statement users. The emphasis is on the user's point of view, not on accountants' and managers' points of view. Thus, *important information* is a synonym for *material information*.

Financial statement measurements and information in some footnote disclosures are not perfectly accurate. However, you should not leap to the unwarranted conclusion that financial reports are inherently imprecise and inaccurate. Doing so would represent a too-extreme view of the relative accuracy of accounting measurements. Accountants and auditors would prefer to say that financial reports are materially accurate or that they do not contain material misrepresentations or misstatements.

Some numbers are not perfectly accurate because mistakes exist in them, and some are not perfectly accurate because they are based on estimates. Everyone acknowledges that people make mistakes—billing a customer the wrong amount, using the wrong prices to compile an inventory, making a mathematical mistake in a depreciation calculation. Furthermore, many financial measurements are based on estimates—for example, the estimated depreciable lives of fixed assets or the estimated amount of uncollectible accounts receivable. However, this imprecise nature of accounting should not be taken as license to be sloppy about clerical accuracy or negligent judgment in operating an accounting system and in preparing financial statements.

Thus, auditors come upon the scene limited by the nature of accounting. Auditors should not be too concerned with finding the last $1,000 of inventory compilation errors when the allowance for uncollectible receivables can be estimated with only $100,000 accuracy. Some amount of inaccuracy is permitted to exist in financial statements because: (1) Unimportant inaccuracies do not effect users' decisions and hence are immaterial; (2) The cost of finding and correcting small errors is too great; and (3) The time taken to find them would delay issuance of financial statements. As a leading accountant once said, summing up materiality thought: "If it doesn't really matter, don't bother with it."[6]

The FASB started a study of materiality in 1975 by issuing its *Criteria for Determining Materiality* discussion memorandum. The project was closed in 1980 when FASB issued its *Statement on Financial Accounting Concepts No. 2,* "Qualitative Characteristics of Accounting Information" (May 1980), which contained some brief commentary on the subject. Many persons wish that definitive, quantitative guides could be issued, but many also fear the rigidity of such guides. The SEC has expressed percentage guides in a few cases in Regulation S-X, and the FASB has handled materiality directly in a few cases (for example, in connection with capitalization of interest costs).

Auditors, however, are generally left without definitive, quantitative guidelines. The best rules of thumb seem to be that anything less than 5

---

[6] Ernest L. Hicks, "Materiality," *Journal of Accounting Research,* Autumn 1964, p. 158.

percent is probably not material and anything greater than 10 percent probably is material. (A legitimate question, therefore, is 5 percent or 10 percent of *what?*) Some of the more common factors auditors use in making materiality judgments are these:

Absolute Size. An amount of potential misstatement may be important irrespective of any other considerations. Not many auditors use absolute size alone as a criterion because a given amount, say $50,000, may be appropriate in one case and too large or too small in another. Yet, some auditors will say: "$1 million (or some other large number) is material, no matter what."

Relative Size. The relation of potential misstatement to a relevant base number is often used (usually with reference to the 5 percent-10 percent rule of thumb). Potential misstatements in income statement accounts are usually related to net income either before or after taxes. If income fluctuates widely, a "normalized" or average income over recent years may be substituted for the current-year net income, or the relation may be to the trend change of income. The base for nonprofit entities may be gross revenue or contributions or a figure important in the statement of changes in financial position. Potential misstatements in balance sheet accounts may be related to a subtotal number such as current assets or net working capital. Some auditors prefer the total gross margin as a uniform base because it is less subject to year-to-year fluctuations than the net income number.

Nature of the Item or Issue. An important qualitative factor is the descriptive nature of the item or issue. An illegal payment is important primarily because of its nature as well as because of its absolute or relative amount. A misstatement in segment information may be small in relation to the total business but important for analysis of the segment (see AU 435.08). Generally, potential errors in the more liquid assets (cash, receivables, and inventory) are considered more important than potential errors in other accounts (such as fixed assets and deferred charges).

Circumstances. Auditors generally place extra emphasis on lesser permitted misstatement in financial statements that will be used widely (publicly held companies) or by important outsiders (bank loan officers). Auditors' liability is a relevant consideration. When management can exercise discretion over an accounting treatment, auditors tend to exercise more care and use a more stringent materiality criterion. Troublesome political events in foreign countries can also cause auditors to try to be more accurate with measurements and disclosures. However, these matters relate as much to *risk* as they do to financial statement materiality.

Uncertainty.   Matters surrounded by uncertainty about the outcome of future events usually come under more stringent materiality considerations.

Cumulative Effects.   Auditors must evaluate the sum of known or potential misstatements. Considering five different $20,000 mistakes which all increase net income as immaterial is inappropriate when the net income-based materiality limit is $50,000.

Working with Materiality

The accounting and auditing profession has not yet created definite guides for working with the concept of materiality. Each case is considered different, and materiality decisions must be made in each, keeping in mind the factors explained above.

The concept of materiality is used by auditors in three ways: (1) as a guide to *planning the audit program*—directing attention and audit work to the important, uncertain, or error-prone items and accounts; (2) as a guide to *evaluation of the evidence;* and (3) as a guide for making *decisions about the audit report.* An important point is that materiality in auditing is perceived both in terms of potential misstatement (in a planning sense) and in terms of known or estimated misstatement (in an evaluation and reporting decision sense). An account, such as inventory, is not necessarily material in an audit context because of its size or its place in the financial statements. The importance derives from the potential for, and effect of, misstatements or errors that might exist in the account.

Materiality decisions are professional judgments. As such, they should be made objectively and with care; they should be supported with well-considered reasons and user-oriented logic.

EVIDENCE IN AUDITING

After the preliminary planning stage of an engagement, auditors proceed to the task of specifying procedures for gathering evidence. However, before studying these procedures, you need to understand some dimensions of evidence in auditing.

The third field work standard requires auditors to obtain sufficient competent evidential matter as a reasonable basis for an opinion on financial statements. The accounting records (journals, ledgers, accounting policy manuals, and the like) are evidence of the bookkeeping-accounting process but are not sufficient competent supporting evidence for the financial statements. Evidence corroborating these records must be obtained through auditors' direct personal knowledge, examination of documentary material and inquiry. The purpose of gathering and analyzing evidence is to make a decision on whether the financial statements conform to GAAP.

Competence of Evidence

To be considered *competent,* evidence must be valid, relevant and unbiased. The following *hierarchy* of evidential matter will help you understand the relative competence and persuasive power of different kinds of evidence. The hierarchy starts with the strongest form of evidence and proceeds to the weakest.

1. An auditor's *direct, personal knowledge,* obtained through *physical observation* and his or her own *mathematical computations,* is generally considered the most competent evidence.

2. Documentary evidence obtained directly from independent external sources *(external evidence)* is considered very competent.

3. Documentary evidence that has originated outside the client's data processing system but which has been received and processed by the client *(external-internal evidence)* is generally considered competent. However, the circumstances of internal accounting control quality are important.

4. *Internal evidence* consisting of documents that are produced, circulated and finally stored within the client's information system is generally considered low in competence. However, internal evidence is used extensively when it is produced under satisfactory conditions of internal accounting control. Sometimes, internal evidence is the only kind available.

5. *Verbal and written representations* given by the client's officers, directors, owners and employees are generally considered the least competent evidence. Such representations should be corroborated with other types of evidence.

Direct personal knowledge is obtained by auditors making their own calculations and being eyewitnesses (for example, by observing an inventory taking). External documents include confirmations, bank statements and vendors' invoices received directly by auditors from independent persons outside the client organization. External-internal evidence includes many of the same kinds of documents (bank statements, cancelled checks and vendors' invoices), but auditors see them after they have been "tainted" by the client's data processing system. Purely internal evidence includes bank reconciliations, insurance policy files, customer or patient history records, credit records, internal reports, budgets and forecasts, cost distribution worksheets and many other kinds of internal paperwork.

Auditors must be very careful about the competence of evidence. When specifying audit procedures for gathering evidence, the best approach is first to seek the evidence of the highest competence. If physical observation and mathematical calculation are not relevant to the task or are impossible or too costly, then move down the hierarchy to obtain the best evidence available.

Sufficiency of Evidence   Sufficiency is a question of: *How much competent evidence is enough?* The auditing profession has no official standard, leaving the matter of sufficiency to auditors' professional judgment. Realistically, however, audit decisions must be based on enough evidence to stand the scrutiny of other auditors (supervisors and reviewers) and outsiders (such as critics and judges). The real test of sufficiency is whether you can persuade someone else that your evidential base is strong enough to reach the same conclusions you have reached. The fact that important evidence is very difficult or costly to obtain is not an acceptable reason for failing to obtain it.

With these aspects of evidence in mind, you are now ready to study specific audit objectives and general procedures for obtaining evidence.

ASSERTIONS AND OBJECTIVES

As you study this section, keep in mind the following scheme of things: Clients present financial *assertions* for audit, and auditors have the *objective* of obtaining *evidence* about each of them. Auditors obtain evidence by performing *procedures,* which can be described in general and applied in hundreds of specific ways.

Financial Statement Assertions   The overall audit objective is to obtain sufficient competent evidence on which to base a report or opinion. This objective is reached by obtaining evidence and making decisions about five key *assertions* made by management in financial statements. The *practical objectives* of all audits of financial statements are to obtain and evaluate evidence about these five assertions:[7]

  □   Existence or occurrence.
  □   Completeness.
  □   Rights and obligations.
  □   Valuation or allocation.
  □   Presentation and disclosure.

For all practical purposes, these assertions are central points for the organization of audit procedures. However, a single procedure may produce evidence about more than one type of assertion. Auditors develop specific objectives related to specific assertions in various accounts and organize their procedures to obtain specific evidence. (Refer to SAS 31, appendix, AU 326 for an extended example.)

Existence or Occurrence.   The objective related to *existence or occurrence* is to establish with evidence that assets, liabilities, and equities actually exist and that revenue and expense transactions actually oc-

---

[7] *Statement on Auditing Standards No. 31* (AU 326), ''Evidential Matter.''

curred. Thus, auditors will count cash and inventory, confirm receivables and insurance policies, and perform other procedures to obtain evidence related to their specific objectives determining whether cash, inventory, receivables, insurance in force and other assets actually exist. You must be careful at this point, however, because the finding of existence alone generally proves little about the four other assertions.

Cutoff. A special aspect of existence or occurrence is ***cutoff***. Cutoff refers to recognizing assets and liabilities as of a *proper date* and accounting for revenue, expense and other transactions in the *proper period*. Simple cutoff errors can occur: (1) when late December sales invoices are recorded for goods actually not shipped until January; or (2) when cash receipts are recorded through the end of the week (e.g., Friday, January 2) and the last batch for the year should have been processed on December 31. In auditors' jargon, the ***cutoff date*** refers to the client's year-end balance sheet date. Proper cutoff means accounting for all transactions that occurred during a period and neither postponing some recordings to the next period nor accelerating next-period transactions into the current-year accounts.

Completeness. The objective related to ***completeness*** is to establish with evidence that all transactions and accounts that should be presented in the financial reports are included. Thus, auditors' specific objectives include obtaining evidence to determine whether, for example, all the inventory on hand is included, all the inventory consigned-out included, all the inventory consigned-in excluded, all the notes payable reported, and so forth.

Cutoff. The completeness assertion also has a special *cutoff* aspect. Both completeness and cutoff mean that *all* the transactions of a period should be recorded in the proper period and not shifted to another. Incomplete accounting and coincident cutoff errors include such things as: (1) failure to record accruals for expenses incurred but not yet paid, thus understating both expenses and liabilities; (2) failure to record purchases of materials not yet received and therefore not included in the ending inventory, thus understating both inventory and accounts payable; and (3) failure to accrue unbilled revenue through the fiscal year-end for customers on a cycle billing system, thus understating both revenue and accounts receivable.

Rights and Obligations. The objective related to ***rights and obligations*** is to establish with evidence that amounts reported as the assets of the company represent its property rights and the amounts reported as liabilities represent its obligations. In plainer terms, the objective is to obtain evidence about *ownership* and *owership*. You should be careful about *ownership,* however, because the idea should be perceived broadly in economic terms to include assets (rights) for which a company does not actually hold title. For example, an auditor will have a specific objective of obtaining evidence about the amounts capitalized for leased property. Likewise, *owership* should be perceived to include accounting liabilities a company may not yet be legally obligated to pay. For example, specific objectives would be obtaining evidence about the obligations under a capitalized lease or the estimated liability for product guarantees.

Valuation or Allocation.   The objective related to ***valuation or allocation*** is to determine whether proper values have been assigned to assets, liabilities, equities, revenue, and expense. Auditors thus obtain evidence about specific valuations by reconciling bank accounts, comparing vendors' invoices to inventory prices, obtaining lower-of-cost-or-market data, evaluating collectibility of receivables and comparing insurance policy terms to actuarial computations of liabilities. In many cases, preliminary dollar valuation evidence may be obtained concurrently with evidence about existence, but only when the counting unit is dollars. (The counting unit for cash and accounts receivable is dollars, whereas inventory physical quantities are counted first and then unit prices are multiplied to yield an extension and a dollar total.)

Presentation and Disclosure.   In engagements to audit financial statements, auditors must also determine whether accounting principles are properly selected and applied and whether disclosures are adequate. This objective relates to the ***presentation and disclosure*** assertion. Specific objectives include proper current and long-term balance sheet classification, mathematical accuracy of figures, and footnote disclosure of accounting policies. The presentation and disclosure objective is the meeting place for accounting principles and audit reporting standards.

A Compliance Assertion.   *Compliance* with laws and regulations is very important for a business, and disclosure of known noncompliance is usually necessary for presentation and disclosure of financial statements in conformity with generally accepted accounting principles. (See SAS 17, AU 328, *Illegal Acts by Clients.*) Independent auditors work with specific objectives related to financial laws and regulations, such as federal and state securities acts, tax withholding regulations, minimum wage laws, wage and price guidelines, credit allocation regulations, income tax laws and specialized industry regulations. Compliance with legal terms of the company's private contracts (for example, merger agreements and bond indentures) is also important for financial statement presentations.

Compliance with laws and regulations is a special objective characteristic of governmental audits, such as those by GAO, IRS, and state auditors. It is generally an objective for internal auditors with respect to managerial policies.

Summary Financial statement assertions are important and fairly complicated. They are the management assertions subject to audit and the focal points for procedures. When audit procedures are specified, you should be able to relate the evidence produced by each procedure to one or more specific objectives tailored to specific assertions. The secret to writing and reviewing a list of audit procedures is to ask: "Which assertion(s) does this procedure produce evidence about?" Then, "Does the list of procedures (the audit program) cover all the assertions?"

You can simplify the major assertions by calling them *existence, completeness, ownership, valuation* and *presentation.* Just do not forget that each of them has additional aspects.

GENERAL EVIDENCE-GATHERING PROCEDURES Auditors use seven basic types of evidence and seven general procedures to gather it. One or more of these procedures may be used no matter what account balance, internal control procedure, transaction flow or other information is under audit. Auditors arrange and combine the procedures to write an *audit program,* which is basically a *list of procedures.* Exhibit 6–2 shows the seven types of evidence and the procedures most closely related to each.

EXHIBIT 6–2
Types of Evidence and Related Audit Procedures

Types of Evidence	Evidence-Gathering Procedures
1. Auditor's calculations.	1. Recalculation by the auditor.
2. Physical observation, inspection.	2. Observation and examination by the auditor.
3. Statements by independent parties.	3. Confirmation by letter.
4. Statements by client personnel.	4. Verbal inquiry and written representations.
5. Documents prepared by independent parties.	5. Examination of documents (vouching or tracing).
6. Documents prepared by the client.	5. Examination of documents (vouching or tracing).
7. Data interrelationships.	6. Scanning.
	7. Analytical review.

1. Recalculation Recalculation of calculations previously performed by client personnel produces compelling mathematical evidence. A client calculation is either right or wrong. Client calculations performed by computer programs can be recalculated using computer auditing software, with differences printed out for further audit investigation. Mathematical evidence can serve the objectives of both existence and valuation for financial statement amounts that exist principally as calculations; for example, depreciation, pension liabilities, actuarial reserves, statutory bad debt reserves and product guarantee liabilities. Recalculation, in combination with other procedures, is also used to provide evidence of valuation for all other financial data.

2. Physical Observation   Physical observation inspection of tangible assets provides compelling evidence of existence and may provide tentative evidence of condition and valuation. In a strict sense, physical observation is limited to tangible assets and formal documents, such as securities certificates. In a broader sense, the procedure of physical observation is utilized whenever auditors view the client's physical facilities and personnel on an inspection tour, when they watch personnel carry out data processing activities and when they participate in a surprise payroll distribution. Physical observation can also produce a general awareness of events in the client's offices.

3. Confirmation   Confirmation by direct correspondence with independent parties is a procedure widely used in auditing. It can produce evidence of existence and ownership and sometimes of valuation and cutoff. Most transactions involve outside parties, and theoretically, written correspondence could be conducted even on such items as individual paychecks. However, auditors limit their use of confirmation to major transactions and balances about which outside parties could be expected to provide information. A selection of confirmation applications includes:

> Banks—account balances.
> Customers—receivables balances.
> Borrowers—note terms and balances.
> Agents—inventory on consignment or in warehouses.
> Lenders—note terms and balances.
> Policyholders—life insurance contracts.
> Vendors—accounts payable balances.
> Registrar—number of shares of stock outstanding.
> Attorneys—litigation in progress.
> Trustees—securities held, terms of agreements.
> Lessors—lease terms.

The important general points about confirmations are these:

- [ ] The confirmation letter should be printed on the client's letterhead, or a facsimile, and signed by a client officer.
- [ ] The auditor should be very careful to be assured that the source of the recipient's address is reliable and not subject to alteration by the client in such a way as to misdirect the confirmation.
- [ ] The request should seek information the recipient can supply, like the amount of a balance or the amounts of specified invoices or notes.
- [ ] The confirmations should be controlled by the audit firm, not given to client personnel for mailing. *Direct* communication is required by auditing standards.

□ The responses should be returned directly to the audit firm, not to the client.

Auditors should try to obtain replies from all positive confirmations by sending second and third requests to nonrespondents. If there is no response or if the response specifies an exception to the client's records, the auditors should carry out other procedures to audit the account.

4. Verbal Inquiry

Verbal inquiry is a procedure that generally involves the collection of oral evidence from independent parties and client officials. Written (formal) statements must be obtained in response to important inquiries. Auditors use inquiry procedures during the early office and plant tour and when conferences are conducted. Evidence gathered by formal and informal inquiry generally cannot stand alone as convincing, and auditors must corroborate responses with independent findings based on other procedures. An exception to this general rule is a negative statement where someone volunteers adverse information such as an admission of theft or irregularity or use of an accounting policy that is misleading.

5. Examination of Documents

Much auditing work involves gathering evidence by examining authoritative documents prepared by independent parties and by the client. Such documents can provide evidence regarding all five assertions.

Documents prepared by independent outside parties. A great deal of documentary evidence is external-internal in nature. The most convincing documentation is that which has been prepared by other parties and sent to the client. The signatures, seals, engraving, or other distinctive artistic attributes of formal authoritative documents make such sources more reliable (less susceptible to alteration) than ordinary documents prepared by outsiders. Some examples of both types of documents are listed below:

Formal Authoritative Documents	Ordinary Documents
Bank statements	Vendors' invoices
Canceled checks	Customers' purchase orders
Insurance policies	Loan applications
Notes receivable (on unique forms)	Insurance policy applications
Securities certificates	Notes receivable (on standard bank
Indenture agreements	forms)
Elaborate contracts	Simple contracts
Title papers (e.g., autos)	Correspondence

Documents prepared and processed within the entity under audit. Documentation of this type is internal evidence. Some of these documents may be quite informal and not very authoritative or reliable. As a general proposition, the reliability of these documents depends upon the quality of internal accounting control under which they were produced and processed. Some of the most common of these documents are:

Sales invoice copies.

Sales summary reports.

Cost distribution reports.

Loan approval memos.

Budgets and performance reports.

Documentation of transactions with subsidiary or affiliated companies.

Shipping documents.

Receiving reports.

Requisition slips.

Purchase orders.

Credit memoranda.

Transaction logs (computer).

Batch control logs (computer).

Vouching—Examination of Documents.   The important point about *vouching* in the examination of documents is the *direction* of the search for audit evidence. In vouching, an item of financial information is selected from an account (for example, the posting of a sales invoice in a customer's master-file record), then the auditor goes *backward* through the data processing (bookkeeping) system to find the source documentation that supports the item selected. He finds the journal entry or data input list, the sales summary, the sales invoice copy, and finally the shipping documents. Vouching of documents can help auditors decide whether all *recorded data* are adequately supported, but vouching does not provide evidence to show whether all events were recorded. (This latter problem is covered by *tracing*.)

Tracing—Examination of Documents.   *Tracing* in the examination of documents takes the *opposite direction* from vouching. When an auditor performs tracing, he or she selects sample items of basic source documents and *proceeds forward* through the bookkeeping process (whether manual or electronic) to find the final recording of the accounting transactions. Thus, samples of payroll payments are traced to cost and expense accounts, sales invoices to the sales accounts, cash receipts to the accounts receivable subsidiary accounts, and cash disbursements to the accounts payable subsidiary accounts, to name a few examples.

Using tracing, an auditor can contribute evidence to decisions about whether all events were recorded (the completeness assertion), and complement evidence obtained by vouching (the existence/occurrence assertion). However, you must be alert to events that may not have been captured in the source documents and not entered in the system. For example, the search for unrecorded liabilities for raw materials purchases must include examination of invoices received in the period following the fiscal year-end and examination of receiving reports dated near the year-end. In nonmanufacturing businesses, the tracing search for a relevant basic population may include loan-approval files, correspondence with attorneys, life insurance file search, and many other unique data populations.

6. Scanning

Scanning is the way auditors exercise their general alertness to unusual items and events in documentation. A typical scanning directive in an audit program is: "Scan the expense accounts for credit entries, vouch any to source documents."

In general, scanning is an "eyes-open" approach of looking for anything unusual. The scanning procedure usually does not produce direct evidence itself, but it can produce questions for which other evidence must be obtained. Scanning can be accomplished on computer records using computer audit software that selects records to be printed out for further audit investigation. Typical items discovered by the scanning effort include debits in revenue accounts, credits in expense accounts, unusually large accounts receivable write-offs, unusually large paychecks, unusually small sales volume in the month following the year-end, and large cash deposits just prior to year-end. Scanning can contribute some evidence related to the existence of assets and the completeness of accounting records, including the proper cutoff of material transactions.

Scanning is valuable when sampling methods are applied in audit decisions. When a sample is the basis for selecting items for audit, the risk of choosing a sample that does not reflect the entire population of items always exists. Such an event may cause a decision error. Auditors subjectively mitigate this risk by scanning items not selected in the sample in order to guard against decision error.

7. Analytical Review Procedures

Analytical review procedures are useful as an attention director in the audit planning stage and can also produce evidence of financial statement errors and irregularities. Five types of analytical review procedures were listed earlier in this chapter. They may seem very general and "soft" to you. The discussion of analytical review earlier in this chapter and the discussion in SAS 23 (AU 318) are specific only in terms of a few examples, otherwise telling you that a large number of unspecified analytical relationships can be useful, if only you can figure out what they are! Yet, lack of a lengthy list of examples and methods for analytical review is a fact of audit life. You have to be resourceful and innovative to adapt ratios, comparisons, time series analyses, regression analyses and similar approaches to analytical review.

Because analytical review is loosely defined, many auditors consider the evidence it produces to be soft. So auditors, professors and students tend to concentrate on recalculation, observation, confirmation and vouching of documents. These procedures are perceived to produce "hard" evidence—and hard is presumed to be better than soft. However, you should resist this way of thinking. Analytical review procedures are, in fact, quite effective.

Hylas and Ashton collected evidence on errors requiring financial statement adjustment in a large number of audits.[8] They were interested primarily in describing the audit procedures used to detect the errors. Their definition of analytical review was broad. It included data comparisons, predictions based on outside data, analyses of interrelationships among account balances, "reasonableness tests," "estimates" and cursory review of financial statements in the audit planning stage. They also had two procedure categories called "expectations from prior years" (which involves the carry-over of analytical and detail knowledge about continuing audit clients) and "discussions with client personnel."

Their findings were at least mildly surprising. Auditors gave credit for error discovery to analytical review procedures for 27.1 percent of all errors. They gave credit to "expectations" and "discussions" for another 18.5 percent. Altogether, the soft procedures accounted for detection of 45.6 percent of the errors. All of these procedures typically are applied early in the audit, so you should not infer that other kinds of audit procedures would or would not have detected the same errors. The detection success of other procedures depends upon the results of the early-applied procedures because, as this study was designed, even a good physical observation procedure did not get credit for "discovery" of an error that already had been discovered using analytical review.

Auditors must consider the utility of analytical review procedures, especially since such methods are usually less costly than more detailed, document-oriented procedures. The "hard-evidence" procedures, however, have their own pitfalls. Auditors might not be competent to "see" things they are supposed to observe. Clients can manipulate confirmations by giving auditors the addresses of conspirators or by asking customers just to "sign it and send it back." An audit program consists of several different types of procedures, and analytical review procedures deserve a prominent place.

When analytical review is applied to a client's unaudited information, auditors may notice out-of-line conditions and unusual fluctuations. Care must also be taken to notice situations in which changes or fluctuations *should have occurred* but did not. For example, a company may not change its monthly property tax accrual when such taxes have actually been increased. Auditors must also be aware of such general economic conditions as product price changes, local tax rates, and a variety of other matters that contribute to useful analytical review.

---

[8] R. E. Hylas, and R. H. Ashton, "Audit Detection of Financial Statement Errors," *Accounting Review,* October 1982, pp. 751–65.

Fluctuations or changes that are not expected and the absence of expected changes should be investigated first by directing inquiries to knowledgeable managers. All responses should be evaluated, and most responses should lead to application of a specific audit of transaction detail procedures. Sometimes, general knowledge—such as awareness of a strike at a plant or another explanation of lower-than-usual output—is enough followup. However, all management responses and explanations should be corroborated and not taken merely at face value.

Many financial accounts are *paired* in that the data in one is a function of the data in another. Some of these account relationships are item-by-item direct, and others are related in general. For example, each item of interest expense should relate to a specifically identifiable interest-bearing liability. Failure to match an interest payment with a liability may indicate an unrecorded liability and a misstatement in another account as well. Failure to find an interest payment or accrual in accordance with borrowing terms may indicate an understatement of expense, perhaps a default on a debt, and possibly a need for adjustment or an explanatory disclosure. When sales increase, cost of sales should also increase; when inventories and purchases increase, accounts payable usually increase. Some of the major related accounts are these:

Sales—Cost of sales.

Sales—Sales returns.

Sales—Accounts receivable.

Accounts receivable—Bad debts.

Fixed assets—Depreciation.

Investment income—Investments.

Demand deposits—Loans.

Interest expense—Interest bearing liabilities.

Purchases—Accounts payable.

Net income—Income taxes.

Capital stock—Professional fees.

Legal fees—Contingent liabilities.

Insurance expense—Fixed assets.

AUDIT PROGRAMS

The process of making a list of procedures to constitute an audit program is an exercise of the scientific decision methodology emphasized throughout this text. For each segment of an audit, an audit manager faces the basic problem of deciding whether the assertions of economic things and events are fair representations of real things and events. In brief, for each segment auditors must design the program of procedures along the following lines:

1. Recognize the explicit and implicit assertions presented in financial classifications, amounts and supplementary disclosures. Recognize, also, the important controls in the client's internal accounting control system.
2. Identify clearly the pertinent features of the assertions and the key controls and select appropriate procedures that will produce sufficient competent evidence related to existence, completeness, valuation, ownership, presentation and control performance.
3. Write the selected procedures in an instructional form so that senior and assistant accountants will know what to do in order to gather the evidence.

Audit programs are of two types: (1) compliance audit programs with procedures designed to produce evidence about the operation of a client's internal accounting control system and (2) account balance audit programs with procedures designed to produce direct evidence about the account balances. These two types of programs are discussed at greater length in Chapter 8.

USING OTHERS' EXPERTISE/ FIRST-TIME AUDITS

Auditors perform most of the procedural evidence-gathering work themselves. However, an audit team can utilize a client's internal auditors and the expertise of specialists. Additional planning and preparation is necessary on a first-time audit.

Internal Auditors

Considerable engagement efficiency may be realized by working in tandem with internal auditors. Independent auditors should comprehend a client's internal audit activities as they relate to operation of the internal accounting control system. In terms of substantive audit work, internal audit personnel may assist with performance of parts of the audit under the supervision of the independent audit team. However, the responsibility for audit decisions remains with the independent auditors.[9]

Specialists

Specialists are persons skilled in fields other than accounting and auditing—actuaries, appraisers, attorneys, engineers and geologists, for example—who are not members of the audit team. Auditors are not expected to be expert in all fields of knowledge that may contribute information to the financial statements. When specialists are engaged, auditors must know about their professional qualifications and reputations. A specialist should be unrelated to the client, if possible. Auditors must obtain an understanding of a specialist's methods and assumptions. Provided some additional auditing work is done on the accounting information used by

---

[9] *Statement on Auditing Standards No. 9* (AU 322), "The Effect of an Internal Audit Function on the Scope of the Independent Auditor's Examination," explains the broad outlines of utilizing the work of internal auditors.

the specialist, auditors may rely on the specialist's work in connection with audit decisions.[10]

First-Time Audit   A first-time audit usually requires more audit work than a repeat engagement. If the company has never been audited, this additional work includes audit of the beginning-of-the-year account balances. These accounts affect the current-year income and funds flow statements. This work may involve going back to audit several years' transactions that make up permanent accounts—accounts whose balances are carried forward for a long time (for example, fixed assets, patents, bonds payable). If the company has been audited by other auditors, the new first-time auditor may facilitate the audit by asking for information from the previous auditor and by reviewing the previous auditor's working papers concerning the permanent accounts and other matters. In any event, a first-time auditor must obtain an understanding of the new client's business and the company's methods of operation.

WORKING PAPER DOCUMENTATION   An audit is not complete without preparation of proper working paper documentation. Working papers are the auditor's record of compliance with generally accepted auditing standards. They should contain support for the decisions regarding procedures necessary in the circumstances and all other important decisions made during the audit. Even though the auditor is the legal owner of the working papers, professional ethics require that they not be transferred without consent of the client because of the confidential information recorded in them. Detail auditing standards concerning working papers are in SAS 41, AU 339.

Working papers can be classified in three categories: (1) permanent file papers, (2) audit administrative papers and (3) audit evidence papers.

Permanent File Papers   The permanent file contains information of continuing interest over many years' audits of the same client. This file can be used year after year, while each year's current audit evidence papers are filed away once they have served their purpose. Documents of permanent interest and applicability include: (1) copies or excerpts of the corporate charter and bylaws, or partnership agreements; (2) copies or excerpts of continuing contracts such as leases, bond indentures, and royalty agreements; (3) a history of the company, its products and its markets; (4) copies or excerpts of stockholders, directors and committee minutes on matters of lasting interest; and (5) continuing schedules of accounts whose balances are carried forward for several years, such as owners' equity, retained earnings, partnership capital and the like. Copies of prior years' financial statements

---

[10] *Statement on Auditing Standards No. 11* (AU336), "Using the Work of a Specialist," contains more explanation about auditor responsibility when selecting a specialist and referring to the work in the audit report.

and audit reports may also be included. The permanent file is a ready source of information for familiarization with the client by new personnel on the engagement.

Audit Administrative Papers

Administrative papers contain the fruit of the early planning phases of the audit. They usually include the engagement letter, staff assignment notes, conclusions related to understanding the client's business, results of preliminary analytical review, initial assessments of audit risks and initial assessments of audit materiality. Many accounting firms follow the practice of summarizing these data in an engagement *planning memorandum*.

Audit planning and administration also includes work on the preliminary review of internal accounting control and preparation of a written audit program. You will study these topics in subsequent chapters. In general, the following items are usually among the administrative working papers in each year's current file:

1. Engagement letter.
2. Staff assignments.
3. Memoranda of conferences with management.
4. Memoranda of conferences with the directors' audit committee.
5. Preliminary analytical review notes.
6. Initial risk assessment notes.
7. Initial materiality assessment notes.
8. Engagement planning memorandum.
9. Audit engagement time budget.
10. Internal control questionnaire.
11. Management controls questionnaire.
12. Computer controls questionnaire.
13. Internal control system and program flowcharts.
14. Audit program.
15. A working trial balance of general ledger accounts.
16. Working paper record of preliminary adjusting and reclassifying entries.
17. Memoranda of review notes and unfinished procedures (all cleared by the end of the field work).

Audit Evidence Papers

The current-year audit evidence working papers contain the record of the procedures performed, the evidence obtained and the decisions made in the course of the audit. These papers are communications of the quality of the audit, so they must be clear, concise, complete, neat, well indexed and informative. Each separate working paper (or multiple pages that go together) must be complete in the sense that it can be removed from the working paper file and considered on its own, with proper cross-reference available to show how the paper coordinates with other working papers. Working papers may be in the form of magnetic tape and film and photographs as well as on computer- or hand-written paper.

The most important facet of the current audit evidence papers is the requirement that they show the auditors' decision problems and conclusions. The papers must record the propositions that were audited (book values or qualitative disclosures), the evidence gathered about them and the final decision. Auditing standards (SAS 41, AU 339.05) require that the working papers show: (1) The client's accounting records agree or reconcile with the financial statements; (2) The work was adequately planned and supervised; (3) A proper study and evaluation of internal accounting control was conducted; and (4) Sufficient competent evidential matter was obtained as a reasonable basis for an audit opinion. Common sense also dictates that the working papers be sufficient to show that the financial statements conform to GAAP, consistently applied, and that the disclosures are adequate. The working papers should also explain how exceptions and unusual accounting questions were resolved or treated.

EXHIBIT 6–3
Current Working Paper File

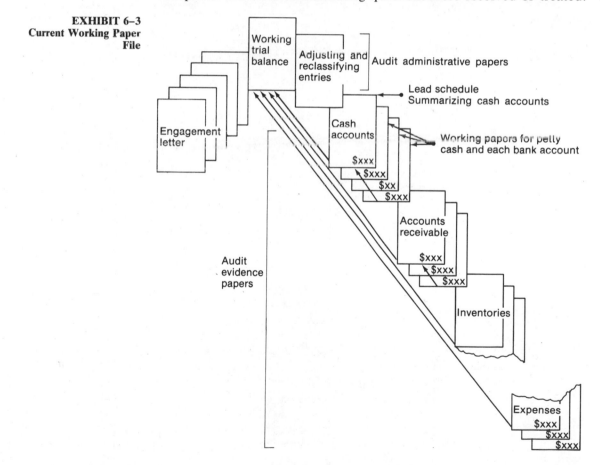

Taken altogether, these features should demonstrate that all the auditing standards were observed.

Working Paper Arrangement and Indexing

Every auditing organization has a different method of arranging and indexing working papers. In general, however, the papers are grouped in order behind the trial balance according to balance sheet and income statement captions. Usually, the current assets appear first, followed by fixed assets, other assets, liabilities, equities, income and expense accounts. The typical arrangement is shown in Exhibit 6–3.

Several working paper preparation techniques are quite important for the quality of the finished product. The points explained below are illustrated in Exhibit 6–4.

EXHIBIT 6–4
Illustrative Working Paper

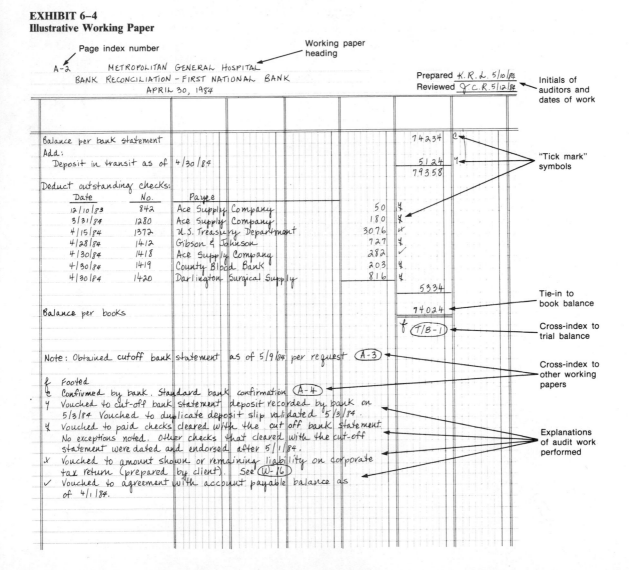

Indexing. Each paper is given an index number, like a book page number, so that it can be found, removed, and replaced without loss.

Cross-indexing. Numbers or memoranda related to other papers carry the index of the other paper(s) so that the connections can be followed.

Heading. Each paper is titled with the name of the company, the period under audit date, and a descriptive title of the contents of the working paper.

Signatures and initials. The auditor who performs the work and the supervisor who reviews it must sign the papers so that personnel can be identified.

Dates of audit work. The dates of performance and review are recorded on the working papers so reviewers of the papers can tell when the work was performed.

Tick marks and explanations. "Tick marks" are the auditor's shorthand for abbreviating comments about work performed. Tick marks must always be accompanied by a full explanation of the auditing work.

CHAPTER SUMMARY

An audit consists of numerous steps that can be divided into several sequential stages, as briefly sketched in Exhibit 1–2 (Chapter 1). This chapter has examined the first two stages—the pre-engagement activities and the planning activities. Pre-engagement work was explained in terms of client acceptance and retention, engagement letters, staff assignment and the understanding of the client's business. These pre-engagement activities can be considered early parts of the audit planning process.

The main planning activities, however, include preliminary analytical review, preliminary assessment of audit risk, and preliminary assessment of materiality. All of these activities are important prerequisites for performing an audit. You will go to the next stage—internal accounting control evaluation activities—in Chapter 7.

This chapter has also given you some necessary conceptual background on audit evidence, emphasizing the relative competence of different kinds of evidence and auditors' needs to seek the best evidence available. The discussion of evidence was followed by explanations of the assertions normally presented for audit attention and the general procedures used to obtain evidence about them. This general discussion is very important. You need to know a small number of general procedures so you can spin off the hundreds of specific procedures applied in various audit areas (for example, cash, receivables, inventory, fixed assets, accounts payable, capital stock). At this stage of your study of auditing, you are better served by learning five basic assertions instead of 500 detailed ones and seven general procedures instead of 7,000 specific ones.

Working papers are a necessary product of every audit. They contain the record of the audit team's work—the controls and assertions audited, the procedures performed, the evidence obtained and the decisions reached. They are the auditor's means of demonstrating that the audit was performed in accordance with GAAS. Most of your on-the-job work in auditing will involve working paper preparation.

SOURCES AND ADDITIONAL READING REFERENCES

Alderman, C. W., and J. W. Deitrick. "Internal Audit Impact on Financial Information Reliability." *The Internal Auditor,* April 1981, pp. 43–56.

Ashton, R. H., and R. E. Hylas. "The Return of 'Problem' Confirmation Requests by the U.S. Postal Service." *Accounting Review,* October 1980, pp. 649–57.

————. "Increasing Confirmation Response Rate." *Auditing: A Journal of Practice and Theory,* Summer 1981, pp. 12–22.

————. "A Study of the Response to Balance and Invoice Confirmation Requests." *Journal of Accounting, Auditing and Finance,* Summer 1981, pp. 325–32.

Boatsman, J. R., and J. C. Robertson. "Policy-Capturing on Some Selected Materiality Judgments." *Accounting Review,* April 1974.

Bremser, Wayne G. "Acceptance and Continuance of Clients." *CPA Journal,* October 1980, pp. 29–35.

Clay, J. R., and D. L. Haskin. "Can Internal Auditors Reduce External Audit Costs?" *The Internal Auditor,* April 1981, pp. 62–69.

Cushing, B. E., D. G. Searfoss, and R. H. Randall. "Materiality Allocation in Audit Planning: A Feasibility Study." *Journal of Accounting Research,* supplement 1979, pp. 172–246.

Davis, G. B., J. Neter, and R. R. Palmer. "An Experimental Study of Audit Confirmations." *Journal of Accountancy,* June 1967, pp. 36–44.

Doege, Richard L. "Photogrammetrics in Auditing." *Journal of Accountancy,* April 1972, pp. 60–63.

Hendricks, Arthur G. "The Initial Audit Engagement." *CPA Journal,* May 1979, pp. 9–17.

Hull, James C. "A Guide to Better Workpapers." *Journal of Accountancy,* February 1969, pp. 44–52.

Hylas, R. E., and R. H. Ashton. "Audit Detection of Financial Statement Errors." *Accounting Review,* October 1982, pp. 751–65.

Jaenicke, Henry R. "A New Approach to Engagement Management." *Journal of Accountancy,* April 1980, pp. 68–78.

Kissinger, John N. "A General Theory of Evidence as the Conceptual Foundation in Auditing Theory: Some Comments and Extensions." *The Accounting Review,* April 1977, pp. 322–39.

Krogstad, J. L., G. Grudnitski, and D. W. Bryant. "PERT and PERT/Cost for Audit Planning and Control." *Journal of Accountancy,* November 1977, pp. 82–91.

Laurie, William F. "Alice through the Looking Glass: Trying New Evaluation Techniques." *GAO Review,* Summer 1980, pp. 37–41.

McKee, Thomas E. "Developments in Analytical Review." *CPA Journal,* January 1982, pp. 36–42.

Mautz, R. K. "The Nature and Reliability of Audit Evidence." *Journal of Accountancy,* May 1958, pp. 40–47.

Mautz, R. K., and Hussein A. Sharaf. *The Philosophy of Auditing.* American Accounting Association Monograph No. 6, especially chap. 5, "Evidence" and chap. 6, "Due Audit Care," American Accounting Association, 1961.

Munter, P., and T. A. Ratcliffe. "Evidential Matter (Flowchart of SAS 31)." *CPA Journal,* January 1981, pp. 70–76.

Neumann, Frederick L. "The Auditor's Analytical Review—Some Sources of Information." *Journal of Accountancy,* October 1974, pp. 88–92.

Newton, Lauren K. "The Risk Factor in Materiality Decisions." *Accounting Review,* January 1977, pp. 97–108.

Romney, M. B., and W. S. Albrecht. "The Use of Investigative Agencies By Auditors." *Journal of Accountancy,* October 1979, pp. 61–67.

Tipgos, Manual A. "Prior Years' Working Papers: Uses and Dangers." *CPA Journal,* September 1978, pp. 19–25.

Toba, Yoshihide. "A General Theory of Evidence as the Conceptual Foundation in Auditing Theory." *Accounting Review,* January 1975, pp. 7–24.

Ward, D. D., and J. C. Robertson. "Reliance on Internal Auditors." *Journal of Accountancy,* October 1980, pp. 62–73.

Warren, Carl S. "Confirmation Reliability—The Evidence." *Journal of Accountancy,* February 1975, pp. 85–89.

Whittington, R., M. Zulinski, and J. W. Ledwith. "Completeness—The Elusive Assertion." *Journal of Accountancy,* August 1983, pp. 82–92.

REVIEW QUESTIONS

6.1. What sources of information can a CPA use in connection with deciding whether to accept a new audit client?

6.2. What benefits are obtained by having an engagement letter?

6.3. What persons and skills are normally assigned to a "full-service" audit team?

6.4. What are the five types of general analytical review procedures?

6.5. Which official documents and proceedings should an auditor read when performing a preliminary analytical review?

6.6. What are the four audit risks an auditor must consider and what does each involve?

6.7. What is *anchoring* with regard to auditors' judgments about the quality or effectiveness of internal control?

6.8. What benefits are claimed for auditors' preliminary assessment of *materiality* as a matter of audit planning? Is $500,000 a material amount of misstatement to leave uncorrected in financial statements?

6.9. How are external, external-internal, and internal documentary evidence generally defined?

6.10. List and briefly explain the five major assertions that can be made in financial statements and auditors' objectives related to each.

6.11. What is meant by "vouching," "tracing," and "scanning"?

6.12. What can auditors do to help the effectiveness of confirmation requests?

6.13. Are analytical review procedures very effective for discovering errors and irregularities?

6.14. What information would you expect to find in a permanent audit file? In the front of a current working paper file?

6.15. What is considered the most important content of the auditor's current audit working papers?

EXERCISES AND PROBLEMS

6.16. **Pre-Engagement and Planning Activities**
Reference to SAS 7, AU 315 and to interpretations of the independence rules of conduct are necessary for a good response to this problem.

Johnson, Inc., a closely held company, wishes to engage Norr, CPA, to examine its annual financial statements. Johnson is generally pleased with the services provided by its current CPA, Diggs, but thinks the audit work is too detailed and interferes excessively with Johnson's normal office routines. Norr has asked Johnson to inform Diggs of the decision to change auditors, but Johnson does not wish to do so.

Required:
a. List and discuss the steps Norr should follow before accepting the engagement.
b. What additional procedures should Norr perform on this first-time engagement over and beyond those that would be performed on the Johnson engagement in succeeding years?

6.17. **Planning Activities**
In the late spring, you are advised of a new assignment as in-charge accountant of your CPA firm's recurring annual audit of a major client, the Lancer Company. You are given the engagement letter for the current audit covering the calendar year ended next December 31, and a list of personnel assigned to this engagement. It is your responsibility to plan and supervise the audit.

Required:
Discuss the necessary preparation and planning for the Lancer Company annual audit prior to beginning field work at the client's office. In your discussion, include the sources you should consult, the type of information you should seek, and the preliminary plans and preparation you should make, but *do not discuss internal control evaluation or write an audit program.*

6.18. **Engagement Letter**
A CPA has been asked to audit the financial statements of a publicly held company for the first time. All preliminary verbal discussions and inquiries have been completed between the CPA, the company, the predecessor auditor and all other necessary parties. The CPA is now preparing an engagement letter.

Required:
List items that should be included in the typical engagement letter in these circumstances.

(*AICPA* adapted)

6.19. **Analytical Review**
Overall tests and ratios are used during preliminary audit reviews to determine whether any areas need special audit attention in the preliminary audit program. When an auditor notices a significant change in a ratio compared with a prior year, the reasons for the change must be considered. Explain possible reasons for: (*a*) an increase in the rate of inventory turnover—ratio of cost of sales

and average inventory—when LIFO is used and (*b*) an increase in the number of days' sales in receivables—the ratio of credit sales and average daily accounts receivable.

6.20. **Audit Risk Model**

Audit risks for particular accounts and disclosures can be conceptualized in the model: Audit Risk (AuR) = Inherent Risk (IR) × Internal Control Risk (IC) × Detection Risk (D). Use this model as a framework for considering the following situations and deciding whether the auditor's conclusion is appropriate.

1. Ohlsen, CPA, has participated in the audit of Limberg Cheese Company for five years, first as an assistant accountant and the last two years as the senior accountant. He has never seen an accounting adjustment recommended. He believes the inherent risk must be zero.

2. Jones, CPA, has just (November 30) completed an exhaustive study and evaluation of the internal accounting control system of Langs Derfer Foods, Inc. (fiscal year ending December 31). She believes the internal control risk must be zero because no material errors could possibly slip through the many error-checking procedures and review layers used by Lang's.

3. Fields, CPA, is lazy and does not like audit jobs in Philadelphia anyway. On the audit of Philly Mfg. Co., he decided to use detail procedures to audit the year-end balances very thoroughly to the extent that his risk of failing to detect material errors and irregularities should be .02 or less. He gave no thought to inherent risk and conducted only a very limited review of Philly's internal accounting control system.

4. Shad, CPA, is nearing the end of a "dirty" audit of Allnight Protection Company. Allnight's accounting personnel all resigned during the year and were replaced by inexperienced people. The comptroller resigned last month in disgust. The journals and ledgers were a mess because the one computer specialist was hospitalized for three months during the year. Thankfully, Shad thought: "I've been able to do this audit in less time than last year when everything was operating smoothly."

6.21. **Determination of "Planning Materiality"**

During the course of an audit engagement, an independent auditor gives serious consideration to the concept of *materiality*. This concept is inherent in the work of independent auditors and is important for planning, preparing and modifying audit programs. The concept of materiality underlies the application of all the generally accepted auditing standards, particularly the standards of field work and reporting.

Required:

a. Briefly describe what is meant by independent auditors' concept of materiality.

b. What are some common relationships and other considerations used by auditors in judging materiality?

c. Identify how the planning and execution of an audit program might be affected by an independent auditor's concept of materiality.

(*AICPA* adapted)

6.22. **Relative Competence of Evidence**

The third generally accepted auditing standard of field work requires that auditors obtain sufficient competent evidential matter to afford a reasonable basis for an opinion regarding the financial statements under examination. In considering what constitutes sufficient competent evidential matter, a distinction should be made between underlying accounting data and all corroborating information available to the auditor.

Required:

What presumptions can be made about:

a. The relative competence of evidence obtained from external and internal sources?

b. The role of internal accounting control with respect to internal evidence produced by a client's data processing system?

c. The relative persuasiveness of auditor observation and recalculation evidence compared to external, external-internal and internal evidence?

(*AICPA* adapted)

6.23.   Relative Competence of Evidence

1. Classify the following evidential items by *type* (direct knowledge, external, and so on), and rank them in order of competence.

   a. Amounts shown on monthly statements from creditors.

   b. Amounts shown "paid on account" in the voucher register.

   c. Amount of "discounts lost expense" computed from unaudited supporting documents.

   d. Amounts shown in letters received directly from creditors.

2. Classify the following evidential items by *type* (direct knowledge, external, and so on) and rank them in order of competence.

   a. Amounts shown on a letter received directly from an independent bond trustee.

   b. Amounts obtained from minutes of board of directors' meetings.

   c. Computation of bond interest and amortization expense when remaining terms and status of bond are audited.

   d. Amounts shown on cancelled checks.

6.24.   Financial Assertions and Audit Objectives

You were engaged to examine the financial statements of Ronlyn Corporation for the year ended June 30.

On May 1, two months before the fiscal year-end, the corporation borrowed $500,000 from Second National Bank to finance plant expansion. The long-term note agreement provided for the annual payment of principal and interest over five years. The

existing plant was pledged as security for the loan.

Due to unexpected difficulties in acquiring the building site, the plant expansion did not begin on time. To make use of the borrowed funds, management decided to invest in stocks and bonds, and on May 16, the $500,000 was invested in securities.

Required:

What are the audit objectives for the audit of the investments in securities at June 30?

(*AICPA* adapted)

6.25.   Financial Assertions

The assertions described in SAS 31 (AU 326) and in the chapter are very important, and auditors specify procedures designed to obtain evidence about them. If an assertion turns out to be false, an error or irregularity exists in the financial statements. For the separate *effects* listed below, explain what false assertions could be involved:

a. Overstatement of assets.

b. Understatement of revenue, current assets, net income and tax liability.

c. Understatement of assets, understatement of liabilities, no effect on retained earnings.

d. Understatement of assets and liabilities and overstatement of retained earnings.

6.26.   Audit Procedures

Auditors frequently refer to the terms "standards" and "procedures." Standards deal with measures of the quality of performance. Standards specifically refer to the generally accepted auditing standards expressed in the *Statements on Auditing Standards*. Procedures relate to the acts performed by auditors to gather evidence. Procedures specifically refer to the methods or techniques used by auditors in the conduct of the examination. Procedures are also expressed in the *Statements on Auditing Standards*.

Required:

List seven different types of procedures that auditors can use during an audit of financial statements and give an example of each.

6.27. Confirmation Procedure

A CPA accumulates various kinds of evidence upon which to base the opinion on financial statements. Among this evidence are confirmations from third parties.

Required:

a. What is an audit confirmation?

b. What characteristics of the confirmation process and the recipient are important if a CPA is to consider the confirmation evidence competent?

6.28. Audit Procedure Terminology

Identify the types of procedure(s) employed in each situation described below (vouching, tracing, recalculation, observation and so on):

1. An auditor uses computer software to select vendors' accounts payable with debit balances and compares amounts and computation to cash disbursements and vendor credit memos.

2. An auditor examines property insurance policies and checks insurance expense for the year. The auditor then reviews the expense in light of changes and ending balances in fixed-asset accounts.

3. An auditor uses computer software to test perpetual inventory records for items that have not been used in production for three months or more. The client states that the items are obsolete and have already been written down. The auditor checks journal entries to support the client's statements.

4. An auditor tests cash remittance advices to see that allowances and discounts are appropriate and that receipts are posted to the correct customer accounts in the right amounts and reviews the documents supporting unusual discounts and allowances.

5. An auditor observes the client taking a physical inventory. A letter is also re-

ceived from a public warehouseman stating the amounts of the client's inventory stored in the warehouse. The company's cost-flow assumption, FIFO, is then tested by the auditor's computer software program.

6.29. First-Time Audit

Z. Summers was assigned to the audit of a new client that had never been audited before. The engagement letter specified that the audit report would cover the statement of financial position, the statement of results of operations and retained earnings, and the statement of changes in financial position of the current year. No comparative financial statements will be issued. Consequently, Z decided to do no audit work on the beginning balances of cash, accounts receivable, inventory, fixed assets, accounts payable, and long-term debt.

Required:

a. What is wrong with Z's reasoning?

b. What would he do about beginning balances if they had been audited in prior years by: (1) His firm? (2) Another CPA firm?

6.30. Audit Working Papers

The preparation of working papers is an integral part of a CPA's audit of financial statements. On a recurring engagement, a CPA reviews his audit programs and working papers from his prior audit while planning his current audit to determine their usefulness for the current engagement.

Required:

a. (1) What are the purposes or functions of audit working papers?

   (2) What records may be included in audit working papers?

b. What factors affect the CPA's judgment of the type and content of the working papers for a particular engagement?

c. To comply with generally accepted auditing standards, a CPA includes certain evidence in his working papers, for example, "evidence that the audit was planned and work of assistants was supervised and reviewed.'' What other evidence should a CPA include in audit working papers to comply with generally accepted auditing standards?

d. How can a CPA make the most effective use of the preceding year's audit programs in a recurring audit?

(AICPA adapted)

DISCUSSION CASES

6.31. Client Selection

You are a CPA in a regional accounting firm that has 10 offices in three states. Mr. Shine has approached you with a request for an audit. He is president of Hitech Software and Games, Inc., a five-year-old company that has recently grown to $20 million in sales and $10 million in total assets. Mr. Shine is thinking about "going public" with a $9 million issue of common stock, of which $5 million would be a secondary issue of shares he holds. You are very happy about this opportunity because you know Mr. Shine is the new president of the Symphony Society board and has made quite a civic impression since he came to your medium-size city seven years ago. Hitech is one of the growing employers in the city.

Required:

a. Discuss the sources of information and the types of inquiries you and the firm's partners can make in connection with accepting Hitech as a new client.

b. Does the AICPA require any investigation of prospective clients?

c. Suppose Mr. Shine has also told you that 10 years ago his closely-held hamburger-franchise business went bankrupt, and upon investigation you learn from its former auditors (your own firm) that Shine played "fast and loose" with franchise-fee income recognition rules and presented such difficulties that your office in another city resigned from the audit (before the bankruptcy). Do you think the partner in charge of the audit practice should accept Hitech as a new client?

6.32. Analytical Review

Staff accountants of E.Z. Campbell & Company, CPAs, are planning the preliminary audit program for the examination of Model Manufacturing Company accounts for the year ended February 28, 1985. You have obtained the company's third-quarter financial statements dated November 30, 1984, and your task is to analyze significant ratios and trends in order to understand Model's business and determine whether audit efforts should be concentrated in any particular areas. The financial statements as of November 30, 1984 and 1983, and for the nine months ending on each of these dates are condensed in Exhibit 6.32–1.

Model's sales are all on credit—no cash sales. A review of the monthly financial statements has shown that the November 30 balances are comparable to the monthly averages for each year.

The controller figures the allowance for uncollectible accounts receivable each month and has provided the following information. (See Exhibit 6.32–2.)

The controller ordinarily figures the allowance for uncollectible accounts as 2 percent, 5 percent and 15 percent of each of the past due categories, and she has been fairly accurate for the last three years. As of November 30, 1984, she explains that a new discount chain customer let a $40,000 account go past due, but the amount is considered fully collectible. This customer has purchased and paid for $685,000 of goods since December 1983.

Required:

a. Compute the accounts receivable turnover ratio. Identify and explain proce-

EXHIBIT 6.32–1
Balance Sheet

Assets

	1984	1983
Cash.	$ 12,000	$ 15,000
Accounts receivable, net.	93,000	50,000
Inventory	72,000	67,000
Other current assets	5,000	6,000
Plant and equipment, net of depreciation	60,000	80,000
Total assets	$ 242,000	$ 218,000

Equities

	1984	1983
Accounts payable	$ 38,000	$ 41,000
Federal income tax payable	30,000	14,400
Long-term liabilities	20,000	40,000
Common stock.	70,000	70,000
Retained earnings	84,000	52,600
Total equities	$ 242,000	$ 218,000

Income Statements

	1984	1983
Net sales	$1,684,000	$1,250,000
Cost of goods sold	927,000	710,000
Gross margin on sales	757,000	540,000
Selling and administrative expenses	682,000	504,000
Income before federal income taxes	75,000	36,000
Income tax expense	30,000	14,400
Net income	$ 45,000	$ 21,600

EXHIBIT 6.32–2

	1984	1983
Current accounts	$40,000	$30,000
Accounts 30–60 days past due.	47,653	12,000
Accounts 60–90 days past due.	4,000	5,000
Accounts over 90 days past due	2,000	4,105
Allowance for uncollectible accounts	(653)	(1,105)
	$93,000	$50,000

dures that might be used to audit the accounts receivable.

b. Compute the current ratio. Review its composition and discuss whether any additional audit attention appears necessary.

c. Compute percent of sales and ratios using costs, expenses, and taxes, and discuss whether any additional audit attention appears necessary.

6.33. **Analytical Review**

Kermit Griffin, an audit manager, had begun a preliminary analytical review of selected statistics related to the Majestic Hotel. His objective was to obtain an understanding of this hotel's business in order to draft a preliminary audit program. He wanted to see whether he could detect any troublesome areas or questionable accounts that might require special audit attention. Unfortunately, Mr. Griffin caught the flu and was

EXHIBIT 6.33–1

AP-6   Majestic Hotel   Prepared by KG
                          Preliminary Analytical Review   Reviewed by _____
                                 FYE 3/31/85

The Majestic Hotel, East Apple, New Jersey, compiles operating statistics on a calendar year basis. Hotel statistics, below, were provided by the controller A. J. Marselli, for 1984. The parallel column contains industry average statistics obtained from Welsch's Hotel Industry Guide.

		Majestic	Industry
Sales:	Rooms	60.4%	63.9%
	Food and beverages	35.7	32.2
	Other	3.9	3.9
Costs:	Rooms department	15.2%	17.3%
	Food and beverages	34.0	27.2
	Administrative and general	8.0	8.9
	Management fee	3.3	1.1
	Advertising	7.7	3.2
	Real estate taxes	3.5	3.2
	Utilities, repairs, maintenance	15.9	13.7
Profit per sales dollar		17.4%	25.4%
Rooms dept. ratios to rooms sales $			
	Salaries and wages	18.9%	15.7%
	Laundry	1.0	3.7
	Other	5.3	7.6
Profit per rooms sales $		74.8%	73.0%
Food/Beverage ratios to F/B Sales $			
	Cost of food sold	42.1%	37.0%
	Food gross profit	57.9%	63.0%
	Cost of beverages sold	43.6%	29.5%
	Beverages gross profit	56.4%	70.5%
	Combined gross profit	57.7%	64.6%
	Salaries and wages	39.6%	32.8%
	Music and entertainment	—	2.7%
	Other	13.4	13.8
Profit per F/B Sales $		4.7%	15.3%
Average annual % room occupancy		62.6%	68.1%
Average room rate per day		$160.00	$120.00
Number of rooms available per day		200	148

hospitalized. From his sickbed, he sent you the schedule (shown in Exhibit 6.33–1) he had prepared. He has asked you to write a memorandum identifying areas of potential errors and irregularities or other matters that the preliminary audit program should cover.

Required:

Write a memorandum describing Majestic's operating characteristics compared to the "industry average" insofar as you can tell from the statistics. Does this analytical review identify any areas that might present problems in the audit?

6.34. **Preliminary Materiality Assessment**

Longneck, Inc., manufactures baby bottles and other glass containers. As of September 30 this year, sales volume amounted to $14,353,812. The company sells to a variety of wholesale and retail distributors and wrote 28,400 sales invoices for the nine-month period ended September 30. Summarized financial statements for the nine-month periods ended September 30, 19X0 and 19X1 (current year) are shown below (000 omitted).

Kaye Clark, CPA, is about to begin an audit of this sales total as a part of the interim audit work. The audit program specifies selection of a sample of sales invoices and: (1) comparison of the quantities billed thereon to shipping records of quantities shipped, (2) comparison of prices used thereon to authorized price lists, and (3) measurement of dollar-value errors discovered.

Assets	19X1	19X0
Cash	$ 1,525	$ 1,198
Accounts receivable	3,190	2,622
Inventory	2,785	2,680
Fixed assets (net)	4,500	4,500
	$12,000	$11,000

Liabilities and Equity	19X1	19X0
Accounts payable	$ 1,039	$ 1,000
Long-term debt @ 10%	2,500	2,000
Capital stock	6,500	6,500
Retained earnings	1,961	1,500
	$12,000	$11,000

Income Statement	19X1	19X0
Sales	$14,354	$13,482
Returns and allowances*	418	285
Net sales	13,936	13,197
Cost of goods sold	8,356	8,039
General and administrative	3,903	3,642
Interest	175	150
Income taxes @ 42%	631	574
Net income	871	792
Dividends	701	632
Retained	$ 170	$ 160

Statement of Changes	19X1	19X0
Net income	$ 871	$ 792
Depreciation	500	500
From operations	1,371	1,292
Debt financing	500	–0–
Total sources	1,871	1,292
Fixed-asset additions	500	–0–
Dividends	701	632
Net changes	$ 670	$ 660

* Analysis of Sales Returns and Allowances, 9 months ended 19X1 and 19X0:

Returned merchandise	$ 33	$ 33
Sales discounts	215	202
Billing error corrections	170	50
	$418	$285

Required.

In order to design an audit plan, Ms. Clark must decide upon an amount of misstatement considered material. As a general guideline, her audit manager believes any misstatement less than 5 percent is probably not material, and any misstatement of more than 10 percent certainly is material. She must prepare two working papers showing:

a. Explanation of why a sales account overstatement of $300,000 would be considered material.

b. Derivation of a smaller sales account overstatement that would be considered material.

6.35. **Working Paper Review**

The schedule in Exhibit 6.35–1 was prepared by the controller of World Manufacturing Inc., for use by the independent auditors during their examination of World's year-end financial statements. All procedures performed by the audit assistant were

EXHIBIT 6.35–1
Marketable Securities (World Manufacturing, Inc., Year Ended December 31, 1984)

Description of Security			Serial No.	Face Value of Bonds	Gen. Ledger 1/1	Purch. in 1984	Sold in 1984	Cost	Gen. Ledger 12/31	12/31 Market	Dividend and Interest		
											Pay Date(s)	Amt. Rec.	Accruals 12/31
Corp. Bonds	%	Yr. Due											
A	6	91	21-7	10000	9400a				9400	9100	1/15 7/15	300b,d 300b,d	275
D	4	83	73-0	30000	27500a				27500	26220	12/1	1200b,d	100
G	9	98	16-4	5000	4000a				4000	5080	8/1	450b,d	188
Rc	5	85	08-2	70000	66000a		57000b	66000					
Sc	10	99	07-4	100000		100000e			100000	101250	7/1	5000b,d	5000
					106900	100000	57000	66000	140900	141650		7250	5563
					a,f	f	f	f	f,g	f		f	f
Stocks													
P 1,000 shs. Common			1044		7500a				7500	7600	3/1 6/1 9/1 12/1	750b,d 750b,d 750b,d 750b,d	250
U 50 shs. Common			8530		9700a				9700	9800	2/1 8/1	800b,d 800b,d	667
					17200				17200	17400		4600	917
					a,f				f,g	f		f	f

Legends and comments relative to above

a = Beginning balances agreed to 1980 working papers.
b = Traced to cash receipts.
c = Minutes examined (purchase and sales approved by the board of directors).
d = Agreed to 1099.
e = Confirmed by tracing to broker's advice.
f = Totals footed.
g = Agreed to general ledger.

noted in the bottom "Legend" section, and it was initialed properly, dated and indexed, and then submitted to a senior member of the audit staff for review. Internal control was reviewed and is considered to be satisfactory.

Required:

a. What information essential to the audit of marketable securities is missing from this schedule?

b. What essential audit procedures were not noted as having been performed by the audit assistant?

(*AICPA* adapted)

CHAPTER 7

PROFESSIONAL STANDARDS SOURCES		
Compendium Section	**Document Reference**	**Topic**
AU 320	SAS 1	Auditor's Study and Evaluation of Internal Control
AU 322	SAS 9	Effect of an Internal Audit Function on the Independent Auditor's Examination
AU 323	SAS 20	Required Communication of Material Weaknesses in Internal Accounting Control
AU 324	SAS 44	Special Purpose Reports on Internal Accounting Control at Service Organizations
AU 642	SAS 30	Reporting on Internal Accounting Control
AU 722	SAS 36	Review of Interim Financial Information
AR 100	SSARS 1	Compilation and Review of Financial Statements

Internal Control Theory and Review Techniques

The preceding chapter introduced several planning steps performed early in an audit engagement. The study and evaluation of internal accounting control is next. This chapter covers control definitions and the evaluation process and explains control characteristics and objectives. Your learning objectives for these topics are to be able to:

☐ Write an essay or memo explaining primary and secondary reasons for conducting a proper study and evaluation of an audit client's existing system of internal accounting control.

☐ Define and discuss administrative and accounting control.

☐ Analyze the costs and benefits of controls in specific case situations.

☐ Explain the three phases of a proper study and evaluation of internal accounting control in relation to alternative audit strategies (plans).

☐ Apply your knowledge of the characteristics of reliable control systems in analyses of specific case situations.

☐ Associate the seven categories of specific control objectives with the four operative objectives expressed in generally accepted auditing standards.

☐ Write an appropriate report on internal accounting control for a given fact situation.

ACCOUNTING SYSTEMS AND CONTROL SYSTEMS

You must understand the major distinction between accounting systems and an internal accounting control system. An *accounting system* is a set of tasks that process transactions, records them in journals and ledgers (either computerized or manual), and produces financial statements.

Accounting is a production function for collecting, summarizing and reporting information. An *internal accounting control system,* however, is a set of techniques (both computerized and manual) imposed on the accounting system for the purpose of preventing, detecting and correcting errors and irregularities that might enter it and flow through to the financial statements. Thus, *internal accounting control* is a function which has the broad objectives of safeguarding assets and enhancing the reliability of financial statements.

An accounting system performs accounting functions, but it does not necessarily guarantee the accuracy of financial statements. If the purpose of a task is to *create* financial accounting data, the task is part of the accounting system. Otherwise, if the purpose of a task is to *check the accuracy* or *review* the processing of accounting information, the task is part of the control system.

Management versus Auditor Responsibility

An entity's management is responsible for designing, installing, and operating an accounting system. Likewise, management is responsible for establishing and maintaining a system of internal accounting control. Continuous supervision and modification, when necessary, are elements of the management responsibility.

An audit team is not responsible for designing an effective control system for a client. "Design" refers to formulating the plan of organization and the control procedures and records. Accounting firms undertake control design as MAS engagements but consider such work to be separate and apart from the audit engagement responsibility. The audit team is responsible for designing a proper study and evaluation of the existing internal control system, not for designing the system itself.

REASONS FOR CONDUCTING A STUDY AND EVALUATION

The primary reason for conducting a proper study and evaluation of a client's existing internal accounting control system is to give the auditors a basis for finalizing the details of the account balance audit program. At this point, you need a glimpse of what lies ahead in the next chapter in regard to audit programs. An *audit program* includes a specification (list) of procedures needed to obtain evidence about the assertions in financial statements. Each procedure should have identifiable characteristics of *nature, timing* and *extent* as well as a direct association with one or more financial statement assertions. Take the following account balance auditing procedure as an example:

> Select 500 inventory item records from the perpetual inventory system, and on December 31, 19XX, accompany client personnel when they count the physical inventory (both onsite and at customers holding consignments), and record the counts of the selected items. Compare the counts to the final inventory compilation used in the financial statements.
> This procedure exhibits:

Objective: Obtain evidence about the assertions of the existence of the inventory.

Nature: Direct personal knowledge by physical observation.

Timing: Client's fiscal year-end date.

Extent: 500 inventory item records.

The procedures in a final audit program are determined by the auditors' evaluation of the reliance that can be placed on particular internal accounting control procedures used by the client. This evaluation is an assessment of the ***internal control risk***—defined in the preceding chapter as the probability that the client's control policies and procedures will *fail* to detect material errors and irregularities, provided any enter the accounting system in the first place. When auditors decide an internal control system is working well, hence internal control risk is relatively small, they can *restrict* (adjust) the nature, timing and extent of subsequent procedures.

Restricting Audit Procedures

Taking the physical observation example above, the ***restrictions*** associated with excellent control could be these: *(1)Nature.* Conduct physical observation of inventory on hand but obtain confirmations from customers holding inventory on consignment. *(2)Timing.* Conduct the observation on November 30, 19XX, without insisting that the client move the count date to December 31. *(3)Extent.* Select 250 inventory item records from the perpetual inventory system, instead of 500.

Constructive Suggestions

A secondary purpose for conducting a study and evaluation of existing internal control is to be able to make constructive suggestions for improvements. Auditors become involved in system design work in a minor way by making suggestions in a management letter given to the client. Officially, the profession considers these suggestions a part of the audit function and does not define the work as a MAS consultation. Clients are free to decide whether to act upon the suggestions.

Material Weakness Report

Another purpose of the study and evaluation is to report to management and the board of directors or its audit committee any discovery of material weaknesses in internal accounting control. A ***material weakness*** is defined in auditing standards as *a condition in which the specific control procedures or the degree of compliance with them do not reduce to a relatively low level the risk that errors or irregularities in amounts that would be material to the financial statements being audited may occur and not be detected within a timely period by employees in the normal course of performing their assigned functions* (SAS 1, AU 320.77).

Even though the report of material weaknesses is required by auditing standards, auditors who fail to report to the client can nevertheless sign an unqualified audit opinion, thus stating that the audit was conducted in accordance with generally accepted auditing standards (SAS 20, AU 323.02). The Auditing Standards Board considers the report important but only incidental to the proper study and evaluation of internal control in connection with the audit of financial statements because management is responsible for designing and maintaining the control system, as was discussed earlier.

CONTROL DEFINITIONS

A perfect system of accounting control is one that prevents, detects and corrects all errors and irregularities. A reliable system, however, may be short of perfection. An auditor's problem, according to the theory in the standards of field work, is to find out how much reliance, if any, can be placed on the control system.

Administrative and Accounting Control

Two dimensions of internal control are administrative controls and accounting controls. Independent auditors are most interested in the accounting controls, but not to the complete exclusion of the administrative controls.

Administrative controls include the plan of organization and the procedures and records involved in the decision processes leading to management's authorization of transactions. Such authorization is a management function directly associated with the responsibility for achieving the objectives of the organization and is the starting point for establishing the accounting control over transactions.

Accounting controls consist of the plan of organization and the procedures and records concerned with the **broad objectives** of safeguarding assets and enhancing the reliability of financial records. Consequently, accounting control is designed to provide reasonable assurance that the following *operative objectives* are met:

a. Transactions are executed in accordance with management's general or specific authorization.
b. Transactions are recorded as necessary (1) to permit preparation of financial statements in conformity with generally accepted accounting principles or any other criteria applicable to such statements and (2) to maintain accountability for assets.
c. Access to assets is permitted only in accordance with management's authorization.
d. The recorded accountability for assets is compared with the existing assets at reasonable intervals and appropriate action is taken with respect to any differences.[1]

In an audit engagement, the distinction between administrative controls and accounting controls may be difficult to make. The distinction

---

[1] SAS 1 (AU 320.27-320.29) and SAS 30 (AU 642.04). Companies registered under the Securities Exchange Act of 1934 are required by law to maintain internal control systems having these characteristics. Refer to the discussion of the Foreign Corrupt Practices Act of 1977 in Chapter 4.

should not be made artificially in order to avoid dealing with some controls that may be labeled "administrative." Accounting controls of primary interest are the methods and procedures bearing directly and importantly on the reliability of financial records. Administrative controls, in contrast, generally relate only indirectly to the accounts.

For example, a company may have a system for planning, approving, and controlling expenditures on major advertising projects. The parts of the system concerning approval and payment of these expenses are accounting controls that impact directly on the amount shown in the expense account. At the same time, the company may maintain marketing analyses of the sales generated by the advertising projects. These analyses serve as administrative controls for the purpose of evaluating the effectiveness of the marketing effort and for planning future promotions. An independent auditor normally would not be concerned with these marketing analyses. However, such records might prove useful to explain unusual sales fluctuations in connection with the audit of the sales revenue accounts.

Other administrative controls—accomplished through such devices as budgets, statistical production analyses, quality control data, investments analysis and maintenance schedules—are in a class of controls with the marketing analyses mentioned above. Usually, these data are not a part of the transaction-processing accounting system itself. Yet, they may turn out to be useful in resolving questions that arise during an audit. A thorough understanding of the client's business is not possible without an understanding of the administrative controls.

Reasonable Assurance   Accounting control systems are subject to cost/benefit considerations. Systems possibly could be made perfect, or nearly so, at great expense. An inventory could be left unlocked and unguarded (no control against theft and no control expenses), or a fence could be used; locks could be installed; lighting could be used at night; television monitors could be put in place; armed guards could be hired. Each of these successive safeguards cost money, as does extensive supervision of clerical personnel in an office. At some point, the cost of protecting the inventory from theft (or of supervisors' catching every clerical error) exceeds the benefit of control. Hence, control systems generally do not provide absolute assurance that the objectives of internal accounting control are satisfied. Reasonable assurance is enough, and according to auditing standards: "The concept of reasonable assurance recognizes that the cost of internal control should not exceed the benefits expected to be derived" (SAS 1, AU 320.32).

Material Weakness   Notwithstanding the common sense of the concept of reasonable assurance, auditors must be careful to determine whether a system contains a material weakness in internal accounting control. Business managers can make estimates of benefits to be derived from controls and weigh them against the cost. Managers are perfectly free to make their own judgments about the necessary extent of controls. Managers can decide the degree of business risk they are willing to tolerate (refer to SAS 30, AU 642.05).

Auditors, however, are obligated to report material weakness they discover, and the definition of material weakness does not depend on the same concept of reasonable assurance. In other words, managers may decide that certain controls are not cost-beneficial, but a material weakness can exist nevertheless. A material weakness, according to the auditing standards definition depends on three criteria: (1) more than a relatively low level of risk that material errors or irregularities may occur; (2) such errors or irregularities may not be detected within a timely period; and (3) employees may not detect the errors in the normal course of performing their regular jobs.

Determining the appropriate "level of risk" is a matter of auditors' professional judgment. Discerning the "materiality" of potential errors or irregularities is also a matter of judgment coupled with materiality criteria. What constitutes a "timely period" is open to interpretation. One view is that failure to provide ways and means to detect errors or irregularities as often as financial statements are issued (say, quarterly) is a sign of material weakness. Employees performing their regular jobs include internal auditors who are involved in systematic and continuous control tasks. The independent auditors are not employees, and their work ordinarily does not satisfy the timeliness criterion. So, independent auditors' work does not plug the gap left by a material weakness.

Understanding these criteria of risk—*failure to detect, timeliness* and *regular jobs*—is important. When independent auditors evaluate internal accounting control and find near-material or material weaknesses, the account balance audit program probably will need to be extended and expanded.

PHASES OF A "PROPER" STUDY AND EVALUATION

The word "proper" in the second AICPA standard of field work is a term of art. A study and evaluation of existing internal control is ***proper*** as long as it coordinates with the final audit program. A study and evaluation has three phases, and the work can be stopped after any one of them and still be considered "proper."

Exhibit 7–1 puts the internal control study and evaluation in perspective. You can consider the preliminary review phase to be part of the planning activities. The preliminary review leads to the auditor's design of a preliminary plan of audit procedures for obtaining evidence about the major assertions presented in the financial statements. After the preliminary review, the audit team can halt the study and evaluation of internal control for the efficiency or effectiveness reasons explained in the next section. However, if the auditors want to rely on controls, the review must be completed.

EXHIBIT 7–1
Three Phases of Internal Control Study and Evaluation

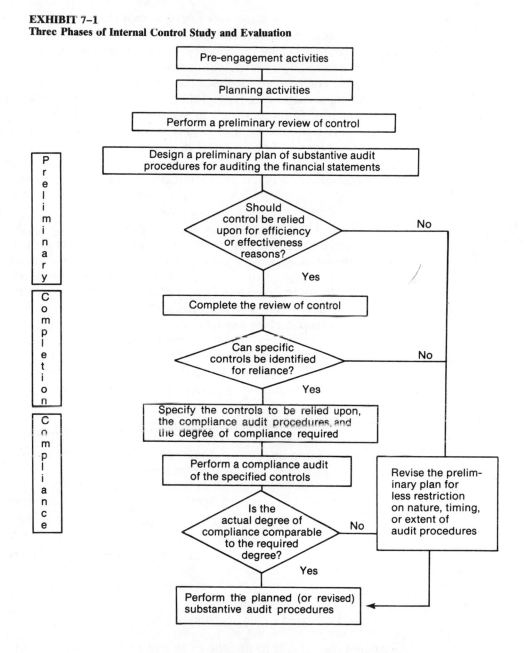

After the review is completed (phase two), auditors must determine whether any *specific controls* can be identified for reliance. Suppose a company's controls over keeping perpetual inventory records contains this procedure: "A copy of the bill of lading (shipping document) is matched with each sales invoice before inventory is removed from the perpetual inventory records." (This procedure controls the error of recording inventory issues and cost of goods sold incorrectly). If no such specific controls can be identified, the auditors might halt the study and evaluation of internal control, revise the audit plan to include more work on the inventory observation, and then proceed with the audit.

If specific controls are identified for reliance, the company's *compliance* with them must be audited. This compliance auditing (phase three) consists of procedures designed to produce evidence of how well the controls worked in practice. If they pass the auditor's criteria for reliance (the required degree of compliance), they can be relied upon. If they fail the test, the auditors final conclusion is to revise the audit plan to take the lack of control into account and then proceed with the audit work.

PRELIMINARY REVIEW PHASE

The preliminary review phase may occur early, along with the audit planning, preliminary analytical review and preliminary assessment of risk. The preliminary review work gives auditors an overall acquaintance with the control environment and the flow of transactions through the accounting system. It can be considered a part of the planning activity of understanding the client's business. It should produce general knowledge of the control environment along these lines:

- ☐ The client's organizational chart.
- ☐ Methods used to communicate responsibility and authority.
- ☐ Methods used to supervise the accounting and the control systems.
- ☐ The work assignments of internal auditors, if any.

It should also produce general knowledge of the flow of transactions through the accounting system along these lines:

- ☐ The various classes of significant accounting transactions.
- ☐ The types of material errors and irregularities that could occur.
- ☐ Methods by which each significant class of transactions is:
  Authorized.
  Executed.
  Initially recorded.
  Processed in the accounting system.

Auditors can decide to stop the study and evaluation work at this point for either of two reasons, both of them coordinated with the final audit program. First, the audit team might conclude that no more evidence is needed to show that control is too poor to justify restrictions of subsequent audit procedures. This conclusion is equivalent to assessing internal control risk at or near 1.0 and specifying extensive procedures such as the inventory observation procedure illustrated earlier. Essentially, this decision is a matter of audit *effectiveness.*

Second, the audit team might decide that more time and effort would be spent evaluating controls than could be saved by relying on them, providing the controls turn out to be working well. In this case, the conclusion is also equivalent to assessing internal control risk at or near 1.0, but this time because of the auditors' lack of knowledge about the controls and not because they have decided controls are poor. The result is the same, however—extensive subsequent procedures are specified. For example, suppose the study and evaluation of controls over the accuracy of perpetual inventory quantities would take 40 hours. If controls were excellent, suppose then the restricted inventory observation procedure would take 30 hours less to perform. The additional work on controls is not economical. The decision to stop work on controls in this case is a matter of audit *efficiency*—deciding not to work 40 hours in order to save 30 hours.

Working paper documentation of a decision not to rely on the controls and not to restrict subsequent procedures can consist only of a memorandum of the reasons for stopping the study and evaluation work after the preliminary review phase. The memorandum should contain an explanation of the effectiveness-related or efficiency-related decisions discussed above. When the review is continued, additional documentation, discussed in the next section, is required.

COMPLETING THE REVIEW OF A SYSTEM

The continuation of the review phase is the audit team's chance to get more acquainted with the organization and gather more information on the accounting and control procedures prescribed. This work produces specific knowledge regarding controls, in terms of:

☐ Specific control objectives.

☐ Specific control procedures.

It should also produce specific knowledge about the flow of transactions that will allow the auditors to:

☐ Group transactions into classes.

☐ Identify points in the data processing where errors or irregularities could occur.

Information obtained in the full review provides the basis for a preliminary evaluation of the system and for decisions about compliance auditing procedures. Methods and procedures for obtaining review phase information include inquiries, examination of client documents and observation of the data processing. Audit documentation of the auditors' understanding of the system can take the form of *questionnaires, narratives* and *flowcharts*.

Internal Control Questionnaire and Narrative

The most efficient means of gathering evidence about internal accounting control is to conduct a formal interview with a knowledgeable manager, using the checklist type of *internal control questionnaire.* Exhibit 7–2 illustrates the type of questions appropriate for a large enterprise. Questionnaires are also tailored for use in computer-based information systems, and the questions are designed to produce information about the operation of the computer installation and the individual data processing subsystems.

Internal control questionnaires are designed to help the audit team obtain evidence about the division of duties, the system of authorization, objectives and techniques, supervision, and many practices that are considered good error-checking routines. Answers to the questions, however, are *not competent and sufficient enough* for final conclusions about the reliability of internal accounting controls. In fact, none of the evidence collected during the review-completion phase is sufficient for final decisions to rely on controls. The review phase findings must be corroborated with compliance evidence.

Evidence obtained through the interview-questionnaire process is hearsay evidence because its source is generally a single person who, while knowledgeable, is still not the person who actually does the control work. This person may give answers that reflect what he or she *believes* the system should be, rather than what it *really* is. The person may be unaware of informal ways in which duties have been changed or may be innocently ignorant of the system details. Nevertheless, interviews and questionnaires are useful when a manager tells of a weak feature. An admission of weak control is fairly convincing.

A strong point about questionnaires is that they are complete, usually containing hundreds of questions dealing with most conceivable points of internal control interest. Armed with such a checklist, an auditor is less likely to forget to cover some important point. Also, questions generally are worded such that a "No" answer points out some weakness or control deficiency, thus making analysis easier.

However, you should be aware that questionnaires have disadvantages. Sometimes, it is tempting to complete the questionnaire for the current-year audit while using the prior year's questionnaire as a crutch. This shortcut might cause an auditor to miss a change in the system. Mechanically checking off "Yes" and "No" answers with cursory comments in the "Remarks" column—a manifestation of viewing the questionnaire as just another form to fill out—does not contribute much to a careful decision about the reliability of internal accounting control. The quality of subsequent audit work may suffer. Also, since questionnaires may be standardized and thus contain a large number of questions, many of the queries inevitably will not be applicable to a particular client.

One way to tailor these inquiry procedures to a unique system is to write a *narrative description* of each important control subsystem. Such a narrative would appear very much like the text portion of the problems at

EXHIBIT 7–2
Internal Control
Questionnaire for Sales
and Accounts Receivable

Client *Kingston Company* Audit Date *December 31, 1985*
Names and Positions of Client Personnel Interviewed: *Mr. Samuel Carloy*
(controller), Mr. Julian Grace (Chief Accountant)
Auditor *Harold Brooly (Senior Accountant)* Date Completed *September 17, 1985*
Reviewed by *Titus Balstrode (Manager)* Date Reviewed *September 20, 1985*

Question	NA	Yes	No	Remarks*
				Answer
SALES:				*Billing clerk matches invoice with sales order, enters prices, extends, and foots. Sends daily batches to keypunch for EDP preparation.*
1. Briefly describe method of recording sales.				
2. Are customers' orders subjected to review and approval before invoice is prepared:				
a. By sales or order department?		√		
b. By credit department?		√		
3. Are blank invoices prenumbered?		√		
4. Are blank invoices available only to authorized personnel?		√		
5. Are sales and order department personnel denied custodial access to assets?		√		
6. Are bill of lading forms prenumbered?		√		
7. Are back orders or pending files reviewed periodically? How often?		√		*Weekly.*
8. Are invoices checked for accuracy of:				
a. Quantities billed?		√		
b. Prices used?		√		
c. Mathematical calculations?		√		
d. Credit terms?		√		
9. Are completed invoices compared with customer orders?		√		*By billing clerk.*
10. Are returned items cleared through the receiving department?		√		
11. Does the system provide control over:				
a. Sales to officers and employees?		√		
b. Sales to subsidiaries and affiliates?		√		
c. Scrap and waste sales?		√		
d. Sales of equipment?		√		
e. COD sales?	√			
f. Cash sales?		√		
12. Are there accuracy checks on data prepared for EDP departments:				
a. Control totals?			√	*Control totals are prepared but not used for control*
b. Key verification?		√		
13. List and describe programmed EDP controls. *Self-checking customer code.* *Limit check on sales amount*				*Unique code for each customer for sales over $5,000*

* In the case of a "No" answer, the "Remarks" column should (1) cross-reference to the audit program steps designed to recognize the weakness or to a supporting memorandum which explains related adequate controls or lack of importance of the item and (2) indicate whether the item is to be included in the draft of the letter to management on internal accounting control.

EXHIBIT 7–2
(concluded)

Question	NA	Yes	No	Remarks*
Accounts receivable:				*EDP of daily document batches*
1. Are cash postings made simultaneously with the posting of the cash receipts records by means of a machine bookkeeping device? (If not, give brief description of method used.)		√		
2. Are the duties of the accounts receivable bookkeeper separate from any cash funtions?		√		
3. If there is more than one accounts receivable bookkeeper, are the account sections for which they are responsible changed from time to time?		√		
4. Are monthly statements sent to all customers?		√		
5. Are statements independently checked to accounts and kept under control to ensure their being mailed by someone other than the accounts receivable bookkeeper?			√	*Monthly statements are maintained prepared, and mailed by the AR department*
6. Are customer accounts regularly balanced with control?		√		
7. Are the accounts aged periodically for review?		√		
8. Are accounts independently confirmed by client's personnel with customers?			√	*No internal auditors*
9. Are credit memoranda approved by proper authority and are they under numerical control?		√		
10. Is approval of credit department a prerequisite to payment of customer credit balances?		√		
11. Are delinquent accounts periodically reviewed by an officer?		√		*Only every six months*
12. Are write-offs of bad debts and adjustment credits approved by an officer?		√		
13. Is proper control exercised over bad debts after they have been written off?		√		
14. Are allowances for discounts in violation of regular terms of sale specifically authorized by a responsible official?		√		
15. Is the collection department independent of and does it constitute a check on accounts receivable bookkeepers?		√		
16. Is the management of the credit department completely divorced from the sales department?		√		
17. Are there accuracy checks on data prepared for EDP departments?		√		*Control totals are prepared but not used for control*
18. Are there post-processing accuracy checks on EDP output?				
a. Comparison of sales and accounts receivable control account entries.		√		
b. Comparison of control account entry to subsidiary detail.		√		
19. List and describe programmed EDP controls. *Self-checking customer code Limit check on sales amount Count hash and batch totals*				*Unique code for each customer for sales over $5,000 Control totals are generated by computer processing*

the end of the chapter which describes data processing and control procedures. The narrative description may be efficient in audits of very small businesses, although concurrent use of specialized questionnaires is also recommended. The greatest drawbacks to the narrative description is that its writing takes time and skill; the evaluation of what is described requires experience and insight; and as the years pass, its revision becomes physically cumbersome. Also, with any major change the entire narrative must be rewritten.

In summary, the formal inquiry to gather evidence about internal accounting control can be documented with a questionnaire, with a narrative description, or with both. In any event, auditors should make sufficient notes of weak points and design the audit program accordingly. For all other points of importance that appear to be reliable, objective evidence must still be obtained, but this work can be limited to those controls that will be relied upon when substantive procedures are performed.

The questionnaire section shown in Exhibit 7–2 covers accounts receivable and sales transaction control matters. This part of the questionnaire relates to the fact situation described in Problem 7.13 at the end of this chapter. At this point, a reading of Problem 7.13 is recommended.

Internal Control System Flowcharts

Another method for documenting auditors' understanding of the accounting and control systems is to construct a flowchart or diagram. Flowcharting is used widely by auditors. The advantages of flowchart diagrams can be summarized by an old cliche: "A picture is worth a thousand words." Flowcharts can enhance auditors' evaluations, and annual updating of a chart is relatively easy (compared to narrative descriptions), with additions or deletions to the symbols and lines.

The alleged disadvantages of flowcharting are its greater time requirement and greater expertise in a rather unique art form. However, the greater time requirement contributes to a much better internal accounting control evaluation and hence possibly to a better and more efficient overall audit. As for the required expertise, the disadvantage is largely illusory and may be overcome by study and practice.

Construction of a flowchart takes time because it cannot be completed before an auditor has consulted firsthand all the operating personnel involved in the system and gathered samples of relevant client documents. Thus, the information for the flowchart, like the narrative description, involves a lot of legwork and observation. When the flowchart is complete, however, the result is an easily evaluated, informative description of the system.

Exhibit 7–3 contains a few simple flowchart symbols used in further illustrations and problem solutions. For any flowcharting application, the chart must be understandable to a reasonably knowledgeable audit supervisor. He or she should not need to consult a lengthy index of symbols to decipher a flowchart.

EXHIBIT 7–3
Abbreviated Set of
Standard Flowcharting
Symbols

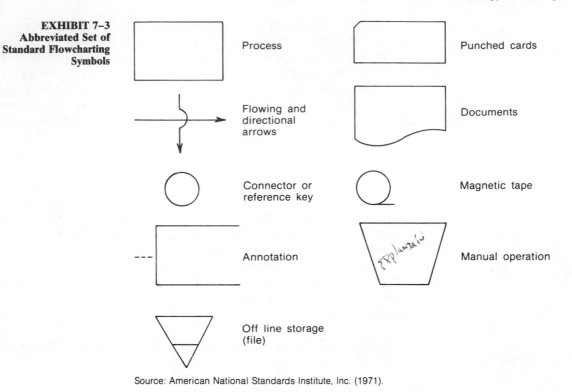

Process

Punched cards

Flowing and
directional
arrows

Documents

Connector or
reference key

Magnetic tape

Annotation

Manual operation

Off line storage
(file)

Source: American National Standards Institute, Inc. (1971).

Before proceeding to flowchart drawing techniques, you should be aware of some elementary cautions. First, a flowchart should be drawn with a template and ruler: A messy chart is hard to read. Second, the starting point in the system should, if possible, be placed at the upper left-hand corner. It is frustrating to pick up a chart and have to hunt around for the place to start. The flow of procedures and documents should be from left to right and from top to bottom, as much as is possible. A chart that has lines going back and forth is hard to decipher. Narrative explanations should be written on the face of the chart as annotations or written in a readily available reference key.

All of these cautions emphasize one main point: The flowchart should communicate all relevant information and evidence about division of duties, authorization, and control procedures in an understandable, visual form. Exhibit 7–4 contains a flowchart representation of the data processing system for the illustrative sales-accounts receivable system described in Problem 7.13.

In Exhibit 7–4, you can see some characteristics of flowchart construction and some characteristics of this data processing system. By reading *down* the columns headed for each department, you can see that transaction initiation authority (both credit approval and sales invoice prepara-

EXHIBIT 7–4
Sales Transaction Processing System Flowchart

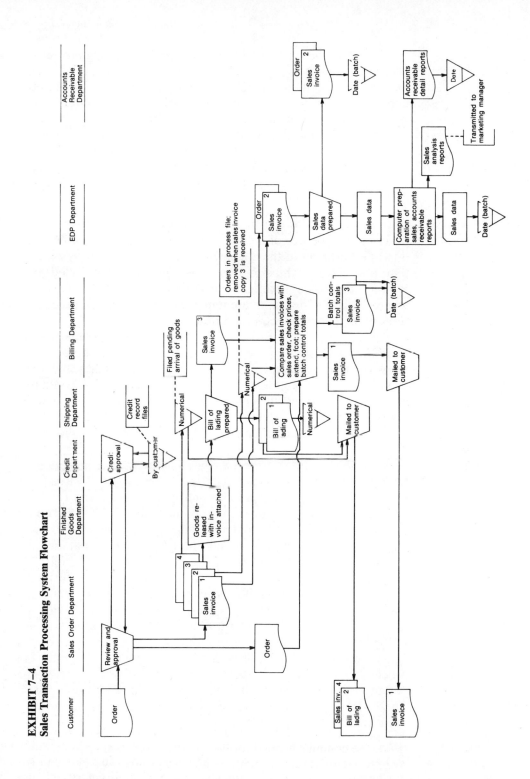

tion), custody of assets, and transaction recordkeeping are separated appropriately. Notice also that all the invoice-completion procedures, including preparation of a batch control total, are performed in the billing department. There is no apparent double check on data accuracy, although both the batched invoice Copy 2 and the computer report on accounts receivable are eventually filed in the accounts receivable department. Also, the chart shows that the *batch control total is not used*. Notice that all documents have an intermediate or final resting place in a file. This flowchart feature gives the auditor information about where to find audit evidence later.

Program Flowcharts Another type of flowcharting, called ***program flowcharting,*** is utilized to describe the features of a computer program. A program flowchart is an important element in the documentation of a computer system. The system flowchart in Exhibit 7–3 contains a process box labeled ''Computer Preparation of Sales and Accounts Receivable Reports.'' This is the place where program flowcharts are important for describing precisely the nature of computer programs and processing.

The flowchart of a program is a step-by-step explanation of all the operations that are supposed to be performed by the computer. Auditors need to know how to read and review simple flowcharts that document a client's computer programs. A portion of a program that could be used to process sales and accounts receivable transactions illustrated in this chapter is presented in Exhibit 7–5. This program flowchart is part of the documentation needed to complete the system flowchart shown in Exhibit 7–4.

Auditors can review the computer program in connection with the review of internal accounting control in two ways: (1) Read the coded program instructions for proper controls and logic; and (2) Review the program flowchart for proper controls and logic. The first method requires considerable expertise in computer languages and much diligence in poring over a printout of the computer program. The second method avoids the need to know the programming language but still requires careful study to perform a critical analysis of the program. Both methods are tentative because the auditor is reading and reviewing documents that *purport* to be the real system. These two methods of review have the same tentative evidential weight as an internal control questionnaire. In Exhibit 7–5, you can see that the computer generates control totals that can be compared for agreement to totals prepared prior to computer processing. Also, you can see two kinds of validity tests—customer number and large-scale limit tests—that are typical of programmed controls. These and other matters of review and objective examination are covered in more detail in Chapter 9.

Preliminary Evaluation After completing the review phase, the audit team should thoroughly understand the client's business and the accounting and control tasks. Furthermore, the audit team can make a preliminary evaluation of

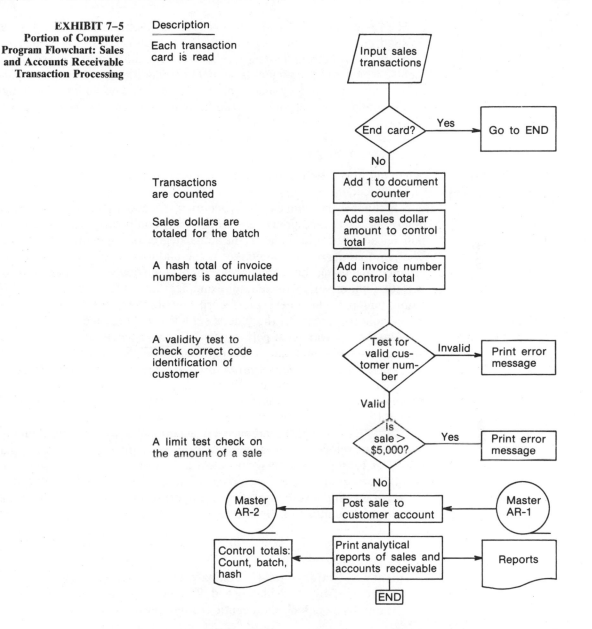

EXHIBIT 7–5
Portion of Computer Program Flowchart: Sales and Accounts Receivable Transaction Processing

Description

Each transaction card is read

Transactions are counted

Sales dollars are totaled for the batch

A hash total of invoice numbers is accumulated

A validity test to check correct code identification of customer

A limit test check on the amount of a sale

strengths and weaknesses.[2] **Strengths** are specific controls that may be relied upon and would need to be audited for compliance. **Weaknesses** are the lack of controls in particular areas, and subsequent audit procedures should be designed to take them into consideration.

---

[2] Accounting firms have different methods for constructing flowcharts. The illustrations in this textbook take the approach of describing an accounting subsystem completely. Some accounting firms use more efficient methods to flowchart only the documents, information flows and controls considered important for the audit.

The review phase of the study and evaluation of internal control is not finished until the auditors *analyze* the flowchart and other evidence for signs of control strengths and weaknesses. Reliable control system elements, which will be subject to compliance auditing, and control weaknesses may be found by analyzing the flowchart. The auditors' findings and preliminary conclusions should be written up for the working paper files.

COMPLIANCE AUDITING

When auditors reach the third phase of a proper study and evaluation of internal accounting control, they will have identified specific controls on which reliance is planned. In order to rely upon them, auditors must determine: (1) the required degree of company compliance with the control policies and procedures and (2) the actual degree of company compliance. The *required degree of compliance* is the auditors' decision criterion for reliance. Knowing that compliance cannot realistically be expected to be perfect, auditors might decide, for example, that evidence of using bills of lading (shipping documents) to record inventory reductions and cost of goods sold 96 percent of the time is sufficient for reliance.

Now the auditors must perform *compliance procedures* to estimate the actual degree of compliance. A compliance procedure is a two-part statement. Part one is an *identification of the data population* from which all items or a sample of items will be selected for audit. Part two is an expression of an *action* taken to produce relevant evidence. In general, the action is: (1) determining whether the selected items correspond to a standard (for example, mathematical accuracy) and/or (2) determining whether the selected items agree with information in another data population. For example, auditors can select a sample of inventory issues recorded in the perpetual records, *recalculate* the recordings for mathematical accuracy, and *vouch* the issues to supporting bills of lading (comparing the physical quantities shown in each). The two-part statement thus is:

Part One: Identifies population of inventory issues recorded in the perpetual records.

Part Two: Actions are: (1) compare to a standard of mathematical accuracy by recalculating and (2) compare to another data population by vouching the quantity to the bill of lading.

This example procedure produces evidence about compliance with the control procedure—controlling inventory recordkeeping accuracy by requiring a supporting bill of lading for inventory issues. As described, the procedures illustrate *reperformance*—the auditors perform again the arithmetic and the comparison the inventory recordkeeper was supposed to have performed. Some accountants, however, believe mere *observation* is enough—the auditors just look to see whether the inventory recordkeeper signed or check-marked the bill of lading to indicate it had been used. They maintain that reperformance is not necessary.[3]

Specific compliance procedures need not be performed if the account balance audit program for a particular account does not depend upon the specific control that could be tested. If, for example, a company had a policy of counting inventory on a cycle basis each month and correcting the perpetual records, the detail vouching of inventory issues to supporting bills of lading would probably not be necessary. Auditors can decide not to rely on controls for some accounts (as in this example related to inventory), and in the same engagement decide to rely upon other controls, for example, the controls related to accounts receivable for the same client. Control reliance is not an all-or-nothing proposition for the audit taken as a whole.

Some compliance procedures depend upon *documentary evidence,* like the inventory issue supported by a bill of lading illustrated above. Documentary evidence in the form of signatures, initials, checklists, reconciliation working papers and the like provide better evidence than procedures that leave no documentary tracks. Some control techniques, such as segregation of employees' duties, may leave no documents behind. In this case, the best kind of procedure—reperformance of control operations—cannot be performed, and the second type of compliance procedure—observation—must be used. This procedure amounts to an auditor's unobtrusive eyewitness observation of employees at their jobs performing control operations.

Auditing standards require application of compliance procedures to samples of transactions and controls executed throughout the period under audit. The reason for this requirement is that the conclusions about controls will be generalized to the whole period under audit.

SUMMARY AND CONCLUSIONS

A study and evaluation of internal accounting control is "proper" as long as it coordinates with the final audit plan. The final audit plan includes the specification (list) of **_substantive audit procedures_** which are defined in Chapter 6 as the transaction detail audit and analytical review procedures designed to produce evidence about the major assertions in financial statement numbers and footnote disclosures. A "proper" study and evaluation of internal accounting control can end with the preliminary review, but the final audit plan will require a great deal of substantive procedural work. A "proper" study and evaluation can end with the completed review, but the final audit plan will still require a great deal of substantive procedural work. The reliance on control that justifies auditors' significant restriction (relaxation) of substantive procedural work is "proper"

---

[3] When you go to work for an accounting firm, one preference will prevail, but the authors believe good evidence requires reperformance, where feasible.

only after the third phase of study and evaluation—compliance auditing—has been completed and evaluated.

Since preparation of the final audit plan is the primary aim and purpose, the study and evaluation of internal accounting control must be documented in audit working papers. The documentation for a preliminary review is light—only a memorandum explaining the reasons for stopping the study and evaluation work is required. When auditors rely on controls, the documentation should include internal control questionnaires, narrative descriptions, flowcharts, specifications of controls and compliance criteria, and the evidence produced by compliance procedures.

You have studied compliance and substantive procedures as if they were easily distinguishable. Be advised, however, that the seven general procedures described in Chapter 6 can be applied either as compliance procedures or as substantive procedures. Actually, you would be better advised to think in terms of compliance and substantive *purposes* of a procedure instead of compliance and substantive procedures. A single procedure may produce both compliance and substantive evidence and thus serve both purposes (hence the name *dual-purpose tests,* SAS 39 [AU 350.43]). For example, the selection of inventory issue entries could have been used: (1) to vouch the issue to the supporting bill of lading and (2) to calculate the correct dollar amount of cost of goods sold. The first datum is relevant information about control compliance. The second is dollar-value information that may help measure an amount of error in the book balance of cost of goods sold. Another example is the confirmation of accounts receivable procedure. This procedure has a primary substantive purpose, but when confirmation replies tell about significant or systematic errors, the evidence is relevant to control evaluation as well as to dollar-value measurement. Most audit procedures serve dual purposes and yield evidence about controls and about financial statement assertions.

You can put the phases of a study and evaluation of internal accounting control in a summary form with the following logical approach (adapted from SAS No. 1, AU 320.74):

1. For each significant class of transactions, think what types of errors or irregularities could occur with material impact on financial statements.

2. Determine what specific accounting control objectives, techniques, and procedures could be used to prevent or detect such errors and irregularities.

3. Determine whether management has identified these control objectives and has prescribed control procedures to accomplish them. (Review phase work.)

4. Determine whether the necessary control procedures are being followed satisfactorily. (Compliance audit work.)

5. Evaluate any weaknesses—material and otherwise—in order to:
   a. Plan the nature, timing and extent of other auditing procedures in light of the weakness.
   b. Inform management (and perhaps the board of directors) and make recommendations for improvement.

This chapter so far has explained the purposes, definitions, phases of work and audit plan implications of the study and evaluation of internal accounting control. The remainder of the chapter explains the characteristics and objectives of control systems.

RELIABLE INTERNAL CONTROL SYSTEMS

Characteristics of reliable internal control systems are:

1. Personnel of a quality commensurate with their responsibilities.
2. A plan of organization which provides appropriate segregation of functional responsibilities.
3. A system of authorization, objectives and procedures, and supervision adequate to provide accounting control over assets, liabilities, revenue and expenses.
4. Control over access to assets and over access to important documents and blank forms.
5. Periodic comparison of records with actual assets and liabilities and action to correct differences.

Quality of Personnel

The most important feature of control is the people who make the system work. Auditors have very limited means for discovering whether a client's personnel are *competent.* Auditors do not administer intelligence tests, dexterity tests or knowledge exams to determine directly whether personnel possess a degree of competence commensurate with their responsibilities. Perhaps the best that can be said is auditors generally can identify the very capable people and the very incapable people. Unfortunately, these two extremes occur with too little frequency to be of much practical help in audits. The next best means of assessing competence is to observe and audit the output generated by the people. Their output is direct evidence of their work and indirect evidence of their abilities.

A company's personnel problems sometimes create internal accounting control problems. High turnover in accounting jobs means that inexperienced people are doing the accounting and control tasks. Inexperienced people generally make more mistakes than experienced people. New accounting officers and managers (financial vice president, controller, chief accountant, plant accountant, data processing manager) may not be familiar enough with company accounting and may make technical and judgmental errors. Sometimes, accounting officers and employees are fired because they refuse to go along with improper accounting desired by a higher level of management. In general, accounting personnel changes *may* be a warning signal.

Segregation of Responsibilities

A very important characteristic of reliable internal control is an ***appropriate segregation of functional responsibilities***. Sometimes this characteristic is called ***division of duties***. Four kinds of functional responsibilities should be performed by different departments, or at least by different persons on the company's accounting staff:

1. Authorization to execute a transaction. This duty belongs to people who have authority and responsibility for initiating the recordkeeping for transactions. Authorization may be general, referring to a class of transactions (for example, all purchases), or it may be specific (for example, sale of a major asset).
2. Recording of the transaction. This duty refers to the accounting and recordkeeping function (bookkeeping) which, in some organizations, may be delegated partially to a computer system.
3. Custody of assets involved in the transaction. This duty refers to the actual physical possession or effective physical control of property.
4. Periodic reconciliation of existing assets to recorded amounts. This duty refers to the comparison of "recorded accountability for assets" with the existing assets at regular intervals and taking appropriate action with respect to any differences (see SAS 1, AU 320.44).

According to auditing standards, incompatible functions are combinations of functions that place a person alone in a position to perpetuate and conceal errors and irregularities in his or her normal job (SAS 1, AU 320.37). The idea underlying the division of duties characteristic is that no one person should have control of two or more of the functional responsibilities. The first and fourth ones are *management* functions, the second is an *accounting* function, and the third is a *custodial* function. If different departments or persons are forced to deal with these different elements of transactions, then two benefits accrue: (1) perpetration of irregularities is made more difficult because it would require collusion of two or more persons, and most people hesitate to seek the help of others to perpetrate wrongful acts and (2) by acting in a coordinated manner (handling different aspects of the same transaction), innocent errors are more likely to be found and flagged for correction. The latter point is a variation on the cross-check or "two heads are better than one" idea of error detection.

System of Authorization, Objectives and Procedures, and Supervision

The third characteristic of reliable internal control is the most technical one. It contains several important features. Many auditors consider one or all of these features important characteristics of control systems.

Authorization According to Management Criteria. Every management is responsible for establishing, operating, maintaining and improving its control system. Management must establish criteria for *recognizing* transactions in the accounting system and for supervisory *approval* of transactions. A control system should permit accounting to proceed only for authorized transactions and should bar unauthorized transactions.

An authorization may be general and may be delegated to a fairly low level of management. For example, (1) all shipments amounting to more than $1,000 in value require credit approval and (2) all sales can be recorded in the accounting department upon receipt of a copy of a shipping ticket. Some authorizations may be quite tacit. For example, listing the payments received on account when the mail is opened may be sufficient "authorization" to accept and record cash receipts. Some authorizations may be very important and defined specifically by the board of directors. For example, sales of major assets or responsibility for signing the company name to a loan agreement may be authorized specifically in the minutes of the board of directors.

Auditors must be alert to know how each major class of transactions enters the accounting system. Authorization should occur at or near that time, and some system of authorization should exist. Transactions should not enter the accounting system in a haphazard or accidental way.

Objectives and Procedures. As a minimum, a company should have a chart of accounts and some written definitions and instructions about classification of transactions. In larger businesses, such material is incorporated in computer systems documentation, computer program documentation, systems and procedures manuals, flowcharts of transaction processing, and various paper forms. A company's internal auditors and systems staff often review and evaluate this documentation. Independent auditors may review and study this work instead of doing the same tasks over again.

Accounting manuals and other such documentation should contain statements of control objectives, policies and procedures. Management should approve statements of specific control objectives and assure that appropriate procedures are used to accomplish them. Control objectives can be detailed and specific. For your purposes, however, they can be generalized in the seven categories shown in Exhibit 7–6.

Each of these objectives is accomplished by using one or more control procedures. (You should be careful not to confuse the **client's control procedures** for achieving control objectives with an **auditor's compliance procedures** for obtaining evidence about control performance.) The client's control procedures are related closely to the specific objectives illustrated in Exhibit 7–6.

Validity refers to control designed to ensure that *recorded* transactions are ones that *should* have been recorded. The client's procedure can be to require matching of shipping documents with sales invoices before a sale is recorded. This procedure is supposed to prevent the recording of undocumented (possibly fictitious) sales.

EXHIBIT 7–6
Internal Accounting
Control Objectives

Category	General Objective	Example of Specific Objective (Accounts Receivable/Sales)
Validity.	Recorded transactions are valid and documented.	Recorded sales are supported by invoices and shipping documents.
Completeness.	All valid transactions are recorded, and none are omitted.	All shipping documents are prenumbered and matched with sales invoices daily.
Authorization.	Transactions are authorized according to company policy.	Credit sales over $1,000 are given prior approval by the credit manager.
Accuracy.	Transaction dollar amounts are properly calculated.	Sales invoices contain correct quantities and prices and are mathematically correct.
Classification.	Transactions are properly classified in the accounts.	Sales to subsidiaries and affiliates are classified as intercompany transactions.
Accounting.	Transaction accounting is complete.	All sales on credit are charged to customers' individual accounts.
Proper period.	Transactions are recorded in the proper period.	Sales of the current period are charged to customers in the current period, and sales of the next period are charged in the next period.

Completeness refers to control designed to ensure that valid transactions are *not omitted* from the accounting records. If sales are represented by shipments, then no shipping documents should be left unmatched. A requirement of periodic accounting for the number sequence of *prenumbered* shipping documents is a control procedure designed to achieve the completeness objective. A *completeness error* refers to *full omission* of a transaction.

Authorization refers to control intended to ensure that transactions are approved before they are recorded. Credit approval for a sale transaction is an example. Sometimes, you may need to ponder the nature of authorization for some transactions. For example, what "authorization" is needed to record a cash receipt? Usually none—companies are happy to accept payments—but a sales manager may need to approve a good customer taking a discount after the discount period has elapsed.

Accuracy refers to control designed to ensure that dollar amounts are figured correctly. A manual or computer check for billing the same quantity shipped, at the correct list (or approved) price, with correct multiplication and addition of the total, is intended to control for accuracy. (This objective, rather than the completeness one, covers errors of billing at too low a price or for a smaller quantity than shipped.)

Classification refers to control intended to ensure that transactions are recorded in the right accounts, charged or credited to the right customers (including classification of sales to subsidiaries and affiliates, as mentioned in Exhibit 7–6), entered in the correct segment product line or inventory description, and so forth. *Classification* might be confused with *accuracy,* but remember that accuracy refers to the accounting numbers.

Accounting is a general category encompassing control designed to ensure that the accounting process for a transaction is completely performed and in conformity with GAAP. For example, a clerk can balance the total of customers' receivables with the control account to determine whether all charges and credits to the control account have also been entered in individual customers' accounts. (*Classification* is the control over whether the entries got into the right customers' accounts, and *accuracy* is the control category related to use of correct numbers.) Control over *accounting,* in general, is a useful category if you cannot identify a control problem in one of the other categories.

Proper period means control over accounting for transactions in the period in which they occur. This control objective is very closely related to the *cutoff* aspect of the *existence* and *completeness* assertions discussed in Chapter 6. Procedurally, the client's accountants must be alert to the dates of transactions in relation to month-, quarter- and year-end.

Clients use numerous control procedures, and altogether these procedures constitute the heart of the technical control system. Each of these control objectives could be stated in the negative, for example: *Authorization*— ''Unauthorized transactions shall not be recorded.'' Viewed in this way, one can see that a *deviation* (an auditor's term for an *error*) from a policy could arise when the related control procedure is not followed. Thus, each category of objectives also has a related deviation that can result from: (1) failure to specify adequate procedures or (2) failure to perform specified procedures.

Supervision.   You can readily imagine a client's management of clerks and computers to carry out the accounting and control tasks. Equally important is management's provision for supervision of the work of clerks and data processing equipment. A supervisor could, for example, oversee the credit manager's performance or could periodically compare the sum of customers' balances to the accounts receivable control account total. Supervisors or department heads can correct errors found by the clerical staff and make or approve accounting decisions. Supervision is important as a means of monitoring and maintaining management's system of internal accounting control.

Controlled Access   Physical access to assets and important records, documents and blank forms should be limited to authorized personnel. Assets such as inventory and securities should not be available to persons who have no need to handle them. Likewise, access to cost records and accounts receivable records should be denied to people who do not have a recordkeeping responsibility for them.

Some blank forms are very important for accounting and control, and their availability should be restricted. Someone not involved in accounting for sales should not be able to pick up blank sales invoices and blank shipping orders. A person should not be able to obtain blank checks (including computer-paper blank checks) unless he or she is involved in cash disbursement activities. Sometimes, access to blank forms is the equivalent of access to, or custody of, an important asset. For example, someone who has access to blank checks has a measure of actual custody and access to cash.

Controlling access to assets and documents is one way to prevent errors and irregularities. As a practical matter, this feature is closely related to the segregation of functional responsibilities. It speaks to the point of keeping the ways and means of causing errors or perpetrating irregularities out of the hands of unauthorized persons.

Periodic Comparison   Management has responsibility for the *recorded accountability* for assets and liabilities. Managements should provide for periodic comparison of the recorded amounts with independent evidence of existence and valuation. Internal auditors can perform periodic comparison on a regular basis, as can other persons on an accounting staff. However, the people who perform these periodic comparisons should not also have responsibility for authorization of related transactions, accounting or recordkeeping, or custodial responsibility for the assets.

Periodic comparisons may include counts of cash on hand, reconciliation of bank statements, counts of securities, confirmation of accounts receivable and accounts payable, and other such comparison operations undertaken to determine whether accounting records—the *recorded accountability*—represent real assets and liabilities. A management that performs frequent periodic comparisons has more opportunities to detect errors in the records than a management that does not. The frequency, of course, is governed by the costs and benefits. One should not try to count, compare or confirm assets with great frequency (say, weekly) unless they are especially susceptible to loss or error or unless they are unusually valuable.

Subsequent action to correct differences is also important. Periodic comparison and action to correct errors lowers the risk that material errors remain in the accounts. Such comparisons should be a normally assigned function of internal auditors and other employees.[4]

---

[4] Alderman and Deitrick have described how companies with active internal auditors have fewer financial statement adjustments recommended by independent auditors than companies without active internal auditors. See "Internal Audit Impact of Financial Information Reliability," *The Internal Auditor,* April 1981, pp. 43–56.

INTERNAL CONTROL IN SMALL BUSINESS

The foregoing explanations of internal control characteristics and features contain an underlying thread of bureaucratic organization theory and a large-business orientation. A company must be large and employ several people (about 10 or more) to have a theoretically appropriate segregation of functional responsibilities and its accompanying high degree of specialization of work. Supervision requires people. The paperwork necessary in most business systems is extensive. Control theory also suggests that people perform in accounting and control *roles* and do not engage in frequent personal interaction across functional responsibility boundaries. None of these theoretical dimensions fit small business very well.

Auditors should be careful to recognize the bureaucratic, large-business orientation of internal control theory. When the business under audit is small, some allowances must be made for size, the number of people employed, and the control attitude expressed by important managers and owners.

The key person in internal control in a small business is the owner-manager. Because the business is small, it does not exhibit the complexity that creates demand for elaborate internal control. A diligent owner-manager may be able to oversee and supervise all the important authorization, recordkeeping, and custodial functions. He or she may also be able to assure satisfactory data processing accuracy. Thus, an auditor evaluating internal accounting control will study the extent of the owner-manager's involvement in the operation of the information system and evaluate the owner-manager's competence and integrity. This latter task emphasizes the importance of the "competent personnel" quality characteristic of internal control theory. Internal control questionnaires designed specifically for small businesses contain more items related to the owner-manager and other key personnel than the large-business questionnaire shown in Exhibit 7–2.

As a small business begins to grow from, say, four people to 10 or 15, the transition to more formalized internal control tends to lag behind. The owner-manager may become overburdened with control duties and may tacitly delegate these to others. The intermediate-size stage represents a turning point where both owner-manager and auditor need to be very careful. At this point, measures such as limited specialization and surety bonding of employees may help make the transition, and an auditor may offer many suggestions to the owner-manager as an added service.

REPORTING ON INTERNAL CONTROL

Auditing standards for reporting on internal control have existed in the official literature since 1971. The social-political events that led to the Foreign Corrupt Practices Act of 1977 and a favorable recommendation made by the Commission on Auditors' Responsibilities (1978) both led to greater interest in internal control reports. Managers and boards of directors have been encouraged to make their own reports on internal accounting control, and auditors have been encouraged by the SEC to become associated with such public reports.[5] Even so, public reports on internal accounting control are not commonplace.[6]

Public and Restricted Reports

The heightened interest in such reports prompted the Auditing Standards Board to review existing auditing standards. As a consequence, SAS 30, "Reporting on Internal Accounting Control" (AU 642), was issued in 1980. This standard contains guidance for the following:

☐ Public reports on control in effect as of a specific date.

☐ Public reports on control in effect during a specified period of time.

☐ Reports for restricted use based on the study and evaluation of control conducted as a part of an audit.

☐ Reports for restricted use based on criteria established by regulatory agencies.

☐ Special purpose reports for restricted use, based on a review without tests of compliance or based on application of limited agreed-upon procedures.

The standard report on internal accounting control based on a special study is shown in Chapter 1 (Exhibit 1–1). Reports based on the study and evaluation conducted as a part of an audit, and not specifically for the purpose of rendering a report on the entire control system, should contain a scope paragraph explanation that the scope of work was limited. The conclusions paragraph should contain a disclaimer of opinion on the control system taken as a whole. However, negative assurance can be given about material weakness conditions, and additional paragraphs should disclose any known material weaknesses (SAS 30, AU 642.49–53).

The report content in these two engagement situations may be summarized and compared as follows:

---

[5] In 1980, the SEC expressed the belief that managements' comments in its own report on controls were "other information" (see SAS 8, AU 550) and that auditors had a responsibility to disclose any material weaknesses management did not disclose. This event prompted the Auditing Standards Board to issue an interpretation (AU 9550) stating that auditors are responsible for seeing whether a management report contains a material misstatement of fact or fails to be complete insofar as known material weaknesses in internal accounting control are concerned. In 1983, the SEC expressed satisfaction with managements' tendency toward volunteering reports on internal accounting control and decided not to require such reports. At the same time, the SEC dropped its consideration of requiring some form of auditor association with management's comments on control. At the time, the SEC was in a "deregulation mode" and loath to enact new requirements.

[6] Internal control reports by independent auditors have appeared in some bank financial statements and are required by certain government agencies and by the SEC with regard to controls of brokers over securities held for customers. See D. R. Carmichael, "Opinions on Internal Control," *Journal of Accountancy*, December 1970, pp. 47–53.

Special Control Report Engagement	**Report Based on Audit Work**
1. Scope paragraph description of the engagement.	1. Scope paragraph description of limitation on study and evaluation performed for purpose of audit.
2. Date to which the opinion relates.	2. Date to which the audit report relates.
3. Statement about management responsibility for the system.	3. Same statement.
4. Statement about broad objectives and inherent limitations of internal accounting control.	4. Same statement.
5. Opinion on the system taken as a whole.	5a. Disclaimer of opinion on system taken as a whole.
	5b. Negative assurance about material weakness.
	6. Statement restricting use of the report to management, a specific regulatory agency, or other specified third party.

When reporting to a regulatory agency, reports modeled on the two forms compared above may be acceptable. If not, a special report can be issued that, among other things, states the accountant's conclusions based on the agency's criteria and restricts use of the report to the agency (SAS 30, AU 642.56). Such reports most often are requested in connection with audits of government grant-holding agencies.

Other special-purpose reports on control systems can be issued, but their scope is generally limited. Such reports should: (*a*) describe the scope of the engagement, (*b*) disclaim an opinion on the system as a whole, (*c*) state the accountant's findings, and (*d*) restrict the report to management or specified third parties (SAS 30, AU 642.61).

Special Reports: Service Organizations

Occasionally, some clients' transactions are handled by a *service organization*—another business that executes and/or records transactions on behalf of the client. Examples of service organizations include: data processing service centers, trust departments of banks, insurers that maintain the accounting records for ceded insurance (reinsurance transactions), mortgage bankers and savings and loan associations that service loans for owners, and transfer agents that handle the shareholder accounting for mutual and money market investment funds. An auditor may need information about the service organization's control over their mutual client's transactions. However, the auditor may not have access to do the work when the service organization is not an audit client. This situation is described in Exhibit 7–7.

In such situations, all the parties concerned—the user auditor and his client organization, and the service auditor and his client (the service organization)—cooperate to try to enable the user auditor to obtain

EXHIBIT 7–7
Special Reports: Service Organization Controls

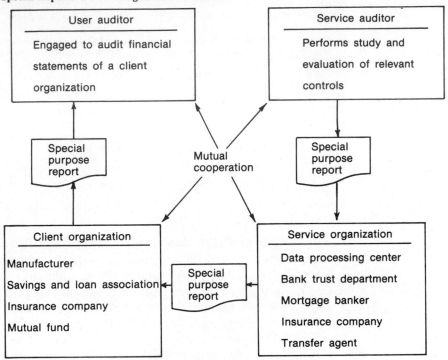

enough information about controls that affect the audit client's transactions. Certain *special-purpose reports on internal accounting control* (described more fully in SAS 44, AU 324) can be relied upon by the user auditor in connection with his study and evaluation of internal accounting controls of the client organization. The reports provide opinions about the service organization's controls as they are applied to the client organization's transactions. Ordinarily, service auditors' reports are not public reports on internal controls. They are used mainly by other auditors.

Conclusion   The auditing standards on conducting engagements and issuing reports on internal accounting control (SAS 30, AU 642 and SAS 44, AU 324) deal with reports that can be used outside the client entity, either publicly or in a restricted distribution. You should be careful not to confuse these reports with the auditors' required communication of material weakness in internal control (SAS 20, AU 323), which is an internal report by a company's auditor to its management and board of directors or audit committee.

SOURCES AND ADDITIONAL READING REFERENCES

Anderson, D. T., H. I. Dycus, and R. B. Welker. "GAAS and the Small Business Audit." *CPA Journal,* April 1982, pp. 10–23.

Brumfield, C. A., R. K. Elliott, and P. D. Jacobson. "Business Risk on the Audit Process." *Journal of Accountancy,* April 1983, pp. 60–68.

Carmichael, D. R. "Behavioral Hypotheses of Internal Control." *Accounting Review,* April 1970, pp. 235–45.

Cohen, G. D., and D. B. Pearson. "Auditing the Client's Judgments." *Journal of Accountancy,* May 1981, pp. 58–64.

Cushing, Barry E. "A Mathematical Approach to the Analysis of Design of Internal Control Systems." *Accounting Review,* January 1974, pp. 24–41.

"Flowchart Symbols and Their Usage in Information Processing." American National Standards Institute, Inc., 1971.

Grollman, W. K., and R. W. Colby. "Internal Control for Small Business." *Journal of Accountancy,* December 1978, pp. 64–67.

A Guide for Studying and Evaluating Internal Accounting Controls. Chicago: Arthur Andersen & Co., 1978.

Konrath, Larry F. "The CPA's Risk in Evaluating Internal Control." *Journal of Accountancy,* October 1971, pp. 53–56.

Loebbecke, J. K., and G. R. Zuber. "Evaluating Internal Control." *Journal of Accountancy,* February 1980, pp. 49–57.

Mautz, R. K., and Donald L. Mini. "Internal Control Evaluation and Audit Program Modification." *Accounting Review,* April 1966, pp. 283–91.

Mock, T. J. and J. L. Turner. *Internal Accounting Control Evaluation and Auditor Judgment.* Auditing Research Monograph No. 3. New York: AICPA, 1981.

Mock, T. J., and J. J. Willingham. "An Improved Method of Documenting and Evaluating a System of Internal Accounting Controls." *Auditing: A Journal of Practice & Theory,* Spring 1983, pp. 91–99.

Morris, W., and H. Anderson. "Audit Scope Adjustment for Internal Control." *CPA Journal,* July 1976, pp. 15–20.

Raiborn, D. D. *Audit Problems Encountered in Small Business Engagements.* Auditing Research Monograph No. 5. New York: AICPA, 1982.

Rea, Richard C. "A Small Business Internal Control Questionnaire." *Journal of Accountancy,* July 1978, pp. 53–54.

Rennie, Robert. "Flow Charts for Audit Purposes." *The Quarterly,* (Touche Ross & Co., March 1965), pp. 13–22.

Serlin, Jerry E. "Amendment of Auditors' Study and Evaluation of Internal Control." *Journal of Accounting, Auditing and Finance,* Summer 1983, pp. 358–64.

REVIEW QUESTIONS

7.1. What are the differences between an *accounting system* and an *internal accounting control* system?

7.2. What are the primary and secondary reasons for conducting a proper study and evaluation of an audit client's existing system of internal accounting control?

7.3. What is a *substantive audit procedure?* Define and explain the *nature, timing* and *extent* features of substantive audit procedures in general.

7.4. In concept, what is a *material weakness in internal accounting control?*

7.5. What distinction can be made between *administrative control* and *accounting control?*

7.6. Must a preliminary review phase of a proper study and evaluation of internal accounting control always be followed by the completion and compliance audit phases? Explain.

7.7. What are the advantages and disadvantages of documenting internal accounting control by using: (1) an internal control questionnaire, (2) a narrative memorandum, and (3) a flowchart?

7.8. What are the general guides for preparing system flowcharts? Discuss them.

7.9. What, in general, is a *compliance procedure?* A *substantive procedure?* A *dual-purpose procedure?*

7.10. What associations can be shown connecting the two *broad objectives* of internal accounting control (safeguarding assets and enhancing the reliability of financial records), the four *operative objectives* (refer to AU320.28), and the *characteristics of reliable internal control systems* including the seven *categories* of general internal accounting control *objectives* (refer to Exhibit 7–6)? Hint: Prepare a memorandum with three columns, the leftmost listing the two broad objectives, opposite each of them the *operative objectives* most closely related, and in the rightmost column the *control characteristics* and general *objectives categories* most closely related to each of the operative objectives.

7.11. Is the general theory of internal control embodied in the basic characteristics of reliable internal control systems equally applicable to large and small enterprises? Discuss.

7.12. What three kinds of engagements can produce an auditor's written report on internal accounting control intended for external use? Describe the reports in general terms.

EXERCISES AND PROBLEMS

Problem 7.13 is a comprehensive internal control study and evaluation exercise. The solutions are given as exhibits in the chapter. The narrative fact situation should be studied and related to the exhibits, so you can obtain some familiarity with the process of translating a description of a system into working paper documentation.

7.13. **Comprehensive Study and Evaluation Description**
The Kingston Company operates as a regional wholesale distributor of small home

appliances. The company ships electric toothbrushes, carving knives, can openers and many other items to large and small retail outlets in a six-state area. The sales order, billing and shipping procedures are standardized for efficient operation and have been described by the controller and observed by the senior accountant on the audit as follows:

1. *Sales order department and credit department:* Customer orders are received

in the mail and over the telephone by sales order clerks, who review the order requests. The clerks show the orders to the credit department supervisor, giving estimates of the amounts, and approval for credit is written on the order. If credit is not approved, a customer is requested to forward a 75 percent advance payment before shipment. After credit approval is obtained, or a payment received, a four-copy sales invoice is prepared. Copy 1 (customer copy) and Copy 2 (billing copy) are sent to the billing department. Copy 4 (packing list copy) is sent directly to the shipping department where it is held pending movement of goods out of inventory. Copy 3 (shipping copy) is sent to the finished-goods warehouse location.

2. *Finished goods warehouse:* Products are removed from shelves and bins only upon receipt of invoice Copy 3. It is the authorization for personnel to gather the order and move it to the shipping department where it will be packed properly. Copy 3 is attached to the goods as they are sent to shipping.

3. *Shipping department:* When the products are received for packing, invoice Copy 4 is taken from the pending file and quantities actually shipped are entered on Copies 3 and 4. A prenumbered bill of lading is filled out in two copies for shipments by common carrier truckers. Copy 2 of the bill of lading and invoice Copy 4 are packed with the shipment. Invoice Copy 3 is transmitted to the billing department. Bill of lading Copy 1 is filed numerically in the shipping department.

4. *Billing department:* When invoice Copy 3 is received, Copies 1 and 2 are taken from an orders-in-process file, and unit prices, according to a current price list, are entered. The invoice is compared to the original customer order and invoice Copy 3 and all the arithmetic is com-

pleted. Invoice Copy 1 is mailed to the customer. The customer order and invoice Copy 2 are stapled together, and a daily batch is accumulated, for which the billing clerks obtain control totals for number of invoices, a hash total of invoice numbers, and a batch total of sales dollar amounts. Copy 3 of sales invoices corresponding to the batch are filed chronologically with the control totals attached. The prenumbered numerical sequence of invoices is not checked because invoices seldom come from shipping in the sequence they were prepared by the sales order department. The daily batches are forwarded to the keypunch department for card and input preparation.

5. *Keypunch and data processing:* Keypunch operators prepare data cards with relevant dates, customer code numbers, shipping document data, quantities, and prices. Computer operator personnel then take the cards and perform the daily sales analysis and accounts receivable updating runs. The customer order and invoice Copy 2 are sent to the accounts receivable department and filed in sales invoice numerical order. Sales analyses and accounts receivable detail reports are transmitted to marketing managers and accounts receivable accounting clerks, respectively. (The general accounting office also receives summary reports for general ledger bookkeeping purposes. The accounts receivable department periodically analyzes the accounts for an aged trial balance and mails monthly statements.)

Required:

To perform a proper study and evaluation of internal accounting controls, an auditor must first review the system, then perform compliance tests to determine whether the system actually operates effectively.

a. Design an internal control questionnaire for the sales and accounts receivable information processing subsystem. (See Exhibit 7–2 in the text.)

b. Construct a flowchart to describe the internal accounting control over sales and accounts receivable transactions. (See Exhibit 7–4 in the text.)

7.14. Costs and Benefits of Control

The following questions and cases deal with the subject of cost-benefit analysis of internal accounting control. Some important concepts in cost-benefit analysis are:

1. *Measurable benefit.* Benefits or cost savings may be measured directly or may be based on estimates of expected value. An *expected loss* is an estimate of the amount of a probable loss multiplied by the frequency or probability of the loss-causing event. A measurable benefit can arise from the reduction of an expected loss.

2. *Qualitative benefit.* Some gains or cost savings may not be measurable, such as company public image, reputation for regulatory compliance, and customer satisfaction.

3. *Measurable costs.* Controls may have direct costs such as wages and equipment expenses.

4. *Qualitative cost factors.* Some costs may be indirect, such as lower employee morale created by overcontrolled work restrictions.

5. *Marginal analysis.* Each successive control feature may have marginal cost and benefit effects on the control problem.

Case A:

Porterhouse Company has numerous bank accounts. Why might management hesitate to spend $10,000 (half of a clerical salary) to assign someone the responsibility of reconciling each account every month for the purpose of catching the banks' accounting errors? Do other good reasons exist to justify spending $10,000 each year to reconcile bank accounts monthly?

Case B:

Harper Hoe Company keeps a large inventory of hardware products in a warehouse. Last year, $500,000 was lost to thieves who broke in through windows and doors. Josh Harper figures that installing steel doors with special locks and burglar bars on the windows at a cost of $25,000 would eliminate 90 percent of the loss. Hiring armed guards to patrol the building 16 hours a day at a current annual cost of $75,000 would eliminate all the loss, according to officials of the Holmes Security Agency. Should Josh arrange for one, both or neither of the control measures?

Case C:

The Merry Mound Cafeteria formerly collected from each customer as he or she reached the end of the food line. A cashier, seated at a cash register, rang up the amount (displayed on a digital screen) and collected the money. Management changed the system, and now a clerk at the end of the line operates an adding machine and gives each customer a paper tape. The adding machine accumulates a running total internally. The customer presents the tape at the cash register on the way out and pays.

The cafeteria manager justified the direct cost of $10,000 annually for the additional salary and $500 for the new adding machine by pointing out that he could serve four more people each weekday (Monday through Friday) and 10 more people on Saturday and Sunday. The food line now moves faster and customers are more satisfied. (The average meal tab is $6, and total costs of food and service are considered fixed.) "Besides," he said, "my internal accounting control is better." Evaluate the manager's assertions.

Case D:

Assume, in the Merry Mound situation cited above, that the better control of separating cash custody from the end-of-food line recording function was not cost-beneficial, even after taking all measurable benefits into consideration. As an auditor, you believe the cash collection system deficiency is a material weakness in internal accounting control, and you have written it as such in your report on internal control, which Merry Mound's central administration engaged you to deliver. The local manager insists on inserting his own opinion on the cost-benefit analysis in the preface to the document that contains your opinion on the internal accounting control system. Should you, in your report, express any opinion or evaluation on the manager's statement?

7.15. **Control Characteristics**

The following four short cases represent separate fact situations bearing on internal controls under specific conditions.

a. Suppose you find during a review of internal accounting control procedures that the client's clerks responsible for accounting for construction contract costs were: (1) all hired within the last six weeks, (2) not trained in accounting methods used by the company, and (3) had no previous accounting employment. What effect would this knowledge have on your evaluation of the existing system of internal control and your substantive auditing procedures related to construction costs?

b. The warehouse inventory of your client consists of CB radios, audio accessories, batteries, cables and antennae. The warehouse is located three blocks from the company's retail store outlet. It is a wood frame building, and items are stored on open shelves. There is no permanent staff at the warehouse, but employees go there almost every two hours to remove items upon customers' requests. Each night, the main door is carefully locked by the watchman who patrols the retail store area. Do the physical safeguards over this inventory appear to be adequate?

c. Marketable securities owned by the client are kept locked in the treasurer's desk drawer. The treasurer instituted this practice seven years ago. He has been with the company for 10 years and works so diligently that he never has had time for a vacation. Do these circumstances suggest any possibility that errors or irregularities may have occurred?

d. The client has experienced several instances of having paid a vendor's invoice twice. The errors become known when vendors' monthly statements show both payments for one charge. What may have happened, and what control procedure appears to be absent?

7.16. **Cash Receipts Control**

Sally's Craft Corner was opened in 1979 by Sally Moore, a fashion designer employed by Bundy's Department Store. Sally is employed full-time at Bundy's and travels frequently to shows and marts in New York and San Francisco. She enjoys crafts, wanted a business of her own, and saw an opportunity in Billmore, Colorado, a city with a population of about 100,000. The Corner now sells regularly to about 300 customers, but business only began to pick up in 1983. The staff presently includes two sales people and four office personnel, and Sally herself helps out on weekends.

Sales have grown, as has the Corner's reputation for quality crafts. The history is as follows:

	Sales	Discounts and Allowances	Net Sales
1979	$16,495	$ 500	$15,995
1980	18,575	550	18,025
1981	17,610	520	17,090
1982	18,380	570	17,810
1983	23,950	950	23,000
1984	29,470	1,480	27,990
1985	37,230	2,230	35,000

With an expanding business and a need for inventory, the Corner is now cash poor. Prices are getting higher every month, and Sally is a little worried. The net cash flow is only about $400 per month after allowance of a 3 percent discount for timely payments on account. So she has engaged you as auditor and asks for any recommendations you might have about the cash flow situation. The Corner has never been audited before.

During your preliminary review of internal accounting control, you have learned the following about the four office personnel:

Janet Bundy is the receptionist and also helps customers. She is the daughter of the Bundy Department Store owner and a long-time friend of Sally's and helped her start the Corner. They run around together when Sally is in town. She opens all the mail, answers most of it herself, but turns over payments on account to Sue Kenmore.

Sue Kenmore recently graduated from high school and started working as a bookkeeper-secretary at the Corner in 1983. She wants to go to college but cannot afford it right now. She is very quiet in the office, but you have noticed she has some fun with her friends in her new Porsche. In the office, she gets the mailed-in payments on account from Janet, takes payments over the counter in the store, checks the calculation of discounts allowed, enters the cash collections in the cash receipts journal, prepares a weekly bank deposit (and mails it), and prepares a list (remittance list) of the payments on account. The list shows amounts received from each customer, discount allowed, and amount to be credited to customer's account. She is also responsible for approving the discounts and credits for merchandise returned.

Ken Murphy has been the bookkeeper-clerk since 1979. He also handles other duties, among them: He receives the remittance list from Sue, posts the customers' accounts in the subsidiary ledger, and gives the remittance list to David Roberts. Ken also prepares and mails customers' monthly statements. Ken is rather dull, interested mostly in hunting on weekends, but is a steady worker. He always comes to work in a beat-up pickup truck—an eyesore in the parking lot.

David Roberts is the bookkeeping super-visor. He started work in 1980 after giving up his small practice as a CPA. He posts the general ledger (using the remittance list as a basis for the cash received entries) and prepares monthly financial statements. He also approves and makes all other general ledger entries and reconciles the monthly bank statement. He reconciles the customer subsidiary records to the accounts receivable control account each month. David is very happy not to have to contend with the pressures he experienced in his practice as a CPA.

Required:

a.   Draw a simple flowchart of the cash collection and bookkeeping procedures.

b.   Identify any material weakness in internal accounting control. Explain any reasons why you might suspect that errors or irregularities may have occurred.

c.   Recommend corrective measures you believe necessary and efficient in this business.

7.17.   **Compliance Procedure Specifications**
In order to conduct a compliance audit of a client's internal accounting control procedures, auditors design a ***compliance audit program.*** This audit program is a list of compliance procedures to be performed, and each is directly related to an important client control procedure. Auditors perform the compliance procedures in order to obtain evidence about the actual performance of the controls.

The controls listed below relate to a system for processing sales transactions. (The descriptions are based on the fact situation in Problem 7.13, so you may want to read it again.) Each item below leads you along the path of the "logical approach" of internal control evaluation by indicating an error or irregularity that could occur and by specifying a control procedure that could prevent or detect it. You are to write the audit program of compliance procedures by specifying the one best compliance procedure that would produce evidence about the client's performance of the control procedure. You are also required to identify the control objective (see Exhibit 7–6) satisfied by the client's control procedure. Remember: A compliance procedure is a two-part statement consisting of: (1) identification of a data population from which a sample can be drawn and (2) expression of an action to take.

a. The company wants to avoid the practice of selling goods on credit to bad credit risks. Poor credit control eventually could create problems with estimating the allowance for bad debts and create a potential error by overstating the realizable value of accounts receivable. Therefore, the control procedure is: Each customer order is to be reviewed and approved for 30-day credit by the credit department supervisor. The supervisor then notes the decision on the customer order, which is eventually attached to Copy 2 of the sales invoice and filed by date in the accounts receivable department. (Even though the sales invoices are prenumbered, they are entered chronologically in the sales journal because orders are not always shipped in sales invoice numerical order.) The company used sales invoices numbered 20,001 through 30,000 during the period under review.

b. The company considers sales transactions complete when shipment is made. The control procedures are: Shipping department personnel prepare shipping documents in duplicate (sending one copy to the customer and filing the other copy in numerical order in the shipping department file). The shipping clerk marks up Copy 3 of the invoice indicating the quantity shipped, the date and the shipping document number and sends it to the billing department where it is taken as authorization to complete the sales recording. Copy 3 is then filed in a daily batch in the billing department file. These procedures are designed to prevent the recording of sales: (1) for which no shipment is made or (2) before the date of shipment.

c. The company wants to control unit pricing and mathematical errors that could result in overcharging or undercharging customers, thus producing the errors of overstatement or understatement of sales revenue and accounts receivable. The accounting procedures are: Billing clerks use a catalog list price to price the shipment on invoice Copies 1, 2 and 3. They compute the dollar amount of the invoice. Copy 1 is sent to the customer. Copy 2 is used to record the sale and later is filed in the accounts receivable department by date. Copy 3 is filed in the billing department by date.

d. The company needs to classify sales to subsidiaries apart from other sales so the consolidated financial statement eliminations will be accurate. That is, the company wants to avoid the error of understating the elimination of intercompany profit and therefore overstating net income and inventory. The control procedure is: A billing supervisor reviews each invoice Copy 2 to see whether the billing clerk imprinted sales to the company's four subsidiaries with a big red "9" (the code for intercompany sales). The supervisor does not initial or sign the invoices.

e. The company wants assurance that all shipments get billed to the customers. The control procedures are: Shipping supervisors are under instructions to make sure that no shipment goes out before shipping documents are prepared. The chief supervisor regularly reviews his pending file of invoice Copy 4, which was sent from the sales order department when the sales invoice was prepared. Any Copy 4 that stays in the file too long is followed up because a shipment may have gone out earlier without all the paperwork being prepared. The chief supervisor has told you that usually the lag is explained because the shipping documents were prepared and Copy 3 was sent to the billing department, but the shipping clerk just forgot to pull Copy 4 and pack it in the shipment. Also, the billing department supervisor reviews her pending file of Copies 1 and 2 (sent to billing at the same time Copy 4 was sent to shipping), and she inquires with the shipping supervisor about old invoices never completed. (The Shipping Department used bills of lading documents in the numerical sequence 70,001 through 80,400 during the period under audit.)

f. The company wants to maintain accurate books and records, especially keeping the accounts receivable subsidiary records balanced with the accounts receivable control account. The control procedure is to check the computer-produced customer accounts each week and check off the sales invoice journal for each invoice properly posted to the

right customer's account. Monthly, the accounts receivable supervisor reconciles the total of the subsidiary records to the control account. Differences are investigated until the two are in balance.

7.18.   **Compliance Procedures and Errors/Irregularities**

The four questions below are taken from the internal control questionnaire in Exhibit 7–2. For each question, state (a) one compliance procedure you could use to find out whether the control technique was really used and (b) what error or irregularity could occur if the question were answered "No," or if you found the control was not effective?

1.   Are blank (sales) invoices available only to authorized personnel?

EXHIBIT 7.19–1 **Internal Control** **Questionnaire—Inventory** **XYZ Company,** **December 31, 19XX**		**Yes**	**No**	**Remarks**
	1. Are purchase orders (PO) authorized by a responsible official?	X		Copy of PO used as Receiving Report?
	2. Is access to the warehouse restricted?	X		Warehouse clerks only.
	3. Are receiving reports (RR) given to the inventory recordkeeper as authority to post additions of materials?	X		Incoming materials inspected, counted, and RR completed.
	4. Does the inventory recordkeeper account for the numerical sequence of receiving reports?		X	
	5. Are issuance orders (IO) authorized by the production staff?	X		IO's are prepared from production orders.
	6. Are issuance orders (IO) given to the inventory recordkeeper as authority to post issuances of materials?	X		Warehouse clerks approve IO's.
	7. Does the inventory recordkeeper account for the numerical sequence of issuance order?		X	
	8. Does a supervisor review for proper inventory posting dates—date of receipt and date of issuance?	X		Control is confirmed by the monthly cycle counts.
	9. Is inventory counted periodically and compared to perpetual records? Differences investigated and corrected?	X		Monthly cycle count by internal auditors. Perpetual records updated.
	10. Describe the inventory valuation method:			

A current file of the three most recent purchases (quantity and unit price) is maintained on the computer. This file is used to price the inventory quantities at FIFO on quarterly and annual reporting dates.

2. Are (sales) invoices checked for the accuracy of quantities billed? Prices used? Mathematical calculations?

3. Are the duties of the accounts receivable bookkeeper separate from any cash functions?

4. Are customer accounts regularly balanced with the control account?

7.19. **Control Procedures and Compliance Procedures**

The objective of this exercise is to help you learn to link concepts and objectives of internal accounting control with the major assertions in financial statements. The actual links are specific audit procedures and the evidence they produce. You should use SAS 1 (AU 320) ''Auditor's Study and Evaluation of Internal Control'' and SAS 31 (AU 326) ''Evidential Matter,'' especially the appendix in SAS 31. The requirements will take you step-by-step through the linking exercise.

The account being audited is a client's inventory of raw materials. It consists of 1,000 different kinds of materials valued at a total FIFO cost of $150 million, which amounts to 20 percent of current assets and 5 percent of total assets. The company maintains detail perpetual inventory records in physical quantities only. Its control procedures are shown in the answers to the questionnaire in Exhibit 7.19–1.

Required:

a. Complete the three-column presentation begun below. For each of the operative control objectives in the left column, associate one or more specific control objectives (authorization, validity, completeness and so forth) in the middle column, and in the third column identify the company's control procedure that most closely relates to each.

b. For each of the first nine control procedures in the questionnaire, specify one compliance audit procedure that will produce the best evidence of the performance of the control. You can assume the existence of necessary document files, and you can use one sample selection to accomplish more than one compliance procedure. (The objective is to determine how accurately the perpetual records are maintained.)

c. The comptroller says the accounts payable clerks are very careful to maintain a price file with the quantities and unit prices of the three most recent purchases. Since this file will be used to determine the FIFO inventory cost for the financial statements, you must determine whether the clerks have really been careful enough. What two compliance audit procedures would provide the best evidence for you to determine whether the file is reasonably up-to-date? (You can assume the price file identifies quantities and unit prices by date and vendor name, and a separate alphabetic accounts payable file contains all the actual vendor invoices received by the company.)

Operative Control Objectives	Specific Control Objectives	Control Procedures (Questionnaire)
Transactions executed according to authorization.	Purchases authorized. Issuances authorized.	1. PO prepared. 3. RR prepared. 5. IO prepared.
Transaction recording permits accounting in conformity with GAAP.		
Access to assets permitted only as authorized.		
Recorded accountability compared with existing assets and differences acted upon.		

d. Most of the compliance audit procedures can also contribute substantive-
purpose evidence, making them *dual-
purpose procedures*. For each of the
first four of the major financial statement assertions (excluding presentation
and disclosure), associate: (1) one or
more of the specific control objectives
identified in requirement (*a*), middle
column, and (2) one or more of the compliance audit procedures specified in
your response to requirement (*b*).

7.20. **Internal Accounting Control Reports**
The president of Taurus Corporation, Clar-
ence Best, has engaged the CPA firm of
Able Associates to perform a special study
of Taurus's internal accounting control system and express an opinion on the system.

Able Associates completed the regular annual audit last month.
Required:
a. Describe: (1) management's responsibility for the internal accounting control
system, (2) the broad objectives of internal accounting control, and (3) the inherent limitations of internal accounting
control systems, as set forth in a report
on internal accounting control.

b. Explain the differences between: (1) the
objectives of the work, (2) the scope of
the work, and (3) the content of the report Able Associates will render in this
engagement in comparison to the objectives, scope, and report content Able
would have observed if the report had
been produced in conjunction with the
regular annual audit.

DISCUSSION CASES

7.21. **"Proper" Study and Evaluation**
The 12 partners of a regional-sized CPA firm
met in special session to discuss audit engagement efficiency. Jones spoke up, saying: "We all certainly appreciate the firm-
wide policies set up by Martin and Smith,
especially in connection with the audits of
the large clients that have come our way
recently. Their experience with a large national firm has helped build up our practice.
But I think the standard policy of conducting reviews and compliance tests of internal
accounting control on all audits is raising
our costs too much. We can't charge our
smaller clients fees for all the time the staff
spends on this work. I would like to propose
that we give engagement partners discretion
to decide whether to do a lot of work on
internal control. I may be an old mossback,
but I think I can finish a competent audit
without it." Discussion on the subject continued but ended when Martin said, with
some emotion: "But we can't disregard generally accepted auditing standards like
Jones proposes!"

What do you think of Jones's proposal
and Martin's view of the issue? Discuss.

7.22. **Starting the "Logical Approach"**
The first thing you are asked to do in a "logical approach" to the study and evaluation of
internal accounting control is to imagine
what types of errors or irregularities could
occur with regard to each significant class of
transactions. Assume a company has the
significant classes of transactions listed below. For each one, identify one or more errors or irregularities that could occur and
specify the accounts that would be affected
if proper controls were not specified or were
not followed satisfactorily.

1. Credit sales transactions.
2. Raw materials purchase transactions.
3. Payroll transactions.
4. Equipment acquisition transactions.
5. Cash receipts transactions.
6. Leasing transactions.
7. Dividend transactions.
8. Investment transactions (short-term).

7.23. **Control Concepts and Definitions**

The Simon Blfpstk Construction Company has two divisions. The president, Simon, manages the roofing division. Simon has delegated authority and responsibility for management of the modular manufacturing division to John Gault. The company has a competent accounting staff and a full-time internal auditor. Unlike Simon, however, Gault and his secretary handle all the bids for manufacturing jobs, purchase all the materials without competitive bids, control the physical inventory of materials, contract for shipping by truck, supervise the construction activity, bill the customer when the job is finished, approve all bid changes, and collect the payment from the customer. With Simon's tacit approval, Gault has asked the internal auditor not to interfere with his busy schedule.

Required:

Discuss this fact situation in terms of internal control and identify *irregularities* that could occur.

7.24. **Preliminary Review**

Sunken Chest, Inc., your audit client, is a wholesaler of diamonds. The business consists entirely of: (1) a purchasing function—diamond buyers operating in several countries under the direction of the vice president for acquisition, (2) a marketing function—salesmen soliciting orders from retailers in the U.S. and Canada under the direction of the vice president for marketing, and (3) a headquarters administration function—receiving, safekeeping, courier and accounting personnel under the direction of the vice-president for administration. J.R. Sunken is president and chairman of the board, and he directs all operations. The company has no internal auditors.

Required:

a. Prepare a simple organization chart. What else would you seek to learn about Sunken Chest, Inc., in your preliminary review of internal accounting control?

b. Identify the types of transactions you think would be important (material) in Sunken Chest's business.

c. Suppose your preliminary audit plan calls for doing accounts receivable confirmation as of Sunken Chest's December 31 year-end date and other related procedures shortly thereafter. The 50 customers have large balances, and you plan to confirm them all. The time budget for this work is 150 hours. The $20 million total accounts receivable is one half of total assets. You have estimated that further evaluation of internal accounting control after your preliminary review on November 30 would take about 50 hours, and you might then be able to reduce the planned year-end confirmation and other work by about 20 hours. Write a memorandum for the working-paper file explaining your decision relating to further work on internal accounting control in these circumstances.

CHAPTER 8

	PROFESSIONAL STANDARDS SOURCES	

Compendium Section	Document Reference	Topic
AU 312	SAS 47	Audit Risk and Materiality in Conducting an Audit
AU 320	SAS 1	Auditor's Study and Evaluation of Internal Control
AU 326	SAS 31	Evidential Matter
AU 350	SAS 39	Audit Sampling
AU 1020	SAS 45	Omnibus 1983: Substantive Tests Prior to the Balance Sheet Date

Audit Sampling and Program Planning

You are now well along the way toward learning how to conduct an audit. You have studied the pre-engagement activities, the planning activities and the process of conducting a proper study and evaluation of internal accounting control. The remaining activities are audit program execution (starting in Chapter 13) and reporting (starting in Chapter 20). This chapter and the next four chapters, however, deal with some auditing methods and other technical considerations important for finalizing an audit program and for carrying out the details of audit program execution.

Application methods are ways and means of planning the details of audit procedures, organizing their performance, and evaluating the evidence they produce. This chapter deals with audit sampling methods and considerations related to audit risk. (*Other technical considerations* concern computer auditing and the mathematical details of statistical sampling, covered in subsequent chapters.) To put these methods and other technical considerations in the context of the principal audit activities, refer to the review of elements of a public accounting audit engagement in Exhibit 8–1. (This Exhibit adds some details to Exhibit 1–2 which you ought to review at this time.)

Your learning objectives with regard to audit sampling are to be able to:

- ☐ Define and explain the many terms unique to audit sampling, including the fundamental technical differences between statistical and nonstatistical sampling.

- ☐ Identify audit work considered audit sampling and distinguish it from work not considered audit sampling.

- ☐ Develop a simple audit plan and program for compliance audit of a client's internal accounting control procedures including:

Specification of objectives, deviation conditions,
populations and sampling units.
Sample size determination and sampling unit selection.

☐ Evaluate compliance audit evidence when given a specific
fact situation.

☐ Develop a simple audit plan and program for audit of an
account balance, including:
Specification of objectives and population definitions.
Sample size determination and sampling unit selection.

☐ Evaluate monetary error evidence when given a specific
fact situation.

☐ Review and evaluate the nature, timing and extent of
procedures in compliance audit and account balance audit
programs and write a simple audit program.

**INTRODUCTION
TO AUDIT
SAMPLING**

Generally accepted auditing standards define *audit sampling* as *the application of an audit procedure to less than 100 percent of the items within
an account balance or class of transactions for the purpose of evaluating
some characteristic of the balance or class* (SAS 39, AU 350.01). In an
earlier chapter, you encountered the sampling idea incorporated in the
explanation of a compliance procedure which was defined as a two-part
statement consisting of: (1) an identification of the data population from
which all items or a sample of items will be selected for audit and (2) an
expression of an action taken to produce relevant evidence. To understand the definition of audit sampling, you must keep the following definitions in mind: *Audit procedure* refers to actions described as general audit
procedures in Chapter 6 (recalculation, physical observation, confirmation, verbal inquiry, vouching, tracing, scanning and analytical review).
An *account balance* refers to a control account made up of many constitu-
ent items, for example, an accounts receivable control account representing the sum of customers' accounts, an inventory control account representing the sum of various goods in inventory, a sales account
representing the sum of many sales invoices, or a long-term debt account
representing the sum of several issues of outstanding bonds. A *class of
transactions* refers to a group of transactions having common characteristics, such as cash receipts and cash disbursements, but which are not
simply added together and presented as an account balance in financial
statements.

Other definitions: A *population* is the set of all the elements that constitute the account balance or class of transactions of interest. Each of the
elements is a *population unit,* and when an auditor selects a sample, each

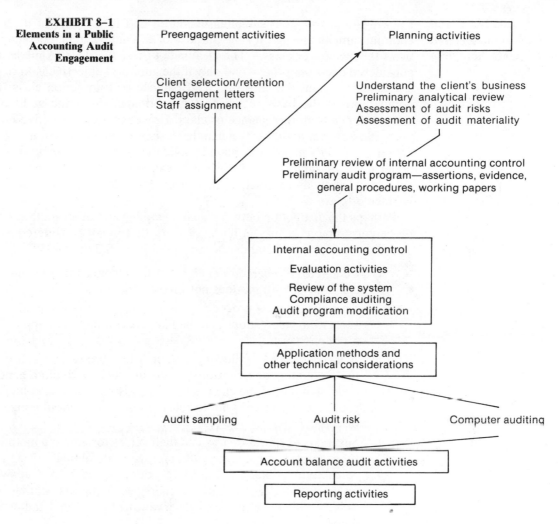

**EXHIBIT 8–1
Elements in a Public
Accounting Audit
Engagement**

Preengagement activities

Client selection/retention
Engagement letters
Staff assignment

Planning activities

Understand the client's business
Preliminary analytical review
Assessment of audit risks
Assessment of audit materiality

Preliminary review of internal accounting control
Preliminary audit program—assertions, evidence,
general procedures, working papers

Internal accounting control

Evaluation activities

Review of the system
Compliance auditing
Audit program modification

Application methods and
other technical considerations

Audit sampling   Audit risk   Computer auditinq

Account balance audit activities

Reporting activities

element selected is called a sampling unit. A *sampling unit* can be a customer's account, an inventory item, a debt issue, a cash receipt, a canceled check and so forth. A *sample* is a set of sampling units.

Sampling and the Extent of Auditing

Three aspects of auditing procedures are important—their nature, timing and extent. *Nature* is best perceived in terms of the description of the seven general procedures. *Timing* is a matter of *when* procedures are performed. More will be said about timing later in this chapter. Audit sampling is concerned primarily with matters of *extent*—the *amount* of work done when the procedures are executed. In the context of auditing standards, *nature and timing* relate most closely to the competence of evidential matter, while *extent* relates most closely to the sufficiency of evidential matter.

Inclusions and Exclusions Related to Audit Sampling

Look again at the audit sampling definition and to the part of it about auditing sampling being "for the purpose of evaluating some characteristic of the balance or class." The meaning of these words is: A method is considered *audit sampling* if and only if the auditors' objective is to reach a conclusion about the entire account balance or transaction class (the population) on the basis of the evidence obtained from the audit of a sample drawn from the balance or class. However, this restrictive interpretation does not necessarily mean that a sample-based procedure application is the *only* means of obtaining evidence about a balance or class under audit. A sample-based procedure can be, and often is, combined with other methods to obtain sufficient evidence for a decision about a balance or class.

Perhaps the distinction between audit sampling and other methods can be perceived more clearly in terms of work that is *not* considered audit sampling subject to the standards expressed in SAS 39 (AU 350).

- ☐ Complete (100 percent) audit of all the elements in a balance or class, by definition, does not involve sampling.
- ☐ Analytical review procedures, in the nature of overall comparisons, ratio calculations and the like, are normally not applied on a sample basis.
- ☐ A *walk-through*—following one or a few transactions through the accounting and control systems in order to obtain a general understanding of the client's systems—is not audit sampling because the objective is not to reach a conclusion about a balance or class.
- ☐ Several procedures do not lend themselves to sampling methods, for example, verbal inquiry of employees, obtaining written representations, obtaining inquiry responses in the form of answers on an internal control questionnaire, scanning accounting records for unusual items, and observation of personnel and procedures.[1]

Why Auditors Sample

Auditors utilize audit sampling when: (1) The nature and materiality of the balance or class does not demand a 100 percent audit; (2) a decision must be made about the balance or class; and (3) the time and cost to audit 100 percent of the population would be too great. So, the response to *why auditors sample* is that they need to perform efficient audits on a timely basis and cannot do so by auditing 100 percent. The two sampling designs used by auditors are *statistical sampling* and *nonstatistical sampling*.

Statistical Sampling

Auditors define *statistical sampling* as *audit sampling that uses the laws of probability for selecting and evaluating a sample from a population for*

---

[1] *Audit Sampling,* Audit and Accounting Guide (AICPA, 1983), pp. 1–3.

the purpose of reaching a conclusion about the population. The essential points of this definition are: (1) A statistical sample is selected at random *and* (2) Statistical calculations are used to measure and express the results. Both conditions are necessary for a method to be considered statistical sampling rather than nonstatistical sampling.

A ***random sample*** is a set of sampling units chosen in such a way that each population item has an *equal likelihood* of being selected in the sample. You can use a random sample in a "nonstatistical sampling" design—provided some method other than statistical calculation is used to express the results. However, you cannot use statistical calculations with a nonrandom sample. The mathematical laws of probability are not applicable for nonrandom samples, and basing such calculations on a nonrandom sample would be wrong.

A statistical calculation of sample size is *not* necessary for a method to be considered statistical sampling. You can use a "magic number"—any sample size you wish. However, a preliminary estimate of sample size can be calculated using statistical models. (More on this subject later in Chapters 11 and 12.) A sampling method is *statistical* by virtue of random selection of the sample coupled with statistical calculation of the results.

Nonstatistical Sampling

A good definition of ***nonstatistical sampling*** is *audit sampling in which auditors do not utilize statistical calculations to express the results.* The sample selection technique can be random sampling or some other selection technique not based on mathematical randomness. Auditors are fond of saying that nonstatistical sampling involves "consideration of sampling risk in evaluating an audit sample without using statistical theory to measure that risk." "Consideration" in this context means "giving sampling risk some thoughtful attention" without direct knowledge or measurement of its magnitude.

Sampling and Nonsampling Risk

Be careful not to confuse sampling and nonsampling risk with statistical and nonstatistical sampling. They are not related. When auditors perform procedures on a sample basis and obtain sufficient evidence, *a conclusion about the population characteristic can still be wrong.* For example, suppose an auditor selected 100 sales invoices for audit and found no errors or irregularities in any of them. The conclusion that a significant incidence of error and irregularities does *not* exist in the entire population of sales invoices from which the sample was drawn might be wrong. How, you say? Simple: The sample might not reflect the actual condition of the population. No matter how randomly or carefully the sample was selected, it might not be a good representation of the extent of errors and irregularities actually in the population.

Sampling risk is defined as *the probability that an auditor's conclusion based on a sample might be different from the conclusion based on an audit of the entire population.* You could audit a sample of sales invoices and decide, based on the sample, that the population of sales invoices contained few errors and irregularities. However, suppose some auditors with more time could audit *all* the sales invoices and find a large number of errors and irregularities. In such a case, your sample-based decision would have been proved wrong. Your sample apparently did not represent the population very well. *Sampling risk* expresses the probability of making a wrong decision based on sample evidence, and *it exists in both statistical and nonstatistical sampling methods*. You cannot escape it in audit sampling. With statistical sampling, you can measure it, and you can control it by auditing sufficiently large samples. With nonstatistical sampling, you can "consider" it without measuring it. However, "considering" sampling risk without measuring it requires experience and expertise. Special aspects of sampling risk are discussed later in the sections on auditing control compliance and account balances.

Nonsampling risk is *all other risk other than sampling risk*. You need to refer to the audit risk model (Chapter 6) to grasp the breadth of this definition:

$$\textbf{\textit{Risk Model:}} \quad AuR = IR \times IC \times DR$$

Nonsampling risk can arise from:

☐ Misjudging the inherent risk (IR). An auditor who mistakenly believes few material errors or irregularities occur in the first place will tend to do less work and therefore the nature, timing and extent of procedures might fail to detect problems.

☐ Misjudging the control risk (IC). An auditor who is too optimistic about the ability of controls to prevent, detect and correct errors and irregularities will tend to do less work, with the same results as misjudging the inherent risk.

☐ Poor choice of procedures and mistakes in execution—related to detection risk (DR). Auditors can select procedures inappropriate for the objective (for example, confirming recorded accounts receivable when the objective is to find unrecorded accounts receivable), can fail to recognize errors or irregularities when vouching supporting documents, or can sign off as having performed procedures when the work actually was not done.

Therefore, nonsampling risk is also the possibility of making a wrong decision. *It exists both in statistical and nonstatistical sampling*. The problem is that nonsampling risk cannot be measured. Auditors control it—and believe it is reduced to a negligible level—through adequate planning and supervision of audit engagements and personnel, by having policies and procedures for quality control of their auditing practices, and by having internal monitoring and external peer review of their own quality control systems.

One other important distinction is important: External critics (judges, juries, peer reviewers) have few grounds for criticizing auditors who fall victim to sampling risk, provided an audit sampling application is planned and executed reasonably well. Auditors are more open to criticism and fault-finding when erroneous decisions result from nonsampling risk.

Sampling Methods and Applications

Audit sampling is a method for executing audit actions. It is concerned mostly with the amount of work performed and the sufficiency of audit evidence obtained. Audit sampling terminology contains many new concepts and definitions. The ones presented above, however, are general and apply to all phases of audit sampling. You need to know them so you can "speak the language."

Auditors design audit sampling to deal with: (1) auditing control compliance and (2) auditing account balances. The next two major sections of this chapter explain these two designs. Each of the sections is organized in terms of: (1) planning, (2) performing and (3) evaluating audit sampling.

This chapter is presented in general terms, avoiding the mathematics of sampling, along the same lines as SAS 39 (AU 350) and the AICPA audit and accounting guide entitled *Auditing Sampling*. If you want to crunch numbers, Chapter 11 (Attribute Sampling) and Chapter 12 (Variables Sampling) should appeal to your technical needs. These two chapters are actually lengthy appendixes to this chapter. Their coverage is limited mostly to technical details. Topics are arranged in parallel order, so if you want more technical details about a particular topic, you can find most of them covered in Chapters 11 and 12.

AUDITING CONTROL COMPLIANCE

Auditors must judge the internal control risk to determine the nature, timing and extent of other audit procedures. Final evaluations of internal control are based on evidence obtained in the review and compliance audit phases of a study and evaluation. (Refer to Chapter 6.) Auditors' judgments of internal control risk are hard to describe because they always depend entirely upon the circumstances in each specific situation. The judgments are usually very specific. For example, an auditor might learn that a company's validity control procedure to prevent recording of fictitious sales is to require the bookkeeper to match a shipping order with each sales invoice before recording a sale—good control, as specified. Now suppose the compliance audit procedure of selecting recorded sales invoices and vouching them to shipping orders shows a number of mistakes (invoices without supporting shipping orders)—poor control as performed. Sales might be overstated. One way to take this control deficiency into account is to perform more extensive work on accounts receivable using confirmation and inquiries and analytical review related to collectibility. (If sales are overstated, one result could be overstatement of receivables.)

This example relates a specific control (the validity-related control procedure of matching sales invoices with shipping orders) to a specific set of other procedures directed toward a possible problem (overstatement of sales and receivables). In a more general sense, auditors reach judgments about control risk along the lines shown in Exhibit 8–2. Some

EXHIBIT 8–2
Auditor's Assessment of Control Risk

Reliance on Internal Control	Judgment Expression of Control Risk	
	Nonquantitative	Quantitative
High: Excellent control, both as specified and in compliance.	Low.	10%–30%
Moderate: Good control, but lacks something in specification or compliance.	Moderate.	20%–70%
Low: Deficient control, either in specification or compliance or both.	High.	60%–100%

situations may call for a nonquantitative expression, and auditors sometimes need a quantitative expression. The quantitative ranges overlap so you will not get the idea that auditors really can put exact numbers on their evaluations.

Audit sampling can be used as a method and plan for conducting the compliance audit procedures. The application of sampling in compliance auditing is a structured, formal approach embodied in seven steps. The seven-step structure helps auditors plan, perform and evaluate compliance audit work. It also helps auditors accomplish an eighth step—careful documentation of the work—by showing each of the seven areas to be described in the working papers. The first seven steps are:

1.   Specify the objectives.
2.   Define the deviation conditions.
3.   Define the population.
4.   Determine the sample size.
5.   Select the sample.
6.   Perform the compliance-purpose procedures.
7.   Evaluate the evidence.

Plan the Procedures   Compliance audit procedures are always directed toward producing evidence of the client's performance of his own control procedures. Thus, auditors' compliance-purpose procedures should produce evidence about the client's achievement of the seven control objectives (described in Chapter 7 as *validity, completeness, authorization, accuracy, classification, accounting and proper period.*)

1. Specify the Objectives. Take a control procedure under the *validity* objective as an example—namely the client's procedure of requiring a shipping order to be matched with a sales invoice before a valid sale is recorded. The specific objective of an auditor's compliance audit procedure would be: *Determine whether recorded sales invoices are supported by matched shipping orders.* The compliance procedure itself would be: *Select a sample of recorded sales invoices and vouch them to supporting shipping orders.*

The matching of sales invoices to shipping orders in the example is a *key control*—it is *important*. Auditors should identify and audit only the key controls. Incidental controls that are not important will not be relied upon and need not be audited for compliance. Auditing them for compliance just wastes time if they really do not have much impact on the control risk evaluation.

2. Define the Deviation Conditions. The terms *deviation, error* and *exception* are synonyms. They all refer to a departure from a prescribed internal accounting control procedure in a particular case, for example, an invoice is recorded with no supporting shipping order. Defining the deviation condition at the outset is important, so the auditors doing the work will know a deviation when they see one. As an assistant accountant, you would prefer to be instructed: "Vouch recorded sales invoices to supporting shipping orders and document cases where the shipping order is missing" instead of "Vouch recorded sales invoices for any mistakes." The latter instruction does not define the deviation condition well enough.

The example we are using is oversimplified. However, this vouching procedure for compliance evidence can be used to obtain evidence about several control objectives at the same time. The invoice can be compared to the shipping order for evidence related to other control objectives: *authorization* (shipping order properly authorized), *accuracy* (sales invoice quantities match the shipping order quantities), *classification* (the type of goods sold is classified in the right product line sales account), and *proper period* (shipment date matches the sales record date).

Time for some more terminology: Compliance audit sampling also is called *attribute sampling*. Attribute sampling is audit sampling in which auditors look for the *presence* or *absence* of a control condition. In response to the audit question: "For each sales invoice in the sample, can a matched shipping order be found?" the answer can be only "Yes" or "No." With this definition, auditors can count the number of deviations and use the count when evaluating the evidence.

3. Define the Population. The specification of compliance audit objectives and the definition of deviation conditions usually define the *population,* which is the set of all elements in the balance or class of transactions. In the example case, the population consists of all the recorded sales invoices, and each invoice is a *population unit*. In *classical attribute sampling,* a *sampling unit* is the same thing as a *population unit*.[2]

Population definition is important because audit conclusions can be made only about the population from which the sample was selected. For example, evidence from a sample of recorded sales invoices (the population for our illustrative procedure) *cannot* be used for a conclusion about *completeness*. Controls related to the completeness objective (in this case, control over failure to invoice goods shipped) can only be audited by sampling from a population representing goods shipped (the shipping order file) and *not* by sampling from the population of recorded invoices.

A complicating factor in population definition is the timing of the audit work. Generally accepted auditing standards advise that compliance audit procedures ideally should be applied to transactions executed throughout the period under audit because auditors want to reach a conclusion about control during the entire period (SAS 1 AU 320.70). However, auditors often perform compliance procedures at an *interim date*—a date some weeks or months before the client's year-end date—and at that time the entire population (say, recorded sales invoices for the year) will not be available for audit. Nothing is wrong with doing the work at an interim date, but auditors still cannot ignore the remaining period between the interim date and the year-end. The problem can be handled several ways, including: (1) stop the work if the conclusion at interim is that control is deficient, control risk is high, and other procedures will not be restricted; (2) extend the attribute sample into the remaining period and continue the work later; or (3) evaluate the specific circumstances and decide whether other procedures will produce enough evidence about the maintenance of control so that detailed compliance auditing need not be continued. Of course, the length of the remaining period, whether it is three months or three weeks, makes a difference.

Another complicating factor in population definition is the need to determine the correspondence of the physical representation of the population to the population itself. The *physical representation of the population* is the *auditor's frame of reference for selecting a sample*. It can be a journal listing of recorded sales invoices, a file drawer full of invoice copies, a magnetic disk file of invoices, or another physical representation. The sample will actually be selected from the physical representation, so it must be complete and correspond with the actual population. The physical representation of the recorded sales invoice population as a list in a journal is fairly easy to visualize. However, an auditor should make sure that periodic listings (for example, monthly sales journals) are added correctly and posted to the general ledger sales accounts. Now, a

---

[2] *Dollar-unit sampling,* however, defines a different sampling unit. Dollar-unit sampling (DUS) is discussed in Chapters 11 and 12.

selection of individual sales invoices from the sales journal is known to be from the complete population of recorded sales invoices. You should be careful, however. Other physical frames may not be so easy to assess for complete correspondence to a population of interest.

Perform the Procedures

The sample size determination and sample selection steps explained in this section can be considered planning steps, but since they require a little more action, they can also be considered performance. The distinction is not crucial. They are merely the next things to do.

4. Determine the Sample Size. Sample size—the number of population units to audit—should be determined thoughtfully. Some auditors operate on the "magic number theory" (for example, select 30). Be careful, however, because a "magic number" may or may not satisfy the need for enough evidence. A "magic number" might also be too large. Auditors must consider four influences on sample size: Sampling risk, tolerable rate, expected population deviation rate and population size.

Sampling Risk. Earlier, sampling risk was defined as the probability that an auditor's conclusion based on a sample might be different from the conclusion based on an audit of the entire population. In other words, when using evidence from a sample, an auditor might reach a wrong conclusion. He or she might decide controls are very reliable when, in fact, they are not, or decide controls are not very reliable when, in fact, they are not so bad. The more you know about a population (from a larger sample), the less likely you are to reach a wrong conclusion. Thus, the larger the sample, the lower the sampling risk of making either of the two decision errors. More will be said about these risks in the section on evaluation.

In terms of our example, the important sampling risk is the probability that the sample will reveal few or no recorded sales invoices without supporting shipping orders when, in fact, the population contains many deviations. This result leads to the erroneous conclusion that the control worked well. The probability of finding few or no deviations when many exist is reduced by auditing a larger sample. Thus, sample size varies inversely with the amount of sampling risk an auditor is willing to take.

Tolerable Rate. Auditors should have an idea of what rate of deviation can exist, yet the control can still be relied upon (that is, the auditor need not expand other planned audit procedures for reason of control performance deficiency). In other words, in light of the fact that perfection is not necessary, how many sales invoices in the population could be unsupported without triggering the extra work to audit for material sales overstatement? Suppose 10,000 invoices are in the population. A criterion for reliable control performance deviation could be expressed as "not many." How many? How about 500? A *tolerable rate* is *the ratio of the number of deviations to the population size that could exist without trig-*

gering additional audit work. In this example, the tolerable rate is 500/ 10,000 = 5 percent. An auditor would need to audit a larger sample if only 200 deviations (2 percent) could be tolerated and a smaller sample if 700 deviations (7 percent) could be tolerated. Sample size varies inversely with the tolerable rate. Some auditors will express the tolerable rate as a number (necessary for statistical calculation of sample size), while others will not put a number on it.

Expected Population Deviation Rate.   Auditors usually know or suspect some control performance conditions. Sometimes, they have last year's audit experience with the client; sometimes, they have information from a predecessor auditor. They know some things about the client's personnel, the working conditions and the general control environment. This knowledge contributes to an ***expectation about the population deviation rate,*** which is an *estimate of the ratio of the number of expected deviations to population size.* Suppose the auditors discovered 1 percent deviation in last year's audit. The expected population deviation rate could then be 1 percent.

The expected rate is important in a commonsense perspective. If auditors had reason to expect more deviations than they could tolerate, there would be no reason to perform any compliance-purpose procedures. Thus, the expected rate must be less than the tolerable rate. Also, the closer the expected rate is to the tolerable rate, the larger the sample would need to be to reach a conclusion that deviations do not exceed the tolerable rate. Consequently, the sample size varies directly with the expected deviation rate (especially in terms of larger samples when the expected rate nears the tolerable rate). Some auditors will express the expected rate as a number (necessary for statistical calculations of sample size), while others will not put a number on it.

Population Size.   Common sense probably tells you that samples should be larger for bigger populations (a direct relationship). Strictly speaking, your common sense is accurate. As a practical matter, however, an appropriate sample size for a population of 100,000 units may be only two or three sampling units larger than an appropriate sample size for a 1000-unit population. Not much difference! The power of the mathematics of probability is at work. The explanations in Chapter 11 are based on populations of 1000 or more. However, you will need to be careful and make extra calculations when dealing with populations of fewer than 1000 units.

The preceding discussion of sample size determinants is intended to give you a conceptual understanding of the four influences on sample size. These influences are applicable to both statistical and nonstatistical sampling. A summary is presented in Exhibit 8–3. For further information about how to *calculate* a sample size, refer to Chapter 11.

   5.   Select the Sample.   Auditing standards express two requirements for samples: (1) Sampling units must be selected from the population to

EXHIBIT 8–3
Sample Size Relationships:
Compliance Auditing

	Predetermined Sample Size Will Be	
Sample Size Influence	High Rate or Large Population	Low Rate or Small Population
1. Acceptable sampling risk . . . . Smaller.		Larger.
2. Tolerable deviation rate . . . . Smaller.		Larger.
3. Expected population deviation rate. . . Larger.		Smaller.
4. Population size. . . . . Larger.*		Smaller.*

* Effect on sample size is quite small for populations of 1000 or more.

which an audit conclusion will apply, ideally from transactions executed throughout the period under audit and (2) A sample must be representative of the population from which it is drawn. In this context, *a representative sample* is one that *mirrors the characteristics of the population.* Auditors, however, cannot guarantee representativeness. After all, that is what sampling risk is all about—the probability that the sample might not mirror the population well enough.

Auditors can try to attain representativeness by selecting random samples. A sample is considered ***random*** if *each unit in the population has an equal probability of being included in the sample.* Intentional or accidental exclusion of a segment of a population can render a sample nonrepresentative. A popular way to select random samples is to associate each population unit with a unique number (easily done if the population units are prenumbered documents), then obtain a selection of random numbers to identify the sample units. You can use a printed random number table (see Appendix 11–A) or a computerized random number generator to obtain a list of random numbers. This method is known as ***unrestricted random selection.***

Another popular method is called ***systematic random selection.*** You need to know the population size and have a predetermined sample size in order to use it. The process is: (1) obtain a random starting place in the physical representation (list of sales invoices recorded in a sales journal, for example) and select that unit, then (2) count through the file and select every kth unit, where k = population size/sample size. For example, if 10,000 invoices are listed and you want a sample of 200, first (1) use a random number table to get a starting place, say at invoice #9000, then (2) select every kth = 10,000/200 = 50th invoice. So the next would be #9050, then #9100 . . . , then #10,000, then #50, #100, and so on. (At the end of the list, you cycle back through the invoices #1–#8,999.) Most systematic samples are selected using five or more random starts, as described in Chapter 11.

Sample selection is the first step where a distinction between statistical and nonstatistical audit sampling is crucial. *For statistical sampling evaluation, the sample must be random.*

In nonstatistical plans, auditors sometimes use sample selection methods whose randomness and representativeness cannot be evaluated readily. ***Haphazard selection*** refers to *any unsystematic way of selecting sam-*

ple units, for example, closing your eyes and dipping into a file drawer of sales invoices to pick items. The problem is that you may pick only the dog-eared ones that stick out, and they may be different from most of the other invoices in the drawer. Also, you cannot describe your method so someone else can **replicate** it—*reperform your selection procedure and get the same sample units.* Another method is **block sampling,** which is the practice of *choosing segments of contiguous transactions,* for example, choosing the sales invoices processed on randomly chosen days, say February 3, July 17 and September 29. Implicitly, the block sampling auditor has defined the population unit as a business day (260 of them in a year) and has selected three—not much of a sample. Block sampling is undesirable because it is hard to get a representative sample of blocks efficiently. When you have enough blocks, you have a huge number of invoices to audit for compliance.

6. Perform the Compliance-Purpose Procedures. Now you are ready to obtain the evidence. Few words are needed to describe it: For example, for each sales invoice in the sample, look (vouch) to see that a shipping order is attached. To make it seem more complicated, you might need to walk over to another file to pull the shipping order, or you might need to run a computer program to find it on a magnetic disk file. Yet, this is the most time-consuming part of the work. You also need to document your findings. In some cases, a memo explaining that no deviations were found might do. In other cases, a schedule of invoices checked off for several different deviations would be good documentation, accompanied by notes of your follow-up and explanation about deviations. The performance of audit procedures is not complete until you follow up each deviation and obtain an explanation.

7. Evaluate the Evidence   Compliance audit sampling is undertaken to provide evidence of whether a client's internal accounting control procedures are being followed satisfactorily. Compliance evidence therefore is very important in the combination of evidence from review and compliance procedures that yields a conclusion about internal control risk. When auditors evaluate sample-based evidence about compliance, they run the sampling risks of making one of two decision errors—overreliance or underreliance. These two risks are further refinements of the idea of sampling risk presented earlier.

The **risk of overreliance** is the probability that the sample evidence supports the auditor's planned degree of reliance on the control when the actual (but unknown) compliance rate does *not* justify such reliance. Overreliance can lead to auditors' failure to do additional work that should be done. Overreliance creates a threat to the *effectiveness* of the audit.

The **risk of underreliance** is the probability that the sample does not support the auditor's planned degree of reliance on the control when the actual (but unknown) compliance rate *would* support this reliance. Under-reliance tends to trigger more audit work than was originally planned. Underreliance threatens the *efficiency* of the audit.

Audit efficiency is certainly important, but audit effectiveness is considered more important. For this reason, auditing standards require auditors to allow for a low level of risk of overreliance. These risks and decisions are illustrated in Exhibit 8–4. Keeping these risks in mind, the

EXHIBIT 8–4
The Compliance Audit
Sampling Decision Matrix

Decision Alternatives (based on sample evidence)	Unknown Actual Deviation Rate	
	Less Than Tolerable Rate	Greater Than Tolerable Rate
The deviation rate is less than the tolerable rate, so the control is performed satisfactorily.	Correct decision	Overreliance decision error
The deviation rate is greater than the tolerable rate, so the control is not performed satisfactorily.	Underreliance decision error	Correct decision

evaluation of evidence consists of calculating the sample deviation rate, comparing it to the tolerable rate and following up all the deviations discovered.

Calculate the Deviation Rate.   The first piece of hard evidence is the sample deviation rate. Suppose an auditor selected 200 recorded sales invoices and vouched them to shipping orders, finding one without a shipping order. The sample deviation rate is $1/200 = 0.5$ percent. This is the best single-point estimate of the actual, but unknown, deviation rate in the population. However, you cannot say that the deviation rate in the population is *exactly* 0.5 percent. Chances are the sample is not *exactly* representative, so the actual but unknown population deviation rate could be lower or higher.

Judge the Deviation Rate in Relation to the Tolerable Rate and the Risk of Overreliance.   Suppose the auditor in the example believed the tolerable rate was 3 percent. (300 invoices could be unsupported in the population before additional work on sales overstatement would be triggered.) In a nonstatistical sampling application, this auditor is supposed to think about the sample deviation rate (0.5 percent) in relation to the tolerable rate (3 percent), and he or she is supposed to think about the risk (of overreliance) that the actual, but unknown, deviation rate in the population exceeds 3 percent. The decision in a nonstatistical evaluation depends on the auditor's experience and expertise.

In a statistical sample evaluation, an auditor does things that are more explainable in a textbook. He or she establishes decision criteria by (1) assigning a number to the risk of overreliance, say 10 percent, and (2) assigning a number to the tolerable rate, say 3 percent. Then, a statistical table is used to calculate a *sampling error-adjusted upper limit,* which is the *sample deviation rate adjusted upward to allow for the idea that the actual population rate could be higher.* In this example, the adjusted limit (call it CUL for "computed upper limit") is about 2 percent. This finding can be interpreted to mean: "The probability is 10 percent that the actual but unknown population deviation rate is greater than 2 percent." The decision criterion was: "The actual but unknown population deviation rate needs to be 3 percent or lower, with 10 percent risk of overreliance." So, the decision criterion is satisfied, and the control will be relied upon.[3]

Follow up All the Deviations.   All the evaluation described so far has been mostly *quantitative* in nature, involving counts of deviations, deviation rates, and tolerable rate and risk judgment criteria. *Qualitative* evaluation is also necessary in the form of following up all the deviations to determine their nature and cause. A single deviation can be the tip of the iceberg—the telltale sign of a more pervasive deficiency. Auditors should try to determine whether a deviation is merely a mistake or an intentional irregularity. Auditors are obligated by the concept of due audit care to investigate known deviations so nothing important and within grasp will be overlooked.

The qualitative evaluation is sometimes called *error analysis* because each error or exception to a prescribed control procedure is investigated to determine its nature, cause, and probable effect on financial statements. The analysis is essentially judgmental and involves auditors' determination of whether the exception is: (1) a pervasive error in principle made systematically on all like transactions or just a mistake on the particular transaction; (2) a deliberate or intentional control breakdown rather than unintentional; (3) due to misunderstanding of instructions or careless inattention to control duties; or (4) directly or remotely related to a money amount measurement in the financial statements. You can see that different qualitative perceptions of the seriousness of an exception would result from error-analysis findings.

When the decision criteria are not satisfied and the preliminary conclusion is that the control being audited *cannot* be relied upon, the auditors need to decide what to do next. The deviation follow-up can give auditors comfort for deciding to do more account balance audit work by changing the nature, timing and extent of other audit procedures; that is, by not

---

[3] Changing the example to suppose four deviations were found creates a problem for the nonstatistical sampler. He or she must think harder about the evidence in relation to the tolerable rate and acceptable risk. The statistical sampler can measure the CUL at about 4 percent, which is greater than the 3 percent tolerable rate at 10 percent risk of overreliance. The control fails the decision criterion test. Chapter 11 contains more information about making these calculations using statistical tables.

limiting the work in reliance on particular internal control procedures. If the audit manager hesitates to make this commitment to do more audit work, he or she can enlarge the sample and perform the compliance audit procedure on more sample units in hopes of deciding that the control in question is really good enough. However, when faced with the preliminary "non-reliance" decision, you should *not* manipulate the quantitative evaluation by raising the tolerable rate or the risk of overreliance. Supposedly, these two decision criteria were carefully determined in the planning stage, so now only new information would be a good basis for easing them.

AUDITING ACCOUNT BALANCES

When audit sampling is used in auditing account balances, the feature of interest is the *monetary amount* of the population units, not the presence or absence of control deviations, as is the case with compliance audit sampling. Compliance auditing is a part of the study and evaluation of internal accounting control. *Substantive tests of details auditing* is the *performance of procedures to obtain direct evidence about the balances and disclosures in the financial statements*.

Substantive-purpose procedures include (1) analytical review procedures and (2) test (audit) of details of transactions and balances. Analytical review procedures are usually not applied on a sample basis. So, substantive-purpose procedures for auditing *details* are the normal means of doing account balance audit sampling.

Risk Model Expansion

Up to now you have worked with a conceptual risk model that incorporated a term for "detection risk"—DR. The detection risk is actually a combination of two more risks: *Analytical review risk (AR)* is the probability that analytical review procedures will *fail* to detect material errors, and *tests of detail risk (TD)* is the probability that detailed substantive audit procedures will *fail* to detect material errors. The two types of procedures are considered independent, so detection risk is DR = AR × TD, and the expanded risk model is:

$$AuR = IR \times IC \times AR \times TD$$

This model is still a conceptual tool. The expansion of it did not make auditing any less judgmental. It can now be used to help you conceptualize some elements of audit sampling for auditing the details of account balances. First, recognize that auditors exercise professional judgment in assessing the inherent risk (IR), control risk (IC) *and* the analytical review risk (AR). If these three risks are given, you can then manipulate the model to express the test of details risk (TD):

$$TD = \frac{AuR}{(IR \times IC \times AR)}$$

More about
Sampling Risk   Substantive-purpose procedures are performed to produce the evidence
necessary to enable an auditor to conclude that an account balance is or is
not fairly presented in conformity with GAAP. So, auditors run the sampling risks of making one of two decision errors. The test of details (TD)
risk is an expression of the *risk of incorrect acceptance,* which is the
decision to accept a balance as being materially accurate when, in fact
(unknown to the auditor), the balance is *materially misstated.* The other
decision error risk is the *risk of incorrect rejection,* which is the decision
that a balance *is* materially misstated, when in fact, it *is not.* These sampling risk relationships are shown in Exhibit 8–5.

EXHIBIT 8–5
The Account Balance
Audit Sampling Decision
Matrix

Decision Alternatives (based on sample evidence)	Unknown Actual Account Balance Is	
	Materially Accurate	Materially Misstated
The book value of the account is materially accurate.	Correct decision	Incorrect acceptance
The book value of the account is materially mis-stated.	Incorrect rejection	Correct decision

Incorrect Acceptance.   The risk of incorrect acceptance is considered
the more important of the two decision error risks. When an auditor
decides an account book balance is materially accurate (hence needs no
adjustment or change), the audit work on that account is considered finished, the decision is documented in the working papers, and the audit
team proceeds to work on other accounts. When the account is, in fact,
materially misstated, an unqualified opinion on the financial statements
may well be unwarranted. Incorrect acceptance damages the *effective-*
ness of the audit.

Incorrect Rejection.   When an auditor decides an account book balance is materially misstated (hence needing an adjustment), the audit
work on that account is generally not complete and further investigation
may be warranted. The *audit risk,* however, is that the book balance
really is a materially accurate representation of the (unknown) actual
value. At this point, the event of *incorrect rejection* is about to be realized, and the audit manager may be inclined to recommend an adjustment
that is not needed.

However, incorrect rejection is not considered to be as serious an error
as incorrect acceptance. When auditors first begin to think a balance may
contain a material misstatement, efforts will be made to determine why
the misstatement occurred and to estimate the amount. Thus, *more* evidence will be sought by the audit team or provided by the client. The data

will be reviewed for a source of systematic error. The amounts of discovered errors will be analyzed carefully. Client personnel may be assigned to do a complete analysis to determine a more accurate account balance.

If the initial decision was, in fact, an error of incorrect rejection, this other work should allow the auditors to determine whether the recorded amount is really misstated or the sample was not representative. Hence, incorrect rejection is not considered as serious as incorrect acceptance because steps will be taken to determine the amount of error and the erroneous decision has a chance to be reversed. Incorrect rejection thus affects the *efficiency* of an audit.

Materiality and Tolerable Error

Determining a threshold for the materiality of misstatements in financial statements is a tough problem under any circumstances. Audit sampling for substantive audit of particular account balances adds another wrinkle. Auditors must also decide upon an amount of **tolerable error,** which is a judgment of the *maximum monetary error that may exist in an account balance or class of transactions without causing the financial statements to be materially misstated.* Audit risk (AuR in the risk model), therefore, is the risk that all the audit work on an account balance will *not* result in discovery of actual error that exceeds tolerable error.

Auditors must judge the materiality of misstatement overall, then assign a part of that amount to all the account(s) and account groupings. Suppose, for purposes of illustration, an audit manager decided that an income-before-taxes misstatement of $100,000 would be material. Using the "top-down approach," he or she needs to decide where parts of this *allowable misstatement* can exist, so that audit work can be directed to the important areas. Suppose the manager can justify allocating $20,000 to cost of goods sold, $50,000 to sales, $30,000 to expenses taken all together, and zero to income tax expenses (it will be figured exactly). The allocations suggest that each of these accounts and account groups could be overstated (or understated) by these amounts. Even if all the misstatements were in the same direction, they would still only add up to the $100,000 considered material.[4]

If sales are overstated, chances are that some of the error has resulted in overstatement of the accounts receivable. The audit manager can reason that part of the material amount assigned to sales can also be assigned to the accounts receivable audit work. Now, suppose the manager decides a good way to audit for sales overstatement is to audit the receivables for overstatement. If the receivables are audited with allowance for $25,000 of error, that will take care of part of the audit for sales overstate-

---

[4] The materiality allocation does not need to be strictly additive, as suggested in this example. Another method is to assign amounts so that the square root of the sum of the squared amounts allocated does not exceed the amount ($100,000 in the example) considered material for the financial statements taken as a whole. For this example, this method produces a result of $61,644 = $(20,000^2 + 50,000^2 + 30,000^2)^{1/2}$.

ment. This $25,000 is the ***tolerable error*** planned for the audit of the accounts receivable on a sample basis.

Audit sampling for the audit of account balances is structured much like the steps you studied in connection with compliance audit sampling. As the steps are explained, an example related to auditing receivables is used. Remember, the example used with regard to compliance audit sampling was the audit of a control procedure designed to prevent the recording of sales invoices without shipping orders. Now we move on to the next stage of work that can produce independent evidence of sales overstatement resulting from a breakdown of the control or from other causes. The seven-step structure explained in the next sections helps auditors plan, perform and evaluate account balance detail audit work. It also helps auditors accomplish an eighth step—careful documentation of the work—by showing each of the seven areas to be described in the working papers. The first seven steps are:

1. Determine the audit objective.
2. Define the population.
3. Choose an audit sampling method.
4. Determine the sample size.
5. Select the sample.
6. Perform the substantive-purpose procedures.
7. Evaluate the evidence.

Plan the Procedures   Substantive audit procedures are always directed toward producing evidence about the client's financial assertions—existence or occurrence, completeness, rights and obligations, valuation of allocation, and presentation and disclosure (SAS 31, AU 326; and Chapter 6). Most substantive procedures can simultaneously produce some evidence about controls, so they can also be called dual-purpose procedures. For instance, the accounts receivable confirmation and follow-up procedures described in the example hereafter can give the auditors new information about control performance over sales and related accounts receivable transactions and enable them, perhaps, to revise their judgments about control risk. However, the example and the discussion concentrate on the audit sampling and not on the dual-purpose possibilities.

1. Specify the Objectives. When performing accounts receivable confirmation on a sample basis, the specific objective is to decide whether the client's assertions about *existence, rights (ownership),* and *valuation* are materially accurate. In this context, the auditing is viewed as ***hypothesis testing***—the auditors hypothesize that *the book value is materially accurate as to existence, rights and valuation.* The evidence will enable them to accept or reject the hypothesis. The most important characteristic of interest is the *monetary error* an auditor might find when comparing the recorded balances to the balances he or she determines from the evidence.

Accountants can use similar sampling methods for a ***dollar-value estimation objective,*** which is the job of *helping a client obtain an estimate of an amount.* Examples include estimation of inventory LIFO indexes and data for current cost accounting information. In dollar-value estimation, the objective is to develop a basic measurement, not to audit the balance or amount. Audit sampling, in the following discussion, adopts the objective of hypothesis testing.

2.   Define the Population.   Auditors need to be sure the definition of the population matches the objectives. Defining the population as the recorded accounts receivable balances suits the objective of obtaining evidence about existence, rights and valuation. This definition also suits the ancillary objective of obtaining evidence about sales overstatement. In the case of accounts receivable, each customer's account balance is a population unit. However, if the objectives were expressed in terms of evidence about completeness and sales understatement, the *recorded* accounts receivable would be the wrong population.

Ordinarily, the sampling unit is the same as the population unit. Sometimes, however, it is convenient and easier to define the sampling unit as a smaller part of a population unit. For example, if the client's accounting system keeps track of individual invoices charged to customers, an auditor might want to audit a sample of invoices by confirming them with customers instead of working with each customer's balance.

Since a sample will be drawn from a physical representation of the population (for example, a printed trial balance or magnetic disk file of customers' accounts), the auditors must determine whether it is complete. Footing the trial balance and reconciling it to the control account total will accomplish the job.

In the jargon of audit sampling related to account balances, *subdividing* the population is known as ***stratification.*** Auditing standards require auditors to use their judgment to determine whether any population units should be removed from the population and audited separately (not sampled) because taking sampling risk (risk of incorrect acceptance or incorrect rejection) with respect to them is not justified. Suppose the accounts receivable in our example amounted to $679,500, but 10 of the customers had balances of $25,000 or more, for a sum of $300,000. The next largest account balance is less than $10,000. The 10 accounts could be considered ***individually significant items*** because each of them exceeds the tolerable error amount, and they should be removed from the population and audited completely. This decision creates two strata—10 accounts totaling $300,000 and all the others totaling $379,500.

3. Choose an Audit Sampling Method. You already have been introduced to statistical and nonstatistical sampling methods. At this point, an auditor must decide which to use. If he or she chooses statistical sampling, another choice needs to be made. In statistical sampling, *classical variables sampling* methods which utilize *normal distribution theory* are available. *Dollar-unit sampling* (known also as probability-proportional-to-size (PPS) and cumulative monetary amount (CMA)), which utilizes *attribute sampling theory,* can also be used. Some of the technical characteristics of these methods are explained more fully in Chapter 12.

Perform the Procedures
Figuring sample size for account balance auditing requires consideration of several influences. Actually, the main reason for figuring a sample size in advance is to help guard against underauditing (not obtaining enough evidence) and overauditing (obtaining more evidence than needed). Another important reason is to control the cost of the audit. An arbitrary sample size *could* be used to perform the accounts receivable confirmation procedures, but if it turned out to be too small, sending and processing more confirmations might be impossible before the audit report deadline. Alternative procedures could then become costly and time-consuming. A predetermined sample size is not as important in other situations where the auditors can increase the sample simply by choosing more items available for audit in the client's office.

4. Determine the Sample Size. Whether using statistical or nonstatistical sampling methods, auditors first need to establish *decision criteria* related to the risk of incorrect acceptance, the risk of incorrect rejection and the tolerable error. Also, auditors need to consider the variability within the population. The three criteria and the variability information are determined *before* any evidence is obtained from a sample.

a. **Risk of Incorrect Acceptance (TD).** This risk is assessed in terms of the entire audit process. The risk model can be your guide. An acceptable risk of incorrect acceptance depends upon the assessments of inherent risk, control risk, and analytical review risk. The risk of incorrect acceptance varies *inversely* with the combined product of the other risks.

Suppose, for example, two different auditors independently assess the client's business control system and their own analytical review procedures and arrive at the following conclusions. (Assume both auditors believe an appropriate audit risk (AuR) is 0.05):

Auditor A believes the inherent risk is high (IR = 1.0), the control system is moderately effective (IC = 0.50) and analytical review procedures will not be performed (AR = 1.0). Audit procedures need to be planned so that the risk of incorrect acceptance will be about 10 percent.

$$TD = \frac{AuR}{IR \times IC \times AR} = \frac{0.05}{1.0 \times 0.50 \times 1.0} = 0.10$$

Auditor B believes the inherent risk is high (IR − 1.00), the control system is very effective (IC = 0.20) and analytical review procedures will not be performed (AR = 1.00). Audit procedures need to be planned so that the risk of incorrect acceptance will be about 25 percent.

$$TD = \frac{AuR}{IR \times IC \times AR} = \frac{0.05}{1.0 \times 0.20 \times 1.0} = 0.25$$

Use the model with caution. The lesson you should learn from these examples is that Auditor A's account balance sampling work can support less risk than that of Auditor B. Since *sample size varies inversely with the risk of incorrect acceptance,* Auditor A's sample will be larger. In fact, when the internal accounting control is more reliable (that is, the internal control risk is lower, as in Auditor B's evaluation), the acceptable risk of incorrect acceptance (TD) is higher. Thus, Auditor B's sample can be smaller than Auditor A's sample.

b. **Risk of Incorrect Rejection.** Like the risk of incorrect acceptance, the risk of incorrect rejection exists both in statistical and nonstatistical sampling applications. It can be controlled, usually by auditing a larger sample. So, sample size varies *inversely* with the risk of incorrect rejection.

c. **Tolerable Error.** The tolerable error—associated with the overall materiality of misstatements—must also be considered in nonstatistical as well as statistical sampling applications. In statistical sampling, tolerable error must be expressed as a dollar amount. The sample size varies *inversely* with the amount of the tolerable error for an account.

d. **Variability within the Population.** Auditors using nonstatistical sampling must take into account the degree of dispersion among unit values in a population. The typical skewness of some accounting populations needs to be taken into account. *Skewness* is the concentration of a large proportion of the dollar amount in an account in a small number of the population items. In our illustration, $300,000 (44 percent) of the total accounts receivable is in 10 customers' accounts while the remainder is in 8,300 customer accounts.

As a general rule, auditors should be careful about populations whose unit values range widely, say from $1 to $10,000. Obtaining a *representative sample* in such a case, as you might imagine, would take a larger sample than if the range of the unit values were only from $1 to $500. Sample size should vary *inversely* with the magnitude of the variability of population unit values. Populations with high variability should be stratified (see Chapter 12, Appendix 12–C).

Auditors using classical statistical sampling methods must obtain an estimate of the population **standard deviation,** which is a measure of the population variability. When using dollar-unit sampling, the variability is taken into account by the method of sample selection, and no separate calculation needs to be made.

These four influences plus the influences of population size on sample size are summarized in Exhibit 8–6.

Sample Size Influence	Predetermined Sample Size Will Be	
	High Rate or Large Amount	Low Rate or Small Amount
1. Risk of incorrect acceptance.	Smaller.	Larger.
2. Risk of incorrect rejection..	Smaller.	Larger.
3. Tolerable error..	Smaller.	Larger.
4. Population variability..	Larger.	Smaller.
5. Population size.	Larger.	Smaller.

5.   Select the Sample.   As was the case with compliance audit samples, account balance samples must be representative. Nothing is new about the selection methods. You can use unrestricted random selection and systematic selection (with five or more random starts) to obtain the random samples necessary for statistical applications. Haphazard and block selection methods have the same drawbacks as they have in compliance audit samples.

6.   Perform the Substantive-Purpose Procedures.   The procedures (audit program list) contemplated in our example of the audit of accounts receivable are these:

☐   Send a positive confirmation to each customer selected in the sample. (A typical audit procedure.)

☐   Investigate exceptions reported by customers and determine a correct amount for the balances.

☐   Send second and third requests to nonrespondents.

☐   For nonresponding customers, vouch the balance to the sales invoices and cash receipts that make the balance.

☐   For nonresponding customers vouch balance to payments received on account after the confirmation date. (An alternative audit procedure.)

The confirmation procedure should be performed for all the sampling units. The other procedures should be performed as necessary to complete the evidence relating to existence, rights and valuations. The important thing is to audit *all* the sample items. You cannot simply discard one that is hard to audit in favor of adding to the sample a customer whose balance is easy to audit. This action might bias the sample. Sometimes, however, you will be unable to audit a sample unit. Suppose a customer did not respond to the confirmation requests, sales invoices supporting the balance could not be found, and no payment was received after the confirmation date. Auditing standards contain the following guidance (AU 350.25):

☐ If considering the entire balance to be in error will not alter your evaluation conclusion, then you do not need to work on it any more. Your evaluation conclusion might be to *accept the book value,* as long as the account counted in error is not big enough to change the conclusion. Your evaluation conclusion might already be to *reject the book value,* and considering another account in error just reinforces the decision.

☐ If considering the entire balance to be in error would change an *acceptance* evaluation to a *rejection* evaluation, you need to do something about it. Since the example seems to describe a dead end, you may need to select more accounts (expand the sample), perform the procedures on them (excluding confirmation), and reevaluate the results.

7. Evaluate the Evidence   You should be concerned first with *quantitative* evaluation of the evidence. *Qualitative follow-up* is also important and is discussed later. The basic steps in quantitative evaluation are these:

☐ Figure the total amount of actual error found in the sample. This amount is called the *known error.*

☐ *Project* the known error to the population. The projected amount is called the *likely error.*

☐ Compare the likely error (also called the *projected error*) to the tolerable error for the account and consider the:

Risk of incorrect acceptance that likely error could be less than tolerable error even though the actual error in the population is greater; or the *Risk of incorrect rejection* that likely error could be greater than tolerable error even though the actual error in the population is smaller.

Amount of Known Error.   Now you need some illustrative numbers. Hypothetical audit evidence from a sample is shown in Exhibit 8–7. The example cited earlier said total accounts receivable is $679,500, and $300,000 of the total is in 10 large balances which are to be audited separately. Assume the remainder is in 8,300 customer accounts whose balances range from $1 to $6,870. Assume also that the audit team selected 100 accounts and applied the confirmation or vouching procedures listed earlier in the chapter to each of them. The evidence showed

EXHIBIT 8–7 Hypothetical Sample Data	Sample Item	Audited Amount	Recorded Amount	Difference* (Audited − Recorded)
	1	$ 45	$ 50	$ −5
	2	26	25	1
	3	100	100	0
	4	37	35	2
	.	.	.	.
	.	.	.	.
	.	.	.	.
	100	17	20	−3
	Sums:	$4,400	$4,500	$−100
	Averages:			
	Audited amount:	$44		
	Recorded amount:		$45	
	Difference:			$−1

* A negative difference is an account *overstatement*, and a positive difference is an account *understatement*.

$−100 of actual error representing overstatement of the recorded amounts (Exhibit 8–7). This amount is the ***known error*** for this sample of 100 customer accounts.

Project the Known Error to the Population. The key requirement for projecting the known error to the population is that *the sample must be representative*. If the sample is not representative, a projection produces a nonsense number. Take an extreme example: Remember that all of the 10 largest accounts ($300,000 in total) were audited. Suppose one of them contained a $600 disputed amount. Investigation showed the customer was right, management agreed, so the $600 is the amount of known error. If an auditor takes this group of 10 accounts as being representative of the population, one calculation method would project a total misstatement of $498,600 compared to the recorded accounts receivable total of $679,500. This projection is neither reasonable nor appropriate.

The method used to project the known error to the population consisted of calculating the average known error and multiplying it by the population size. The average in the case cited above is $60 ($600 error/10 accounts in the group), and the whole population size is 8,310 accounts. Thus, by projection: $60 × 8,310 accounts = $498,600 misstatement. However, this number does not mean anything. The 10 large accounts are not representative of the entire population of 8,310 accounts. Nothing is wrong with the calculation *method*. The nonrepresentative "sample" is the culprit in this absurd result.

A projection based on a sample applies only to the population from which the sample was drawn. Consider the sample of 100 accounts from the population of 8,300. The average difference is $ −1 (overstatement of the recorded amount), so the ***projected likely error*** is $−8,300 (overstatement), provided the sample is representative. This projection method is called the ***average difference method*** expressed in equation form as:

$$\text{Projected Likely Error (Average difference method)} = \left[\frac{\text{Dollar amount of error in the sample}}{\text{Number of sampling units}}\right] \times \left[\text{Number of population units}\right]$$

In the example:

$$\text{Projected Likely Error (Average difference method)} = \frac{\$-100}{100} \times 8,300 = \frac{\$-8,300}{\text{(overstatement)}}$$

How can you tell whether a sample is representative? You cannot guarantee representativeness, but you can try to attain it by selecting a random sample and by carefully subdividing ***(stratifying)*** the population according to an important characteristic, such as the size of individual customers' balances. When the population is stratified, each stratum is more homogeneous than the population as a whole, and the known error in each can be projected. Combining them into a single projection, however, is best done with statistical calculations, as described in Chapter 12, Appendix 12–C.

You can also inspect the sample to see whether it shows the characteristics of the population. In the example, for instance, the average recorded amount of the population is $45.72 ($379,500/8,300); the average in the illustrative sample is $45. You can also look to see whether the sample contains a range of recorded amounts similar to the population which ranged from $1 to $6,870. With statistics, you can calculate the standard deviation of the sample and compare it to the standard deviation of the population. (A computer helps!)

Another projection method takes into account the fact that the average recorded amount in the sample may turn out to be quite different from the population average. If you have reason to believe that the size of differences is directly related to the size of the customers' accounts, you can project (nonstatistically) using the ***ratio method,*** expressed in equation form as:

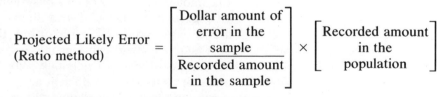

$$\text{Projected Likely Error (Ratio method)} = \left[\frac{\text{Dollar amount of error in the sample}}{\text{Recorded amount in the sample}}\right] \times \left[\text{Recorded amount in the population}\right]$$

In the example:

$$\text{Projected Likely Error (Ratio method)} = \frac{\$-100}{\$4,500} \times \$379,500 = \frac{\$-8,433}{\text{(overstatement)}}$$

The first term in this equation is the *ratio of error to recorded amount*. So, the representativeness of the ratio is crucial. Auditors must be very careful to discern the representativeness of the average difference and the ratio. They also need to be very careful about the adequacy of the sample size. You can see that small samples which produce large or small difference amounts can distort both the average difference and the ratio, thus distorting the projected likely error. One way to exercise care is to take the sampling risks into account.

Consider Sampling Risks.   The risks of making wrong decisions (incorrect acceptance or incorrect rejection) exist in both nonstatistical and statistical sampling. The smaller the sample, the greater the risks—both of them. Common sense tells you the less you know about a population because of a small sample, the more risk you run of making a wrong decision.

The problem is to "consider" the risk that the projected likely error ($8,300 overstatement in the example using the average difference method) could have been obtained even though the actual total error in the population is *greater* than the tolerable error ($25,000 in the example). Auditing guidance suggests you can use your experience and professional judgment to "consider" the risk. If the likely error is considerably less than tolerable error, chances are good that actual error is not greater than tolerable error. However, when likely error is close to tolerable error (say, $20,000 compared to $25,000), the chance is not so good, and the risk of incorrect acceptance might exceed the acceptable risk (TD) an auditor initially established as a decision criterion.

A similar situation exists with respect to the risk of incorrect rejection. Suppose the sample results had produced a projected likely error of $30,000 overstatement. Now the question is: "What is the risk that this result was obtained even though the actual error in the population is $25,000 or less?" Again, the judgment depends on the size of the sample and the kinds and distribution of errors discovered. Auditors take the rejection decision as a serious matter and conduct enough additional investigation to determine the amount of adjustment required. Hence, the risk of incorrect rejection is mitigated by additional work necessary to determine the amount and nature of an adjustment. In the example, if the sample of 100 customers' accounts had shown total error of $361.45 (yielding the $30,000 projected error using the average difference method), most auditors would consider the evidence insufficient to propose a significant adjustment. (Incidentally, however, correction of the $361.45 should not by itself be a sufficient action to satisfy the auditors.)

When using nonstatistical sampling, auditors utilize their experience and expertise to take risks into account. Statistical samplers can add statistical calculations to these considerations of sampling risk. Further explanation of statistical calculations is in Chapter 12.

Qualitative Evaluation. The numbers are not enough. Auditors are required to follow up each error discovered to determine whether it arose from: (*a*) misunderstanding of accounting principles; (*b*) simple mistakes or carelessness; (*c*) an intentional irregularity; or (*d*) management override of an internal accounting control procedure. Auditors also need to relate the errors to their effect on other amounts in the financial statements. For example, overstatements in accounts receivable may indicate overstatement of sales revenue.

Likewise, you should not overlook the information that can be obtained in account balance auditing about the performance of internal accounting control procedures—the dual-purpose characteristic of auditing procedures. Errors (or absence of errors) discovered when performing substantive procedures can help confirm or contradict an auditor's previous conclusion about internal control risk. If many more errors arise than expected, the control risk conclusion may need to be revised, and more account balance auditing work may need to be done.

Knowledge of the source, nature and amount of monetary errors is very important. Such knowledge is required to explain the situation to management and to direct additional work to areas where adjustments are needed. The audit work is not complete until the qualitative evaluation and follow-up is done.

Evaluate the Amount of Error. Auditing standards require the aggregation of *known error* and *projected likely error* (SAS 47, AU 312.28). The aggregation is the sum of: (*a*) known error in the population units identified for 100 percent audit (in the example, the 10 accounts totaling $300,000, with $600 overstatement discovered) and (*b*) the projected likely error for the population sampled (in the example, the $8,300 overstatement projected using the average-difference method). The theory underlying (*b*) is that the projected likely error is the best single estimate of the amount that would be determined if *all* the accounts in the sampled population had been audited. You can see the importance of sample representativeness in this regard. This aggregation ($8,900 overstatement in the example) should be judged in combination with other errors found in the audit of other account balances to determine whether the financial statements taken as a whole need to be adjusted, and if so, in what amount.

The evaluation of amounts is not over yet, however. One thing that *cannot* be said about the projected likely error is that it is the *exact* amount that would be found if all the units in the population were audited. The actual amount might be more or less, and the problem arises from *sampling error*—the amount by which an actual error total could differ from a projected likely error amount as a result of the sample not being exactly representative. Of course, auditors are most concerned with the possibility that the actual total error might be considerably *more* than the

projected likely error. The possibility affects the risk of incorrect acceptance.

This sampling phenomenon gives rise to the concept of *possible error*
(the third kind, in addition to known and likely error), which is interpreted
in auditing standards as the *further error remaining undetected* (SAS 47,
AU 312.32). Nonstatistical auditors resort to experience and professional
judgment to consider additional possible error. Statistical auditors, however, can utilize some statistical calculations to measure possible error, as
explained in Chapter 12.

AUDIT PROGRAMS

In Chapter 6, audit programs were described as lists of audit procedures
which tell auditors what steps to take to obtain evidence. *Compliance
audit programs* consist of procedures designed to produce evidence about
the effectiveness of a client's internal accounting control procedures. The
audit procedures listed therein are compliance-purpose procedures.

Account balance audit programs consist of procedures designed to
produce evidence about the account balances. The procedures listed
therein are substantive-purpose procedures. The next two sections contain lists of specific procedures you may expect to see in audit programs.

Compliance Auditing

You have studied the review phase of the study and evaluation of internal
control and should know that the company's specific control procedures
are learned at that time. Continuing with the example of the audit of
accounts receivable, assume the company has specified controls designed
to meet the general control objectives (validity, completeness, authorization, accuracy, classification, accounting, and proper period). The following compliance procedures can be performed to determine how well the
control procedures were performed on the transactions that affect accounts receivable:

1. Select a sample of recorded sales invoices and:
    a. Vouch them to supporting shipping orders (evidence of *validity*).
    b. Vouch them to notation of credit approval in credit files (evi-
        dence of *authorization*).
    c. Compare the quantities shipped to the quantities billed, look up
        the authorized unit prices, recalculate the amounts billed (evi-
        dence of *accuracy*).
    d. Note the type of product shipped and determine proper classifica-
        tion in the right product-line revenue account (evidence of *classi-
        fication*).
    e. Compare the shipment date with the revenue recognition (record-
        ing) date (evidence of *proper period*).
    f. Trace the invoice to posting in the general ledger control account
        and in the correct customer's account (evidence of *accounting*).

2. Select a sample of shipping orders and:
   a. Trace them to recorded sales invoices (evidence of *completeness*).
   b. The procedures in 1*b*, 1*c*, 1*d*, 1*e*, and 1*f* also could be performed on the sales invoices produced by this sample. However, the work need not be duplicated.

3. Select a sample of recorded cash receipts and:
   a. Trace them to deposits in the bank statement (evidence of *validity*).
   b. Vouch discounts taken by customers to proper approval or policy (evidence of *authorization*).
   c. Recalculate the cash summarized for a daily deposit or posting (evidence of *accuracy*).
   d. Trace the deposit to the right cash account (evidence of *classification*).
   e. Compare the date of receipt to the recording date (evidence of *proper period*).
   f. Trace the receipts to postings in the correct customers' accounts (evidence of *accounting*).

4. Select a sample of daily cash reports or another source of original cash records and:
   a. Trace to the cash receipts journal (evidence of *completeness*).
   b. The procedures in 3*b*, 3*c*, 3*d*, 3*e*, and 3*f* could also be performed on this cash receipts sample. However, the work need not be duplicated.

5. Scan the accounts receivable for postings from sources other than the sales and cash receipts journals (for example, general journal adjusting entries, credit memos). Vouch a sample of such entries to supporting documents (evidence of *validity, authorization, accuracy,* and *classification*).

This list describes the **nature** of the procedures. Each one is a specific application of one of the general procedures described in Chapter 6.

Account Balance Auditing

The basic assertions in a presentation of accounts receivable are that they *exist,* they are *complete* (no receivables are unrecorded), the company has the *right* to collect the money, they are *valued* properly at net realizable value, and they are *presented and disclosed properly.* Substantive-purpose procedures that will produce evidence relevant to these assertions include:

1. Confirm a sample of the receivables, investigate exceptions and follow up nonrespondents by vouching sales charges and cash receipts to supporting documents (evidence of *existence, rights,* and *valuation*).

2. Obtain an aged trial balance of the receivables. Audit the aging accuracy on a sample basis. Calculate and analyze the age status of the accounts and the allowance for uncollectible accounts in light of current economic conditions and the company's collection experience (evidence of *valuation*).

3. Discuss past due accounts with the credit manager. Obtain credit reports and financial statements for independent analysis of large overdue accounts (evidence of *valuation*).

4. Vouch receivables balances to cash received after the cutoff date (evidence of *existence, rights and valuation*).

5. Distinguish names of trade customers from others (officers, directors, employees, affiliates) and determine that the two classifications are reported separately (evidence of *presentation and disclosure*).

6. Read loan agreements and note any pledge of receivables, sales with recourse or other restrictions or contingencies related to the receivables (evidence of *presentation and disclosure*).

7. Obtain written representations from the client concerning pledges for collateral, related party receivables, collectibility and other matters relating to accounts receivable (detail assertions in writing).

This list describes the **nature** of the procedures. Each one is a specific application of one of the general procedures described in Chapter 6. However, this list has no procedure dealing explicitly with the *completeness* assertion. You can obtain completeness evidence with the dual-purpose nature of the completeness procedures done in the compliance audit work (see compliance procedures 2 and 4). The list also contains no analytical review procedures based on interrelationships with budget, forecast, industry or historical data. More specific situational facts would need to be known in order to be specific about analytical review work.

Timing of Compliance Audit Procedures

Earlier in the chapter, you learned that auditors can perform the compliance audit procedures at an *interim date*—a date some weeks or months before the client's year-end date. When compliance auditing is timed early, an audit manager must decide what to do about the remaining period (for example, the period October through December after doing compliance auditing in September for a December 31 year-end audit).

Auditing standards suggest that the decision turns on a number of factors: (1) The results of the work at interim might, for example, indicate poor control performance and no justification for reliance; (2) inquiries made after interim may show that a particular control procedure has been abandoned or improved; (3) the length of the remaining period may be short enough to forego additional work, or long enough to suggest a need for continuing the compliance audit; (4) the dollar amounts affected by the control procedure may have been much larger or much smaller than before; (5) evidence obtained about control as a by-product of performing substantive procedures covering the remaining period may show enough about control performance that separate work on the control procedure performance might not be necessary; or (6) work performed by the company's internal auditors might be relied upon with respect to the remaining period.

Depending upon the circumstances indicated by these sources of information, an audit manager can decide to: (1) continue the compliance audit work because knowledge of the state of control performance is necessary to justify reliance and restriction of other audit work or (2) stop further compliance audit work because (a) compliance evidence derived from other procedures provides a sufficient basis for reliance or (b) information shows the control has failed, reliance is not justified, and other work will not be restricted. Whatever the final judgment, considerations of audit effectiveness and efficiency should always be uppermost in the audit manager's mind.

Timing of Substantive Audit Procedures

Account balances can also be audited, at least in part, at an interim date. When this work is done before the company's year-end date, auditors must extend the interim-date audit conclusion to the balance sheet date. The process of *extending the audit conclusion* amounts to nothing more (and nothing less) than performing substantive-purpose audit procedures on the transactions in the remaining period and on the year-end balance to produce sufficient competent evidence for a decision about the year-end balance.

Substantive procedures must be performed to obtain evidence about the balance after the interim date. You cannot audit a balance (say, accounts receivable) as of September 30, then without further work accept the December 31 balance. Internal control must be well specified and performed adequately. If the company's internal control over transactions that produce the balance under audit are not particularly reliable, you should time the substantive detail work at year-end instead of at interim. If reliance on internal control is not intended, then the substantive work on the remaining period will need to be extensive.

If rapidly changing business conditions might predispose managers to misstate the accounts (try to slip one by the auditors), the work should be timed at year-end. In most cases, careful *scanning of transactions* and *analytical review comparisons* should be performed on transactions that occur after the interim date.

As an example, accounts receivable confirmation can be done at an interim date. Subsequently, efforts must be made to ascertain whether controls continued to be reliable. You must scan the transactions of the remaining period, audit any new large balances, and update work on collectibility, especially with analysis of cash received after the year-end.

Audit work is performed at interim for two reasons: (1) To spread the accounting firm's workload so not all the work on clients is crammed into

December and January; (2) To make the work efficient and enable companies to report audited financial results soon after the year-end. Some well-organized companies with well-planned audits report their audited figures as early as five or six days after their fiscal year-ends.

SUMMARY   Throughout several chapters, you have studied the *nature* of audit procedures. The audit programs—the lists of procedures just presented—merely describe the work to be done in terms of the nature of the procedures. When, as an assistant auditor, you are given an audit program, it is up to you to be able to perceive the evidence the procedures will produce and what relevance it has for decisions about control procedure performance and about financial assertions.

The list of procedures is only part of an audit plan. A plan also involves matters of *timing* and *extent* of procedures applications. Timing was discussed in terms of work done at an interim date and work done in the remaining period between an interim date and the company's year-end. The extent of work involves the subject of *audit sampling*—matters concerning the amount of work done and the question: "How much evidence is enough?" This chapter and Chapters 11 and 12 deal with the terminology, design and technology of audit sampling.

The process of planning an audit begins with the pre-engagement and familiarization activities (Chapter 6), continues in the study and evaluation of internal accounting control (Chapter 7), and is completed in this chapter with the specifications for timing and sampling. Next, in Chapters 9 and 10, the special features of auditing in a computer environment are added to this sequence of events.

SOURCES AND   Akresh, Abraham D. "Statistical Sampling in Public Accounting." *CPA Journal,*
ADDITIONAL   July 1980, pp. 20–26.
READING
REFERENCES   Bailey, Larry P. "Impact of SAS 39 on Nonstatistical Sampling." *CPA Journal,*
                         June 1982, pp. 38–47.

Ijiri, Y., and R. S. Kaplan. "A Model for Integrating Sampling Objectives in Auditing." *Journal of Accounting Research,* Spring 1971, pp. 73–87.

Taylor, Robert G. "Error Analysis in Audit Tests." *Journal of Accountancy,* May 1974, pp. 78–82.

Warren, C. S., S. V. N. Yates, and G. R. Zuber. "Audit Sampling: A Practical Approach." *Journal of Accountancy,* January 1982, pp. 62–72.

REVIEW QUESTIONS

8.1.   Why do auditors sample?

8.2.   What are the primary distinctions between statistical and nonstatistical sampling?

8.3.   What is *nonsampling risk?*

8.4.   What are *compliance procedures* in general, and what purpose do they serve?

8.5. Why must an audit sample be representative of the population from which it is drawn?

8.6. How can an auditor specify the specific objectives of compliance audit procedures?

8.7. In compliance auditing, why is it necessary to define a compliance deviation in advance? Give seven examples of compliance deviations.

8.8. What judgments must an auditor make when deciding upon a sample size for compliance audit sampling? Describe the influence of each judgment on sample size.

8.9. What criterion must be met if a sample is to be considered random?

8.10. Name and describe four sample selection methods.

8.11. Why should auditors be more concerned in compliance auditing with the risk of overreliance than with the risk of underreliance?

8.12. Write the expanded risk model. What risk is implied for "test of detail risk" when: Inherent risk = 1.0, internal control risk = 0.40, analytical review risk = 0.60, audit risk = 0.048, tolerable error = $25,000, and the estimated standard deviation of errors in the population = $25.00?

8.13. When auditing account balances, why is an incorrect acceptance decision considered more serious than an incorrect rejection decision?

8.14. What should be the relationship between tolerable error in the audit of an account balance and the amount of monetary error considered material to the overall financial statements?

8.15. What general set of audit objectives can you use as a frame of reference to be specific about the particular objectives for the audit of an account balance?

8.16. What audit purpose is served by stratifying an account balance population and by removing some units from the population for 100 percent audit attention?

8.17. What is the influence on sample size of the risk of incorrect acceptance, the risk of incorrect rejection, the tolerable error, the population variability and the population size?

8.18. What kind of evidence evaluation consideration should an auditor give to the dollar amount of a population unit that cannot be audited?

8.19. What are the three basic steps in quantitative evaluation of monetary amount evidence when auditing an account balance?

8.20. What are two methods of *projecting the known error to the population?*

8.21. The projected likely error may be calculated, yet further error might remain undetected in the population. How can auditors account for the further error when completing the quantitative evaluation of monetary evidence?

8.22. What two types of audit programs are ordinarily used as written plans for audit procedures?

8.23. What important decision must be made when compliance auditing is performed and internal control is evaluated at an interim date several weeks or months before the client's fiscal year-end date?

8.24. What additional considerations are in order when auditors plan to audit account balances at an interim date several weeks or months before the client's fiscal year-end date?

8.25. What important audit question is embodied in auditors' references to the *extent* of audit procedures?

EXERCISES AND PROBLEMS

8.26. **Sampling and Nonsampling Audit Work**
The accounting firm of Mason & Jarr performed the work described in each separate case below. The two partners are worried

about properly applying standards regarding audit sampling (SAS 39, AU 350). They have asked your advice.

Required:

Write a report addressed to them, stating whether they did or did not observe the essential elements of audit sampling standards in each case.

a. Mason selected three purchase orders for raw materials from the LIZ Corporation files. He started at this beginning point in the accounting process and traced each one through the accounting system. He saw the receiving reports, purchasing agent's approvals, receiving clerks' approvals, the vendors' invoices (now stamped PAID), the entry in the cash disbursement records, and the cancelled checks. This work gave him a firsthand familiarity with the cash disbursement system, and he felt confident about understanding related questions in the internal control questionnaire completed later.

b. Jarr observed the inventory taking at SER Corporation. She had an inventory list of the different inventory descriptions with the quantities taken from the perpetual inventory records. She selected the 200 items with the largest quantities and counted them after the client's shop foreman had completed his count. She decided not to check out the count accuracy on the other 800 items. The shop foreman miscounted in 16 cases. Jarr concluded the rate of miscount was 8 percent, so as many as 80 of the 1000 items might be counted wrong. She asked the foreman to recount everything.

c. CSR Corporation issued seven series of short-term commercial paper notes near the fiscal year-end to finance seasonal operations. Jarr confirmed the obligations under each series with the independent trustee for the holders, studied all seven indenture agreements, and traced the proceeds of each issue to the cash receipts records.

d. At the completion of the EH & R Corporation audit, Mason obtained written representations, as required by auditing standards, from the president, the chief financial officer and the controller. He did not ask the chief accountant at headquarters or the plant controllers in the three divisions for written representations.

8.27. **Compliance Procedure Objectives and Control Deviations**
This exercise asks you to specify compliance audit procedure objectives and define deviations in connection with planning the compliance audit of Kingston Company's internal accounting controls. For each control cited below, state the objective of an auditor's compliance procedure and the definition of a deviation from the control. (In problem 7.17, the requirement was to specify the control objectives and write compliance procedures related to these controls.)

a. The credit department supervisor reviews each customer's order and approves credit by making a notation on the order.

b. The billing department must receive written notice from the shipping department of actual shipment to a customer before a sale is recorded. The sale record date is supposed to be the shipment date.

c. Billing clerks carefully look up the correct catalog list prices for goods shipped and calculate and recheck the amounts billed on invoices for the quantities of goods shipped.

d. Billing clerks review invoices for intercompany sales and mark each one with the code "9," so they will be posted to intercompany sales accounts.

e. Shipping clerks are supposed to notify the billing department of all shipments so that none fail to be billed to customers.

f. Accounting personnel are supposed to make sure all invoices are charged to customers' accounts receivable, balance the subsidiary list of customers' balances to the control account monthly, and review any error reports of out-of-balance conditions.

8.28. **Relevant Populations for Validity and Completeness Evidence**

Below are listed a number of populations of business documents. If you are auditing for evidence of compliance with control over the *validity* of transactions, which populations would you sample, and what would be the logical sampling unit? If you are auditing for evidence of compliance with control over the *completeness* of transactions, which populations would you sample, and what would be the logical sampling unit? Explain your choices.

a. Shipping orders filed in the shipping department.

b. Sales invoices listed in a sales journal.

c. Twelve monthly totals of sales posted in a general ledger.

d. Daily lists of cash received filed in the cashier's office.

e. Raw materials receiving reports filed in the receiving department.

f. Perpetual inventory records of 10,000 different kinds of materials and parts.

g. Cash disbursements listed in a cash disbursements journal.

h. Payroll amounts recorded in individual employees' earnings records (records of each paycheck and amounts withheld kept for tax reporting purposes).

i. Files of life insurance applications and policies kept by a life insurance company.

8.29. **Timing of Compliance Audit Procedures**

Auditor Magann was auditing the authorization control over cash disbursements. She selected cash disbursement entries made throughout the year and vouched them to paid invoices and cancelled checks bearing the initials and signatures of people authorized to approve the disbursements. She performed the work on September 30, when the company had issued checks numbered

from 43921 to 52920. Since 9,000 checks had been issued in nine months, she reasoned that 3,000 more could be issued in the three months before the December 31 year-end. About 12,000 checks had been issued last year. She wanted to take one sample of 100 disbursements for the entire year, so she selected 100 random numbers in the sequence 43921 to 55920. She audited the 80 checks in the sample that were issued before September 30, and she held the other 20 randomly selected check numbers for later use. She found no deviations in the sample of 80—a finding that would, in the circumstances, cause her to evaluate the control as reliable and assign a low (20 percent) control risk to the probability that the system would permit improper charges to be hidden away in expense and purchase/inventory accounts.

Required:

Take the role of Magann and write a memo to the audit manager (dated October 1) describing the audit team's options with respect to evaluating control performance for the remaining period, October–December.

8.30. **Evaluation of Compliance Audit Evidence**

The Kingston Company system of accounting and control over sales transactions is described in problem 7.13 (Chapter 7). The exercises below are derived from the Kingston Company system. You may need to review the system description and flowchart before you do these exercises.

a. Customer credit is approved by the credit department supervisor. She reviews a customer's order and the estimated amounts, and she refers to her credit files on each customer when deciding whether to approve credit. Effective compliance with the credit approval control procedure depends upon having good, up-to-date credit files on the 5,000 regular customers. You have selected 120 files for review. A deviation is defined in terms of a file not being up-to-date. You expect as many as 6 percent of the files may be out of date, but you believe you can rely upon the credit approval control in terms of the planned work on accounts receivable collectibility if as many as 10 percent are out of date. Subjectively, you are not too concerned about the risk of overreliance. What is your evaluation of the credit files if you find: (1) 3 files not up-to-date? (2) 7 files not up-to-date? (3) 13 files not up-to-date?

b. Kingston Company made 10,000 shipments during the year, and therefore created 10,000 bill of lading documents (shipping orders). Shipping clerks are supposed to file one copy in the shipping department and send a copy of the sales invoice to the billing department as notification of shipment. The billing department holds another copy of the invoice awaiting this notification, and billing clerks are supposed to exercise control over failure to bill shipments by making inquiry about old invoices they are holding. You want to audit this control over completeness by selecting bills of lading from the shipping department file and tracing them to recorded sales invoices. You really expect that no more than 1 percent (100) shipments failed to get billed, but even a 3 percent failure rate would not cause you to expand the work on sales and inventory. (If shipments are not recorded as sales, then cost of goods sold is not recorded, inventory is not reduced, and the recorded amount of inventory might be overstated.) The risk of overreliance is not trivial, so you select 200 bills of lading for your audit sample. What is your evaluation of the completeness control

if you find (1) one shipment not recorded as a sale? (2) four shipments not recorded as sales? (3) six shipments not recorded as sales?

8.31. **Evaluation of Compliance Audit Evidence**
The Kingston Company has several control procedures specified to control validity, authorization, accuracy and proper period in relation to recording sales. (You may benefit by rereading problem 7.13 for the Kingston Company system description.) You have decided to audit a sample of 60 recorded sales invoices, looking for deviations of: (a) absence of a supporting shipping order (bill of lading); (b) lack of credit approval; (c) use of wrong product unit price; (d) arithmetic mistakes; and (e) shipment date later than sales recording date. Eight thousand invoices were issued during the year.

Based on prior years' audit experience at Kingston, you expect the deviation rate in the population of sales invoices to be about 5 percent for credit approval noted on the invoices and no more than 1 percent for the other deviations. You believe the rest of your audit work on sales and accounts receivable could proceed as planned if the deviation rate were no more than 10 percent for the credit approvals and no more than 5 percent for the other deviations. Your audit plan does not place heavy reliance on internal control anyway. Control risk is tentatively judged at 60 percent, so you are not too concerned about the risk of overreliance.

Required:
Prepare three worksheets, one each for Case I, Case II and Case III. In the top half

		Number of Deviations		
Types of Deviations		**Case I**	**Case II**	**Case III**
a.	Absence of a supporting shipping order.	0	2	4
b.	Lack of credit approval noted on the sales invoice.	2	4	2
c.	Wrong unit price used to price the products sold.	0	2	0
d.	Invoice arithmetic incorrect	0	2	0
e.	Shipment date later than sales record date	0	4	2

of each worksheet, present a schedule showing the nonstatistical evaluation of the quantitative evidence. In the bottom half of the worksheet, give a brief explanation of your audit conclusions and the effect on the audit plan.

Qualitative Follow-Up Evidence

a. Missing shipping orders were all explained as sales on consignment, and Kingston requires these customers to pick up the goods themselves.

b. Lack of credit approval in all cases occurred on sales less than $1,000.

c. The unit prices that differed from the catalog were all higher.

d. Arithmetic errors were both overcharges and undercharges.

e. No uniform explanation for different dates was offered.

8.32. **Analysis of Test of Detail Risk Relationships**
Prepare a table showing the test of detail risk (TD) for all combinations of internal control risk = 0.10, 0.30, 0.50 and 1.0, analytical review risk = 0.10, 0.30, 0.50 and 1.0, when the inherent risk is 1.0 and audit risk is 0.05.

Prepare another table showing the test for detail (TD) risk for the combinations above, but this time let inherent risk = 0.50.

8.33. **Determining a Risk of Incorrect Acceptance**
Longneck, Inc., was introduced in problem 6.34 (Chapter 6) as a manufacturer of baby bottles and other glass containers. Financial information about the company is in problem 6.34.

Kaye Clark is planning a sampling application to audit the nine-month sales total of Longneck, Inc. The study and evaluation of internal accounting control has shown: (1) 400 invoices out of 28,400 issued in the nine months have been cancelled or reversed on the books at the insistence of customers because they were double-billings of previously issued invoices ($320,000 total debited to the sales account) and (2) about 10 percent of the invoices show corrections inserted by review clerks who check invoices for quantity and pricing errors.

Raven, the engagement manager, believes the accounting control system is deficient and believes its effectiveness for detecting aggregate material sales overstatement is no better than 50 percent. However, accounts receivable confirmations to be mailed as of December 31 represent a "supplementary procedure" (i.e., like an analytical review element in the audit risk model) for detecting sales overstatement, and properly designed, the confirmations could be as much as 80 percent effective. The sales account accuracy is quite important, and Raven believes an audit risk for this work of no greater than 0.02 is appropriate.

Required:

a. Given Raven's maximum criteria, what maximum risk of incorrect acceptance appears to be appropriate for this application?

b. Use the expanded risk model to justify a smaller risk of incorrect acceptance.

8.34. **Quantitative Evaluation of Monetary Evidence**
When Kaye Clark audited the sales invoices of Longneck, Inc., she selected 200 invoices at random from the entire population of 28,000. Her objective was to determine the appropriate (audited) amount of each one, taking into account the use of correct product prices, selling terms and invoice arithmetic. The recorded sales total for the 28,000 invoices was $14,353,812.

Required:

For each of the four different cases described below, project the known error to the population (i.e., calculate the projected likely error) using (a) the average difference method and (b) the ratio method.

		Case		
	(1)	**(2)**	**(3)**	**(4)**
Recorded amount in sample	$102,600	$102,200	$70,200	$160,000
Audited amount determined in sample	$101,800	$100,200	$71,260	$158,000
Known error in sample . .	$−800	$−2,000	$1,060	$−2,000
Number of sample units with errors	80	100	80	80

8.35. Quantitative Evaluation of Monetary Evidence

When Kaye Clark audited 200 of Longneck, Inc.'s 28,000 invoices, she was able to calculate an amount of projected likely error (Problem 8.34). When this audit work was planned, she had decided the amount of tolerable error should be $300,000, the risk of incorrect acceptance should be fairly low (say, around 10 percent) and the risk of incorrect rejection should be moderate (say, around 20 percent). The total amount of recorded sales was $14,353,812.

Required:

Using the average difference and ratio projection methods, she calculated the likely error amounts given below. For each different case, your task is to evaluate the likely error, taking the tolerable error, the risk of incorrect rejection, and the risk of incorrect acceptance into consideration.

		Case		
Projected Likely Error	**(1)**	**(2)**	**(3)**	**(4)**
Average difference method . . .	$−112,000	$−280,000	$148,400	$−280,000
Ratio method.	$−111,921	$−280,897	$216,738	$−179,423
Number of sample units with errors	80	100	80	80

8.36. Audit Programs

The first generally accepted auditing standard of field work requires, in part, that "the work is to be planned adequately." An effective tool that aids the auditor in adequately planning the work is an audit program.

Required:

What is an audit program, and what purposes does it serve?

(*AICPA*)

8.37. Analysis of an Audit Program

Assigned to audit plant asset balances, an assistant auditor began by footing the equipment subsidiary ledgers and reconciling the total to the general ledger account. She checked the mathematical accuracy for the depreciation expense calculation (fixed percent on declining base), giving due consideration to additions and retirements of equipment noted in the subsidiary ledgers. Depreciation expense was traced to the trial balance and the income statement. All amounts were mathematically accurate, and the auditor concluded no adjustments were necessary.

Required:

a. What are the auditor's objectives with specific reference to plant equipment?

b. What evidence-gathering procedures did the auditor rely on in determining the propriety of plant asset balances? Explain.

c. Does the evidence gathered by the auditor afford a reasonable basis for her conclusion? Explain.

d. How might the auditor obtain *firsthand* evidence of the existence of plant assets?

8.38. **Compliance and Account Balance Audit Programs**

Coil steel comprises half the inventory of the Watermore Manufacturing Company. At the beginning of the year, the company installed a system to control coil steel inventory. The coil steel is kept inside the plant in a special storage area. When coils are received, a two-part tag is prepared. The tag is prenumbered, and each part provides for entry of supplier's name, receiving report number, date received, coil weight and description. Both parts of the tag are prepared at the time the material is received and weighed and the receiving report prepared. The "A" part of the tag is sent to the stock records department with the receiving report. The stock records department files the tags numerically by coil width and gauge. Using the receiving report, the stock records department also maintains perpetual stock cards on each width and gauge by total weight. In a sense, the cards are a control record for the tags. No material requisitions are used by the plant, but as coils are placed into production, the A part of the tag is re-moved from the coil and sent to stock records as support for the production report, which is the basis for entries on the perpetual inventory cards.

When the A part of the tag is received by the stock records department, it is matched with the "B" part of the tag and the A part is destroyed. The B part is stamped with the date of use, processed, and retained in a "Consumed" file by width and gauge.

The coils are neatly stacked and arranged, and all tags are visible.

Physical inventories are taken on a cycle basis throughout the year. About one twelfth of the coil steel inventories are counted each month. The coil steel control account and the perpetual stock cards are adjusted as counts are made. Internal control over inventories is considered good.

In previous years, the client had taken a complete physical inventory of coil steel at the end of the year (December 31), but only the cycle counting will be done this year. You audited the financial statements last year and are planning the audit for the current year.

Required:

a. Write an audit program for the compliance audit of control procedures relating to the coil steel inventory. Assume you plan to do this work in late December.

b. Write an audit program for evidence about the existence and cost valuation of the coil steel inventory.

(*AICPA* adapted)

CHAPTER 9

PROFESSIONAL STANDARDS SOURCES		
Compendium Section	**Document Reference**	**Topic**
AU 311*	SAS 22	Planning and Supervision
AU 318*	SAS 23	Analytical Review Procedures
AU 320*	SAS 1	The Auditor's Study and Evaluation of Internal Control
AU 326*	SAS 31	Evidential Matter

* As amended by SAS 48 (July 1984). "The Effects of Computer Processing On the Examination of Financial Statements."

Auditing in a Computer Environment

On many engagements, auditors will encounter computer processed accounting transactions. The decreased costs of data processing equipment, the widespread availability of computer service bureaus and the development of inexpensive microcomputers have made automated processing available even to small companies. Computer systems also have become increasingly complex. Thus, a field of special auditing technology known as "computer auditing" has arisen.

The presence of a computer system affects three areas of an audit: (1) the planning, (2) the proper study and evaluation of internal control and (3) the gathering of evidence on details of transactions and account balances. The first two of these areas, in a *simple* computer environment, is the subject of this chapter. The third, how to use the computer to perform substantive audit work and the control concerns and audit techniques of *advanced* computer systems is examined in Chapter 10.

Your learning objectives for this study and evaluation of internal accounting control in a computer environment are to be able to:

- ☐ Explain how a computer accounting system differs from a manual accounting system.
- ☐ Explain the differences among: (*a*) auditing around the computer, (*b*) auditing through the computer and (*c*) auditing with the computer.
- ☐ List and discuss the additional matters the auditor should consider in planning when a computer is used.
- ☐ Describe how the preliminary phase and the completion of the review of internal accounting control are affected by computer processing.

□ Explain the difference between general controls and application controls.

□ Identify and explain: (*a*) functional responsibilities that should be segregated, (*b*) system documentation that should exist, (*c*) data and program file access controls and (*d*) hardware controls.

□ List and describe the purpose of application controls.

□ Compute a check digit, given the starting data and the method.

□ Explain how the auditor might perform the compliance audit of computerized controls, especially how parallel simulation and test data are used.

**COMPUTER
ENVIRONMENT**

An auditing text cannot fully describe all the complexities of how computers process business transactions. This text assumes that you have had a course in computer concepts and general computer data processing. The purposes of this section are: to *review* the basic elements of computer systems, to *define* some terms which will be subsequently used, and to *describe* some of the control considerations unique to automated systems.

Although the term "computer auditing" has a certain mystique, there is no fundamental difference between computer auditing and the auditing described elsewhere in this book. To be more specific, when a computer is used to process the transactions:

The definition of auditing is not changed.

The purposes of auditing are not changed.

The generally accepted auditing standards are not changed.

The assertions of management embodied in financial statements are not changed.

The internal accounting control objectives are not changed.

The requirement to gather sufficient competent evidential matter is not changed.

The independent auditor's report on financial statements is not changed.

Therefore, everything you have learned from previous chapters is valid, only the method of processing and storing accounting data has changed. When the automation of transactions becomes complex, auditing organizations need to employ audit specialists who understand computer technology and who are aware of basic audit purposes. These "computer auditors" are members of the audit team and are called upon when the need for their skills arises, just as statistical sampling specialists or SEC specialists are available when their expertise is needed. A general, single-volume audit text cannot prepare you to be a computer auditor. All auditors however, should have enough familiarity with computer processing and controls to enable them to complete the audit of simple systems and to interface with computer auditor specialists.

Elements of a Computer-Based System

In a manual accounting system, transaction processing can be followed readily and is typically supported by paper documents—approvals, vouchers, invoices and records of accountability, such as perpetual inventory records. Similar documents often exist in a computer system, but in many cases are available only in machine-sensible form. Further, the basic records (ledgers and journals) of a computer-based accounting system are frequently machine-sensible data files that cannot be read or changed without a computer.

A computer-based system includes the following elements:

1. *Hardware*—The physical equipment or devices that constitute a computer. These may include the central processing unit, card reader, tape drives, disk devices, printers, terminals and other devices.
2. *Software:*
    a. *System programs*—Programs that perform generalized functions for more than one application. These programs, sometimes referred to as supervisory programs, typically include: "operating systems," which control, schedule and maximize efficient use of the hardware; "data management systems," which perform standardized data-handling functions for one or more application programs; and "utility" programs that can perform basic computer operations. System programs are generally developed by the hardware supplier or by software development companies and are typically tailored by each user to suit individual requirements.
    b. *Application (user) programs*—Sets of computer instructions that perform data processing tasks. These programs are usually written within the organization or purchased from an outside supplier.
3. *Documentation*—A description of the system and its controls in relation to input, data processing, output, report processing, logic, and operator instructions.
4. *Personnel*—Persons who manage, design, program, operate or control data processing systems.
5. *Data*—Transactions and related information entered, stored and processed by the system.
6. *Controls*—Procedures designed to assure the proper recording of transactions and to prevent or detect errors or irregularities.[1]

---

[1] AICPA, *The Auditor's Study and Evaluation of Internal Control in EDP Systems* (New York, 1977), p.5.

According to auditing standards, the establishment and maintenance of a system of internal control is an important responsibility of management (SAS 1, AU 320.31). The controls included as elements of a computer-based system are part of that responsibility. The audit team's responsibility is to study and evaluate the existing controls. Management can meet its responsibility and assist auditors in the following ways: (1) by ensuring documentation of the systems is complete and up-to-date, (2) by maintaining a system of transaction processing that includes an audit trail and (3) by making computer resources and knowledgeable personnel available to the auditors to help them understand and audit the system.

Control Considerations in Computer-Based Systems

The method used to process accounting transactions will affect a company's organizational structure and will influence the procedures and techniques used to accomplish the broad objectives of internal control (as discussed in Chapter 7). When computers are used, special control considerations are relevant for evaluating the control environment and control procedures. *Statements on Auditing Standards Number 48,* "The Effects of Computer Processing on the Examination of Financial Statements," lists the following characteristics that distinguish computer processing from manual processing:

☐ *Transaction trails*. Some computer systems are designed so that a complete transaction trail useful for audit purposes might exist only for a short period of time or only in computer-readable form. (A transaction trail is a chain of evidence provided through coding, cross-references, and documentation connecting account balances and other summary results with the original transactions and calculations.)

☐ *Uniform processing of transaction*. Computer processing uniformly subjects like transactions to the same processing instructions. Consequently, computer processing virtually eliminates the occurrence of random errors normally associated with manual processing. Conversely, programming errors (or other similar systematic errors in either the computer hardware or software) will result in all like transactions being processed incorrectly when those transactions are processed under the same conditions.

☐ *Segregation of functions*. Many internal accounting control procedures, once performed by different individuals in manual systems, may be concentrated in computer systems. Therefore, individuals who have access to the computer may be in a position to perform incompatible functions. As a result, other control procedures may be required in computer systems to achieve the degree of control ordinarily accomplished by segregating functions in manual systems. These may include such techniques as use of password control procedures to prevent incompatible functions from being performed by individuals who have access to assets and access to records through an online terminal.

☐ *Potential for errors and irregularities.* The potential for individuals, including those performing control procedures, to gain unauthorized access to or alter data without visible evidence, as well as gain access (direct or indirect) to assets, may be greater in computerized accounting systems than in manual systems. Less human involvement in handling transactions processed by computers can reduce the potential for observing errors and irregularities. Errors or irregularities made in designing or changing application programs can remain undetected for long periods of time.

☐ *Potential for increased management supervision.* Computer systems offer management a wide variety of analytical tools that may be used to review and supervise the operations of the company. The availability of these additional controls may enhance the entire system of internal accounting control on which auditors may wish to place reliance. For example, traditional comparisons of actual operating ratios with those budgeted, as well as reconciliation of accounts, are frequently available for management review on a more timely basis when such information is computerized. Additionally, some programmed applications provide computer operating statistics that may be used to monitor the actual processing of transactions.

☐ *Initiation or subsequent execution of transactions by computer.* Certain transactions may be automatically initiated or certain transactions may be automatically executed by a computer system. The authorization of these transactions or procedures may not be documented in the same way as those in a manual accounting system, and management's authorization of those transactions may be implicit in its acceptance of the system's design.

The controls described in this chapter relate to a *simple* computer system, although many of the controls are applicable to more advanced systems described in Chapter 10. A **simple system** is one where all processing occurs at a central processing facility in a **batch** mode. Batch processing (also called serial or sequential processing) means that all records to be processed are collected in groups (batches) of like transactions. The computer operator (or the operating system) obtains the programs and master files from the computer library. Following the instructions in the run manual, all like transactions are then processed utilizing the same programs and the same master files. For example, all payroll records are run at one time and the input is in the form of punched cards containing employees' identification numbers and hours worked. The programs edit and validate the input and match good transactions against the employee master file for pay rate and deduction information. Programs execute the processing to compute the payroll, print checks, update year-to-date records, and summarize payroll information for management. After completion of the run, the programs and files are returned to storage (magnetic) and the output of checks and reports is distributed.

Batches may be collected at a central computer site or other locations. Input transactions may be entered via terminals and stored on magnetic tape or disks rather than cards. Regardless of these modifications, the *batch* processing is characterized by grouping like transactions to be processed in batches, all using the same programs. The master files take the place of subsidiary and general ledger accounts in manual systems. The batches of transactions are similar to journals in a manual system. All transactions in a batch may be listed in printed output. However, the detail of transactions is usually not printed and the familiar journal is nonexistent. Instead, summary entries are prepared for updating general ledger master files.

Master files contain records of two general types of fields—*static* fields such as employee number and pay rate and *dynamic* fields such as year-to-date gross pay or account balances. Most of the computer processing of accounting data involves changing these fields in the master file records. The dynamic fields are changed in *update* processing as was described for batch processing of payroll. Update processing does not change the static fields. The static fields are changed by *file maintenance* processing which will add or delete entire records (for example, add a new employee) or change fields (for example, new pay rate). Auditors are concerned with authorization and controls over *both* types of changes.

EVALUATION APPROACHES FOR COMPUTER SYSTEMS

When businesses started using computers, two terms were coined to describe the nature of auditing work on computer systems. The first term, *auditing around the computer* came to mean that auditors were attempting to isolate the computer—to treat it like a "black box"—and to find audit assurance by vouching data from output to source documents and tracing data from source documents to output. As long as the computer was used as a speedy calculator, this method was generally considered adequate. In fact, it may be satisfactory today if the computer system is used simply as a calculator and printer. Nothing inherently is wrong with auditing around the computer if auditors are satisfied with controls and are able to gather sufficient evidence. Auditing around the computer becomes unacceptable if this approach is used because of lack of auditor expertise regarding computer processing.

The second term that evolved is *auditing through the computer*. It refers to the auditor's actual evaluation of the hardware and software to determine the reliability of operations that could not be viewed by the human eye. *Auditing through* has become more common in practice because more and more computer systems do not operate as speedy calculators but have significant control procedures built into their systems. Thus, ignoring a computer system and the controls built into it would amount to ignoring important characteristics of internal accounting control.

More recently, two new terms have been used to describe the auditor's approach to computer systems: (1) *auditing without the computer* and (2) *auditing with the computer.* The first approach consists of using visible evidence such as the input source data, the machine-produced error listings, the visible control points (for example, use of batch totals) and the detailed printed output. The second approach, when auditing a *simple* computer system, refers to such audit techniques as: (1) the use of the client's computer hardware and software to process real or simulated transactions or (2) the use of specialized audit software to perform other audit tasks.

PLANNING

In addition to the audit planning considerations you learned in Chapter 6, auditors should consider the methods employed by a client to process significant accounting information, including the use of outside organizations, such as data processing service centers. The client's methods influence the design of the accounting system and the nature of the internal accounting control procedures.

The degree to which computer processing is used in significant accounting applications as well as the complexity of the processing may also influence the nature, timing and extent of audit procedures. Accordingly, when evaluating the effect of a client's computer processing on an examination of financial statements, auditors should consider matters such as:

- □ The extent to which the computer is used in each significant accounting application.
- □ The complexity of the computer operations used by the entity, including the use of an outside service center.
- □ The organizational structure of the computer processing activities.
- □ The availability of data.
- □ The computer-assisted audit techniques to increase the efficiency of audit procedures.
- □ The need for specialized skills.[2]

---

[2] *Statement on Auditing Standards No. 48* (AU 311.09), ''The Effects of Computer Processing on the Examination of Financial Statements,'' amending *Statement on Auditing Standards No. 22.*

The Extent to Which the Computer Is Used

The extent to which the computer is used in each significant accounting application should be considered in audit planning. Significant accounting applications are those relating to accounting information that can materially affect the financial statements. Computers are used to process applications that relate to such information, and the audit team may need computer-related skills to understand the flow of transactions. The nature, timing and extent of audit procedures may also be affected by the level of computer use.

The Complexity of Computer Operations

The complexity of the computer operations used by a client, including the use of an outside service center, should be considered in audit planning. When assessing the complexity of computer processing, the audit manager should consider his or her training and experience relative to the methods of data processing used by the client. If significant accounting applications are processed at outside service centers, it may be necessary to coordinate audit procedures with service auditors. (Refer to Chapter 7 for a discussion of "service auditors.")

Other matters may be considered when assessing the complexity of computer processing. The computer hardware utilized by the entity may show the degree of complexity involved. The degree to which various computerized systems appear to share common files or are otherwise integrated may also be considered because these characteristics may cause all such integrated systems to be considered significant accounting applications. In some computerized systems, a transaction trail may be available only in computer-readable form, only for short periods of time, and possibly in a complex form.

The Organizational Structure of Computer Processing

The organizational structure of a client's computer processing activities can have significant effects on how the auditor plans to conduct the work. Clients may have significant differences in the way these activities are organized. The degree of centralization inherent in the organizational structure especially may vary.

A highly centralized organizational structure will generally have all significant computer processing activities controlled and supervised at a central location. The control environment, the computer hardware, and the computer systems may be uniform throughout the company. Auditors may be able to obtain most of the necessary computer processing information by visiting the central location. At the other extreme, a highly decentralized organizational structure generally allows various departments, divisions, subsidiaries or geographical locations to develop, control and supervise computer processing activities in an autonomous fashion. In this situation, the computer hardware and the computer systems will usually not be uniform throughout the company. Thus, auditors may need to visit many locations to obtain the necessary audit information. To assess the potential for appropriate segregation of functions, auditors may wish to consider the number of people involved with computer processing activities within the company, as well as the apparent level of computer-related knowledge possessed by these personnel.

The Availability of Data

Computer systems provide an ability to store, retrieve and analyze much more data than is practical in manual systems. Input data, certain computer files and other data required by the auditor team may exist only for short periods of time or only in computer-readable form. In some computer systems, input documents may not exist at all because information is entered directly. The data-retention policies adopted by a client may require auditors to arrange for some information to be retained for review. Alternatively, auditors may need to plan to perform audit procedures at a time when the information is still available.

In addition, certain information generated by the computer system for management's internal purposes may be useful in performing analytical review procedures and other audit procedures. For example, due to the ease of storage, the client may save sales information by month, by product and by salesman. Such information can be used with analytical review procedures in determining if the revenue accounts are reasonable.

The Use of Computer-Assisted Audit Techniques

Computer-assisted audit techniques (described in Chapter 10) may be used to increase the efficiency of certain audit procedures and also may provide auditors with opportunities to apply certain procedures to an entire population of accounts or transactions. The use of these techniques requires advance planning and may require individuals with specialized skills as members of the audit team.

The Need for Specialized Skills

In determining the need for specialized computer skills on the audit team, all aspects involved in evaluating the effect of a client's computer processing should be considered. In planning the engagement, the audit manager may conclude that certain specialized skills are needed to consider the effect of computer processing on the audit, to understand the flow of transactions, or to design and perform audit procedures. For example, specialized skills relating to various methods of data processing, programming languages, software packages or computer-assisted audit techniques may be needed. Audit managers and partners should possess sufficient computer knowledge to know when to call on specialists and to understand and supervise the specialists' work.

COMPUTER SYSTEM REVIEW

The purpose of the review of a system (as explained in Chapter 7) is to obtain sufficient knowledge and understanding about the accounting system and the internal control system to: (a) determine whether internal control procedures provide a basis for reliance thereon in determining the nature, timing and extent of substantive audit procedures and (b) aid in designing substantive procedures. (SAS 1, AU 320.52.) The review of the computer system consists of the preliminary phase and the completion of the review.

Preliminary Phase   The preliminary phase should be designed to provide an understanding of the control environment and the flow of transactions through the accounting system. The ***understanding of the control environment*** should provide a general knowledge of: (*a*) the organizational structure, (*b*) the methods used by the client to communicate responsibility and authority and (*c*) the methods used by management to supervise the system, including the existence of an internal audit function, if any. Each of these elements of the control environment may be affected by computer processing.

Control Environment—The Organizational Structure.   The auditors' understanding of the organizational structure of a company should include an understanding of the organization of its computer function. This understanding should contribute to the overall assessment of whether reliance on internal controls may be possible. In reviewing the organizational structure of a company's computer function, auditors should obtain and evaluate:

☐   A description of the company's computer resources, including details of computer equipment used, the use of an outside service center, if any, and locations from which the computer resources can be accessed.

☐   A description of the organizational structure of computer operations as it relates to personnel within the computer department, and the interaction with personnel in other departments.

The description of computer resources should give auditors: (1) an overview of computer-operating activities, (2) knowledge of access to computer resources used to process accounting information and (3) knowledge of company policies about access only by authorized personnel. Auditors should inquire about the division of responsibilities between systems and programming staff and operations personnel in order to assess the planned segregation of duties. The existence and organization of the control function and its assigned responsibilities should be understood. Auditors should identify the position the computer function has in the overall organization structure, as well as understand the interaction between user departments and the computer department.

Control Environment—Methods Used to Communicate Responsibility and Authority.   In connection with understanding the methods used by the client to communicate responsibility and authority, the auditor should obtain information about the existence of: (*a*) accounting and other policy manuals including computer operations and user manuals and (*b*) formal job descriptions for computer department personnel. Related user personnel job descriptions may also be helpful. Auditors should also gain an understanding of how the client's computer resources are managed and how priorities for their use are determined. Auditors should also gain an understanding of the extent to which other departments within the company have a clear understanding of how they must comply with computer processing related standards and procedures.

Control Environment—Methods Used by Management to Supervise the System. As part of the review's preliminary phase, auditors should learn what procedures management uses to supervise the computer operation, including:

- ☐ The existence of systems design and documentation standards and the extent to which they are in use.
- ☐ The existence and quality of procedures for system and program modification, systems acceptance approval and output modification (such as changes in reports or files).
- ☐ The procedures limiting access to authorized information, particularly with respect to sensitive information.
- ☐ The availability of financial and other reports, such as budget/performance reviews for use by management.
- ☐ The existence of an internal audit function and the degree to which it is involved in reviewing computer-produced accounting records and related controls and its involvement in systems development control evaluation and testing.

After the audit team gains an understanding of the control environment, the preliminary phase of the review should be continued by obtaining an understanding of the flow of transactions.

Understanding the Flow of Transactions. An understanding of the flow of transactions through the accounting system is required to support the design of substantive audit procedures whether the auditor decides to complete or not complete the review of internal accounting control. Gaining an understanding of the flow of transactions for each significant accounting application begins with referring to the client's description of the accounting applications. If a computer system is used in significant accounting applications, descriptions should include the user's manuals and instructions, file descriptions, system flowcharts and narrative descriptions. However, auditors only need to consider system flowcharts that indicate the major inputs and outputs and principal processing steps.

The audit team may find that internal audit personnel or other client personnel have already prepared documentation relating to the flow of transactions. This documentation may be adequate for purposes of understanding the accounting system. Early in the planning phase, the internal auditors and others should be consulted to determine if they have documentation that can be useful.

**Completing the
Review of a System**   The distinction between the preliminary phase of the review and completing the review of a system is useful for your understanding of the review process. However, regardless of the theory of internal control reviews, most auditors in practice will do the two together.

Completing the review when a computer is used involves:

☐ Identifying specific control objectives based on the types of errors and irregularities which may be present in significant accounting transactions.

☐ Identifying the points in the flow of transactions where specific types of errors or irregularities could occur.

☐ Identifying specific control procedures designed to achieve the control objectives.

☐ Identifying the interdependent control procedures which must function for an identified specific control procedure to be effective.

☐ Evaluating the design of control procedures to determine whether it provides a reasonable basis for reliance and whether compliance audit procedures on them might be cost-effective.

Identifying *specific control objectives* is no different than in a manual data processing system. However, the process of *identifying the points in the flow of transactions where error or irregularities could occur* is different in a computer system in comparison to a manual system. For example, when a computer is used, the following are processes where errors or irregularities could occur:

1. Activities related to source data preparation are performed, which cause the flow of transactions to include authorization and initial execution.

2. Non-computerized processing procedures are applied to source data, such as manual summarization of accounting data (preparation of batch totals).

3. Source data are converted into computer-readable form.

4. Input files are identified for use in processing.

5. Information is transferred from one computer program to another.

6. Computer-readable files are used to supply additional information to augment information relating to individual transactions (for example, tables of approved vendors).

7. Transactions are initiated by the computer.

8. Output files are created or master files are updated.

9. Master files are changed (records added, deleted or modified) outside the normal flow of transactions within each cycle through file maintenance procedures.
10. Output reports or files are produced.
11. Errors identified by control procedures are corrected.
12. Output, including reports and terminal displays, are utilized by client personnel.

Once the audit team has identified the points where an error or irregularity might occur, specific control objectives can be related to such points. For example, one possible error or irregularity might involve billing customers with incorrect prices because a wrong file has been used. One way to state a control objective which relates to this type of error or irregularity is "appropriate price information is used during the billing process."

Once points where errors or irregularities could occur in flow of transactions are identified within a client's accounting system, auditors should focus on *specific control procedures which may prevent or detect such errors or irregularities*. Control procedures should be considered in terms of specific control objectives. For example, for the objective of using appropriate price information, one control procedure might be, "the billing application program should identify the correct price file through matching the file name in the program to the name on the header label." (Header labels are described subsequently.) When one or more specific control procedures are determined to be adequate to achieve a specific objective, the auditors need not consider other control procedures that pertain to the same control objective.

In a computerized accounting system, control procedures may have characteristics that differ from manual control procedures designed to accomplish the same control objectives. For example, in a manual system, approval for payment is usually indicated by affixing an authorized signature to a source document, such as an invoice, to indicate approval for payment. In a computerized system, however, approval can be accomplished by utilizing an approved password that releases a transaction by assigning a special code to it. The password would provide access to programs which permit initiating a specific type of transaction or changing existing data. In such a case, although the control objective is identical in the manual and computerized systems, the methods used to achieve the objective and the visible evidence of conformity with authorized procedures differ considerably, and the impact on the audit approach may be significant.

If specific controls (application controls) upon which the auditor intends to rely are identified, a review should be made of general or interdependent control procedures which must also function properly for reliance to be placed on the application controls. The general and application controls are discussed in the following sections.

The *evaluation of the design* at the end of the review is the same as in a manual system. The information gathered about the client's internal control system and about the accounting system should enable the auditor to reach one of the following conclusions:

☐ Control procedures designed to prevent or detect errors or irregularities appear to provide a basis for reliance, and these control procedures can apparently be audited for compliance in a cost-effective manner. In this case, the auditors would continue with compliance auditing as discussed in this chapter.

☐ Control procedures appear to provide a basis for reliance, but compliance auditing would not be cost-effective. In this case, the auditors would not rely on controls but would concentrate attention on the substantive audit procedures.

☐ Control procedures do not appear to be sufficient to prevent or detect material errors or irregularities. If this is the case, the auditors would also not rely on controls but concentrate on substantive audit procedures.

If at any time during the review internal control procedures do not appear to provide a basis for reliance, the auditors should proceed with the design of substantive audit procedures. In making this evaluation, it may be possible to identify specific control procedures which provide a basis for reliance with regard to some but not all transaction types or transaction cycles. In such situations, the auditors may achieve certain audit objectives through a combination of compliance and substantive auditing while other audit objectives may be achieved through substantive procedures alone.

GENERAL CONTROL

All of the desired internal control characteristics discussed in Chapter 7 apply equally to computer systems. However, an additional dimension of control is present, created by the removal of data processing from the traditional accounting function and by the complex technology involved.

According to SAS 48 (AU 320), "The Effects of Computer Processing on the Examination of Financial Statements," internal accounting control procedures may be classified into two types—general controls and application controls. *General controls* relate to all or many computerized accounting activities, such as controls over access to computer programs and data files. *Application controls* relate to individual computerized accounting applications, such as programmed validation controls for verifying customers' account numbers and credit limits. The general controls are presented first because they are usually reviewed early in the audit.

**Organization and
Physical Access**

The proper segregation of functional responsibilities—authority to authorize transactions, custody of assets, recordkeeping, and periodic comparison—is as important in computer systems as in manual systems. However, computer systems involve functions such as systems analysis, programming, data conversion, library functions and machine operations that are unique. Therefore, a further separation of duties is recommended.

The essential division of duties are among the functions of analyst, programmer, and operator. The duties associated with these and other roles are defined as follows:

Systems Analyst.   Analyzes requirements for information. Evaluates the existing system and designs new or improved data processing. Outlines the system and prepares specifications which guide the programmers. Prepares documentation of the application system.

Programmer.   Flowcharts the logic of the computer programs required by the overall system designed by the systems analyst. Codes the logic in the computer program. Prepares documentation of the program.

Computer Operator.   Operates the computer according to written operating procedures for each application system found in the computer operation instructions.

Data-Conversion Operators.   Prepares data for machine processing. Previously, these individuals operated keypunch machines and produced punched cards. Now, these operators usually convert visible source data to magnetic tape or disk, operate optical-character reading equipment and use data transmission terminals.

Librarian.   Two types of librarian functions may be found in a computer facility—one for system and program documentation and the other for the actual program and data files. The purpose of the system/program documentation library is to maintain control over documentation of the design and operation stages of computer information systems. The purpose of the program/data library is to maintain control over the data files and programs actually used from day to day. In many systems, this library function is done automatically with software.

Control Group.   The control group receives input from user departments, logs the input and transfers it to data conversion, reviews documentation sequence numbers, reviews and processes error messages, monitors actual processing, compares control totals to computer output and distributes output.

Separation of the duties performed by analysts, programmers and operators is important. The general idea is that anyone who designs a processing system should not also do the technical programming work, and anyone who performs either of these tasks should not also be the computer operator when "live" data is being processed. Persons performing each function should not have access to the others' work, and only the computer operators should have access to the equipment. Computer systems are susceptible to manipulative handling and the lack of separation of duties along the lines described should be considered a serious weakness in general control.

Illustration.   A programmer employed by a large savings and loan association wrote a special subroutine that could be activated by throwing a switch on the computer console. The computation of interest on deposits and certificates was programmed to truncate calculations at the third decimal place. The special subroutine instructed the program to accumulate the truncated mills, and when processing was complete, to credit the amount to the programmer-operator's savings account. Whenever this person was on duty for the interest-calculation run, she could "make" several hundred dollars! She had to be on duty to manipulate the control figures "properly" so that the error of overpaying interest on her account would not be detected by the control group. She was a programmer with computer operation duties.

Physical security and limited access to files and computer equipment are important. (Note: Access may be via a terminal far removed from the computer.) Access controls help prevent improper use or manipulation of data files, unauthorized or incorrect use of computer programs, and improper use of the computer itself. The librarian function or librarian software should control access to systems documentation and access to program and data files by using a check-out log or password to record use by authorized persons. Someone in possession both of documentation and data files would have enough information to alter data and programs for his or her own purposes.

Locked doors, security passes, passwords, and check-in logs (including logs produced by the computer) can be used to limit access to the computer system hardware. Having definite schedules for running computer applications is another way to detect unauthorized access, because the computer systems software can produce reports that can be compared to the preset schedule. Variations can then be investigated for unauthorized use of computer resources.

Weakness or absence of organizational and access controls decrease the overall integrity of the computer system. The audit team should be uncomfortable when such deficiencies exist and should weigh their impact in the overall evaluation of internal accounting controls.

Some typical questions asked by auditors are shown in the box below. A full set of questions, of which these are a part, is one method of reviewing and documenting the review of the organization and access control of a computer facility.

**ORGANIZATION AND PHYSICAL ACCESS
SELECTED QUESTIONNAIRE ITEMS**

Preliminary

Prepare or have the client prepare a "Computer Profile" which should include an organization chart, hardware and peripheral equipment, communication network, major application processes (batch or online), significant input and output files, software used and a layout of the data center.

Organization

Are the following functions performed by different individuals so that proper segregation of duties exist between:

a. Application programming, computer operation and control of data files?
b. Application programming and control and reconciliation of input and output?
c. Computer employees and users who initiate transactions and authorize changes to master files?

Are computer operators rotated periodically from shift to shift?
Are programmers and systems analysts rotated periodically from application to application?

Data and Procedural Control

Is there a separate group within the computer department to perform control and balancing of input and output?
Are there written procedures for setting up input for processing?
Is there a formal procedure for distribution of output to user departments?

Access Controls

Is access to the computer room restricted to authorized personnel?
Are operators restricted from access to program and application documentation?
Does access to online files require that specific passwords be entered to identify and validate the terminal user?

Documentation and Systems Development

Documentation is the means of communicating the essential elements of the data processing system. The following purposes may be served by computer system documentation:

☐ Provide for management review of proposed application systems.

☐ Provide explanatory material for users.

☐ Instruct new personnel by providing background on previous application systems and serve as a guideline for developing new applications.

- ☐ Provide the data necessary for answering inquiries about the operation of a computer application.
- ☐ Serve as one source of information for an evaluation of internal control.
- ☐ Provide operating instructions.
- ☐ Simplify program revision by providing details of processing logic.
- ☐ Supply basic information for planning and implementing audit software or other auditing techniques.[3]

Auditors review the documentation to gain an understanding of the system and to determine whether the documentation is adequate. Of utmost importance in this area of the review is whether *system development* and *documentation standards* have been established by the client. Unless written standards exist, it is very difficult to determine whether the systems development controls and the documentation are adequate. Auditors must impose their own standards if none exist in the company. The ***system development and documentation standards manual*** prepared by management should contain standards which ensure: (1) proper user involvement in the systems design and modification process, (2) review of the specifications of the system, (3) approval by user management and data processing management and (4) minimum controls and auditability.

Armed with the manual describing systems development standards, auditors will first evaluate the standards to determine whether they are adequate and then review the documentation to determine whether the standards are followed. This review actually accomplishes a compliance audit of systems development standards (and development controls) as well as providing an understanding of how a particular system works.

Auditors are interested in specific items in each of the parts of the systems documentation—systems description, problem definition, program descriptions, acceptance-testing records, computer operator instructions, user department manual, change and modification log, and listing of controls. For example, the ***systems description*** usually contains system flowcharts, description of all inputs and outputs, record formats, lists of computer codes, and control features. The computer system flowcharts can frequently be adapted to audit working paper flowcharts where the flow of transactions can be followed and control points noted (similar to the manual flowcharts illustrated in Chapter 7). Copies of record formats of significant master files are frequently obtained for use in computer-assisted audit techniques (described later in Chapter 10).

The ***program description*** should contain a program flowchart, a listing of the source code (such as COBOL) and a record of all program changes.

---

[3] Gordon B. Davis, Donald L. Adams, and Carol A. Schaller, *Auditing & EDP,* 2d ed. (New York: AICPA, 1983), p. 59.

Auditors should review this documentation to determine whether programmed controls, such as edits, exist. (Edit controls are described later in this chapter.)

The *acceptance testing records* may contain test data that can be used by auditors when performing their own compliance audit procedures. The *users' manual* should indicate manual procedures and controls in the user departments that submit transactions and receive the output. The *log of changes and modifications* is important to auditors because it should provide assurance that the application systems have been operating as described for the period under review and that all changes and modifications have been authorized.

The *controls* section of the documentation is also very important. Here all the computer controls described in other sections are repeated along with manual controls that affect the application. Careful review of this section should provide a complete overview of the entire control over the processing of transactions in a particular application and how the general controls are carried out in that application.

**DOCUMENTATION AND SYSTEMS DEVELOPMENT
SELECTED QUESTIONNAIRE ITEMS**

Development

Does a written priority plan exist for development of new systems and changes to old systems?

Does the design and development of a new system involve the users as well as computer personnel?

Is there a formal review and approval process at the end of each significant phase in developing a new system?

Documentation

Do written standards exist for documentation of new systems and for changing documentation when existing systems are revised?

Does the following documentation exist for each application?

System flowchart.

Record layouts.

Program edit routines.

Program source listing.

Operator instructions.

Approval and change record.

Hardware Controls   Modern computer equipment is highly reliable. Machine malfunctions that can go undetected are relatively rare. You are not expected to be a computer systems engineer, but you should be familiar with some of the hardware controls so they will not escape your attention and so you can converse knowledgeably with computer personnel.

The most important hardware control now incorporated in all computers is a *parity check*. The parity check ensures that the coding of data internal to the computer has not changed when it is moved from one internal storage location to another. An additional hardware control commonly found is an *echo check*. It involves a magnetic read after each magnetic write "echoing" back to the sending location and comparing results. Many computers also contain dual circuitry to perform arithmetic operations twice. Auditors (and management) cannot do much about the absence of such controls but should be concerned primarily with operator procedures when such errors occur. Modern computers are largely self-diagnostic. Therefore, written procedures should exist for all computer malfunctions, and all malfunctions should be recorded along with their causes and resolutions.

Another significant area of auditor interest is the *preventive maintenance*. Review of this area should determine whether maintenance is scheduled and whether the schedule is followed and documented. Maintenance is frequently under contract with the computer vendor. In such cases, auditors should review the contract as well as the record of regular maintenance work. Other general evidence on hardware reliability may be obtained from a review of operating reports and downtime logs.

Data File and Program Control and Security

Controls over physical access to the computer hardware were described in conjunction with organization controls. Equally important and sensitive is control over access, use and security of the data files and programs. Since magnetic storage media can be erased or written over, controls are necessary to ensure that the proper file is being used and that the files and programs are appropriately backed up. *Backup* involves a systematic retention system (some of which is offsite, away from the main computer) of files, programs and documentation so that master files could be reconstructed in case of accidental loss and processing could continue at another site if the computer center were lost to fire or flood.

Some of the more important security and retention control techniques and procedures are:

External Labels.   These labels are paper labels on the outside of a file (punched cards, portable disk packs or magnetic tapes). The label identifies the contents, such as "Accounts Receivable Master File," so that the probability of using the file inappropriately, for example in a payroll run, is minimized.

Header and Trailer Labels.   These labels are special internal records on magnetic tapes and disks. They are magnetic records on the tape or disk, but instead of containing data, they hold label information similar to the external file label. Therefore, the header and trailer labels are sometimes called *internal labels*. Their function is to serve as controls to prevent use of the wrong file during processing. The header label will contain the name of the file and relevant identification codes. The trailer label gives a signal that the end of the file has been reached, and sometimes these trailer labels are designed to contain accumulated control totals to serve as a check on loss of data during operation.

File Security.   Security is enhanced by many physical devices, such as storage in fireproof vaults, in remote locations and in computer-readable, printed or microfilm form. In the majority of cases, the exposure to risk of loss warrants insurance on program and data files.

File Retention.   Retention practices are closely related to file security, but, in general, retention may provide the first line of defense against relatively minor loss, while security generally consists of all measures taken to safeguard files against total loss. In essence, the problem is how to reconstruct records and files once they have been damaged. One of the most popular methods is the "grandfather-father-son" concept. This involves the retention of backup files, such as the current transaction file and the prior master file from which the current master file can be reconstructed. Exhibit 9–1 illustrates the file retention plan. Particularly impor-

EXHIBIT 9–1
Grandfather, Father, and
Son in Magnetic Tape
Files

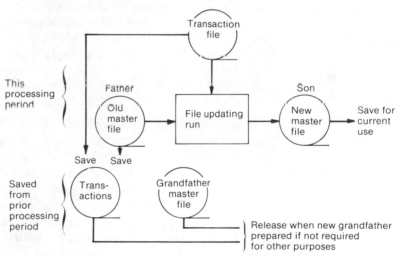

Source: Gordon B. Davis, Donald Adams, and Carol A. Schaller, *Auditing and EDP* (New York: AICPA, 1983), p. 128.

tant files may be retained to the great-grandfather generation if considered necessary.

Disk files are more difficult to reconstruct than tape files because the process of updating old records with new information is "destructive." The old or superceded data on a record is removed (destroyed) when new data is entered in the same place on a disk. One means of reconstruction is to have a disk file "dumped" onto tape periodically (each day or each week). This file copy, along with the related transaction file also retained, can serve as the father to the current disk file (son).

APPLICATION CONTROLS

Application control features are categorized as: (1) input controls, (2) processing controls and (3) output controls. The weakest point in computer systems is input—the point at which transaction data is transformed from hard-copy source documents into machine-readable cards, tape or disk, or when direct entry is made with a communication device such as a remote terminal. When undetected errors are entered originally, they may not be detected during processing, and if detected, they are troublesome to correct. Processing control refers to error-condition check routines written into the computer program. Output control refers primarily to control over the distribution of reports, but feedback on errors and comparison of input totals to output totals are also part of this "last chance" control point.

Input Controls

Input controls are designed to provide reasonable assurance that data received for processing by the computer department have been authorized properly and converted into machine-sensible form, and that data have not been lost, suppressed, added, duplicated or otherwise improperly changed. These controls also apply to correction and resubmission of data initially rejected as erroneous. The following control areas are particularly important.

Input Authorized and Approved.　Only properly authorized and approved input should be accepted for processing by the computer center. Authorization is usually a clerical (non-computer) procedure involving a person's signature or stamp on a transaction document. However, some authorizations can be general (for example, a management policy of automatic approval for sales under $500), and some authorizations can be machine-controlled (for example, automatic production of a purchase order when an inventory item reaches a predetermined reorder point).

Check Digits.　Numbers are often used in computer systems in lieu of customer names, vendor names, and so forth. One common type of number-validation procedure is the calculation of a *check digit*. A check digit is an extra number, precisely calculated, that is tagged onto the end of a basic identification number, such as an employee number. The basic code with its check digit is sometimes called a *self-checking number*. An electronic device can be installed on a keypunch or the calculation can be programmed. The device or the program calculates the correct check digit and compares it to the one on the input data. When the digits do not match, an error message is indicated on the keying device or printed out on an input error report. Check digits are used only on identification numbers (not quantity or value fields) and detect coding errors or keying errors such as the transposition of digits (for example, coding 387 as 837).[4]

A check digit test will only indicate that an identification number is valid, not that the number exists in the master file. A comparison of the transaction identification number to the master file numbers would be necessary to determine whether a matching record exists.

Data Conversion. Conversion of data into machine-sensible form is a source of many errors. Control procedures include the following:

Key Verification. Verification involves rekeying the data. When a datum is keyed differently the second time, the verifier machine locks (or cuts a notch in the card), and the operator can investigate the reason. Since this is a duplicate keying operation, it is usually only done on very sensitive data or on a sample basis.

Record Counts. Counts of records are tallies of the number of transaction documents submitted for data conversion. The known number submitted can be compared to the count of records produced by the data-conversion device (for example, the number of punched cards or count of magnetic records coded). A count mismatch indicates a lost item or one converted twice. Record counts are used as **batch control totals** and also are used during processing and at the output stage—whenever the comparison of a known count can be made with a machine-generated count.

Batch Number Totals. These totals are used in the same way as record counts, except the batch total is the sum of some important quantity

---

[4] One check digit algorithm is the "Modulus 11 Prime Number" method.

a. Begin with a basic identification number: 814973.
b. Multiply consecutive prime number weights of 19, 17, 7, 13, 7, 5, 3 to each digit in the basic code number:

$$\begin{array}{cccccc} 8 & 1 & 4 & 9 & 7 & 3 \\ 19 & 17 & 13 & 7 & 5 & 3 \\ \hline \end{array}$$
$$= 152 + 17 + 52 + 63 + 35 + 9 = 328$$

Note: the sequence of weights is the same for all codes in given system.
c. Add the result of the multiplication = 328.
d. Determine the next higher multiple of 11, which is 330.
e. Subtract the sum of the multiplication $(330 - 328 = 2)$. This is the check digit.
f. New account number: 8149732.

Now if this number is entered incorrectly, say it is keypunched as 8419732, the check digit will not equal 2 and an error will be indicated. (Source: J. G. Burch, Jr., F. R. Strater, Jr., and G. Grudniski, *Information Systems: Theory and Practice,* 2d ed. (Santa Barbara, Calif.: Hamilton Publishing, 1979), p. 181.

or amount (for example, the total sales dollars in a batch of invoices). Batch totals also are useful during processing and at the output stage.

Batch Hash Totals.   These totals are similar to batch number totals, except the **hash total** is not meaningful for accounting records (for example, the sum of all the invoice numbers on invoices submitted to the keying operator).

Edit or Validation Routines.   Various computer-programmed editing or validation routines can be used to detect data conversion errors. Some of these are:

Valid Character Tests.   These tests are used to check input data fields to see if they contain numbers where they are supposed to have numbers, and alphabetic letters where they are supposed to have letters.

Valid Sign Tests.   Sign tests check data fields for appropriate plus or minus signs.

Missing Data Test.   These edit tests check data fields to see if any are blank when they must contain data for the entry to be correct.

Sequence Tests.   These tests check the input data for numerical sequence of documents when sequence is important for processing, such as in batch processing. This validation routine can also check for missing documents in a prenumbered series.

Limit or Reasonableness Tests.   These tests are very important. They are computerized checks to see whether data values exceed or fall below some predetermined limit. For example, a payroll application may have a limit test to flag and reject any weekly payroll time record of 50 or more hours. The limit tests are a computerized version of *scanning,* the general audit procedure of reviewing data for indication of anything unusual which might turn out to be an error.

Error Correction and Resubmission.   Errors should be subject to special controls. Usually, the computer department is responsible only for correcting its own errors (keying errors, for example). Other kinds of errors, such as those due to improper coding, should be referred to and handled by the user departments. It is a good idea to have a control group log the contents of error reports in order to monitor the nature, disposition, and proper correction of rejected data. Unless properly supervised and monitored, the error-correction process itself can become a source of data input errors.

Some typical questionnaire items that may be asked during a review of input controls are shown in the box that follows. These questions should be asked about each significant accounting application where the computer is used (payroll processing, sales invoice processing, and so forth).

INPUT CONTROLS—SELECTED QUESTIONNAIRE ITEMS

Authorization of Transactions

Have procedures been established to assure that only authorized transactions are accepted such as: (*a*) Written approval on source documents? (*b*) General authorizations to process all of a user's transactions? or (*c*) Use of identification numbers, security codes and passwords for remote terminal users?

Completeness of Input

Are control totals established by the user prior to submitting data for processing? Does someone verify that input data is received on a timely basis from the user and physically controlled in the computer center?

Data Conversion

Have procedures been established to exercise proper control over processing rejected transactions including: (*a*) Positive identification of rejected records? (*b*) Review of the cause of rejection? (*c*) The correction of rejected records? (*d*) Review and approval of the correction? and (*e*) Prompt reentry of the correction at a point where it will be subjected to the same input controls as the original data?

Processing Controls

Processing controls are designed to provide reasonable assurance that data processing has been performed as intended without any omission or double counting of transactions. Many of the processing controls are the same as the input controls but are used in the actual processing phases rather than at the time input is checked. Other important control areas include:

Run-to-Run Totals.   Movement of data from one department to another or one processing program to another should be controlled. One useful control is run-to-run totals. *Run-to-run* refers to sequential processing operations—runs—on the same data. These totals may be batch record counts, financial totals, and/or hash totals obtained at the end of one processing step. The totals are passed to the next step and compared to corresponding totals produced at the end of the second step.

Control Total Reports.   Control totals—record counts, financial totals, hash totals, and run-to-run totals—should be produced during processing operations and printed out on a report. Someone (the control group, for example) should have the responsibility for comparing and/or reconciling them to input totals or totals from earlier processing runs. Loss or duplication of data thus may be detected. For example, the total of the balances in the accounts receivable master file from the last update run, plus the total of the credit sales from the current update transactions, should equal the total of the balances at the end of the current processing.

File and Operator Controls. External and internal labels are means of assuring that the proper files are used in applications. The systems software should produce a log to identify instructions entered by the operator and to make a record of time and use statistics for application runs. These logs should be reviewed by supervisory personnel.

Limit and Reasonableness Tests. These tests should be programmed to assure that illogical conditions do not occur: for example, depreciating an asset below zero or calculating a negative inventory quantity. These conditions, and others considered important, should generate error reports for supervisory review. Other logic and validation checks, such as the ones described earlier under the heading of input edit checks, can also be used during processing.

Some typical questionnaire items that might be asked about processing controls are shown in the box below.

PROCESSING CONTROLS—SELECTED QUESTIONNAIRE ITEMS

Completeness

Are programmed control procedures (run-to-run totals) included in each job step during the processing cycle?

Do application programs test the terminal identification and/or password for access authorization to that specific program?

Are control totals maintained on all files and are these verified by the update or file maintenance application program each time a file is used in processing?

File Control

Do application programs check for internal header and trailer labels?

Are tape or disk files subjected to adequate onsite and offsite backup support?

Are test data files documented, up-to-date and kept separate from live data files?

Output Controls   Output controls are the final check on the accuracy of the results of computer processing. These controls should also be designed to assure that only authorized persons receive reports or have access to files produced by the system. Typical output controls include:

Control Totals. Control totals produced as output should be compared and/or reconciled to input and run-to-run control totals produced during processing. An independent control group should be responsible for the review of output control totals and the investigation of differences.

Master File Changes. These changes should be reported in detail back to the user department from which the request for change originated, because an error can be pervasive. For example, changing selling prices incorrectly can cause all sales to be priced wrong. Someone should compare computer-generated change reports to original source documents for assurance of correct data.

Output Distribution.   Output should be distributed only to persons authorized to receive it. A distribution list should be maintained and used to deliver report copies. The number of copies produced should be restricted to the number needed.

Some typical questionnaire items that might be asked about output controls are shown below.

OUTPUT CONTROLS—SELECTED QUESTIONNAIRE ITEMS

Are input control totals reconciled to output totals?
Are input changes to master files compared item by item to output reports of these changes?
Do written distribution lists exist for all output reports from each application?
Are all output files appropriately identified with internal and external labels?

Evaluation   Apparent weaknesses in any of the input, processing and output controls are matters of concern. However, absence of a control at the input stage may be offset by other controls at later stages. For example, if check digits are not calculated when the input is prepared, but all the identification numbers are compared to master file numbers and non-matches are rejected and printed in an error report, the control is likely to be satisfactory and effective. Of course, it is usually more efficient to catch errors early rather than late, but control can still be considered reliable for the accounting records and financial statements. Internal auditors, however, may be very interested in *when* controls are applied, since they are concerned about the efficiency of computer operations.

Material weaknesses in manual and computer controls become a part of the independent auditor's evaluation of internal accounting control. Lack of input controls may permit data to be lost or double counted; poor processing control can permit accounting calculation, allocation and classification errors to occur; poor output controls over distribution of reports and other output (negotiable checks, for example) can be the source of errors and irregularities that could make financial statements materially misleading.

The purpose of the internal control review is to gain an understanding of the flow of transaction processing and to determine strengths (controls) that can be relied upon and weaknesses (lack of controls) that need to be considered in designing substantive audit procedures. In a computer environment, the *general controls* must be reviewed if any *application system* contains computer controls which are to be relied upon. Based on the audit documentation (working papers) of the computer controls *and man-*

ual controls, the audit manager must determine which controls appear to be the ones he can rely upon. The audit documentation may consist of questionnaires, such as those illustrated in this chapter, and flowcharts. The general controls and the controls of each application system to be relied upon are subject to compliance auditing to determine whether the controls operate as described.

COMPLIANCE AUDITING OF COMPUTER CONTROLS

In the simple batch systems described in this chapter, adequate evidence of control performance frequently exists in the printed output and logs. For example, input error reports for a few days will usually contain examples of each type of error that the edit routines are designed to detect. A sample of each type of error can be traced to the error log maintained by the computer control group and to evidence of correction and resubmission. Likewise, printed documentation may exist of compliance with authorized procedures required for execution of transactions or for changes to master files.

However, external auditors occasionally must use the computer as an audit tool to test the controls within the application programs of even simple systems. (Internal auditors also frequently utilize these techniques.) Thus, a consideration of the use of the computer as an "auditor's assistant" in compliance audit procedures is the next topic for study.

General Approaches To Using The Computer In Compliance Auditing Procedures

Auditors can take one of three approaches to utilizing the computer as a compliance auditing tool: (1) use the computer to select transactions and manually audit the actual transaction processing, (2) audit the processing programmed controls with simulated data and (3) audit the programmed controls with live data reprocessed with an audit program. The computer can be used to select samples (usually statistical) of transactions for manual vouching and tracing. Auditor-designed computer programs can also be prepared (using generalized audit software described in Chapter 10) to compare various transaction files. For example, open vendor invoice files can be compared to purchase order files. Further, various automatic authorizations can be computer selected for manual verification, such as automatic credit limits in accounts receivable files or reorder points in inventory files. The auditing of programmed controls with simulated data is generally referred to as *test data,* while the reprocessing of live data to test program controls is called *parallel simulation.* These techniques are described in more detail in the following sections.

Test Data

The basic concept of test data is that once a computer is programmed to handle transactions in a certain logical way, it will faithfully handle every transaction exactly the same way. Therefore, the audit team need only prepare a limited number of simulated transactions (some with "errors" and some without) to determine whether each control operates as described in the program documentation.

A *test deck* is a sample of one of each possible combination of data fields that may be processed through the real system. *Test deck* is a term that refers to the earliest days of computer system operation when all input was prepared on punched card media. Today, simulated test data can be on tape or disk as well as on punched cards. Or, test data may be entered into an online system through computer terminals. The purpose of using test data is to determine whether controls operate as described in questionnaire responses and program flowcharts. Test transactions may consist of abstractions from real transactions and of simulated transactions generated by the auditors' imagination. The auditors must prepare a worksheet listing each transaction and the predicted output based on the program documentation. Then, these test transactions must be converted to the normal machine-sensed input form, and arrangements must be made to process the transactions with the actual program used for real transactions.

Auditors must be very familiar with the nature of the business and the logic of the programs to anticipate all data combinations that might exist as transaction input or which might be generated by processing. They must be able to assign degrees of audit importance to each kind of error-checking control method. Further, they must ensure that the test data do not get commingled with real transactions and change the actual master files.

Consider an example of processing sales transactions using the illustration that was begun earlier in Chapter 7. Assume also that the objective of the test is to check the controls over accuracy of input data. The problem is to assemble a set of transactions that includes important error conditions in order to determine whether the input and processing controls can detect them.

For example, the audit team can create hypothetical transactions with the following conditions:

No customer code number.

Invalid customer code number (wrong check digit).

Bill of lading document number not in field.

Sale amount greater than $5,000. (The client assumes no sales invoice will ever be greater than $5,000.)

Sale amount equal to zero.

Sale amount less than zero.

These six conditions generate many possible combinations of transactions. An example of 15 of them is shown in a decision table presented with Case 9.19 (Exhibit 9.19–1) at the end of this chapter. Computerized *test data generators* are also available to help develop the simulated transactions. The auditors know that transactions having no customer number or no bill of lading document number (missing data test), an invalid customer code number (self-checking number test), a sale amount greater than $5,000 (limit test), a sale amount equal to zero (missing data test), or a sale amount less than zero (sign test) should produce error messages, and transactions with valid conditions should not. The auditors arrange to run these simulated transactions on the client's system and to find out whether the controls operate.

Test data are processed at a single point in time along with the client program that is supposed to have been in use during the period under audit. Following the analysis of test output, the audit manager must still make an inference about processing throughout the entire period. In order to do so, he or she must be satisfied by a review of documentation that any program changes have been authorized and correctly made.[5] Some auditors occasionally perform test data procedures on an irregular, surprise basis.

Parallel Simulation   In parallel simulation, the audit team prepares a computer program (utilizing generalized audit software described in Chapter 10) to duplicate the logic and controls of the client's program. The result of the auditors' processing of real data is compared with the result of the real data processed by the actual application system. The concept of this method is illustrated in Exhibit 9–2.

Auditors have the options of: (1) using the client's real program for tests, (2) having client personnel write special audit programs to perform tests or (3) writing their own special audit programs. The first option requires test data utilization. The second option requires close supervision and testing. The third option requires significant programming expertise on the audit staff or close liaison with expert independent programmers.

However, following the advent of generalized audit software in the mid-1960s, the third option has become much more attractive. The generalized audit software programs consist of numerous prepackaged subroutines that can perform most tasks needed in auditing and business applications. The auditor's programming task consists of writing on preprinted specification forms simple instructions that call up one or more of the subroutines. Thus, there is no need to write complete, complex programs, and the expertise to use the generalized software can be acquired in one week of training. (You will get a closer examination of these programs and their capabilities in Chapter 10.)

Using the generalized audit program capabilities, an auditor can con-

---

[5] AICPA, *Controls Over Using and Changing Computer Programs,* Computer Services Guideline, (New York: AICPA, 1979).

EXHIBIT 9–2
System Concept of
Parallel Simulation

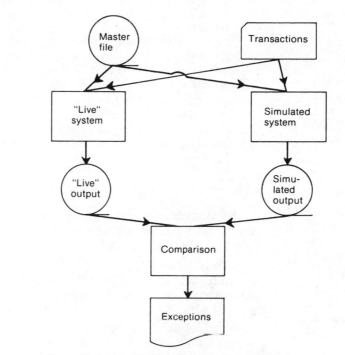

Source: W. C. Mair, "New Techniques in Computer Program
Verification," *Tempo* (Touche Ross & Co., Winter 1971–72), p.
14.

struct a system of data processing that will accept the same input as the
real program, use the same files and attempt to produce the same results.
This simulated system will contain all the controls the auditor believes
appropriate, and in this respect the thought process is quite similar to the
logic that goes into preparing test data. The simulated-system output is
then compared to the real system output for correspondence or difference, and at this point the audit evidence is similar to the evidence obtained by using test data with the real program. Conclusions can be
reached about the error-detection capabilities of the real system.

The first audit application of parallel simulation may be very costly,
although it will probably be more efficient than auditing without the computer or utilizing test data. Real economies are realized, however, in
subsequent audits of the same client.

The audit team must take care to determine that the real transactions
selected for processing are "representative." Thus, some exercise in random selection and identification of important transactions may be required in conjunction with parallel processing. The following illustration
is based on the illustrative sales-accounts receivable system described in
Problem 7.13.

Illustration. A simulation of a manufacturer's sales invoice and accounts receivable processing system revealed that invoices which showed no bill of lading or shipment reference were processed and charged to customers with a corresponding credit to sales. Further audit of the exceptions in the sample showed that the real data processing program did not contain a missing-data test and did not provide error messages for lack of shipping references. This finding led to (1) a more extensive test of attributes based on the sales invoice population with comparison to shipping documents and (2) a more extensive audit of accounts receivable for customers who were charged with such sales.

The ultimate goal of the methods of compliance auditing is to reach a conclusion about the actual operation of controls in a computer system. This conclusion allows the audit manager to determine the reliability of the data processing system and provide logical grounds for restricting or extending the scope of subsequent account balance audit procedures. This internal control decision is crucial particularly in computer systems because subsequent audit work may be performed using magnetic files produced by the computerized information system. The data processing control over such files is important since their content is utilized later in computer-assisted work.

SOURCES AND ADDITIONAL READING REFERENCES

AICPA. *Audits of Service-Center Produced Records,* especially chapter 2, "Evaluating Controls at Service Centers," New York, 1974.

_____. *Equity Funding, Report of the Special Committee,* New York, 1975.

_____. *The Auditor's Study and Evaluation of Internal Control in EDP Systems,* Auditing and Accounting Guide, New York, 1977.

_____. *Report of the Special Advisory Committee on Internal Accounting Control,* New York, 1979.

_____. *Controls Over Using and Changing Computer Programs,* Computer Services Guideline, New York, 1979.

Burns, D. C., and J. K. Loebbecke. "Internal Control Evaluation: How the Computer Can Help." *Journal of Accountancy,* August 1975, pp. 60–70.

Canadian Institute of Chartered Accountants. *Computer Control Guidelines and Computer Audit Guidelines,* Toronto, Canada, 1975.

Cerullo, Michael J. "Post-Implementation Evaluation of Computer Systems." *CPA Journal,* May 1982, pp. 45–51.

Davis, Gordon B., Donald L. Adams, and Carol A. Schaller. *Auditing & EDP,* 2d ed., AICPA, 1983.

EDP Auditors Foundation for Education and Research. *Control Objectives,* Carol Stream, Ill. 1983.

General Accounting Office. *Evaluating Internal Controls in Computer Based Systems,* Washington D.C., 1981.

Helms, Glenn L., and Ira R. Weiss. "Auditor Involvement in the System Development Life Cycle." *The Internal Auditor,* December 1983, pp. 41–44.

Loebbecke, J. K., J. F. Mullarkey, and G. R. Zuber. "Auditing in a Computer Environment." *Journal of Accountancy,* January 1983, pp. 68–78.

Macchiaverna, P. R. *Auditing Corporate Data-Processing Activities,* New York, The Conference Board Inc., 1980.

Porter, S. Thomas, and William E. Perry. *EDP: Controls and Auditing,* Boston: Kent Publishing Co., 1984

Rittenberg, L. E., and G. B. Davis. "The Roles of Internal and External Auditors in Auditing EDP Systems." *Journal of Accountancy,* December 1977, pp. 51–58.

Sardinas, J., J. G. Burch, and R. Asebrook, *EDP Auditing: A Primer,* New York: John Wiley & Sons, 1981.

Schlegel, F. A. "A Test Data Generator." *Internal Auditor,* January-February 1976, pp. 80–86.

Watne, Donald A., and Peter B. B. Turney. *Auditing EDP Systems,* Englewood Cliffs, N. J.: Prentice-Hall, 1984.

Weber, Ron. *EDP Auditing: Conceptual Foundations and Practice,* New York: McGraw-Hill, 1982.

REVIEW QUESTIONS

9.1 Distinguish between auditing "through the computer" and auditing "with the computer."

9.2. In addition to the planning items considered in a manual accounting system, what additional matters should be considered when computer processing is involved?

9.3. Describe how the *understanding of the control environment* (the organizational structure, methods used to communicate responsibility and authority and methods used to supervise the system) is affected when a computer is used in data processing.

9.4. What duties should be segregated within the computer department?

9.5. What is the difference between an external label and an internal label in magnetic file media? What is the purpose of each?

9.6. What aspects of documentation, file security and retention-control procedures are unique to computer systems?

9.7. What does an auditor need to know about computer hardware controls?

9.8. What is a self-checking number? Can you give an example of one of your own?

9.9. Describe five types of edit or validation controls and give an example of each for fields on a sales invoice input.

9.10. What is the difference between the computerized audit compliance procedures of *test data* and *parallel simulation?*

9.11. Define an "audit trail." How might a computer system audit trail differ from one in a manual system?

EXERCISES AND PROBLEMS

9.12. Audit around versus Audit through Computers.

CPAs may audit "around" or "through" computers in the examination of financial statements of clients who utilize computers to process accounting data.

Required:

a. Describe the auditing approach referred to as auditing "around" the computer.

b. Under what conditions does the CPA decide to audit "through" the computer instead of "around" the computer?

c. In auditing "through" the computer, the CPA may use "test data."

(1) What is the "test data" compliance audit procedure?

(2) Why does the CPA use the "test data" procedure?

d. How can the CPA be satisfied that the computer program tested by him or her is actually being used by the client to process its accounting data?

(*AICPA* adapted)

9.13. Computer Internal Control Questionnaire Evaluation.

Assume that when conducting the review of internal accounting control for the Denton Seed Company, you checked "No" to the following questionnaire items (selected from those illustrated in the chapter):

Does access to online files require specific passwords to be entered to identify and validate the terminal user?

Are control totals established by the user prior to submitting data for processing? (Order entry application subsystem)

Are input control totals reconciled to output control totals? (Order entry application subsystem)

Required:

Describe the error(s) or irregularity(ies) that could occur due to the weakness indicated by the lack of control.

9.14. Check Digit.

Suppose that a credit sale was made to John Q. Smyth, customer account number 8149732. The last digit is a check digit calculated by the "Modulus 11 Prime Number" method. The data entry operator made an error and keyed in the customer number as 8419732.

Required:

a. Calculate the check digit for the number that was keyed in.

b. How would the self-checking number control detect this data input error.

9.15. Explain Computer Controls.

At a meeting of the corporate audit committee attended by the general manager of the products division and yourself, representing the internal audit department, the following dialogue took place:

Jones (committee chair): Mr. Marks had suggested that the internal audit department conduct an audit of the computer activities of the products division.

Smith (general manager): I don't know much about the technicalities of computers, but the division has some of the best computer people in the company.

Jones: Do you know whether the internal controls protecting the system are satisfactory?

Smith: I suppose they are. No one has complained. What's so important about controls anyway, as long as the systems works?

Jones turns to you and asks you to explain computer controls.

Required:

Address your response to the following points:

a. State the principal objective of achieving control over: (1) input, (2) processing and (3) output.

b. Give at least three methods of achieving control over the following: (1) source data, (2) processing and (3) output.

9.16. File Retention and Backup

You have audited the financial statements of the Solt Manufacturing Company for several years and are making preliminary plans for the audit for the year ended June 30. This year, however, the company has installed and used a computer system for processing a portion of its accounting data.

The following output computer files are produced in the daily processing runs:

1. Cash disbursements sequenced by check number.

2. Outstanding payables balances (alphabetized).

3. Purchase journals arranged by (a) account charged and (b) vendor.

Vouchers and supporting invoices, receiving reports and purchase order copies are filed by vendor code. Purchase orders and checks are filed numerically.

Company records as described above are maintained on magnetic tapes. All tapes are stored in a restricted area within the computer room. A grandfather-father-son policy is followed in retaining and safeguarding tape files.

Required.

a. Explain the grandfather-father son policy. Describe how files could be reconstructed when this policy is used.

b. Discuss whether company policies for retaining and safeguarding the tape files provide adequate protection against losses of data.

(AICPA adapted)

9.17. Separation of Duties and General Controls

You are engaged to examine the financial statements of Horizon Incorporated which has its own computer installation. During the preliminary review, you found that Horizon lacked proper segregation of the programming and operating functions. As a result, you intensified the study and evaluation of the system of internal control surrounding the computer and concluded that the existing compensating general controls provided reasonable assurance that the objectives of the system of internal control were being met.

Required:

a. In a properly functioning computer environment, how is the separation of the programming and operating functions achieved?

b. What are the compensating general controls you most likely found?

(AICPA adapted)

9.18. Payroll Audit Procedures, Computer and Sampling.

You are the senior auditor in charge of the annual audit of Onward Manufacturing Corporation for the year ending December 31. The company is of medium size, having only 300 employees, but the payroll system work is performed by a computer. All 300 employees are union members paid by the hour at rates set forth in a union contract, a copy of which is furnished to you. Job and pay rate classifications are determined by a joint union-management conference and a formal memorandum is placed in each employee's personnel file.

Every week, clock cards prepared and approved on the shop area are collected and transmitted to the payroll department. The total of labor hours is summed on an adding machine and entered on each card. Batch and hash totals are obtained for the following: (1) labor hours and (2) last four digits of social security numbers. These data are keypunched onto cards and sent to the computer department. The clock cards (with cost classification data) are sent to the cost accounting department.

Payroll checks are written by the computer as follows: As each person's card is processed, the social security number is matched to a table (in a separate master table file) to obtain job classification and pay rate data, then the pay rate is multiplied by the number of hours and the check is printed. (Ignore payroll deductions for the following requirements.)

Required:

a. What audit procedures would you recommend to obtain evidence that payroll data are accurately totaled and transformed into machine-readable cards? What deviation rate might you expect? What tolerable error rate would you set? What "items" would you sample?

What factors should be considered in setting the size of your sample?

b. What audit procedures would you recommend to obtain evidence that the pay rates are appropriately assigned and used in figuring gross pay? In what way, if any, would these procedures be different if the gross pay were calculated by hand instead of on a computer?

DISCUSSION CASES

9.19. **Illustrative Case Continued—Kingston Company, Preparation of Test Data.**
This case is a continuation of the fact situation presented in Problem 7.13 at the end of Chapter 7 and Case 8.30 at the end of Chapter 8. Additional requirements related to internal control compliance audit procedures are given below. The controls tested are illustrated in the form of a decision table.

Required:

a. Prepare the simulated transactions for using test data to evaluate the edit controls over sales invoices input identified in this chapter in the material under "Test Data." See Exhibit 7–2 and 7–4 in Chapter 7 for the related internal control questionnaire and flowchart. (See Exhibit 9.19–1 for a decision table solution to this requirement.)

b. Assume that when the test data was run through Kingston's edit program, test transactions (3), (8), (11) and (14) failed to produce an error message that no bill of lading number was in the field. What effect could this weakness (non-compliance of a control) have on the audit? In other words, what financial statement accounts would be affected which would require changing the nature, timing or extent of substantive audit procedures?

9.20. **Control Weaknesses and Recommendations—Louisville Sales Corporation.**
George Beemster, CPA, is examining the financial statements of the Louisville Sales

Corporation, which recently installed a computer. The following comments have been extracted from Mr. Beemster's notes on computer operations and the processing and control of shipping notices and customer invoices:

To minimize inconvenience, Louisville converted without change its existing data processing system, which utilized tabulating equipment. The computer company supervised the conversion and had provided training to all computer department employees (except keypunch operators) in systems design, operations, and programming.

Each computer run is assigned to a specific employee, who is responsible for making program changes, running the program and answering questions. This procedure has the advantage of eliminating the need for records of computer operations because each employee is responsible for her or his own computer runs.

At least one computer department employee remains in the computer room during office hours, and only computer department employees have keys to the computer room.

Systems documentation consists of those materials furnished by the computer company—a set of record formats and program listings. These and the tape library are kept in a corner of the computer department.

EXHIBIT 9.19–1
Kingston Company, Test Data Transactions: Computer Controls Tests (December 31, 1985)

Conditions	Test Data Transactions														
	(1)	(2)	(3)	(4)	(5)	(6)	(7)	(8)	(9)	(10)	(11)	(12)	(13)	(14)	(15)
Customer code number in field	n	y	y	y	y	y	y	n	n	n	y	y	y	y	y
Customer number is valid	y	n	y	y	y	y	y	n	n		n	n	n	n	y
Bill of lading document number in field .	y	y	n	y	y	y	y	n	y	y	n	y	y	n	y
Sale Amount < 5,000	y	y	y	n 5,500				y	n 5,001		y	n 9,999		n 11,000	y
Sale amount = 5,000					n 5,000								n 5,000		
Sale amount = 0						n 0									
Sale amount < 0							n –100			n –5,000					
Actions															
Error messages	X	X	X	X	X	X	X	X	X	X	X	X	X	X	
No error message															X

Document count control total = 15.
Sale dollar batch control for test = $77,220 positive amounts.
           5,100 negative amounts.
           $72,120

y = valid condition.
n = invalid condition.

The company considered the desirability of programmed controls but decided to retain the manual controls from its existing system.

Company products are shipped directly from public warehouses which forward shipping notices to general accounting. There, a billing clerk enters the price of the items and accounts for the numerical sequence of shipping notices from each warehouse. The billing clerk also prepares daily adding machine tapes ("control tapes") of the units shipped and the unit prices.

Shipping notices and control tapes are forwarded to the computer department for keypunching and processing. Extensions are made on the computer. Output consists of invoices (in six copies) and a daily sales register. The daily sales register shows the aggregate totals of units shipped and unit prices which the computer operator compares to the control tapes.

All copies of the invoice are returned to the billing clerk. The clerk mails three copies to the customer, forwards one copy to the warehouse, maintains one copy in a numerical file, and retains one copy in an open invoice file that serves as a detail accounts receivable record.

Required:

Describe weaknesses in internal control over information and data flows and the procedures for processing shipping notices and customer invoices, and recommend improvements in these controls and processing procedures. Organize your answer sheet with two columns, one headed "Weaknesses," and the other "Recommended Improvements."

(*AICPA* adapted)

9.21. **Flowchart Control Points.**
Each number on the flowchart in Exhibit 9.21–1 locates a control point in the labor processing system. Make a list of the control points, and for each point describe the type or kind of internal control feature which ought to be specified.

EXHIBIT 9.21–1

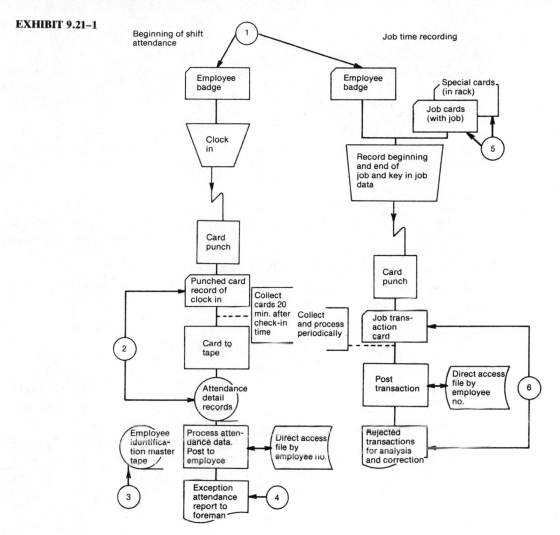

CHAPTER 10

---

* As amended by SAS 48 (July, 1984), "The Effects of Computer Processing on the Examination of Financial Statements."

Auditing Advanced Computer Systems and Using Generalized Audit Software

LEARNING OBJECTIVES The advanced computer environment frequently makes use of traditional computer control and audit techniques impractical. The summary of advanced computer characteristics, control and audit techniques in this chapter is presented to provide you with a fundamental background of terminology and audit techniques. When advanced computer systems are encountered in the data processing environment, a computer audit expert would normally join the audit team. However, every auditor should understand enough to communicate with the computer audit specialist to achieve the basic objectives of the audit. You can learn these technical features of advanced computer systems! They are not as complex as accounting for such complicated items as earnings per share, foreign currency translation and capitalized leases, which you have mastered, and computers are more fun. Many of these advanced features are encountered in minicomputer or microcomputer systems used by small businesses.

Your learning objectives related to auditing advanced computer systems and using audit software are to be able to:

☐ List and describe the four features that characterize "advanced" computer systems.

☐ Give a brief explanation of "time-sharing," "online" systems, "real-time" systems and "distributed processing."

☐ Describe the characteristics of minicomputer installations.

☐ Discuss the control considerations of minicomputer systems.

☐ List and briefly describe six techniques applicable to auditing advanced computer systems.

☐ Give the advantages of generalized audit software packages.

357

□ Give examples of audit procedures that can be performed on a computer using generalized audit software.

□ List and explain the principal phases of a generalized audit software application.

□ List what a person must have access to in order to perpetrate a computer fraud.

ADVANCED SYSTEMS   Simple batch computer systems as described in Chapter 9 deal with one component of an organization at a time, such as payroll or billing. Advanced applications involve immediate update utilizing a company-wide database and perform multiple functions simultaneously. Of course, you will encounter variations between simple batch and the most advanced systems. For example, terminals may be used for data entry, but the transactions are collected on disks for batch update. Terminals may be used to inquire about the status of balances (for example, perpetual inventory), while update is done by batch. Further, while some processing may be updated immediately, such as order entry, other applications in the same company, such as payroll which has a natural periodic cycle, could be batch processed.

Advanced systems have been described by many terms such as *online, real-time, remote entry and distributed processing*. The problem with such terms from an audit point of view is that they describe hardware and software technology and do not focus on how accounting transactions are processed. For purposes of evaluating control, advanced systems are those systems (large or small) that possess one or more of the following characteristics:

Data communications.

Data integration.

Automatic transaction initiation.

Unconventional or temporary audit trail.[1]

Data Communications   Data communications are a combination of electronic communications and the computer. The complexity of data communication networks may vary from a few remote terminals linked to a minicomputer to a complex network utilizing time-sharing, online, real-time and distributed processing systems (terms defined in the box following). The main change is that programs, transactions and data files can be introduced, maintained, mod-

---

[1] AICPA, *Management Control and Audit of Advanced EDP Systems*, Computer Services Guidelines (New York, 1977), p. 5.

ADVANCED COMPUTER TERMS

Time-sharing

A processing system with a number of independent, relatively slow speed terminal devices. The user has the impression that he or she is the sole user due to the slowness of input/output, when in reality the computer is sharing its time with a number of users. Time-sharing may be owned or utilized by many organizations. (The company providing the service for many users is called a service bureau.)

Online

Online is used with two different meanings. Data files are said to be online if they are electronically available to the central processor and can be accessed without operator intervention. Online also refers to a user who is connected to the central processor as described above under time-sharing. Data processing is also termed *online* (or direct access or random) when transactions can be input into computer processing from the point of origin without first being sorted.

Real-time

Real-time has a variety of meanings. Real-time can refer to a quick response in a time-shared system, such as is necessary for airline reservations. Real-time in an accounting and production sense means that the system evaluates information and feeds back (returns signals) in time to take action.

Distributed Processing

Distributed processing refers to the situation when two or more computers handle the data processing. This is an extension of time-sharing, except that the terminal can be connected to one of a number of computers. Minicomputers may be located at a remote site to handle local processing and to maintain local files with summary data transactions transmitted to a central location.

---

ified or accessed at locations distant from the central data processing installation.

These types of systems are said to be *transaction-driven* or *event-driven* because the individual transaction triggers the processing activity and updates all relevant files. In contrast, a batch system could be said to be program-driven because a specific program must be loaded into the computer to process all transactions that fit that program and its related files. In a transaction-driven system, the transaction code part of the message becomes the most sensitive part because it initiates all subsequent actions.

Control Implications. Control standards in advanced communication systems are difficult to maintain, yet controls at all locations that can access the system are essential. Especially crucial are procedures for identification and authorization of all users. Control weaknesses at any one location may compromise the control elsewhere.

Data Integration   In batch processing, each application system has its own files. For example, the payroll processing utilizes the payroll master file. Some of the same information (such as employee numbers, pay rates) may also be maintained on personnel files and labor cost accounting files. Further, the master files in a batch system tend to become the property of a particular user department. Periodic review must be made of identical fields in various user department files to ensure they are the same and to reconcile differences.

Advanced systems frequently include a new part of the system software called a ***database management system (DBMS)*** and an integrated "master file" called the ***database.*** The database contains all the information formally maintained in separate user department files. A particular piece of data, such as an employee number, is stored only once (data integration), but through the DBMS it is made available to all programs (payroll, personnel, cost accounting) that need that data. Thus, ***data redundancy*** (same data stored in several separate files) is eliminated. Since the traditional files of all the same record format do not exist, the concept of a *field* in a record no longer applies. The individual pieces of information (employee number, address, pay rate, balance) are called ***data elements*** and are *logically combined* by the DBMS to provide programs with the *records* necessary for the particular processing. The information in the database becomes a company-wide resource rather than belonging to a particular user department. The DBMS separates the database from users' programs, online updates and online inquires, thus achieving data independence.

Control Implications.   The DBMS contains controls that restrict access to the database. The database is composed of individual data elements (fields), each with a unique storage space in the database. The entire population of data elements is called the ***schema.*** Authorized users (including computer programs) can be limited to only those portions of the database (called ***sub-schema***) that are needed. Thus, authorized employees in the payroll department might be able to enter the weekly hours that update year-to-date gross pay but are precluded from changing the pay rate.

Responsibility must be delegated for establishing, assigning and maintaining the authorization procedures. This responsibility is usually assigned to a ***database administrator (DBA)*** function. The DBA is responsible for determining who should have access to each data element (define each user's sub-schema). Further, responsibility must be assigned by the DBA to users for each data element in the database. The DBA function should have the following responsibilities:

☐   Design the content and organization of the database, including logical data relationships, physical storage strategy and access strategy.

☐ Protect the database and its software, including control over access to and use of the data and DBMS and provisions for backup and recovery in the case of errors or destruction of the database.

☐ Monitor the performance of the DBMS and improve efficiency.

☐ Communicate with the database users, arbitrate disputes over data ownership and usage, educate users about the DBMS, and consult users when problems arise.

☐ Provide standards for data definition and usage and documentation of the database and its software.[2]

Since the DBA should have such extensive responsibilities, this function should be segregated from the other computer functions of systems development, programming, operations and users described in Chapter 9.

When auditors encounter a DBMS, the following accounting controls should be evaluated:

DBMS Accounting Control	Audit Consideration
Segregation of data administration functions	Segregation of data administrator from incompatible functions
	Segregation of duties within data administration, if possible
User data controls	User responsibility for data
	User review of all changes
	Periodic review and comparison with physical counts and other evidence of correct data values
Accuracy controls	Use of standard data editing and validation procedures
Error-correction controls	Use of procedures for error correction
Access controls	Use of procedures to limit access to authorized programs to authorized personnel only[3]

Automatic Transactions Initiation

Automatic transaction initiation, present in some batch systems, is usually more extensive in advanced systems. Transactions can be initiated to write invoices, checks, shipping orders and purchase orders, without human review.

Control Implications. Without a human-readable document indicating the transaction event, the correctness of automatically initiated transactions is difficult to judge. Authorization of transactions occurs when cer-

---

[2] Gordon B. Davis, Donald L. Adams, and Carol A. Schaller, *Auditing & EDP*, AICPA (1983), p. 109.

[3] Davis et al., *Auditing & EDP*, p. 111.

tain *flags* are installed in programs or records (for example, inventory quantity falling below reorder point). Therefore, authorization is more difficult to trace to the proper person. Controls must be designed into the system to insure the genuineness and reasonableness of automatically initiated transactions and to prevent or detect erroneous transactions.

Unconventional or Temporary Audit Trail

The audit trail of frequent printouts in simple systems and the hard copy source documents supporting keyed data entry gradually disappear as systems become more advanced. They are replaced by sensor-based data collection input and microfilm or machine-readable output. All advanced systems need an audit trail in case of transmission interruption or power surge; however, the retention period may be short and the information available only in complex machine-readable form.

Control Implications.   Audit and control specifications for an audit trail need to be established at the time a system is designed or evaluated for lease or purchase. The loss of hard-copy documents and reports and the temporary nature of the audit trail may require external auditors to alter both the timing and nature of audit procedures. Greater cooperation and coordination are required between external and internal auditors.

A transaction-oriented environment is represented in Exhibit 10–1. The transaction processor keeps track of the remote input terminal source of messages, performs preliminary message editing, checks authority and identifies the transaction type. Based on the transaction code, a particular transaction module (such as the payroll update program) is initiated.

EXHIBIT 10–1
Transaction-Oriented Environment

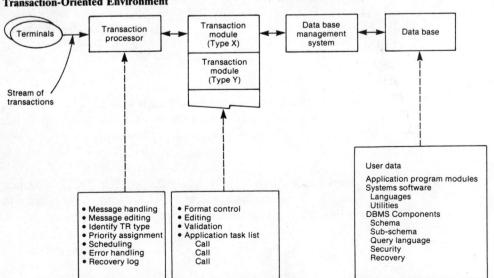

These modules *edit* the transactions (as explained in Chapter 9) for input errors. A *query-only* transaction (no change to data elements in the database) will involve less complex transaction modules. All transactions must pass through the DBMS where access authorization is tested and certain data elements are made available for the return trip through the various steps. Such systems require complex hardware and software.

ACCOUNTING CONTROLS IN A MINICOMPUTER ENVIRONMENT

The term *minicomputer* is used herein to describe a family of computers that includes small business computers, microcomputers and intelligent terminals. These small computers can have any or all of the characteristics of advanced systems.

Computer activity involving minicomputers should be included in the study and evaluation of internal accounting control. Since the control objectives do not change, the internal control questionnaires illustrated in Chapter 9 and the audit techniques discussed in Chapter 9 and this chapter are relevant, but may have to be tailored to the minicomputer installation. The following explanations are designed to assist you in appreciating how the questionnaires, flowcharts and audit techniques may have to be modified by directing attention to potential problems and controls normally affecting minicomputers.

Major Characteristics: Minicomputers

Minicomputers may be elements of a distributed system or a stand-alone system doing all the data processing for a business. The latter is considered here. The control environment, and not the computer technology, is the important aspect for auditors. The control considerations described would be applicable to computer installations with the following characteristics:

☐ *Lack of segregation of functions between the EDP department and users.* Personnel in the user department initiate and authorize source documents, enter data into the system, operate the computer, and use the output reports.

☐ *Location of the computer.* The computer is generally located in the same area as the user department.

☐ *Lack of segregation of functions within the EDP department.* There is a limited number of "technical" data processing personnel.

☐ *Limited knowledge of EDP.* The supervisor responsible for data processing has limited knowledge of EDP.

In addition, the following characteristics are found in many minicomputer environments.

☐ *Utility programs.* Utility programs are used extensively to enter and to change data.

☐ *Diskettes.* Diskettes are used extensively for file storage.

☐ *Terminals*. Terminals are used for transaction data entry, inquiry, and other interactive functions.

☐ *Software packages*. Purchased software packages are used extensively rather than internally developed application software.

☐ *Documentation*. Available system, program, operation and user documentation may be limited or nonexistent.[4]

In a minicomputer installation having these characteristics, the most significant control weakness is a lack of segregation of duties. This potential weakness may be compounded by the lack of controls in the operating system and application programs. Simply turning on the system and using a terminal may provide access to all the files and programs with no record of usage.

Control Considerations and Techniques

Most of the control problems can be traced to the lack of segregation of duties and lack of computerized controls. It follows that most of the auditors' control considerations and techniques are designed to overcome these deficiencies. Auditors should consider the entire control structure including manual controls and look for compensating controls that might offset apparent weaknesses. The various control considerations and techniques are discussed under major groups that are similar to the general controls discussed in Chapter 9—organizational, operations and processing, and systems development and modification.

Organizational Controls.   The environment in a minicomputer installation is similar to the one-person bookkeeping department because the systems analysis, design and programming operations can be performed by one or two people. The main controls involve limiting the concentration of functions to the extent possible and establishing proper supervision. The situation is a computerized version of *internal control in a small business* as described in Chapter 7. You should review that section at this time if you do not recall it. The implementation of the other controls discussed below will help offset control weaknesses caused by lack of segregation of duties.

Operation and Processing Controls.   With online minicomputer installations, the most important controls are those over online data (accounting transactions) entry. These control techniques include:

Restricting Access to Input Devices.   Terminals may be physically locked and keys controlled. The utilization of various levels of passwords to access files, initiate changes and invoke programs should be strictly followed.

---

[4] AICPA, *Audit and Control Considerations in a Minicomputer or Small Business Computer Environment,* Computer Services Guidelines (1981), p. 1.

Standard Screens and Computer Prompting. The computer can be programmed so that when a particular function is called, a standard screen format appears. The operator must complete all blanks as prompted by the computer, thus ensuring complete transactions are entered before they are processed.

Online Editing and Sight Verification. The input edit and validation controls discussed in Chapter 9 can be programmed to occur at time of input. In some installations, the data on the screen is not released until the data has been sight verified and the operator signals the computer to accept the entire screen.

The processing can be controlled by artificially creating the files equivalent to the grandfather-father-son retention concept found in batch systems. The procedures that could ensure that the data processed are in balance, an adequate audit trail is maintained, and recovery is possible (and also provide audit files) include the following:

Transaction Logs. Transaction entry through the terminal should be captured automatically in a computerized log. The transaction logs (for each terminal or each class of terminals) should be summarized into the equivalent of batch totals (counts of transactions by class, financial totals or hash totals).

Control Totals. Master files should contain records that accumulate the number of records and financial totals. The update processing automatically should change these control records.

Balancing Input to Output. The summary of daily transactions and the master file control totals from the minicomputer should be balanced to manual control totals maintained by the user department. If this external balancing is not feasible, techniques similar to the auditor's analytical review procedures can be employed to test for reasonableness.

Audit Trail. The transaction logs and periodic dumps of master files should provide an audit trail and means for recovery. In addition, some minicomputer installations have systems software which can provide a log of all files accessed and all jobs processed.

Systems Development and Modification. The control objectives and techniques in a minicomputer installation are no different than on a larger system, even though the environment is different. Many application programs will be purchased from computer manufacturers or software vendors not completely familiar with online control techniques. Purchased programs should be reviewed carefully and tested before acquisition and implementation.

The programming languages most frequently used in minicomputers (RPG, Basic) are easily learned and programming ability may develop within the user group. Some minicomputers have "menu-type" macro-instructions which are simple to use without technical training. Further, the programming is in an ***interpretative*** language, which means it remains in the computer program library in source code form which is easy to change. Development standards and modification authorization become even more important than in larger systems. Since most programming will be done through terminals, special passwords should be required to access programs, and only authorized personnel should be issued these passwords.

Generalized audit software is not available for minicomputers. However, in many cases utility extract programs or the simplified programming and retrieval systems can be used by auditors to create tailored audit software.

CONTROL AND AUDIT OF ADVANCED SYSTEMS

As explained in the beginning of Chapter 9, the internal control and audit objectives do not change when the environment changes from manual to computer data processing. However, the techniques of control must be adapted to the different environment and new audit techniques and procedures developed. The control features are summarized in the box following.

CONTROL FEATURES

To achieve the control objectives in an advanced computer environment, the system should be designed to provide the following features:

1. *User identification.* The system should have the capability to uniquely identify each of the persons using the system.
2. *Request Authorization.* The system should be able to determine if the processing or information request of a user is authorized.
3. *Activity Logging.* The system should be capable of recording all user activity (such as the number of attempted log-ons, inquiries and the like), as well as recording information about the processes executed.

Source: AICPA, *Management Control and Objectives of Advanced Systems*, p. 11.

Audit Tools and Techniques

The audit of advanced computer systems usually involves computer audit specialists with advanced technical proficiency. However, "general" auditors must possess some knowledge of the tools and techniques available in order to coordinate the specialist work with the other procedures to achieve the audit objectives. Auditors also need to know the available techniques in order to advise clients of the control concerns and potential audit aids. Most of the tools and techniques discussed below need to be designed into the system. Auditors should become more involved in reviewing systems at the development stage to ensure adequate controls are installed and auditability is possible.

The tools and techniques applicable to auditing in an advanced computer environment can be classified as those that: (1) operate online on a real-time basis with live data, (2) operate on historical data, (3) utilize simulated or dummy data and (4) utilize program analysis techniques.

Techniques Using Live Data.   In most cases, these techniques require special audit modules to be designed and coded into programs at the time of development. These *audit hooks* allow auditors to select specific transactions of audit interest before or during processing and save them for subsequent audit follow-up. (Program modules solely for audit or maintenance purposes are called *audit hooks,* the same concepts used for fraudulent purposes are called *trap doors.*)

Tagging Transactions.   Transactions selected by the auditor are "tagged" with an indicator at input. A computer trail of all processing steps of these transactions in the application system can be printed out or stored in computer file for subsequent evaluation.

Audit Files.   Auditor-selected transactions are written to a special file for later verification. Two methods may be employed. *Systems control audit review file (SCARF)* is a method in which auditors build into the data processing programs special limit, reasonableness or other audit tests. These tests produce reports of transactions selected according to the auditor's criteria, and the reports are delivered directly to the auditor for review and follow-up. The SCARF procedure is especially attractive to internal auditors. A *sample audit review file (SARF)* technique is similar to SCARF, except that instead of programming auditors' test criteria, a random-sampling selection scheme is programmed. The report of sample transactions can be reviewed by auditors after each production run. The SARF method is efficient for producing representative samples of transactions processed over a period by the computer.

Snapshot.   A "picture" of main memory of data elements is taken before and after selected decision-making processes and printed out for auditor use. The auditor can trace and verify the decision process utilizing the results.

Monitoring Systems Activity.   Hardware or software is available which can analyze activity within a computer. These monitors were designed to determine efficiency. However, they may be applied for audit purposes to determine who uses elements of the system and for what operations.

Extended Records.   Special programs provide an audit trail of an individual transaction by accumulating the results of all application programs that contributed to the processing of a transaction. The accumulated results are stored either as additional fields of the transaction record or in a separate audit file. Thus, auditors can follow the flow of a transaction without reviewing several files at various times and stages of processing.

Techniques Using Historical Data.   These techniques are generally designed to give auditors access to machine-sensible files. The *parallel* *simulation* concept of reprocessing data and comparing results to original processing explained in Chapter 9 is included among this class of techniques. Also included is *generalized audit software* which will be discussed later in this chapter.

Techniques Using Simulated or Dummy Data.   The *test data* concept explained in Chapter 9 is a technique that fits in this class, although it is generally used in simple batch computer systems. An extension of the test data concept has been expanded for use in advanced computer systems under the name of integrated test facility.

Integrated Test Facility (ITF).   The "minicompany" approach is a technique used by clients' program maintenance personnel, although it can be used by auditors. It involves creating a dummy department or branch complete with records of employees, customers, products, receivables, payables and other accounts. The ITF has master file records, carefully coded (such as, "99"), included among the real master file records. Simulated transactions (test data) are inserted along with real transactions, and the same application program(s) operate on both the test data and the real transactions. Since the auditor knows what the ITF output should be, the actual results of processing (output reports, error reports) can be reviewed to determine whether the application program is functioning properly.

A great deal of care is required when ITF is used because the fictitious master file records, the transactions and the account outputs are placed in the system and in the business records. The account amounts and other output data must be reversed or adjusted out of the financial statements. Also, care must be taken not to damage or misstate any of the real master file records and account balances.

Program Analysis Techniques.   Numerous software packages are used by computer technicians for documentation, debugging and analysis. These tools can also be used for audit purposes in certain situations. Programs exist to take the source code (for example, COBOL) and produce flowcharts or decision tables which can be used to understand the logic of an application program. *Cross-reference* programs provide printed listings of every occurrence of each name used in an application program or a list of every file used in an application system. Auditors can use these listings to follow the flow of transactions and identify significant data files. *Program analysis* software can be utilized by auditors to identify potential trap doors created for fraudulent use.[5]

These audit tools and techniques are summarized in Exhibit 10–2. The Techniques Matrix should be studied carefully, especially the purposes,

---

[5] For more detail on the audit techniques in advanced systems see Davis et al, *Auditing & EDP,* chapter 16 or Institute of Internal Auditors, *Systems Auditability & Control Study.*

advantages and disadvantages. The next section of this chapter will focus on how auditors can use the computer to assist in auditing historical computer accounting records.

GENERALIZED AUDIT SOFTWARE

Generalized audit software programs are a set of functions that may be utilized to read, compute and operate on machine-readable records. Audit software provides access to audit evidence that would otherwise be unavailable. This part of the chapter builds upon the computer-related concepts and terminology introduced in Chapter 9 and the first section of this chapter. However, the emphasis is shifted from the evaluation of internal control to the techniques of using the computer to assist with gathering substantive evidential matter about transaction details and account balances.

Auditing with the Computer

The audit problems following evaluation of internal accounting control in a computer environment are to gain access to machine-readable detail records, to select samples of items for manual audit testing, to perform calculations and analyses of entire data files and to produce hard-copy reports of the work performed. Generalized audit software packages were first developed by CPA firms in the mid-1960s for specific application to audit engagements and have been improved and adapted to the advanced technology. The essential advantages of a generalized audit software package are:

Original programming is not required. The generalized package consists of a set of preprogrammed editing, operating and output subroutines.

The required programming is easy. A simple, limited set of programming instructions using preprinted specification forms is used to call up the subroutines in the package.

Training time is short. About one week of intensive training is sufficient to learn how to program using the specification forms.

For special-purpose analysis of data files, the generalized software is more efficient than special programs written from scratch because of the little time required for writing the instructions to call up the appropriate functions of the generalized software package. Also, the same software can be used on various clients' computer systems. Control and specific tailoring are achieved through the auditor's own ability to program and operate the system. A large number of generalized programs are currently available through CPA firms and consulting firms.[6]

---

[6] For a list of these and their capabilities, see IIA, *How to Acquire and Use Generalized Audit Software*, Appendix 2, pp. 43–52.

EXHIBIT 10–2
Techniques Matrix

Technique	Capability Supplied By	Used By	Data Used	Purpose	Advantages	Disadvantages
Tagging transactions.	Vendor or application system designer.	Auditors and managers.	Live accounting.	Compliance and substantive audit.	Full range of selectivity.	Adds to overhead of system, special programming.
Audit files.	System designer.	Auditors and control personnel.	Live accounting and system.	Compliance and substantive audit.	Specified transactions logged for audit review.	Cost.
Snapshot.	Systems designer.	Programmers and auditors.	Live system.	Review system, logic.	Aids understanding flow of transaction processing.	Special programming.
Monitoring.	Vendor.	Auditors and managers.	Live system.	Review actual system activity.	Shows what has happened.	Requires technical knowledge to interpret.

Technique	Developer/source	Users	Data	Purpose	Advantages	Limitations
Generalized audit software.	Vendor and system designer, software house, manufacturer or audit firm.	Auditors and managers.	Historical and live.	Compliance and substantive audit. Perform wide variety of audit procedures.	Retrieves data for audit purposes. Relatively easy to use, not expensive.	Requires some programming knowledge by auditor. Presently limited to types of files that can be accessed.
Simulation.	Auditors, internal and external with program copy.	Auditors.	Historical.	Determine accuracy of data processed, compliance audit.	Permits comparison with real processing.	Extensive use can be large consumer of machine resources.
Extended records.	Design of client application.	Auditors and managers.	Historical.	Provide complete trail for audit and management purposes.	Provides complete account history.	Very costly use of machine resources at present.
Integrated test facility.	Auditors, mostly internal.	Auditors.	Simulated.	Compliance audit.	Relatively inexpensive.	Must be "backed out" very carefully.
Progam analysis techniques.	Special software, contractor or vendor.	Auditors and programmers.	Usually simulated.	Authentication of program operation. Check of key points in program execution.	Gives better understanding of application; gives assurance controls are functioning.	Needs auditor knowledge of programming, may be expensive; useful only in certain circumstances.

Source: Adapted from AICPA, *Management Control and Objectives of Advanced Systems,* p. 24.

Audit Procedures
Performed by
Generalized Audit
Software

A computer application captures and generates voluminous amounts of data that are usually only available on machine-readable records. Generalized audit software (GAS) can be used to access the data and organize it into a format useful to the audit team. Audit software can be used to accomplish six basic types of audit tasks.[7]

1. *Examine and review records based on auditor criteria* to determine quality, completeness, consistency and correctness. This is the computer version of *scanning* the records for exceptions to the auditor's criteria. For example, scan: (*a*) accounts receivable balances for amounts over the credit limit, (*b*) inventory quantities for negative or unreasonably large balances, (*c*) payroll files for terminated employees.

2. *Testing calculations and making computations* can be done by the computer with more speed and accuracy than by hand. The audit software can be used to test the accuracy of client computations and to perform analytical review to evaluate the reasonableness of account balances. Examples of this use are: (*a*) recalculate extensions on inventory items, (*b*) compute file totals, (*c*) compare budgeted, standard and prior-year data with current-year data.

3. *Comparing data on separate files* can be accomplished by GAS to determine if compatible information is in agreement. Differences can be printed out for investigation and reconciliation. Examples are comparing: (*a*) payroll details with personnel records, (*b*) current and prior inventory to details of purchases and sales and (*c*) paid vouchers to check disbursements.

4. *Selecting and printing audit samples,* using statistical or judgmental criteria, for manual audit procedures is a common use of GAS. Most audit software has subroutines that will perform the quantitative analysis of statistical samples described in Chapters 11 and 12. Selected items can be printed for auditor's workpapers or printed in special format such as confirmation requests. Examples include: (*a*) accounts receivable balances for confirmation, (*b*) fixed asset additions or disposals for vouching, and (*c*) inventory items for observation.

5. *Summarizing, resequencing and reformatting data* can be done with GAS in a variety of ways. Examples of this are: (*a*) preparing general ledger trial balances, (*b*) resequencing inventory items by location to facilitate observations and (*c*) summarizing inventory turnover statistics for obsolescence analysis.

6. *Comparing audit evidence from manual procedures* to company records can be done more efficiently with GAS. The audit evidence

---

[7] The classification of audit tasks and examples are modified from AICPA, *Computer Assisted Audit Techniques,* and IIA, *How to Acquire and Use Generalized Audit Software* cited in the Sources and Additional Reading References at the end of the chapter.

must be converted to machine-readable form and then can be compared to the company records on computer files or auditor files of sample items. Examples are: (*a*) comparing inventory test counts with perpetual records and (*b*) comparing adjusted audit balances on confirmed accounts receivable to the audit file of book balances.

Using Generalized Audit Software

For the most part, the widely used GAS packages are very similar. Regardless of the particular GAS used, five distinct phases are involved in developing a GAS application: (1) define audit objectives, (2) plan the application, (3) design the application, (4) code and test the application and (5) process the application and evaluate the results.

   1.   **Define the Audit Objective.** The first step in applying GAS is to determine specific audit objectives. These objectives are related to the overall audit approach of reliance on internal control and the nature, timing and extent of procedures to gather audit evidence that you have learned from previous chapters. Using GAS should be viewed as a special tool to allow auditors a means to accomplish their objectives, not an objective in itself. For example, the general audit objectives might be to test management's assertions that the accounts receivable balance represents detail accounts which exist, are complete and are valued correctly (see Chapter 6 for the financial statement assertions). Based on these general objectives, specific procedures may include: foot the accounts subsidiary ledger master file, select a sample of accounts for confirmation, prepare an aged trial balance, and investigate accounts with overdue balances.

   2.   **Feasibility and Planning.** Feasibility should be considered in three ways: (1) Is the use of audit software technically feasible? (2) Are alternative ways to accomplish the audit task available? (3) Which of the alternatives is the most practical and economical? If the use of GAS is technically feasible, other considerations as listed in the box below must be weighed.

FEASIBILITY CONSIDERATIONS

Nature of the audit area and audit approach.
Significance of audit effort and timing.
Availability and sequence of data.
Extent of client data center cooperation.
Availability of qualified audit software staff.
Costs and benefits.

Source: AICPA, *Computer-Assisted Audit Techniques*, p. 9.

Audit software may be the most practical way to achieve the audit objective, but it is seldom the only way. Audit resources (qualified people and their time) must be allocated carefully to achieve efficient and effective results. Using GAS requires considerable investment in time and effort and may be efficient only when repeated use is anticipated on return engagements. Obviously the data must be available. The desired files, especially detailed transaction files, are often retained only for a short period of time. The availability of data files and the degree of client cooperation would normally be determined during the general and application controls review.

After determining the feasibility of using GAS, the audit manager should determine specifically how it will be used, establish control procedures for all subsequent steps and arrange the logistics with the data center. Specific planning steps are listed in the box below.

PLANNING STEPS

Set application objectives.

Determine reports and other output requirements.

Review content, accessibility, etc., of client files.

Identify client personnel to provide technical assistance.

Determine computer supply needs.

Prepare GAS application budgets and timetables.

Source: AICPA, *Computer-Assisted Audit Techniques*, p.10.

The planning phase is also the time to define the workpapers which will document the GAS application. The audit manager should determine what computer output representing coding and testing should be retained in the workpapers (note: the computer output may be in the form of computer-readable workpapers, such as magnetic tape audit files).

3. Application Design.   Developing a GAS application is not unlike the client's procedures for developing a new application system. The steps and documentation described for the client's system development, as described in Chapter 9, generally apply to the auditor's development of a GAS application. A complete description of the application phase is beyond the scope of this book and would be undertaken only by specially trained audit staff. In summary, the application design expands the ideas developed during the feasibility and planning stage into detailed descriptions necessary for preparing coded computer instructions. The documentation of the application design phase includes the GAS application system flowchart, logic descriptions, detailed report layouts, list of control points and procedures, record formats and a test plan. Frequently, the auditor must obtain a computer dump of a few records of each client file to be used to ensure subsequent coding is based on accurate information. The application must be thoroughly tested with sample client data or simulated data until the audit manager is confident the GAS application works as desired. The client's file should not be used for testing, and the auditor should obtain a copy for testing purposes. The time to determine the test plan is during the application design (not after coding).

4. Coding and Testing. Most GAS packages have an extensive repertoire of powerful instructions to facilitate processing data files and preparing audit output. The coding is done on specially designed forms and involves parameter concepts. Each parameter sheet will have a code that will be keyed into the beginning columns of a record and each column will have a special meaning.

Coding converts the application design into specific operational requirements (computer language) of the package in use. As coding progresses, the sequence and the logic should be challenged and reviewed. The coding must be converted to a machine-readable form, all syntax errors removed (errors due to failure to follow the rules of the package), and it must be compiled (converted into the hardware machine language like any computer program).

Once the coding errors are removed, the logic must be tested. Testing is very similar to the test data approach used in compliance auditing of client programs described in Chapter 9. The test plan defined in the design phase should be extensive enough to test each logic path and anticipate all variations of client data.

5. Processing and Evaluation. The processing phase involves: (1) verifying that the status of the client file has not changed, (2) obtaining an auditor copy of the file, (3) processing the GAS application against the copy of the client's file(s) and (4) reviewing results, updating working papers and retaining audit files. The audit team should carefully monitor and control the actual processing and output. Control procedures established during the design phase should be followed. Planned totals should be compared to results and the totals logged on control working papers. The audit manager should review the output for reasonableness and clarity. Finally, the documentation workpapers of the application must be completed and filed. Special care must be taken to leave adequate documentation for subsequent use on a repeat engagement. (In a sense, this documentation is the "audit trail of the audit.") The working papers will frequently contain a list of suggested modifications for next year's audit.

In summary, following the feasibility and planning phase, a GAS application should be designed to achieve specific audit objectives. Further, the reliability of general application computer controls, the availability of client files, access to the computer and technical assistance, estimated costs and the availability of GAS-trained audit staff must be evaluated. The noncomputer-trained auditor should be actively involved in the definition of audit objectives and the application plan. The computer auditor will utilize the application design to link the coding and testing to the planning phase. Results of testing should be reviewed by the audit manager. In the processing phase, audit software is run under control of the computer auditor to process copies of client files and produce audit results.

Planning and testing are the most critical tasks in the development of a GAS application. If planning is not adequate, the audit objectives may not be achieved. Problems are likely to occur in subsequent phases and require excessive time and effort to correct. Testing must be adequate or the probability of success is low. Once processing is commenced, it is extremely difficult to correct errors and deficiencies.

Not all GAS will operate in a database environment. The technology to adapt the GAS to use the DBMS is beyond this text.[8] However, the easiest solution is to request the client to create a file that the GAS can read from the desired data elements of the database at the desired point in time.

Many larger companies have internal auditors skilled in using GAS. Independent auditors may utilize their work and reports of these internal "computer auditors."[9]

Generalized Audit Software Limitations

Notwithstanding the powers of the computer, several general auditing procedures are outside its reach. The computer cannot observe and count physical things (inventory, for example), but it can compare numerous auditor-made counts to the computer records.

The computer cannot examine external and internal documentation, and thus it cannot vouch accounting output to sources of basic evidence. An exception would exist in an advanced computer system that stored the basic source documents only on magnetic media. The auditor would have to test the controls over creation of the files, but then would have no choice but to treat the file as a basic "document" source.

However, when manual vouching is involved, computer-assisted selection of sample items is a great efficiency. Finally, the computer cannot conduct an inquiry in the limited sense that the inquiry procedure refers to questionnaires and conversations.

---

[8] For information on how to adapt the GAS to interface with the DBMS, see Davis et al., *Auditing & EDP,* Chapter 17, "Audit Tools and Techniques for Database Management Systems."

[9] In some circumstances, an independent auditor may utilize the work and reports of the internal auditor. Refer to SAS 9 (AU322), "The Effect of an Internal Audit Function on the Scope of the Independent Auditor's Examination."

COMPUTER ABUSE   Computer fraud is a matter of concern for managers and investors as well as auditors. A more general term which includes computer fraud is ***computer abuse.*** It has been defined as follows:

> Any incident associated with computer technology in which a victim suffered or could have suffered loss and a perpetrator by intention made or could have made gain.[10]

This definition of computer abuse is broad enough to include such acts as intentional damage or destruction of a computer, use of the computer as a tool to assist in a fraud, and using the mystique of a computer to promote business. Computers indeed have been damaged by vandals, an abuse best prevented by physical security measures. A computer was used by perpetrators of the Equity Funding fraud to print thousands of fictitious records and documents that otherwise would have occupied the time of hundreds of clerks. Some services (such as "computerized" dating services) have promoted business on the promise of using computers when none are actually used.

However, in a business environment, you would be concerned particularly with acts of computer abuse that could result in theft or embezzlement of assets or material misstatements in published financial statements. To perpetrate computer abuses, persons must have access to one or more of the following:

☐ The computer itself, or a terminal.

☐ Data files.

☐ Computer programs.

☐ System information.

☐ Time and opportunity to convert assets to personal use.

The most important preventive controls are those that limit access to computers, data files, programs and system documentation to the minimum number of persons needed to operate the computer system for legitimate business purposes. Definition of duties, segregation of functional responsibilities, dual-person access, enforced vacations for computer personnel, physical security and electronic security (for example, access-code "passwords") are all methods of limiting access to computer resources.

Computer experts generally agree that an ingenious programmer can commit theft or misappropriation of assets that would difficult, if not impossible, to detect. Nonetheless, such abuses generally produce an unsupported debit balance in some asset account, although this is not always the case. For example, someone might manipulate the computer

---

[10] Donn B. Parker, *Crime by Computer* (New York: Charles Scribner's Sons, 1976), p. 12.

to cause purchased goods to be routed to his own warehouse. In this case, the business inventory balances would probably be overstated. One bank employee caused checking account service charges to be credited to his own account instead of to the appropriate revenue account. In this case, the service charge revenue account would be less than the sum of charges to the checking account customers. Thorough auditing of accounting output records might result in detection of computer-assisted frauds such as these.

Non-computer auditing methods, as well as some computer-assisted methods, may be employed to try to detect computer abuse. Direct confirmations with independent outside parties, analytical review of the output of the system for typical relationships, and comparison of output with independently maintained files may reveal errors and irregularities in computer-produced accounting records. However, all too often auditors and managers are surprised by computer abuses reported to them by conscious-stricken participants, anonymous telephone messages, tragic suicides or other haphazard means. Nevertheless, you as an auditor working in a computer environment are expected to possess the expertise required to identify serious computer control weaknesses. When such weaknesses are believed to exist, the best strategy is to use the services of a computer specialist to help plan and execute technical procedures for further study and evaluation of the computer control system.

Computer abuse is a glamorous topic and attracts newspaper headlines. However, studies have shown that the majority of problems in computer processing are the errors that are not detected and corrected utilizing the controls described in this chapter.

SOURCES AND ADDITIONAL READING REFERENCES

AICPA. *Report of The Joint Database Task Force*. New York, 1983 (Also members of the Task Force: The Canadian Institute of Chartered Accountants, Toronto, Ontario and The Institute of Internal Auditors, Altamonte Springs, Florida.)

————. *Audit and Control Considerations in an On-Line Environment*. Computer Services Guidelines, New York, 1983.

————. *Audit and Control Considerations in a Minicomputer or Small Business Computer Environment*. Computer Services Guidelines, New York, 1981.

————. *Computer-Assisted Audit Techniques*. Audit and Accounting Guide, New York, 1979.

————. *Management, Control and Audit of Advanced EDP Systems*. Computer Services Guidelines, New York, 1977.

Allen, Brandt. "Embezzler's Guide to the Computer." *Harvard Business Review*, July-August 1975, pp. 79–89.

————. "The Biggest Computer Frauds: Lesson for CPAs." *Journal of Accountancy*, May 1977, pp. 52–63.

Capote, Arnold P. "Methods for Auditing the Reliability of Computerized Applications." *The Journal of Accounting, Auditing and Finance,* Fall 1981, pp. 42–62.

Cerullo, Michael J. "Controls for Data Base Systems." *CPA Journal,* January 1982, pp. 30–35.

Dasher, Paul E., and W. Ken Harmon. "Assessing Microcomputer Risks and Controls for Clients." *The CPA Journal,* May 1984, pp. 36–41.

Davis, Gordon B., Donald L. Adams, and Carol A. Schaller. *Auditing & EDP,* 2d ed. AICPA, 1983, New York.

Davis, Keagle W. "The Information Systems Auditor of the 1980s." *Management Accounting,* March 1981, pp. 40–47.

Dowell, C., and James Arthur Hall. "EDP Controls With Audit Cost Implications." *The Journal of Accounting, Auditing and Finance,* Fall 1981, pp. 30–40.

Hubbert, James F. "Computer Personnel Frauds." *Journal of Accountancy,* August 1979, pp. 44–50.

Institute of Internal Auditors. *How to Acquire and Use Generalized Audit Software.* Modern Concepts of Internal Auditing Series, Altamonte Springs, Fla., 1979.

————. *Systems Auditability & Control Study.* Altamonte Springs, Fla., 1977.

Loebbecke, James K., John F. Mullackey, and George Zuber. "Auditing in a Computer Environment." *The Journal of Accountancy,* January 1983, pp. 68–78.

Lainhart, J. W., and B. R. Snyder. "A Simultaneous-Parallel Approach to Testing Computerized Systems." *GAO Review,* Summer 1977, pp. 29–37.

Mack, Kenneth. "Computer Fraud and Fidelity Bonding." *CPA Journal,* October 1982, pp. 18–23.

Mason, J. O., and J. J. Davies. "Legal Implications of EDP Deficiencies." *CPA Journal,* May 1977, pp. 21–24.

Norris, Daniel M., and Charles R. Litecky. "Minicomputer Control Evaluation." *Information Systems & Management Consulting,* Summer 1983, pp. 6–7.

Parker, Donn B. *Crime by Computer,* New York: Charles Scribner's Sons, 1976.

Porter, W. Thomas, and William E. Perry. *EDP: Controls and Auditing,* 4th ed. Boston: Kent Publishing Co., 1984.

Reneau, J. H. "Auditing in a Data Base Environment." *Journal of Accountancy,* December 1977, pp. 59–65.

Romney, Marshall. "Fraud and EDP." *CPA Journal,* November 1976, pp. 23–28.

Shearon, W., E. Butler, and J. Benjamin. "Audit Aspects of Small Computer Systems." *CPA Journal,* August 1980, pp. 17–21.

Simkin, Mark G. "Computer Crime: Lessons and Direction." *CPA Journal,* December 1981, pp. 10–16.

Stone R. L. "Who Is Responsible for Computer Fraud?" *The Journal of Accountancy,* February 1975, pp. 35–38.

Timko, Ronald J. "Controlling Microcomputers—Don't Overreact" *The Internal Auditor,* December 1983, pp. 20–22.

Tobison, G. L., and G. B. Davis. "Actual Use and Perceived Utility of EDP Auditing Techniques." *The EDP Auditor,* Spring 1981, pp. 1–34.

Tussing, R. T., and G. L. Helms. "Training Computer Audit Specialists." *Journal of Accountancy,* July 1980, pp. 71–74.

Vanecek. M. T., and G. Scott. "Data Bases—The Auditor's Dilemma." *CPA Journal,* January 1980, pp. 26–36.

Vanecek, M. T., R. F. Zant, and C. S. Guynes. "Distributed Processing: A New Tool for Auditors." *Journal of Accountancy,* October 1980, pp. 75–83.

Weeb, Richard D. "Audit Planning—EDP Considerations." *Journal of Accountancy,* May 1979, pp. 65–75.

Weber, Ron. *EDP Auditing: Conceptual Foundations and Practices,* New York: McGraw-Hill, 1982.

————. "Audit Trail System Support in Advanced Computer-Based Accounting Systems." *Accounting Review,* April 1982, pp. 311–25.

REVIEW QUESTIONS

10.1. What are the characteristics of advanced computer systems?

10.2. Why are advanced computer systems said to be "transaction-driven," while batch systems can be said to be "program-driven?"

10.3. How can each department "own" their computer data files when data processing is accomplished in a simple batch system, but would lose ownership if a database management system is in use?

10.4. What are the responsibilities of the Database Administration function?

10.5. What controls should be evaluated when a database is used instead of master files?

10.6. What is an audit trail? How is the audit trail changed in advanced computer systems? What are the audit implications of a computer-based audit trail?

10.7. What is the difference between the test data technique described in Chapter 9 and the integrated test facility technique?

10.8. What are the major characteristics and control problems in minicomputer installations?

10.9. Which of the advanced audit tools and techniques would be used for compliance audit procedures? Which for substantive audit procedures?

10.10. Evaluate the following statement made by a client's data processing manager. "Who cares if we use identification numbers and passwords to access the inventory database and the update programs as long as the computer maintains a transaction log?"

10.11. "The use of the test data technique or the integrated test facility technique to test application controls is unprofessional. We don't enter fake transactions into a client's manual system. Why should we do it in their computer system?" Evaluate this position and question posed by an audit partner.

10.12. What is generalized audit software?

10.13. What general audit tasks may be performed with the assistance of generalized audit software?

10.14. Why are the testing and planning tasks the most critical when using generalized audit software?

10.15. What are the phases of developing an application using generalized audit software? What are the noncomputer auditor's responsibilities in each phase?

10.16. What advantages are derived from using generalized audit software to perform recalculations? To select samples and print confirmations?

10.17. Evaluate the following statement by a senior *computer auditor*. "The time to be thinking about generalized audit software procedures is during the review of the application."

10.18. "We should not leave the firm's generalized audit software on the client's computer system. This would be no different than leaving our audit program with the client. Likewise, we should not rely on the client's generalized audit software package." Evaluate this statement made by an audit partner.

10.19. List the five things a person must have access to in order to commit a computer fraud.

EXERCISES AND PROBLEMS

10.20. **Advanced Computer Systems Controls**

The Department of Taxation of one state is developing a new computer system for processing state income tax returns of individuals and corporations. The new system features direct data input and inquiry capabilities. Identification of taxpayers is provided by using the social security number for individuals and the federal identification number for corporations. The new system should be fully implemented in time for the next tax season.

The new system will serve three primary purposes as described below:

1. Data will be input into the system directly from tax returns through terminals located at the central headquarters of the Department of Taxation.

2. The returns will be processed using the main computer facilities at central headquarters. The processing includes:

   a. Verification of mathematical accuracy.

   b. Auditing the reasonableness of deductions, tax due, etc., through the use of edit routines; these routines also include a comparison of the current year's data with the prior year's data.

   c. Identification of returns which should be considered for audit by revenue agents of the department.

   d. Issuing refund checks to taxpayers.

3. Inquiry service will be provided taxpayers upon request through the assistance of tax department personnel at five regional offices. A total of 50 terminals will be placed at the regional offices. A taxpayer will be allowed to determine the status of his/her return or get information from the last three years' returns by calling or visiting one of the department's regional offices.

The State Commissioner of Taxation is concerned about data security over and above protection against natural hazards such as fire and flood. He is concerned with protection against the loss or damage of data during data input or processing or the improper input or improper processing of data. In addition, the Tax Commissioner and the State Attorney General have discussed the general problem of data confidentiality which may arise from the nature and operation of the new system. Both individuals want to have all potential problems identified before the system is fully developed and implemented so that the proper controls can be incorporated into the new system.

Required:

a. Describe the potential confidentiality problems that could arise in each of the following three areas of processing and recommend the corrective actions(s) to solve the problem.

(1) Data input.

(2) Processing of returns.

(3) Data inquiry.

b. The State Commissioner of Taxation wants to incorporate controls to provide data security against the loss, damage or improper input or use of data during data input and processing. Identify the potential problems (other than of natural hazards such as fire and floods) for which the Department of Taxation should develop controls and recommend the possible controls for each problem identified.

(*CMA* adapted)

10.21. **GAS Application—Phases and Documentation**

The phases and documentation of developing a GAS application are very similar to the phases and documentation when the client develops a new computer system. Refer to Chapter 9 and prepare a table of the phases and the related documentation when the client develops a new system. Based on the material in Chapter 10, prepare a table of the phases and the related documentation when the auditor develops a GAS application. Organize your answer as follows:

Client's System Development	
Phases	**Documentation**

Auditor's GAS Application	
Phases	**Documentation**

10.22. **GAS Application—Receivables Confirmation**

You are using generalized audit software to prepare accounts receivable confirmations during the annual audit of the Eastern Sunrise Services Club. The company has the following data files:

> Master file—debtor credit record.
>
> Master file—debtor name and address.
>
> Master file—account detail.
>
>> Ledger number.
>>
>> Sales code.
>>
>> Customer account number.
>>
>> Date of last billing.
>>
>> Balance (gross).
>>
>> Discount available to customer (memo account only).
>>
>> Date of last purchase.

The discount field represents the amount of discount available to the customer if the customer pays within 30 days of the invoicing date. The discount field is cleared for expired amounts during the daily updating, and you have determined that this is properly executed.

Required

List the information from the *data files* shown above that you would include on the confirmation requests. Identify the file from which the information can be obtained.

10.23. **GAS Application—Fixed Assets**

You are supervising the audit field work of Sparta Springs Company and need certain information from Sparta's fixed-asset records which are maintained on magnetic disk. The particular information is: (1) Net book value of assets, so that your assistant can reconcile the subsidiary ledger to the general ledger control accounts. The general ledger contains an account for each asset *type* at each plant *location* and (2) sufficient data to enable your assistant to find and inspect selected assets.

Record layout of the fixed-asset master file:

Asset number.

Description.

Asset type.

Location code.

Year acquired.

Cost.

Accumulated depreciation, end of year (includes accumulated depreciation at the beginning of the year plus depreciation for year to date).

Depreciation for year to date.

Useful life.

Required:

a. From the data file described above, list the information needed to verify correspondence of the subsidiary detail records with the general ledger accounts. Does this work complete the audit of fixed assets?

b. What additional data is needed to enable your assistant to inspect the assets?

10.24   GAS Application—Inventory

Your client, Boos & Becker, Inc., is a medium-sized manufacturer of products for the leisure-time activities market (camping equipment, scuba gear, bows and arrows, and the like). During the past year, a minicomputer system was installed, and inventory records of finished goods and parts were converted to computer processing. Each record on the inventory master file contains the following information:

Item or part number.

Description.

Size.

Quantity on hand.

Cost per unit.

Total value of inventory on hand at cost.

Date of last sale or usage.

Quantity used or sold this year.

Reorder point (quantity).

Economic order quantity.

Code number of major vendor.

Code number of secondary vendor.

In preparation for year-end inventory, the client has two identical sets of pre-printed, prepunched inventory cards prepared from the master file. One set is for the client's inventory counts, and the other is for your use to make audit test counts. The following information has been key-punched into the cards and printed on their face:

Item or part number.

Description.

Size.

Unit of measure code.

In taking the year-end count, the client's personnel will write the actual counted quantity on the face of each card. When all counts are complete, the counted quantity will be keypunched into the cards. The cards will be processed against the master file, and quantity-on-hand figures will be adjusted to reflect the actual count. A computer listing will be prepared to show any missing inventory count cards and all quantity adjustments of more that $100 in value. These items will be investigated by client personnel, and all required adjustments will be made. When adjustments have been completed, the final year-end balances will be computed and posted to the general ledger.

Your firm has available a generalized audit software package that will run on the client's computer and can process both cards and the disk master file.

Required:

a. In general and without regard to the facts above, discuss the nature of generalized audit software packages and list the various audit uses of such packages.

b. List and describe at least five ways a GAS package can be used to assist in all aspects of the audit of the inventory of Boos & Becker, Inc. (For example, the package can be used to read the inventory master file and list items and parts with a high unit cost or total value. Such items can be included in the test counts to increase the dollar coverage of the audit verification.) Hint: think of the normal audit procedures in gathering evidence on inventory when the client makes a periodic count, then think of how the GAS could help in this particular client situation.

(AICPA adapted)

DISCUSSION CASES

10.25. Internal Control Considerations in a Microcomputer Environment

Introduction

The second standard of field work requires that an audit include "a proper study and evaluation of the existing internal control as a basis for reliance thereon and for the determination of the resultant extent of the tests to which auditing procedures are to be restricted."

Given the increasing use of microcomputers by many businesses today, auditors must be cognizant of the potential internal control weaknesses inherent in a microcomputer environment. Such knowledge is crucial if the auditor is to make a proper assessment of the related controls and to plan an effective and efficient audit approach.

Required:

In the following case study, assume you are participating in the audit of Chicago Appliance Company and the background information below has been obtained during the planning phase. You have been asked to: (1) consider the potential effects on internal control that have been introduced by the microcomputer application and (2) assess how those internal control effects may alter the audit plan for the current year.

Background Information

Chicago Appliance is a wholesale distributor of electric appliances. The company's sales in each of the last two years have been approximately $40,000,000. All accounting applications are handled at the company's corporate office.

The data processing operations have historically centered around an onsite minicomputer. The computer applications include accounts payable and cash disbursements, payroll, inventory, and general ledger. Accounts receivable and fixed-asset records have been prepared manually in the past. Internal controls in all areas have been considered strong in the last few years.

During the past year, financial management decided to automate processing of sales, accounts receivable and fixed-asset transactions and accounting. Management also concluded that purchasing a microcomputer and related available software was more cost-effective than increasing the minicomputer capacity and hiring a second computer operator. The controller and accounting clerks have been encouraged to find additional uses for the microcomputer and to "experiment" with it when they are not too busy.

The accounts receivable clerk is enthusiastic about the microcomputer, but the fixed-asset clerk seems somewhat apprehensive about it because he has no prior experience with computers. The accounts receivable clerk explained that the controller had purchased a "very easy to use" accounts receivable software application program for the microcomputer which enables her to input the daily information regarding billings and payments received quickly and easily. The controller has added some programming of his own to the software to give it better report-writing features.

During a recent demonstration, the accounts receivable clerk explained that the program required her to only input the customer's name and invoice amount in the case of billings, or the customer's name and check amount in the case of payments. The microcomputer then automatically updates the respective customer's account balance. At the end of every month, the accounts receivable trial balance is printed and reconciled by the clerk to the general ledger balance. The reconciliation is reviewed by the controller.

The fixed-asset program was also purchased from an outside vendor. The controller indicated that the software package had just recently been put on the market and that it was programmed to compute tax depreciation based on recent changes in the federal tax laws. He also stated that because of the fixed-asset clerk's reluctance to use the microcomputer, he had input all the information from the fixed-asset manual records. He indicated, however, that the fixed-asset clerk would be responsible for the future processing related to the fixed-asset files and for generating the month-end and year-end reports used to prepare the related accounting entries.

The various accounts receivable and fixed-asset diskettes are all adequately labeled as to the type of program or data file. They are arranged in an organized manner in a diskette holder located near the microcomputer.

(Adapted from a case contributed by Price Waterhouse to *The Auditor's Report,* Summer 1983.)

10.26. **Lapping via Terminal and Other Defects in a New System**
VBR Company has recently installed a new computer system which has online, real-time capability. Terminals are used for data entry and inquiry. A new cash re-

ceipts and accounts receivable file maintenance system has been designed and implemented for use with this new equipment. All programs have been written, tested, and the new system is being run in parallel with the old system. After two weeks of parallel operation, no differences have been observed between the two systems other than keypunch errors on the old system.

Al Brand, data processing manager, is enthusiastic about the new equipment and system. He reveals that the system was designed, coded, compiled, debugged and tested by programmers utilizing online terminals installed specifically for around-the-clock use by the programming staff. He claimed that this access to the computer saved one third in programming elapsed time. All files, including accounts receivable, are online at all times as the firm moves toward a full database mode. All programs, new and old, are available at all times for recall into memory for scheduled operating use or for program maintenance. Program documentation and actual tests confirm that data entry edits in the new system include all conventional data error and validity checks appropriate to the system.

Inquiries have confirmed that the new system conforms precisely to the flowcharts, a portion of which are shown following (Exhibit 10.26–1). A turnaround copy of the invoice is used as a remittance advice (R/A) by 99 percent of the customers. If the R/A is missing, the cashier applies the payment to a selected invoice. Sales terms are net 60 days, but payment patterns are sporadic. Statements are not mailed to customers. Late payments are commonplace and are not vigorously pursued. VBR does not have a bad debt problem because bad debt losses average only 0.5 percent of sales.

Before authorizing the termination of the old system, Cal Darden, controller, has requested a review of the internal control features which have been designed for the

EXHIBIT 10.26–1
VBR Company System Flowchart

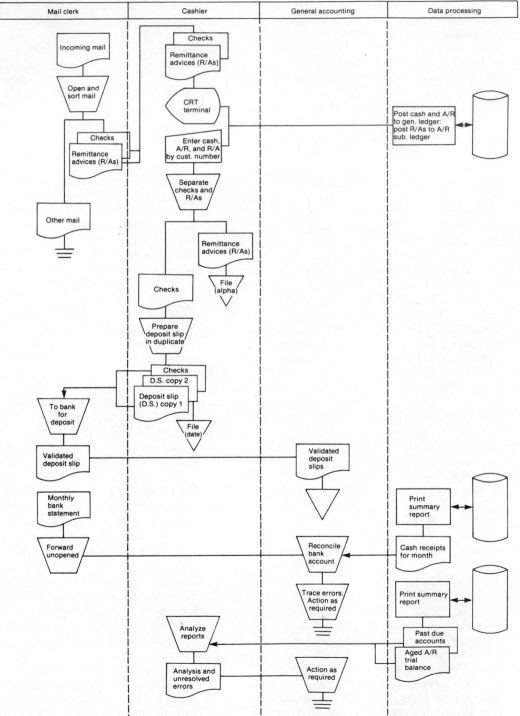

new system. Security against unauthorized access and fraudulent actions, assurance of the integrity of the files and protection of the firm's assets should be provided by the internal controls.

Required:

a. Describe how fraud by lapping of accounts receivable could be committed in the new system and discuss how it could be prevented. (Fraud by lapping of accounts receivable is accomplished by an individual who has access to both cash receipts and the accounts receivable records. The cash receipts of one customer are taken, and subsequent cash receipts for another customer are posted to the first customer's account. Thus, a payment entry is made, and differences between customer and company records can be explained by timing differences. The lapping continues as cash receipts of a third customer are posted to the second customer's accounts and so forth.)

b. Based upon the description of VBR Company's new system and the systems flowchart that has been presented:

(1) Describe any other defects which exist in the system.

(2) Suggest how every other defect you identified could be corrected.

(CMA adapted)

10.27. **Kingston Company—Continued: GAS and Online Controls.**
This problem is a continuation of the fact situation presented in Problem 7.13 at the end of Chapter 7. Additional requirements were requested in Cases 8.30 and 9.19 at the end of those chapters. Assume the Kingston Company maintains the accounts receivable subsidiary ledger in a computer master file. The audit manager has decided to stratify the population of 2,600 receivable accounts and send positive confirmations to the 150 accounts with the largest

balances and negative confirmations to a random sample of 220 of the remaining accounts.

Required:

a. Assume you are going to use a GAS package to select and prepare the confirmations. List the steps (in general terms) required in the following phases: (1) defining the audit objective, (2) planning, and (3) application design.

b. Assume that the Kingston Company has decided the current order, billing and shipping system described in Exercise 7.13 is obsolete and is considering converting to an advanced computer system. They envision this upgrading as the first step to a completely integrated online database system. Outline, in general terms, the control implications of converting to an advanced system and recommend controls and audit techniques that should be considered before development work begins.

10.28. **Rock Island Quarry—Evidence Collection in an Online System**
Your firm has audited the Rock Island Quarry Company for several years. Rock Island's main revenue comes from selling crushed rock to construction companies from several quarries owned by the company in Illinois and Iowa. The rock is priced by weight, quality and crushed size.

Past Procedure:

A purchasing contractor's or a Rock Island's truck had to display a current certified empty weight receipt or be weighed in. The quarry yard weigh master recorded the empty weight on a handwritten "scale ticket" along with the purchasing construction company name, the truck number and date. After the truck was loaded, it was required to leave via the scale where the loaded weight and rock grade were recorded on the "scale tickets." Weekly, the scale tickets were sorted by grade and manually recorded on a summary sheet which was forwarded to the home office. Scale tickets were prenumbered and accounted for in the home office.

Revenue (and receivables) audit procedures involved evaluating the controls at selected quarries (rotated each year) and a statistical sample of vouching weight tickets to weekly summaries. Weekly summaries were traced through pricing and invoicing to the general ledger on a sample basis and general ledger entries vouched back to weekly summaries on a sample basis. Few material discrepancies were found.

New Procedure:

At the beginning of the current year, Rock Island converted to a distributed network of microcomputers to gather the information formally entered manually on the "weight ticket." This conversion was done with your knowledge, but without your advice or input. Now all entering trucks must weigh in. The yard weigh master enters *NEW* on the terminal keyboard, and a form appears on the screen that is similar to the old weight ticket, except the quarry number, transaction number, date and incoming empty weight are *automatically* entered. Customer and truck number are keyed in. After the weigh-in, the weigh master enters *HOLD* through the terminal. The weight ticket record is stored in the microcomputer until weigh-out.

When a truck is loaded and stops on the scale, the weigh master enters *OLD*, and a directory of all open transactions appears on the screen. The weigh master selects the proper one and enters *OUT*. The truck out-weight and the rock weight is computed and entered automatically. The weigh master must enter the proper number for the rock grade. The weigh master can not change any automatically entered field. When satisfied the screen weight ticket is correct, the weigh master enters *SOLD,* and the transaction is automatically transmitted to the home office computer and the appropriate accounting database elements are updated. One copy of a scale ticket is printed and given to the truck driver. There is *no written evidence* of the sale kept by Rock Island.

Required:

It is now midyear for Rock Island, and you are planning for this year's audit.

a. What controls (manual and computer) should you look for in this system for recording quarry sales?

b. The computer programs that process the rock sales and perform the accounting reside at the home office and at the quarries. What implications does this have on your planned audit procedures?

c. What are you going to do to gather substantive audit evidence now that there are no written "weight tickets?"

C H A P T E R 1 1

PROFESSIONAL STANDARDS SOURCES		
Compendium Section	Document Reference	Topic
AU 312	SAS 47	Audit Risk and Materiality in Conducting an Audit
AU 320	SAS 1	Auditor's Study and Evaluation of Internal Control
AU 350	SAS 39	Audit Sampling

Compliance Auditing with Attribute Sampling

LEARNING OBJECTIVES

This chapter contains more technical details on some, but not all, of the topics introduced in Chapter 8. Here you will find more specific coverage of how to do statistical sampling in the compliance audit of internal accounting control procedures. After studying this chapter in conjunction with Chapter 8, you should be able to:

☐ Explain more fully the role of professional judgment in assigning numbers to risks of overreliance and underreliance and to tolerable rate.

☐ Calculate the effect on sample size of subdividing a population into two relevant populations.

☐ Use graphs and tables to determine sample size, given all the necessary specifications.

☐ Use your imagination to overcome difficult sampling unit selection problems.

☐ Use evaluation tables to calculate statistical results (CUL) of evidence obtained through compliance audit procedures.

☐ Use the discovery sampling evaluation table for assessment of audit evidence.

The assessment of sampling risk is an exercise of professional judgment. When using statistical sampling methods, auditors must quantify the two risks of decision error. The more important one is the risk of overreliance. Even so, not much is known about the sensitivity of the audit taken as a whole to overreliance on internal accounting control.

RISK OF OVERRELIANCE: A PROFESSIONAL JUDGMENT

The first effect of overreliance is to cause the auditors to judge internal control risk to be lower than it really is. However, control risk judgments themselves tend to be fairly crude. For example, suppose an auditor makes the mistake of overreliance and judges the control risk to be moderate (say, 0.50), when, in fact, a more informed decision would have been to judge internal control less favorably and let internal control risk be high (say, 0.90). In the example below, assume inherent risk is judged at 1.0 and the other planned audit work is believed to have a detection risk of 0.10. Then:

Plan: $AuR = IR (=1.0) \times IC (=0.50) \times DR (=0.10) = 0.05$
Judgment: $AuR = IR (=1.0) \times IC (=0.50) \times DR (=0.10) = 0.05$
Actual: $AuR = IR (=1.0) \times IC (=0.90) \times DR (=0.10) = 0.09$

The inherent risk element in the model muddies the waters. Who is to say that it should not be less than 1.0 in the plan? Nevertheless, ignoring the problems of reality, the theory asks auditors to decide what amount of risk they want to take of relying too much on internal control—to the extent of almost doubling the overall audit risk (from 0.05 to 0.09).

The conceptual difficulty of controlling audit risk, as this example illustrates, is very realistic. In practice, the problem is not so much what number to assign to the risk of overreliance as it is a matter of being careful not to brush aside some evidence of deficient control performance. Auditors can be found at fault for not paying proper attention to signs of problems that should trigger additional audit work. Auditing standards suggest a low level of risk of overreliance. Practicing auditors tend to permit it to be from 20 percent to 1 percent, depending on the circumstances.

RISK OF UNDERRELIANCE: A PROFESSIONAL JUDGMENT

Auditors usually do not say much about the risk of underreliance. An explanation of it depends upon your knowing more about statistical evaluation, so you will be well advised to skip this section, read the remainder of the chapter and then return.

Compliance audit sampling as explained in SAS 39 (AU 350) and in this textbook has a potentially serious drawback. The methods concentrate on controlling the risk of overreliance in order to avoid erroneous decisions that could reduce the *effectiveness* of audits. Erroneous decisions leading to underreliance should also be avoided in the interest of audit *efficiency*.

Take, for example, a compliance audit of 80 sales invoices. The problem is this:

Suppose the sample size of 80 invoices was based on a zero expected population deviation rate and a 3 percent tolerable rate, with 10 percent risk of overreliance.

Finding no deviations in the sample would yield a CUL of 3 percent, and finding 1 or more deviations would yield a CUL of 5 percent or more (refer to Appendix 11–C.3). For all practical purposes, zero is a maximum *acceptance number*.

The probability of finding 1 or more deviations when the actual population deviation rate is 3 percent is 0.91. Thus, the risk of underreliance is 91 percent.

You can compute the risk of underreliance for the case where finding one deviation is important by using this formula:

Risk of underreliance = Probability that one or more deviations
will be found in a sample of size n
($=80$) for a given population
deviation rate ($=3\%$)
$$= 1 - (1 - \text{Rate})^n$$
$$= 1 - (1 - 0.03)^{80}$$
$$= 0.913$$

The 91.3 percent risk of underreliance is high. This situation illustrates a pitfall in using small samples. Statistically, finding even one deviation can cause a sample evaluation to exceed the tolerable rate. In fact, you have a risk of underreliance even when the population deviation rate is *less* than the tolerable rate. Using the formula above, the risk of underreliance is 80 percent if the population deviation rate is 2 percent, 55 percent if the population rate is 1 percent, and 7.7 percent if the population rate is .1 percent.

The only way to guard against the underreliance decision error and thus control its risk is to audit a larger sample. This strategy permits discovery of one or more exceptions without making CUL exceed your tolerable rate. The concept is that even a good control will have a few deviations.

For example, instead of selecting 80 items where discovery of 1 deviation would indicate ineffective control performance, select 140 invoices where discovery of 1 deviation still leaves the CUL equal to the tolerable rate at 3 percent (see Appendix 11–C.3). Now the risk of underreliance has been reduced to a risk less than 91.3 percent because you have the flexibility to find one deviation without exceeding the 3 percent tolerable rate criterion. Larger samples would reduce the risk even further, which is a *benefit*. The *cost* of reducing the risk of underreliance is the cost of auditing more sampling units.

TOLERABLE RATE: A PROFESSIONAL JUDGMENT The tolerable rate is the maximum frequency of deviation *in the population* that auditors are willing to accept without altering planned reliance on the client's control procedures. You should notice that the concept associates the tolerable rate with the planned reliance and therefore with the amount of other audit work. If the other audit work is quite heavy and not much reliance on control is planned, an auditor might assign a fairly high tolerable rate (say, 20 percent), if he or she decides to perform compliance auditing at all.

Some illustrative tolerable rates are shown in Exhibit 11–1. The overlapping rates indicate that general guidance can only go so far. Judgments always depend on the specific fact circumstances.

EXHIBIT 11–1
Illustrative Control
Reliance and Tolerable
Rate Relationships

Planned Degree of Reliance	Tolerable Rate
Substantial reliance on the internal accounting control.	2%–7%
Moderate reliance on the internal accounting control.	6%–12%
Little reliance on the internal accounting control.	11%–20%
No reliance on the internal accounting control.	Omit the compliance audit procedures.

Source: *Audit Sampling.* Auditing and Accounting Guide (AICPA, 1983), p. 32

Suppose an auditor wants to attain a reasonable audit risk for a decision about whether sales are overstated, and suppose a $50,000 or smaller overstatement of the $2 million of recorded sales would be considered immaterial. The auditor wants to do the work efficiently, so he plans to rely on the client's control procedures that requires matching a shipping order to a sales invoice before the invoice is recorded. Ten thousand invoices whose individual values do not have a very wide range are recorded. How many can be unsupported by shipping orders without causing the matching control to be considered ineffective?

Consider another concept before trying to answer the question. An unsupported sales invoice (in general, a control deviation) does not necessarily mean the sale was fictitious. Of course, follow-up evaluation of deviations will help settle the question. Nevertheless, an account such as sales could be *exposed* to control deviations without the deviations having a direct effect on the amount of sales shown in the audited income statement. This exposure is known jocularly as the **smoke/fire concept.** A conflagration normally has more smoke than fire. Hence, transactions may be exposed to more control deviations that might at first seem warranted in light of the $50,000 materiality amount. So how much? Some auditors suggest the exposure could be two or three times materiality.

Now you are ready for a simple approach to answering the question about the control of matching shipping orders to sales invoices. Assume you accept the smoke/fire concept and would permit as much as $150,000 in sales to be exposed through lack of supporting shipping documents. Since the average invoice amount is $200 ($2 million sales/10,000 invoices), this suggests that as many as 750 invoices (7.5 percent of the total) could be exposed. So, a rough cut at judging the tolerable rate is to set it at about 7 or 8 percent. Be careful, however. This example depends a great deal on the assumptions that the invoice amounts do not differ very much and that the average invoice amount is well centered at $200. (In statistical terms, the variance of the invoice amounts is not large.)

MORE ABOUT DEFINING THE POPULATION(S)

Auditors can exercise flexibility when defining population(s). Populations are not always what they seem to be. Accounting populations are often *skewed,* meaning that *much of the dollar value in a population is in a small number of population units*. For example, the *80/20 "rule"* is that *80 percent of the value tends to be in 20 percent of the units*. Many inventory and accounts receivable populations have this skewness. Sales invoice, cash receipts and cash disbursements populations may be skewed, but usually not as much as inventory and receivables.

Subdividing a Population

Theoretically, a client's internal accounting control procedures should apply to small-dollar transactions and items as well as to large-dollar ones. Nevertheless, many auditors believe evidential matter is better when more dollars are covered by compliance auditing procedures. This inclination can be accommodated in a sampling plan by subdividing a population according to a relevant characteristic of interest. For example, sales transactions might be subdivided into foreign and domestic; accounts receivable might be subdivided into sets of customers with balances of $5,000 or more and those with smaller balances; payroll transactions might be subdivided into supervisory payroll (salaried) and hourly payroll.

Nothing is wrong with this kind of subdividing. However, you must remember that (1) an audit conclusion based on a sample applies only to the population from which the sample was drawn and (2) the sample should be representative—random for statistical sampling. If the 10,000 invoices represent 2,000 foreign sales and 8,000 domestic sales, and you want to subdivide the population this way, you will have two populations. You can establish decision criteria of acceptable risk of overreliance and tolerable deviation rate for each population. You can also estimate an expected population deviation rate for each one. Suppose your specifications are these:

	Foreign	Domestic
Risk of overreliance	5%	10%
Tolerable rate	5%	5%
Expected population deviation rate	2%	1%
Then:		
Sample size (Appendix 11–B)	160	60

As long as you evaluate the two samples separately, everything is fine. However, you cannot add the two samples together and evaluate the combination in terms of the whole sales invoice population. Why? Because the "sample" of 220 is not random. Each foreign-sales invoice had a 160/2000 chance of being in the sample, and each domestic-sale invoice had a 60/8000 chance. Each invoice did not have an equal likelihood. Therefore, the "sample" of 220 is not random, and it should not be taken as "representative" of the whole population of 10,000 sales invoices.

Dollar-Unit Sampling (DUS)

In dollar-unit sampling, the population is cleverly defined as the number of *dollars* therein. For example, if the client had $2 million of recorded sales, the population is defined to consist of 2 million one-dollar units. A DUS sample selection method then consists of a random selection of individual $1 units. The effect of this plan is to skew the selection to the large-dollar units (sales invoices) because when a "dollar" is selected in the sample, it *hooks* the entire invoice (which is known as the *logical unit*). Thus, a $10,000 sales invoice is 10 times more likely to be selected in a sample than a $1,000 invoice because the first one has 10 times more dollar units than the second. This method provides an auditor's dream world—random selection of high-dollar items, large dollar coverage for the compliance audit, and statistical support as well.

The skewness in the sample to large-dollar invoices, which at first glance seems to deny randomness, is accommodated in the technique for mathematical evaluation of the results. Space does not permit a full explanation of DUS. However, a brief discussion and example are given in Appendix 12–E (Chapter 12).

SAMPLE SIZE DETERMINATION

When you have assigned numbers to the acceptable risk of overreliance and the tolerable deviation rate and have estimated the expected population deviation rate, you can "calculate" a sample size using the graphs in Appendix 11–B. Locate the graph for your risk of overreliance, use the bar for expected population deviation rate, and find the intersection of the bar with the tolerable rate at the bottom of the graph. Then read the sample size at the left or right margin. The graph is a little crude, so exact calculation of a sample size such as 423 is not possible, but such exactness is not required for audit purposes. For example, suppose you are going to conduct a compliance audit procedure to obtain evidence about the sales invoice-shipping orders matching control (the example used throughout Chapters 8 and 11). Assume your acceptable risk of overreliance is 10 percent, your tolerable deviation rate is 5 percent, and your expected population deviation rate is 1 percent.

Your predetermined sample size is about 60 (Appendix 11–B.3). In this case, with a population of 10,000 invoices, the graph presents no problems with population size.[1]

A LITTLE MORE ABOUT SAMPLING UNIT SELECTION METHODS

Audit sampling can be wrecked on the shoals of auditors' impatience. Planning an imaginative selection method takes a little time, and auditors are sometimes in a big hurry to grab some units and audit them. A little imagination goes a long way. For example, suppose an auditor of a newspaper needs to audit the controls over the completeness of billings—specifically, the control procedure designed to ensure that customers were billed for classified ads printed in the paper. You have seen classified ad sections, so you know they consist of different-size ads, and you know that ad volume is greater on weekends than on weekdays. How can you get a random sample that can be considered representative of the printed ads?

The physical frame of printed ads defines the population. You probably cannot obtain a population count (size) of the number of ads. However, you know the paper was printed on 365 days of the year, and the ad manager can probably show you a record of the number of pages of classified ads printed each day. Using this information, you can determine the number of ad pages for the year, say 5,000. For a sample of 100 ads, you can choose 100 random numbers to obtain a random page. Then you can choose a random number between one and eight to identify one of the eight columns on the page, and another random number between 1 and 500 (the number of lines on a page). The column-line coordinate identifies an ad on the random day. (This method approximates randomness because larger ads are more likely to be chosen than smaller ads. In fact, the selection method probably approximates a DUS-like sample selection.)

You can judge the representativeness by noticing the size of the ads selected. Also, since you will know the number of Friday-Saturday-Sunday pages (say, 70 percent of the total, or 3,500 pages), you can expect about 70 of the ads to come from weekend days. A little imagination and perception go a long way.

---

[1] If you are dealing with a population with fewer than 1,000 units, you can adjust the sample size determined in the graph like this:

$$n = \frac{n'}{1 + (n'/N)}$$

where

n' = Sample size found in Appendix 11–B
N = Population size
n = Sample size adjusted for population size

Random Number Table

The simplest, although most time-consuming, sampling unit selection device is a table of random digits. (See Appendix 11–A). This table contains rows and columns of digits from 0 to 9 in random order. When items in the population are associated with numbers in the table, the choice of a random number amounts to choice of a sampling item, and the resulting sample is random. Such a sample is called an ***unrestricted random sample***. For example, in the population of 10,000 sales invoices, assume the first invoice in the year was 32059 and the last one was 42058. By obtaining a random start in the table and proceeding systematically through it, 100 invoices may be selected for audit.[2] Assume that a random start is obtained at the five-digit number in the second row, fifth column—number 29094—and that the reading path in the table is down to the bottom of the column then to the top of the next column, and so on. The first usable number and first invoice is 40807, the second is 32146, and so forth. Note that several of the random numbers were skipped because they do not correspond with the invoice number sequence.[3] A page of random digits like the one in Appendix 11–A can be annotated and made into your sample selection working paper that documents the selection.

Suppose you need to audit the newspaper publisher's control over the validity of sales billings—specifically, the control procedure to ensure a classified ad was actually printed for each billing to a customer. (In this case, the printed ad is equivalent to the "shipping orders" cited as the supporting documents in the sales validity control compliance procedure in the examples in Chapters 8 and 11.) With a sample of invoices, you can find (vouch) the billing to a printed ad.

Systematic Random Selection

Another selection method used commonly in auditing because of its simplicity and relative ease of application is *systematic selection*. This method is employed when direct association of the population with random numbers is cumbersome. Systematic selection consists of: (*a*) dividing the population size by the sample size, obtaining a quotient k (a "skip interval"), (*b*) obtaining a random start in the population file, and (*c*) selecting every k^{th} unit for the sample. A file of credit records provides a good example. These may be filed alphabetically with no numbering system. Therefore, to select 50 from a population of 5,000, first find $k = 5,000/50 = 100$, then obtain a random start in the set of physical files and pull out every 100th one, progressing systematically to the end of the file

---

[2] A random start in a table may be obtained by poking a pencil at the table, or by checking the last four digits on a $100 bill to give row and column coordinates for a random start.

[3] Most auditors will not allow the same sample item to appear twice in a selection—duplicate selections are counted only once. Strictly speaking, this amounts to *sampling without replacement* and the hypergeometric probability distribution is appropriate instead of the binomial distribution. The binomial probabilities are exact only when each sample item is *replaced* after selection, thus giving it an equally likely chance of appearing in the sample more than once. For audit purposes, the practice of ignoring the distribution is acceptable because the difference is mathematically insignificant.

and returning to the beginning of the file to complete the selection. This method only approximates randomness, but the approximation can be improved by taking more than one random start in the process of selection. When more than one start is used, the interval k is changed. For example, if five starts are used, then every 500th item would be selected. Five random starts give you five systematic passes through the population, and each pass produces 10 sampling items, for a total of 50.

Auditors usually require five or more random starts. You can see that when the number of random starts equals the predetermined sample size, the "systematic" method becomes the same as the unrestricted random selection method. Multiple random starts are a good idea because a population may have a nonrandom order that could be imbedded in a single-start systematic method.

Computerized Selection

Most audit organizations have computerized random number generators available to cut short the drudgery of poring over printed random number tables. Such routines can print a tailored series of numbers with relatively brief turnaround time. Even so, some advance planning is required, and knowledge of how a random number table works is useful.

STATISTICAL EVALUATION

To accomplish a statistical evaluation of compliance audit evidence, you must know the tolerable rate and the acceptable risk of overreliance. These are your **decision criteria**—the *standards for evaluation in the circumstances*. You also need to know the size of the sample that was audited and the number of deviations. Now you can use the evaluation tables in Appendix 11–C.

The procedure is this: (1) Find the evaluation table for your acceptable risk of overreliance, (2) Find your sample size in the left margin, (3) Read across and find the *number of deviations* in the table, then (4) Read up to the top of the column for the sampling error-adjusted upper limit ("CUL"). Your result is expressed: The probability is 10 percent (the *risk of overreliance* when you read the 10 percent table) that the population deviation rate is greater than the CUL (the *sampling error-adjusted upper limit*). If CUL (Computed Upper Limit) is less than your tolerable rate, you can conclude that the population deviation rate is low enough to meet your decision criterion, and you can rely upon the control. If CUL exceeds your tolerable rate, you can conclude that the population deviation rate may be higher than your decision criterion, and you cannot rely upon the control.

The **computed upper limit** found in the table is the product of a *statistical calculation that takes sampling error into account*. You know a sample deviation rate (number of deviations/sample size) cannot be expressed as the *exact* population deviation rate. According to common sense and statistical theory, the actual but unknown population rate might be lower or higher. Since auditors are mainly concerned with the risk of overreliance, the *higher* limit is calculated to show how high the rate may be.

Auditing standards tell you to "consider the risk that your sample deviation rate can be lower than your tolerable rate for the population even though the actual population rate exceeds the tolerable rate." In statistical evaluation, you accomplish this consideration by holding the risk of overreliance constant at the acceptable level while computing CUL (reading the evaluation table), then comparing CUL to your tolerable rate.

Example of Satisfactory Results

Suppose you have selected 200 recorded sales invoices and vouched them to supporting shipping orders. You have found no shipping orders in one case. When you follow up, no one could explain the missing documents, but nothing about the sampling unit appears to indicate an intentional irregularity. You have already decided a 10 percent risk of overreliance and a 3 percent tolerable rate adequately define your decision criteria for the compliance audit of this control.

1. Find Appendix 11–C.3—the evaluation table for 10 percent risk of overreliance.
2. Find the sample size, 200, in the left margin.
3. Read across to the number 1, for 1 deviation.
4. Read up to find CUL at the top of the column, finding 2 (2 percent).

Audit Conclusion: The probability is 10 percent that the population deviation rate is greater than 2 percent. This finding satisfies your decision criteria.

Example of Unsatisfactory Results

The situation is the same as above, except you found four cases of missing shipping orders.

1. Find Appendix 11–C.3—evaluation table for 10 percent risk of overreliance.
2. Find the sample size, 200, in the left margin.
3. Read across to 4 deviations.
4. Read up to find CUL, which is 4 (4 percent).

Audit Conclusion: The probability is 10 percent that the population deviation rate is greater than 4 percent. This finding exceeds your tolerable rate criterion of 3 percent.

DISCOVERY SAMPLING

Discovery sampling is essentially another kind of sampling design directed toward a specific objective. However, discovery sampling statistics also offer an additional means of evaluating the *sufficiency* of audit evidence in the event that no deviations are found in a sample.

A discovery sampling table is shown in Appendix 11–D. A discovery sampling plan deals with this kind of question: *If I believe some important kind of error or irregularity might exist in the records, what sample size will I have to audit to have assurance of finding at least one example?* Ordinarily, discovery sampling is used for designing procedures to search for such things as examples of forged checks or intercompany sales improperly classified as sales to outside parties. However, discovery sampling may be used effectively whenever a low deviation rate is expected. Auditors must quantify a desired ***probability of one occurrence,*** which is *1 minus a relevant risk of overreliance,* and must specify a tolerable deviation rate that is called a ***critical rate of occurrence.*** Generally, the *critical rate* is very low because the deviation is something very sensitive and important.

The probability of one occurrence in this case represents the desired probability of finding at least one occurrence (example of the deviation) in a sample. In Appendix 11–D, you can read down a specified critical rate column to the specified probability of one occurrence, then read the required sample size at the left margin. This discovery sampling table expresses a type of cumulative binomial probability of finding one or more deviations in a sample of a particular size, if the population deviation rate is equal to a given critical occurrence rate.

Suppose that in the compliance audit of recorded sales, you are especially concerned about finding an example of a deviation if as few as 50 outright fictitious sales (intentional irregularities) existed in the population of 10,000 recorded invoices (a critical rate of .5 percent). Furthermore, suppose you want to achieve at least .99 probability of finding at least one. Appendix 11–D indicates a required sample of 900 recorded sales invoices. If a sample of this size were audited and no fictitious sales were found, you could conclude that the actual rate of occurrence in the population was *less than* .5 percent with .99 probability of being right.

This feature of discovery sampling evaluation provides the additional means of evaluating the *sufficiency* of audit evidence whenever a sample turns up zero deviations. You can read across from the sample size audited (say, 200) to a probability that, in your judgment, represents reasonable assurance. Then, reading up the column, the "critical rate" is found. Suppose 200 sales invoices were audited and no deviations of missing shipping orders were found. The discovery sampling table shows that if the population deviation rate were 2 percent, the probability of including at least one deviation in a sample of 200 is 0.98. None was found, so with .98 probability, you can believe that the occurrence rate is 2 percent or less.

SUMMARY   Statistical sampling for attributes provides quantitative measures of deviation rates and risks of overreliance. The statistics support auditors' judgments of factors that influence the assessment of control risk. The most important judgments are the numbers assigned to the tolerable rate of deviations, the risk of overreliance, and the risk of underreliance. With these specifications and an estimate of the deviation rate in the population, a preliminary sample size can be predetermined by calculation. However, nothing is magic about a predetermined sample size. It will turn out to be too few, just right, or too many, depending upon the evidence produced by it and the statistical evaluation supported by it.

The easy part of attribute sampling is the statistical evaluation. The hard parts are (1) specifying the controls for audit and defining deviations, (2) quantifying the decision criteria, (3) using imagination to find a way to select a random sample, and (4) associating the quantitative evaluation with the assessment of control risk. The structure and formality of the steps involved in statistical sampling force auditors to plan the procedures exhaustively. This same structure and formality also contribute to good working paper documentation because they clearly identify the things that should be recorded in the working papers. Altogether, statistical sampling facilitates auditors' plans, procedures and evaluations of defensible evidence.

SOURCES AND ADDITIONAL READING REFERENCES

Akresh, A. D., and D. R. Finley. "Two-Step Attribute Sampling in Auditing." *CPA Journal,* December 1979, pp. 19–24.

Akresh, A. D., and G. R. Zuber. "Explaining Statistical Sampling." *Journal of Accountancy,* February 1981, pp. 50–56.

Bailey, Larry P. "Impact of SAS 39 on Nonstatistical Sampling." *CPA Journal,* June 1982, pp. 38–47.

Brumfield, C. A., R. K. Elliott, and P. D. Jacobson. "Business Risk and the Audit Process," *Journal of Accountancy,* April 1983, pp. 60–69.

Elliott, R. K., and J. R. Rogers. "Relating Statistical Sampling to Audit Objectives." *Journal of Accountancy,* July 1972, pp. 46–55.

Finley, D. R. "Controlling Compliance Testing with Acceptance Sampling." *CPA Journal,* December 1978, pp. 30–35.

Hansen, D. R., and T. L. Shaftel. "Sampling for Integrated Audit Objectives." *Accounting Review,* January 1977, pp. 109–23.

Ijiri, Yuji, and R. S. Kaplan. "A Model for Integrating Sampling Objectives in Auditing." *Journal of Accounting Research,* Spring 1971, pp. 73–87.

Johnson, K. P., and H. R. Jaenicke. *Evaluating Internal Control.* New York: John Wiley & Sons, 1980, 649 pages.

Roberts, Donald M. "A Statistical Interpretation of SAP No. 54." *Journal of Accountancy,* March 1974, pp. 47–53.

Smith, Kenneth. "Internal Control and Audit Sample Size." *Accounting Review,* April 1972, pp. 260–69.

Tracy, John A. "Bayesian Statistical Methods in Auditing." *Accounting Review,* January 1969, pp. 90–98.

Warren, C. S., S. V. N. Yates, and G. R. Zuber. "Audit Sampling: A Practical Approach." *Journal of Accountancy,* January 1982, pp. 62–72.

REVIEW QUESTIONS

11.1. If inherent risk (IR) is assessed as 0.90 and the detection risk (DR) implicit in an audit plan is 0.10, what audit risk (AuR) is implied when internal control risk is judged to be 0.10, 0.50, 0.70, 0.90 and 1.0?

11.2. What professional judgment and estimation decisions must be made by auditors when applying statistical sampling in compliance audits? Explain them.

11.3. What considerations are important when an auditor decides upon an acceptable risk of overreliance?

11.4. What considerations are important when an auditor decides upon an acceptable risk of underreliance?

11.5. What is the probability of finding one or more deviations in a sample of 100 units if the deviation rate in the population is only .5 percent?

11.6. What is the connection between a preliminary assessment of control risk and a judgment about tolerable rate, both made prior to performing compliance audit procedures?

11.7. When you subdivide a population into two populations for attribute sampling compliance auditing, how do the two samples compare to the one sample that would be drawn if the population had not been subdivided?

11.8. What steps are involved in selecting a sample using the systematic random selection method?

11.9. What is the auditing interpretation of the sampling error-adjusted sample deviation rate (CUL)?

11.10. What is the proper interpretation of the *probability* contained in the Discovery Sampling table in Appendix 11–D?

EXERCISES AND PROBLEMS

11.11. **Risk of Underreliance**

When you audited Kingston Company's performance of its control procedures (in problem 8.31), you found certain numbers of deviations, as shown in Case II. Your acceptable risk of overreliance is 5 percent. This quantitative evidence indicating control deficiencies now subjects you to a risk of underreliance. Calculate the risk of underreliance based on the presumption that only 5 percent of invoices in the population actually lack credit approval and the population deviation rate for the others actually is only 2 percent. (Hint: You will need to use the equation Risk = $1 - (1 - \text{rate})^n$ and the Poisson approximation discussed in Appendix Note 11–C.)

11.12. **Tolerable Rate Determination**

Kaye Clark, CPA, is planning to audit compliance with the credit approval policy by the credit manager of Longneck, Inc. The company issued 28,000 sales invoices during the year for a total of $14,353,812. Kaye believes a misstatement as large as $300,000 in this account could still be considered immaterial. The credit approval procedure is evidenced by the credit manager's notation on each customer order. If approval consideration is not noted, presumably the sale is subject to credit risk, and accounts receivable collectibility evaluation might become an audit problem if such deviations are widespread.

Required:

Assume Kaye accepts the smoke/fire concept of thinking about how many dollars in an account can be "exposed" to control deviations before the control would be considered ineffective. Assume also that she believes the exposure could be three times the $300,000 amount considered material for the sales account. Write a memo to the working paper file explaining the estimate of the tolerable deviation rate for compliance auditing of the credit approval control.

11.13. **Sample Size Relationships**
For the specifications of acceptable risk of overreliance, tolerable deviation rate and expected population deviation rate shown below, prepare tables showing the appropriate sample sizes. (Use the graphs in Appendix 11–B.)

a. Tolerable deviation rate = 0.05. Expected population deviation rate = zero. Acceptable risk of overreliance = 0.01, 0.05, 0.10.

b. Acceptable risk of overreliance = 0.10. Expected population deviation rate = 0.01. Tolerable deviation rate = 0.10, 0.08, 0.05, 0.03, 0.02.

c. Acceptable risk of overreliance = 0.10. Tolerable deviation rate = 0.10. Expected population deviation rate = 0.01, 0.02, 0.04, 0.07, 0.09.

d. Expected population deviation rate = 0.02

	Risk of Overreliance	Tolerable Rate
(i)	0.01	0.10
(ii)	0.05	0.08
(iii)	0.10	0.05

e. Place a second sample size column in *a, b,* and *c* (prepare a second table for

d), and figure the sample size when the population contains only 500 units.

11.14. **Exercises in Sample Selection**
a. Sales invoices beginning with number 0001 and ending with number 5,000 are entered in a sales journal. You want to choose 50 invoices for audit. Start at row 5, column 3 of the random number table in Appendix 11–A and select the first five usable numbers, using the first four digits in the column.

b. There are 9,100 numbered checks in a cash disbursements journal, beginning with number 2,220 and ending with number 11,319. You want to choose 100 disbursements for audit. Start at row 11, column 1 of the table of random digits in Appendix 11–A and select the first five usable numbers.

c. During the year, the client wrote 45,200 vouchers. Each month, the numbering series started over with number 00001, prefixed with a number for the month (January = 01, February = 02, and so on), so that the voucher numbers had seven digits, the last five of which were in overlapping series. You want to choose 120 vouchers for audit. Evaluate each of the following suggested selection methods:

(1) Choose a month at random and select 120 at random in that month by association with a five-digit random number.

(2) Choose 120 usable seven-digit random numbers.

(3) Select 10 vouchers at random from each month.

d. Explain how you could use systematic sampling to select the first five items in each case above. For case (*c*), assume the random start is at voucher 03-01102.

11.15. **Imagination in Sample Selection**
The text illustrated a problem of selecting a sample of classified ads printed in a news-

paper. Auditors often need to be imaginative when figuring out how to obtain a random sample. For each of the cases below, explain how you could select a sample having the best chance of being random.

a. You need a sample of recorded cash disbursements. The client used two bank accounts for general disbursements. Account #1 was used during January–August and issued checks numbered 3633–6632. Account #2 was used during May–December and issued checks numbered 0001–6000. (Hint: for purposes of random number selection and check identification, convert one of the numerical sequences to a sequence that does not overlap the other.) In Appendix 11–A, start at row 1, column 2, and select the first five random checks, reading down column 2.

b. You need a sample of purchase orders. The client issued prenumbered purchase orders in the sequence 9,000–13,999 (5,000 of them). You realize if you just select five-digit random numbers from a table, looking for numbers in this sequence, 95 percent of the random numbers you scan will be discards because a table has 100,000 different five-digit random numbers. (The computer is down today!) How can you fiddle with this sequence to reduce the number of discards. (Hint: you can reduce discards to zero.) In Appendix 11–A, start at row 30, column 3, and select the first five random purchase orders, reading down column 3.

c. You need a sample of perpetual inventory records so you can go to the warehouse and count the quantities while the stockclerks take the physical inventory. The perpetual records have been printed out in a control list showing location, item description and quantity. You have a copy of the list. It is 75 pages long, with 50 lines to a page (40 lines on the last page). Find

an efficient way to select 100 lines for your compliance audit of the client's counting procedure.

d. You need to determine whether an inventory compilation is complete. You plan to select a sample of physical locations, describe and count the inventory units, and trace the information to the inventory compilation (control list, as in c above). The inventory consists of tools, parts and other hardware material shelved in a large warehouse. The warehouse contains 300 rows of 75-foot long shelves, each of which has 10 tiers. The inventory is stored on these shelves. Find an efficient way to select 100 sampling units of physical inventory for count and tracing to the inventory listing.

11.16.   **CUL Calculation Exercises**
These two exercises exhibit relations among CUL, number of deviations, sample size, and sample deviation rate.

a. Assume six auditors have audited samples of cash disbursement transactions, and each one found three deviations from the company's authorization control procedure. Their acceptable risk of overreliance was 0.05. For their samples of 60, 80, 100, 120, 180 and 320, prepare a table showing the relation among CUL, number of deviations, sample size and sample deviation rate. (Hint: the columns in the table can be (1) Number of Deviations/ Sample Size, (2) Sample Deviation Rate, (3) CUL for Risk of Overreliance = 0.05 for sample sizes of 60, 80, 100, 120, 180 and 320. The rows identified under the first column should be (1) 3 deviations/60, (2) 3/80, (3) 3/100, (4) 3/120, (5) 3/180 and (6) 3/320.) Interpret the CUL and derive three other relationships from the table.

b. Assume six auditors have audited samples of cash disbursement transactions and each one found a sample deviation rate of 5 percent from the company's authorization control procedures. Their acceptable risk of overreliance was 0.10. For their samples of 60, 80, 100, 120, 180 and 320, prepare a table showing the relation among CUL, number of deviations, sample size and sample deviation rate. (Hint: the columns in the table can be (1) Sample Rate, (2) Number of Deviations/Sample Size, (3) CUL for Risk of Overreliance = 0.10 for sample sizes of 60, 80, 100, 120, 180, 320. The rows identified under the second column should be (number of deviations)/(sample size) of samples of 60, 80, 100, 120, 180, 320.) Interpret the CUL and derive two other relationships from the table.

11.17. **CUL Calculation Exercises**
Using the tables in Appendix 11–C, find the computed upper limit (CUL) for each case below:

	(a)	(b)	(c)
Risk of overreliance.	.01	.05	.10
Sample size	300	300	300
Deviations	6	6	6
Sample deviation rate. . . .	—	—	—
Computed upper limit. . . .	—	—	—

	(d)	(e)	(f)
Risk of overreliance.	.05	.05	.05
Sample size	100	200	400
Deviations	2	4	8
Sample deviation rate. . . .	—	—	—
Computed upper limit. . . .	—	—	—

	(g)	(h)	(i)
Risk of overreliance.	.05	.05	.05
Sample size	100	100	100
Deviations	10	6	0
Sample deviation rate. . . .	—	—	—
Computed upper limit. . . .	—	—	—

11.18. **Quantitative Evaluation**
The exercises in this set expand the data given in problem 8.30. The additional data enable you to make statistical evaluation calculations. Your task is to evaluate the apparent effectiveness of the control procedures, much like you did in 8.30, but this time using the calculated upper limit (CUL) and a quantified risk of overreliance.

Required:
a. When you audited the sample of 120 credit files, you found three out-of-date files. Your tolerable deviation rate criterion is 10 percent, and your acceptable risk of overreliance is 10 percent. What is your evaluation of the suitability of the population? What would be your evaluation if you had found seven deviations? Thirteen deviations?

b. When you audited the sample of 200 bills of lading, you found one that had not been recorded as a sale. The related invoice was crumpled at the bottom of the billing department pending file. Your tolerable deviation rate is 3 percent, and your acceptable risk of overreliance is 5 percent. What is your evaluation of the effectiveness of Kingston's completeness control? What would be your evaluation if you had found four deviations? Six deviations?

11.19. **Quantitative Evaluation**
The requirements in this problem expand the data given in problem 8.31. The additional data enable you to make statistical evaluation calculations. Your task is to evaluate the apparent effectiveness of the control procedures, much like you did in 8.31, but this time using the calculated upper limit (CUL) and a quantified risk of overreliance (10 percent under the circumstances).

Required:
a. Take the same quantitative and qualitative evidence given in problem 8.31. Prepare three worksheets, one each for Case I, Case II and Case III. Present a statistical evaluation of the

EXHIBIT 11.19–1
Compliance Sampling Data Sheet

Client _____ By _____

Period covered _____ Date _____

Define the objective(s) _____

_____

_____

_____

Population description _____

Random selection procedures _____

_____

Definition of Deviations	Risk Over-reliance	Toler-able Rate	Expected Deviation Rate	Sample Results				
				Sample Size	Devia-tions	Sample Rate	CUL	
1.								
2.								
3.								
4.								
5.								
6.								
7.								
8.								
9.								
10.								

Audit Conclusions
A. Effect on audit plan: _____

_____

_____

_____

B. Recommendation to management: _____

_____

C. Other action: _____

quantitative evidence and give a brief explanation of your audit conclusions and the effect on the audit plan. You can use copies of the "Compliance Sampling Data Sheet" worksheet form shown in Exhibit 11.19–1.

b. Suppose your audit plan involved considerable reliance on the controls, to the extent that you want to justify an assessment of control risk at 30 percent instead of the 60 percent stated in problem 8.31. In this situation, you are more concerned about the risk of overreliance and want to use a 1 percent risk instead of 10 percent. Prepare the worksheet required in *a* for Case I, using a 1 percent risk of overreliance.

11.20. Missing Documents

Assume that when you audited Kingston Company's performance of its control procedures (problem 8.31, Case II), you had a problem with missing documents. After selecting random numbers for the sequence of sales invoices issued during the year, you found all of them listed (by date) in the sales journal. For two of them, however, you could find no invoice copy. No one could explain the missing documents. The quantitative evidence given in Case II treats the missing ones as deviations. Had they simply been omitted from the sample, the number of deviations in Case II would be a = 0, b = 2, c = 0, d = 0, e = 4. Prepare a comparative schedule showing the statistical results if you (1) treat the missing documents as deviations on all the controls and (2) omit the missing documents from the sample. (For statistical calculation purposes, you can read the evaluation table for a sample size of 60 in both cases.) You will accept a 10 percent risk of overreliance.

11.21. Discovery Sampling

Using the discovery sampling table in Appendix 11–D, fill in the missing data in each case below.

	(a)	(b)	(c)
Critical rate of occurrence. . . .	.4%	.5%	1.0%
Required probability	99	99	99
Sample size (minimum).	—	—	—

	(d)	(e)	(f)
Critical rate of occurrence . . .	2.0%	1.0%	.5%
Required probability	—	—	—
Sample size (minimum)	240	240	240

	(g)	(h)	(i)
Critical rate of occurrence. . . .	—	—	—
Required probability	70	85	95
Sample size (minimum).	300	460	700

DISCUSSION CASES

11.22. Tom's Misapplied Application

Tom Barton, an assistant accountant with a local CPA firm, has recently graduated from the Other University. He studied statistical sampling for compliance auditing in college and wants to impress his employers with his knowledge of modern auditing methods.

He decided to select a random sample of payroll checks for audit, using a tolerable rate of 5 percent and an acceptable risk of overreliance of 5 percent. The senior accountant told Tom that 2 percent of the checks audited last year had one or more errors in the calculation of net pay. Tom decided to audit 100 random checks. Since supervisory personnel had larger paychecks than production workers, he selected 60 of the larger checks and 40 of the others. He was very careful to see that the selections of 60 from the April payroll register and 40 from the August payroll register were random.

The audit of this sample yielded two deviations, exactly the 2 percent rate experienced last year. The first was the deduction of federal income taxes based on two exemptions for a supervisory employee, when his W-4 form showed four exemptions. The other was payment to a production employee at a rate for a job classification one grade lower than his actual job. The worker had been promoted the week before, and Tom found that in the next payroll he was paid at the higher correct rate.

When he evaluated this evidence, Tom decided that these two findings were really not control deviations at all. The withholding of too much tax did not affect the expense accounts, and the proper rate was paid the production worker as soon as the clerk caught up with his change orders. Tom decided that having found zero deviations in a sample of 100, the computed upper limit at 5 percent risk of overreliance was 3 percent, which easily satisfied his predetermined criterion.

The senior accountant was impressed. Last year he had audited 15 checks from each month, and Tom's work represented a significant time savings. The reviewing partner on the audit was also impressed because he had never thought that statistical sampling could be so efficient, and that was the reason he had never studied the method.

Required:

Identify and explain the mistakes made by Tom and the others.

11.23. **Inventory Recordkeeping Control**

The raw material inventory records of Abbott Mills are maintained on a perpetual basis. Five hundred different types of chemical materials are kept in stock. When raw materials are issued for production, an Issuance Slip (Copy 1) is sent to the inventory control department, where it is used to update the perpetual records.

Each perpetual inventory record has space for showing the name of the material, date of each issue, the issuance slip number, issuance slip quantity, unit cost, total dollar amount issued, and the quantity and dollar balance. Each issuance slip had on it the name of the chemical, the issuance slip number and date, the foreman's and the warehouser's authorizing signatures, the quantity issued, the unit cost and the total dollar amount issued.

As of November 15, issuance slips numbered from 60,000 to 90,000 had been used since the fiscal year began January 1. Your audit manager is interested in knowing how accurately inventory control personnel have posted the issuance slips to the perpetual raw materials records. Your assignment is to select a sample of the filed Copy 1 of the issuance slips and trace them to the perpetual records. The audit manager requires application of attribute sampling.

Required:

Copy the "compliance sampling data sheet" shown in Exhibit 11.19–1 (or use a blank form supplied by your instructor) and fill in the following:

a. Client, your name, period covered, date of work.

b. Define the objectives of the compliance procedure.

c. Describe the population from which the sample is to be drawn.

d. Identify the sampling unit.

e. Describe the random selection procedures.

f. Define the deviations.

g. Assuming the acceptable risk of overreliance is 1 percent, the tolerable rate is 5 percent, and the expected deviation rate in the population is zero, determine the planned sample size.

h. Assuming you actually audit 100 issuance slips and find no deviations, figure the computer upper limit. Repeat the calculation, assuming you find one deviation in each case.

i. Express both sample results in terms of the effect on the audit plan and any recommendations to management.

APPENDIX 11-A

Table of Random Digits

32942	95416	42339	59045	26693	49057	87496	20624	14819
07410	99859	83828	21409	29094	65114	36701	25762	12827
59981	68155	45673	76210	58219	45738	29550	24736	09574
46251	25437	69654	99716	11563	08803	86027	51867	12116
65558	51904	93123	27887	53138	21488	09095	78777	71240
99187	19258	86421	16401	19397	83297	40111	49326	81686
35641	00301	16096	34775	21562	97983	45040	19200	16383
14031	00936	81518	48440	02218	04756	19506	60695	88494
60677	15076	92554	26042	23472	69869	62877	19584	39576
66314	05212	67859	89356	20056	30648	87349	20389	53805
20416	87410	75646	64176	82752	63606	37011	57346	69512
28701	56992	70423	62415	40807	98086	58850	28968	45297
74579	33844	33426	07570	00728	07079	19322	56325	84819
62615	52342	82968	75540	80045	53069	20665	21282	07768
93945	06293	22879	08161	01442	75071	21427	94842	26210
75689	76131	96837	67450	44511	50424	82848	41975	71663
02921	16919	35424	93209	52133	87327	95897	65171	20376
14295	34969	14216	03191	61647	30296	66667	10101	63203
05303	91109	82403	40312	62191	67023	90073	83205	71344
57071	90357	12901	08899	91039	67251	28701	03846	94589
78471	57741	13599	84390	32146	00871	09354	22745	65806
89242	79337	59293	47481	07740	43345	25716	70020	54005
14955	59592	97035	80430	87220	06392	79028	57123	52872
42446	41880	37415	47472	04513	49494	08860	08038	43624
18534	22346	54556	17558	73689	14894	05030	19561	56517
39284	33737	42512	86411	23753	29690	26096	81361	93099
33922	37329	89911	55876	28379	81031	22058	21487	54613
78355	54013	50774	30666	61205	42574	47773	36027	27174
08845	99145	94316	88974	29828	97069	90327	61842	29604
01769	71825	55957	98271	02784	66731	40311	88495	18821
17639	38284	59478	90409	21997	56199	30068	82800	69692
05851	58653	99949	63505	40409	85551	90729	64938	52403
42396	40112	11469	03476	03328	84238	26570	51790	42122
13318	14192	98167	75631	74141	22369	36757	89117	54998
60571	54786	26281	01855	30706	66578	32019	65884	58485
09531	81853	59334	70929	03544	18510	89541	13555	21168
72865	16829	86542	00396	20363	13010	69645	49608	54738
56324	31093	77924	28622	83543	28912	15059	80192	83964
78192	21626	91399	07235	07104	73652	64425	85149	75409
64666	34767	97298	92708	01994	53188	78476	07804	62404
82201	75694	02808	65983	74373	66693	13094	74183	73020
15360	73776	40914	85190	54278	99054	62944	47351	89098
68142	67957	70896	37983	20487	95350	16371	03426	13895
19138	31200	30616	14639	44406	44236	57360	81644	94761
28155	03521	36415	78452	92359	81091	56513	88321	97910
87971	29031	51780	27376	81056	86155	55488	50590	74514
58147	68841	53625	02059	75223	16783	19272	61994	71090
18875	52809	70594	41649	32935	26430	82096	01605	65846
75109	56474	74111	31966	29969	70093	98901	84550	25769
35983	03742	76822	12073	59463	84420	15868	99505	11426

Source: The Rand Corporation, *A Million Random Digits with 100,000 Normal Deviates* (Glencoe: Free Press, 1955), p. 102.

APPENDIX 11–B.1

Graph for Computing Sample Size—1 Percent Risk of Overreliance

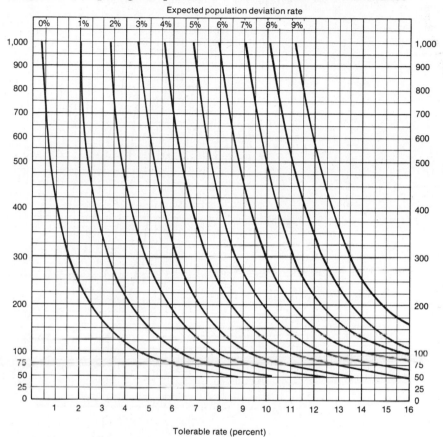

This graph is based upon an infinite population size. If the population is small (1,000 or less), slightly smaller sample sizes than those indicated by the graph are adequate.
Source: Used with permission of the American Group of CPA firms.

APPENDIX 11–B.2

Graph for Computing Sample Size—5 percent Risk of Overreliance

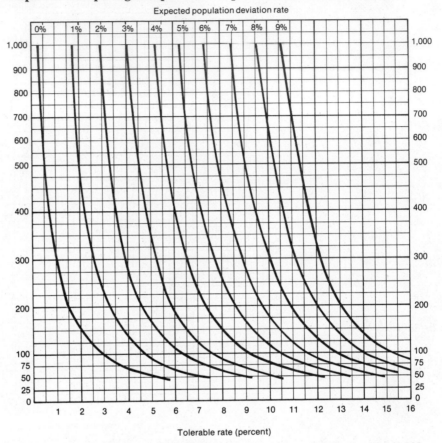

This graph is based upon an infinite population size. If the population is small (1,000 or less), slightly smaller sample sizes than those indicated by the graph are adequate.
Source: Used with permission of the American Group of CPA firms.

APPENDIX 11–B.3

Graph for Computing Sample Size—10 Percent Risk of Overreliance

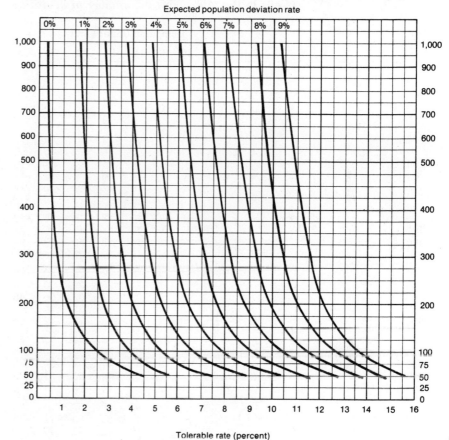

Tolerable rate (percent)

This graph is based upon an infinite population size. If the population is small (1,000 or less), slightly smaller sample sizes than those indicated by the graph are adequate.
Source: Used with permission of the American Group of CPA firms.

APPENDIX 11–C.1

Evaluation Table—1 Percent Risk of Overreliance
(Cells in the table show the *number of deviations*)

Sample Size	Computed Upper Limit																				
	1	2	3	4	5	6	7	8	9	10	12	14	16	18	20	25	30	35	40	45	50
10																			0		
20																0	1		2	3	4
30													0			1	3	4	5	6	8
40											0		1		2	3	5	7	8	10	12
50									0			1	2		3	5	7	9	11	13	16
60								0			1	2	3		4	7	9	12	14	17	20
70							0			1	2	3	4	5	6	9	11	14	18	21	24
80						0			1		2	4	5	6	7	10	14	17	21	25	29
90				0				1		2	3	5	6	7	9	12	16	20	24	29	33
100				0			1		2	3	4	6	7	9	10	14	19	23	28	33	37
120			0		1	2			3	4	6	8	9	11	13	18	24	29	35	40	46
140			0	1	2	3			4	5	7	10	12	14	16	22	29	35	42	48	55
160			0	1	2	3		5	6	7	9	12	14	17	20	27	34	41	49	56	64
180			0	1	2	3	4	6	7	8	11	14	17	20	23	31	39	47	56	65	73
200			0	1	3	4	5	7	8	10	13	16	19	23	26	35	44	54	63	73	83
220			0	2	3	5	6	8	10	11	15	18	22	26	30	39	50	60	70	81	92
240		0	1	2	4	6	7	9	11	13	17	21	25	29	33	44	55	66	78	89	101
260		0	1	3	5	6	8	10	12	14	19	23	27	32	36	48	60	72	85	97	110
280		0	2	3	4	7	9	12	14	16	21	25	30	35	40	53	65	79	92	106	120
300		0	2	4	6	8	10	13	15	18	23	28	33	38	43	57	71	85	99	114	129
320		0	2	4	7	9	11	14	17	19	24	30	35	41	47	61	76	91	107	122	138
340		1	3	5	7	10	13	15	18	21	26	32	38	44	50	66	82	98	114	131	148
360		1	3	6	8	11	14	16	19	22	28	35	41	47	54	70	87	104	122	139	157
380		1	3	6	9	12	15	18	21	24	30	37	44	50	57	75	93	111	129	148	166
400		1	4	7	10	13	16	19	22	26	32	39	46	54	61	79	98	117	136	156	176
420		2	4	7	10	14	17	20	24	27	35	42	49	57	64	84	103	124	144	164	185
460	0	2	5	8	12	15	19	23	27	31	39	47	55	63	72	93	114	136	159	181	204
500	0	3	6	10	13	17	21	26	30	34	43	52	60	70	79	102	125	149	174	198	223
550	0	3	7	11	15	20	24	29	34	38	48	58	68	78	88	113	139	166	192	219	247
600	0	4	8	13	17	22	27	32	37	43	53	64	78	86	97	125	153	182	211	241	271
650	0	4	9	14	19	25	30	36	41	47	58	70	82	94	106	136	167	198	230	262	294
700	1	5	10	16	21	27	33	39	45	51	64	76	89	102	115	148	181	215	249	283	318
800	1	7	13	19	25	32	39	46	53	60	74	89	103	118	133	171	209	248	287	326	366
900	2	8	15	22	29	37	45	53	61	69	85	101	118	135	152	194	237	281	325	369	414
1,000	2	9	17	25	34	42	51	60	69	78	96	114	133	151	170	218	266	314	363	412	462

Source: Adapted from "Tables of the Cumulative Binomial Probability Distribution," from *The Annals of the Computation Laboratory of Harvard University*, vol. 35.

APPENDIX 11–C.2

Evaluation Table—5 Percent Risk of Overreliance
(Cells in the table show the *number of deviations*)

Sample Size	1	2	3	4	5	6	7	8	9	10	12	14	16	18	20	25	30	35	40	45	50
																Computed Upper Limit					
10																	0		1		
20												0				1	2	3		4	5
30										0			1		2	3	4	5	7	8	10
40								0				1	2		3	5	6	8	10	12	14
50						0				1		2	3	4	5	7	9	11	13	16	18
60				0			1				2	3	4	5	6	9	11	14	17	20	23
70					0		1		2		3	4	5	7	8	11	14	17	20	24	27
80			0			1		2		3	4	5	7	8	9	13	16	20	24	28	32
90				0		1		2	3	4	5	6	8	9	11	15	19	23	27	32	36
100			0		1		2	3		4	6	8	9	11	13	17	22	26	31	36	41
120				0	1	2	3	4	5	6	8	10	12	14	16	21	27	33	38	44	50
140			0	1	2	3	4	5	6	7	10	12	14	17	19	26	32	39	46	52	59
160		0	1	2	3	4	5	6	8	9	12	14	17	20	23	30	38	45	53	61	69
180		0	1	2	3	5	6	8	9	11	14	17	20	23	26	35	43	52	60	69	78
200		0	1	3	4	6	7	9	11	12	16	19	23	26	30	39	48	58	68	77	87
220		0	2	3	5	7	8	10	12	14	18	22	25	29	33	44	54	64	75	86	97
240		1	2	4	6	8	10	12	14	16	20	24	28	33	37	48	59	71	83	94	106
260		1	3	4	7	9	11	13	15	17	22	26	31	36	41	53	65	77	90	103	116
280		1	3	5	7	10	12	14	17	19	24	29	34	39	44	57	71	84	98	111	125
300	0	1	3	6	8	11	13	16	18	21	26	31	37	42	48	62	76	91	105	120	135
320	0	2	4	6	9	11	14	17	20	22	28	34	40	45	51	66	82	97	113	128	144
340	0	2	4	7	10	12	15	18	21	24	30	36	42	49	55	71	87	104	120	137	151
360	0	2	5	8	10	13	17	20	23	26	32	39	45	52	59	76	93	110	128	146	163
380	0	2	5	8	11	14	18	21	24	28	34	41	48	55	62	80	98	117	135	154	173
400	0	3	6	9	12	15	19	22	26	29	37	44	51	59	66	85	104	123	143	163	183
420	0	3	6	9	13	16	20	24	27	31	39	46	54	62	70	90	110	130	151	171	192
460	0	4	7	11	15	18	22	26	31	35	43	51	60	68	77	99	121	143	166	188	211
500	1	4	8	12	16	21	25	29	34	38	47	56	66	75	84	108	132	157	181	197	221
550	1	5	9	14	18	23	28	33	38	43	53	63	73	83	94	120	146	173	200	227	255
600	1	6	10	15	20	26	31	36	42	47	58	69	80	92	103	132	161	190	219	249	279
650	2	6	12	17	23	28	34	40	46	52	64	76	88	100	112	143	175	207	239	271	303
700	2	7	13	19	25	31	37	43	50	56	69	82	95	108	122	155	189	223	258	292	327
800	3	9	15	22	29	36	43	51	58	65	80	95	110	125	141	179	218	257	296	336	376
900	4	10	18	26	34	42	50	58	66	74	91	108	125	142	159	203	247	291	335	379	424
1,000	4	12	20	29	38	47	56	65	74	84	102	121	140	159	178	227	275	324	374	423	473

Source: Adapted from "Tables of the Cumulative Binomial Probability Distribution," from *The Annals of the Computation Laboratory of Harvard University*, vol. 35.

APPENDIX 11–C.3

Evaluation Table—10 Percent Risk of Overreliance
(Cells in the table show the *numbers of deviations*)

Sample Size	Computed Upper Limit																				
	1	2	3	4	5	6	7	8	9	10	12	14	16	18	20	25	30	35	40	45	50
10																0		1		2	
20											0				1	2		3	4	5	6
30								0				1		2		4	5	6	8	9	10
40					0					1		2	3		4	6	7	9	11	13	15
50				0				1			2	3	4	5		8	10	12	15	17	19
60				0			1		2		3	4	5	6	7	10	13	15	18	21	24
70				0		1		2		3	4	5	6	8	9	12	15	18	22	25	29
80			0		1		2		3	4	5	6	8	9	10	14	18	22	25	29	33
90			0		1	2		3	4		6	7	9	11	12	16	20	25	29	33	38
100			0	1		2	3	4		5	7	9	10	12	14	19	23	28	33	38	43
120		0		1	2	3	4	5	6	7	9	11	13	15	17	23	29	34	40	46	52
140		0	1	2	3	4	5	6	7	9	11	13	16	18	21	27	34	41	48	54	61
160		0	1	2	4	5	6	8	9	10	13	16	19	22	25	32	40	47	55	63	71
180		0	2	3	4	6	7	9	10	12	15	18	22	25	28	37	45	54	63	71	80
200		1	2	4	5	7	8	10	12	14	17	21	24	28	32	41	51	60	70	80	90
220		1	2	4	6	8	10	12	13	15	19	23	27	31	35	46	56	67	78	89	99
240	0	1	3	5	7	9	11	13	15	17	21	26	30	35	39	50	62	74	85	97	109
260	0	1	3	5	8	10	12	14	17	19	24	28	33	38	43	55	68	80	93	106	119
280	0	2	4	6	8	11	13	16	18	21	26	31	36	41	46	60	73	87	101	114	128
300	0	2	4	7	9	12	14	17	20	22	28	33	39	45	50	64	79	93	108	123	138
320	0	2	5	7	10	13	16	18	21	24	30	36	42	48	54	69	85	100	116	132	148
340	0	3	5	8	11	14	17	20	23	26	32	38	45	51	58	74	90	107	123	140	157
360	0	3	6	9	12	15	18	21	25	28	34	41	48	55	61	79	96	113	131	149	167
380	0	3	6	9	13	16	19	23	26	30	37	44	51	58	65	83	102	120	139	158	177
400	1	4	7	10	14	17	21	24	28	31	39	46	54	61	69	88	107	127	146	166	186
420	1	4	7	11	14	18	22	26	29	33	41	49	57	65	73	93	113	134	154	175	196
460	1	4	8	12	16	20	24	28	33	37	45	54	63	71	80	102	124	147	170	192	215
500	1	5	9	13	18	22	27	31	36	40	50	59	69	78	88	112	136	160	185	210	235
550	2	6	10	15	20	25	30	35	40	45	55	66	76	87	97	124	150	177	204	232	259
600	2	7	12	17	22	28	33	39	44	50	61	72	84	95	107	135	165	194	224	253	283
650	2	8	13	19	24	30	36	42	48	54	66	79	91	104	116	147	179	211	243	275	308
700	3	8	14	20	27	33	39	46	52	59	72	85	99	112	126	159	194	228	262	297	332
800	4	10	17	24	31	38	46	53	61	68	83	99	114	129	145	183	222	262	301	341	381
900	4	12	20	28	36	44	52	61	69	78	95	112	129	146	164	207	251	296	340	385	430
1,000	5	13	22	31	40	49	59	68	77	87	106	125	144	164	183	232	280	330	379	429	479

Source: Adapted from "Tables of the Cumulative Binomial Probability Distribution," from *The Annals of the Computation Laboratory of Harvard University*, vol. 35.

APPENDIX NOTE 11–C

Poisson Approximation of Computed Risk

The tables in Appendix 11–C contain probabilities calculated using the binomial equation. The binomial equation approximates fairly closely the hypergeometric equation which is mathematically accurate for finite populations and for sampling-without-replacement methods. The hypergeometric equation is even more difficult to solve than the binomial equation.

The *Poisson distribution* approximates fairly closely the binomial distribution, and it is easier to calculate using one of the popular pocket calculators capable of raising numbers to a power. Auditors can use the equation shown below to calculate risk because the Poisson distribution is a limiting case of the binomial distribution when the population is large and the deviation rate is low (commonly found in audit situations).

$$p_p(x;np) = \frac{e^{-np}(np)^x}{x!}$$

where

$$p_p(x;np) = \text{Poisson probability of finding exactly } x \text{ number of deviations in a sample having } np \text{ expected number of deviations}$$
$$e = \text{Base of natural logarithms, approximately 2.718}$$
$$n = \text{Sample size}$$
$$p = \text{Hypothesized deviation rate}$$
$$x = \text{Number of deviations}$$

The *computed risk* of finding a given number of deviations is a cumulative function:

$$\text{Computed Risk} = \sum^{x} \frac{e^{-np}(np)^x}{x!}$$

For example, consider the illustration in Chapter 11 concerning the risk of underreliance. When the procedure of vouching a random sample of 80 invoices to supporting shipping orders was performed, the auditor found no deviations (no cases of missing shipping orders). The example says the probability (risk) is 10 percent that the actual population deviation rate is equal to, or less than, 3 percent (found in Appendix 11–C.3). Using the Poisson approximation formula, the computed risk of finding zero deviations when the actual deviation rate in the population is 3 percent is:

$$\text{Computed Risk} = \sum^{x=0} \frac{2.718^{-(80 \times .03)}(80 \times .03)^0}{0!} = 0.091$$

The computed risk probability of finding no deviations in a sample of 100 when the population deviation rate is 3 percent is 9.1 percent. Therefore, the risk of underreliance is $1 - 9.1\% = 90.9$ percent. That is, the probability is .909 of finding 1 or more deviations in a sample of 100 when the actual population deviation is 3 percent. If the actual population rate were only 2 percent, the Poisson probability (computed risk) of finding zero deviations in a sample of 80 would be 20.2 percent. So the risk of underreliance would be $1 - 20.2\% = 79.8$ percent.

Turning to the problem of *controlling* the risk of underreliance in the same example, suppose you decided to sample 140 units so finding 1 deviation could still give you a CUL of 3 percent at 10 percent risk of overreliance (Appendix 11–C.3). The Poisson probability of finding two or more deviations when the actual population deviation rate is less than 3 percent (say, 2 percent) is 0.7689, calculated as follows:

1. First calculate the probability (risk) of finding 0 and 1 deviations:

$$P_p(0 : 140 \times .02) = [2.718^{-2.8}(2.8)^0]/0! = 0.0608$$
$$P_p(1 : 140 \times .02) = [2.718^{-2.8}(2.8)^1]/1! = \underline{0.1703}$$
$$P_p(x = 0,1 : 1.40 \times .02) = 0.2311$$

2. Calculate the probability (risk) of finding two or more deviations: Since the probability of finding 0 or 1 is 0.2311, the probability of finding 2 or more is $0.7689 = 1 - 0.2311$.

Thus, the risk of underreliance when the actual population deviation rate is a little less than the tolerable rate is improved to 76.89 percent with a sample of 140, from the 79.8 percent risk with a sample of 80. The improvement is not much, but the example points out how a larger sample size reduces risk.

APPENDIX 11–D

Discovery Sampling Table*

Sample Size	Critical Rate of Occurrence							
	.1%	.2%	.3%	.4%	.5%	.75%	1%	2%
50	5%	10%	14%	18%	22%	31%	40%	64%
60	6	11	17	21	26	36	45	70
70	7	13	19	25	30	41	51	76
80	8	15	21	28	33	45	55	80
90	9	17	24	30	36	49	60	84
100	10	18	26	33	40	53	64	87
120	11	21	30	38	45	60	70	91
140	13	25	35	43	51	65	76	94
160	15	28	38	48	55	70	80	96
200	18	33	45	56	64	78	87	98
240	22	39	52	62	70	84	91	99
300	26	46	60	70	78	90	95	99+
340	29	50	65	75	82	93	97	99+
400	34	56	71	81	87	95	98	99+
460	38	61	76	85	91	97	99	99+
500	40	64	79	87	92	98	99	99+
600	46	71	84	92	96	99	99+	99+
700	52	77	89	95	97	99+	99+	99+
800	57	81	92	96	98	99+	99+	99+
900	61	85	94	98	99	99+	99+	99+
1,000	65	88	96	99	99	99+	99+	99+
1,500	80	96	99	99+	99+	99+	99+	99+
2,000	89	99	99+	99	99+	99+	99+	99+

* Probability, in percent, of including at least one deviation in a sample for populations between 5,000 and 10,000.
Source: Used with permission of Ernst & Whinney.

CHAPTER 12

PROFESSIONAL STANDARDS SOURCES		
Compendium Section	**Document Reference**	**Topic**
AU 312	SAS 47	Audit Risk and Materiality in Conducting an Audit
AU 326	SAS 31	Evidential Matter
AU 350	SAS 39	Audit Sampling
AU 1020	SAS 45	Omnibus: Substantive Tests Prior to the Balance Sheet Date

Account Balance Auditing with Variables Sampling

LEARNING OBJECTIVES This chapter contains more technical details on some, but not all, of the topics introduced in Chapter 8. You will find more specific coverage of how to do statistical sampling when auditing the details of the monetary amount of account balances with substantive-purpose procedures. After studying this chapter in conjunction with Chapter 8, you should be able to:

- ☐ Explain the professional judgments involved in the risk model used to determine a preliminary risk of incorrect acceptance.

- ☐ Calculate the cost trade-offs involved in a judgment about the risk of incorrect rejection.

- ☐ Calculate predetermined sample sizes, given particular fact situations.

- ☐ Perform a quantitative evaluation of monetary error evidence by projecting the known error and calculating the risks of incorrect acceptance and incorrect rejection.

- ☐ Discuss the relative merits of alternatives for determining an amount by which a monetary balance should be adjusted.

The statistics of account balance auditing is known as *variables sampling,* referring to measurement of a continuously variable dollar amount. In contrast, the statistics of compliance auditing, known as *attribute sampling,* refers to measurement of just the presence or absence of an attribute—a control deviation. In variables sampling, the dollar amount or error is measured, and its value can range continuously from zero to a larger number.

The best way to proceed is to take the stream of ideas in Chapter 8 and add statistical calculations to them. The numbers used in this chapter come from the example presented in Chapter 8, along with some other numbers assumed for purposes of illustration.

RISK OF INCORRECT ACCEPTANCE

To continue the Chapter 8 example of the audit of accounts receivable, assume the audit manager made these judgments:

Acceptable audit risk (AuR) 0.03
Inherent risk (IR) 1.00
Control risk (IC) 0.30
Analytical review risk (AR) 0.50

The expanded risk model suggests a risk of incorrect acceptance (TD) arising from audit of the details of customers' balances of 0.20, judged as follows:

$$TD = \frac{AuR}{IR \times IC \times AR} = \frac{0.03}{1.0 \times 0.3 \times 0.5} = 0.20$$

RISK OF INCORRECT REJECTION

An initial incorrect rejection decision will create an audit *inefficiency* because additional work will be done to determine the amount of an adjustment. Barring a subsequent incorrect rejection conclusion, the auditors will discover that the recorded amount was materially accurate all along. When planning the size of an audit sample, the judgment about the acceptable risk of incorrect acceptance amounts to an incremental cost analysis.

You can minimize the risk by auditing a large sample—spending time and effort at the beginning. Alternatively, you can take more risk, save the initial time and effort, and take your chances about needing to do more auditing later.

An example of estimating the early cost versus late cost trade-off would go something like this:

1. A low risk of incorrect rejection is chosen as a "base." For example, if this risk is 0.10, an appropriate sample size would be 264 customer accounts.[1]

2. The variable cost of auditing each sampling unit in the initial sample is estimated, say at $10 per unit for a total of $2,640.

3. An "alternative" risk of incorrect acceptance larger than the "base" needs to be compared. So, for an alternative risk of 50 percent, the sample size is 100.

---

[1] Sample size calculations are explained later, but for the record, 264 was calculated using the finitely corrected formula shown in Equation 3B.

4. The variable cost for an initial sample of 100 is $1,000.

5. The initial cost savings of a sample of 100 compared to a sample of 264 is $1,640, ($2,640 − $1,000).

6. If an incorrect rejection decision is made based on an initial sample of 100 units, an additional sample of as many as 164 units may be needed (bringing the total audit effort up to the "base" of 264 units).

7. Assume the variable cost of auditing the items in a second sample is higher, say $15 per unit, for an added cost of $2,460, ($15 × 164).

8. The incremental probability of the incorrect rejection decision is 40 percent (0.50 − 0.10), thus the expected additional cost could be $984, (40% × $2,460).

9. The cost saving with a risk of 50 percent is $656, ($1,640 − $984), when compared with the initial audit sample of 264 units, so a risk of 50 percent appears to be efficient.

10. The maximum adverse cost is the additional cost of auditing the 164 units later—$820, ($5 additional cost per unit × 164 units)—if the incorrect rejection decision is made initially but reversed with the evidence from the audit of 164 more units.

The cost trade-off is based on probabilities, and these are sometimes hard to grasp. The analysis illustrated above shows that a risk of 50 percent *can* be more efficient than a risk of 10 percent with repeated trials using samples of 100. However, auditors do not perform repeated trials—only one sample of 100 units constitutes the first audit work. An audit manager may prefer to incur the $1,640 additional cost in the first phase of work in order to avoid any possibility of an additional $820 cost of subsequent work. Assessment of the risk depends entirely on the auditor's preferences.

SAMPLE SIZE CALCULATIONS

The two basic choices of sampling methods are *classical variables sampling* and *dollar-unit sampling*. Classical variables sampling requires an estimate of the standard deviation of the population, whereas dollar-unit sampling does not. Classical variables sampling depends upon statistical characteristics of the normal distribution.

Classical Variables Sampling

First a revelation: *There's nothing magic about a predetermined sample size calculated using a complicated equation.* You can audit and evaluate any size sample so long as you select it randomly and use the statistical mathematics correctly. The best reason for trying to calculate sample size in advance is to guard against significant underauditing (too small an arbitrary sample size) and against significant overauditing (too large an arbitrary sample size). By now, you should realize an auditor has plenty of latitude in several judgments—audit risk, inherent risk, control risk, analytical review risk, risk of incorrect acceptance and risk of incorrect rejection—to justify a sample size *before* the audit work is done. Anyway, some auditing organizations advise their auditors to calculate sample size, then add 10 percent more units as a "safety factor."

Normal Distribution Theory.   Classical variables sampling relies on normal distribution theory. Basically, when a statistic is distributed normally about its mean, the normal curve looks like this:

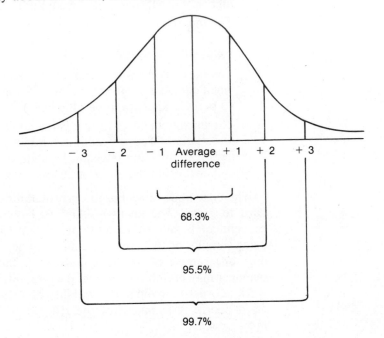

In account balance audit sampling, the statistic of interest is the dollar amount of difference between the unit amount determined by an auditor (the "audited amount") and the unit amount recorded in the books (the "recorded amount"). These *difference amounts* exist in a population, and they have a distribution around an average difference. If the distribution is normal, 68.3 percent of the differences lie in the range ±1 standard deviation from the average, 95.5 percent lie in the range ±2 standard deviations, and 99.7 percent lie in the range ±3 standard deviations. The 1, 2 and 3 can be understood as the *coefficients representing the risk of incorrect rejection*.

Look again at the normal curve. If 95.5 percent of the differences lie between ±2 standard deviations, then 2.25 percent lies above +2 standard deviations, 2.25 percent lies below −2 standard deviations, and 97.75 percent (95.5% + 2.25%) lies *below* +2 standard deviations. This one-tail view of the curve is the viewpoint of the risk of incorrect acceptance, and

+2 can be understood as the *coefficient representing 1 minus the risk of incorrect acceptance.*

A NOTE ABOUT READING APPENDIX 12–A AND APPENDIX 12–B

These two tables of areas under the normal curve are different. Appendix 12–A is a "two-tail" table. When you have a coefficient for the risk of incorrect rejection (say 0.67), read 0.6 at the left margin and across to the .07 column. The entry in the cell, .5029, is the value for the risk of incorrect rejection. When you know the risk and want to find the coefficient for a risk, say of 0.10: Find the cell value closest to it (.1010) and read the coefficient at the left margin and top of the column to find 1.64. Interpolation for exact values is not necessary.

Appendix 12–B is a "one-tail" table and the following holds:

For a coefficient for the risk of incorrect acceptance with a plus sign, the value in the cell is 1 minus the risk of incorrect acceptance.

For a coefficient for the risk of incorrect acceptance with a minus sign, the value in the cell is the risk of incorrect acceptance.

For example, for a coefficient = .84, find 0.8 at the left margin, read over to the .04 column, and find the cell entry .7995. The risk of incorrect acceptance associated with the coefficient of 0.84 is .2005 (20.05 percent). For the coefficient −1.0, read 1.0 at the left margin, and in the .00 column the value is .8413 (round to 0.84), which is the value for the risk of incorrect acceptance. When you have a known risk less than 0.5 (say, 0.06) and want to find the coefficient: Find the closest cell value for 1 minus the risk of incorrect acceptance (0.94 = 1 − .06), and read the coefficient at the left margin and top (1.56). When your known risk of incorrect acceptance is greater than 0.5 (say, 0.60) and want to find the coefficient: Find the closest cell value for the risk and read the coefficient at the left margin and top, remembering the coefficient is a negative number (−0.25).

Calculating the Standard Deviation and Standard Error. The *standard deviation* of the differences can be calculated using this equation:[2]

$$S_d^2 = \frac{\sum_{i=1}^{n} (d_i - \bar{D})^2}{n - 1} \tag{1A}$$

where

$i = 1, \ldots, n$ = index identifying each sampling unit

S_d = standard deviation of the difference statistic

n = sample size

d = signed difference of the audited amount minus the recorded amount of each sampling unit

$\bar{D}$ = average difference, the sum of d_i divided by n

---

[2] Equation **1A** can also be expressed in this form:

$$S_d^2 = \frac{\sum_{i=1}^{n} (d_i)^2 - n\bar{D}^2}{n - 1} \tag{1B}$$

When the distribution is a *distribution of averages of sample differences taken from numerous samples of the same size,* the normal distribution describes the shape of the curve for the *distribution of sample averages.* In this case, the standard deviation measure is the **standard error of the mean,** calculated by this equation:

$$S_{\bar{D}} = \frac{S_d}{\sqrt{n}} \tag{2}$$

An estimate of the standard deviation is used in the sample size formula. The standard error of the mean is used in making the evaluation calculations.

Calculating Sample Size.   The formula for sample size calculation is:

$$\text{Sample Size} = n = \frac{[S_d(Z_\alpha + Z_\beta)]^2}{(TE/N)^2} \tag{3A}$$

where

S_d = estimated standard deviation of the differences in the population, as defined

Z_α = coefficient representing the risk of incorrect rejection (Appendix 12–A)

Z_β = coefficient representing the risk of incorrect acceptance (Appendix 12–B)

TE = tolerable error, as defined

N = population size

You can use this equation to visualize how changes in the elements influence the sample size (refer to Exhibit 8–6, Chapter 8). The two risk coefficients—Z_α and Z_β—both become *smaller numbers* as their respective risks become *higher.* Thus for higher risks, sample size is smaller because the numerator becomes smaller, and vice versa. When tolerable error is larger, the denominator becomes larger. For larger tolerable error, sample size is smaller, and vice versa. When population size is larger, the term in the denominator *(TE/N)* becomes smaller. So, for a larger population, the sample size is larger, and vice versa.

You need to use an *estimate of the standard deviation of the differences* to calculate a sample size. This estimate is difficult because making it requires auditors to guess the dollar amount of error in the population. The bases for guesses can include knowledge of the extent of error found in prior years' audits, knowledge of adjustments the client may have made during the current year, estimates of the effects of internal control failures, or just "feelings" about the extent of error. Sometimes advice is given to audit a *pilot sample*—a random selection of 50 sampling units— and measure the amount of error. All of these methods are tentative and preliminary, however.

Once you have a guess about the amount of error in the population, figure the population unit average. The standard deviation of the differences can be as much as 10 to 20 times as large. Suppose, for the illustrative population of accounts receivable, an auditor thinks $10,000 total error might exist. The population average, thus, is about $1.20 ($10,000/ 8,300 customer accounts). The standard deviation could be between $12 and $24. So, suppose he or she decides to use $20 as a nice but conservative estimate.

When calculating sample size, you should use the formula shown below (Equation 3B). It is *finitely corrected,* meaning that it incorporates the population size in such a way that sample sizes larger than the population size cannot be produced. (The first formula is not finitely corrected, and it *can* produce sample sizes larger than the population size!)

$$\text{Sample Size (finitely corrected)} = n = \frac{N[S_d(Z_\alpha + Z_\beta)]^2}{N(TE/N)^2 + [S_d(Z_\alpha + Z_\beta)]^2} \quad \textbf{(3B)}$$

For an example of sample size calculation, take the calculation of n = 264 used earlier in the illustration of the assessment of the risk of incorrect rejection. In that case:

$S_d = \$20$

$Z_\alpha = 1.645$, the coefficient for a 10 percent risk of incorrect rejection (Appendix 12–A)

$Z_\beta = 0.84$, the coefficient for a 20 percent risk of incorrect acceptance (Appendix 12–B)

$TE = \$25,000$

$N = 8,300$ customer accounts

$$\text{Sample Size (finitely corrected)} = n = \frac{8,300[\$20(1.645 + 0.84)]^2}{8,300(\$25,000/8,300)^2 + [\$20(1.645 + 0.84)]^2}$$
$$= 263.6$$

By now you should be thoroughly aware of the fact that a sample size calculation is based on auditors' judgments and estimates. A predetermined sample size is particularly tentative as a result of the process of estimating the standard deviation.

Dollar-Unit Sampling (DUS)

This sampling methodology is well suited for audit sampling applications. DUS is used widely by many accounting firms both for compliance auditing (attribute sampling) and account balance auditing (variables sampling). The unique feature of DUS is its definition of the population as the number of dollars in an account balance or class of transactions. Thus, the illustrative accounts receivable total of $379,500 becomes a population of 379,500 dollar units instead of a population of 8,300 customer accounts.

Earlier, you saw the definition of *stratification* in terms of a plan for subdividing the 8,300 accounts into groups *(strata)* according to the size of the customers' balances. This definition permits a statistically valid sample selection to be skewed to include more of the high-dollar balances. This design gives auditors protection against incorrect acceptance by justifying the audit coverage of a large proportion of the dollars in the total. DUS automatically accomplishes a high degree of stratification.

You must determine a sample size in advance to use DUS. Technical details about figuring a DUS sample size are in Appendix 12–D. Judgments about audit risk, inherent risk, control risk, analytical review risk, incorrect acceptance risk and incorrect rejection risk are all applicable.

For illustrative purposes, however, assume an appropriate sample size is 100. Theoretically, the sample is 100 of the $1 units in the population. One sample selection method is systematic. You find the quotient k = population size/sample size = 379,500/100 = 3,795. With one random start, you select every 3,795th dollar unit. Each time a $1 unit is selected, it *hooks* the **logical unit** that contains it—in this case, the customer's account. Obviously, *all* customer accounts with balances of $3,795 or more will be in the sample. Also, larger accounts have a greater likelihood of selection. These phenomena of the selection method give DUS its high degree of stratification. With a selection of 100 dollars, you could hook a large dollar amount, say as much as $190,000 of the $379,500 total. Since the average account balance is $45.72 ($379,500/8300), a customer-account selection of 100 accounts should produce about $4,572 of dollar coverage (100 × $45.72), so the DUS sample that covers $190,000 is highly stratified by comparison.

A particular advantage of DUS is that you do not need to make a guess about the standard deviation of errors. DUS does not depend upon normal distribution theory. Its underlying statistics is the same as attribute sampling theory. However, you must make an estimate of the expected amount of error in the population in order to plan a large enough sample.

The high degree of stratification is taken into account in the statistical evaluation calculations. Since these calculations involve some new ideas, they are saved for Appendix 12–D. The subject is not relegated to an appendix because it is unimportant. For the time being, we need to continue with the development of audited-recorded amount difference calculations.

PROJECT THE KNOWN ERROR

The whole point of quantitative evidence evaluation is to extend the findings from the sample to the entire population. The example in Chapter 8 assumed you audited 100 customer accounts and found total known error of −$100 (overstatement error). Now that you know the direction of the error (overstatement), you can drop the minus sign. A *simple extension* can be used to project the known error, using either the *average difference method* or the *ratio method* described in Chapter 8. The average difference method is used in further examples to produce a single point estimate of the population difference:

$$\text{Projected Likely Error} \atop \text{(Average difference method)} = \frac{\$100}{100} \times 8,300 = \$8,300 \atop \text{(overstatement)}$$

To this projection from the sample, you add the error ($600) found in the accounts audited separately. Now the total projected likely error in the example is $8,900.

You are supposed to "compare" this point estimate to the tolerable error ($25,000) and "take sampling risk into account." However, as you might suspect, taking risk into account involves other calculations.

CONSIDER SAMPLING RISK Your problem is to figure the probability that you could have obtained a projected likely error (point estimate) of $8,300 overstatement when in fact the total amount of overstatement in the population is $25,000.[3] This probability is the maximum risk of incorrect acceptance if you decide to accept the recorded amount of $379,500 as materially accurate and requiring no adjustment. In order to calculate the risk, you must first calculate the *standard error of the average in the sample of 100 customer accounts*. This standard error is no longer an estimate like the estimate of the standard deviation used to predetermine a sample size. It is based on actual data from the sample.

First, you should have 30 or more actual differences in the sample. A standard error calculation is a tricky proposition, and it is especially suspect (subject to bias) when based on only a few differences. Next, the procedures are these:

1. Calculate the standard error using Equation 2. Data for this calculation come from the sample, as assumed below.

(a) Sample Item	(b) Audited Amount	(c) Recorded Amount	(d) Difference (b) − (c)	(e) Average Difference	(f) [(d) − (e)]²
1	$ 45	$ 50	$ −5	$−1	$ 16
2	26	25	1	−1	4
3	100	100	0	−1	1
4	37	35	2	−1	9
.	.	.	.	.	.
.	.	.	.	.	.
.	.	.	.	.	.
100	17	20	−3	−1	4
Sums	$4,400	$4,500	$−100		$89,100

Equation 1A: $S_d^2 = \$89,100/(100 - 1) = 900$

and

$S_d = 30$

Equation 2: $S_{\bar{D}} = \$30/10 = \$3$

---

[3] Actually, the risk problem relates to possible population error of $24,400, since you have already found $600 in the accounts audited separately. To keep the example clean, we will continue to use $25,000. However, do not forget about the other $600 of known error. It appears later in the section on determining the amount of an adjustment.

2. Figure the distance between tolerable error ($25,000) and projected likely error ($8,300). It is $16,700.

3. Convert this distance to an average: $16,700/8300 = $2.01

4. Calculate a *sample-based coefficient of the risk of incorrect acceptance* by dividing the average distance by the standard error of the average. The result is 0.67 = $2.01/$3. This 0.67 is Z_β based on the sample data.

5. Find this $Z_\beta = 0.67$ in Appendix 12–B. Its associated cell value is .7486. Since the cell value is 1 minus the risk of incorrect acceptance, the risk evident in the sample is .2514 or 25.14 percent.

This *risk based on the sample data* at 25.14 percent exceeds your *planned risk* of 20 percent. The maximum probability that total error could equal or exceed $25,000, as far as you now know, does not meet the decision criterion you established when planning this part of the audit. So, your tentative decision should lean toward rejection, and now you run the risk of *incorrect rejection*. Before we turn to some calculations, however, look at some reasons your sample data appear to have failed the test.

Sample Size Too Small

If these same results (projected likely error of $8300 overstatement and standard deviation of $30) had been obtained with a sample of 200 customer accounts, then the risk of incorrect acceptance would be about 17 percent. More information—a larger sample—would have met your risk criterion. You can verify this risk calculation using steps four and five listed above.

Variability Greater than Expected

You based the sample size of 100 on a guess that the standard deviation would be about $20. In the sample, it turned out to be $30. You should not be surprised. Guessing at the standard deviation is a pitfall. Besides, different samples of 100 could produce a wide range of standard deviations. The standard deviation is subject to what some samplers call "bounce," meaning it is unpredictable. Furthermore, you have no good way of knowing whether $30 is a good representation because you have no way of knowing the actual standard deviation of errors for the population. All the population errors are not known and available for a calculation.

However, if the 100-unit sample had turned up a standard deviation of $18, then the risk of incorrect acceptance would be about 13 percent. In contrast to the original deviation of $30 related to the same $−1 average difference, the new assumption of a smaller standard deviation means that the range of the size of the differences is "tighter" around the average. You can verify the calculation of 13 percent risk using steps four and five listed above.

Observations

Once you have predetermined a sample size, as long as you audit the calculated number of sampling units, your decision outcome is dependent largely upon two elements: (1) The actual amount of error and (2) the standard deviation in the sample data. The closer the actual average difference in the sample is to the average amount of error you expected and the closer the sample standard deviation is to the estimate you used to calculate sample size, the more likely your decision will be to accept the recorded amount as materially accurate. The sample-based risk of incorrect acceptance is more likely to be less than your criterion established at the beginning.

Calculating the Upper Error Limit. The three examples can be put in another perspective by calculating an ***upper error limit (UEL)*** of monetary error. The UEL is the largest amount of monetary error you can calculate, using the coefficient for your decision criterion risk of incorrect acceptance ($Z_\beta = 0.84$ for 20 percent risk of incorrect acceptance used in the example). You can interpret it like this: "The probability that monetary error in the population exceeds UEL is equal to the risk of incorrect acceptance." If UEL exceeds your tolerable error, then the risk of incorrect acceptance is *greater* than your decision criterion for the risk, and your decision should lean toward rejection.

$$UEL = N(|\bar{D}| + Z_\beta S_{\bar{D}}) \qquad \textbf{(4)}$$

Basic Example: $n = 100$, $S_d = \$30$, average error $= \$-1$

$$UEL = 8300 \left(|\$-1| + 0.84 \frac{\$30}{\sqrt{100}} \right) = \$29{,}216$$

Interpretation. The probability is 0.20 that error in the population exceeds $29,216, which is more than the $25,000 tolerable error.

First Variation: $n = 200$, $S_d = \$30$, average error $= \$-1$

$$UEL = 8300 \left(|\$-1| + 0.84 \frac{\$30}{\sqrt{200}} \right) = \$23{,}090$$

Interpretation: The probability is 0.20 that error in the population exceeds $23,090, which is less than the $25,000 tolerable error.

Second Variation: $n = 100$, $S_d = \$18$, average error $= \$-1$

$$UEL = 8300 \left(|\$-1| + 0.84 \frac{\$18}{\sqrt{100}} \right) = \$20{,}850$$

Interpretation: The probability is 0.20 that error in the population exceeds $20,850, which is less than the $25,000 tolerable error.

CONSIDER THE OTHER SAMPLING RISK   Audit work on the audit of details of an account balance can be considered finished when the statistical calculations produce an UEL less than tolerable error at the criterion risk of incorrect rejection. You can accept the recorded amount as materially accurate, assured by the careful planning of the sampling application and the statistical support for having met your risk criterion. However, if your preliminary decision is to reject the recorded amount, you need to consider the "other" sampling risk—the risk of incorrect rejection.

You can "consider" this risk by calculating the probability that the average error ($-1 in the example) *could* have come from a sampling distribution of average errors from D ($+1) to −D ($−1) normally distributed around zero average error. (The fact that you have found $100 of overstatement error in a sample does not mean the population error is not zero. Other understatement errors could exist to cause the *average error* to be zero.) Remember that the standard deviation in the basic example sample was $30. The steps are these:

1. Divide the absolute value of the average difference by the sampling error of the average ($1/$3 = 0.33).
2. The result (0.33 in the example) is the coefficient Z_α for the risk of incorrect rejection.
3. Find this Z_α = 0.33 in Appendix 12–A. Its associated cell value is .7414. Therefore, the risk of incorrect rejection is 74.14 percent, far more than the 50 percent criterion established when the audit sample size was planned.

Now you are in a pickle. Since the standard deviation in the sample turned out to be $30, your sample size is too small to satisfy the statistical criteria.[4] If you accept the recorded amount as materially accurate, your risk of incorrect acceptance is too high. If you reject it, your risk of incorrect rejection is too high. You need to audit more sampling units, obtain more evidence, and build the basis for a supportable decision.

DETERMINING THE AMOUNT OF AN ADJUSTMENT   The problem with determining the amount to recommend for adjustment is troublesome because auditors usually do not know the exact amount of error in an account. (An exception exists when audit teams or client personnel perform a 100 percent review and correct all errors.) As long as the evidential base is a random sample, the three measurable aspects of monetary error are: (1) known error, (2) likely error and (3) possible error.[5]

---

[4] If you had planned for a standard deviation of $30 at the outset, sample size would have been 220.

$$n = \frac{8,300[\$30(0.67 + 0.84)]^2}{8,300(\$25,000/8,300)^2 + [\$30(0.67 + 0.84)]^2} = 220$$

where

   Z_α = 0.67 is the coefficient for the 50 percent risk of incorrect rejection decided upon in the incorrect rejection cost trade-off analysis

[5] SAS 47 (AU 312.32), *Audit Risk and Materiality in Conducting an Audit,* refers to possible error as "further error remaining undetected."

Quantitative Known error and the projected likely error have already been discussed.
Considerations *Possible error* is the *additional undiscovered error that might exist in the population and not be reflected in the sample findings*. It is a measure of sampling error. It is calculated by: *Possible Monetary Error* = UEL − Likely Error. Since UEL is a statistical calculation based on an audit criterion for the risk of incorrect acceptance, you can see that possible monetary error is also dependent on the auditor's judgment about this risk.

So, in the example, you now have the following information based on the sample from 8,300 customer accounts:

Known error = $100 overstatement
Likely error = $8,300 overstatement
Possible error = $20,916 overstatement in addition to likely error (29,216 − $8,300) based on 20 percent risk of incorrect acceptance

As a practical matter, auditors would not use these data to recommend an adjustment because the sample size is not large enough to yield enough information. (Witness the earlier discussion of sampling risks of both decision errors based on these data.) However, for illustrative purposes, several measures of adjustment amounts can be derived from the data. Various sources have suggested the following:

Adjust in the amount of the known error, in this case $700 ($100 in the sample plus $600 in the 10 other accounts). Usually, the actual amount of known error is smaller than the tolerable error.

Adjust in the amount of the most likely error, in this case $8,900. The point estimate is considered the best single-value measurement available for this purpose.

Also adjust in the amount of the possible error, in this case another $20,916. This amount is the largest one an auditor can measure using the risk of incorrect acceptance. It contains an element of statistical measurement that auditors may or may not be willing to accept for adjustment purposes.

Adjust by the amount of tolerable error when the sum of likely error and possible error exceeds tolerable error, in this case $25,000. This kind of rule is somewhat arbitrary and is subject to question when the sum exceeds 2 × tolerable error.

Adjust by the amount the sum of likely error and possible error exceeds tolerable error, in this case $4,816 ($29,816 − $25,000). The theory here is that the amount of error left in the account balance after adjustment will not exceed tolerable error ($25,000). Not much theory exists to support this measure, which may be somewhat arbitrary.

Nonquantitative Considerations

You can see that much latitude exists for determining the amount of an adjustment to recommend. Oftentimes the amount recommended for one account depends upon adjustment amounts recommended for other accounts. Auditors typically consider the findings in other audit areas when recommending adjustments.

The special characteristics of the accounts must also be considered. For example, the net $100 overstatement is the illustrative accounts receivable data may consist of $1,000 overcharges to customers or failure to record discounts and $900 of sales that were underbilled or simply not invoiced to customers. Management may make a policy decision not to try to recover the underbilled or unbilled amounts, so the audit manager must then deal with $1,000 of overstatement in the sample instead of a $100 net overstatement. Other accounts may be different. For example, both overstatements and understatements in an inventory valuation may be adjustable simply by correcting the records, and no one needs to take customer relations into account.

Determining the amount of an adjustment may be difficult. Auditors consider not only the quantitative measures of error but also management policy and their findings in other audit areas.

Now that the lack of a definitive guide on "how to figure the amount of an adjustment" has revealed the lack of science in auditing, we can close the discussion with one definite statement: The $600 of overstatement error found in 10 large accounts audited separately should be adjusted in the client's books. As a general rule and a necessary condition for an unqualified audit opinion, all errors discovered in accounts or subsets of accounts audited completely should be adjusted, provided the amounts are material.

SUMMARY

Statistical sampling requires knowledge of the underlying statistical calculations and relationships and a certain amount of faith in the mathematics. Auditors are entitled to hold a statistical result at arm's length and study it for its face validity. However, deciding to disregard an adverse statistical result because it does not give an auditor a good "feeling" is dangerous. Auditors must make decisions about account balances with care and with the best evidential base reasonably obtainable.

The list of steps below is a summary of steps common to both statistical and nonstatistical audit sampling. The steps marked with an asterisk are the ones where models, quantifications and explicit calculations are needed for statistical sampling applications.

1. Recognize the financial assertions subject to audit and specify the objectives of the substantive-purpose procedures.

*2. Decide the amount of tolerable error appropriate in the audit of the account balance.

*3. Use the expanded risk model to estimate the allowable risk of incorrect acceptance.

*4. Calculate cost trade-offs to decide upon an acceptable risk of incorrect rejection.

*5. Decide whether to use classical variables sampling or dollar-unit sampling.

6. Define the population of data and stratify it for efficiency. Identify units for separate 100 percent audit attention.

*7. When classical variables sampling is used, estimate the standard deviation of the population values.

*8. Predetermine the sample size.

*9. Select a random sample.

10. Perform the audit procedures on each unit in the sample.

11. Project error amounts to the population. Calculate *likely error*.

*12. Calculate the sample-based risks of incorrect acceptance and/or incorrect rejection.

*13. Calculate the upper error limit (UEL), as a basis for estimating *possible error*.

14. Determine the amount, if any, to adjust the balance.

Judging from the placement of the asterisks (*) in the list above, you can see that *all sampling* depends upon good objectives specification at the outset and upon a judgment about adjustment at the end. In between, the statistical methodology requires that numbers be assigned to auditors' judgments. Calculated numbers serve in place of the ambiguous "considerations" characteristic of nonstatistical sampling and evidence evaluation. The whole point of sampling is to make good decisions efficiently, and statistical methods contribute some measurements to focus auditors' judgments.

SOURCES AND ADDITIONAL READING REFERENCES

Introduction and Application

Akresh, A., and G. R. Zuber. "Exploring Statistical Sampling." *Journal of Accountancy,* February 1981, pp. 50–56.

Elliot, R. K., and J. R. Rogers. "Relating Statistical Sampling to Audit Objectives." *Journal of Accountancy,* July 1972, pp. 46–55.

Kinney, William R., Jr. "A Note on Compounding Probabilities in Auditing." *Auditing: A Journal of Practice and Theory,* Spring 1983, pp. 13–22.

Leslie, D. A., A. D. Teitlebaum, and R. J. Anderson. *Dollar-Unit Sampling: A Practical Guide for Auditors.* Toronto: Copp Clark Pitman, 1979, 409 pages.

Pushkin, Ann B. "Presenting Beta Risk to Students." *Accounting Review,* January 1980, pp. 117–22.

Roberts, Donald M. "Statistical Interpretation of SAP No. 54." *Journal of Accountancy,* March 1974, pp. 47–53.

Warren, Carl S. "Audit Risk." *Journal of Accountancy,* August 1979, pp. 66–74.

Zuber, G. R., R. K. Elliott, W. R. Kinney, Jr., and J. L. Leisenring. "Using Materiality in Audit Planning." *Journal of Accountancy,* March 1983, pp. 42–55.

Research Papers and Advanced Sources

Baker, R. L., and R. M. Copeland. "Evaluation of the Stratified Regression Estimator for Auditing Accounting Populations." *Journal of Accounting Research,* Autumn 1979, pp. 606–17.

Barkman, Arnold. "Within-Item Variation: A Stochastic Approach to Audit Uncertainty." *Accounting Review,* April 1977, pp. 450–64.

Cochran, Wm. G. *Sampling Techniques,* 3rd ed. New York: John Wiley & Sons, 1977.

Felix, W. L., Jr., and R. A. Grimlund. "A Sampling Model for Audit Tests of Composite Accounts." *Journal of Accounting Research,* Spring 1977, pp. 23–41.

Gartska, Stanley J. "Models for Computing Upper Error Limits in Dollar-Unit Sampling." *Journal of Accounting Research,* Autumn 1977, pp. 179–92.

Gartska, S. J., and P. A. Ohlson. "Ratio Estimation in Accounting Populations with Probabilities of Sample Selection Proportional to Size of Book Value." *Journal of Accounting Research,* Spring 1979, pp. 23–59.

Hansen, D. R., and T. L. Shaftel. "Sampling for Integrated Objectives in Auditing." *Accounting Review,* January 1977, pp. 109–23.

Ijiri, Y., and R. S. Kaplan. "A Model for Integrating Sampling Objectives in Auditing." *Journal of Accounting Research,* Spring 1971, pp. 73–87.

Johnson, J. R., R. A. Leitch, and J. Neter. "Characteristics of Errors in Accounts Receivable and Inventory Audits." *Accounting Review,* April 1981, pp. 270–93.

Kaplan, Robert S. "A Stochastic Model for Auditing." *Journal of Accounting Research,* Spring 1973, pp. 38–46.

————. "Statistical Sampling in Auditing with Auxiliary Information Estimators." *Journal of Accounting Research,* Autumn 1973, pp. 238–58.

————. "Sample Size Computations for Dollar-Unit Sampling." *Journal of Accounting Research,* Supplement 1975, pp. 126–33.

Kinney, Wm. R., Jr. "A Decision Theory Approach to the Sampling Problem in Auditing." *Journal of Accounting Research,* Spring 1975, pp. 115–32.

————. "Decision Theory Aspects of Internal Control System Design/Compliance and Substantive Tests." *Journal of Accounting Research,* Supplement 1975, pp. 14–37.

————. "Integrating Audit Tests: Regression Analysis and Partitioned Dollar-Unit Sampling." *Journal of Accounting Research,* Autumn 1979, pp. 456–75.

Loebbecke, J. K., and J. Neter. "Considerations in Choosing Statistical Sampling Procedures in Auditing." *Journal of Accounting Research,* Supplement 1975, pp. 38–68.

Neter, J., and J. K. Loebbecke. *Behavior of Major Statistical Estimators in Sampling Accounting Populations.* Auditing Research Monograph no. 2. New York: AICPA, 1975.

Roberts, Donald M. *Statistical Auditing.* New York: AICPA, 1978.

Smith, K. A. "The Relationship of Internal Control Evaluation and Audit Sample Size." *Accounting Review,* April 1972, pp. 260–69.

Teitlebaum. A. D., and C. F. Robinson. "The Real Risks in Audit Sampling." *Journal of Accounting Research,* Supplement 1975, pp. 70–97.

REVIEW QUESTIONS

12.1. If audit risk (AuR) is 0.015, inherent risk (IR) is 0.50, control risk (IC) is 0.30 and analytical review risk (AR) is 0.50, what test of detail risk (TD) is suggested by the expanded risk model?

12.2. Which elements in the risk model are *not* a product of an auditor's professional judgment? Which ones are determined by auditors in relation to specific circumstances?

12.3. Why is the risk of incorrect acceptance considered more critical than the risk of incorrect rejection in connection with audit decisions about an account balance?

12.4. What considerations are important for determining the risk of incorrect rejection?

12.5. If nothing is magic about a predetermined sample size, why should auditors go to the trouble of calculating the size in advance?

12.6. What basic statistical characteristics distinguish classical variables sampling methods from the dollar-unit sampling method?

12.7. If you audit 100 customer accounts receivable balances and find 37 errors to the extent that the sum of the squared deviations of each sampling unit from the average error amount is $121,275, what is the standard deviation (S_d) of the differences?

12.8. What is the standard error of the mean for the sample described in review question 12.7?

12.9. What are the coefficients (Z_β) of these risks of incorrect acceptance: 0.71, 0.50, 0.40, 0.29, 0.22, 0.20, 0.16. 0.14, 0.11, 0.10, 0.08, 0.07, 0.06, 0.05?

12.10. What are the coefficients (Z_α) of these risks of incorrect rejection: 0.50, 0.40, 0.20, 0.10, 0.05?

12.11. What is the unique feature of dollar-unit sampling insofar as sample selection is concerned?

12.12. How does dollar-unit sampling automatically accomplish a high degree of stratification?

12.13. What is the amount of projected likely error for these data: Recorded amount of units in the sample = $500,000; Recorded amount for the population = $4,500,000; Dollar amount of error found in a sample of 472 units = $17,500?

12.14. What is the amount of projected likely error for these data: Recorded amount for the population of 4,000 units = $4,500,000; Dollar amount of error found in a sample of 472 units = $17,500?

12.15. What general reasons usually explain why sample-based evidence can indicate material misstatement in an account balance, thus failing the decision criteria of tolerable error and acceptable risk of incorrect acceptance?

12.16. What is the general formula for calculating the upper error limit (UEL) based on average difference statistics and relying upon normal distribution theory? What is the UEL for these data: average difference =

-8.00; sample size $= 625$; standard deviation of sample differences $= \$50.00$; risk of

incorrect acceptance $= 10$ percent; population size $= 7,900$.

EXERCISES AND PROBLEMS

12.17.   Risk of Incorrect Rejection

Kaye Clark, CPA, needs to determine the risk of incorrect rejection to use in auditing a sales invoice population that has 28,000 sales invoices (N) and a standard deviation of $63 ($S_d$). Decisions have already been made on audit risk (AuR) = 0.02, the test of details detection risk (TD) = 0.20 and the tolerable error (TE) = $300,000.

Write two memos to the working paper file documenting your decision in the following two separate cases. (Use sample size calculation Equation 3A.)

a. The variable cost of auditing a sampling unit is $10 if the work is done with the initial sample selection and $25 if done later. The alternatives in question are risks of incorrect rejection of 0.10 and 0.20. Which is preferable?

b. The variable cost of auditing a sample item is $10 if the work is done with the initial sample selection and $25 if done later. The audit manager believes a minimum risk of incorrect rejection of 0.10 and a maximum of 0.25 are appropriate. However, she is willing to gamble on a maximum adverse cost of $1,000. What risk of incorrect rejection fits these requirements?

12.18.   Effect of Risk Relationships on Sample Size

In problem 8.32, the requirements were to prepare tables showing the test of detail risk (TD) for certain combinations of internal control risk (IC) and analytical review risk (AR) while inherent risk (IR) and audit risk (AuR) were held constant. These tables are abbreviated below.

1.   When IR = 100 percent and AuR = 5 percent.

	AR			
	10%	30%	50%	100%
IC		TD		
10%	*	*	*	50%
30	*	55%	33%	16
50	*	33	20	10
100	50%	16	10	5

* (IR × IC) is less than AuR.

2.   When IR = 50 percent and AuR = 5 percent.

	AR			
	10%	30%	50%	100%
IC		TD		
10%	*	*	*	*
30	*	*	66%	33%
50	*	66	40	20
100	*	33	20	10

* (IR × IC) is less than AuR.

Required:

a. Notice how the acceptable risk of overreliance (TD) is twice as large when the inherent risk (IR) is one half as large. Prepare these same tables with sample sizes instead of TD risk in the cells. Use sample size Equation 3A. Assume the population consists of 28,000 units totaling $14,353,812, the estimated standard deviation is $63, the tolerable error is $300,000, and the risk of incorrect rejection is 10 percent ($Z_\alpha = 1.645$).

b. Write an explanation of the auditing theory and generally accepted auditing standards treatment of the cells in the tables with an asterisk.

12.19. Effect of Risk Relationships on Sample Size

Kaye Clark, CPA, is preparing a sampling plan for the audit of 28,000 sales invoices totaling $14,353,812. The estimated standard deviation of this population is $63, and a $300,000 misstatement is considered material. Ms. Raven, the audit manager, asks Kaye to show her the effect of various risk specifications on the predetermined sample size.

Required:

a. Prepare a table in the format shown below, entering sample sizes where indicated. Use sample size Equation 3A, but if the predetermined sample size exceeds 1,400, recalculate the sample size using the finitely corrected form shown in Equation 3B.

b. Write an explanation of the effect on sample size of the risk of incorrect rejection and the finitely corrected sample size calculation.

Comparative Sample Sizes

Risk of Incorrect Acceptance	Z_β	Risk of Incorrect Rejection	
		10% = 1.645 Z_α	20% = 1 28 Z_α
.71	−.54		
.50	0		
.40	.25		
.29	.55		
.22	.77		
.20	.84		
.16	.99		
.14	1.08		
.11	1.23		
.10	1.28		
.08	1.41		
.07	1.48		
.06	1.555		
.05	1.645		

12.20. Quantitative Projection of Known Error

When Kaye Clark audited 400 sales invoices from the population of 28,000 recorded by Longneck, Inc., she obtained the following results:

Total difference in the sample . . .	$−4,000
Sum of the squared differences between each unit difference and the average difference. . . .	$89,775
Number of invoices with errors	100

Required:

a. Calculate the standard deviation and the standard error of the mean.

b. Project the known error to the population by calculating the (projected) likely error. Describe your result.

c. Compare the likely error to the tolerable error of $300,000 at the level of 20 percent risk of incorrect acceptance by calculating UEL. What is your conclusion? Why? What would be the comparison if the risk of incorrect acceptance had been 10 percent? 5 percent?

12.21. Risk of Incorrect Rejection

Kaye Clark audited 400 of the 28,000 sales invoices recorded by Longneck, Inc., in the total recorded amount of $14,353,812. She found 100 errors amounting to a total overstatment error of $4,000. When this known error was projected to the population using the average difference method, the likely error was calculated to be $280,000.

Kaye's tolerable error for this part of the work was $300,000. She also had an acceptable risk of incorrect acceptance of 5 percent as a planned decision criterion.

When sampling error was considered, Kaye found her sample data showed an upper error limit of $314,545. She also calculated a probability of 17 percent that the total overstatement error in the population was $300,000 or more. (The standard error of the average difference was $0.75.)

Required:

a. Verify the calculation of UEL and risk cited in the last paragraph above.

b. If Kaye makes the preliminary decision that the recorded sales amount is materially overstated based on these criteria and data, what is her risk of incorrect rejection? Explain the risk in these circumstances.

12.22. **Quantitative Evaluation**
Kaye Clark, CPA, audited the sales total of Longneck, Inc., for the nine months ended September 30, by selecting 200 invoices at random and determining the actual invoice amount for each one. Twenty-eight thousand invoices totaling $14,353,812 were recorded during the period. Clark's criteria for deciding about the recorded total were

tolerable error = $300,000, risk of incorrect rejection = .20, risk of incorrect acceptance = .10.

Required:
Assume the results shown in the table below were obtained in independent samples of 200 invoices each. Using measurements of differences, give your preliminary decision on whether: (1) the recorded amount is materially accurate or (2) the recorded amount is materially misstated. Write up your decisions in good working paper form.

	Case				
	(1)	(2)	(3)	(4)	(5)
Recorded amount in sample. . .	$102,600	$102,200	$70,200	$160,000	$102,600
Audited amount determined in sample	$101,800	$100,200	$71,260	$158,000	$101,800
Number of sample units with errors	80	100	80	80	80
Standard deviation of sample differences	$25	$25	$25	$60	$100

12.23. **Adjusting the Accounts**
Kaye Clark, CPA, completed the audit of 200 sales invoices recorded by Longneck, Inc. She is now ready to determine what amount of adjustment, if any, might be suggested by the quantitative evidence. She also realizes that further work might be necessary.

Required:
a. Prepare a working paper explaining possible adjustment recommendations and/or further work for the data in the independent cases 2, 3, and 5 in problem 12.22.
b. For each of these three cases, write the adjusting entry. (Other financial information for Longneck, Inc., is given in problem 6.34. You will need to refer to those financial statements to know about other accounts that might need

to be adjusted with the entries required here.)

12.24. **Questions and Problems for Appendix 12–C, Stratified Sampling**
a. How does a sample stratified on recorded book values accomplish a protective sampling objective?
b. Using the illustrative population data given in the table in Appendix 12–C, calculate the stratified sample size. Use tolerable error = $25,000, risk of incorrect rejection = 0.10 and risk of incorrect acceptance = 0.20.
c. Using the illustrative population data, allocate the sample calculated in (b) on the basis of relative dollar amount in each stratum.
d. Use the hypothetical data below to calculate the stratified average of the differences.

Stratum	Population Size	Sample Size	Sample Audited Values	Sample Book Values
0	78	78	$88,452	$90,000
1	1,100	236	29,028	29,500
2	1,211	115	5,635	5,520
3	3,241	155	3,720	3,951
4	2,770	47	423	376

e. Using the results in (d), project the known error to the population.

f. Assume the stratified standard error of the mean is $6,200 for the differences. (This standard error is already finitely corrected and multiplied by the population size.) Decide whether the book value is materially accurate according to the decision criteria set forth in (b) above.

g. Using the projected likely error from (e) and the standard error of the mean datum from (f), calculate the UEL based on risk of incorrect acceptance = 20 percent.

12.25. **Questions and Problems for Appendix 12–D Dollar-Unit Sampling**

a. Explain the difference between the sampling unit in DUS and the sampling unit in other variables sampling methods.

b. Explain the relationship of the attributes statistics CUL (Chapter 11) and the DUS-based UEL factor (e.g., for zero errors in a sample of 100, CUL = 3 percent at 10 percent risk of overreliance, Appendix 11–C.3, and UEL factor = 2.31).

c. To audit a population of $14,353,812 with criteria of risk of incorrect acceptance = 10 percent and tolerable error = $300,000, what minimum sample size is required if no errors are expected? If one 100 percent error is expected?

d. Show whether a total UEL in dollars at 5 percent risk of incorrect acceptance for a sample of 301 from a population of $14,353,812 when four errors with tainting percentages of 90 percent, 80 percent, 40 percent, and 10 percent is different from a total UEL in dollars (5 percent risk of incorrect acceptance) when no errors are found in the sample. Compare these results to a sample of 301 when four errors with tainting percentages of 80 percent, 40 percent, 10 percent and 5 percent are found. ($300,000 may be considered a material misstatement.)

e. Assume that Kaye Clark selected a proper dollar-unit sample of 200 invoices from the 28,000 recorded by Longneck, Inc., for the nine-month period ended September 30. The total book value recorded was $14,353,812. When the audit of the sample was complete, Kaye had discovered five errors of overstatement (Exhibit 12.25–1) and no errors of understatement.

Required:

1. Evaluate the sample results relative to a criterion of 10 percent risk of incorrect acceptance. The

EXHIBIT 12.25–1

Index _____

LONGNECK, INC.
Audit of Sales Invoices
December 31, 19x1

By _____
Date _____
Reviewed _____

Invoice Number	Book Value	Audit Value	Remarks
100	746.93	597.54	Wrong unit price
633	1,002.00	951.90	Discount not credited
1912	400.00	360.00	2 discounts not credited
2515	20,500.00	19,475.00	Discount not credited
2700	10,000.00	6,000.00	Wrong unit price

amount of misstatement considered material is $300,000.

2. What is the probability of Kaye's finding five or more 100 percent errors if 585 of them existed in the 28,000 invoices. (Assume the sample for this purpose is an unrestricted sample of 200 invoices, from the 28,000 invoices, not a dollar-unit sample.)

DISCUSSION CASE

12.26. **Audit Planning Strategy**

As a senior accountant, you are in charge of planning the audit of finished mix fertilizer inventory at Abbot Mills, Inc., as of December 31. Preliminary information obtained on November 24 indicates the inventory consists of 2,800 different kinds of products held in various quantities at various unit production costs. The company plans to conduct the physical count of this inventory on November 30, and your audit team will observe the counting and test-count a sample of items to decide whether the counting is done accurately.

Your audit manager has decided that the audit risk of failing to find a material misstatement of $300,000 should be 5 percent. The inventory measurement is considered quite important. To be on the conservative side of auditing theory, and in light of your knowledge of Abbot's business and personnel, you both decide the inherent risk of material error entering the accounting system should be treated as 100 percent.

The inventory book value as of November 24 is $3 million. The prior-year working papers show the standard deviation of differences was $350 in a sample of 150 inventory types where 80 dollar-value differences were found. The average difference last year was $−50 (overstatement).

The audit manager does not consider analytical review procedures to be very effective for detecting material errors as small as $300,000 in Abbot's situation. At best, the risk of missing material error with analytical review procedures could be 90 percent, although the planned gross margin ratio comparisons might be as much as 50 percent effective for showing potential problems of inventory overstatement in amounts of $500,000 or more.

Last year, the audit team evaluated internal accounting control and observed the inventory-taking on November 30. The internal accounting control work took 25 hours and the former audit senior evaluated control risk at 30 percent—a rating of "good but not excellent" on the firm's scale of control evaluation.

The audit of each inventory type takes about 30 minutes. Last year, 75 hours were spent auditing the 150 sample items. The follow-up review as of December 31 took 20 hours. The time budget for this year's work is 75 hours.

However, you know that internal accounting control seems to have gotten worse this year. Presently, you would evaluate the risk at 70 percent at best—a "poor and less than fair" rating.

Required:

Assume you have two choices: (1) Evaluate internal accounting control with compliance tests and decide whether to observe the inventory on November 30, after which a follow-up review as of December 31 would be necessary, taking 8 hours, or (2) do not evaluate internal accounting control any further, assign it a risk evaluation of 1.0 (unreliable), and insist that the client perform the physical inventory on December 31, in which case you would not have to do the 8 hours' follow-up work.

You figure the "best case" is that with 15 hours work on internal accounting control, you might be able to raise the internal control risk evaluation to 50 percent—a "fair but less than good" rating. The "worst case" is that the 15 hours work would confirm your 70 percent evaluation, and you would have to request the physical inventory be taken on December 31.

For this part of the requirement, assume that the risk of incorrect rejection is set at 10 percent if you do the variables sampling work on November 30 and at 5 percent if you do the work on December 31.

Use the standard deviation of $350 for planning purposes. Do not finitely correct the sample size calculations. Evaluate your options and document your audit strategy on a "best/worst case" basis. (Ignore whatever time budget might be assigned to the analytical review procedure.)

APPENDIX 12–A

Areas in Two Tails of the Normal Curve at Selected Values of Z_α from the Arithmetic Mean

This table shows the black areas.

Z_α	.00	.01	.02	.03	.04	.05	.06	.07	.08	.09
0.0	1.0000	.9920	.9840	.9761	.9681	.9601	.9522	.9442	.9362	.9283
0.1	.9203	.9124	.9045	.8966	.8887	.8808	.8729	.8650	.8572	.8493
0.2	.8415	.8337	.8259	.8181	.8103	.8026	.7949	.7872	.7795	.7718
0.3	.7642	.7566	.7490	.7414	.7339	.7263	.7188	.7114	.7039	.6965
0.4	.6892	.6818	.6745	.6672	.6599	.6527	.6455	.6384	.0312	.6241
0.5	.6171	.6101	.6031	.5961	.5892	.5823	.5755	.5687	.5619	.5552
0.6	.5485	.5419	.5353	.5287	.5222	.5157	.5093	.5029	.4965	.4902
0.7	.4839	.4777	.4715	.4654	.4593	.4533	.4473	.4413	.4354	.4295
0.8	.4237	.4179	.4122	.4065	.4009	.3953	.3898	.3843	.3789	.3735
0.9	.3681	.3628	.3576	.3524	.3472	.3421	.3371	.3320	.3271	.3222
1.0	.3173	.3125	.3077	.3030	.2983	.2937	.2801	.2846	.2801	.2757
1.1	.2713	.2670	.2627	.2585	.2543	.2501	.2460	.2420	.2380	.2340
1.2	.2301	.2263	.2225	.2187	.2150	.2113	.2077	.2041	.2005	.1971
1.3	.1936	.1902	.1868	.1835	.1802	.1770	.1738	.1707	.1676	.1645
1.4	.1615	.1585	.1556	.1527	.1499	.1471	.1443	.1416	.1389	.1362
1.5	.1336	.1310	.1285	.1260	.1236	.1211	.1188	.1164	.1141	.1118
1.6	.1096	.1074	.1052	.1031	.1010	.0989	.0969	.0949	.0930	.0910
1.7	.0891	.0873	.0854	.0836	.0819	.0801	.0784	.0767	.0751	.0735
1.8	.0719	.0703	.0688	.0672	.0658	.0643	.0629	.0615	.0601	.0588
1.9	.0574	.0561	.0549	.0536	.0524	.0512	.0500	.0488	.0477	.0466
2.0	.0455	.0444	.0434	.0424	.0414	.0404	.0394	.0385	.0375	.0366
2.1	.0357	.0349	.0340	.0332	.0324	.0316	.0308	.0300	.0293	.0285
2.2	.0278	.0271	.0264	.0257	.0251	.0238	.0288	.0232	.0226	.0220
2.3	.0214	.0209	.0203	.0198	.0193	.0188	.0183	.0178	.0173	.0168
2.4	.0164	.0160	.0155	.0151	.0147	.0143	.0139	.0135	.0131	.0128
2.5	.0124	.0121	.0117	.0114	.0111	.0108	.0105	.0102	.00988	.00960
2.6	.00932	.00905	.00879	.00854	.00829	.00805	.00781	.00759	.00736	.00715
2.7	.00693	.00673	.00653	.00633	.00614	.00596	.00578	.00561	.00544	.00527
2.8	.00511	.00495	.00480	.00465	.00451	.00437	.00424	.00410	.00398	.00385
2.9	.00373	.00361	.00350	.00339	.00328	.00318	.00308	.00298	.00288	.00279

Z_α	.0	.1	.2	.3	.4	.5	.6	.7	.8	.9
3	.00270	.00194	.00137	$.0^{3}967$	$.0^{3}674$	$.0^{3}465$	$.0^{3}318$	$.0^{3}216$	$.0^{3}145$	$.0^{4}962$
4	$.0^{4}413$	$.0^{4}413$	$.0^{4}267$	$.4^{4}171$	$.0^{4}108$	$.0^{5}680$	$.0^{5}422$	$.0^{5}260$	$.0^{6}159$	$.0^{6}958$
5	$.0^{6}573$	$.0^{4}340$	$.0^{6}199$	$.0^{6}116$	$.0^{7}666$	$.0^{7}380$	$.0^{7}214$	$.0^{7}120$	$.0^{8}663$	$.0^{8}364$
6	$.0^{8}197$	$.0^{8}106$	$.0^{9}565$	$.0^{9}298$	$.0^{9}155$	$.0^{10}803$	$.0^{10}411$	$.0^{10}208$	$.0^{10}105$	$.0^{11}520$

From Frederick E. Croxton, *Tables of Areas in Two Tails and in One Tail of the Normal Curve,* Copyright, 1949, by Prentice-Hall, Inc.

APPENDIX 12–B

Cumulative Standardized Normal Distribution

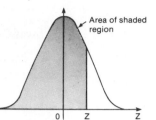

Area of shaded region

x	.00	.01	.02	.03	.04	.05	.06	.07	.08	.09
.0	.5000	.5040	.5080	.5120	.5160	.5199	.5239	.5279	.5319	.5359
.1	.5398	.5438	.5478	.5517	.5557	.5596	.5636	.5675	.5714	.5753
.2	.5793	.5832	.5871	.5910	.5948	.5987	.6026	.6064	.6103	.6141
.3	.6179	.6217	.6255	.6293	.6331	.6368	.6406	.6443	.6480	.6517
.4	.6554	.6591	.6628	.6664	.6700	.6736	.6772	.6808	.6844	.6879
.5	.6915	.6950	.6985	.7019	.7054	.7088	.7123	.7157	.7190	.7224
.6	.7257	.7291	.7324	.7357	.7389	.7422	.7454	.7486	.7517	.7549
.7	.7580	.7611	.7642	.7673	.7704	.7734	.7764	.7794	.7823	.7852
.8	.7881	.7910	.7939	.7967	.7995	.8023	.8051	.8078	.8106	.8133
.9	.8159	.8186	.8212	.8238	.8264	.8289	.8315	.8340	.8365	.8389
1.0	.8413	.8438	.8461	.8485	.8508	.8531	.8554	.8577	.8599	.8621
1.1	.8643	.8665	.8686	.8708	.8729	.8749	.8770	.8790	.8810	.8830
1.2	.8849	.8869	.8888	.8907	.8925	.8944	.8962	.8980	.8997	.9015
1.3	.9032	.9049	.9066	.9082	.9099	.9115	.9131	.9147	.9162	.9177
1.4	.9192	.9207	.9222	.9236	.9251	.9265	.9279	.9292	.9306	.9319
1.5	.9332	.9345	.9357	.9370	.9382	.9394	.9406	.9418	.9429	.9441
1.6	.9452	.9463	.9474	.9484	.9495	.9505	.9515	.9525	.9535	.9545
1.7	.9554	.9564	.9573	.9582	.9591	.9599	.9608	.9616	.9625	.9633
1.8	.9641	.9649	.9656	.9664	.9671	.9678	.9686	.9693	.9699	.9706
1.9	.9713	.9719	.9726	.9732	.9738	.9744	.9750	.9756	.9761	.9767
2.0	.9772	.9778	.9783	.9788	.9793	.9798	.9803	.9808	.9812	.9817
2.1	.9821	.9826	.9830	.9834	.9838	.9842	.9846	.9850	.9854	.9857
2.2	.9861	.9864	.9868	.9871	.9875	.9878	.9881	.9884	.9887	.9890
2.3	.9893	.9896	.9898	.9901	.9904	.9906	.9909	.9911	.9913	.9916
2.4	.9918	.9920	.9922	.9925	.9927	.9929	.9931	.9932	.9934	.9936
2.5	.9938	.9940	.9941	.9943	.9945	.9946	.9948	.9949	.9951	.9952
2.6	.9953	.9955	.9956	.9957	.9959	.9960	.9961	.9962	.9963	.9964
2.7	.9965	.9966	.9967	.9968	.9969	.9970	.9971	.9972	.9973	.9974
2.8	.9974	.9975	.9976	.9977	.9977	.9978	.9979	.9979	.9980	.9981
2.9	.9981	.9982	.9982	.9983	.9984	.9984	.9985	.9985	.9986	.9986
3.0	.9987	.9987	.9987	.9988	.9988	.9989	.9989	.9989	.9990	.9990
3.1	.9990	.9991	.9991	.9991	.9992	.9992	.9992	.9992	.9993	.9993
3.2	.9993	.9993	.9994	.9994	.9994	.9994	.9994	.9995	.9995	.9995
3.3	.9995	.9995	.9995	.9996	.9996	.9996	.9996	.9996	.9996	.9997
3.4	.9997	.9997	.9997	.9997	.9997	.9997	.9997	.9997	.9997	.9998

The entries from 3.49 to 3.61 all equal .9998. The entries from 3.62 to 3.89 all equal .9999. All entries from 3.90 and up equal 1.0000.

From Alexander M. Mood, *Introduction to the Theory of Statistics*, Copyright 1950, McGraw-Hill. Used with permission of McGraw-Hill Book Co.

APPENDIX 12–C

Stratified Sample Selection

Stratified sampling is *not* another statistical estimator like differences and dollar-units. Stratified sampling is a *sample selection strategy* designed to enhance efficiency and accomplish coverage of dollar amounts in audit sampling.

WHY USE STRATIFIED SAMPLING
One important audit sampling objective is *protective sampling*. It has the objective of selecting items randomly to obtain the greatest coverage of dollar amounts for the purpose of guarding auditors from missing material errors. This objective is based on the reasonable premise that the largest overstatement errors can occur in the largest dollar-value population items. Stratified sampling skews the sample item selection toward the high-dollar items. Therefore, it covers more dollars than unstratified, unrestricted random selection, which gives every item an equal chance of selection regardless of size. Stratified samples, however, can be evaluated statistically.

Stratified selection, when strata are based on recorded amounts, tends to include a large proportion of items from strata with large standard deviations (the high-value items). When the finite correction factor is applied properly, this selection design reduces the standard error of the sample and enables an estimator to be more efficient.

For example, if an auditor selected all 100 accounts receivable over $10,000 for audit, the finitely corrected standard error for this stratum would be:

$$S = S' \sqrt{1 - \frac{n}{N}} = 0, \text{ when } n = N$$

The zero standard error for the stratum would be combined with nonzero standard errors for other strata, and the stratified standard error will be smaller than the standard error that would be calculated from an unstratified sample of the same total size. Hence, statistical measurements can be more precise and therefore more efficient.

Almost all practical sampling applications employ stratified designs. The strategy is easily used with machine-readable records and computer assistance. The important additional considerations in stratified sampling are: (1) how to define the relevant strata and (2) how to apportion the total sample to the strata.

DEFINING THE RELEVANT STRATA

Segments (strata) of a population may be identified by professional judgment.[6] Auditors must decide what characteristics of a population are most relevant for the objectives of the audit. The general objective of auditing an account balance calls for stratification of the population units by their dollar balances. Dollar value stratification usually has the effect of differentiating among segments of the population on the basis of relative standard deviation.

For example, suppose that the illustrative accounts receivable population had the following characteristics.[7]

Stratum	Book Value Interval	Number of Account	Total Dollar Amount	Standard Deviation in Stratum	Sample Size
0	$512–$6,870	78	$ 90,000	$1,100.00	78
1	64– 512	1,000	123,500	224.00	236
2	32– 64	1,211	60,000	16.00	115
3	16– 32	3,241	81,000	8.00	155
4	1– 16	2,770	25,000	7.50	47
Strata 1–4		8,222	$289,500		
Total population		8,300	$379,500	$ 133.00	631

Computer programs for optimal stratification are available. A "quick-and-dirty" definition scheme is to stratify items so each stratum contains an approximately equal recorded total amount. Auditors usually identify a top stratum which will be audited 100 percent, as shown in the table above. At least four or five strata should be used. Sometimes auditors use as many as 20 strata.

ALLOCATING THE SAMPLE TO STRATA

The calculation of an optimal sample size for stratified sampling is slightly different:

$$n = \frac{\left(\sum\limits^{k} N_h S_h\right)^2}{\left(\dfrac{TE}{Z_\alpha + Z_\beta}\right)^2 + \sum\limits^{k} N_h S_h^2}$$

---

[6] Optimal stratification rules are available, but are beyond the scope of this textbook. See W. G. Cochran, *Sampling Techniques,* 3rd ed. (New York: John Wiley & Sons, 1977); and Donald M. Roberts, *Statistical Auditing* (New York: AICPA, 1978), chapter 6.

[7] For reference purposes, these data are adaptations from Population 1 used in *Auditing Research Monograph No. 2.* See citation in the Sources and Additional Reading References at the end of this chapter.

where

h = number of the stratum, $h = 1, 2, \ldots k$
N_h = stratum population size in the hth stratum
S_h = standard deviation in the hth stratum

The standard deviation used in this calculation can be the estimated standard deviation (for each stratum) of the recorded book values, the difference estimator, the ratio estimator, or the regression estimator. Methods are available for making preliminary estimates, but they are beyond the scope of this appendix.[8]

The sample can be allocated to strata using mathematically optimal methods. Or, the sample can be allocated in proportion to the book values in the strata (as shown in the right-hand column of the data illustrated in the table). However, each stratum should have a sample of at least 30 items.

MATHEMATICAL CALCULATIONS   When the evidence is evaluated, the average of the stratified statistic (difference) is weighed by the population size in each stratum:

$$\bar{D} = \frac{\sum_{h=0}^{k} (N_h \bar{D}_h)}{N}$$

where

$\bar{D}_h$ = Mean of differences in the hth stratum

The stratified average may then be used to calculate the projected likely error by simple extension in the manner illustrated in Chapter 12 for averages based on the unstratified samples. Equations to calculate stratified ratio and regression point estimates are more complex and are beyond the scope of the appendix.[9]

Since strata sample sizes can be very large in proportion to strata population sizes, common practice is to apply finite correction to the calculation of standard error of the estimate. The stratified standard error expressed in total dollars is:

$$S = \sqrt{\Sigma N_h^2 \left(1 - \frac{n_h}{N_h}\right) \frac{S_h^2}{n_h}}$$

where

S_h = Standard deviation in the hth stratum

---

[8] See Donald M. Roberts, *Statistical Auditing* (New York: AICPA, 1978), chap. 5.
[9] See Roberts, *Statistical Auditing*, chap. 6.

This standard error can be used in evaluating the evidence and calculating possible error in the same manner illustrated in Chapter 12 for unstratified statistics. Equations to calculate stratified error for ratio and regression statistics are more complex and are beyond the scope of this appendix.[10]

APPENDIX 12–D

Dollar-Unit Sampling

Dollar-unit sampling (DUS) is a modified form of attributes sampling that permits auditors to reach conclusions about dollar amounts. Variations are called *combined attributes-variables* sampling (CAV), *cumulative monetary amount* sampling (CMA), and sampling with *probability proportionate to size* (PPS).

Recall from Chapter 11 the discussion of the point that compliance audit of control procedures based on attribute statistics did not directly incorporate dollar measurements. Hence, conclusions were limited to decisions about the rate of control deviations.

DUS is a sampling plan that corresponds dollar amounts to attribute statistics. It facilitates conclusions about dollar balances and totals and about the exposure of dollar amounts to control deviations. The method has been discussed extensively by Canadian authorities[11] and is used by many U.S. accounting firms. The method purports to overcome difficulties inherent in other sampling plans, such as:

☐   Unstratified sampling plans may call for large sample sizes.

☐   Classical statistics estimators suffer problems of bias because a sufficient number of differences may not be found in a sample to permit proper use.

☐   Complex stratification plans are not necessary. DUS accomplishes stratification by automatically selecting a large proportion of high-value items.

The beauty of attribute statistics is that they do not require the assumptions about the normal distribution, as do all the classical statistical methods. The problem is in *pricing* the results. DUS has overcome this problem.

However, DUS sampling also has some disadvantages. They include:

☐   The DUS pricing of errors is conservative (high) because rigorous mathematical proof of DUS upper error limit calculations has not yet been accomplished.

---

[10] See Roberts, *Statistical Auditing,* chap. 6.

[11] Leslie, Tietlebaum, and Anderson, *Dollar-Unit Sampling,* as cited in the Sources and Additional reading References at the end of Chapter 12.

□ DUS is not designed to evaluate financial account *understatement* very well. (No sampling estimator is considered very effective for understatement error, however.)

□ Expanding a dollar-unit sample is difficult when preliminary results indicate a decision that a balance is materially misstated.

USE OF DOLLAR-UNIT SAMPLING (DUS)

The use of DUS in compliance and account balance auditing can be inferred from the advantages and disadvantages indicated above. DUS is clearly the best method to use for auditing account balances that have a high expectation of no errors or very few errors, and where the greatest risk of error is the risk that the book value is overstated. In all other situations, such as (1) the expectation of many errors, (2) very little basis to estimate the number of errors, or (3) the expectation of both the understatement and overstatement of book values, caution is advised. A careful evaluation of the audit situation and alternative sampling methods is recommended before selecting DUS.

SELECTING THE SAMPLE

The trick that enables DUS to correspond dollar amounts to attribute statistics is to define the population as individual $1 units, each of which is an item subject to being included in the sample. For example, the 8,300 accounts receivable totaling $379,500 would be defined as 379,500 dollar units. (Imagine the accounts being represented by 379,500 dollar bills spread out on a table.)

Now imagine drawing a sample of 100 individual $1 items (disregarding for the moment which customers' accounts turn up in the sample). Assume an auditor wants to select 100 dollar units for audit. Basically, the selection process is to obtain a random starting point and select every 3,795th *dollar* as a sample item. (This is a type of *systematic selection*.) This method assures that the largest customer's account ($6,870) will be included in the sample, and in fact, all larger *customer accounts* have a greater likelihood of selection than smaller ones because the former contain more dollar units. (For example, a $2,000 customer account is 10 times more likely to contain a dollar chosen in the sample than another customer's $200 account.) This selection is still random, however, because the theoretical sampling unit is the dollar, not the customer. The effect is a very high degree of stratification of the population.

Other methods are available for selecting dollar unit samples. A computer is convenient but not always necessary.

SAMPLE SIZE CALCULATION

The basic equation for calculation of DUS sample size is:

$$n = \frac{RA \times RF}{TE}$$

where

TE = tolerable error considered material
RA = total recorded amount (book value)
RF = a DUS *risk factor* related to the risk of incorrect acceptance. Risk factors when zero errors are expected are:

Risk of Incorrect Acceptance	Risk Factor[12]
20%	1.61
15%	1.90
10%	2.31
5%	3.00
2.5%	3.69
1%	4.61

In the accounts receivable example (Chapter 12), with risk of incorrect acceptance = 0.20, the DUS sample size would be 24:

$$n = \frac{RA \times RF}{TE} = \frac{379{,}500 \times 1.61}{25{,}000} = 24$$

This calculation of sample size, however, holds some dangers. While the calculation controls the risk of incorrect acceptance, a very high risk of incorrect rejection exists. For example, if 6.5 percent of the dollars in the accounts receivable are 100 percent fictitious (a total overstatement of $24,667.50 = 0.065 \times \$379,500$, almost equal to the $25,000 tolerable error), the probability of finding at least one such dollar in the sample is 0.80.[13] Thus, with a sample of 24 dollar units (representing 24 different customer accounts) from a materially accurate balance, there is an 80 percent chance that the decision will be that the balance is not materially accurate. (Discovering one 100 percent error would cause the upper error limit to be about $47,400 which is greater than TE = $25,000.)

DUS samplers usually take some precautions to control both risks simultaneously. The effect is to select samples larger than those given by the equation shown above. Some auditors recommend a minimum sample of 100 for this purpose.

The important thing about sample size calculation is that it produces the average sampling interval (ASI):

$$ASI = \frac{RA}{n} = \frac{TE}{RF}$$

---

[12] In the *Audit Sampling* guide (AICPA, 1983), the risk factor is also called the "assurance factor" and the "reliability factor."

[13] The probability is estimated by $1 - (1 - \text{rate})^n = 1 - (1 - .065)^{24} = 0.80 =$ the probability of including at least one occurrence of a 100 percent error in a sample of 24 dollar units when the proportion of such occurrences in the population is 6.5 percent.

The ASI is very useful in pricing the sample results and performing the quantitative analysis of evidence.

PRICING THE RESULTS

The problem with attribute sampling is expression of the results in terms of a deviation rate instead of in dollars. In an audit context, expressing results in dollars is generally conceded to be more meaningful.

Suppose 100 customer accounts had been selected at random and none were found in error. Attribute statistics would enable an auditor to say at most 3 percent (CUL, Appendix 11–C.2) were in error with 5 percent risk of incorrect acceptance. So what does this proportion mean in terms of dollars?

One assumption is to price the 249 accounts (3% × 8,300) at the value of the largest account(s). Using the largest account of $6,870 and the next largest ones, assume that this measure amounts to $200,000. This amount is huge in relation to the $379,500 book value and is clearly unreasonable.

Another assumption is to price the 249 accounts at the average book value (RA/N = $379,500/8,300 = $45.72), which results in a measure of $11,385 = 249 × $45.72. This result is more reasonable, but is still based on a pricing assumption.

Dollar-unit sampling makes only one assumption: The maximum amount of overstatement in a sample item cannot exceed the book value of the sample item itself. Otherwise, the pricing is based on attribute statistics.

When a dollar-unit sample is audited, determinations are made of: (1) the dollar amount of difference between the audit value and the book value of the *logical unit*—the account or invoice—that contains the sampled dollar and (2) the ratio of the difference to the recorded amount of the logical unit. This ratio is called the *tainting percentage* and can be positive (indicating understatement) or negative (indicating overstatement). The simplest DUS pricing evaluation occurs when no errors are found in the sample. In this case, the pricing of the upper error limit (UEL in dollars) is:

$$\text{UEL in dollars} = \text{RF} \times \text{ASI}$$

In our example of n = 100, RF = 1.61 and ASI = $3,795, the attributes-type UEL converts to a UEL in dollars of $6,110 = 1.61 × 3,795.[14] This UEL in dollars is interpreted as the dollar amount of error in the population, subject to a 20 percent risk that the total population error might be larger.

When one or more errors are found, they are arrayed in order of their tainting percentages for purposes of evaluation. A table based on Poisson

---

[14] If the sample size 24.4398 (= ($379,500 × 1.61)/$25,000) had been used, the ASI would have been $15,527.95 (= $379,500/24.4398), and the UEL based on zero errors would be exactly $25,000 (= 1.61 × $15,527.95). Instead, the sample size of 100 is used as an illustration.

probabilities is consulted for the risk factor and the "precision gap widening (PGW)" factors, as shown below. (The risk factor plus 1.0 plus the PGW factor(s) gives the UEL factors shown in the table. For example, if one error is found and evaluation is made at 20 percent risk of incorrect acceptance, the UEL factor = 1.61 + 1.0 + 0.39 = 3.00.)

Table of Selected UEL and PGW Factors

| Number of Sample Errors | Risk of Incorrect Acceptance | | | | | |
| | 20 percent | | 10 percent | | 5 percent | |
	UEL	PGW	UEL	PGW	UEL	PGW
0*	1.61	—	2.31	—	3.00	—
1	3.00	.39	3.89	.58	4.75	.75
2	4.28	.28	5.33	.44	6.30	.55
3	5.52	.24	6.69	.36	7.76	.46
4	6.73	.21	8.00	.31	9.16	.40
5	7.91	.18	9.28	.28	10.52	.36

* Basic risk factor.
Source: Adapted from D. Leslie, A. Teitlebaum, and R. Anderson, *Dollar-Unit Sampling* (Toronto: Copp Clark Pitman, 1979.)

For example, suppose three errors were found, and their tainting percentages were 90, 80, and 75 percent. All three were errors of overstatement in the book value. The DUS evaluation scheme uses the taintings and the PGW factors as shown in the table below. (These data are based on an assumed sample size of 100 and an ASI of $3,795.)

	Basic Error, Likely Error, and PGW Factors	× Tainting Percentage ×	Average Sampling Interval =	Dollar Measurement
1. Basic error	1.61	100%	$3,795	$6,110
2. Most likely error				
1st error	1.00	90	3,795	$3,416
2nd error	1.00	80	3,795	3,036
3rd error	1.00	75	3,795	2,846
Projected likely error				9,298
3. Precision gap widening				
1st error	.39	90	3,795	$1,332
2nd error	.28	80	3,795	850
3rd error	.24	75	3,795	683
				2,865
Total upper error limit (20 percent risk of incorrect acceptance)				$18,273

DUS evaluation provides ways to calculate the UEL in dollars when both overstatement and understatement errors are found. While not particularly complicated, these evaluations are too involved for adequate explanation in this short appendix.

USING DUS   Dollar-unit sampling can be used to audit any population denominated in dollars for which a book value of sample logical units (for example, customers' accounts receivable or sales invoices) is available. DUS can also be used in compliance auditing to yield a "dollarized" attribute conclusion which measures the number of dollars exposed to control deviations.

The method is powerful and efficient. A computer is not necessary, but many audit organizations have computer software or time-sharing access to facilitate DUS sample selection and evaluation. Independent and internal auditors, having learned the other methods of variables sampling evaluation, are now learning how to use DUS. It is fast becoming a major statistical sampling tool.

PART 3

Audit Program Applications

CHAPTER 13

		PROFESSIONAL STANDARDS SOURCES

Compendium Section	Document Reference	Topic
AU 311	SAS 22	Planning and Supervision
AU 9311		Interpretations: Planning and Supervision
AU 320	SAS 1	The Auditor's Study and Evaluation of Internal Control
AU 333	SAS 19	Client Representations
AU 335	SAS 45	Related Parties

Revenue Cycle

The overall objective of gathering evidence is to provide the audit team with reasonable assurance that the financial statements do not contain material misstatements. This reasonable assurance can be gained in two general approaches which parallel the second and third field standards. Auditors can rely on the *controls* in the system processing the transactions to give assurance that material errors which lead to material misstatements could not occur (that is, the study and evaluation of internal control). The other approach is to rely on the audit of the *results* of the processing system—the account balances—to give assurance that material errors did not occur (that is, gathering sufficient competent evidential matter by auditing the balances).

These two approaches are not mutually exclusive. They are interdependent approaches toward the same objective. However, to conduct an efficient audit, the planned reliance on each approach must be made for each client and for each major area. The two approaches viewed together imply that the amount of evidential matter (third field standard) will vary inversely with reliance on internal control. Further, the combination of the two approaches should provide a reasonable basis for the opinion, although the proportion of assurance derived from the two approaches will vary among cases (SAS 1, AU 320.82). The material on the application of audit techniques in the chapters in Part 3 is organized around these two approaches.

When planning the audit, two other considerations must be understood: flow of transactions and timing of the audit work. Auditors must understand the system that processes each significant class of transactions (a point emphasized in Chapter 7). Audit firms have found that one efficient way to accomplish this review of control procedures and techniques is to classify transactions into "cycles" of related activities. While the number and composition of cycles may vary from company to company, certain cycles are common to every company. The audit team is concerned with control procedures throughout the cycle, from the initiation of the transaction between the entity under audit and outside parties to the final financial reporting of the transaction. Therefore, the understanding of transaction flows must include activities that are not part of the formal accounting system, such as accepting sales orders, selecting vendors, and hiring personnel.

Frequently, the study and evaluation of internal control is accomplished before year-end. This *interim work* allows an audit manager to evaluate the controls within each cycle, audit those to be relied upon as part of interim work, and make modifications to the preliminary program of procedures to be performed after year-end. The audit work can then be scheduled to take advantage of the manpower available within the audit firm and provide evidence for evaluation of control in the processing of transactions before the account balances are ready to be audited.

The material in Part 3 has been organized as follows and gives consideration both to the cycle concept and the normal interim work:

A. The review of the flow of transactions and the internal controls, compliance auditing and evaluation of controls are organized around four cycles:

Chapter 13   Revenue Cycle (sales—receivables—cash receipts).

Chapter 14   Acquisition and Expenditure Cycle (purchasing—inventory and fixed assets—payables—cash disbursements).

Chapter 15   Personnel and Payroll Cycle (hiring—payroll—labor distribution—accruals).

Chapter 16   Conversion Cycle (production planning—cost accounting—property accounting—inventory management).

B. Evidence-gathering procedures related to the details of account balances:

Chapter 17   Current Assets, Current Liabilities and Related Accounts.

Chapter 18   Long-Term Assets, Equities and Related Accounts.

C. Wrapping up the audit: Evidence-gathering procedures related to other revenue and expenses, completion of the field work and audit review procedures are covered in Chapter 19.

LEARNING OBJECTIVES   The four major learning objectives in this chapter are linked to the tools and techniques described in previous chapters. Your objectives, which relate to the revenue cycle, are to understand:

☐ A business approach to the review of the revenue cycle.

☐ The flow of transactions in a typical revenue cycle, the effect on specific accounts and the elements of control within the revenue cycle.

☐ Audit procedures used to gather evidence regarding the compliance with control procedures.

☐ Evaluation of the controls (strengths) and lack of controls (weaknesses) to determine the effect upon the nature, timing and extent of procedures for auditing account balances.

The explanation of each of these four topics is intended to enable you to relate the background material described in previous chapters to the revenue cycle.

The study and evaluation of internal accounting controls in the revenue cycle is presented as a systematic approach which relates all audit work to overall objectives and to specific objectives of each step. The transactions typically classified as part of the revenue cycle are those which flow through the following business activities:

Receiving and accepting customer orders.

Order entry.

Credit granting.

Delivering goods and services.

Relieving inventory records for goods shipped.

Billing.

Determining cost of sales.

Cash receipts.

Collection activities on delinquent accounts.

Notice that this *cycle approach* encompasses the activities from the initial sales source through the formal accounting recording to the cash collections.

A BUSINESS APPROACH   A broad view of operations is very helpful in the planning stage of an audit engagement, as stated succinctly in SAS 22 (AU 311.07):

> The auditor should obtain a knowledge of matters that relate to the nature of the client's business, its organization, and its operating characteristics. Such matters include, for example, the type of business, types of products and services, capital structure, related parties, locations, and production, distribution and compensation methods. The auditor should also consider matters affecting the industry in which the entity operates, such as economic conditions, government regulations and changes in technology, as they relate to his examination. Other matters, such as accounting practices common to the industry, competitive conditions and, if available, financial trends and ratios should also be considered by the auditor.

Relating this broad statement to the revenue cycle, auditors should obtain an in-depth understanding of the client's marketing function, credit policies, sales valuation, related accounting policies and compliance with applicable laws.

Marketing

Comprehending the marketing function is central to understanding the occurrence of revenue-producing transactions and the existence of cash and receivables balances. Further, the marketing function is pervasive in that production plans, inventory management and research and development programs are also affected by marketing operations.

One of the first things that auditors should understand is the company's product or service and the manner in which it is exchanged. Outright sales create few accounting and auditing problems, but other exchange methods, such as leasing, franchising, film distribution and construction contracting can cause special revenue-recognition problems.[1] Auditors should be aware of marketing forecasts, industry trends, market share analyses and performance monitoring reports that relate to the client's product or service.

Credit Policies and Office Procedures

The credit policies of the company and the terms and types of accounts must be understood for an informed audit. Auditors should become familiar with the system of control provided by the office procedures for sales order origination, credit approval, billing, shipping and collection. For example, if these office procedures are scattered in many branch locations, an entirely different audit plan would be adopted than had they been centralized in a home office.

Sales Valuation

With respect to sales valuation, the various accounting methods of revenue recognition become of paramount importance. For example, lease and franchise contract terms should be read with care. When the client is in the construction business and the percentage-of-completion method is used, construction sites should be visited for a firsthand view of progress.

Marketing policies for pricing should be understood. For example, any long-term, fixed-price sales commitments should be reviewed in the light of expected costs over the term of the contract. Likewise, the policy and experience with returns and allowances should be reviewed. These will affect the valuation of net sales.

Accounting Policies

Accounting principles applicable to all companies require separate disclosure of receivables from directors, officers, subsidiaries, and affiliates. Auditors should, as a matter of familiarization, inquire about such trans-

---

[1] Technical discussion of special accounting issues can be found in AICPA audit and accounting guides on subjects such as "Accounting for Franchise Fee Revenue," "Accounting for Retail Land Sales," "Banks," "Fire and Casualty Insurance Companies," "Hospitals," "Construction Contractors," and other titles available from the AICPA Publications Division.

actions with related parties.[2] In the light of industry practices and the company's liquidity position, inquiry should also be made if any receivables have been sold, assigned or pledged as collateral.

Further, the SEC has rules for disclosures relating to liquidity. For example, among these rules is the requirement that any cash balance held as a compensating balance pursuant to a formal agreement should be segregated on the balance sheet. Compensating balances not embodied in formal agreements should be disclosed in a footnote. A review of cash management planning can reveal such formal and informal arrangements.

Public companies must report sales and profits by segments in accordance with FASB *Statement No. 14*. Therefore, the auditor must be alert to client products that might qualify as separate segments. Several preceding comments on leases, franchises and construction revenues are also relevant to the requirement that all significant accounting policies be disclosed (see APB *Opinion No. 22*).[3]

Legal Compliance

The Truth in Lending Act must be observed by any company with receivables. A review of disclosures made to debtors can provide evidence of compliance with this law.

Companies that sell products must observe the Robinson-Patman Act (dealing with fair pricing), the antitrust acts (relevant to market activities) and various laws governing the use of alcohol and drugs in production. The collection and payment of sales and excise taxes on sales is another area where compliance is particularly relevant.

REVIEW PHASE: FLOW OF TRANSACTIONS AND ELEMENTS OF CONTROL

A proper study and evaluation of internal control, as required by the second field standard, is divided into three phases. These phases, described in Chapter 7 and shown in Exhibit 7–1, are: (a) preliminary review, (b) completion of the review, and (c) compliance auditing procedures.

In this and the following chapters, no attempt is made to distinguish between the preliminary and the completion phases of the review, although most of the material applies to the completion phase where *specific controls* are identified for reliance. Understanding *the flow of transactions through the accounting system* is considered an integral part of the review. However, most students are not familiar with the common steps, significant documents and appropriate controls in the flow of transactions in the major transaction cycles. Therefore, the approach in this and subsequent chapters is to provide a model illustration with flowcharts

---

[2] As required by FASB *Statement No. 57*, "Related Party Disclosures," and by *Statements on Auditing Standards No. 45* (AU 1020), "Omnibus Statement: Related Parties" and *Statement on Auditing Standards No. 19* (AU 333), "Client Representations."

[3] "Disclosure of Accounting Policies." See also "Segment Information" (SAS 21, AU 435).

and narrative descriptions. Thus, the material that follows is a combination of an example of the flow of transactions through the revenue cycle and an example of the review of common controls in that cycle.

The review of the revenue cycle is primarily a process of obtaining information about the flow of transactions and control procedures *the client thinks are in effect*. The primary purpose is to identify control procedures (*strengths*) that the audit team may choose to rely upon and lack of controls (*weaknesses*) which will affect subsequent testing. Secondary objectives of the review are: (1) to identify populations of documents which give evidence of compliance with procedures (where documents are filed, in what order, prenumbered, cross-reference numbers), (2) to identify evidence that may be used in substantive procedures and (3) to identify nonmaterial weakness which should be mentioned in the management letter.

The documentation of the review takes one of three forms: a narrative description, an internal control questionnaire or a flowchart. The following flowcharts and questionnaires are illustrative of this working paper documentation. You should understand that the preparation of review working papers such as flowcharts is a *means to an end,* not the end itself. Therefore, as the auditor prepares these working papers, the purpose of the review—to identify controls that may be relied upon—must always be kept in mind. In practice, the control objectives illustrated in this chapter as part of the evaluation are considered throughout the review.

Frequently, auditors will prepare additional working papers to document the strengths and weaknesses identified in the flowcharts or questionnaires. The strengths, which will be relied upon, are further identified for compliance auditing. The weaknesses are evaluated for their possible impact on specific financial statement items and the consequent effect on substantive procedures. These working papers, sometimes called *bridging working papers* because they "bridge" the review findings and the next audit steps, take many forms and are not illustrated herein.

The understanding of the transaction flow is obtained through interviews, observation and collecting sample documents. A technique frequently employed is to *walk through* a transaction from its initiation to its recording in the accounting records, sometimes called a "sample of one." The revenue cycle walk-through involves following a sale from the initial order through credit approval, billing and shipment of goods to the entry in the sales journal and subsidiary account receivable records. Sample documents are collected and each department involved is questioned about its specific duties.

The flowchart exhibits in this chapter present model organizational systems for control of sales, cash receipts, and accounts receivable. Each flowchart illustrates the segregation of functions considered characteristic of satisfactory internal control. You should thoroughly understand the flow of the transactions by studying each flowchart and the interconnections between the flowcharts. You may need to review the standard flowchart symbols described in Exhibit 7–3 in Chapter 7. Exhibits 13–3, 13–5 and 13–8 contain internal control questionnaire items typical of these systems. Actual internal control questionnaires are designed with columns for the auditor to check Yes, No, or Not Applicable and a Remarks column to write comments (as illustrated in Chapter 7, Exhibit 7–2). The questions are worded such that a No answer points out a control weakness. "No" answers are usually cross-referenced in the Remarks column to: (1) audit program steps designed to recognize the weakness or a memorandum which explains compensating controls or the lack of importance of the item and (2) a working paper memorandum of all items to be included in the management letter comments on internal accounting control. The questionnaires illustrated in this chapter contain only the questions. Taken together, the flowcharts and the questionnaire items describe desirable control features for each of the three revenue cycle systems: sales, cash receipts and accounts receivables.

Sales Procedures   Exhibit 13–1 depicts part of a sales procedure system. The external stimulus for a sales transaction is shown originating with the customer. Thus, a customer's purchase order may exist as a basic file document evidencing the existence of an actual order. Thereafter, the internal data processing system takes over. The flowchart description of such a sales document processing system begins with the operations shown in Exhibit 13–1.

Sales invoice blanks should be controlled in a sales order section of the sales department and issued only on receipt of a stimulus, such as a customer's written or telephoned purchase order. Prenumbered sales in-

EXHIBIT 13–1
Sales Invoice Origination

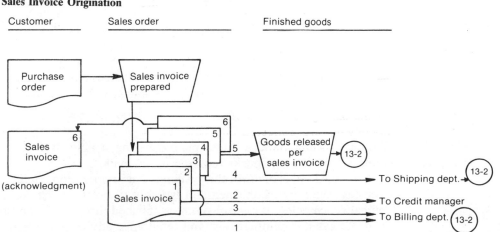

voice forms should be used so that someone can check the numbering sequence for missing invoices. If a credit sale is involved, approval of credit should be obtained from a separate credit department prior to the final preparation of the sales invoice.

Copies of the approved invoice are then distributed as authority for other departments to act:

Copies 1 and 3 go to the billing department as authority for billing (after matching with the shipping copy).

Copy 2 goes to the credit manager for credit approval (before the other copies are released).

Copy 4 (packing list copy) goes to the shipping department as authority to pack and ship.

Copy 5 goes to an inventory location as authority to release goods to the shipping department.

Copy 6 is returned to the customer as an acknowledgement of the order.

According to the flowchart, as each action is carried out, copies of the invoice document are transmitted in parallel so that accounting awareness of activities follows the activities themselves. Notice also that segregation of functional responsibilities is maintained among: (1) authority to initiate a transaction, (2) physical custody of assets and (3) responsibility for account recordkeeping.

The sales invoice documents of authorization continue along their way through the shipping, billing and accounts receivable bookkeeping departments shown in Exhibit 13–2.

Eventually, copies 1, 4 and 6 of the invoice are sent to the customer, and copies 2, 3 and 5 are filed in the credit, billing and accounts receivable departments as documentary evidence of the entire process that produced accounting records of a sale and an associated account receivable. Following this flow of documents, duties, operations and files should give the auditor a thorough understanding of the internal accounting control system. In particular, the flowchart should enable the auditor to identify and locate important *files of accounting records*. Knowledge of these files becomes very important for designing compliance and substantive audit procedures. Typical internal control questionnaire (ICQ) items are shown in Exhibit 13–3.

Cash Receipts Exhibit 13–4 depicts a cash receipts processing system. It describes pro-
Procedures cedures for handling checks received in the mail.

When the mail is opened, the system is put in operation. Initial control over cash must be established and is likely to be the most sensitive to control deficiencies. If control is not established through (1) a cash register or (2) a daily remittance list and remittance advice document, subse-

**EXHIBIT 13–2
Accounting for Sales
Invoices**

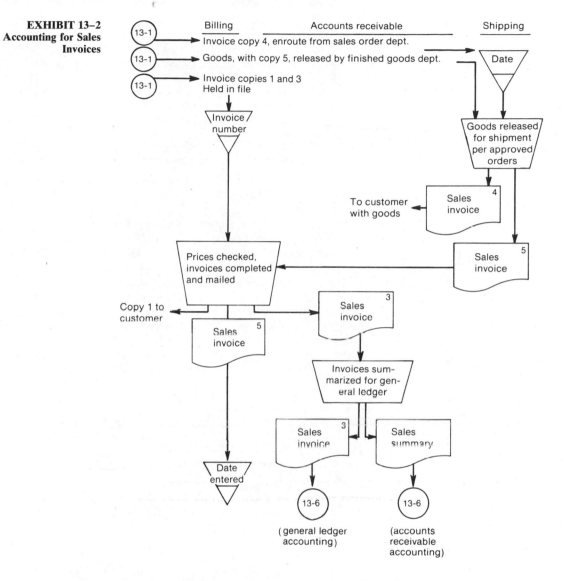

quent data processing control features may not be able to detect omission of data in a timely manner.

Throughout the data processing, the custody of cash and the record-keeping functions should be kept separate. Receipts should be deposited daily and intact. (No money is removed from the cash received.) Thus, basic documentary evidence of mail cash receipts exists in files in the form of remittance lists, bank deposit slips, remittance advice copies, the accounts receivable subsidiary records, and the accounts receivable and cash control accounts. Periodic reconciliation of the accounts receivable

EXHIBIT 13–3
Internal Control
Questionnaire—Sales
System

1. Are sales invoice blanks prenumbered? Controlled in the sales order department?

2. Are all credit sales approved by the credit department prior to shipment?

3. Is the credit department independent of the sales department?

4. Are sales prices and terms based on approved standards? Are deviations from standard approved by a responsible officer?

5. Are prenumbered bills of lading or other shipping documents prepared or completed in the shipping department?

6. Are shipping quantities checked against invoice quantities in the billing department? Explain alternate procedures, if any.

7. Are numerical sequences of invoices and shipping documents checked in the billing department?

8. Are sales invoices checked for error in the billing department for prices, credit terms, extensions and footing, freight allowances and checked with customers' orders?

9. Is there an overall check on arithmetic accuracy of period sales data by a statistical or product-line analysis?

10. Are periodic sales data reported directly to general ledger accounting independent of accounts receivable accounting?

11. Are returned sales credits and other credits supported by documentation as to receipt, condition and quantity, and approved by a responsible officer?

12. Are sales of the following types controlled by the same procedures described above? Sales to employees, COD sales, disposals of property, cash sales and scrap sales.

13. Are detail records maintained on a computer system? If so, complete relevant portions of the computer internal control questionnaire.

EXHIBIT 13–4
Initial Cash Receipts
Control

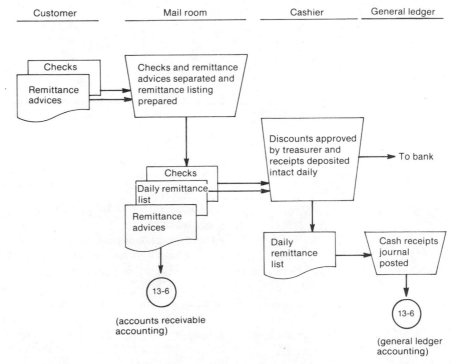

subsidiary ledger with the control account and monthly statements sent to customers should detect errors of posting and errors of an omitted remittance from the daily list and bank deposit.

Not shown in the flowchart, but important for satisfactory control, is the reconciliation of the bank statement. The reconciliation should be done by someone not otherwise responsible for handling cash or cash records. In some companies, the internal auditors do the reconciliations. Internal auditors may also be involved in control functions such as review of access to cash registers, deposit slips and other cash records. Typical ICQ items about cash receipts are provided in Exhibit 13–5.

A wide variety of cash receipts transactions may occur in addition to those associated with normal sales. Other receipts may arise from dividends and interest on investments, proceeds from sale of assets or scrap

EXHIBIT 13–5
Internal Control
Questionnaire—Cash
Receipts System

A. General.
  1. Are receipts deposited daily, intact and without delay?
  2. Does the cashier control cash from the time it is received in his or her department until deposit?
  3. Does someone other than the cashier or accounts receivable bookkeeper take the deposits to the bank?
  4. Is a duplicate deposit slip retained by the internal auditor or someone other than the employee making up the deposit?
  5. Are the duties of the cashier entirely separate from recordkeeping for notes and accounts receivable? From general ledger recordkeeping?
  6. Is the cashier prevented from obtaining access to receivables records or monthly statements?
  7. Are all other cash funds (for example, petty cash) and securities handled by someone other than the cashier?
  8. Is any employee having custody of client cash funds prevented from having custody of nonclient funds (such as credit union or benefit funds)?
  9. Do branch offices collect cash? Are withdrawals from branch office accounts controlled by a central office?
  10. Are rents, dividends, interest and similar receipts accounted for by accrual or other means so that their nonreceipt would be noticed? Explain.
  11. Is a bank reconciliation performed monthly by someone who does not have cash custody or recordkeeping responsibility?

B. Mail and Currency Receipts.
  1. Is mail opened by someone other than the cashier or accounts receivable recordkeeper? Are daily remittance lists and remittance advices prepared by this person?
  2. Is the daily remittance list compared to the daily deposit by someone other than the cashier?
  3. Are the daily remittance lists and deposit slips compared to the cash receipts book and accounts receivable credits regularly?
  4. Are currency receipts controlled by mechanical devices? Are machine totals checked by the internal auditor?
  5. Are prenumbered sales or receipts books used? Is the numerical sequence checked by the accounting department?
  6. Are detail transaction records maintained on a computer system? If so, complete relevant portions of the computer internal control questionnaire.

materials, proceeds from loans or other financing transactions and similar sources. With regard to these receipts, the basic control characteristics of segregation of responsibilities, system of authorization and system of error-checking routines should exist.

Accounts Receivable Procedures

The accounts receivable recordkeeping is an end point for aspects of both sales and cash receipts transactions, resulting in the maintenance of subsidiary accounts receivable records. Notice that no actual cash (checks, currency or coin) appears in the custody of personnel who perform the operations shown in Exhibit 13–6.

The general ledger segment of the flowchart in Exhibit 13–6 also describes maintenance of accounts receivable, cash and sales control accounts.

EXHIBIT 13–6
Accounts Receivable and
General Ledger
Accounting

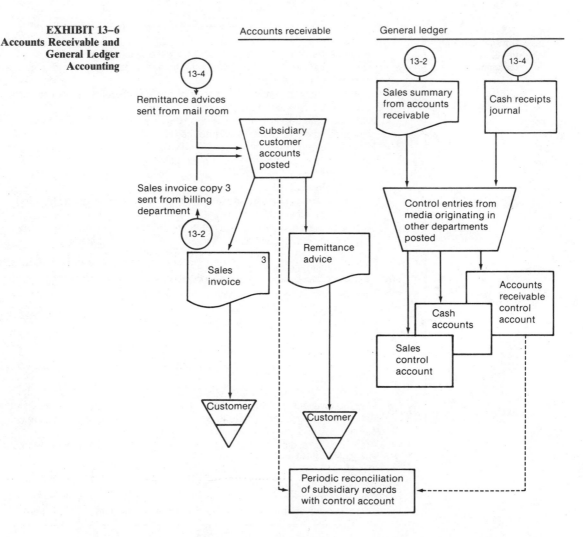

Noncash credits to accounts receivable (such as, sales returns and allowances, settlement of disputed bills) are shown in Exhibit 13–7. These accounting controls are of particular interest to an auditor. The credit manager's authorization of noncash credits should be in conformity with company policy and should be supported by suitable explanations.

EXHIBIT 13–7
Credit Memo Procedure

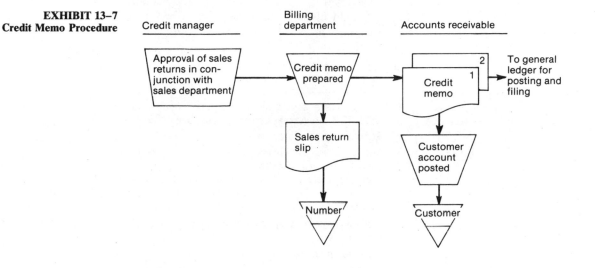

Five accounts receivable control procedures other than the normal processing of charges and credits are important:

1. *Sales returns* Authority to approve credit for a return should rest with the credit manager, and evidence of the physical return should exist (for example, a sales return receiving slip). The credit manager should not handle cash or keep records relative to the credit memo documents.

2. *Collection effort.* The accounts receivable department should analyze the accounts (for example, using an aged trial balance) and transmit this information to the credit manager for follow-up.

3. *Account write-offs.* The collection effort should be coordinated with the write-off authority that requires final approval of the treasurer.

4. *Monthly statements.* The mailing of monthly statements is an important regular activity that enhances the control process. The mailing should be handled only by the accounts receivable department and should include all accounts each month.

5. *Internal auditors.* The internal auditors may serve as control points in a second-level control over accounts written off and may occasionally conduct a review of credit memos and aged accounts receivable

schedules. The internal auditors may also conduct periodic surprise confirmation of accounts as an audit procedure. The auditors should be especially alert to transactions involving officers, directors, affiliates and subsidiaries.

Receivables that arise from sources other than sales (such as advances to officers, insurance claims, returned goods claims, deposits and prepayments) should also be authorized in connection with the activity that causes them. These other activities could involve the notes receivable system, the cash disbursement system, the purchasing-receiving system, or another method of authorization.

EXHIBIT 13–8
Internal Control
Questionnaire—Accounts
and Notes Receivable

1. Are customers' subsidiary records maintained by someone who has no access to cash? Is the cashier denied access to the records?

2. Are customers' records balanced monthly with the general ledger account?

3. Are customers' statements mailed monthly? Is the mailing controlled by the accounts receivable department? Are differences noted by customers routed to someone outside the accounts receivable department?

4. Are delinquent accounts listed periodically for review by someone other than the credit manager?

5. Are written-off accounts kept in a memo ledger or credit report file for periodic access?

6. Are credit memo documents prenumbered and controlled?

7. Are noncash credits, discounts allowed after discount date and return credits subject to approval by a responsible officer?

8. Are returned goods checked against receiving reports?

9. Is management of the credit department functionally separated from the sales department?

10. Are direct confirmations of accounts and notes obtained periodically by the internal auditor?

11. Are notes authorized by a responsible official? Are large loans or advances to related persons approved by the directors?

12. Are notes receivable under the custody of someone other than the cashier or accounts receivable recordkeeper?

13. Is custody of negotiable collateral in the hands of someone not responsible for handling cash or keeping records?

14. Are detailed records of accounts and notes transactions maintained on a computer system? If so, complete relevant portions of the computer internal control questionnaire.

EVALUATION OF
REVENUE CYCLE
CONTROL

When the review phase is completed, usually by a junior audit team member, the audit manager must evaluate the revenue cycle control to determine the degree of reliance. The audit manager will use a systematic framework to determine the strength of the controls in the cycle. The internal accounting control objectives listed in Exhibit 7–6 (Chapter 7)

	General Objectives	Examples of Specific Objectives
EXHIBIT 13–9 **Internal Accounting** **Control Objectives** **Revenue Cycle (Sales)**	1. Recorded sales are *valid* and documented.	Customer purchase orders support invoices. Bills of lading or other shipping documentation exist for all invoices. Recorded sales in sales journal supported by invoices.
	2. Valid sales transactions are *recorded* and none omitted.	Invoices, shipping documents and sales orders are prenumbered and numerical sequence is checked. Overall comparisons of sales are made periodically by a statistical or product-line analysis.
	3. Sales are *authorized* according to company policy.	Credit sales approved by credit department. Prices used in preparing invoices are from authorized price schedule.
	4. Sales invoices are *accurately* prepared.	Invoice quantities compared to shipment and customer order quantities. Prices checked and mathematical accuracy independently checked after invoice prepared.
	5. Sales transactions are properly *classified*.	Sales to subsidiaries and affiliates classified as intercompany sales and receivables. Sales returns and allowances properly classified.
	6. Sales transaction *accounting* is proper.	Credit sales posted to customers' individual accounts. Sales journal posted to general ledger account. Sales recognized in accordance with generally accepted accounting principles.
	7. Sales transactions are recorded in the *proper period*.	Sales invoices recorded on shipment date.

provide such a framework. These objectives are stated in specific terms for sales in Exhibit 13–9. A similar evaluation of cash receipts and accounts receivable by specific objectives would be performed by the audit manager.

The audit manager must decide which systems in the revenue cycle contain enough strengths (controls) to rely upon and determine the proper degree of reliance. Also, the weaknesses (absence of desired controls) must be evaluated in terms of their possible monetary impact on financial statements. Appropriate substantive procedures must be specified to gather evidence for reasonable assurance that material errors did not occur, even though the control weaknesses imply that errors could occur. Note that reliance is expressed in terms of degrees, not as an absolute (that is, control/no control). Some firms use ranking systems such as: excellent (heavy reliance), good (some reliance), fair (minimum reliance) and poor (no reliance).

COMPLIANCE AUDITING

In most organizations, revenue and cash receipts transactions are numerous. Compliance auditing of the details of transactions to determine the effectiveness of internal accounting control involves sampling techniques for choosing transactions for audit and for evidence evaluation.

Audit Procedures

Exhibit 13–10 contains a selection of compliance audit procedures. These steps are designed to enable the audit team to obtain objective evidence

EXHIBIT 13–10
Audit Program—Selected
Compliance Auditing
Procedures

A. Sales.
  1. Trace a sample of shipping documents to related sales invoices.
  2. Scan sales invoices for missing numbers in the sequence.
  3. Select a sample of recorded sales invoices:
     a. Perform recalculations to verify arithmetic accuracy.
     b. Vouch to supporting shipping documents. Note dates and quantities.
     c. Vouch prices to approved price lists.
     d. Vouch credit approval.
     e. Trace posting to general ledger and proper customer account.
  4. Observe customer order handling and invoice preparation work.

B. Cash Receipts.
  1. Select a sample of recorded cash receipts:
     a. Vouch to duplicate deposit slip and remittance list.
     b. Trace to bank statement.
     c. Trace posting to general ledger accounts.
     d. Trace posting to subsidiary accounts.
  2. Select a sample of remittance lists (or daily cash reports):
     a. Trace to cash receipts journal.
     b. Trace journal posting to general ledger.
     c. Trace to bank statement.
  3. Observe the work habits of cashiers and clerks and their use of cash registers.

C. Accounts Receivable.
  1. Trace sales invoices to accounts receivable posting (procedure A-3e above).
  2. Trace cash receipts to accounts receivable posting (procedure B-1d above).
  3. Select a sample of credit memos.
     a. Review for proper approval.
     b. Trace to posting in customers' accounts.
  4. Select a sample of customers' accounts.
     a. Vouch debits to supporting sales invoices.
     b. Vouch credits to supporting cash receipts documents and approved credit memos.
  5. Observe mailing of monthly customer statements.

about the effectiveness of controls and about the reliability of accounting records. These records contain the basic numbers that appear in the financial statements under audit.

The sales transaction compliance procedures include procedures to determine whether the specific objectives listed in Exhibit 13–9 were achieved. The following indicates the relationship between the sales control objectives and the compliance procedures:

Control Objectives	Compliance Procedures
Recorded sales valid.	A-3b vouch invoices to shipping documents.
Valid sales recorded.	A-1 trace shipping documents to sales invoices and A-2 scan for missing invoice numbers.
Sales authorized.	A-3c vouch prices to approved price lists and A-3d vouch to credit approval.
Invoice accurately prepared.	A-3a perform recalculations.
Proper accounting.	A-3e trace posting to customer account.
Proper period.	A-3b note dates on shipping documents.

Likewise, the cash receipts compliance procedures are designed to provide evidence that: (1) recorded cash receipts are supported by documentary evidence and properly posted to accounts (procedure B-1) and (2) that cash received is being recorded and accounted for properly (procedure B-2).

The accounts receivable compliance procedures are designed to provide evidence of proper posting of charges and credits to customers' accounts (procedures C-1, C-2 and C-3) and of whether charges and credits recorded in customers' accounts are properly supported by underlying documents (procedure C-4).

Taken together, these procedures audit the accounting for transactions in two directions. One direction determines whether all transactions that occurred were recorded (none omitted), and the other direction is to determine whether recorded transactions actually occurred (were valid). An example of the first direction is the examination of a sample of shipping documents (from the file of all shipping documents) to determine whether invoices were prepared and recorded. An example of the second direction is the examination of a sample of sales invoices (from the file representing all recorded sales) to determine whether supporting shipping documents exist to verify the fact of an actual shipment. In many instances, compliance procedures applied to the attributes of control consist of these two directions. The contents of one file are compared with the contents of another. The example is illustrated below. (The A-1 and A-3b codes correspond to the compliance procedures in Exhibit 13–10.)

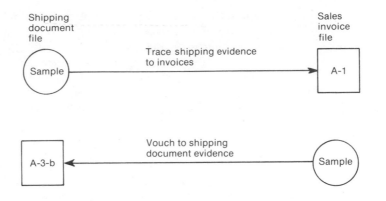

Many of the compliance procedures can be characterized as steps taken to verify the content and character of sample documents from one file with the content and character of documents in another file.

REEVALUATION OF CONTROL

When the compliance auditing is complete and documented in the working papers, the audit manager must reevaluate the controls that are to be relied upon. If more errors (lack of compliance with a control procedure) were found than specified as the maximum tolerable (the tolerable rate), the degree of control must be downgraded, perhaps from excellent to good. Likewise, the subsequent audit procedures must be changed in terms of their nature, timing, and extent. For example, assume that after the review phase, the audit manager considered internal accounting control in the revenue cycle to be "excellent." Based on this degree of reliance, an audit program was prepared to confirm receivables a month before year-end with negative confirmations on a random sample of 10 percent of the accounts. However, after completing the compliance procedures, controls were reevaluated down to "good." The audit program could be changed to confirm receivables at year-end (change timing), utilize positive confirmations on the 10 percent of the largest accounts (change nature), and utilize negative confirmations on 20 percent of the remaining accounts (change extent).

Judgments and conclusions about the degree of reliance vested in the existing accounting control system and effect on the nature, timing and extent of subsequent audit procedures will be discussed in Chapters 17 and 18. The purpose of conducting a proper study and evaluation of internal control in the revenue cycle is to determine the final audit program for auditing the account balances controlled by it—cash, accounts receivable, sales and sales returns/allowances.

REVIEW QUESTIONS

13.1. What is the primary purpose of "reviewing" the internal controls in the revenue cycle.

13.2. Explain how a "walk-through" is done. What is the purpose of the walk-through?

13.3. Why should the auditor take a "business approach" to auditing the revenue cycle?

13.4. What features of the internal control system for sales would be expected to prevent the omission or double counting of sales data?

13.5. What feature(s) of a cash receipts internal control system would be expected to prevent: (a) an employee's absconding with company funds and replacing the funds during audit engagements with cash from the employee pension fund and (b) the cash receipts journal and recorded cash sales from reflecting more than the amount shown on the daily deposit slip?

13.6. What is the purpose of the evaluation of the controls in the revenue cycle by the audit manager after the review phase, before compliance auditing?

13.7. What is the meaning of a strength in the transaction processing controls of the revenue cycle? A weakness? Why are weaknesses not subject to compliance auditing?

13.8. Assume the audit manager, after the review phase, evaluated the sales system of the revenue cycle as excellent, but chose not to rely upon these controls. What justification is there for not relying on controls when the evaluation at this point is excellent?

13.9. What features of an accounts receivable internal control system would be expected to prevent an employee from embezzling cash through the creation of fictitious credit memos?

13.10. What procedures might internal auditors use to ensure the controls in the accounts receivable system are functioning?

13.11. What are the goals of dual-direction sampling in regard to an audit of accounts receivable?

13.12. Why is it necessary to evaluate the controls after the compliance audit of the revenue cycle when an evaluation was already made after the review phase?

13.13. Assume the audit manager's evaluation of the cash receipts internal control system after the review phase was "good" (some reliance). Upon completion of the compliance auditing where fewer errors than expected were found, the audit manager re-evaluated the system as "excellent" (heavy reliance). Would the preliminary audit program be changed as to nature, timing and extent of subsequent procedures?

13.14. What are the objectives of internal accounting control? Express each objective in specific terms to apply to cash receipts.

13.15. Evaluate the following statement by a manager of an audit firm: "When an organization uses a computer-based sales order-entry system, the computer will take the place of a number of employees who formerly handled the sales orders and subsequent activities. Consequently, there will be no separation of duties controls for the auditor to rely on." Consider which functions are separated in a manual system and which should be separated in a computer system.

EXERCISES AND PROBLEMS

13.16. Cash Receipts: Control Objectives and Control Examples
Prepare a table similar to Exhibit 13–9 (Internal Accounting Control Objectives) for cash receipts.

13.17. ICQ Items Matched to Control Objectives
The internal accounting control objectives listed in Chapter 7 are: (1) validity, (2) completeness, (3) authorization, (4) accuracy, (5) classification, (6) accounting, and (7) proper period. Refer to Exhibit 13–3 and prepare a table matching the questionnaire questions to the seven control objectives. (Hint: see Exhibit 14–7 for format.)

13.18. ICQ Items: Objectives and Errors from Control Weaknesses
Refer to the internal control questionnaire on cash receipts (Exhibit 13–5) and assume the answer to each question is "No." Prepare a table matching the questions to the seven control objectives (See Exhibits 7–6 and 13–9) and the "errors" that could occur because of the absence of the control. The column headings of your table should be:

Control Objective	Question	Possible Error due to Weakness

13.19. Documentary Evidence For Compliance Procedures
One of the secondary purposes of the review phase is to identify populations of documents that might be used in the compliance auditing phase of the proper study and evaluation of internal control. Refer to the sales and accounts receivables flowcharts in this chapter (Exhibits 13–2 and 13–6). For each file symbol:

a. Identify the documents filed and the sequence of filing.

b. Describe what documentary evidence might exist that indicates compliance with a control procedure.

c. Describe how an auditor could be sure the population was complete prior to selecting a sample.

13.20. Compliance Audit Procedures: Control Objectives and Control Procedures
Each of the following audit procedures might be performed during compliance auditing of the controls in the revenue cycle. For each procedure: (*a*) identify the internal accounting control objective(s) being addressed and (*b*) identify the internal control procedure (strength) being tested. (Hint: see Exhibit 13–9.)

1. Scan sales invoices for missing numbers in sequence.

2. Trace a sample of remittance advices to the duplicate deposit slips, and deposit slips to the bank statement and to posting in the cash receipts journal.

3. Review a sample of credit memos and trace to postings in customers' accounts.

4. Vouch a sample of accounts receivable postings to: (*a*) sales invoices, (*b*) credit memos and (*c*) cash receipts documents (remittance advices).

5. Examine a sample of sales invoices for indication of credit approval.

6. Select a sample of sales invoices and compare prices to approved price list, compare quantities to shipping documents and recompute all mathematics.

13.21. ICQ Items: Control Characteristic, Compliance Procedure and Possible Error or Irregularity
Listed below is a selection of items from the internal control questionnaires shown in the chapter.

1. Are sales invoice blanks prenumbered? Controlled in the sales order department?

2. Are sales invoices checked for error in the billing department as to prices, credit terms, extensions and footings,

freight allowances, and checked with customers' orders?

3. Is a bank reconciliation performed monthly by someone who does not have cash custody or recordkeeping responsibilities?

4. Is mail opened by someone other than the cashier or accounts receivable recordkeeper? Are daily remittance advices and/or remittance lists prepared by this person?

Required:

For each one:

a. Identify the control characteristic to which it applies (such as, segregation of duties—authorization of transactions, access to assets and recordkeeping duties, sound error-checking practice, and so on).

b. Specify one compliance procedure an auditor could use to determine whether the control was operating effectively.

c. Using your business experience, your logic and/or your imagination, give an example of an error or irregularity that could occur if the control were absent or ineffective.

13.22. **Internal Control Questionnaire for Book Buy-Back Cash Fund**

Taylor, a CPA, has been engaged to audit the financial statements of University Books, Incorporated. University Books maintains a large, revolving cash fund exclusively for the purpose of buying used books from students for cash. The cash fund is active all year because the nearby university offers a large variety of courses with varying starting and completion dates throughout the year.

Receipts are prepared for each purchase, and reimbursement vouchers are periodically submitted to replenish the fund.

Required:

Construct an internal control questionnaire to be used in evaluating the system of internal control of University Books' buy-

ing back books using the revolving cash fund. The internal control questionnaire should elicit a yes or no response to each question. *Do not discuss the internal controls over books that are purchased.*

(*AICPA* adapted)

13.23. **Internal Control Weaknesses and Recommendations**

The customer billing function of the Wheaton Paint Company, a small paint manufacturer, is accomplished by a receptionist, an accounts receivable clerk and a secretary who also serves as a cashier. The company's paint products are sold to wholesalers and retail stores. The following describes *all* of the procedures performed by the employees of the Wheaton Paint Company pertaining to customer billings:

1. The mail is opened by the receptionist who gives the customers' purchase orders to the accounts receivable clerk. Fifteen to 20 orders are received each day. Under instructions to expedite the shipment of orders, the accounts receivable clerk at once prepares a five-copy sales invoice form which is distributed as follows:

   (a) Copy 1 is the customer billing copy and is held by the accounts receivable clerk until notice of shipment is received.

   (b) Copy 2 is the accounts receivable department copy and is held for ultimate posting of the accounts receivable records.

   (c) Copies 3 and 4 are sent to the shipping department.

   (d) Copy 5 is sent to the storeroom as authority for release of the goods to the shipping department.

2. After the paint order has been moved from the storeroom to the shipping department, the shipping department prepares the bills of lading and labels the cartons. Sales invoice Copy 4 is inserted in a carton as a packing slip.

After the trucker has picked up the shipment, the customer's copy of the bill of lading and Copy 3, on which are noted any undershipments, are returned to the accounts receivable clerk. The company does not "back order" in the event of undershipments; customers are expected to reorder the merchandise. Wheaton's copy of the bill of lading is filed by the shipping department.

3. When Copy 3 and the customer's copy of the bill of lading are received by the accounts receivable clerk, copies 1 and 2 are completed by numbering them and inserting the quantities shipped, unit price, extensions, discounts and totals. The accounts receivable clerk then mails Copy 1 and the copy of the bill of lading to the customer. Copies 2 and 3 are stapled together.

4. The individual accounts receivable ledger cards are posted by the accounts receivable clerk by a bookkeeping-machine procedure whereby the sales register is prepared as a carbon copy of the postings. Postings are made from Copy 2, which is then filed, along with staple-attached Copy 3, in numerical order. Monthly, the general ledger clerk summarizes the sales register for posting to the general ledger accounts.

   Required:
   a. List and discuss the internal control weaknesses in the Wheaton Paint Company's procedures for customer billings and related accounting.
   b. For each weakness, recommend changes to overcome the internal control weakness.

13.24. **Compliance Audit Procedures For Cash Receipts**
You are the in-charge auditor examining the financial statements of the Gutzler Company for the year ended December 31. During late October, you, with the help of

Gutzler's controller, completed an internal control questionnaire and prepared the appropriate memoranda describing Gutzler's accounting procedures. Your comments relative to cash receipts are as follows.

All cash receipts are sent directly to the accounts receivable clerk with no processing by the mail department. The accounts receivable clerk keeps the cash receipts journal; prepares the bank deposit slip in duplicate; posts from the deposit slip to the subsidiary accounts receivable ledger; and mails the deposit to the bank.

The controller receives the validated deposit slips directly (unopened) from the bank. She also receives the monthly bank statement directly (unopened) from the bank and promptly reconciles it.

At the end of each month, the accounts receivable clerk notifies the general ledger clerk by journal voucher of the monthly totals of the cash receipts journal for posting to the general ledger.

Each month, with regard to the general ledger cash account, the general ledger clerk makes an entry to record the total debits to cash from the cash receipts journal. In addition, the general ledger clerk on occasion makes debit entries in the general ledger cash account from sources other than the cash receipts journal; for example, funds borrowed from the bank.

Certain standard auditing procedures listed below have already been performed by you in the audit of cash receipts:

Total and cross-total all columns in the cash receipts journal.

Trace postings from the cash receipts journal to the general ledger.

Examine remittance advices and related correspondence to support entries in the cash receipts journal.

Required:
Considering Gutzler's internal control over cash receipts and the standard audit-

ing procedures already performed, list all other auditing procedures which should be performed to obtain sufficient audit evidence regarding cash receipts control and give the reasons for each procedure. Do not discuss the procedures for cash disbursements and cash balances. Also, do not discuss the extent to which any of the procedures are to be performed. Assume adequate controls exist to assure that all sales transactions are recorded. Organize your answer sheet as follows:

Other Audit Procedures	Reason for Other Audit Procedures

(*AICPA* adapted)

13.25. Cash Receipts: Weaknesses and Recommendations

The Pottstown Art League operates a museum for the benefit and enjoyment of the community. During hours when the museum is open to the public, two volunteer clerks positioned at the entrance collect a $5 admission fee from each nonmember patron. Members of the Art League are permitted to enter free of charge upon presentation of their membership cards.

At the end of each day, one of the clerks delivers the proceeds to the treasurer. The treasurer counts the cash in the presence of the clerk and places it in a safe. Each Friday afternoon, the treasurer and one of the clerks deliver all cash held in the safe to the bank and receive an authenticated deposit slip that provides the basis for the weekly entry in the cash receipts journal.

The board of directors of the Pottstown Art League has identified a need to improve their system of internal control over cash admission fees. The board has determined that the cost of installing turnstiles, sales booths, or otherwise altering the physical layout of the museum will greatly exceed any benefits that may be derived. However, the board has agreed that the sale of admission tickets must be an integral part of its improvement efforts.

Required:

The board of directors has requested your assistance. Prepare a report for presentation and discussion at their next board meeting which identifies the weaknesses in the existing system of cash admission fees and suggests recommendations.

(*AICPA* adapted)

DISCUSSION CASE

13.26. Charting Inc.—Flowchart and Bridging Workpaper

Charting Inc., a new audit client of yours, processes its sales and cash receipts documents in the following manner:

1. *Payment on account.* The mail is opened each morning by a mail clerk in the sales department. The mail clerk prepares a remittance advice (showing customer and amount paid) if one is not received. The checks and remittance advices are then forwarded to the sales department supervisor, who reviews each check and forwards the checks and remittance advices to the accounting department supervisor.

The accounting department supervisor, who also functions as credit manager in approving new credit and all credit limits, reviews all checks for payments on past-due accounts, then forwards the checks and remittance advices to the accounts receivable clerk, who arranges them in alphabetical order. The remittance advices are posted directly to the accounts receivable ledger cards. The checks are endorsed by rubber stamp with the company name and totaled. The total is posted to the cash receipts journal. The remittance advices are filed chronologically.

After receiving the cash from the previous day's cash sales, the accounts receivable clerk prepares the daily deposit slip in triplicate. The third copy of the deposit slip is filed by date, and the second copy and the original accompany the bank deposit.

2. *Sales*. Salesclerks prepare sales invoices in triplicate. The original and second copy are presented to the cashier. The third copy is retained by the salesclerk in the sales book. When the sale is for cash, the customer pays the salesclerk, who presents the money to the cashier with the invoice copies.

A credit sale is approved by the cashier from an approved credit list after the salesclerk prepares the three-part invoice. After receiving the cash or approving the invoice, the cashier validates the original copy of the sales invoice and gives it to the customer. At the end of each day, the cashier recaps the sales and cash received and forwards the cash and the second copy of all sales invoices to the accounts receivable clerk.

The accounts receivable clerk balances the cash received with cash sales invoices and prepares a daily sales summary. The credit sales invoices are posted to the accounts receivable ledger, then all invoices are sent to the inventory control clerk in the sales department for posting to the inventory control cards. After posting, the inventory control clerk files all invoices numerically. The accounts receivable clerk posts the daily sales summary to

the cash receipts journal and sales journal and files the sales summaries by date.

The cash from cash sales is combined with the cash received on account to comprise the daily bank deposit.

3. *Bank deposits*. The bank validates the deposit slip and returns the second copy to the accounting department where it is filed by date by the accounts receivable clerk.

Monthly bank statements are reconciled promptly by the accounting department supervisor and filed by date.

Required:

a. Construct a flowchart for the sales and cash receipts system of Charting Inc. (Hint: the column headings, left to right, are Sales Department Clerks, Cashier, Sales Department Supervisor, Accounting Department Supervisor and Accounts Receivable Clerk.)

b. Put a reference symbol on the flowchart for strengths and weaknesses and number each. For example, [S1], [W1].

c. Prepare a workpaper listing the strengths and weaknesses (a bridging workpaper). For example, [W6] validated deposit slips returned by the bank are not compared to entries in the sales journal; [S1] mail clerk prepares a remittance advice.

(AICPA adapted)

CHAPTER 14

PROFESSIONAL STANDARDS SOURCES		
Compendium Section	Document Reference	Topic
AU 320	SAS 1	Auditor's Study and Evaluation of Internal Control
AU 901	SAS 1	Public Warehouses—Controls and Auditing Procedures for Goods Held

Acquisition and Expenditure Cycle

LEARNING OBJECTIVES

This chapter has four major objectives related to the tools and techniques described in earlier chapters. After completing this chapter, you should understand with relation to the acquisition and expenditure cycle:

- A business approach to understanding the acquisition and expenditure cycle including the acquisition of fixed assets.

- The flow of transactions in a typical acquisition and expenditure cycle, how specific accounts are affected and the elements of control within the cycle.

- Audit procedures used to gather evidence regarding the compliance with control procedures.

- Evaluation of the controls (strengths) and lack of controls (weaknesses) to determine the effect upon the nature, timing and extent of procedures for auditing account balances.

The discussion and explanation of each of these four topics should enable you to sharpen your awareness of audit objectives, relevant evidence, relevant audit procedures and the application of audit methodology to the specific acquisition and expenditure subset of accounts.

Some programs used in audit field work contain separate sections for procedures related to fixed asset acquisitions, inventories and cost of sales. The cash disbursement audit procedures are generally combined with procedures for auditing cash receipts transactions and cash balances. However, in this text, cash disbursement audit procedures are grouped with inventory, purchasing and cost-of-sales procedures in order to illustrate the flow of a transaction from purchase to account payable and inventory (or fixed assets) and thence to payment of the liability.

In order to understand this flow of transactions by grouping related activities in a cycle, consider the following as typical functions of the acquisition and expenditure cycle:

Requisitioning—requests for goods, services or other assets.

Authorization—especially for fixed assets.

Vendor selection.

Obtaining information on pricing and other specifications.

Purchasing—placing the order.

Receiving, inspecting and accepting assets.

Maintaining the inventory and fixed-asset subsidiary records.

Accounting for accounts payable.

Cash disbursements accounting.

Accounting for cash discounts, returned goods and other adjustments.

Notice that many of these functions do not require formal entries in the accounting records but are still part of the flow of transactions. Auditors, unlike accountants, are concerned with the entire flow of transactions and especially with the controls over each step in this flow.

A BUSINESS APPROACH

Auditors must recognize the danger of becoming so involved in the detail procedures of an audit that major issues which could result in material misstatements in the financial statements escape attention. This danger can be overcome through understanding the client from a manager's perspective. Of special interest to the acquisition and expenditure cycle are the client's marketing and production activities, purchasing and disbursing procedures and the fixed asset acquisition procedures.

Marketing and Production

The areas of purchasing, inventories and cost of sales are closely related to the marketing function. As discussed in the previous chapter, in consideration of sales and receivables, auditors should become familiar with the client's product. It is important to know whether the product is produced or purchased complete, whether it is perishable, whether it is produced by job order or in a continuous process, whether it is produced on contract only or for shelf inventory or—in nonmanufacturing businesses—whether there is any physical product at all. The size and frequency of sales orders also may be considered in this familiarization with the product.

Marketing plans, when coordinated with production and purchasing plans, should also reveal the composition of purchase sources. Items purchased from only a few suppliers present different auditing problems than when suppliers are numerous and purchases are scattered. Knowledge of major types of purchases can facilitate auditors' subsequent concentration of procedures on the most important elements of cost. The existence of a computer-based purchasing-inventory system that automatically produces standard purchase orders will have an impact on subsequent auditing procedures.

The overview of the product and the major suppliers and major customers should also enable auditors to discern the major cost elements in inventories and cost of sales. Some products are materials cost-intensive, others may be labor cost-intensive and others may be low cost (with heavy expenditures on promotion and advertising). Knowledge of the mix of product-line sales and their related gross margins, as well as knowledge of the cost element mix, can contribute to understanding inventories and cost of sales.

Auditors should also become familiar with the receiving and shipping operation. Receiving practices are important because receiving operations establish initial control over inventories (both as to quantity and quality). Observations of shipping and selling operations can provide auditors with information regarding inventory on consignment or stored in public warehouses off the client's premises. A tour of inventory storage areas can help in later planning for the observation of a physical inventory count.

Purchasing and Disbursing

Auditors will want to learn about organization structure—whether the acquisition and expenditure functions are centralized at a headquarters' level or decentralized in several locations. The extent to which the purchasing function coordinates with the disbursement function is also important. Some companies centralize authority for creation of liabilities through a "purchasing-control" department, while others allow the authority to acquire supplies and services to be dispersed among operating managers. For example, the authority to contract for advertising and promotion may rest with the sales manager without approval from a purchasing department.

The system of accounting for disbursements is of interest to the auditor. A system that provides for monthly payment of vendors' accounts requires different auditing attention than one that pays individual invoices by due dates (as in a voucher system). A computer system that integrates check-writing capabilities with liability records poses still different auditing problems.

In general, auditors are interested in the major types and dollar volumes of purchases—information that may flow from a familiarization with the product and the manufacturing process. In this connection, information about purchasing department procedures for obtaining prices will be useful. The practice of buying regularly from a small number of suppliers has different implications in comparison to practices of soliciting bids or searching continuously among numerous suppliers for the lowest price.

General and specific economic conditions such as price changes, labor conditions (both in the client's and in suppliers' plants) and market price changes should be related to the circumstances of the engagement. An increase in inventory investment could be the result of higher prices; low inventory turnover could be the result of stockpiling as a hedge against anticipated strikes in suppliers' plants. On the other hand, both of these conditions could also result from having obsolete, worn or worthless items in the inventory. Attention to market prices and relative product costs will be essential to later determinations of lower-of-cost-or-market inventory values. Special attention to the prices paid to affiliated companies or persons for inventory items is necessary in order to value inventory properly. Knowledge of a new labor contract will certainly affect the audit of labor cost inputs.

Fixed Asset Acquisition   The nature and utilization of fixed assets varies widely among companies. A broad business approach provides familiarity with the type of assets, related maintenance schedules and associated expenses that are characteristic of the assets of a particular client. Equally important is the nature of the data processing system for asset records.

Auditors must recognize that some assets in productive use may not be formally recorded in asset accounts. Leased assets may be recorded only as rental expense. Some recorded assets may not be "fixed" in the meaning of "in productive use;" for example, assets held for future disposal, excess capacity and unrecorded dispositions. Amounts recorded as assets may, in fact, be repair and maintenance expenses, and amounts expensed may be properly capitalized as fixed assets.

During a preliminary plant tour and in the course of conversational inquiries, auditors should observe the quantity and size of assets, their location and apparent physical condition and the activity surrounding them. Auditors should ask executives about the ownership or leasing of property.

Further preliminary evidence of existence may be gained by a review of internal management reports. Typical reports include: capital expenditure proposals, capital budgets, construction cost or acquisition cost post-analyses, maintenance and repair reports, reports of sales or retirements, and insurance and property tax analyses. A general awareness of social-political-economic forces may also indicate that certain assets may have been acquired or disposed. For example, newspaper reports of consumer groups' complaints about product quality or safety could have caused management to change production methods and equipment. Ecological controversies could have prompted installation of pollution control equipment. In the case of multinational companies, reports of political unrest in foreign countries may predict problems with future expropriation of assets.

REVIEW PHASE: FLOW OF TRANSACTIONS AND ELEMENTS OF CONTROL

The primary objective of the review phase is to determine the strengths that can be relied upon and the weaknesses that will require extended substantive procedures. To accomplish a review, however, you must be familiar with the common procedures, significant documents and appropriate controls. In this section, the flow of transactions and appropriate controls will be described and illustrated with flowcharts. These simplified flowcharts can be considered examples of the flowcharts auditors might prepare to document the understanding of the systems within this cycle.

The understanding of the transaction flow of the acquisition and expenditure cycle is obtained through interviews, observations and collecting sample documents. For example, the auditors may "walk through" the cash disbursements system—obtaining a sample voucher and check form, questioning people regarding their duties, and observing such procedures as control of document-number sequence, separation of duties, posting to accounting records, cancellation of documents after payment, and the sequence of document files.

The flowchart exhibits in this chapter illustrate model organizational systems for control of purchase, inventory, fixed asset, liability and cash disbursement transactions. Each flowchart shows the segregation of functions considered characteristic of satisfactory internal accounting control. You should understand thoroughly the flow of transactions by studying each flowchart and the interconnection between them. Exhibits 14–3, 14–5, 14–7, 14–9 and 14–12 contain internal control questionnaire items typical of these systems. The questionnaires presented in this chapter do not contain the columns necessary for complete workpapers, but have been condensed to contain only the questions for illustrative purposes. (See Exhibit 7–2, Chapter 7, for the complete questionnaire format.) Taken together, the flowcharts and the questionnaire items describe desirable control features for each of the five systems of the acquisition and expenditure cycle: purchasing, inventory, fixed assets, cash disbursements, and accounts and notes payable.

The material that follows is a combination of an example of the flow of transactions through the acquisition and expenditure cycle and an example of the review of the common controls in that cycle. Your understanding of the flow of transactions should acquaint you with the common documents and procedures in the systems within this cycle. Remember that the review is just the first step of a proper study and evaluation of internal control. The auditor is seeking significant controls that would prevent material errors which can be relied upon to restrict subsequent substantive audit procedures. These subsequent audit procedures are presented in Chapters 17 and 18.

Purchasing Procedures

Exhibit 14–1 illustrates part of a purchasing-procedure system, the preparation of the purchase order. The internally generated authority for a purchase is shown as a requisition originating in the stores (inventory)

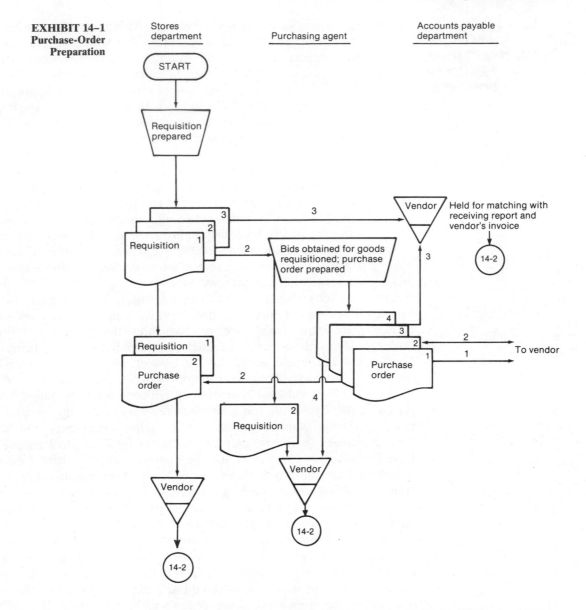

EXHIBIT 14–1 Purchase-Order Preparation

location. In other systems, the requisition may be originated by a production supervisor, by a sales back order signal, or by a computer system that automatically produces a requisition when an inventory item falls to a programmed reorder point quantity.

The requisition (or capital budget for fixed assets) serves as an authorization for purchase order preparation. The purchase order is prepared by the purchasing agent who is segregated from the authorizing department. The purchasing agent obtains bids (or selects a vendor from an authorized vendor list) and prepares the purchase order. Purchase order copies are distributed and used as follows:

Copy 1 and 2—to the vendor, copy 2 is returned as acknowledgment of the order.

Copy 2—to stores inventory to acknowledge the purchase requisition and to be held until the receiving report and the goods arrive (see Exhibit 14–2).

Copy 3—to accounts payable to be held and matched with the receiving report and vendor's invoice (see Exhibit 14–2).

Copy 4—attached to the requisition and filed in purchasing for future reference.

As shown in Exhibit 14–2, while an order is in process, pending purchase order files of goods ordered but not yet received are kept in the stores and accounts payable departments. After the goods are received, these open purchase-order files are emptied by matching the purchase orders with the receiving report copies.

Exhibit 14–2 illustrates the procedures when the goods and the vendors' invoices are received. The receiving report is prepared when goods are received. Copy 1 is sent to the purchasing agent and later to the inventory accounting department (Exhibit 14–4). Copy 2 is filed for reference in the receiving department. Copies 3 and 4 move with the goods to stores. After a recount of the goods, the stores department matches the copies to the related requisition and purchase order and initials copy 3 as an indication that the goods were placed in inventory. Copy 3 is forwarded to accounts payable.

The vendor's invoice is received by the purchasing department where it is reviewed for terms, prices and quantities and compared to the purchase requisition, purchase order and receiving report. Then copy 1 of the invoice is initialed to indicate it is correct and transmitted to the accounts payable department where it may be held pending receipt of copy 3 of the receiving report (if that copy has been delayed in processing). Copy 2 of the invoice is attached to the related requisition and purchase order and filed in purchasing for future reference. Thus, at any one time the accounts payable department may be holding invoices not matched with receiving reports, receiving reports not yet matched with invoices, and purchase orders not matched with either receiving reports or invoices.

At year-end these various pending files contain relevant information for the audit of proper cutoff. Purchase orders and invoices unmatched with receiving reports may represent inventory in transit, depending on freight and title terms. In both cases, liabilities may be unrecorded. Receiving reports unmatched with invoices could also represent unrecorded liabilities. When all documents have been approved and matched, a pay-

EXHIBIT 14–2
Receiving, Invoice Processing

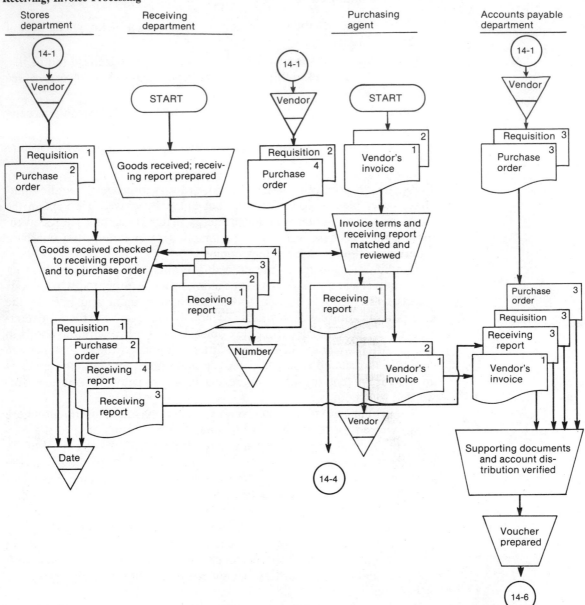

able voucher is prepared, the liability and inventory are formally recorded, and the voucher enters the cash disbursement procedure system (Exhibit 14–6). Copy 1 of the receiving report is used to update inventory records as shown in Exhibit 14–4.

Notice that throughout the purchasing system, the custody of goods (receiving and stores departments), the authority to initiate a transaction (purchasing department), and the bookkeeping (accounts payable and inventory records departments) are kept separate. Typical internal control questions about the purchasing system are provided in Exhibit 14–3. The

EXHIBIT 14–3
Internal Control
Questionnaire—Purchasing
and Receiving System

1. Is the accounts payable ledger or open voucher register balanced periodically with the general ledger control account?
2. Are vendors' monthly statements checked against accounts payable or unpaid vouchers?
3. Is there a purchasing department independent of the accounting department, receiving department and shipping department?
4. Are all purchases made only on the basis of approved purchase requisitions?
5. Are all purchases, whether for inventory or expense, routed through the purchasing department?
6. Are the purchase order forms prenumbered and controlled?
7. Are competitive bids received and reviewed for certain items?
8. Are purchase prices approved by a responsible purchasing officer?
9. Are quantity and quality of goods received determined at time of receipt by receiving personnel independent of the purchasing department?
10. Are receiving report forms prenumbered and controlled?
11. Are receiving report copies transmitted to inventory custodians? To purchasing? To the accounting department?
12. Is the accounts payable department notified of goods returned to vendors?
13. Are returned goods cleared through the shipping department procedures?
14. Are unmatched invoices reviewed frequently by inquiry with receiving?
15. Are unmatched receiving reports reviewed frequently and investigated for proper recording?
16. Are vendors' invoices registered immediately upon receipt?
17. Are vendors' invoices first checked by the purchasing department against purchase orders and receiving reports?
18. Is there an adequate system for recording partial deliveries on a purchase order?
19. Are invoices approved for payment by a responsible officer?
20. Are invoices checked for quantities, prices and terms in the accounts payable department against purchase orders and receiving reports?
21. Are purchases made for employees cleared through the regular purchases procedures?
22. Are all purchases (materials, services, expenses) routed through the accounts payable record and not directly through cash disbursements?
23. Are purchasing and receiving procedures automated in a computer system? If so, complete relevant portions of the computer internal control questionnaire.

answers to these questions provide the auditor further understanding and identification of control strengths and weaknesses. If records are maintained on a computer system, the transaction data (requisition, purchase order, receiving report and invoice) would be transformed into machine-readable media when received by the accounts payable department. The pending files would then exist on magnetic tapes or disks.

Inventory Procedures and Cost of Goods Sold

Exhibit 14–4 shows an abbreviated set of documents and procedures for updating perpetual inventory records. This system will be more fully illustrated in the discussion of the Conversion Cycle in Chapter 16. The additions to inventory flow from the purchasing procedures flowchart in

**EXHIBIT 14–4
Inventory Procedures
Flowchart**

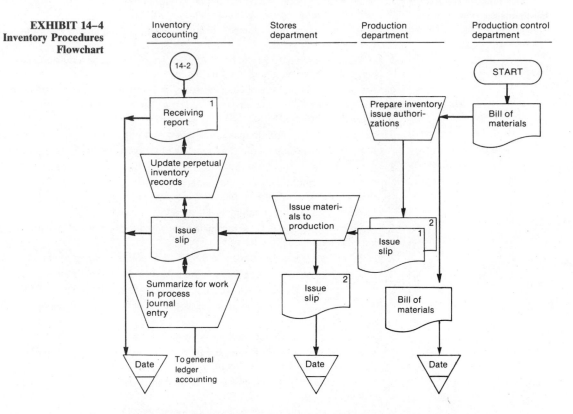

Exhibit 14–2. Inventory issues to production are originated in a production control department or engineering department with a specification (bill) of materials to be used in manufacture. This bill of materials, or issue slips prepared from it, serves as the stores custodian's authorization to release inventory. The issue slips are then forwarded to inventory accounting where the perpetual records are updated for the issues and a summary is prepared and priced for a general ledger entry.

Authorizations to release finished goods to the shipping department are affected by sales invoices as described in Chapter 13. Finished goods inventory records would be updated for such issues and summaries would be prepared for a cost of goods sold journal entry.

Notice in Exhibit 14–4 that the functions of inventory receipt and issue authorization, physical custody and recordkeeping are performed in different departments. Relevant internal control questionnaire items that further highlight good inventory control practices are presented in Exhibit 14–5.

EXHIBIT 14–5
Internal Control
Questionnaire—Inventory
System

1. Are perpetual inventory records kept up-to-date for raw materials? Supplies? Work in process? Finished goods?

2. Are such perpetual records subsidiary to general ledger control accounts?

3. Do the perpetual records show quantities only? Quantities and prices?

4. Are inventory records maintained by someone other than the inventory custodian?

5. Are inventory records maintained on a computer system? If so, complete relevant portions of the computer internal control questionnaire.

6. Are designated inventory custodians held responsible for physical control over various categories of inventory?

7. Do inventory custodians notify the accounting department of all additions to and issues from inventory?

8. Are issues made only on authority of bills of material and sales invoices?

9. Is there effective control over inventory out on consignment? In outside warehouses? In public warehouses?

10. Is merchandise or materials on consignment-in (that is, not the property of the client) physically segregated and under effective accounting control?

11. Is there a periodic review for overstocked, slow-moving or obsolete inventory? Have any adjustments been made during the year?

12. If standard costs have been used for inventory pricing, have they been reviewed for current applicability?

Cash Disbursement
Procedures

The cash disbursement system shown in Exhibit 14–6 presumes that all purchases of inventory items, fixed assets, materials and services expenses (e.g., rent, utilities, advertising) are routed through the purchasing department for approval prior to the preparation of a voucher. However, in many businesses, authority to purchase may be vested in several officers (for example, advertising manager, maintenance personnel) and supporting documents for receipt or use of goods and services may come to the accounts payable department from sources other than the purchasing department to be matched with an invoice. Decentralized control over purchase authority and invoice transmission may create difficulties in keeping up-to-date records of liabilities.

As shown in Exhibit 14–6, all the supporting documentation is gathered in a voucher that is recorded by the accounts payable department in

EXHIBIT 14–6
Cash Disbursements
System

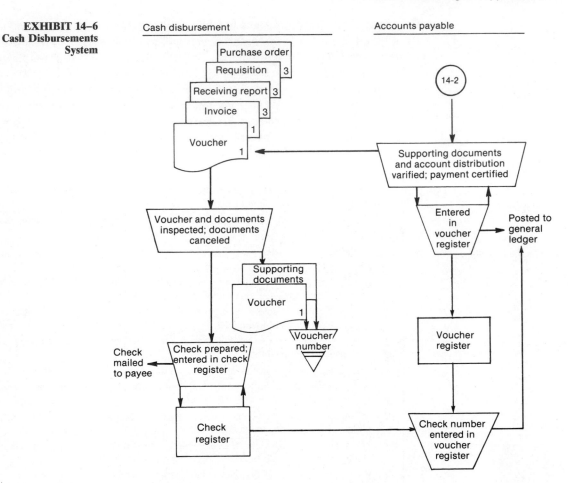

a vouchers payable register. When payment is made, a record of payment is entered in the register. Periodically, the open items should be balanced to the liability control account in the general ledger. The voucher is used to record various charges to inventory and expense accounts, with a summary entry transmitted to general ledger accounting.

The voucher original is sent to the cash disbursement section prior to the due date for check preparation. The officer responsible for signing checks should review the documentation, approve the voucher, sign the check and then stamp the voucher "paid" so that it cannot be paid a second time in error. The check register is summarized periodically for entries to cash and payables in the general ledger. The authorizing documentation for a cash disbursement originates entirely outside the cash disbursement function. Later, when the bank statement is received, it should be reconciled independently by other personnel not involved in the cash disbursements procedures. Relevant internal control questionnaire items, organized by control objectives, further highlight good cash disbursements practices and are presented in Exhibit 14–7. Note the questions have been organized by the control objectives stressed throughout this book.

Note that in the illustrated cash disbursements system, the functions of authorization, physical custody of cash and recordkeeping are performed

EXHIBIT 14–7
Internal Control
Questionnaire—Cash
Disbursement System
(questions organized by
internal accounting control
objectives)

A. *Recorded transactions valid and documented*
  1. Are all disbursements except petty cash made by check?
  2. Are check signers prohibited from drawing checks to cash?
  3. Is the signing and/or countersigning of blank checks prohibited?
  4. Are voided checks mutilated and retained for inspection?
  5. Are vouchers and other supporting documents reviewed by the check signer?
  6. Are the voucher and supporting documents stamped or impressed "paid" to prevent duplicate payment before being returned to accounts payable for filing?
  7. If the original entry is through the cash disbursements journal, is voucher documentation prepared and filed?
  8. Are checks mailed directly by the signer and not returned to the accounts payable for mailing?

B. *All valid transactions recorded and none omitted*
  9. Are check forms prenumbered and under control?
  10. Is the numerical sequence of checks reviewed in the reconciliation process?

C. *Transactions authorized in accordance with company policy*
  11. Do checks require two signatures? Is there dual control over machine signature plates?
  12. Are check signers persons who have no access to accounting records, cash receipts or bank reconciliations?
  13. Are check signing and other cash disbursements procedures automated on computer equipment? If so, complete the relevant portions of the computer internal control questionnaire.

D. *Transaction dollar amounts accurately and properly calculated*
  14. Are bank accounts reconciled by personnel independent of cash custody or recordkeeping?

E. *Transactions properly classified*
  15. Is there an accounting manual and employee approval for determining distribution of invoice charges to general ledger accounts?
  16. Is the distribution of charges double-checked periodically?
  17. Are payroll checks and dividend checks drawn on separate bank accounts?
  18. Are special disbursement accounts such as for payroll and dividends kept on an imprest basis?

F. *Transaction accounting complete and in the proper period*
  19. Are cash disbursements entered in the check register and voucher journal as of the date signed and mailed?

in different departments. The authorization is the invoice approved by purchasing (Exhibit 14–2), the cash disbursements procedures represent the custody of cash, and recordkeeping is done in accounts payable.

Many companies have automated their ordinary cash disbursements procedures with computer equipment. Generally, the automation involves transferring the voucher data onto magnetic tapes or disks. Daily, the file is searched for the voucher due dates, these vouchers are automatically removed from the vouchers payable master file, and checks are printed and signed by machine. In such a computer system, the human approval procedures take place prior to the time data is transformed to machine-readable media. The check-signing control is achieved by special controls over blank check forms, controls over the disbursement computer program and control over the check signature plate. Other programmed controls such as valid-code and limit-test checks may also be used as safeguards.

Fixed-Assets Procedures Many of the procedures and responsibilities for purchasing, inventory and cash disbursements apply to fixed assets. Internal accounting controls

EXHIBIT 14–8
General Flowchart: Fixed-Asset Transactions

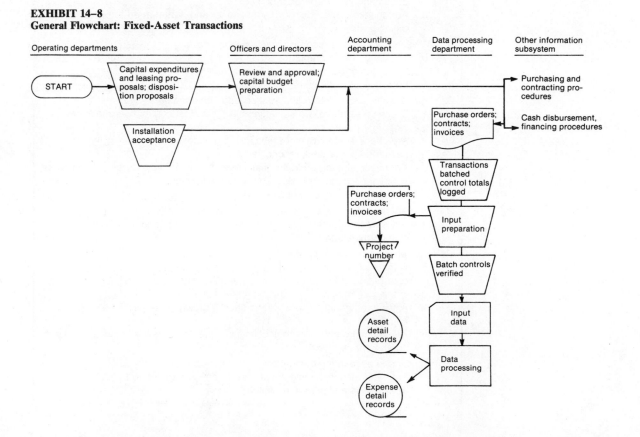

over fixed assets and related accounts transactions are usually not elaborate because most companies do not have a large enough volume of such transactions to merit the cost of specialized controls. (Exceptions would include large capital-intensive companies and businesses that rent or lease tangible property such as automobiles, trucks and trailers.)

Functional responsibilities that should be delegated to separate departments or management levels are:

Planning and approval of capital expenditures.

Data processing of documents evidencing delivery or construction and payment.

Physical custody and operating responsibility for use of assets.

Authority to idle, sell or otherwise take assets out of production.

A flowchart of the system of authorization, custody and recordkeeping may be constructed in order to explain control over fixed asset transactions. Exhibit 14–8 contains a very general representation of such a control system. The flowchart may be analyzed in conjunction with the internal control questionnaire items (Exhibit 14–9) to give a complete picture of important control features.

EXHIBIT 14–9
Internal Control
Questionnaire—Fixed
Assets and Related
Accounts

1. Are detailed property records maintained for the various units of fixed assets? When were subsidiary records last balanced with the general ledger accounts?

2. Are capital expenditure and leasing proposals prepared for review and approval by the board of directors or by responsible officers?

3. When actual expenditures exceed authorized amounts, is the excess approved as in question 2? Describe policy.

4. When was the last physical inspection and inventory? Was it complete?

5. When was the last analysis of insurance coverage? Did it include an appraisal of asset values?

6. When was the last analysis of property tax renditions?

7. Is there an accounting policy for distinguishing capital additions from repairs and maintenance expenses? Explain.

8. Are memorandum records of leased assets maintained?

9. Is approval of a designated officer or director required for disposal, dismantling or idling a productive asset? For terminating a lease or rental?

10. Are procedures devised to assure that recording new assets causes inquiry about accounting for disposal of replaced assets? Describe procedures.

11. Are procedures devised to assure notifying the accounting department of asset disposals when there are no replacements? Describe procedures.

12. Is there a uniform policy for assigning depreciation rates, useful lives and salvage values? Describe policy.

13. Describe procedures and analyses performed by internal auditors in the past year.

At each point in the flowchart where an explanation of some action is given, the auditor may expect to find documentary evidence. For example:

Operating personnel may prepare analytical proposals.

The directors' minutes and capital budget should contain approvals of expenditures.

Some documentation of installation, acceptance and readiness should have been prepared.

Orders and approvals for disposal should be in evidence.

The related subsystems for purchasing, cash disbursements and cash receipts should generate appropriate documentation related to those features of a transaction.

Notice that the flowchart in Exhibit 14–8 presumes that the transaction and property records are captured on computer media. Thus, some means of reading these records and using the computer are going to be required. The review of internal accounting control should include a review of computer-based general and applications controls. A selection of questionnaire items for a computer review is shown in Exhibit 14–10. These

EXHIBIT 14–10
Selected Questionnaire Items—Computer General and Application Controls

A. *General Controls.*
   1. Are computer operators and programmers excluded from participating in the input and output control functions?
   2. Are programmers excluded from operating the computer?
   3. Is there a computer librarian who is independent of computer operations, systems, programming and users?
   4. Are computer personnel restricted from initiating, authorizing or independently processing entries or adjustments to the general ledger master file or the subsidiary ledger master files?
   5. Is access to the computer room restricted to authorized personnel?
   6. Are systems, programs and data files stored in a fireproof area?
   7. Can current files, particularly master files, be reconstructed from files stored in an off-site location?

B. *Application Controls.*
   1. Is conversion of data to machine-readable form done on the basis of up-to-date written instructions?
   2. Are important data fields key verified?
   3. Are batch control totals used to reconcile computer-processed data to input control data?
   4. Is the computer department responsible for correcting errors in data arising in computer operations?
   5. Are edit tests used in computer processing—missing data tests, limit and range tests, check digits, valid codes and proper sequence?
   6. Does the computer print an error log? Is this returned to data preparation or users for correction of errors?
   7. Is computer output reviewed for reasonableness, accuracy and legibility before distribution to users?

items serve the purpose of providing information about general controls and application controls. A good design of general controls gives the auditor some comfort that computer operations are well planned and organized. A good set of application controls gives some comfort that material errors may be prevented or detected promptly. The applications controls should be tested for compliance. An auditor can review instructions, sample key-verified cards, observe the use of batch totals and review error logs for evidential matter concerning the effective operation of computer controls.

Accounts and Notes Payable Procedures

In the account grouping of liabilities and owners' equity, internal accounting control systems and procedures may be classified three ways depending on the volume and nature of transactions:

1. *Accounts payable and notes payable.* Internal control systems and procedures are generally fairly elaborate with document authorization, recordkeeping and custody responsibilities designed to handle numerous transactions.

2. *Derivative liabilities, for example, sales and excise taxes, income taxes, payroll taxes.* These transactions are generally controlled within the system that controls the basic transactions from which the liabilities are derived. For example, the sales transaction control system, the tax planning function and the payroll system essentially control the related liabilities for sales and excise taxes, income taxes and payroll taxes. Controls over payroll transactions will be discussed in Chapter 15.

3. *Long-term debt and capital stock.* Transactions in these accounts are generally few in number and large in amount and may be handled on a special-event basis rather than as a part of an elaborate system of procedures. Oftentimes, stockholder records are under the control of independent registrars, transfer agents and dividend disbursing agents. Controls over these transactions will be discussed in Chapter 18.

As a practical matter, questionnaires are generally relied upon heavily to analyze internal control over most liability and equity transactions. However, for more elaborate control systems flowchart descriptions may be quite useful.

Even in cases where the system of internal control procedures is not elaborate, the audit team is still interested in the existence of satisfactory control that provides for:

A plan of organization that assigns high-level responsibility for review and approval of major financing transactions.

A system of accounting data processing that is independent of the review and approval level.

A system of accounting review to check for errors in data processing.

In the area of accounts and notes payable, these features may be bureaucratized to a large extent. For infrequent debt and equity transactions, the system may not be especially well defined.

EXHIBIT 14–11
General Flowchart: Accounts and Notes Payable Procedures

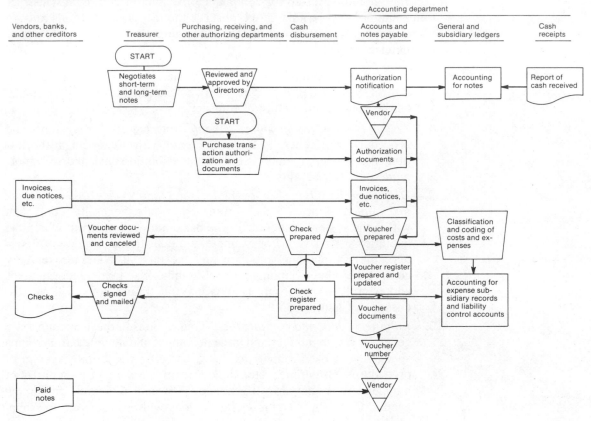

Exhibit 14–11 contains features relating to purchases, accounts payable and cash disbursements. Parts of Exhibit 14–11 are a combination of elements of the purchasing system and the cash disbursement system. Notice that the essential characteristic of the system is the separation of authorization and approval to initiate a transaction from the responsibility for recordkeeping.

The authorization documents may be multicopy and may pass through several departments as in the case for materials purchases. On the other hand, the authorizations may be less formal and nonstandardized as may be the case with loans or purchases of some services (e.g., consultants' studies). Whatever specific forms, documents or procedures are used, auditors would consider a system well controlled if for every transaction that created a liability there was an initial general or specific written authorization on file. Additional audit work will have to be performed, to the extent that authorizing documents are missing.

Recordkeeping control procedures should exist to double-check the coding and classification of costs and expenses represented by account and note payable obligations. Cash disbursement procedures should be controlled in such a way as to ensure proper payment of all liabilities and duplicate payment of none. Additional internal control questionnaire items over purchases and cash disbursements are contained in Exhibit 14–12.

EXHIBIT 14–12
Internal Control
Questionnaire—Accounts
and Notes Payable

1. Are direct borrowings on notes payable authorized by the directors? The treasurer?
2. Are two or more authorized signatures required on notes?
3. Are notes payable records kept by someone who cannot sign notes or checks?
4. Are paid notes canceled, stamped "paid" and filed?
5. Is the voucher register or subsidiary of open accounts payable and notes payable periodically reconciled with the general ledger control account(s)?
6. Are vendors' statements and bank due notices compared with records of unpaid liabilities?
7. Are any adjustments made as a result of this comparison? Are adjustments approved by a responsible officer?

EVALUATION OF ACQUISITION AND EXPENDITURE CYCLE CONTROL

The review phase is usually completed (updated in the case of a repeat engagement) by a junior audit team member. The audit manager will evaluate the working paper documentation to determine the proper degree of reliance, using a systematic framework such as that presented in Exhibit 7–6 (Chapter 7). These objectives are stated in specific terms for purchases in Exhibit 14–13. Similar evaluation would be made for the other systems in the acquisition and expenditure cycle (inventory, fixed asset, cash disbursements, payables).

The audit manager must decide which systems in the acquisition and expenditure cycle contain enough strengths to rely upon and the degree of reliance. Also, the weaknesses must be evaluated in terms of their possible monetary impact on financial statements, and appropriate substantive procedures must be specified to gather evidence for reasonable assurance that material errors did not occur even though the control weaknesses imply errors could occur. Note, however, the audit manager will usually evaluate each system separately. For example, controls in the purchasing procedures may be evaluated as "excellent" (heavy reliance), controls in the cash disbursements procedures evaluated as "good" (some reliance), while controls over notes payable evaluated as "poor" (no reliance).

EXHIBIT 14–13 Internal Accounting Control Objectives (Purchases)	General Objectives	Examples of Specific Objectives
	1. Recorded purchases are *valid* and documented.	Recorded vouchers in the voucher register supported by completed vouchers. Voucher for purchases of inventory (or fixed assets) supported by vendor invoices, receiving reports, purchase orders and requisitions (or approved capital budget).
	2. Valid purchase transactions are *recorded* and none omitted.	Requisitions, purchase orders, receiving reports and vouchers are prenumbered and numerical sequence is checked. Overall comparisons of purchases are made periodically by statistical or product-line analysis.
	3. Purchases are *authorized* according to company policy.	All purchase orders are supported by requisitions from proper persons (or approved capital budgets). Purchases made from approved vendors or only after bids are received and evaluated.
	4. Purchase orders are *accurately* prepared.	Completed purchase order quantities and descriptions independently compared to requisitions and vendors' catalogs.
	5. Purchase transactions are properly *classified.*	Purchases from subsidiaries and affiliates classified as intercompany purchases and payables. Purchase returns and allowances properly classified. Purchases for repairs and maintenance segregated from purchases of fixed assets.
	6. Purchase transaction *accounting* is complete and proper.	Account distribution on vouchers proper and reviewed independent of preparation. Freight-in included as part of purchase and added to inventory (or fixed-assets) costs.
	7. Purchase transactions are recorded in the *proper period.*	Perpetual inventory records updated as of date goods are received.

COMPLIANCE AUDITING

In most manufacturing businesses, acquisition and expenditure cycle transactions are numerous. Compliance audit of the details of transactions to determine the effectiveness of internal accounting control involve sampling techniques for choosing transactions for examination and for evaluating the evidence. Recall that only strengths (effective control procedures) are audited for compliance and only for those systems the auditors are relying upon.

Compliance Audit Procedures For Inventory Purchases, Cost of Sales and Cash Disbursements

Exhibit 14–14 contains a selection of compliance audit procedures. These steps are designed to enable auditors to obtain objective evidence about the effectiveness of controls and about the reliability of accounting records (such as purchases totals, inventory accounts, cost of sales, and expense account balances). These records contain the basic numbers that appear in the financial statements under audit.

EXHIBIT 14–14
Audit Program—Selected Compliance Testing Procedures

A. *Inventory Purchases and Issues.*
  1. Select a sample of receiving reports.
    a. Vouch to related purchase orders, and note the missing receiving reports (missing numbers).
    b. Trace to inventory record posting of additions.
  2. Select a sample of materials issue slips.
    a. Vouch to supporting authorization (signature, production report or bill of materials properly approved).
    b. Trace to inventory record posting of issues.
  3. Select a sample of shipping documents (finished goods) and trace to inventory record posting of issues.
  4. Select a sample of inventory item perpetual records:
    a. Vouch additions to receiving reports.
    b. Vouch issues to issue slips, production reports or bills of materials (or to shipping documents for finished goods).
  5. Observe work habits of purchasing and receiving department personnel.

B. *Cost of Sales.*
  1. With the sample of issues in A–2 above:
    a. Review the accounting summary of quantities and prices for mathematical accuracy.
    b. Trace posting of amounts to general ledger.
  2. Obtain a sample of cost of goods sold entries in the general ledger and vouch to supporting summaries of finished goods issues.
  3. Review (recalculate) the appropriateness of standard costs, if used, to price inventory issues and cost of goods sold. Review the disposition of variances from standard costs.

C. *Cash Disbursements and Other Expenses.*
  1. Select a sample of cash disbursement vouchers (or cash disbursement check numbers):
    a. Scan for missing documents (missing numbers).
    b. Vouch supporting documentation for evidence of accurate mathematics, correct classification, proper approval and cancellation of documents.
    c. Trace disbursement debits to general and subsidiary ledger accounts.
  2. Select a sample of recorded expenses from various accounts and vouch them to: (a) canceled checks and (b) supporting documentation.

The inventory-related compliance procedures include procedures to determine whether the maintenance of inventory records achieves specific control objectives. The following indicates this relationship between the objectives and compliance procedures:

Control Objectives	Compliance Procedures
Recorded inventory valid.	A–4a vouch recorded additions to receiving reports.
	A–4b vouch recorded issues to material issue slips, etc.
Valid inventory recorded.	A–1 trace receiving reports to perpetual records.
	A–2 trace material issue slips to perpetual records.

Notice that the tests run in two directions from basic transaction files (A–1, A–2 and A–3) to the perpetual records and from the perpetual records (A–4) to the basic transaction files. A diagram of this two-way test design is shown below. (The codes in the boxes refer to the procedures in Exhibit 14–14.)

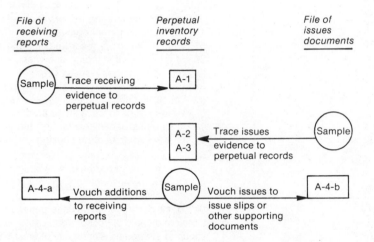

The cost of sales compliance procedures are designed to complete the tracing procedure started with the sample of inventory issue slips (or other issue documentation). This time, however, the procedure B–1 involves determining whether the issue documents were properly summarized, priced and posted to the cost of sales account. The other direction (B–2) is to vouch recorded cost of sales entries to supporting documentation.

The cash disbursement compliance procedures are designed to help the auditor determine whether cash disbursements were properly authorized and processed (C–1) and whether recorded debit entries from vouchers or cash disbursements are properly supported by the underlying documentation (C–2).

Many beginning auditors and students have difficulty designing audit procedures, especially for compliance auditing. A useful approach is to realize that all audit procedures are directly related to audit objectives, as was illustrated for inventory. The control objectives listed frequently in this text provide a framework to list the necessary procedures; then the procedures can be organized by document samples, as was done with the illustrative procedures in Exhibit 14–14. To provide an example of this relationship of procedures to control objectives, study Exhibit 14–15. Notice that a procedure may satisfy more than one objective.

EXHIBIT 14–15
Internal Accounting Control Objectives—Related to Audit Program Procedures

General Objectives	Procedures per Exhibit 14–14
1. Recorded transactions are *valid* and documented.	A–4a, A–4b, B–2, C–1b
2. All valid transactions are *recorded*.	A–1a, A–1b, A–2b, A–3, A–5, B–1b, C–1a, C–1c
3. Transactions are *authorized*.	A–2a, C–1b
4. Transactions are *accurately* prepared.	B–1a, B–3, C–1b
5. Transactions are properly *classified*.	C–1b, B–3
6. Transaction *accounting* complete and (7) in the *proper period*.	B–3, C–2

Compliance Audit Procedures for Fixed Assets

Compliance audit of transaction details is relevant in the case of fixed assets only when the transactions are numerous. When there are only a few major transactions, an audit of all of them will constitute a complete audit of recorded amounts and sampling will not be necessary. In either event, audit procedures should include an examination of evidential matter in the files.

Compliance auditing of computer application controls illustrated in Exhibit 14–10 may include the following:

Obtain and read instructions for conversion of data to machine-readable form.

Select a sample of punched cards and inspect them for evidence of key-verification.

Obtain and review check-off sheets showing the proper use of batch control totals.

Obtain and review error logs and error-correction reports.

Prepare and run test data to determine whether programmed edit tests are working properly.

Observe computer personnel review of output and trace distribution to list(s) of authorized recipients.

Compliance Audit Procedures for Liabilities

The compliance audit of transaction details is more extensive in the accounts and notes payable transactions than in other accounts in the liabilities and owner equity grouping. Some aspects of these procedures have already been encountered in connection with an examination of purchase and cash disbursement transactions. In Exhibit 14–16, portions

A. *Notes Payable.*
  1. Read director's and finance committee's minutes for authorization of financing transactions (such as short-term notes payable, bond offerings).
  2. Select a sample of paid notes:
     a. Recalculate interest expense for the period under audit.
     b. Trace interest expense to general ledger account.
     c. Vouch payment to canceled checks.
  3. Select a sample of notes payable:
     a. Vouch to authorization by directors or finance committee.
     b. Vouch cash receipt to bank statement.
B. *Accounts Payable.*
  1. Select a sample of open accounts payable and vouch to supporting documents of purchase (vendor's invoices).
  2. Trace debits arising from accounts payable transactions for proper classification.
  3. Select a sample of accounts payable entries recorded after the balance sheet date and vouch to supporting documents for evidence of proper cut-off—evidence that a liability should have been recorded as of the balance sheet date.

of earlier compliance audit procedures are abstracted and set in the context of an audit of liability transactions. To the extent that sufficient audit procedures have already been performed during the audit, these procedures will not have to be repeated.

Each of the compliance procedures in Exhibit 14–16 (except A–1) describes one or more attributes relevant for the design of audit samples. However, in the event that note transactions are few in number, they may be audited 100 percent. If such is the case, the compliance procedures will have been adapted to accomplish a large part of the substantive audit of the notes payable and interest expense balances.

REEVALUATION OF CONTROL

The audit manager must reevaluate the evidence obtained during the compliance audit phase for each system and compare the conclusions with the tentative conclusions made after the review phase. If more errors (lack of compliance with a control procedure) were found than specified as the maximum tolerable rate, the degree of control must be downgraded. For example, assume the audit manager, after the review phase, considered internal control over perpetual inventory records in the purchases and sales systems to be "excellent." Accordingly, in the sampling audit procedures of testing postings to these records, the tolerable rate of errors to total postings was established at 2 percent, with a low risk of overreliance (5 percent). Based on this degree of reliance, the audit manager agreed that the client's cyclical count of a portion of the physical inventory was acceptable and the preliminary substantive tests audit program called for observation of one of these cycle counts with few test counts.

However, assume that when the results of the sample compliance procedures were completed, the evaluation was that the population of postings could contain as many as 10 percent errors at the desired risk of overreliance (5 percent). The audit manager may now revise the audit program to require the client to make a complete count at year-end under observation of the audit team making many test counts. Thus, based on evidence from compliance audit procedures, the subsequent audit procedures were altered in nature (observation of complete physical inventory count versus partial count), timing (year-end versus interim) and extent (many test counts versus few).

These judgments and conclusions on the degree of reliance that can be vested in the existing accounting control systems will be addressed again in Chapters 17 and 18 where substantive year-end audit procedures are discussed. Descriptions of major deficiencies, control weaknesses and inefficiencies may be incorporated in a management letter to the client.

REVIEW QUESTIONS

14.1. Explain the auditor's interest in general and specific economic conditions with regard to the objective of determining whether inventories are properly valued.

14.2. What are the primary functions which should be segregated in a purchasing system?

14.3. Identify the users and uses of the receiving report.

14.4. How can the situation in which the same supporting documents are used for a duplicate payment be prevented?

14.5. Describe a "walk-through" of a purchase transaction. What sample documents would be collected? Why?

14.6. In the receiving and invoice processing system described in this chapter, the purchasing agent is described as the one who matches quantities, description and amounts on the invoice to the purchase order and receiving report. In many companies, this procedure is done by an accounts payable clerk. What other accounts payable functions should be separated from the clerk who does this matching? If an accounts payable clerk does the matching,

the purchasing function should be informed of receipt of goods. Why?

14.7. What features of the acquisition and expenditure cycle would be expected to prevent an employee's abstracting cash through creation of fictitious vouchers?

14.8. In fixed-asset management, which functional responsibilities should be delegated to separate departments or management levels?

14.9. What unusual transactions would auditors look for when scanning the fixed-assets records?

14.10. The essential characteristic of the liabilities control system is to separate the authorization and approval to initiate a transaction from the responsibility for recordkeeping. What would constitute the authorization for notes payable? What documentary evidence could auditors examine as evidence of this authorization?

14.11. What is the primary control to ensure all valid transactions are recorded and none omitted? How could auditors gather evidence that this control was operating in the case of cash disbursements?

14.12. Why would internal control over fixed assets of a computer leasing company be important? Refer to Exhibit 14–9, Internal Control Questionnaire, Fixed Assets and Related Accounts; design additional questions for a fixed-asset internal questionnaire that would be appropriate for a computer-leasing company.

14.13. Explain the difference in the audit manager's evaluation of controls following the review phase and following the compliance auditing of controls in the acquisition and expenditure cycle.

14.14. Assume that an audit manager decides to utilize sampling for the compliance audit of the voucher and cash disbursements system of two different clients, Mean Green Company and Burnt Orange Company. After the review phase of each, the audit manager concluded the controls for the system of Mean Green could be rated as "poor" (no reliance), while those of Burnt Orange were "excellent" (considerable reliance). For which client would the audit team design a compliance auditing program? Why?

14.15. Evaluate the following statement made by a client's purchasing manager: "We have computerized the purchasing/inventory/payables system. The most important part of our system is people; however, they are also our greatest problem."

EXERCISES AND PROBLEMS

14.16. **ICQ Items Matched to Control Objectives**
Refer to Exhibit 14–7 and 14–3. Reorganize the questions in Exhibit 14–3, Purchasing and Receiving System, under internal control objectives as was done in Exhibit 14–7 for cash disbursements. List the control objectives followed by the questions that relate to that objective. For example: Cash disbursement transactions *valid* and documented. (Questions 1, 16 and 23.) Note that some of the questions relate to more than one objective.

14.17. **Cash Disbursements: Control Objectives and Control Examples**
Prepare a table similar to Exhibit 14–13 (General Objectives and Examples of Specific Objectives—Purchases) for Cash Disbursements. Refer to the cash disbursement flowchart (Exhibit 14–6) and the ICQ (Exhibit 14–7) for examples of control techniques.

14.18. **Inventory ICQ Items: Objectives and Errors From Control Weaknesses**
Refer to the internal control questionnaire for the inventory system (Exhibit 14–5) and assume the answer to each question is "No." Prepare a table matching the questions to the seven control objectives (see Exhibit 7–6 and 14–7). Using your business experience, logic and imagination, give an example of an error (or irregularity) that could occur if the control was absent or ineffective. For example: Question 8— Issues made only on bills of material or invoice? Relates to the objective that inventory transactions are valid. The possible error (or irregularity) is that unauthorized issues could be made. Organize your table as follows:

Control Objective	Question Number	Possible Errors Due to Weaknesses

14.19. **Client Procedures When Deviation in Controls Occur**
Notice that the flowcharts in this chapter and Chapter 13 do not indicate the procedures that are followed in the case of an exception. For example, in the text material on receiving report and invoice processing (Exhibit 14–2 and the accompanying text material), (1) the stores department is to compare the goods received to the attached bill of lading and to their copies of the purchase order and receiving report.

However, nothing is stated about what should be done if the quantities, description or part number do not agree. Similarly, in the purchasing department, (2) the procedure "invoice terms and receiving report matched (to the vendors invoice) and reviewed" by the purchasing agent, and (3) the procedure "supporting documents and account distribution verified" in the accounts payable department are left undefined if there is a deviation.

a. Describe what would be a proper procedure in the event of a deviation or exception in each of these three cases.

b. Indicate for each case what evidence auditors could gather to show whether the procedure in (a) was actually followed.

c. Describe how these procedures could be added to the flowchart and questionnaire documentation of the control review.

14.20. **Purchase Control Objectives Related to Possible Errors and Compliance Audit Procedures**
Each of the seven control objectives could be stated in the negative, for example, Authorization: "Unauthorized transactions should not be recorded." Viewed in this way, one can see that an exception (an auditor's term for an error) to a policy could exist if the related control procedure were not followed. For example, "an unauthorized purchase transaction could be made and booked." Thus, each category of objectives also has a related "error" that can result from: (1) failure of the client to install adequate control procedures or (2) failure of client's personnel to perform specified control procedures. For each of the objectives listed in the table of General Objectives and Examples of Specific Objectives—Purchases (Exhibit 14–13):

a. Reword the general objectives in the negative.

b. For each general objective, indicate the exception or error that could occur

if the client did not have control procedures to accomplish that objective.

c. For each general objective, indicate at least one compliance audit procedure that would reveal an error in the client's controls that are listed as examples in Exhibit 14–13. See Exhibit 14–14 for examples of compliance audit procedures over purchase control techniques.

14.21. **Documentary Evidence For Purchasing Compliance Procedures**
One of the purposes of the review phase is to identify populations of documents that might be used in the compliance audit procedures. Refer to the flowcharts on the purchasing system in the chapter (Exhibits 14–1 and 14–2). For each file symbol:

a. Identify the population and the sequence of filing.

b. Describe what documentary evidence of compliance with a control procedure might exist.

c. Describe how auditors could be confident the population was complete prior to selecting a sample.

14.22. **Payables ICQ Items: Control Objectives, Compliance Procedures, and Possible Errors or Irregularities**
Listed below is a selection of items from the internal control questionnaire on payables shown in the chapter.

1. Is direct borrowing on notes payable authorized by the directors? The treasurer?

2. Are notes payable records kept by someone who cannot sign notes or checks?

3. Are vendors' statements and bank due notices compared with records of unpaid liabilities?

4. Are paid notes canceled, stamped "paid" and filed?

Required:
For each one:

a. Identify the control system characteristic to which it applies (e.g., segregation of duties—authorization of transactions, access to assets and recordkeeping duties; sound error-checking practice; and so on).

b. Specify one compliance audit procedure an auditor could use to determine whether the control was operating effectively.

c. Using your business experience, logic and/or imagination, give an example of an error or irregularity that could occur if the control was absent or ineffective.

14.23. **Purchasing Control Procedures**
Long, CPA, has been engaged to examine and report on the financial statements of Maylou Corporation. During the review phase of the study of Maylou's system of internal accounting control over purchases, Long was given the following (Exhibit 14.23–1) document flowchart for purchases.

Required:
a. Identify the procedures relating to purchase requisitions and purchase orders that Long would expect to find if Maylou's system of internal accounting control over purchases is effective. For example, purchase orders are prepared only after giving proper consideration to the time to order and quantity to order. Do not comment on the effectiveness of the flow of documents as presented in the flowchart or on separation of duties.

b. What are the factors to consider in determining—
   (1) The time to order?
   (2) The quantity to order?
                              (*AICPA* adapted)

14.24. **Compliance Procedures For Cash Disbursements**
The Runge Controls Corporation manufactures and markets electrical control systems—temperature controls, machine controls, burglar alarms and the like. Electrical and semiconductor parts are acquired from outside vendors and systems are assembled in Runge's plant. The company, of course, incurs other administrative and operating expenditures. Liabilities for goods and services purchased are entered in a vouchers-payable journal, at which time the debits are classified to the asset and expense accounts to which they apply.

The company has specified control procedures for approving vendor invoices for payment, for signing checks, for keeping records and for reconciling the checking accounts. The procedures appear to be well specified.

You are the senior auditor on the engagement and need to specify a program (list) of compliance procedures to audit the effectiveness of the controls over cash disbursements.

Required:
Using the seven general internal accounting control objectives, specify two or

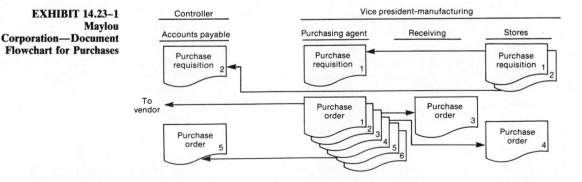

EXHIBIT 14.23–1
Maylou
Corporation—Document
Flowchart for Purchases

more compliance procedures to audit the effectiveness of typical control procedures. (Hint: from one sample of recorded cash disbursements, you can specify procedures related to several objectives. See Exhibit 14–14 for examples of compliance procedures over cash disbursements.) Organize your list according to the example shown below for the "completeness" objective.

Completeness Objective	Compliance-Procedures Program
All valid cash disbursements are recorded and none omitted.	Determine the numerical sequence of checks issued during the period and scan the sequence for missing numbers.
	Scan the accounts payable records for amounts that appear to be too long outstanding (indicating liabilities for which payment may have been made but not recorded properly).

DISCUSSION CASES

14.25. **Peabock Co.: Incomplete Flowchart, Control Procedures**

Peabock Co. is a wholesaler of soft goods. The inventory is composed of approximately 3,500 different items. The company employs a computerized batch processing system to maintain its perpetual inventory records. The system is run each weekend so that the inventory reports are available on Monday morning for management use. The system has been functioning satisfactorily for the past 15 months, providing the company with accurate records and timely reports.

The preparation of purchase orders has been automatic as a part of the inventory system to ensure that the company will maintain enough inventory to meet customer demand. When an inventory item falls below a predetermined level, a record of the item is written. This record is used in conjunction with the vendor file to prepare the purchase orders.

Exception reports are prepared during the update of the inventory and the preparation of the purchase orders. These reports list any errors or exceptions identified during the processing. In addition, the system provides for management approval of all purchase orders exceeding a specified amount. Any exceptions or items requiring management approval are handled by supplemental runs on Monday morning and are combined with the weekend results.

A system flowchart of Peabock Co.'s inventory and purchase-order procedure appears following.

Required:

a. The illustrated system flowchart (Exhibit 14.25–1) of Peabock Co.'s inventory and purchase-order system was prepared before the system was fully operational. Several steps which are important to the successful operations of the system were inadvertently omitted from the chart. Now that the system is operating effectively, management wants the system documentation complete and would like the flowchart corrected. Describe the steps which have been omitted and indicate where the omissions have occurred. The flowchart does not need to be redrawn.

b. In order for Peabock's inventory/purchase order system to function properly, control procedures would be included in the system. Describe the type of control procedures Peabock

EXHIBIT 14.25–1
Peabock Company—Inventory and Purchase Order Procedure 12/31/85

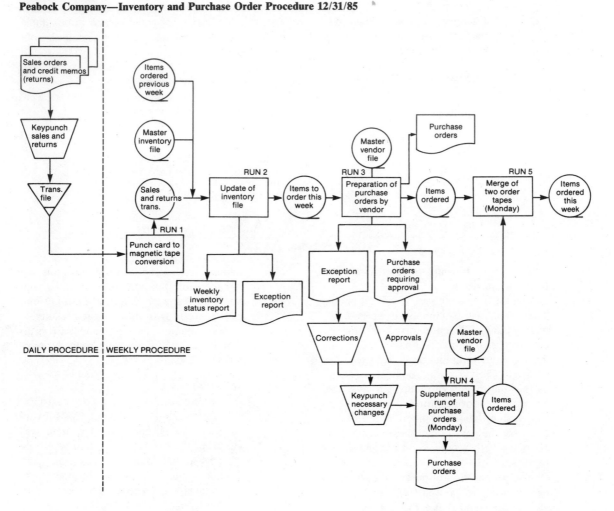

Co. would use in its system to assure proper functioning and indicate where these procedures would be placed in the system.

(*CMA* adapted)

14.26. Dunbar Camera: Control Evaluation and Financial Impact of Weaknesses

Dunbar Camera Manufacturing, Inc., is a manufacturer of high-priced precision motion picture cameras in which the specifications of component parts are vital to the manufacturing process. Dunbar buys valuable camera lenses and large quantities of

sheet metal and screws. Screws and lenses are ordered by Dunbar and billed by the vendors on a unit basis. Sheet metal is ordered by Dunbar and billed by the vendors on a weight basis. The receiving clerk is responsible for documenting the quality and quantity of merchandise received.

A review of the system of internal control indicates that the following procedures are being followed:

Receiving Report:
1. Properly approved purchase orders, which are prenumbered, are filed numerically. The copy sent to the receiv-

ing clerk is an exact duplicate of the copy sent to the vendor. Received merchandise is recorded on the duplicate copy by the receiving clerk.

Sheet metal:

2. The company receives sheet metal by railroad. The railroad independently weighs the sheet metal and reports the weight and date of receipt on a bill of lading (waybill), which accompanies all deliveries. The receiving clerk only checks the weight on the waybill to the purchase order.

Screws:

3. The receiving clerk opens cartons containing screws, then inspects and weighs the contents. The weight is converted to number of units by means of conversion charts. The receiving clerk then checks the computed quantity to the purchase order.

Camera Lenses:

4. Each camera lens is delivered in a separate corrugated carton. Cartons are counted as they are received by the receiving clerk and the number of cartons is checked to the purchase orders.

Required:

a. Explain why the internal control procedures as they apply individually to receiving reports and the receipt of sheet metal, screws and camera lenses are adequate (strengths) or inadequate (weaknesses). ***Do not discuss recommendations for improvements.***

b. What financial statement distortions may arise because of the weaknesses or inadequacies in Dunbar's system of internal control and how may they occur?

(*AICPA* adapted)

14.27. **Alex Corporation: Control Weaknesses and Recommendations**
Alex Corporation manufactures several lines of machine tools primarily for the automotive industry. As a consequence of the high demand for its products, the firm is currently operating three shifts, five days a week. Maintenance work is done on the weekends unless breakdowns occur that require immediate attention.

The production supervisors have complained that many times the maintenance work is not completed because parts have not been available in the storeroom. The internal audit staff has been asked to review the operating and accounting procedures of the maintenance crew and storerooms. The internal audit staff has identified the facts and observed the procedures described below during its preliminary investigation.

The maintenance crew consist of three persons, each of whom works 12 hours on most Saturdays and Sundays. Two of the three are "on call" during the week for breakdowns. Each person on the maintenance crew reports directly to the production supervisor. At the end of the week, the production supervisor leaves a list of maintenance work to be completed. The maintenance crew leaves the list for the supervisor at the end of the weekend indicating with a check mark the jobs which were completed and giving a reason for those which were not.

Maintenance parts and supplies are stored in a separate locked room. Many of the parts and supplies are very small in size and monetary value. However, there are a large number which are very expensive and quite portable. The production supervisor, the receiving supervisor and all of the maintenance crew members have keys to this room.

Perpetual inventory cards are maintained for all parts and supplies in the maintenance storeroom; the inventory cards are kept in the maintenance storeroom. When ordered parts and supplies are received, the receiving supervisor stores them in the storeroom and records the receipt on the respective perpetual inventory cards. The maintenance crew members record deductions on the inventory cards when they take parts and supplies. Parts and supplies are ordered by the receiving supervisor based upon notes from the maintenance crew members indicating that quantities are low or depleted.

The accounting department uses the perpetual inventory cards at the end of the month to determine the value of the maintenance parts and supplies inventory. The balances indicated on the inventory cards are multiplied by the most recent prices to determine the carrying value of the maintenance inventory.

Required:

Identify the internal control weaknesses and recommend improvements which the internal audit staff should include in its report regarding the operating and accounting procedures of Alex Corporation's maintenance crew and storeroom. Use the following format in preparing your answer.

Weaknesses	Recommendations
1.	1.

Hint: in solving problems such as this (and in evaluating controls in actual practice), utilize the logic suggested in SAS 1 AU 320 which can be paraphrased as follows:

a. Think of everything that could go wrong—the errors and irregularities that could occur (make a list on scratch paper). (Refer to the objectives in Exhibit 7–6: validity, completeness, authorization, accuracy, classification, accounting and proper period.)

b. Determine the control procedures to prevent such errors and irregularities (match to your list in (a) on scratch paper).

c. Compare the ideal controls to the situation described (reread the problem).

d. List the weaknesses—errors and irregularities not covered by existing controls (make margin notes in the narrative of the problem).

(*CMA* adapted)

CHAPTER 15

PROFESSIONAL STANDARDS SOURCES		
Compendium Section	**Document Reference**	**Topic**
AU 320	SAS 1	The Auditor's Study and Evaluation of Internal Control
AU 324	SAS 44	Special-Purpose Reports on Internal Accounting Control at Service Organizations

Personnel and Payroll Cycle

The four major objectives in this chapter are related to the tools and techniques described in Part 2 (Chapters 6–12). After completing this chapter, you should understand:

☐ A business approach to understanding the personnel and payroll cycle.

☐ The flow of transactions in a typical personnel and payroll cycle, how specific accounts are affected and the elements of control within the cycle.

☐ The audit procedures used to gather evidence regarding compliance with control procedures.

☐ Evaluation of the controls (strengths) and lack of controls (weaknesses) to determine the effect upon the nature, timing and extent of procedures for auditing account balances.

The discussion of each of these four topics is intended to enable you to apply the overall concepts on evidence gathering and internal control presented in previous chapters to the transactions in the personnel and payroll cycle. You should be able to understand a systematic approach that relates audit work to general and specific objectives.

Management decisions about payroll and other compensation costs are important because the resources allocated for labor services are usually large. Further, personnel policies and procedures are crucial to a business because people are the most important "asset" of any business, even though this asset is not formally recognized in the financial statements.

The personnel and payroll cycle not only includes transactions which affect the wage and salary accounts, but also the transactions which affect pension benefits, deferred compensation contracts, compensatory stock option plans, employee benefits (such as health insurance), payroll taxes and related liabilities for these costs. However, audit concerns and procedures explained in this chapter will be limited mostly to techniques for reviewing and evaluating transactions and balances of the wage and salary accounts and the related payroll liabilities.

The following are typical functions of the personnel and payroll cycle:

Manpower planning and scheduling.

Personnel selection and termination (hiring and firing).

Labor relations (compensation rates and indirect compensation).

Reporting attendance and work performed.

Payroll accounting (gross pay, deductions, employee benefits, adjustments, related expenses and accruals).

Payroll distribution and disbursement.

Several of these functions consist of interrelated processing tasks that are functions of cycles previously discussed. For example, payroll disbursements may be processed through the normal cash disbursements system and accrued liabilities related to payroll may be subject to the same controls as other current liabilities, as described in Chapter 14.

A BUSINESS APPROACH   An overview of the personnel management system in a client company can contribute significant understanding of payroll and related costs. Such an overview can assist in planning the compliance procedures. In most cases, the overview also contributes to planning the procedures for auditing balances as well.

Auditors should first determine whether the business is labor-intensive or capital-intensive. The absolute magnitude and the percent relationship of payroll costs to total revenue and total expense will inform auditors the degree of importance to attach to the audit of such costs. The data processing system, valuation and legal compliance are the areas of particular interest to auditors.

Data Processing System   The general design of the data processing system is important. Some companies may account for payroll costs in a simple manner to satisfy legal requirements—classifying output in a few accounts for direct labor, indirect labor, sales salaries and executive salaries. The legal requirements include payroll accounting for tax reporting and withholding purposes and inventory-production cost accounting for income tax purposes.

In contrast, other companies may use a complex managerial accounting and reporting system. Of course, such a system must be designed to satisfy basic legal recordkeeping requirements, but the system of reporting, analyzing and controlling costs may be far more elaborate than the simple legalistic-system output. A managerial-oriented system may segment direct and indirect labor into several budgetary categories and may segment costs by responsibility centers or by cost centers. Thus, aggregate sums of related costs (such as direct labor) may not appear in a single account but instead may be subclassified in a wide variety of accounts.

If the system is a simple legalistic one, the opportunities for close managerial control are minimized and auditors will probably have to perform extensive compliance and substantive procedures. On the other hand, a more complex managerial-oriented system provides for closer managerial review and control of errors and out-of-line costs. Thus, auditors may rely on managerial control to some extent, provided they can find evidence that the review-control system is actually used effectively by managers.

In connection with a business approach to understanding the client, auditors can incorporate earlier acquired knowledge of the marketing and production functions. Payroll costs and accounting for standard, repetitive marketing and production operations tend to be more systematized and uncomplicated than when marketing and production is oriented to special orders, special promotions and nonrepetitive operations. A good understanding of the business also contributes insights to relative staff levels in production, marketing, maintenance, administration, and research and development functions. The nature of seasonal fluctuations and the mode of payment (such as hourly, monthly, bonus, commission) can also be discerned through knowledge of marketing and production organization features.

Valuation   For the most part, payroll cost valuation problems are not difficult. However, some compensation costs and benefit programs (such as stock options, bonuses, pension plans) typically involve complex measurement methods and issues.

Auditors should determine how the client sets pay rates. For executives, such determinations may be a matter of record in the directors' minutes, or they may be recorded in reports of periodic salary review committees. In the case of office and production workers, the personnel department generally includes a labor relations and salary administration function. Pay scales for unionized workers may be formalized in a union contract. In general, the more formal the system the better, because objective evidence of basic rates is available in documentary sources.

One type of valuation problem may arise in audits of medium-to-small businesses. The Internal Revenue Code requires that compensation be "reasonable" in order to qualify as a business deduction, otherwise a portion of an unreasonably large salary may be considered a "dividend" paid by a corporation. When this happens, the corporation's income tax liability may be increased materially. Auditors should be alert to unreasonably large salaries, especially when paid to officers who are controlling stockholders.

Pension and stock option cost measurement principles are specified in APB Opinion No. 8[1] and APB Opinion No. 25[2]. The audit of these costs and other costs computed as bonuses, incentive pay and deferred compensation requires that the auditor obtain copies of the plans and contracts in order to understand the valuation problems.

Legal Compliance   Personnel and payroll administration are subject to a wide variety of laws and regulations. The major ones are: federal, state and local income tax withholding regulations; social security withholding and contribution regulations; federal and state unemployment insurance laws; workmen's compensation insurance laws; minimum wage laws; equal employment opportunity laws; industrial safety laws; the federal welfare and pension plans disclosure act and the pension reform act of 1974 (ERISA—Employee Retirement Income Security Act). With almost every session of the U.S. Congress, some form of social legislation impacting on workers—their wages, working conditions, pensions, benefits and so forth—is proposed.

Auditors need to be thoroughly familiar with the laws that produce regular and direct business expenses (such as social security, unemployment insurance, withholding regulations, workmen's compensation insurance). However, the effect of other social legislation concerning employment opportunities and industrial safety are difficult to evaluate in an audit situation and the auditor's duties in such cases are the same as those associated with other kinds of contingencies.

Compliance with plans, contracts and union agreements respecting compensation should be reviewed. These private agreements contain rights and obligations that create liabilities for the company. Failure to comply with one or more provisions of such agreements may mean the client has not recorded compensation cost and a related liability. For example, failure to award stock options, failure to program payment of a cost-of-living wage escalator or failure to pay employees the rate required by their job classifications are errors in compensation cost measurement that result from noncompliance.

**REVIEW PHASE: The functions of a cycle consist of transaction processing tasks, and their
FLOW OF   design should provide for effective control procedures and techniques.
TRANSACTIONS   The auditors' primary objective in understanding and documenting the
AND ELEMENTS   flow of transactions in the review phase of the study and evaluation of
OF CONTROL**   internal control is to determine the strengths that can be relied upon to give reasonable assurance that material errors could not occur. If controls are inadequate, the weaknesses must be evaluated to determine what

---

[1] "Accounting for the Cost of Pension Plans," as amended by SFAS no. 36 (AC 4063).
[2] "Accounting for Stock Issued to Employees" (AC 4062).

substantive procedures are necessary to give reasonable assurance that material errors did not occur. To understand and evaluate the flow of transactions in the personnel and payroll cycle, auditors must be familiar with the common procedures, normal separation of duties and appropriate controls. Questionnaires and flowchart tools may be used to document the review of the overall system for controlling payroll costs.

The study and evaluation of payroll-system control normally takes on added importance because most companies have fairly elaborate and well-controlled personnel and payroll functions. Further, the transactions in this cycle are numerous during the year, yet result in minimum amounts in balance sheet accounts at year-end. (Cash transactions have a similar effect.) Therefore, in most audit engagements, the review of controls and compliance audit of transaction details constitute the major portion of the audit time. Procedures devoted to auditing the payroll-related accounts balances give the auditors assurance that the accounts affected by these transactions do not contain material errors.

When assessing the risk of material errors and irregularities in this cycle, auditors must be aware that most payroll errors or irregularities are one of two types:

1. Recorded employee transactions are not valid; for example, fictitious (or former) employees receive pay checks which are cashed by someone in the client's employ.

2. Recorded attendance transactions are not valid; for example, fictitious hours are included in hours used to determine gross pay for existing employees.

The control characteristics of separation of duties and authorizations (such as hiring, termination and timekeeping) prevent or correct these errors and are therefore especially important in the evaluation of controls in this cycle. A payroll data processing control system should exhibit separation of five functional responsibilities. These responsibilities overlap with the cash disbursements and accounts payable internal control systems.

1. Personnel or Labor Relations Department. Persons independent of the other functions should have transaction initiation authority to add new employees to the payroll, to delete terminated employees, to obtain authorizations for deductions (such as insurance, saving bonds, withholding tax exemptions) and to transmit authority for rate changes to the payroll department.

2. Supervision. All pay base data (hours, job number, absences, time off allowed for emergencies, etc.) should be approved by an employee's immediate supervisor.

3.   Timekeeping and Cost Accounting.   Data on which pay is based (such as hours, piece-rate volume, incentives) should be accumulated independent of other functions. Thus, cost data accumulated can be entered into the cost accounting system.

4.   Payroll Accounting.   Using rate and deduction information supplied by the personnel function and base data supplied by the timekeeping-supervision functions, independent persons should prepare individual paychecks, employee wage and salary records and summary accounting journal entries.

5.   Payroll Distribution.   Actual custody of paychecks and cash should be controlled when distributed to employees so that the checks or cash do not return to persons involved in any of the other four functions.

These functional responsibilities relate primarily to nonsalaried employees of a manufacturing business. For salaried employees, the system is simplified by not having to collect timekeeping data. In nonmanufacturing businesses, the cost accounting operations may be very simple or even nonexistent. The relative importance of each of these five areas should be determined for each engagement in light of the nature and organization of the client's operations.

The flowchart in Exhibit 15–1 illustrates the segregation of functional responsibilities related to employment authorization (personnel department), timekeeping and supervisor's approval. The remaining payroll responsibilities center in the preparation and distribution of checks.

In some companies, the payroll and personnel cycle may begin in the personnel department where the initial interview takes place. Note that hiring authorization forms, job classification forms and pay rate authorization forms are on file in both the personnel and payroll departments. The illustrated system assumes that a job time ticket, noting the employee's department and time indicated thereon, is forwarded to cost accounting as well as payroll.

The payroll and cost accounting activities are illustrated in Exhibit 15–2. Note that four copies of the payroll register are prepared.

Copy 1 is forwarded to accounts payable for preparation of a voucher to transfer funds to the payroll checking account.

Copy 2 is forwarded to general ledger accounting for comparison to the documents from accounts payable (and cash disbursements). In some systems, these first two copies will be replaced by a standard journal voucher containing only summary totals.

Copy 3 is used by the cost distribution department to reconcile to the labor distribution sheet.

Copy 4 is filed in payroll for future reference.

EXHIBIT 15–1
Employment and Timekeeping

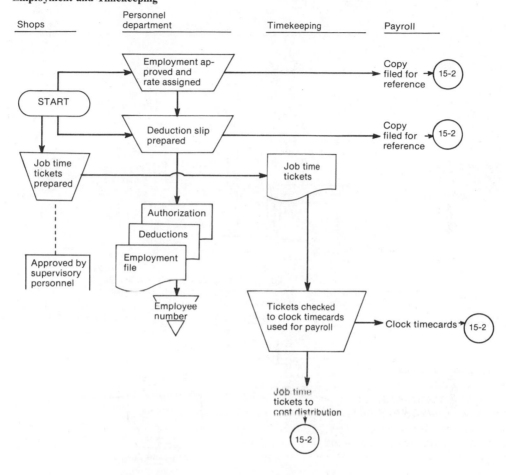

The labor distribution sheet sent to the accounting department (or a journal voucher summarizing the cost accounting) provides the information for entries in the general ledger. This process is developed more fully in the following chapter (see Exhibit 16–4).

The internal control questionnaire (ICQ) illustrated in Exhibit 15–3 provides examples of further controls. You should carefully follow the flow of documents in the illustrated flowcharts and study the questions in the questionnaire to understand the typical controls in this cycle (and to be able to complete the assigned problems). The most common control deficiency in the personnel and payroll cycle is an inadequate separation of duties. If the foreman or supervisor has too many duties (for example, hiring and firing, rate authorization and check distribution) in addition to approving the timecards, the opportunity exists for unauthorized employees or unauthorized hours or pay rates to be entered into the system.

EXHIBIT 15–2
Check Preparation and Cost Accounting

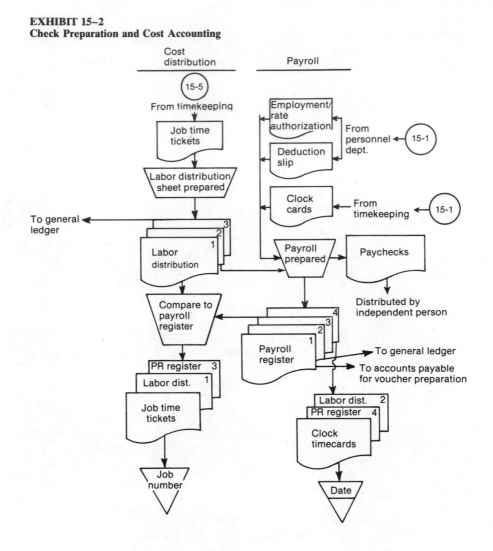

Personnel and payroll procedures produce documentary files that can be sampled in the compliance audit of transaction details. The most important files are: (1) Personnel Department personnel files, (2) rate and deduction authorizations filed in Payroll, (3) job time tickets filed in Cost Distribution and the labor distribution worksheet filed in General Ledger and (4) clock cards filed in Payroll and the payroll listing filed in Accounts Payable. Each of these files coordinate with one or more of the others and can be audited in both directions as suggested in the discussion accompanying Exhibit 15–5.

By reference to the internal control questionnaire and flowchart, several kinds of error-checking procedures may be noted, including:

EXHIBIT 15–3
Internal Control
Questionnaire—Personnel
and Payroll System

1. Are names of employees hired or terminated reported in writing to the payroll department by the personnel department?
2. Is the payroll compared to personnel files periodically? How often? By internal auditors?
3. Are all wage rates determined by contract, agreement or policy and approved by a responsible personnel officer?
4. Are authorizations for deductions, signed by the employees, on file?
5. Are all employees paid by check?
6. Are payroll check blanks prenumbered? Is a special payroll bank account used?
7. Are payroll checks signed by persons who neither prepare the payroll or the checks, nor have custody of the other cash funds, nor keep accounting records?
8. Are checks distributed by someone other than the employee's immediate supervisor?
9. Is the payroll bank account reconciled by someone who does not prepare payrolls, sign checks or distribute paychecks?
10. If payments are made in cash: Is an independent agent such as an armored car service used? Is currency placed in envelopes by employees who do not prepare payrolls? Are receipts obtained from employees?
11. Are unclaimed wages deposited in a special bank account or otherwise controlled by a responsible officer?
12. Is there a timekeeping department (function) independent of the payroll department?
13. Are timekeeping and cost accounting records (such as hours, dollars) reconciled with payroll department calculations of wages and salaries?
14. Are timecards or piece work reports prepared by the employee approved by his or her supervisor? Is a time clock or other electromechanical system used?
15. Are payroll department personnel rotated in their duties? Required to take vacations? Bonded?
16. Is the payroll register sheet signed by the employee preparing it and approved prior to payment?
17. Are payrolls audited periodically by internal auditors?
18. Do internal auditors conduct occasional surprise distributions of paychecks or cash?
19. Is the payroll preparation, check preparation or check signature performed with computer equipment? If so, complete the relevant portions of the computer internal control questionnaire.

Periodic comparison of the payroll to the personnel department files to check for terminated employees not deleted.

Periodic rechecking of wage-rate authorizations.

Payroll bank account reconciliation.

Rotation of employee duties.

Reconciliation of payroll data with cost accounting data.

When the review phase is completed, the audit manager must evaluate the personnel and payroll cycle and its various functions or systems to determine reliance thereon. The audit manager will use a systematic framework, such as illustrated in Exhibit 15–4, to determine the strengths of the client procedures. The objectives listed in Exhibit 15–4 are the same as the ones presented in previous chapters, expressed here in specific terms for the personnel and payroll functions.

**EXHIBIT 15–4
Internal Accounting
Control Objectives
Personnel and Payroll
Cycle**

General Objectives	Examples of Specific Objectives
1. Recorded payroll transactions are *valid* and documented.	Payroll accounting separated from personnel and timekeeping. Time cards indicate approval by supervisor's signature. Payroll files compared to personnel files periodically.
2. Valid payroll transactions are *recorded* and none omitted.	Employees' complaints about pay checks investigated and resolved (written records maintained and reviewed by internal auditors).
3. Payroll names, rates, hours, and deductions are *authorized*.	Names of new hires or terminations reported immediately in writing to payroll by the personnel department. Authorization for deductions kept on file. Rate authorized by union contract, agreement or written policy and approved by personnel officer.
4. Payroll computations contain *correct* gross pay, deductions and net pay.	Payroll computations checked by person independent of preparation. Totals of payroll register reconciled to totals of payroll distribution by general accounting.
5. Payroll transactions are *classified* correctly as direct or indirect labor.	Employee classification reviewed periodically. Overall charges to indirect labor compared to direct labor and total product costs periodically.
6. Payroll transaction *accounting* is complete.	Details of employee withholding reconciled periodically to liability control accounts. Employee tax expense and liabilities prepared in conjunction with payroll.
7. Payroll costs and expenses are recognized in the *proper period*.	Month-end accruals reviewed by internal auditors. Payroll computed, paid and booked in timely manner.

The audit manager must decide which systems contain enough strengths (controls) to rely upon and the degree of reliance. Then specific audit procedures must be designed to gather evidence of whether these controls are operating as described in the review documentation. Alterna-

EXHIBIT 15–5
Audit Program—
Selected Compliance
Audit Procedures

A. *Personnel Files and Compensation Documents.*
  1. Select a sample of personnel files. (If the files are magnetic tape or disk, use generalized audit software to select the sample and print out relevant fields.)
    a. Review personnel files for complete information on employment date, authority to add to payroll, job classification, wage rate and authorized deductions.
    b. Trace pay rate to union contracts or other rate authorization. Trace salaries to director's minutes for authorization.
    c. Trace pay rate and deduction information to payroll department files used in payroll preparation (file likely to be a master file on tape or disk).
  2. Obtain copies of pension plans, stock options, profit sharing and bonus plans. Review and extract relevant portions that relate to payroll deductions, fringe benefit expenses, accrued liabilities and financial statement disclosure.

B. *Payrolls.*
  1. Select a sample of payroll register entries:
    a. Vouch pay rate and deductions to personnel files or other authorizations.
    b. Vouch hours worked to clock timecards. Note supervisor's approval.
    c. Recalculate gross pay, deductions, net pay.
    d. Foot (recalculate addition) a selection of periodic payrolls.
    e. Vouch to canceled payroll check. Examine employees' endorsement.
    Note: Sample selection and the recalculations may be done with generalized audit software.
  2. Select a sample of clock timecards, note supervisor's approval and trace to periodic payroll sheets.
  3. Vouch a sample of periodic payroll totals to payroll bank account transfer vouchers and vouch payroll bank account deposit slip for cash transfer.
  4. Trace a sample of employees' payroll entries to cumulative payroll records maintained for tax reporting purposes. Reconcile total of employees' payroll records with payrolls paid for the year.
    Note: The reconciliation may be started using generalized audit software.
  5. Review computer-printed error messages for evidence of the use of check digits, valid codes, limit tests and other input, processing and output application controls. Investigate correction and resolution of errors.
  6. Trace payroll information to management reports and to general ledger account postings.
  7. Obtain control of a periodic payroll and conduct a surprise distribution of paychecks. (When controls are considered deficient.)

C. *Cost Distribution Reports.*
  1. Select a sample of cost accounting analyses of payroll:
    a. Reconcile periodic (weekly) totals with payroll payments for the same periods.
    b. Vouch to time records (job time tickets).
  2. Trace cost accounting labor cost distributions to management reports and postings in general ledger and subsidiary account(s).
  3. Select a sample of labor cost items in (a) ledger accounts and/or (b) management reports. Vouch to supporting cost accounting analyses.
    Note: Sample selections from accounts management reports and cost accounting analyses may involve using generalized audit software to read computerized database files.

tively, the weaknesses (absent or unreliable controls) must be evaluated in terms of the possible monetary impact on financial statements of material errors that could occur. In this case, appropriate year-end audit procedures must be designed to provide reasonable assurance to detect material errors, if any occurred.

COMPLIANCE AUDITING

Payroll processing is usually one of the first applications to be implemented on a computer because it is basically the same for all businesses and the repetition of like calculations in volume are ideally suited for automation. The files in a personnel and payroll database and the related record fields auditors should expect to find include:
Reference files:

> Personnel master—employee name and number, date hired, education, skills, employment history, withholding factors.
>
> Payroll master—employee number, name, department, address, compensation class, deduction codes.
>
> Compensation table—compensation classes matched to hourly rates.
>
> Deduction tables—deduction codes matched to amounts or formulae.

Dynamic files:

> Employee earning records—employee number, compensation class, gross (YTD), deductions (YTD), net (YTD).
>
> Deduction, withholding and tax—employee number, social security number, tax (YTD and QTD).
>
> "Timecard" transactions—employee number, compensation class, hours (regular and overtime), time period, shop or department.
>
> Cost distribution—job or department, employee number, job or process number, labor costs, benefit costs.

Generalized audit software can be used extensively in the compliance audit of the personnel and payroll cycle. Files can be matched, and unmatched records and differences in common fields can be printed out. Random samples can be selected of table files and printed for vouching to union contracts or other authorizations. Random samples can also be selected for recomputation using the generalized software or printed out as working papers for vouching as indicated in Exhibit 15–5.

In both manual and computer systems, compliance audit of transaction details are highly important because the evidence bears heavily on the reliability of internal management reports and analyses. In turn, reliance on these reports and analyses, along with other analytical relationships, constitutes a major portion of the audit of payroll, compensation costs and cost accounting balances.

Typical compliance audit procedures are illustrated in Exhibit 15–5. Along with the procedures are indications of some ways in which typical manual-oriented procedures may be coordinated with tests in a computer environment.

These compliance procedures are designed to produce evidence of the following:

Adequacy of personnel files, especially the authorizations of pay rate and deductions used in calculating pay. The compliance procedures run in two directions (codes below refer to procedures in Exhibit 15–5).

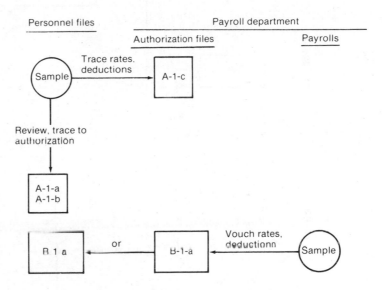

Accuracy of the periodic payrolls recorded in accounts and in employees' cumulative wage records. The compliance procedures tend to center on the periodic payrolls. The diagram on page 530 shows that the sample of employees' paycheck entries and totals from payrolls are both vouched to supporting documents and traced to other records and reports.

Accuracy of cost accounting distributions and management reports. The cost accounting for labor costs must be reasonably accurate because good management reports contribute to cost control. The auditor who wishes to rely on the cost accounting system must determine whether it contains and transmits accurate information. Procedure B–6 is part of this work. Other procedures are shown in the diagram on page 531.

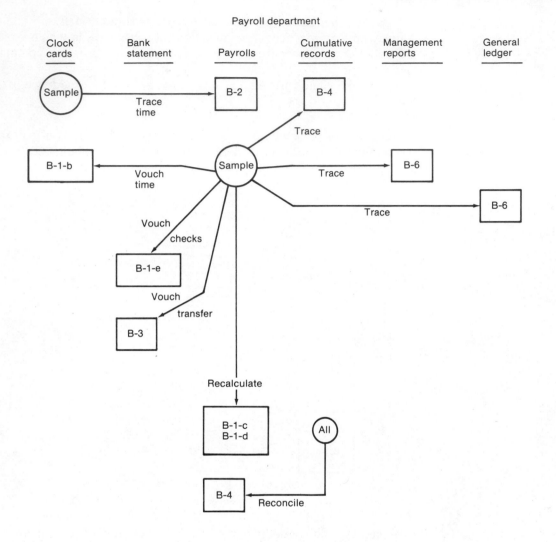

Auditors may perform a surprise observation of a payroll distribution when controls are very weak. Such an observation involves taking control of paychecks and accompanying a client representative as the distribution takes place. Care is taken to see that each employee is identified and that only one check is given to each individual. Unclaimed checks are controlled, and in this manner auditors hope to detect any fictitious persons on the payroll.

Computerized payroll and cost accounting systems are encountered frequently. Their complexity, however, may range from an application of simply writing payroll checks to an integrated system that prepares management reports and cost analyses based on payroll and cost distribution

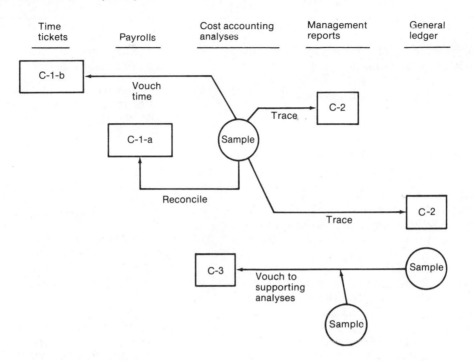

inputs. Computerized audit techniques such as the use of test data are frequently employed to audit controls in such systems, and parallel simulation may be applied efficiently to test an integrated system. Refer to Chapter 9 for an explanation of these computerized procedures.

REEVALUATION OF CONTROL

When the compliance audit is complete and documented in the working papers, the audit manager must reevaluate the controls to be relied upon. The tentative conclusions made after the review phase constitute a hypothesis that will be supported or rejected based upon the evidence from auditing compliance with the controls. If the evidence from the compliance procedures reveals more errors (lack of compliance with a control procedure) than specified as a tolerable rate before the audit procedures were performed, a hypothesis that controls are "excellent" must be rejected and the degree of control (and reliance thereon) downgraded.

Based upon the reevaluation conclusions, the audit manager will reexamine the planned source(s) of reasonable assurance that the financial statements do not contain material errors. This reexamination will result in strengthening the confidence in the preliminary audit program for year-end substantive procedures (when client controls are effective) or requiring that the preliminary audit program procedures be increased in nature, timing and/or extent (when client controls are deficient).

REVIEW QUESTIONS

15.1. What grouping of accounts is associated with the personnel and payroll cycle?

15.2. In a payroll system, what duties should be separated?

15.3. Why might an auditor conduct a surprise observation of a payroll distribution? What should be observed?

15.4. What are the most common errors and/or irregularities in the personnel and payroll cycle? What control characteristics are auditors looking for to prevent or detect these errors?

15.5. Describe a "walk-through" of the personnel and payroll transaction flow from hiring authorization to payroll check disbursement. What document copies would be collected? What controls noted? How would the walk-through be modified if payroll is processed by a computer?

15.6. Assume the processing of payroll is accomplished with a computer utilizing the files described in this chapter. What files could be matched for audit purposes utilizing generalized audit software?

15.7. Why can reevaluation after the compliance audit be referred to as hypothesis testing? What is the hypothesis that is tested? What is the audit impact of rejecting the hypothesis?

15.8. Evaluate the following statement made by an audit senior. "It is impossible to determine who authorizes a transaction when the payroll accounting is computerized."

15.9. Assume you are the audit senior conducting a review of the payroll system of a new client. In the process of interviewing the payroll department manager, she makes the following statement: "We don't need many controls since our payroll is done outside the company by Automated Data Processing, a service bureau." Evaluate her statement and describe the effect of a service bureau on your review of controls. You may want to reread SAS 44 (AU 324), "Special-Purpose Reports on Internal Accounting Control at Service Organizations."

EXERCISES AND PROBLEMS

15.10. **ICQ Items Matched to Control Objectives**
The internal accounting control objectives listed in Chapter 7 are: (1) validity, (2) completeness, (3) authorization, (4) accuracy, (5) classification, (6) accounting, and (7) proper period. Refer to Exhibit 15–3 and prepare a table matching the questionnaire question numbers to the seven control objectives. A question may relate to more than one objective. (Hint: see Exhibit 14–7 for format and refer to Exhibit 15–4 for control procedures related to the objectives.)

15.11. **ICQ Items: Errors That Could Occur From Control Weaknesses**
Refer to the internal control questionnaire on the personnel and payroll system (Ex-

hibit 15–3) and assume the answer to each question is "No." Prepare a table matching the questions to errors or irregularities that could occur because of the absence of the control. Your column headings should be:

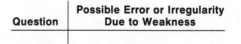

Question	Possible Error or Irregularity Due to Weakness

15.12. **Documentary Evidence For Compliance Procedures**
One of the secondary purposes of the *review phase* is to identify document popula-

tions that might be used in the *compliance audit procedures phase* of the proper study and evaluation of internal control. Refer to the flowcharts in this chapter (exhibits 15–1 and 15–2). For each file symbol:

a. Identify the population and sequence of filing.

b. Describe what documentary evidence might exist of compliance with a control procedure.

c. Relate the file to the audit procedures described in Exhibit 15–5.

15.13. **ICQ Items: Control Objectives, Compliance Procedures, and Possible Errors or Irregularities**

Listed below is a selection of items from the internal control questionnaire shown in the chapter.

1. Are names of employees hired or terminated reported in writing to the payroll department by the personnel department?

2. Are payroll checks signed by persons who neither prepare the payroll or checks, nor have custody of other cash funds, nor keep accounting records?

3. Is there a timekeeping department (function) independent of the payroll department?

4. Are timekeeping and cost accounting records (such as hours, dollars) reconciled with payroll department calculations of wages and salaries?

Required:

For each one:

a. Identify the control objective to which it applies.

b. Specify one compliance audit procedure an auditor could use to determine whether the control was operating effectively.

c. Using your business experience, logic and/or imagination, give an example of an error or irregularity that could occur if the control was absent or ineffective.

15.14. **Evaluation of Controls When Employees Are Paid In Cash**

You are engaged in auditing the financial statements of Henry Brown, a large independent contractor. All employees are paid in cash because Mr. Brown believes this arrangement reduces clerical expenses and is preferred by his employees.

During the audit you find in the petty cash fund approximately $200, of which $185 is stated to be unclaimed wages. Further investigation reveals Mr. Brown has installed the procedure of putting any unclaimed wages in the petty cash fund so that the cash can be used for disbursements. When the claimant to the wages appears, he is paid from the petty cash fund. Mr. Brown contends that this procedure reduces the number of checks drawn to replenish the petty cash fund and centers the responsibility for all cash on hand in one person inasmuch as the petty cash custodian distributes the pay envelopes.

Required:

a. Does Mr. Brown's system provide proper internal control of unclaimed wages? Explain fully.

b. Because Mr. Brown insists on paying salaries in cash, what procedures would you recommend to provide better internal control over unclaimed wages?

(*AICPA* adapted)

15.15. **Compliance Audit Procedures, Evaluation of Possible Diverting of Payroll Funds**

The Generous Loan Company has 100 branch loan offices. Each office has a manager and four or five subordinates who are employed by the manager. Branch managers prepare the weekly payroll, including their own salaries, and pay employees from cash on hand. Employees sign the payroll sheet signifying receipt of their salary. Hours worked by hourly personnel are inserted in the payroll register sheet from timecards prepared by the employees and approved by the manager.

The weekly payroll register sheets are sent to the home office along with other accounting statements and reports. The home office compiles employee earnings records and prepares all federal and state salary reports from the weekly payroll sheets.

Salaries are established by home office job-cvaluation schedules. Salary adjustments, promotions and transfers of full-time employees are approved by a home office salary committee based upon the recommendations of branch managers and area supervisors. Branch managers advise the salary committee of new full-time employees and terminations. Part-time and temporary employees are hired without referral to the salary committee.

Required:

a. Prepare a payroll audit program to be used in the home office to audit the branch office payrolls of the Generous Loan Company. See Exhibit 15–5 for sample audit procedures.

b. Based upon your review of the payroll system, how might payroll funds be diverted?

(*AICPA* adapted)

DISCUSSION CASES

15.16. Croyden Factory Inc., Evaluation of Flowchart For Payroll Control Weaknesses
A CPA's audit working papers contain a narrative description of a segment of the Croyden Factory, Inc., payroll system and an accompanying flowchart as follows:

Narrative:

The internal control system with respect to the personnel department is functioning well and is not included in the accompanying flowchart.

At the beginning of each workweek, payroll clerk no. 1 reviews the payroll department files to determine the employment status of factory employees and then prepares clock timecards and distributes them as each individual arrives at work. This payroll clerk, who is also responsible for custody of the check signature stamp machine, verifies the identity of each payee before delivering signed checks to the foreman.

At the end of each workweek, the foreman distributes payroll checks for the preceding workweek. Concurrent with this activity, the foreman reviews the current week's employee timecards, notes the regular and overtime hours worked on a summary form, and initials the clock timecards. The foreman then delivers all timecards and unclaimed payroll checks to payroll clerk no. 2.

Required:

a. Based upon the narrative and accompanying flowchart, what are the weaknesses in the system of internal control?

b. Based upon the narrative and accompanying flowchart in Exhibit 15.16–1, what inquiries should be made with respect to clarifying the existence of possible additional weaknesses in the system of internal control?

Note: Do not discuss the internal control system of the personnel department.

(*AICPA* adapted)

15.17. Vane Corporation: Control Weaknesses in Computerized Payroll System
The Vane Corporation is a manufacturing concern which has been in business for the past 18 years. During this period, the company has grown from a very small family-owned operation to a medium-sized manufacturing concern with several departments. Despite this growth, a substantial number of the procedures employed by Vane have been in effect since the business was started. Just recently

EXHIBIT 15.16–1
Croyden, Inc., Factory Payroll System

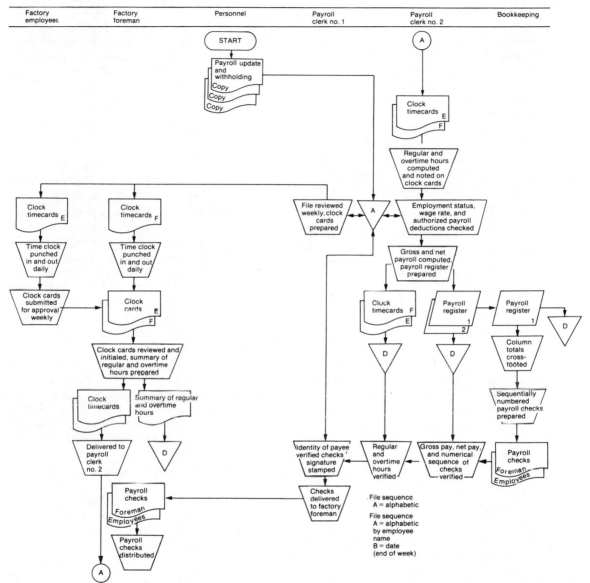

Vane has computerized its payroll function.

The payroll function operates in the following manner. Each worker picks up a weekly timecard on Monday morning and writes in his name and identification number. These blank cards are kept near the factory entrance. The workers write on the timecard the time of their daily arrival and departure. On the following Monday, the factory foremen collect the completed timecards for the previous week and send them to data processing.

In data processing, the timecards are used to prepare the weekly payroll transaction file. This file is used to update the master payroll file which is maintained on magnetic tape sequenced by worker identification number. After the payroll file is updated and the checks are prepared, the checks are written by the computer on the regular checking account and imprinted by a signature plate with the treasurer's signature. The checks are sent to the factory foremen who distribute them to the workers or hold them for the workers to pick up later if they are absent.

The foremen notify data processing of new employees and terminations. Any changes in hourly pay rate or any other changes affecting payroll are usually communicated to data processing by the foremen.

The workers also complete a job time ticket for each individual job they work on each day. The job time tickets are collected daily and sent to cost accounting where they are used to prepare a cost distribution analysis.

Further analysis of the payroll function reveals the following:

1. A worker's gross wages never exceed $300 per week.

2. Raises never exceed 55 cents per hour for the factory workers.

3. No more than 20 hours of overtime is allowed each week.

4. The factory employs 150 workers in 10 departments.

The payroll function has not been operating smoothly for some time, but even more problems have surfaced since the payroll was computerized. The foremen have indicated that they would like a weekly report indicating worker tardiness, absenteeism and idle time, so they can determine the amount of productive time lost and the reason for the lost time. The fol-lowing errors and inconsistencies have been encountered the past few pay periods:

1. A worker's paycheck was not processed properly, because he had transposed two numbers in his identification number when he filled out his timecard.

2. A worker was issued a check for $1,531.80 when it should have been $153.18.

3. One worker's paycheck was not written, and this error was not detected until the paychecks for that department were distributed by the foreman.

4. Part of the master payroll file was destroyed when the tape reel was inadvertently mounted on the wrong tape drive and used as a scratch tape. Data processing attempted to reestablish the destroyed portion from original source documents and other records.

5. One worker received a paycheck for an amount considerably larger than he should have. Further investigation revealed that 84 had been keyed instead of 48 for hours worked.

6. Several records on the master payroll file were skipped and not included on the updated master payroll file. This was not detected for several pay periods.

7. In processing nonroutine changes, a computer operator included a pay rate increase for one of his friends in the factory. This was discovered by chance by another employee.

Required:

Identify the control weaknesses in Vane's payroll procedures and in the computer processing as it is now conducted. Recommend the changes necessary to correct the system. Arrange your answer in the following columnar format:

Control Weaknesses   Recommendations

(*CMA* adapted)

C H A P T E R   1 6

Conversion Cycle

LEARNING
OBJECTIVES The major purpose of the conversion cycle is to transform resources—materials, labor and overhead—into finished products.
Many resources acquired by a company enter **cost pools** in which
they are held, converted, processed, assembled or otherwise used.
The conversion cycle functions manage these pools of resources
such as inventories, depreciable property and equipment, prepaid
insurance and other nonmonetary assets. The cost pool activities are
most extensive in a manufacturing business but exist to some extent
in retail businesses, utilities, real estate companies and health care
institutions. Accounting within the conversion cycle encompasses
the procedures and techniques to account for movement of resources *within the company.*

The four major objectives are related to the tools and techniques
described in Part 2 (Chapters 6–12). After completing this chapter,
you should understand:

- □ A business approach to the conversion cycle.

- □ The flow of transactions in a typical conversion cycle, how
  specific accounts are affected and the elements of control
  within the conversion cycle.

- □ Audit procedures used to gather evidence regarding
  compliance with control procedures.

- □ Evaluation of the controls (strengths) and lack of controls
  (weaknesses) to determine the effect upon the nature,
  timing and extent of procedures for auditing account
  balances.

The explanation of each of these four objectives is intended to
enable you to direct your understanding of audit objectives, relevant

evidence, appropriate audit procedures and the application of audit methodology to the specific subset of conversion cycle accounts.

In this chapter, a manufacturing business is assumed. In order to understand the flow of transactions in the conversion cycle, consider the following as typical functions:

Production planning and control.

Cost accounting.

Inventory planning and control.

Property and deferred cost accounting.

Labor distribution.

These functions are the basic structure for managing, controlling and accounting for the movement of resources *within* the company. All companies have revenue, acquisition and expenditure, and personnel and payroll cycles (discussed in previous chapters), but the conversion cycle is unique to manufacturing or processing. Banks, insurance companies, saving and loan associations, service companies and the like do not have conversion operations.

As you can see from the list of functions, the conversion cycle has several connections with the other cycles. The acquisition and expenditure cycle functions of requisitioning and purchasing inventory and fixed assets provide the resources to be managed and converted in the conversion cycle. The labor distribution function is an output of the personnel and payroll cycle and is listed again as an input to the conversion cycle. The conversion cycle is completed when the finished goods are placed in the final warehousing location. Shipments to customers are part of the revenue cycle.

A BUSINESS APPROACH

In the conversion cycle, it is especially important that auditors understand management's approach to conversion of resources into finished products. Of special interest is the data processing and cost accounting system, valuation of goods-in-process and effectiveness of the operations. The perspective provided by a business approach lends understanding of each unique engagement circumstance to the primary audit objectives.

Data Processing and Cost Accounting

Cost accounting systems differ more than other accounting systems because of the various methods of production, the wide variety of inventories and the degree of accounting detail desired by management. For example, the cost system of a food processor, such as a packaged cereal company, will be completely different from a construction company that builds water towers. In addition to these widely different cost systems (process costing for the cereal company and job order costing for the construction company), many companies utilize a standard costing system. If the cost records are maintained by a computer, as will be the case for many clients, auditors must understand how the cost data processing is accomplished and how the production costing system interfaces with the other data processing systems.

Auditors need to understand the movement of physical goods and the movement of costs. It is especially important to understand that the flow of costs does not always coincide with the flow of physical inventory. Auditors should be concerned with understanding the flow and the controls over the physical inventories from raw materials, to work-in-process, to finished goods. A separate concern is the control over the related cost flow.

Overhead is a troublesome area and subject to manipulation. Auditors must: (1) understand management's method of incorporating deferred costs (depreciation, indirect labor, utilities, insurance) into inventory costs and (2) be able to evaluate whether the methods used are appropriate under the circumstances and in accordance with generally accepted accounting principles.

Auditors need to become familiar with the internal reports produced for management to plan and control the production process, such as the periodic statement of cost of goods manufactured. These internal reports are important elements of control.

Valuation The valuation of work-in-process and finished goods inventories is affected not only by the cost accounting method and techniques used, but also by the depreciation policies and alternative inventory cost methods. Auditors must recognize that manufacturing equipment may be depreciated in a variety of methods from the unit-of-production method to an accelerated method such as sum-of-the-years digits. In regard to manufacturing equipment, auditors need to become familiar with the production technology used by the client and with recent technological changes. Continued use of an obsolete technology may result in the incurrence of costs that cannot be recovered through sale of the product. Management of daily operations should produce analysis of input costs—materials, labor and overhead—that would show any unusual fluctuations which might require greater audit attention. Changes in technology and the purchase of new equipment should be discussed so that auditors can look for changes in cost assignments (such as more overhead and less direct labor). Changes in technology may also alert auditors to look for reevaluation of standard costs, if such a system is used to allocate costs.

Effectiveness Effectiveness is an evaluation objective that is more characteristic of the internal auditor's work than that of the independent auditor. However, an understanding of sales levels, gross margins, seasonal fluctuations and general efficiency of management in avoiding crises—rush orders, back-log snarls and so forth—can be factored into a general understanding of the flow of the product. Inefficiencies and lack of planning may mean that excess costs have been assigned to inventories.

REVIEW PHASE: FLOW OF TRANSACTIONS AND ELEMENTS OF CONTROL

To accomplish a review to identify strengths and weaknesses, auditors must become familiar with the common procedures, significant documents and appropriate controls. In this section, flowcharts will be utilized to describe the flow of transactions and controls. These flowcharts may be considered as examples of the flowcharts auditors might prepare to document their understanding of the systems within this cycle.

The review of the conversion cycle is a process of obtaining and understanding the physical and cost flow through interviews, observations and sample documents (or computer outputs). The primary objective is to identify control procedures (strengths) that may be relied upon and to identify lack of controls (weaknesses) which will affect subsequent audit procedures. Secondary objectives are to identify: (1) populations of documents which give evidence of compliance with procedures and (2) weaknesses in controls which should be communicated in the management letter.

The flowcharts in this chapter show model organizational systems for control of production planning, production, inventories and cost accounting. The related timekeeping and payroll flowcharts are not repeated from Chapter 15; however, the appropriate exhibits in that chapter are cross-referenced. Exhibit 16–5 contains internal control questionnaire items typical of production and cost accounting systems. Taken together, the flowcharts and questionnaire items describe desirable control features for a conversion cycle.

Production Planning

Exhibit 16–1 depicts a separate department to coordinate the production planning with sales forecasts and inventory management. Normally, the production plan must be approved by the top managers of sales and inventory, as well as by the production manager.

The production plan results in production orders. The production orders must then be matched to standard parts lists and standard labor requirement tables (or to contract bid specifications). The bill of necessary materials and manpower planning needs are prepared for each production order, and these documents are transmitted to the production supervisor.

Production Department

The flowchart of the production department (Exhibit 16–2) illustrates the proper separation of duties, with an individual foreman in charge of each job. The production orders, bills of materials and manpower needs are given to a foreman to execute the job production and a job number is

EXHIBIT 16–1
Production Planning and
Control

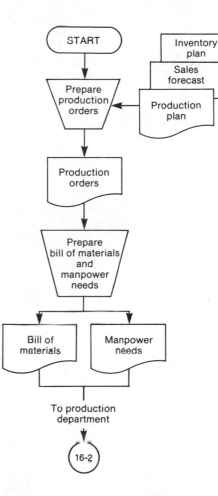

assigned. The job number should be on all subsequent production documents because from this point through production until finished products are put into inventory (or shipped to customers), the job number controls all physical movement and costs. Notice how internal reports of material and labor used are prepared for cost accounting to allow the accounting records to reflect the use of resources in the production process. Notice also that segregation of functional responsibilities is maintained between: (1) authority to initiate a transaction (production supervisor), (2) physical custody of assets, work in process inventory (foreman) and (3) responsibility for recordkeeping (cost accounting).

The foreman prepares two-copy material requisitions. The first copy is sent to raw materials stores as authorization to release materials to production. The second copy is filed pending the receipt of the raw materials and a raw materials issue slip. Not shown on the flowchart is the necessity for the foreman to compare materials received to the requisition and issue

EXHIBIT 16–2
Production Department

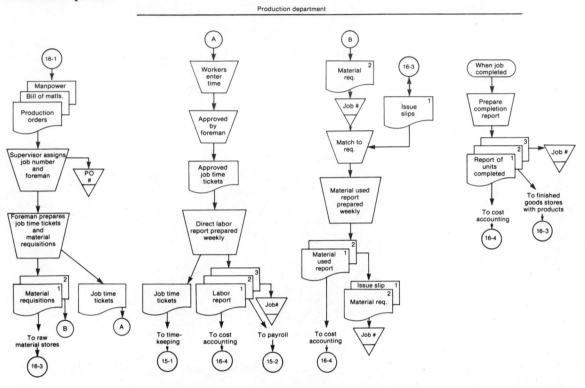

slip. Once accepted, the materials become the responsibility of the foreman and all materials, including scrap, should be accounted for in a materials-used report.

The job time tickets are utilized by the production workers to record
hours spent on each job. These tickets are approved by the foreman and
summarized in the labor report. The labor report and the materials-used
report should be approved by the production supervisor. The job time
tickets are sent to timekeeping to be reconciled to the clock timecards
before being sent to cost accounting (see Exhibit 15–1, Chapter 15). Copy
2 of the labor report is used by payroll to reconcile total hours to the
payroll summary.

When jobs are completed, a three-part completion report is prepared
by the foreman and approved by the production supervisor.

> Copy 1 is forwarded to cost accounting to transfer the job from work in
> process to finished goods inventory.
>
> Copy 2 accompanies the completed products to finished goods stores.
>
> Copy 3 of the completion report remains in production.

All labor reports and materials-used reports (with accompanying material requisitions and issue slips) for the completed job are filed with the third copy of the completed units report. Thus, a file of all completed jobs exists in the production and cost accounting departments.

Stores Department

Throughout the chapters on the various cycles, the flowcharts and internal control questionnaires have illustrated proper controls and separation of duties. However, in Exhibit 16–3, a frequently found control weakness is illustrated. Before reading further, examine these stores department flowcharts to see if you can determine the weakness.

EXHIBIT 16–3
Stores Department

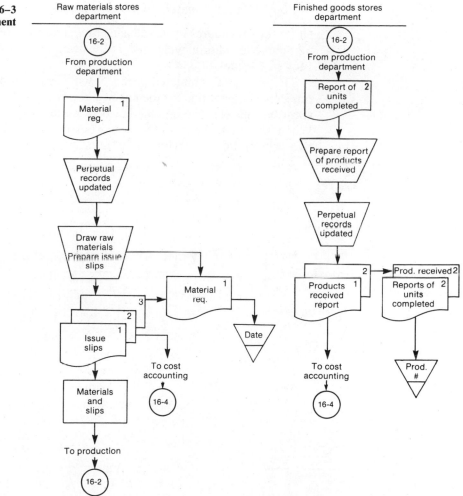

Recall that proper separation of duties requires that physical custody of assets should be segregated from responsibility for record-keeping. That separation of duties is not maintained in this example. The same person maintains the perpetual inventory records and has physical custody of the inventory. Proper separation of these functions is illustrated in Exhibit 14–4, Chapter 14.

Authorization for the raw-materials-stores clerk to release inventory is copy 1 of the material requisition from the production foreman. Raw materials are removed from inventory, perpetual records updated, and a three-part material issue slip is prepared.

Copy 1 of the issue slip accompanies the materials to production.

Copy 2 is transmitted to cost accounting as an independent check on materials used.

Copy 3 with the material requisition is filed.

Note: the procedures for purchasing raw materials are part of the acquisition and expenditure cycle and are illustrated in Exhibits 14–1, 14–2 and 14–4 in Chapter 14.

The arrival of completed products with copy 2 of the units completed report is authorization for the finished goods clerk to update the perpetual records. This clerk counts the finished products and inspects for quality. When accepted, the inventory items become his or her responsibility. A two-part product-received report is prepared to notify cost accounting

EXHIBIT 16–4
Cost Accounting

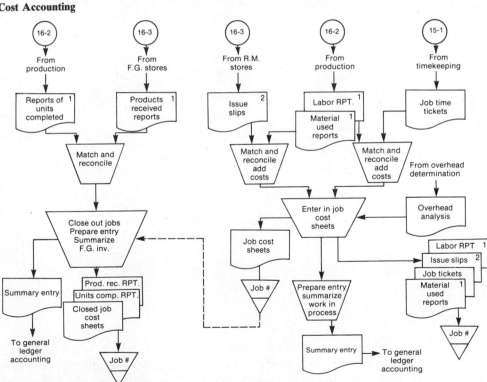

that the finished products were put into inventory. The procedures for releasing finished goods inventory are illustrated in Exhibits 13–1 and 13–2 (Chapter 13). Note that in both stores departments, copies of all documents are maintained to support the authorization of the transactions.

Cost Accounting   Several important control features are illustrated in Exhibit 16–4 where the cost accounting procedures are depicted. Notice that documentation for labor and materials comes from two separate sources for each. This allows an independent check of these important cost items. Further, if differences are recorded and reported to the cost accounting supervisor (as suggested by question 9 of the internal control questionnaire, Exhibit 16–5), a permanent record exists of how well this control works.

EXHIBIT 16–5
Internal Control
Questionnaire, Illustrative
Questions (production and
cost accounting)

1. Are production orders prepared by authorized persons?
2. Are production orders prenumbered? Numerical sequence accounted for? Blank production order forms kept in a secure place?
3. Are bills of materials and manpower needs prepared by authorized persons?
4. Are bills of materials and manpower needs forms prenumbered? Numerical sequence accounted for? Blank forms kept in a secure place?
5. Are material requisitions and job time tickets reviewed by the production supervisor after the foreman prepares them?
6. Are material requisitions and job time tickets prenumbered? Numerical sequence accounted for? Blank forms secure and available only to authorized persons?
7. Are the weekly direct labor and materials used reports reviewed and approved by the production supervisor after preparation by the foreman?
8. Do cost clerks account for numerical sequence of issue slips?
9. Are differences between issue slips and materials used reports recorded and reported to the cost accounting supervisor?
10. Are differences between job time tickets and the labor report recorded and reported to the cost accounting supervisor?
11. Are standard costs used? If so, are they reviewed and revised periodically?
12. Are differences between reports of units completed and products received reports recorded and reported to the cost accounting supervisor?
13. Are summary entries reviewed and approved by the cost accounting supervisor?

Two sources provide a record of completed production: (1) a report from production of units completed and (2) a report from finished goods stores of completed products received and put into inventory. These reports serve as an independent check and allow the cost records to keep pace with the physical movement of finished inventory.

Not shown on the flowchart is the important function of determining costs of work in process (and finished goods) inventory. Since valuation is one of the seven control objectives stressed in the internal control study, auditors must be concerned with proper valuation of inventories. Also not shown on the flowchart is the important process of overhead determination, which is a cost element of manufactured inventories.

Note that the costs maintained in the job sheets are summarized periodically for posting to the general ledger control accounts. The flowchart does not illustrate the control of independent, periodic reconciliation of the work-in-process control account to the open-job cost sheets. As was illustrated in each department, copies of all documents supporting authorization for accounting transactions are maintained in department files.

The internal control questionnaire compliments the flowcharts and illustrates further necessary controls. Flowcharts are essential to follow the flow of the transactions (and the physical movement of inventories) in a conversion cycle, and yet, not all essential concerns of auditors can be charted. The internal control questionnaires provided in previous chapters are fairly standard and could be adapted to most businesses. However, because the conversion cycles of different companies are unique, the audit supervisor will most likely have to prepare internal control questionnaires for each engagement. You should take some time to see how the example questions in Exhibit 16–5 are tailored specifically to the production and cost accounting procedures illustrated in the previous flowcharts.

Recall that the review phase is only the first step of the study and evaluation of internal control. When preparing flowcharts or completing internal control questionnaires, auditors must constantly keep in mind that the purpose is to identify controls that can be relied upon (strengths) or lack of controls (weaknesses) that must be considered in the subsequent audit of balances.

EVALUATION OF CONVERSION CYCLE CONTROL

When the review phase is completed, usually by a junior team member, the audit manager must evaluate the various systems of the conversion cycle to determine reliance thereon. The consideration of control objectives provides a systematic framework to accomplish this evaluation. The seven control objectives that have been emphasized throughout this book are expressed in terms of production transactions along with specific objectives in Exhibit 16–6.

The audit manager normally will prepare a working paper or audit memo of significant strengths and weaknesses. (See problem 16.13 where such a working paper is required for the controls illustrated in this chapter.)

COMPLIANCE AUDITING

In organizations that convert, process or assemble products, the production, inventory and cost accounting transactions are numerous. Compliance auditing of the details of transactions to determine the effectiveness

EXHIBIT 16–6
Internal Accounting Control Objectives (conversion cycle)

General Objectives	Examples of Specific Objectives
1. Recorded production transactions are *valid* and documented.	Cost accounting separated from production, payroll and inventory control. Material usage reports compared to raw material stores issue slips. Labor usage reports compared to job time tickets.
2. Valid production transactions are *recorded* and none omitted.	All documents prenumbered and numerical sequence accounted for.
3. Production transactions are *authorized*.	Material usage and labor usage prepared by foreman and approved by production supervisor.
4. Production job cost transactions *computations* contain *correct figures*.	Job cost sheet entries reviewed by person independent of preparation. Costs of inventory and labor reviewed periodically.
5. Labor and materials are *classified* correctly as direct or indirect.	Production foreman required to account for all material and labor used as direct or indirect.
6. Production *accounting* is complete.	Open job cost sheets periodically reconciled to work-in-process inventory account.
7. Production transactions are recognized in the *proper period*.	Production reports of material and labor used prepared weekly and transmitted to cost accounting. Job cost sheets posted weekly, and summary journal entries of work in process and finished goods prepared monthly.

of internal accounting control involves sampling techniques for choosing transactions for audit and evaluation of the evidence.

The partial audit program in Exhibit 16–7 contains a selection of compliance audit procedures. These steps are designed to enable auditors to obtain objective evidence about the effectiveness of controls and the reliability of accounting records (such as perpetual inventory records and job cost sheets). These records contain the detail of the basic numbers that appear in the financial statements under audit.

The work-in-process inventory procedures include procedures to determine whether the specific objectives listed in Exhibit 16–6 were achieved. These selected procedures are designed to determine whether all recorded transactions are valid (A–2), all valid transactions are recorded and none omitted (A–3, A–4, A–5) and accounting is complete (A–1).

Taken together, these procedures audit the important transactions in two directions. One direction is to determine whether all transactions that occurred were recorded (completeness). The other direction is to determine whether recorded transactions actually occurred (validity). An example of the first direction is auditing a sample of production orders (from

EXHIBIT 16–7
Audit Program—Selected
Compliance Audit
Procedures

A. *Work-in-Process Inventory.*
   1. Reconcile the open job cost sheets to work in process inventory control account.
   2. Select a sample of open and closed job cost sheets:
       a. Recalculate all costs entered.
       b. Vouch labor costs to job tickets and labor reports.
       c. Compare labor reports to summary of payroll for that week.
       d. Vouch material costs to issue slips and materials used reports.
       e. Compare materials used reports to material requisitions and bill of materials.
       f. Vouch overhead charges to overhead analysis schedules.
       g. Trace selected overhead amounts from analysis schedules to cost allocations and to invoices or accounts payable vouchers.
   3. Select a sample of issue slips from the raw materials stores file:
       a. Determine if a matching requisition is available for every issue slip.
       b. Trace to materials used reports and into job cost sheets.
   4. Select a sample of clock timecards from the payroll file. Trace to job time tickets, labor reports and into job cost time sheets.
   5. Select a sample of production orders:
       a. Determine if production order was authorized.
       b. Match to bill of materials and manpower needs.
       c. Trace bill of materials to material requisitions, material issue slips, material-used reports and into job cost sheets.
       d. Trace manpower needs to job time sheets, labor reports and into job cost sheets.
B. *Raw Materials Inventory (see Exhibit 14–14, Chapter 14).*
C. *Finished Goods Inventory (not illustrated).*

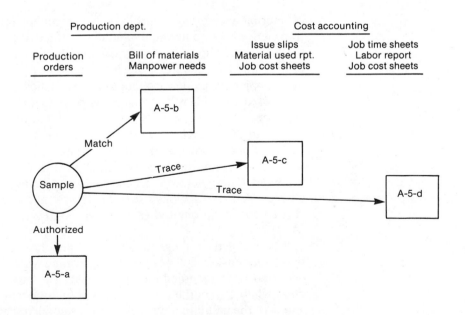

production files representing all production that occurred) to determine whether job cost sheets were prepared and appropriate costs entered representing resources utilized. The example of this direction is illustrated on page 550 (the A–5 codes correspond to the compliance procedures in Exhibit 16–7).

Many of the compliance procedures involve verifying the content and authorization of sample documents from a file in one department, and vouching or tracing the transactions represented by these documents to another file in another department. Auditors can expand the simple illustration given to all the files in the conversion cycle and develop a chart or table showing: the file name and sequence, the location, the information contents of documents and the procedures that could be applied to sample transactions. Problem 16.11 calls for such a table for the files illustrated in this chapter.

An example of the second direction of testing (validity of recorded transactions) is illustrated below. The key documents are the job cost sheets. All of these for open jobs are totaled (recalculated) and reconciled to the general ledger account. Then a sample of open and closed job cost sheets is selected for vouching to the documents that provide evidence that the work-in-process and finished goods inventories represented in these job cost sheets reflects internal transactions that actually occurred.

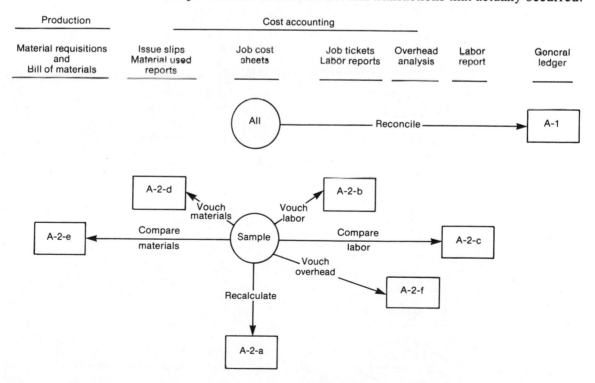

Computerized conversion cycle records are encountered frequently. Their complexity may range from simple batch systems which automate the data processing to transaction-driven, integrated systems which capture the production progress directly from automated devices on the production line. Computer audit techniques such as test data are frequently employed to audit controls in such systems, and generalized audit software may be employed to match data on different files.

REEVALUATION OF CONTROL   Reevaluation of the controls by the audit manager is necessary when the compliance audit is complete and documented in the working papers. As indicated in Chapter 7, the audit manager should specify in advance the maximum tolerable rate of noncompliance with control procedures that can be accepted and still consider the control reliable. If more errors are found than specified, the degree of control must be downgraded (such as from excellent to good) and the subsequent audit procedures changed in nature, timing and extent accordingly. In addition, each noncompliance of control procedures should be evaluated to determine if evidence exists of systematic errors or deliberate irregularities.

The controls illustrated in this chapter bear directly upon the reliability of the perpetual inventory records (including the job cost sheets) and therefore have a major impact on the year-end inventory procedures discussed in the next chapter.

REVIEW QUESTIONS

16.1. What are the functions normally associated with the conversion cycle?

16.2. Why is an understanding of the production process including the related data processing and cost accounting important to auditors performing a proper study and evaluation of internal accounting control?

16.3. Describe a "walk-through" of the conversion transaction flow from production orders to entry in the finished goods perpetual inventory records. (What document copies would be collected? What controls noted? What duties separated?)

16.4. Describe how the separation of: (1) *authorization* of production transactions, (2) *recording* of these transactions and (3) *physical custody* of inventories is maintained between the production, inventory and cost accounting departments illustrated in this chapter.

16.5. What features of the cost accounting system would be expected to prevent the omission or double counting of materials-used or labor-used data?

16.6. Why are weaknesses (lack of desired control procedures) not audited for compliance? Describe how weaknesses may not be detected during the review phase, but discovered during the compliance audit.

16.7. Why is an evaluation recommended before and after compliance auditing? Describe the differences and similarities of the objectives of these two evaluations.

16.8. Evaluate the following statement made by an auditing student: "I do not understand cost accounting. Therefore, I want to get a job with an auditing firm where I will only have to know financial accounting."

EXERCISES AND PROBLEMS

16.9. ICQ Items Matched to Control Objectives
The internal control objectives listed in Chapter 7 are: (1) validity, (2) completeness, (3) authorization, (4) accuracy, (5) classification, (6) accounting and (7) proper period. Refer to Exhibit 16–5 and prepare a table matching the questionnaire question numbers to the seven control objectives. (Hint: see Exhibit 14–7 for format. A question may relate to more than one objective.)

16.10. ICQ Items: Possible Error or Irregularity Due to Weakness
Refer to the internal control questionnaire (Exhibit 16–5) and assume the answer to each question is "No." Prepare a table matching questions to errors or irregularities that could occur because of the absence of the control. Your column headings should be:

Question	Possible Error or Irregularity Due to Weakness

16.11. Documentary Evidence For Compliance Procedures
One of the secondary purposes of the review phase of the study and evaluation of internal accounting control is to identify populations of documents that might be used in gathering evidence on the existence of controls in the compliance auditing phase. Refer to the flowcharts in this chapter (Exhibits 16–2, 16–3 and 16–4) and prepare a table which lists for each file symbol the content of the file and possible compliance audit procedures. Your workpaper should appear as follows (example from Exhibit 16–2):

16.12. Compliance Audit Procedures Related To Controls and Objectives
Each of the following compliance audit procedures might be performed during the compliance audit of the controls in the conversion cycle. For each procedure: (*a*) identify the internal accounting control objective(s) being addressed and (*b*) identify the internal control procedure (strength) being tested.

1. Balance and reconcile detail job cost sheets to the work-in-process inventory control account.

2. Scan closed job cost sheets for missing numbers in the sequence.

3. Vouch a sample of open and closed job-cost-sheet entries to: (*a*) job tickets and labor reports and (*b*) to issue slips and material-used reports.

4. Locate the material issue forms: Are they prenumbered? Kept in a secure location? Available to unauthorized persons?

5. Select several summary journal entries to work-in-process inventory: vouch to weekly labor and material reports and to job cost sheets, trace to control account.

6. Select a sample of the material issue slips in the production department file. Examine for:
   a. Issue date/materials-used report date.
   b. Job number.
   c. Foreman's signature or initials.
   d. Name and number of material.
   e. Raw-material-stores clerk's signature or initials.

EXHIBIT 16.11–1

File Name/ Sequence	Location	Contents	Possible Compliance Procedure
Labor report. job #	Production dept.	Weekly summary of labor hours charged to each job.	Match to copy in cost accounting or payroll. Match to job time tickets in cost accounting. Compare to payroll summary.

f. Matching material requisition in raw-material-stores file, note date of requisition.

7. Determine by inquiry and inspection if cost clerks review dates on report of units completed for accounting in the proper period.

16.13. Evaluation of Answers to ICQ Items

Assume you are the audit manager evaluating the documentation of the review phase presented in this chapter (flowcharts and internal control questionnaire). Further, assume the answers to question numbers 5, 6 and 11 of Exhibit 16–5 were no, and answers to all other questions were yes.

Prepare a workpaper listing: (1) the major strengths you might rely upon and an example of a compliance procedure and (2) the major weaknesses and possible impact on year-end substantive audit work on account balances. Your workpaper should appear as follows (with two examples provided):

EXHIBIT 16.13–1

Strength or Weakness	Compliance Procedure or Impact on Year-end Procedures
Strength: 1. All cost support for sheets documented.	1. Select sample of job cost sheets, vouch labor hours to job time.
Weakness: 1. Raw materials clerk maintains custody of perpetual records.	1. Perpetual records cannot be relied upon, physical count required at year-end with extensive audit test counts.

16.14. Internal Controls: Cash Receipts and Warehousing

Trapan Retailing Inc. has decided to diversify operations by selling through vending machines. Trapan's plans call for the purchase of 312 vending machines which will be situated at 78 different locations within one city and the rental of a warehouse to store merchandise. Trapan intends to sell only canned beverages at a standard price.

Management has hired an inventory control clerk to oversee the warehousing functions and two truck drivers who will periodically fill the machines with merchandise and deposit cash collected at a designated bank. Drivers will be required to report to the warehouse daily.

Required:

What internal controls should the auditor expect to find in order to assure the integrity of the cash receipts and warehousing functions?

(*AICPA* adapted)

16.15. Control Over Departmental Labor-Cost In Job-Cost System

The Brown Printing Company accounts for the services it performs on a job-cost basis. Most jobs take a week or less to complete and involve two or more of Brown's five operating departments. Actual costs are accumulated by job. To ensure timely billing, however, the company prepares sales invoices based on cost estimates.

Recently, several printing jobs have incurred losses. To avoid future losses, management has decided to focus on cost control at the department level. Since labor is a major element of cost, one proposal suggested is the development of a departmental labor-cost report. The report will originate with the payroll department as part of the biweekly payroll. The report will go to an accounting clerk for comparison to total labor-cost estimates by department. If the actual total department labor costs in a payroll period are not much more than the estimated total departmental labor cost during that period, the accounting clerk will send the report to the department foreman. If the accounting clerk concludes that a significant variance exists, the report will be sent to the assistant controller. The assistant controller will investigate the cause, when time is available, and recommend corrective action to the production manager.

Required:

Evaluate the proposal:

a. Give at least three common aspects of control with which the departmental labor-cost report proposal complies. Give an example from the case to support each of the aspects cited.

b. Give at least three common aspects of control with which the departmental labor-cost report proposal does **not** comply. Give an example from the case to support each aspect cited.

(*CIA* adapted)

DISCUSSION CASES

16.16. **Deake Corporation: Property Accounting System**

Deake Corporation is a medium-size, diversified manufacturing company. Recently, Fred Richards was promoted to manager of the Property Accounting Section. Richards has had difficulty in responding to some of the requests from individuals in other departments of Deake for information about the company's fixed assets. Some of the requests and problems Richards has had to cope with are:

1. The controller has requested schedules of individual fixed assets to support the balances in the general ledger. Richards has furnished the necessary information but has always been late. The manner in which the records are organized makes it difficult to obtain information easily.

2. The maintenance manager wished to verify the existence of a punch press which he thinks was repaired twice. He has asked Richards to confirm the asset number and location of the press.

3. The Insurance Department wants data on the cost and book values of assets to include in its review of current insurance coverage.

4. The Tax Department has requested data that can be used to determine when Deake should switch depreciation methods for tax purposes.

5. The company's internal auditors have spent a significant amount of time in the Property Accounting Section recently, attempting to audit the annual depreciation expense.

The property account records that are at Richards' disposal consist of a set of manual books. These records show the date the asset was acquired, the account number to which the asset applies, the dollar amount capitalized and the estimated useful life of the asset for depreciation purposes.

After many frustrations, Richards has realized that his records are inadequate and he cannot easily supply the data when requested. He has decided to discuss his problems with the controller, Jim Castle.

Richards: Jim, something has got to give. My people are working overtime and can't keep up. You worked in Property Accounting before you became controller. You know I can't tell the tax, insurance, and maintenance people everything they need to know from my records. Also, that internal auditing team is living in my area, and that slows down the work pace. The requests of these people are reasonable, and we should be able to answer these questions and provide the needed data. I think we need a computerized property accounting system. I would like to talk to the information systems people to see if they can help me.

Castle: Fred, I think you have a good idea, but be sure you are personally involved in the design of any system so you get all the information you need.

Required:

a.   Identify and justify four major objectives Deake Corporation's computerized property accounting system should possess in order to provide the data necessary to respond to requests for information by company personnel.

b.   Identify the data that should be included in the computer record for each asset included in the property account.

(*CMA* Adapted)

16.17.   **Huron Co.: Computer-based Inventory**

Huron Co. manufactures and sells eight major product lines with 15 to 25 items in each product line. All sales are on credit, and orders are received by mail or telephone. Huron Co. has a computer-based system that employs a hard magnetic disk as a file medium.

All sales orders received during regular working hours are typed immediately on Huron's own sales order form. This typed form is the source document for the terminal keying of a shipment or backorder record for each item ordered. These transaction records are batched and entered into the after-hours processing at night to complete all necessary recordkeeping for the current day and to facilitate the shipment of goods the following day. In summary, an order received one day is to be processed that day and night and shipped the next day. The inventory records are online to answer questions about inventory status.

(Inquiry only is online, data entry is key to disk with batch update at night.)

The daily batch processing which has to be accomplished at night includes the following activities:

1.   Preparing the invoice to be sent to the customer at the time of shipment.

2.   Updating accounts receivable records.

3.   Updating finished goods inventory records.

4.   Preparing a report listing of all items not in inventory and backordered.

Each month the sales department would like to have a sales summary and analysis. At the end of each month, the monthly statements should be prepared and mailed to customers. Management also wants an aging of accounts receivable each month.

Required:

a.   Identify the master files which Huron Co. should maintain in this system to provide for the daily processing. Indicate the data which should be included in each file and the order in which each file should be maintained.

b.   Prepare a systems flowchart of the daily processing required to update the finished goods inventory records and to produce the necessary inventory reports (assume that the necessary magnetic disk devices are available). Use the annotation symbol to describe or explain any facts which cannot be detailed in the individual symbols. (You may want to refer to Chapter 7 for flowchart symbols.)

c.   Describe: (1) the items that should appear in the monthly sales analysis report(s) the sales department should have and (2) the input data and master files that would have to be maintained to prepare these reports.

(*CMA* Adapted)

CHAPTER 17

PROFESSIONAL STANDARDS SOURCES		
Compendium Section	**Document Reference**	**Topic**
AU 318	SAS 23	Analytical Review Procedures
AU 9318		Interpretation: Analytical Review Procedures
AU 326	SAS 31	Evidential Matter
AU 9326		Interpretation: Evidential Matter
AU 327	SAS 16	The Independent Auditor's Responsibility for the Detection of Errors or Irregularities
AU 328	SAS 17	Illegal Acts by Clients
AU 9328		Interpretation: Illegal Acts by Clients
AU 331	SAS 1	Evidential Matter for Receivables and Inventories
AU 9331		Interpretation: Receivables and Inventories
AU 333	SAS 19	Client Representations
AU 9333		Interpretation: Client Representations
AU 339	SAS 41	Working Papers
AU 1020	SAS 45	Related Parties
AU 9509		Interpretation: Using Work of an Outside Inventory-Taking Firm

Current Assets and Liabilities, Related Revenue and Expense

LEARNING OBJECTIVES

Chapters 17 and 18 present the audit procedures for obtaining evidence about the details of account balances that appear in the financial statements. The chapters are organized around the balance sheet accounts, however, the related income statement accounts will be discussed where appropriate. After completing this chapter, in relation to the current asset, current liability and related accounts, you should be able to:

□ Identify specific audit procedures used to gather evidence to ascertain if assertions are materially correct, given the financial statements assertions.

□ Identify the major working paper for each major current account and list common procedures documented on that working paper.

□ Explain the difference between positive and negative forms of confirmations of a client's accounts receivable and the conditions under which each might be used.

□ Describe the auditors' responsibilities in observing the client's count of physical inventory and specific procedures that are normally part of the observation.

□ Explain why the emphasis is on the completeness assertion for the audit of liabilities, rather than the existence assertion, and what procedures might be involved in the search for unrecorded liabilities.

□ Describe the types of fraud or misstatement that might occur in the current accounts.

The audit procedures to gather evidence on account balances are called *substantive procedures*. Some amount of substantive audit procedures *must* follow the evaluation of internal accounting control. Audit teams are not permitted to place total reliance on controls to the exclusion of other procedures. Actually, many of the procedures described in the previous four chapters are of a substantive nature, as well as of a compliance nature. They are used to gather evidence about monetary details of transactions that make up the account balances.

As discussed in Chapter 7, students are best advised to think in terms of compliance and substantive *purposes* rather than compliance and substantive *procedures*. Many audit procedures have dual purposes. Just as the procedures described in previous chapters provide information about the accounting measurements, the procedures in this and the following chapter provide some information about internal accounting control. For example, if accounts receivable confirmations showed numerous exceptions, auditors would be concerned with the controls over the details of sales and cash receipts transactions regardless of previous control evaluations.

This potential confusion over compliance and substantive procedures was the primary reason for the organization of this part of the text. The typical timing of audit procedures also suggests that the material on the flow of transactions be presented separately from the material on account balances. The study and evaluation of internal accounting control is frequently scheduled before the client's year-end (called an "interim working period"), while procedures to gather evidence on account balances are normally scheduled around or after the balance sheet date. Further, you have a good comprehension of account balances from previous accounting courses, but will have difficulty understanding the flow of transactions unless you have had related work experience. The overall audit methodology of two approaches for gaining reasonable assurance that financial statements do not contain material misstatements (reliance on controls over the data processing system and reliance on sample-based audit of the results of processing) further suggests separation of the material.

The following discussion of audit procedures contains specific examples of the evidence-gathering procedures discussed in Chapter 6 (recalculation, observation, confirmation, inquiry, vouching, tracing, scanning and analytical review). You may want to review the general explanation of each of these procedures in Chapter 6 before proceeding further. The material is organized under major accounts by the *assertions* made by management in financial statements (existence or occurrence, completeness, rights and obligations, valuation or allocation, and presentation and disclosure). These assertions become the overall practical objectives for gathering the evidence on each account. From these assertions, auditors develop specific objectives related to specific assertions about each account and organize their procedures accordingly. Because the specific assertions and objectives vary with each client, only illustrative examples of the specific assertions will be provided hereafter.

CASH   In this section, the discussion of audit procedures for examining the balances of cash accounts is organized around the five broad audit objectives of existence, completeness, rights, valuation, and presentation and disclosure. The construction of an audit program should begin with the audit supervisor's explicit recognition that these broad objectives represent assertions by management embodied in the financial statements. The assertions point directly to hypotheses questions that can be tested by gathering sufficient competent evidential matter.

Substantive Audit   A one-to-one relationship between audit objectives and procedures does
Procedures Related   not necessarily exist. Some procedures may satisfy more than one objec-
to Objectives   tive, as will be indicated subsequently. Organizing procedures under objectives is an attempt to illustrate that all procedures are related to one or more objectives and that all evidence-gathering audit work relates to the financial statements. Specific assertions typical of Cash accounts are:

□ Cash is the sum of change funds, petty cash and demand deposit bank accounts.

□ Management has the unrestricted right to use cash for general business purposes.

□ Cash designated for special purposes has been segregated.

□ All restrictions on the use of cash are disclosed.

Existence.   The procedure of obtaining formal statements from outside independent parties is known as ***confirmation***. The standard bank confirmation form is shown in Exhibit 17–1. This confirmation is a request from the client for the bank to report its record of account balances for all deposits of the company. Note that several of the questions relate to information for the audit of direct and contingent liabilities. The *search for unrecorded liabilities* goes on in every audit area and the most is made of every piece of evidence in many audit areas. The confirmed bank balance should be cross-referenced on the bank reconciliation working paper (shown in Exhibit 17–3). Confirmations should be obtained from all banks with which the client did business during the period, even if the checking accounts have been closed, because the company may have notes payable, contingent liabilities or other relationships with such banks.

The second procedure relating to cash that is directly related to existence is the *physical observation* and count of cash funds on hand. Petty cash and undeposited cash receipts are typical cash funds on hand. The

EXHIBIT 17–1

A-4

STANDARD BANK CONFIRMATION INQUIRY
Approved 1966 by
AMERICAN INSTITUTE OF CERTIFIED PUBLIC ACCOUNTANTS
AND
BANK ADMINISTRATION INSTITUTE (FORMERLY NABAC)

ORIGINAL—To be retained by bank.
DUPLICATE—To be mailed to accountant.

April 30, 19 84

Dear Sirs:

Your completion of the following report will be sincerely appreciated. **IF THE ANSWER TO ANY ITEM IS "NONE",
PLEASE SO STATE.** Kindly mail it in the enclosed stamped, addressed envelope <u>direct</u> to the accountant named below.

Report from   Yours truly,

Metropolitan General Hospital
(ACCOUNT NAME PER BANK RECORDS)

(Bank) First National Bank   By Robert Davis
                                                        Authorized Signature

    Main Street   Bank customer should check here if confirma-
                                                     tion of bank balances only (item 1) is desired. ☐

    Austin, Texas   NOTE – If the space provided is inadequate,
                                                     please enter totals hereon and attach a state-
           Gibson Johnson & Co.   ment giving full details as called for by the
           P.O. Box 4486   columnar headings below.
Accountant 4200 North Lamar Blvd. Suite 105
           Austin, Texas 78765

Dear Sirs:

1. At the close of business on _____ April 30 _____ 19 84 our records showed the following balance(s) to the
<u>credit</u> of the above named customer. In the event that we could readily ascertain whether there were any balances to
the credit of the customer not designated in this request, the appropriate information is given below.

AMOUNT	ACCOUNT NAME	ACCOUNT NUMBER	SUBJECT TO WITH-DRAWAL BY CHECK?	INTEREST BEARING? GIVE RATE
$ 74,234	Metropolitan General Hospital	146-2013	Yes	No

2. The customer was directly liable to us in respect of loans, acceptances, etc., at the close of business on that
date in the total amount of $_____ , as follows:

AMOUNT	DATE OF LOAN OR DISCOUNT	DUE DATE	INTEREST RATE	INTEREST PAID TO	DESCRIPTION OF LIABILITY, COLLATERAL, SECURITY INTERESTS, LIENS, ENDORSERS, ETC.
$ 100,000	6-30-82	6-30-84	18%	12-31-83	Unsecured

3. The customer was contingently liable as endorser of notes discounted and/or as guarantor at the close of business
on that date in the total amount of $ None , as below:

AMOUNT	NAME OF MAKER	DATE OF NOTE	DUE DATE	REMARKS
$				

4. Other direct or contingent liabilities, open letters of credit, and relative collateral, were

None

5. Security agreements under the Uniform Commercial Code or any other agreements providing for restrictions, not
noted above, were as follows (if officially recorded, indicate date and office in which filed):

None

Yours truly, (Bank) First National Bank

Date May 3 _____ 19 84   By Alfred E. Newman
                                                        Authorized Signature

Hart Graphics—Austin

count should be made in the presence of the fund custodian and that person's signature should be obtained on a working paper statement that all monies were returned intact. Such a statement protects auditors from accusations of impropriety. All funds should be counted at the same time (simultaneously), and all negotiable assets should be under auditor control so that money or securities cannot be shifted from one location to another to conceal a shortage. Such control may involve simultaneous count by several auditors or control by locking and sealing other funds while one is counted.

The working paper of the count of petty cash should contain a record of all vouchers, checks, bills and other amounts that have not been entered in the accounts. If the amounts are material, an adjusting entry may be required to record them in the period under audit. Auditors should *scan* the evidence of fund activity and authorization signatures for any signs that the fund has been used improperly. Counts of funds at year-end also apply to the audit cutoff objective—a part of the completeness objective.

Completeness.   The client is normally requested to provide a list of all bank accounts and cash funds, which is the starting place to ensure all cash transactions are recorded. Of course, the detailed work described on cash receipts in Chapter 13 and on cash disbursements in Chapter 14 provide auditors with some evidence that all cash transactions are recorded. This understanding of the flow of normal cash transactions should also provide evidence about proper cutoff. If possible, auditors should be present on the client's premises at the end of the last business day to record the last check number issued on each bank account and the last deposit slip number.

When a company has several bank accounts and monies may be transferred from one account to another, a schedule of interbank transfers for several days before and after year-end is prepared. The purpose of this schedule (shown in Exhibit 17–2) is to see that both sides of the transfer transaction are recorded in the same period (and in the proper period); thus, the need for the four dates. This schedule would indicate any attempt at "kiting." *Kiting* is the practice of recording the deposit of an interbank transfer before recording the disbursement—thus, briefly double counting the amount of cash.

Another procedure to ensure completeness is to *scan* bank statements of the year for reportedly inactive accounts to determine whether they are in fact inactive. Cash receipts records and receivables from officers and directors should be scanned for any apparent payment and reborrowing maneuvers designed to avoid reporting such advances in the financial statements.

Analytical review is usually not used as an extensive procedure in the audit of cash. However, comparison of bank balances with prior years

EXHIBIT 17–2
Interbank Transfers

A-5

Eagle Processing Inc.
Schedule of Interbank Transfers
December 31, 1985

Prepared by MfA
Date 1-20-86

check no.	Disbursing Bank				Receiving Bank		
	Bank	Amount	Date per Books	Date per Bank	Bank	Date per Books	Date per Bank
1085	1st National	30,000 ✓	12-31-85 ✗	1-5-86 ⅂	Citizen's National	12-31-85 ✗	1-3-86 ✗
6114	Citizen's National	5000 ✓	12-30-85 ✗	1-4-86 ⅂	1st National	12-30-85 ✗	1-3-86 ✗

✓ Traced to cash disbursements journal.
✗ Checks properly listed as outstanding on bank reconciliations
     (A-1, A-3).
⅂ Vouched checks cleared bank in cutoff bank statements.
✗ Traced to cash receipts journal.
✗ Vouched deposits cleared bank in cut-off bank statements.

Note: We scanned the cash disbursements and cash
     receipts journals for checks to and deposits
     from banks. Found none other than the
     two listed above.

and with monthly balances during the year may reveal an unusually low
(or high or omitted) balance that would require further attention.

Valuation.   The primary workpaper for year-end bank balances is the
bank reconciliation, illustrated in Exhibit 17–3. This reconciliation should
be *recalculated,* the outstanding checks and deposits in transit footed, and
the book balance *traced* to the trial balance (which has been traced to the
General Ledger). The reconciling items should be *vouched* to determine
whether outstanding checks really were not paid and that deposits in
transit actually were mailed before the reconciliation date. The auditors'
information source for vouching the bank reconciliation items is a *cutoff
bank statement.*

The cutoff bank statement is sent by the bank directly to the auditor
and is usually for a 15- or 20-day period following the reconciliation date.
The *vouching* is a matter of comparing checks that cleared in the cutoff
period with the outstanding checklist for evidence that all checks that
were written prior to the reconciliation date were on the outstanding

EXHIBIT 17–3
Bank Reconciliation

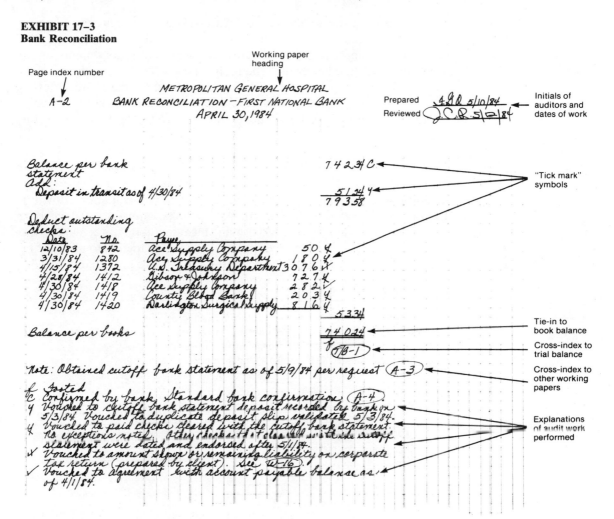

checklist. The deposits shown in transit should be recorded by the bank in the first business days of the cutoff period. If recorded later, the inference is the deposit may have been made up from receipts of the period after the reconciliation date. For large outstanding checks not clearing in the cutoff period, vouching may be extended to other documentation supporting the disbursement.

The combination of all the procedures performed on the bank reconciliation provides evidence of existence, valuation and proper cutoff of the bank cash balances.

Rights, Presentation and Disclosure.   Verbal *inquiries* directed to officers and employees provide evidence of matters not otherwise noted in the accounts and subsidiary records. Cash-related inquiries center on any formal or informal restrictions on availability. By this procedure, auditors can learn of compensating balances, loan agreement requirements or restrictions in foreign banks that should be disclosed. (All significant items learned through inquiries should be included in the client representation letter.) Examination of the minutes of directors' committees, bank confirmations, and formal loan documents may also reveal restrictions on the use of cash.

Main Working Paper

The main working paper for cash balances is the bank reconciliation of the year-end balance. The reconciliation could be a copy of the client's reconciliation or one prepared by the audit team. The reconciliation shown in Exhibit 17–3 is a repeat of Exhibit 6–4 (and the notations of good working paper techniques are repeated to provide meaningful reinforcement of the concepts covered generally in Chapter 6, which are applied to all working papers). Selected substantive procedures for cash are provided in Exhibit 17–4.

EXHIBIT 17–4
Audit Program—Selected
Substantive
Procedures—Cash

1. Prepare or obtain from client, reconciliations of all bank accounts.
2. Ask the client to request cutoff bank statements be mailed directly to the audit firm.
3. Obtain confirmation from banks (standard bank confirmation).
4. Vouch outstanding checks and deposits in transit to checks and deposits cleared in the cutoff statement.
5. Prepare a schedule of interbank transfers.
6. Obtain written representations from the client concerning compensating balance agreements.
7. Count petty cash funds.

CURRENT RECEIVABLES

The internal control evaluation of the sales and cash receipts functions presented in Chapter 13 directly affects the nature, timing and extent of year-end procedures on accounts receivable, notes receivable and sales balances. The more reliable the internal control, the more restricted these procedures can be. Further, in understanding the flow of transactions of the revenue cycle, auditors gain a thorough comprehension of all the transactions and client procedures that affect these balances.

Substantive Audit Procedures Related to Objectives

The overall audit objectives are organized around the assertions of existence, completeness, rights, valuation, and presentation and disclosure. These broad assertions can be broken down to more specific assertions, of which the following are typical of this account group:

☐ Accounts and notes receivable are bona fide claims owed the company.

☐ Accounts and notes receivable are collectible in the normal course of business.

☐ None of the accounts or notes receivable are fictitious.

☐ No accounts or notes receivable have been omitted from the balance sheet.

☐ Sales transactions occurred in the period under audit.

☐ Pledged accounts and notes are disclosed.

☐ Receivables from directors, officers and affiliates are separately disclosed.

The above assertions are not a complete list of all matters of audit interest, but they are illustrative of the types of problems that should be recognized. The next task is to consider the evidence that might support or refute these assertions and then the audit team can select the most efficient procedures for gathering that evidence.

Existence. *Confirmation* of accounts and notes receivable is considered a primary means of obtaining evidence of existence and, to a limited extent, valuation. The accounts and notes to be confirmed may be selected at random or in accordance with a stratification plan consistent with the audit manager's objectives. The area of receivables is one in which the applications of statistical methods may be useful. Generalized audit software to access computer files of accounts receivable may be utilized to select and even print the confirmations.

Confirmation of receivables is one of the procedures formally expressed as a required procedure whenever possible.[1] If receivables confirmation is not practical, the auditors must utilize other audit procedures (such as vouching) to be satisfied that account balances are fairly presented. Confirmations of receivables (and payables) may take several forms. Two widely used forms are *positive confirmation* and *negative confirmation.* An example of a positive confirmation is shown in Exhibit 17–5. The negative confirmation form is simply a request for a response only if something is wrong with the balance. Thus, nonresponses are considered evidence of propriety. Generally, a positive confirmation includes a recitation that an audit is being performed and a request to provide specified information *directly* to the auditors.

The positive form is used when individual balances are relatively large or when accounts are in dispute. Positive confirmations may include either the account balance or specific invoices, depending upon knowledge about how customers maintain their accounting records. The negative form is used mostly when internal control is considered effective, when a large number of small balances are involved and when the client's customers can be expected to consider the confirmations properly. Fre-

---

[1] See "Evidential Matter for Receivables . . ." (SAS 1 AU 331).

EXHIBIT 17–5
Positive Confirmation
Letter

APPLE BLOSSOM COLOGNE COMPANY
Chicago, Illinois

January 5, 1986

Alpha Aroma Company
Lake and Adams
Chicago, Illinois

Gentlemen:

   Our auditors, Anderson, Olds and Watershed, are making their annual audit of our financial statements. Part of this audit includes direct verification of customer balances.

   PLEASE EXAMINE THE DATA BELOW CAREFULLY AND EITHER CONFIRM ITS ACCURACY OR REPORT ANY DIFFERENCES DIRECTLY TO OUR AUDITORS USING THE ENCLOSED REPLY ENVELOPE.

   This is not a request for payment. Please do not send your remittance to our auditors.

   Your prompt attention to this confirmation request will be appreciated.

_____

Parker Shelton, Controller

The balance due Apple Blossom Cologne Company as of December 31, 1985 is $3,600, which originated December 1, 1985, and is due March 1, 1986, bearing interest at 10 percent per annum, is correct except as noted below:

_____

_____

Date: _____

                                By: _____

                             Title: _____

quently, both forms are used by sending positive confirmations on some customers' accounts and negative confirmations on others. Sometimes confirmations are *in blank,* meaning the amount is left blank to be filled in by the recipient. Blank confirmations are most often used to confirm a client's accounts payable. Confirmations should be signed by the client's officers, although they must be controlled in preparation, in mailing and in return by the audit team.

   The *response rate* for positive confirmations is the proportion of the number of confirmations returned to the number requested, generally after the audit team prompts recipients with second and third requests.

Research studies have shown response rate ranging from 66 percent to 96 percent. Recipients seem to be able to detect account misstatements to varying degrees. Studies have shown *detection rates* (the ratio of the number of exceptions reported to auditors to the number of account errors intentionally reported to customers) ranging from 20 percent to 100 percent. Negative confirmations seem to have lower detection rates than positive confirmations. Also, studies show somewhat lower detection rates for misstatements favorable to recipients (that is, an accounts receivable understatement). Overall, positive confirmations appear to be more effective than negative confirmations, but results depend on the type of recipients, the size of the account, and the type of account being confirmed. Effective confirmation practices depend on attention to these factors and on the experience with confirmation results on a particular client's accounts.

Effective confirmation also depends upon using a "bag of tricks" to boost the response rate. Often, auditors merely send out a cold, official-looking request in a metered-mail envelope and expect customers to be happy to respond. However, the response rate can be increased by using: (1) a postcard sent in advance, notifying that a confirmation is coming, (2) special delivery mail, (3) first-class stamp postage (not metered) in an envelope imprinted "Confirmation Enclosed: Please Examine Carefully." These devices increase the cost of the confirmation procedure, but the benefits from better response are greater.[2]

The audit team should endeavor to obtain replies from all positive confirmations by sending second and third requests to nonrespondents. If there is no response or if the response specifies an exception to the client's records, the auditors should carry out *vouching* procedures to audit the account. When sampling is used, all accounts in the sample should be audited. It is improper to substitute an easy-to-audit customer account not in the sample for one that does not respond to a confirmation request.

Confirmation of receivables may be performed at a date other than the year-end. When confirmation is done at an interim date, the audit firm is able to spread work throughout the year and avoid the pressures of overtime that typically occur around December 31. Also, the audit can be completed sooner after the year-end date when confirmation has been done earlier. The primary consideration when sending confirmations of accounts at a date before the balance sheet date is the client's internal control over transactions affecting receivables. When confirmation is performed at an interim date, roll-forward procedures should be performed. Roll-forward procedures may involve an analysis of transactions and supporting details for the period from the confirmation date to the balance sheet date. Unusual changes in accounts should be investigated.

---

[2] AICPA, *Confirmation of Accounts Receivable,* Auditing Procedure Study, 1984, chapter 4.

Auditors must be careful when confirming advances and notes with officers, directors, affiliated companies and subsidiaries. These parties are not independent of client management, thus the confirmation is not like one obtained from an independent, outside party. To obtain persuasive evidence, the audit team may wish to combine the confirmation procedure with other evidence from vouching and inquiry procedures.

Vouching is another procedure to establish existence and valuation of receivables and related sales revenue. Vouching of documentation (sales invoice or shipping evidence) underlying receivables is generally deferred until after confirmation. The procedure is directed toward audit of accounts for which positive confirmations were mailed but replies not received. Vouching may also be carried out to gather evidence about account discrepancies and disputes indicated on confirmation replies. Another application for vouching of receivables lies in the checking of an aged trial balance for proper classification of amounts by age categories. After the year-end, credits recorded in receivables existing at the year-end may be vouched to cash receipts documents for evidence of the existence, rights, valuation and current asset classification of the receivables balances.

Revenue balances might be audited by selecting a sufficient sample of recorded transactions and vouching them to source documents for authenticity. This task has the objective of auditing the balance and not that of testing internal controls. In statistical model terms, a decision model for a dollar balance would be appropriate and not an application of attribute sampling. This vouching would involve examination of the sales invoice (lease contract or other statement of charges), shipping documents, correspondence and the customer's payment record. Auditors should be especially alert to evidence of transactions with related persons or affiliated companies (particularly with regard for proper exchange prices) and for transactions with subsidiary companies subject to elimination in consolidated financial statements.

Notice, however, that the vouching procedure accomplishes only an audit of recorded revenue transactions. Such extensive vouching is not common. Usually auditors combine a limited amount of vouching with other analyses of interrelationships to audit revenue balances.

Scanning is another procedure related to the existence objective. Scanning is a rapid but careful review of records for any unusual transactions. Sales accounts may be scanned for any unusually large individual sales that might deserve additional vouching. The monthly summaries of sales may be reviewed for unusual fluctuations which might signal accounting errors. (One publicly held company reported in an annual report that in December of that year they discovered that sales for the month of November of the prior year had been recorded twice, resulting in a sales overstatement of $5 million and net income overstatement of $3 million, amounting to $1.60 per share—all material amounts.)

Trade accounts and notes receivable should be scanned individually and in total for the period between an interim confirmation date and the fiscal year-end for indications of unusual transactions. This procedure may give auditors reason to vouch the transaction documentation or make additional inquiries about collectibility.

Completeness.   The primary procedure to ensure completeness is to *reconcile* (recalculate) the sum of the subsidiary receivables ledger to the general ledger control account. The aged trial balance is the primary working paper for accounts receivable and the total of the detail of this schedule is traced to the trial balance which has been traced to the general ledger (see Exhibit 17–7).

Analytical review may be used as an overall procedure check on the completeness of receivables and sales. Relationships such as receivables turnover, gross margin ratio and sales/asset ratios can be compared to industry statistics and prior years' statistics of the company for evidence of overall reasonableness. Sales and revenue relationships of prior years' audited data to current year data by product line or other classification is useful for highlighting changes for further investigation. However, auditors must be careful when observing data that indicate little or no change from the prior year when changing economic conditions indicate that changes *should* have occurred.

Account interrelationships can also become a part of the analysis. Sales returns and allowances and sales commissions should vary directly with sales; bad debt expense should vary directly with the amount of sales on credit and accounts receivable balances; freight expenses should vary directly with physical sales volume. As a means of monitoring earlier audit decisions, receivables write-offs should be compared to prior years' allowances for uncollectible accounts.

In general, the various analyses of interrelationships are most useful for auditing sales and revenue account balances. Auditors generally rely on evidence produced from many different tests and analyses rather than on vouching sales and revenue transactions in detail. Confirmation and extensive vouching are relied upon much more heavily for the audit of receivables balances, hence additional evidence from analyses of interrelationships is not as important. However, when a direct relationship exists, such as between notes receivable and interest, all related accounts should be examined at the same time as illustrated in Exhibit 17–6.

Auditing the cutoff of transactions that affect accounts receivable is usually accomplished as part of the inventory procedures and cash procedures.

Valuation.   *Confirmation* of selected receivable balances is a procedure which is also related to the valuation objective. However, the confirmations are evidence only of the gross value of receivables. The remain-

EXHIBIT 17–6

B-10   Notes Receivable, Interest Income Accrued Interest

Munday Seed Mill

12-31-85

Prepared by MFG
Date 1-7-86

Name / Terms	Date of Note	Date Due	Amount 12-31-84	Amount 12-31-85	Interest Income	Accrued Interest
Gertrude Brown 10%, interest ..	7-1-84	7-1-85	10,000	—	500 N ⌇	—
Im N. Debt 11% interest due 1-1-86	1-1-85	1-1-86	—	5,000 I C	550 ⌇	550 ⌇ v
Mr. Greenjeans 10%, interest due 10-1-85 and 4-1-86	4-1-85	4-1-86		15,000 I C	1125 N ⌇	375 ⌇
			10,000 T	20,000 T	2175 T	925 T

T   Agrees with general ledger.
N   Vouched cash receipts to bank deposit slip. (Greenjeans, $750)
⌇   Recalculated interest income and accrued interest
     according to terms of notes.
I   Inspected notes kept in Treasurer's safe
C   Confirmed amount and terms of notes with debtor
     Confirmation replies in working papers B-11, B-12

ing part of the valuation objective for accounts receivable is to evaluate the client's estimate of allowance for uncollectibles to determine if the net realizable value is reasonable.

The information collected in the review of the flow of sales transactions regarding the company's credit policy is relevant to this evaluation. Further, the noncurrent accounts in the aged trial balance should be examined. *Vouching* to subsequent cash receipts will indicate which of these accounts may be troublesome. Discussions with the credit manager regarding long overdue accounts and review of applicable correspondence are common procedures in evaluating the adequacy of the allowance account. For large overdue accounts, auditors should obtain credit reports and financial statements (audited, if available).

EXHIBIT 17-7

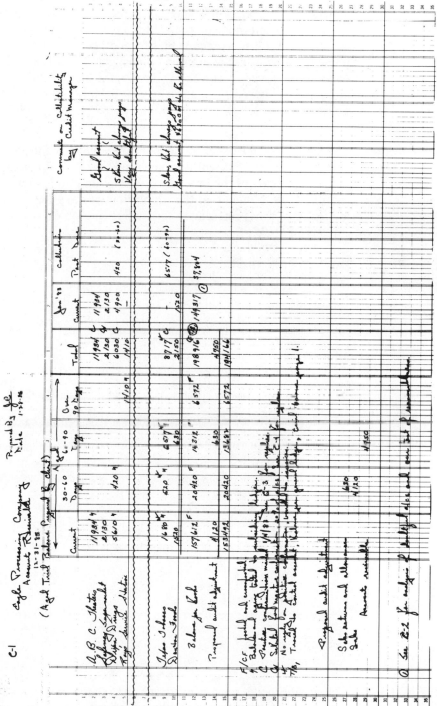

Rights, Presentation and Disclosure. *Inquiries* of management are necessary to determine if receivables have been sold, assigned or pledged as collateral. Further, receivables from officers, directors, affiliated companies and subsidiaries must be investigated and segregated from trade accounts and notes receivables. Finally, the list of detail account balances should be reviewed for material credit balances that need to be reclassified as liabilities.

Major Working Paper

The major working paper for accounts receivable is the aged trial balance. The illustration of this working paper in Exhibit 17–7 indicates with keyed tick marks many of the procedures discussed in this section and listed in Exhibit 17–8. Notice that the supporting working papers such as confirmations are cross-referenced for finding and quick review by the audit supervisor.

EXHIBIT 17–8
Audit Program—Selected Substantive Procedures

> A. Accounts and Notes Receivable.
>   1. Inspect or obtain confirmation of notes receivable.
>   2. Recalculate interest income and accrued interest receivable related to notes.
>   3. Prepare or obtain from client, an aged trial balance of customers' accounts receivable. Reconcile total to the accounts receivable control account.
>   4. Send positive confirmations to all accounts over $X. Select a random sample of all remaining accounts for negative confirmation.
>   5. Recalculate the allowance for uncollectible accounts and discuss past due accounts with the credit manager. Obtain and analyze financial statements of major debtors.
>   6. Obtain written representations from the client concerning pledging of accounts receivable as collateral and as to amounts due from officers and directors.
>
> B. Revenue.
>   1. Select a sample of recorded sales invoices and vouch to underlying shipping documents.
>   2. Select a sample of shipping documents and trace to sales invoices.
>   3. Obtain production records of physical quantities sold and calculate an estimate of sales dollars based on average sale prices.
>   4. Compare revenue dollars and physical quantities with prior year data and industry economic statistics.
>   5. Select a sample of sales invoices prepared a few days before and after the balance sheet date and vouch to supporting documents for evidence of proper cutoff.

INVENTORY

The audit procedures for inventory and related cost of sales accounts are frequently extensive in an audit engagement. Inventory can be one of the company's largest assets.

Substantive Audit Procedures Related to Objectives The construction of an audit program should begin with explicit recognition of the assertions in the inventory accounts (including the aggregations of purchases and issues) and the cost of sales accounts. The assertions point directly to the hypothesis questions that can be tested by gathering sufficient, competent evidential matter. A few of the assertions typical of this account group are:

☐ Inventory is a current asset.

☐ Inventory pledged as collateral is disclosed.

☐ Inventory is owned by the company.

☐ Obsolete and unsalable goods have been written off or written down.

☐ The inventory value does not exceed the applicable measure of market value.

☐ All purchases are for inventory use or for approved business expenditures.

☐ All inventory issues are for production.

The above assertions are not a complete list of all matters of audit interest but are illustrative of the types of problems that should be recognized. The next task is to consider the evidence that might support or refute these assertions and then select the most efficient procedures for gathering that evidence.[3]

Existence, Completeness and Rights. The primary procedure for gathering evidence relative to the audit objectives of the existence and completeness of inventories is ***physical observation.*** It is important to realize that independent auditors are responsible for *observing* the client's count of inventory and *not* responsible for personally making the complete count. Hence the audit procedures involve reviewing the client's plans, observing the count operations and making some test counts for tracing to the inventory compilation. The first task is to learn about the client's inventory-taking instructions (whether oral or written) and review them for the following characteristics:

1. Names of client personnel responsible for the count.
2. Dates and times of inventory taking.
3. Names of client personnel who will participate in the inventory taking.
4. Instructions for recording accurate descriptions of inventory items, for count and double-count, and for measuring or translating physi-

---

[3] For a complete list of inventory assertions, see the appendix to "Evidential Matter" (SAS 31, AU 326).

cal quantities (such as counting by measures of gallons, barrels, feet, dozens).

5. Instructions for making notes of obsolete or worn items.

6. Instructions for the use of tags, punched cards, count sheets or other media devices and for their collection and control.

7. Plans for shutting down plant operations or for taking inventory after store closing hours and plans for having goods in proper places (such as on store shelves instead of on the floor or raw materials in a warehouse rather than in transit to a job.)

8. Plans for counting or controlling movement of goods in receiving and shipping areas if those operations are not shut down during the count.

9. Instructions for compiling the count media (such as tags, punch cards) into final inventory listings or summaries.

10. Instructions for pricing the inventory items.

11. Instructions for review and approval of the inventory count; notations of obsolescence or other matters by supervisory personnel.

These characteristics are indicative of a well-planned counting operation. As the plan is carried out, the independent auditors should be present to observe. Many physical inventories are counted at hours that do not conflict with normal business operations.

When the client's records include reasonably well-controlled perpetual inventory records, auditors' test counting can proceed very much like a compliance audit of transactions. A sample of inventory items can be chosen from the perpetual records for test-counting to ascertain whether recorded inventory was counted. In the inventory locations, the audit team can count a selection of items, record these and later trace them to the perpetual records and inventory summary count sheets to ascertain whether all inventory in place was recorded (in perpetual records) or counted (included in the count compilation). This dual-direction sampling for test counting serves the purpose of auditing the perpetual records and the count compilation for erroneous counts and omissions.

As the counting operations proceed, the auditors can continuously evaluate the frequency of actual count errors by recounting the items counted by client personnel. By this evidence, the auditors can determine whether the count is satisfactorily accurate. If perpetual records are not maintained and inventory is recorded only on a periodic basis, the auditors will need to concentrate attention on the physical goods and sufficient test counts in the field.

The foregoing procedures are applicable to the audit of physical quantities when the auditors are present to observe the count and when the count is made on the year-end date. However, the following situations may occur frequently.

A. Auditors present, physical inventory taken at a date prior or subsequent to year-end date. The auditors can follow the procedures outlined above for observation of the physical count. However, with a time period intervening between the count date and the year-end, additional roll-forward or roll-back auditing procedures must be performed on purchases, inventory additions and issue transactions during that period. The inventory on the count date can be reconciled to the year-end inventory by appropriate addition or subtraction of the intervening receiving and issue transactions.

B. Auditors present, physical inventory taken on a cycle basis or on a statistical plan, but never a complete count on a single date. If a statistical plan is used, the audit manager must understand the sampling plan and evaluate its appropriateness, in addition to making the physical observation. In these kinds of situations, the auditors may be present for some counting operations. The auditors would be present every month (or more frequently) to observe all counts only as an "extended procedure" and only under unusual circumstances. Businesses that count inventory in this manner purport to have accurate perpetual records and carry out the counting as a means of testing the records and maintaining their accuracy. The auditors should arrange to be present during one or two counting operations in order to evaluate the counting plans and their execution. The procedural characteristics enumerated above would be utilized, test counts would be made and the audit team would be responsible for a conclusion concerning the reasonable accuracy of perpetual quantity records.

C. Auditors not present, physical inventory taken by the client. This sort of situation might arise when the audit firm is appointed late or when attempting to audit beginning inventories that had not previously been audited. The auditors should review the client's plan for the count as before. Some test counts should be made and traced to current records to the extent needed for a conclusion about the reliability of perpetual records. If the actual count was recent, intervening transaction activity may be reconciled to the year-end inventory. However, the reconciliation of a year's transactions (to unobserved beginning inventories) may be quite difficult. The auditors may employ procedures utilizing interrelationships such as sales activity, physical volume, price indices and gross profit margins for decisions about reasonableness. Nevertheless, much care must be exercised in "backing into" the audit of a previous inventory.[4]

The auditors should determine where and in what dollar amounts inventories are located off the client's premises, in the custody of consignees or in public warehouses. If amounts are material and if control is not exceptionally strong, the audit team will probably need to visit these locations and conduct onsite test counts. However, if amounts are not

---

[4] See "Evidential Matter for . . . Inventory" (SAS 1, AU 331.01–.02 and 331.09–.16).

material and/or if related evidence is adequate (such as periodic reports, cash receipts, receivables records, shipping records) and if controls are strong, then direct confirmation with the custodian may be considered sufficient competent evidence of the existence of quantities.[5]

Physical observation may also be employed in connection with controlling the *cutoff* when the auditors are present on the year-end date. In the shipping and receiving locations, the numbers of the last receiving report and the last shipping documents may be recorded. A list of items about to be shipped or received, but to be included or excluded from inventory, can be made. These data may be traced later to the inventory compilation, to accounts receivable and payable records, and to sales records as a part of the cutoff audit procedures.

Cutoff problems in inventory are directly related to accounts payable. Unrecorded inventory items (such as goods in transit) oftentimes pertain to liabilities that should have been recorded in the year under audit. Particular problems arise with the reconciliation of a physical inventory count with perpetual inventory records. The auditor must determine whether:

☐ Goods on hand were counted and included in the inventory compilation.

☐ Goods consigned-out or stored in outside warehouses (goods owned but not on hand) were included in the inventory compilation.

☐ Goods in transit (goods actually purchased and recorded but not yet received) were added to the inventory count and included in the inventory compilation.

☐ Goods on hand but already sold (but not yet delivered) were not counted and were excluded from the inventory compilation.

☐ Goods consigned-in (goods on hand but not owned) were excluded from the inventory compilation.

Another procedure which is frequently employed as a test of completeness of inventories and related accounts is *analytical review.* The basic analytical review ratio analyses relevant to inventory and cost of sales accounts are inventory turnover, inventory shrinkage, percentage markups and markdowns and gross margin percentages. These interrelationships are particularly important for businesses that do not identify specific cost of sales to individual sales transactions. These turnovers and rates should be analyzed for interperiod trend data for the client and in relation

---

[5] See "Public Warehouses—Controls and Auditing Procedures for Goods Held" (SAS 1, AU 901).

to industry-wide statistics. Significant variations from trend or from the industry should be investigated further to provide a satisfactory explanation.

For manufacturing operations, the relative ratios of material, labor and overhead in inventory and in cost of goods sold can be computed and analyzed. Variations may be indicative of amounts misclassified in the accounts. For example, repairs and maintenance expense items improperly classified as material purchases in the current year would probably change the relative ratios of the inputs enough for questions to be raised and thus cause additional vouching of materials costs.

Expenses that are functionally related to inventory levels and production activity may be correlated with inventory balances and costs of sales. Insurance and certain property tax expenses relate to the value of inventories, and these policies and assessments may be correlated with the account data. Royalty and license payments for use of production techniques may be indicative of production volume. There may even be a special control system set up to gather such data as a basis for figuring royalty payments due. Warehouse receipts may be associated with some types of goods held in public warehouses, and these would bear the seal of the warehouseman. Some selling commission costs may be correlated with consignment sales, and these amounts may be associated with cost of goods sold through consignment arrangements.

If the audit engagement includes subsidiary companies, the audit team can match intercompany purchases of the buyer with intercompany sales of the seller. If other auditors are involved, this same information may be obtained by communication with the other auditors (with management consent respecting information that might be considered confidential).

Budgets, forecasts, performance reports and variance analysis reports that are a part of the internal management information system should be studied and matched or reconciled to the account data. These reports are generally designed for control purposes to highlight unexpected results and problem areas. Results that differ from expectations and production cost problems are also of interest to auditors. A review of these reports may supply many explanations or lead to further auditing procedures.

In general, several of the analytical relationships may be combined to provide sufficient evidence concerning fair presentation of cost of goods sold. As a practical matter, cost of goods sold is generally audited through a combination of limited vouching and extensive interrelationships analysis. Inventory balances, in contrast, are usually audited with heavy reliance on observation, vouching and recalculation, with much less emphasis on analytical interrelationships.

Valuation or Allocation. The physical observation procedures are principally designed to audit physical quantities and to facilitate notice of obsolete or worn inventory. Other procedures for inventory valuation mainly involve the audit of unit cost prices used to price, extend and total the inventory cost. Essentially, the procedural application involves sampling inventory items grouped under a unit price. (The quantity times cost extension may be defined as a sample item.) Since the quantity has been audited by observation, there remains the audit of the unit price by *vouching* the price to a vendor's invoice. Auditors must consider the inventory cost flow assumption in this procedure (such as FIFO, LIFO, average) in order to identify the appropriate vendor's price.

When inventory consists of manufactured goods, the vouching will be to the cost accounting records and thence to vendor's invoices, payroll cost records, and overhead allocation calculations. To the extent that previous evidence has shown the cost accounting system to be reliable, these vouching applications may be limited. However, auditors should at this point be careful to vouch actual costs sufficiently to reach a conclusion about the reasonableness of standard costs.

Additional attention in vouching operations should be paid to current replacement costs of inventory. If replacement cost prices have fallen below prices used to value the inventory, lower-of-cost-or-market valuation calculations will have to be undertaken. Auditors will then need to obtain selling price data and data on selling costs, costs to complete work in process, and normal profit margin in order to calculate the cost-or-market ceiling and floor limits.

Inventories of a retail store add complications when the inventory is valued by a retail method estimation. In such cases, vouching would be extended to audit the retail price and the cost price and to audit markups and markdowns involved in the retail method calculations.

Vouching should be applied especially to inventory costs associated with purchases from affiliates or subsidiaries. The prices assigned to such goods may be out of line with market prices.[6] Any intercompany profit in inventories would have to be known and eliminated in consolidation.

With regard to cost of goods sold, vouching is a very useful procedure for obtaining specific and detailed evidence. The procedure may in some cases be perceived as a detailed audit of individual cost of goods sold transactions, much like the audit of the value of inventory items. When costs are associated with each sale transaction, the population of recorded data may be defined as the *sales* transactions. With a sample of sales, the related cost of goods sold may be located and then vouched to supporting evidence in vendors' invoices or cost accounting records. The other direction of the test would involve a sample of cost of goods sold entries, vouching to supporting documents, then vouching to recorded sales to determine whether all associated costs and revenues were recorded in the same period.

---

[6] See "Related Parties" (SAS No. 45, AU 1020).

In other situations, cost of sales may not be identified specifically with individual sales transactions. In such cases, overall tests of reasonableness and recalculations (i.e., analytical review) may serve for sufficient audit evidence. Consider the usual calculation of cost of goods sold:

Beginning inventory.	$ 300,000
Purchases (net cost)	4,380,000
	$4,680,000
Ending inventory	650,000
Cost of goods sold	$4,030,000

If observation, vouching, recalculation and other procedures are sufficient to audit beginning and ending inventories and purchases (net of discounts, freight, returns, and the like), the cost of goods sold is also audited in the overall. To the extent that significant items for separate disclosure exist (such as significant shrinkage, theft or casualty losses), then these would have to be identified by other procedures and broken out from the cost of goods sold category. Other procedures for assessing interrelationships relevant to cost of goods sold are covered in sections below.

Recalculations with respect to inventories and cost of sales are performed mostly in connection with price and cost vouching and in auditing the clerical accuracy of inventory compilations. The inventory extensions (quantity times cost) of a sample of items should be recalculated to audit their accuracy, and the entire inventory compilation should be footed. Various quantity transformations (such as units to dozens, gallons to barrels) that match the pricing unit should be recalculated. Multiplying a per-gross price by quantity measured in dozens can create a significant error. Recalculation is also involved in auditing the accuracy of job and process cost accumulations related to cost-price vouching.

The audit of appropriate pricing by FIFO, LIFO and other inventory methods amounts to recalculation procedures. The objective here is to determine whether an appropriate cost flow assumption has been applied appropriately. Similarly, recalculations of percentage-of-completion data such as cost accumulations and percent completion serve to audit the clerical accuracy and valuation measurement.

The retail method of inventory estimation is a more complex sort of calculation involving cost and retail relationships, markups and markdowns, and cost ratios. The retail method calculation should be carefully analyzed for any errors of logic or mathematical inaccuracy.

Direct correspondence with outside parties finds limited use with regard to inventories and practically no use with regard to cost of sales. *Confirmation* of inventory held by consignees or public warehouses may be appropriate under conditions of strong internal control as mentioned earlier. Confirmations may also be used to ascertain the terms of agreements to pledge inventory as security for liabilities and to ascertain or clarify special terms of orders or contracts.

In connection with accounts payable confirmation, if a particular vendor is a large supplier, the purchasing activity as well as the year-end account balance may be confirmed. In this way, a significant portion of the purchases total may be audited by confirmation rather than by extensive vouching of documents.

Initial *inquiries* are very useful in the planning of an audit. Information gained in this way would include the locations of inventory, dates for the physical count, inventory held off premises by consignees and public warehouses, the cost flow assumption used to price cost of goods sold and inventories, and the pledging of inventory as collateral. All of this information leads auditors to other applicable evidence-gathering procedures.

More in the nature of direct evidence, however, would be discussions with knowledgeable client personnel about the status and value of slow-moving inventory, apparently worn, damaged or obsolete inventory, and the existence of large inventory stockpiles. Inquiries may also be directed to learning about any significant purchase commitments.

Questions and discussions may lead to explanations of cost overruns on construction projects or manufacturing jobs. Such responses may help explain fluctuations or changes otherwise evident in cost records or inventory prices. Of course, auditors must be discerning enough to distinguish a factual explanation from an inadequate one. The explanation that "cost of sales increased this year as a result of increased sales and inflation" is one that can be audited. Auditors should be able to ascertain whether inflation did in fact touch the client's inputs (such as materials costs, labor rates) and to ascertain whether sales in fact increased instead of simply being inflated by false entries.

Rights, Presentation and Disclosure.   Inquiries should also include discussions regarding inventory pledged as collateral for loans. However, evidence regarding the pledging of inventory will usually be found when auditing the liabilities. Auditors should also discuss with client personnel the necessity of proper description of the inventory costing method in the accounting policy disclosure footnote.

Major Working Paper   The major working paper for documenting the audit procedures relating to inventory is the compilation schedule. Test counts would be traced to this compilation, pricing vouched to invoices, and all computations recalculated. An example of a simple compilation schedule is illustrated in Exhibit 17–9. Some of the audit procedures discussed are listed in Exhibit 17–10.

EXHIBIT 17–9

D-1 ABC Company Prepared by MbD
Inventory Compilation Date 1-20-86
December 31, 1985

Item	Prepared by Client			Audit Data		
	Quantity	Cost	Amount	Quantity	Cost	Amount
# A 601	8928 √	$ 4.00 √	35712			35712 ≠
# F 60	13920 √	$ 3.40	47328	13920	$ 3.33 ×	46353 ≠
# L 612	17760 √	$ 2.40 √	42624			42624 ≠
# S 801	4560 √	$ 18.00 √	82080			82080 ≠
	Inventory, per client		207744			
Inventory Consigned-out, item #S801			(f/t)	1264 ①	$18	22752 ≠
	Inventory, per audit					227521
						T/B
	√ Agrees with physical observation and count by DW audit staff.					
	√ FIFO cost vouched to vendor's recent invoices, no exceptions.					
	√ Client failed to exclude cash discount taken on last purchase					
	≠ calculated by audit staff.					
	f Footed client's inventory schedule.					
	t Traced to general ledger-physical difference was adjusted					
	to the Inventory over/short expense account.					
	T/B Tied to audit trial balance.					
	① Shipping department records show 1264 units of #S801 shipped to					
	customer December 24 marked "on consignment". Inquiry in					
	billing department revealed this shipping document being					
	held -- no invoice was prepared and no sale was recorded.					
	Recommended Adjusting Journal Entry					
	Inventory		22752			
	Inventory over/short		975			
	Inventory			975		
	Cost of Goods Sold			22752		

EXHIBIT 17–10
Audit Program—Selected
Substantive Procedures

A. Inventory.
   1. Review the client's instructions for physical count of the inventory. If the
       count is based on a statistical sample, review the plan for statistical validity.
   2. Observe the client's counting procedures, determine whether instructions
       are followed. Count a sample of inventory items. Trace these counts to the
       final inventory compilation.
   3. Vouch unit prices to vendors' invoices.
   4. Recalculate extensions and footings of the final inventory compilation.
   5. Determine the applicability of lower-of-cost-or-market valuation on selected
       inventory categories.
   6. Inquire about inventory out on consignment and about inventory on hand
       which is consigned-in from vendors.
   7. Confirm inventories held in public warehouses.
   8. Inquire about obsolete or damaged goods subject to write-down or write-off.
       Scan perpetual records for indications of slow-moving inventory.
   9. Obtain written representations from the client concerning any pledge of
       inventory as collateral.

B. Cost of Sales.
   1. Select a sample of recorded cost of sales entries and vouch to supporting
       documentation.
   2. Select a sample of basic transaction documents (such as sales invoices,
       production reports) and determine whether the related cost of goods sold
       was figured and recorded properly.
   3. Determine whether the accounting costing method used by the client (such
       as FIFO, LIFO, standard cost) was applied properly.
   4. Compute the gross margin rate and compare to prior years.
   5. Compute the ratio of cost elements (such as labor, material) to total cost of
       goods sold and compare to prior years.

CURRENT PAYABLES

When considering assertions and obtaining evidence regarding payables, auditors must put emphasis on completeness and obligations, where most of the emphasis was on existence and rights for assets. Obtaining evidence is more difficult for the completeness assertion. Evidence is usually available to verify an asset exists (or a transaction that is recorded is valid) or that management has certain rights to the use of an asset. Normally, however, little or no evidence exists for incomplete or unrecorded liabilities or obligations (or valid transactions not recorded).

Substantive Audit Procedures Related to Objectives

The construction of an audit program of substantive procedures should begin with auditors' recognition of the explicit and implicit assertions contained in the current liability accounts and disclosures relating to liabilities. The assertions point directly to questions that can be audited by gathering sufficient, competent evidential matter. The general assertions about all accounts (existence, completeness, rights and obligations, valuation, and presentation and disclosure) can be expressed in specific terms for liabilities. For example:

- ☐ All material liabilities are recorded and none omitted.
- ☐ All obligations are recognized and disclosed.
- ☐ Liabilities are properly classified by their contingent or direct nature.
- ☐ Liabilities are properly classified by their current or long-term status.

The substantive year-end procedures in this section will be described primarily with relation to trade accounts payable. However, where appropriate, other liabilities and related accounts, such as purchases, will be included. Of course, the nature, timing and extent of year-end procedures will depend upon the evaluation of controls in the acquisition and expenditure cycle, which was covered in Chapter 14.

Obligations, Existence and Completeness.   The primary audit work at year-end for liabilities involves the *search for unrecorded liabilities* which falls under the completeness objective. There is usually no problem with the existence of the recorded liabilities. The search for unrecorded liabilities goes on in all audit areas, as was illustrated by the questions on the standard bank confirmation. In addition, however, the **tracing** procedures are utilized specifically in this search.

Tracing may be used extensively in the search for unrecorded liabilities. The essence of the search is that the auditor examines the basic file records (such as purchases, receiving reports, payments, vouchers) and traces the data processing to determine whether transactions were recorded in the proper period. The transactions included in the search are ones recorded during the two- or three-week periods both immediately before and immediately after the balance sheet date. Many innocent errors of unrecorded liabilities result from simple cutoff errors and their detection is not difficult.

Auditors may obtain the invoices recorded in the post-year-end period, many of which may have been received for the first time (say, on January 10 for a December 31 year-end). By a combination of tracing from the invoices to the records and vouching from the records to the invoices, cutoff errors (including unrecorded liability errors) can be found. Auditors document these items in the working papers and record their decisions of whether they are material enough to require an adjustment of the accounts. A working paper showing a search based on subsequent cash disbursements is illustrated in Exhibit 17–11.

Another particularly relevant application of tracing procedures involves the examination of IRS audit reports and correspondence and the audit reports of state and local tax authorities. Errors and deficiencies revealed and assessed in such reports should be traced to the accounts to ascertain whether the accounting is correct. Tax audits typically lag and the period of the last completed audit should be disclosed in footnotes to

EXHIBIT 17–11

G-2	Search for Unrecorded Liabilities	ABC Company			Prepared by MB	
		December 31, 1985			Date 1-31-86	

Check No.	Payee	Date	Amount			
1101	Smalltown Utility Co.	1-5-86	733 00	x	December 1985 Utility Bill
1102	Mortons Vendomat	1-6-86	1032 00	x	Christmas Party Costs
1103	Vendorama	1-6-86	7628 00	✓	Inventory Received 12-26-85
1189	Adams Apple	1-31-86	321 00	y	Supplies Received 1-4-86
	✓ Traced to accounts payable balance as of 12-31-85 Properly recorded					
	x Account payable was not recorded in 1985.					
	y Payment on liability arising after 12-31-85.					
	Recommended Adjustment					
	Utility Expense	733				
	Miscellaneous Expense	1032				
	Accounts Payable		1765			

the financial statements. Oftentimes, this review of tax agents' reports reveals some deductions or assessments in dispute. Information on such matters is important for disclosure of contingent liabilities if probable assessments have not already been recorded.

Basic files, vouchers, invoices, receiving reports, cash disbursements, cash receipts and other such records may be *scanned* for unusual amounts. Sometimes when the transaction volume is large in the cutoff period, the items chosen for audit are selected by scanning for amounts larger than a relevant limit (for example, every transaction over $300). An alternative selection method would be random selection, augmented by scanning the items not selected for any unusual characteristics.

Confirmations may also be used to determine the existence and completeness of liabilities. However, there is a great difference between accounts payable confirmation and accounts receivable confirmation. When confirming receivables, the audit team is primarily interested in evidence of the validity of recorded claims on real debtors. The relative risk respecting payables is that they may be omitted or otherwise understated. A confirmation sample of accounts payable with balances greater than zero can only reveal omission of invoices (which could result from cutoff errors), but such a sample would not provide any means of detecting accounts that were entirely omitted.

The accounts payable confirmation sample should include all suppliers with whom the client has done business recently (or at least the major ones), regardless of the size of the balance (even a zero balance) at the confirmation date. With this selection, the confirmation procedure becomes a part of the search for unrecorded liabilities. Similarly, payable amounts that are old, past due, in dispute or have other unusual characteristics should be confirmed.

Analytical review may be utilized to support conclusions about completeness in the current liability accounts. Two different overall interrelationships can be analyzed to support conclusions about transaction activity and account balances. The general level of activity as evidenced by physical production volume, purchasing activity, inventory stockpiling and cost of goods sold amounts should correspond with credits to trade accounts payable. When production, purchases and sales are increasing, accounts payable activity and period-end balances will likely be greater also. These relationships, coupled with the cash position and payment activity, are essential clues to the reasonableness of trade accounts payable totals.

Also in the area of overall relationships, certain liabilities are functions of other basic transactions. Sales taxes are functionally related to sales dollar totals, payroll taxes to payroll totals, excise taxes to sales dollars or volume, and income taxes to income.

Valuation. *Vouching* may be used extensively to gather evidence on the valuation of the recorded balance of accounts payable. In a manner similar to the compliance audit procedures, selected liability balances may be vouched to the documentation of the transaction (or series of transactions) that created the balance. Notice that the procedure differs somewhat from the compliance audit of transactions in that a balance (such as an account payable to a supplier) is selected instead of one purchase from a supplier. Thus, liability balances may be audited by: (1) vouching an accounts payable balance to recent invoices and recent payments, (2) vouching a note or bond payable balance to cash receipts and the loan agreement, (3) vouching payroll tax liabilities to payroll records and tax returns, (4) vouching income tax payable to the income tax return. Additional vouching whereby auditors compare year-end liability amounts to cash payments made in the subsequent period serves the dual purpose of producing evidence of the year-end balance and possible evidence of unrecorded liabilities (if subsequent payment includes an amount not properly recorded at the balance sheet date).

Presentation and Disclosure. Verbal *inquiry* of the proper presentation and disclosure of liabilities is necessary. Auditors are especially concerned that only trade payables are included in the accounts payable balance. The schedule of the detail accounts that make up the total of accounts payable should be *scanned* for unusual nonvendor or interest-bearing accounts and for liabilities to related parties.

Major Working Papers

The major working papers for accounts payable are the (1) trial balance of the subsidiary vendor ledger-detail accounts representing recorded liabilities and (2) the documentation of the specific procedures performed in the search for unrecorded liabilities (see Exhibit 17–11). The evidence of the audit procedures, such as vouching and tracing, are recorded by tick marks on the trial balance in much the same fashion as they were recorded on the trial balance of the detail of accounts receivable. Of course, the schedule is footed and traced through the trial balance into the general ledger. Exhibit 17–12 contains a partial audit program for accounts payable.

EXHIBIT 17–12
Audit Program—Selected Substantive Procedures—Accounts Payable

1. Obtain from the client a trial balance of recorded accounts payable as of year-end. Foot and trace to the general ledger account. Vouch a sample of balances to underlying documents.

2. Conduct a search for unrecorded liabilities by examining vendor's invoices received and cash payments made for a period after year-end.

3. Reconcile vendor's monthly statements at year-end with recorded accounts payable.

4. If concern still exists about possible unrecorded payables, confirm with creditors, especially those with small or zero balances.

PREPAIDS AND ACCRUALS

The prepaid expenses, accrued receivables and accrued liabilities represent differences in timing between cash transactions and the use of goods or services. The audit objectives remain the same: however, the specific procedures may not be extensive due to the limited activity in such accounts and their relative immateriality.

Substantive Audit Procedures Related to Objectives

The prepaids and accruals are frequently audited in conjunction with other accounts, such as accrued sales taxes and commissions, as part of the sales account work (or accrued interest receivable as part of notes receivable work, see Exhibit 17–6). When audited alone, a common procedure is to schedule the entire activity for the year, as will be illustrated in this section with prepaid insurance.

Existence, Completeness, Rights and Obligations.   The verification of the recorded amounts in prepaid insurance and a search for unrecorded amounts can be accomplished with one or two procedures. Sending a *confirmation* letter is preferred because confirmations are more reliable evidence and a letter can also request information about loans to the client (thus, becoming part of the search for unrecorded liabilities). The letter should not only request the face amount and premium cost of the policies in force during the year, but should also request the beneficiaries of the policies. If the insurance is for the benefit of a party other than the client, assets may also be pledged as security, and a disclosure must be made in the financial statements.

Vouching the insurance purchased involves examining the policies held by the company and the invoices for the policies purchased during the year. Evidence on the policies in force at the beginning of the year was obtained in previous audits and should be in last year's working papers.

Establishing cutoff, a common completeness objective, is usually not a separate problem addressed for most prepayments and accruals. The cutoff procedures for cash, sales and purchases will cover these accounts.

Valuation or Allocation.   The valuation of the prepaid insurance begins with the confirmation or examination of the policy contract and invoices. After noting the amount of the premium and length of coverage, the client's computations of the prepaid and expensed amounts can then be *recalculated* (see Exhibit 17–13).

Many liability balances owe both existence and valuation to a calculation. All the accrued expense liabilities (such as accrued interest payable, rent payable, salaries and wages payable) fall into this category as well as sales and excise taxes payable, income tax payable, warranty and guarantee liabilities, deferred installment income and other liability and deferred credit balances.

The audit of such balances may depend in large part on auditor recalculations, supported by appropriate vouching to basic transactions or contract agreements. As suggested in previous discussion, accrued expenses are recalculated with reference to interest rates, wage rates, tax rates, time periods, last payment date and other definitive factors. To the extent that the client has already made these accruals, the recalculation process is relatively simple. In all cases, particularly when the client has not made accruals, the auditor must be alert to the variety of possible accruals so that one is not overlooked and omitted entirely. The short list below contains typical accrual items.

Salaries, wages and bonuses.

Sales commissions.

Royalties.

Real estate and personal property taxes.

Social security and unemployment insurance taxes.

Insurance.

Rents.

Interest.

Compensation cost of stock option plans.

Warranty and guarantee expenses.

EXHIBIT 17–13

F-1

Prepared by JC
1-20-86

Mean Greg Manufacturing Co.
Prepaid Insurance
12/31/85

		1	2	3	4
1	Insurer	Baker Ins.	Rock Price Casualty	Umbrella Surety	Blanket Bonding
4	Policy number	764-23-44 Ⓐ	1976-413 Ⓐ	FBD-1432 Ⓐ	643-XZ-14 Ⓐ
6	Coverage	All autos owned Ⓓ	Plant office bldg. including contents $4,000,000	Blanket Bond $50,000	Blanket Bond $200,000
10	Term	3 years	4 years	one year	one year
11		7/1/84-87	1/1/83-86	3/1/84	3/1/85
13	Unexpired premium 12/31/84	3,000 ⍺	10000 ⍺	800 ⍺	-0-
15	Additions - 1985 (1/1/85)	300 Ⓒ√			9600 √
17	Expensed - 1985	1320 √	5000 √	800 √	8000 √
19	Unexpired premium 12/31/85	1980 T/b	5000 T/b	-0-	1600 T/b

Ⓐ Review copy of insurance contract, in the permanent file added copy of Blanket Bonding policy which replaced Umbrella Surety policy.

√ Computations recalculated.

⍺ PF to prior year workpapers.

√ Vouched to agency invoices.

T/b sum of these total to trial balance - page 6.

Ⓓ Liability 100,000/400,000, collision, comprehensive, uninsured motorist. Additional premium to cover increase in autos owned by company.

Likewise, other prepaid expenses are generally matters of calculation, subject to audit of the bases for items: for example, prepaid interest, rent, taxes, salaries, commissions and the like. Recalculation, following verification of the base data (usually by vouching), can complete the audit of items such as these.

Presentation and Disclosure. Normally this audit objective is not troublesome for prepaids and accruals. Some items may require special disclosure considerations, such as warranty and guarantee accruals, if they are material.

One item relating to insurance that requires disclosure consideration is the adequacy of coverage and the existence of coinsurance. Auditors cannot be expected to be experts on insurance matters, but *inquiry* regarding adequacy of coverage with the client, and possibly an insurance broker, and comparison to industry practice should be done. This information, in conjunction with the understanding by auditors of the general value of the assets, should provide evidence of the adequacy of insurance coverage. Inadequate insurance and self-insurance should be disclosed in the footnotes to the financial statements.

Main Working Paper

When there are few transactions, as is frequently the case with insurance, all transactions for the year can be listed on one working paper. This kind of schedule is commonly referred to as account analysis or input/output analysis and is illustrated in Exhibit 17–13.

Although consideration of audit objectives is very useful in planning the audit and the necessary substantive procedures, the actual audit program is organized by the work areas. Selected procedures from among those discussed covering prepaid and accruals are presented in Exhibit 17–14.

EXHIBIT 17–14
Audit Program—Selected
Substantive
Procedures—Prepaids and
Accruals

1. Prepare or have client prepare, a schedule of all accrued and estimated liabilities (such as accrued interest, wages, taxes)
2. Recalculate accrued amounts.
3. Based on average interest rates and amount of debt outstanding, recalculate interest expense for the period under audit.
4. Recalculate interest income based on average loans receivable outstanding and average interest rate in effect for the year.
5. Vouch payroll taxes payable to tax returns.

MAJOR TYPES OF
FRAUD AND
MISSTATEMENT

Revenue,
Receivables and
Cash

Revenue, receivables and cash transactions provide many of the classic examples of fraud and embezzlement. Sales and other revenue transactions may be deliberately overstated to puff up a poor operating record. Thorough auditing of receivables, alertness for fictitious debtors and careful reconciliation of cash receipts activity can detect most attempts to overstate sales. Understatement of sales to evade income taxes is harder to detect, but when such understatement is attempted, the receivable and cash collection and the related cost of goods sold records must also be suppressed to hide the omission. About the only way to detect a complete omission of sales and related transactions is through some reconciliation of physical activity with recorded dollar amounts. Incomplete omissions might be detected by careful analysis of account interrelationships (such as the gross margin relationship).

Cash is relatively easy to steal, although poor internal accounting controls must exist to make such theft possible. A person who has access both to cash and accounts receivable records may take a cash receipt and then cover it the next day with a payment received for another customer's account. Of course, the second customer does not have credit, so this "lapping" operation must be continued with subsequent receipts from other customers. The telltale sign is that customers listed on the bank deposit slip do not match with customers whose accounts are credited. Surprise confirmation or an enforced vacation policy may prevent such activity, but a proper separation of duties is more effective in the long run. If one person has authority to handle cash receipts and issue credit memoranda on accounts, it may be possible to hide a theft, but then a high level of noncash credits to receivables should alert a careful auditor to further investigation of credit memoranda.

A cashier who prepares the bank deposit and also prepares bank reconciliations may take cash and hide this fact by falsifying the reconciliation. Inflated "deposits in transit" may be covered by receipts of later days, by underfooting the outstanding checklist or by omitting outstanding checks from the reconciliation. Regular audit procedures applied to a bank reconciliation should detect these frauds.

An accounts receivable bookkeeper who has access to cash might record a sale in an amount less than the invoice. When payment is received, the "excess" can be stolen. Audit vouching of sales-receivables entries to invoice documents and detail comparison of deposit slip items to accounts receivable credits would detect these embezzlements. Most times, however, finding such an item could amount to trying to find a needle in a haystack, but independent auditors still need to be aware of possibilities for embezzlement that might be material with relation to financial statements. Internal auditors, however, may be given an assignment to carry out such a detail investigation for the express purpose of finding isolated instances of embezzlement.

Cash disbursement operations can harbor several opportunities for embezzlement. Generally, the process is one of siphoning company funds to a fictitious person or company or to accomplices outside. Fictitious invoices for nonexistent goods or services must reach the check-signing stage with approvals and documents in order. This may involve forged requisitions, purchase orders and receiving reports, or fraudulent approvals by an authorizing manager. A check so issued may be recorded as an expense item and the funds intercepted by the dishonest manager. Alternatively, an accounts payable clerk may simply raise the amount due on an invoice and later recover a share from an accomplice recipient.

Any checks made payable to a bank, to "cash," or to bearer should be investigated and vouched to supporting documents. Checks payable to a bank in repayment of a loan could be intercepted if not mailed directly to the bank, and the interceptor might be able to hide the nonpayment by suppressing due notices, by renewing the note or by covering with a later embezzlement. Thorough confirmation with all bank creditors would likely uncover this kind of scheme. Having checks drawn to cash, stolen, not recorded (so as not to falsify any other account balance), and then underfooting the cash receipts journal is another complex embezzlement. However, this one leaves many tracks—a missing check in the check number sequence, the canceled check in the bank statement, and the erroneous cash journal addition. A proof of cash that reconciles receipts and disbursements activity per the bank statement to receipts and disbursements recorded in the accounts would detect this maneuver easily.

Purchasing and Inventory
Purchasing operations and inventory custody are activities susceptible to fraud and error that can achieve material proportions. Each of these areas is interrelated.

Purchasing embezzlement schemes range from the simple to the complex, and oftentimes the latter is next to impossible to detect with ordinary auditing procedures. A purchasing agent may take a kickback from a supplier. There is virtually no way to uncover this activity. However, if the kickback is sizable, the supplier's price may be raised out of line with market prices (from other suppliers) to cover the kickback. Audit vouching of prices would draw attention only to the one supplier's price, and should be verified by looking them up in a price catalog. Otherwise a general awareness of available market prices and knowledge of prices paid to other vendors might trigger a lower-of-cost or market valuation calculation for goods in inventory. If the purchasing agent buys goods or services for personal use (such as furnishings, home improvements), the agent would have to cover with an authorizing requisition and with some notification of receipt (such as receiving report or use report). These maneuvers would involve either access to blank forms or collusion with other employees.

Some persons authorized to purchase may have an easier time without being constrained by a bureaucratic system of requisitions, receipts and other-person authorizations. Promotion managers, sales representatives, internal news magazine editors and similar persons have cropped up in the news from time to time for having charged personal trips and amenities for their homes and friends as business expenses. Signs of extravagant habits for a person in a less-well-paid position might be a clue for further investigation. However, auditors must be very careful about undertaking an expensive investigation when vague suspicions are the only grounds.

Inventory losses may result from simple theft. Physical safeguards are the best protection against nonemployees. However, an employee who can remove inventory and create an inventory issue authorization (or keep inventory records directly) can cover his or her tracks. Fraudulent overstatement of inventories in order to boost financial position must be perpetrated by deceiving the auditors. History has recorded the practices of nailing empty cartons to shelves (push at them; they do not move; ergo they must be full), by stacking boxes or bales around an empty center (climb to the top and look), and by inserting a full chamber under a measuring hole atop a liquid storage tank, with inventory material in the chamber and water in the remainder of the tank (rattle a rod through the measuring hole to hit the sides of the chamber). These and other deceptions are relatively easy when dishonest persons can predict the auditor's sample selection and degree of suspicion and carefulness.

Production losses may be created by a dishonest inspector who labels good production as defective or as scrap and then is able to remove it. High incidence of such action should become evident in accounting for production quality and inefficiency. Lack of a system for controlling scrap sales and rework operations can make such theft easier, but a sound system of accounting controls, management reports and follow-up action can prevent or detect the dishonest inspector's activity.

Current Liabilities   The kinds of fraud and misstatement connected with current liabilities differ significantly from those associated with current asset accounts. Few employees are tempted to steal a liability, although fictitious liabilities may be created in the records as a means of misdirecting cash payments. Auditors should be alert for such fictions in the same sense that they are alert to the possibility of having fictitious accounts receivable.

Financial statements may be materially misstated by reason of omission or understatement of liabilities. The concern for unrecorded liabilities in all audit areas and the specific procedures suggested in the "search for unrecorded liabilities" are used to discover such omissions and understatements.

SOURCES AND   AICPA. *Confirmation of Accounts Receivable*. Auditing Procedure Study, 1984.
ADDITIONAL
READING   Ashton, Robert H., and Robert H. Hylas. "Increasing Confirmation Response
REFERENCES   Rate." *Auditing: A Journal of Practice and Theory,* Summer 1981, pp. 12–22.

Ashton, Robert H. "The Return of 'Problem' Confirmation Requests by the U.S. Postal Service." *Accounting Review,* October 1980, pp. 649–57.

Braid, Michael. "Counting the Cash." *CPA Journal,* September 1979, pp. 82–84.

Davis, Maurice. "Using Statistical Sampling for Inventory Observations." *CPA Journal,* February 1978, pp. 73–75.

Greenwald, B. M., and C. D. Harnick. "Corporate Tax Review: the Auditor's Approach." *Journal of Accountancy,* May 1974, pp. 63–70.

Horvitz, Jerome S., and Michael Hainkel. "The IRS Summons Power and Its Effect on the Independent Auditor." *Journal of Accounting, Auditing and Finance,* Winter 1981, pp. 114–27.

Krogstad, J. L., and M. B. Romney. "Accounts Receivable Confirmation—An Alternative Auditing Approach." *Journal of Accountancy,* February 1980, pp. 68–74.

Lentine, Lawrence. "Using Ratio Estimation in Observing Inventories. *The CPA Journal,* June, 1981, pp. 24–31.

Sauls, Eugene. "Nonsampling Errors in Accounts Receivable Confirmation." *Accounting Review,* January 1972, pp. 109–15.

Sorkin, Horton L. "Third Party Confirmation Requests: A New Approach Utilizing an Expanded Field." Auditing Symposium IV—*Proceedings of the 1978 Touche Ross/University of Kansas Symposium on Auditing Problems,* pp. 61–72.

Sumutka, Alan R. "1980: Year of Increased Audit Risk." *CPA Journal,* December 1980, pp. 21–27.

Warren, Carl S. "Confirmation Informativeness." *Journal of Accounting Research,* Spring 1974, pp. 158–77.

_____. "Confirmation Reliability—The Evidence." *Journal of Accountancy,* February 1975, pp. 85–89.

_____. "Non-Commercial Organization Confirmation Reliability in Audits-A Credit Union as a Case." *CPA Journal,* February 1974, pp. 67–69.

Whittington, R., M. Zulinski, and J. W. Ledwith. "Completeness—The Elusive Assertation." *The Journal of Accountancy,* August 1983, pp. 82–92.

REVIEW QUESTIONS

Cash

17.1.   What is a cutoff bank statement? How is it used by the auditor?

17.2.   List the information a CPA should solicit in a standard bank confirmation inquiry sent to an audit client's bank.

17.3.   Why should all cash funds be counted at the same time?

17.4.   Why should petty cash be counted in the presence of the fund custodian with that person signing the working paper?

17.5.   What is "kiting?" What procedures do auditors use to detect kiting?

Current Receivables and Related Revenue

17.6.   Distinguish between "positive" and "negative" confirmations. Under what conditions would you expect each type of confirmation to be appropriate?

17.7.   Distinguish between confirmation "response rate" and confirmation "detection rate."

17.8.   What methods can be used to increase response rate of receivable confirmations?

17.9.   From a timing standpoint, when is vouching performed on the documentation underlying receivables balances? Explain.

17.10.   How does the auditor test for sales cutoff?

17.11.   What is "lapping"? What procedures does the auditor employ for its detection?

Inventory and Cost of Sales

17.12.   In the auditor's review of a client's inventory-taking instructions, what characteristics is the auditor looking for?

17.13.   Explain dual-direction sampling in the context of inventory test counts.

17.14.   What procedures are employed to audit inventory when the physical inventory is taken on a cycle basis or on a statistical plan, but never a complete count on a single date?

17.15.   What evidence regarding inventories and cost of sales can the auditor typically obtain from verbal inquiry?

17.16.   In performing an audit, what are the relevant account interrelationships with respect to a retailer's inventory? A manufacturer's inventory?

17.17.   What techniques are relied upon most heavily in an audit of cost of goods sold? Inventory balances?

Current Liabilities

17.18.   Describe the purpose and give examples of audit procedures in the "search for unrecorded liabilities."

17.19.   Explain the difference in approach in confirmation of accounts receivable and accounts payable.

Prepaids and Accruals

17.20.   List the steps for valuation of prepaid insurance.

17.21.   Why should auditors be concerned with insurance coverage?

Other

17.22.   List the major working papers for cash, accounts receivable, inventory, accounts payable and prepaid insurance.

17.23.   Describe the major types of fraud and material misstatement with regard to cash disbursements of which the auditor should be aware. What procedures are generally relied upon to detect such embezzlement?

EXERCISES AND PROBLEMS

Cash

17.24.   **Bank Reconciliation**
The following client-prepared bank reconciliation is being examined by you during an audit of the financial statements of Cynthia Company:

CYNTHIA COMPANY
Bank Reconciliation
Village Bank Account 2
December 31, 1985

Balance per bank (a)		$18,375.91
Deposits in transit (b):		
12/30	$1,471.10	
12/31	2,840.69	4,311.79
Subtotal		22,687.70
Outstanding checks (c):		
837	6,000.00	
1941	671.80	
1966	320.00	
1984	1,855.42	
1985	3,621.22	
1987	2,576.89	
1991	4,420.88	(19,466.21)
Subtotal		3,221.49
NSF check returned 12/29 (d)		200.00
Bank charges		5.50
Error check no. 1932		148.10
Customer note collected by the bank ($2,750 plus $275 interest (e)		(3,025.00)
Balance per books (f)		550.09

Required:

Indicate one or more audit procedures that should be performed in gathering evidence in support of each of the items (*a*) through (*f*) above.

(*AICPA* adapted)

17.25. Sales Cutoff and Cutoff Bank Statement

a. You wish to audit Houston Corporation's sales cutoff at June 30. Describe the procedures you should perform.

b. You obtain a July 10 bank statement directly from the bank. Explain how this cutoff bank statement will be used—

   (1) In your review of the June 30 bank reconciliation.

   (2) To obtain other audit information.

(*AICPA* adapted)

17.26. Cash Transfers

XYZ operates sales divisions in several cities throughout the country. In addition to other activities, the sales divisions are charged with the collection of local receivables; each division maintains a bank account in which all collections are deposited intact. Twice a week, these collections are transferred to the home office by check; no other checks are drawn on this bank account. Except for cash receipts and cash disbursements books, no accounting books are kept at the sales offices, but all cash records are retained by them in their files.

As part of your year-end audit, you wish to include an audit of cash transfers between the sales divisions and the main office. It is intended that your representative will visit all locations.

Required:

a. What are the purposes of the audit of cash transfers?

b. Assuming that your representative has full knowledge of audit procedures for regular cash collection to which he will attend at each location, design only such additional specific audit steps as the representative will be required to perform to audit the cash transfers from each division to the home office.

(*AICPA* adapted)

17.27. Bank Reconciliation—Cash Shortage

The Patrick Company had poor internal control over its cash transactions. Facts about its cash position at November 30 were the following:

The cash account in the books showed a balance of $18,901.62, which included undeposited receipts. A credit of $100 on the bank statement did not appear on the books of the company. The balance according to the bank statement was $15,550.

When you received the cutoff bank statement on December 10, the following canceled checks were enclosed: no. 62 for $116.25, no. 183 for $150.00, no. 284 for $253.25, no. 8621 for $190.71, no. 8623 for $206.80, and no. 8632 for $145.28. The only deposit was in the amount of $3,794.41 on December 7. The first check issued in January of this year was no. 1125.

The cashier handles all incoming cash and makes the bank deposits personally. He also reconciles the monthly bank statement. His November 30 reconciliation is shown below.

Balance, per books, November 30		$18,901.62
Add outstanding checks:		
8621	$190.71	
8623	206.80	
8632	145.28	442.79
		19,344.41
Less undeposited receipts . . .		3,794.41
Balance per bank, November 30		15,550.00
Deduct unrecorded credit . . .		100.00
True cash, November 30		15,450.00

Required:

a. You suspect that the cashier has stolen some money. Prepare a schedule showing your estimate of the minimum and maximum amount of the loss.

b. How did the cashier attempt to conceal the theft, if any?

c. Based only on the information above, name two specific features of internal control apparently missing.

d. If the cashier's October 31 reconciliation is known to be in order and you start your audit on December 5, what specific auditing procedures could you perform to discover the theft?

(*AICPA* adapted)

Receivables and Revenues

17.28. Alternative Procedures
Several accounts receivable confirmations have been returned with the notation that "verification of vendors' statements is no longer possible because our data processing system does not accumulate each vendor's invoices." What alternative auditing procedures could be used to audit these accounts receivable?

(*AICPA* adapted)

17.29. Confirmation and Valuation Procedures
You are auditing the financial statements of your new client, Flinight Manufacturing Company, as of December 31. Flinight makes home kitchen cleaning utensils and markets the products through direct sales to a large network of wholesale distributors located throughout the United States. Some distributors are very successful, purchase a large volume of the products, and tend to have large accounts receivable balances with Flinight. A large number of distributors (about 300) are apparently not able just now to penetrate local markets; hence, their purchases and accounts receivable balances tend to be quite small.

There are only 53 of the large accounts, totaling $530,000, and the 300 or so smaller accounts total $250,000. However, accounts receivable constitutes 60 percent of the company's current assets and about 20 percent of total assets. Flinight's stockholders' equity is $500,000, and the company's income for the year (unaudited) was $300,000 before taxes.

Your assistant points out that fairly small misstatements of the accounts receivable total could be material with relation to other accounting measurements. For example, a 7 percent overstatement of receivables would also be a 4.2 percent current asset overstatement and would cause Flinight to show a small working capital deficit. Also, this 7 percent overstatement would be 18 percent of the net income. Such an overstatement might result from having too small an allowance for doubtful accounts. In fact, the company treasurer has mentioned that some of the larger wholesalers have not been ordering as much lately, and some of them have not paid as quickly as they did six months ago, even missing the 3 percent cash discount. A few have complained about broken boxes received in shipment.

You and your assistant have already obtained evidence that the accounts receivable are properly classified as trade receivables and no sales are made on terms extending beyond 12 months. You are considering the audit procedures to apply in connection with sending confirmations and evaluating the collectibility of the trade receivables.

Required:

a. Identify and describe the two forms of accounts receivable confirmation requests and indicate what factors should be considered in determining when to use each.

b. Assume you receive satisfactory responses to the confirmation requests. Describe how you could evaluate collectibility of the trade accounts receivable.

17.30. Receivables Audit Procedures
The ABC Appliance Company, a manufacturer of minor electrical appliances, deals exclusively with 20 distributors situated at focal points throughout the country. At December 31, the balance sheet date, receivables from these distributors aggregated $875,000. Total current assets were $1,300,000.

With respect to receivables, the auditors followed the procedures outlined below in the course of the annual examination of financial statements:

1. Reviewed the system of internal accounting control and found it to be exceptionally good.
2. Tied detail with control account at year-end.
3. Aged accounts. None were overdue.
4. Examined detail sales and collection transactions for the months of February, July and November.
5. Received positive confirmations of year-end balances.

Required:

You are to criticize the completeness or incompleteness of the above program, giving reasons for your recommendations concerning the addition or omission of any procedures. (Hint: Decide how well the program provides evidence about the existence, valuation, completeness, rights and obligations, and presentation and disclosure assertions.)

(*AICPA* adapted)

17.31   **Procedures to Investigate Lapping**

During the year, Strang Corporation began to encounter cash flow difficulties, and a cursory review by management revealed accounts receivable collection problems. Strang's management engaged you to perform a special investigation. You studied the billing and collection cycle and noted the following:

The accounting department employs one bookkeeper who receives and opens all incoming mail. This bookkeeper is also responsible for depositing receipts, filing remittance advices on a daily basis, recording receipts in the cash receipts journal, and posting receipts in the individual customer accounts and the general ledger accounts. There are no cash sales. The bookkeeper prepares and controls the mailing of monthly statements to customers.

The concentration of functions and receivable collection problems caused you to suspect that a systematic defalcation of customer's payments through a delayed posting of remittances (lapping of accounts receivable) is present. You were surprised to find that no customers complained about receiving erroneous monthly statements.

Required:

Identify the procedures you should perform to determine whether lapping exists. Do not discuss deficiencies in the system of internal control.

(*AICPA* adapted)

17.32   **Rent Revenue**

You were engaged to conduct an audit of the financial statements of Clayton Realty Corporation for the year ending January 31, 1985. The examination of annual rent reconciliation is a vital portion of the audit.

The following rent reconciliation was prepared by the controller of Clayton Realty Corporation and was presented to you. You subjected it to various audit procedures:

CLAYTON REALTY CORPORATION
Rent Reconciliation
For the year ended January 31, 1985

Gross apartment rents (schedule A)	$1,600,800*
Less vacancies (schedule B)	20,500*
Net apartment rentals	1,580,300
Less unpaid rents (schedule C)	7,800*
Total	1,572,500
Add prepaid rent collected (schedule D)	500*
Total cash collected	$1,573,000*

Schedules A, B, C and D are available to you, but have not been illustrated. You have conducted a study and evaluation of the system of internal control and found it could be relied upon to produce reliable accounting information. Cash receipts from rental operations are deposited in a special bank account.

Required:

What substantive audit procedures should you employ during the audit in order to substantiate the validity of each of the dollar amounts marked by an asterisk (*)?

(*AICPA* adapted)

Inventory and Cost of Sales

17.33. **First Audit—Beginning Inventory Proce-**
dures

You are performing an audit of the financial statements of Allright Wholesale
Sales, Inc., for the year ended December
31, 1985. Allright has been in business for
many years but has never had its financial
statements audited. You have gained satisfaction with respect to the ending inventory and are considering alternative audit
procedures to gain satisfaction with respect to management's representations
concerning the beginning inventory which
was not observed.

Allright sells only one product (bottled
One Star beer) and maintains perpetual inventory records. Allright takes physical inventory counts monthly. You have already
confirmed purchases with the manufacturer and have decided to concentrate on
evaluating the reliability of perpetual inventory records and performing analytical
review procedures to the extent that prior
years' unaudited records will enable such
procedures to be performed.

Required:

What are the audit procedures, including analytical review procedures, you
should apply in evaluating the reliability of
perpetual inventory records and gaining
satisfaction with respect to the January 1,
1985 inventory?

(*AICPA* adapted)

17.34. **Sales/Inventory Cutoff**

Your client took a complete physical inventory under your observation as of December 15 and adjusted the inventory control account (perpetual inventory method)
to agree with the physical inventory. You
have decided to accept the balance of the
control account as of December 31, after
reflecting transactions recorded therein
from December 16 to December 31, in connection with your examination of financial
statements for the year ended December
31.

Your examination of the sales cutoff as
of December 15 and December 31 disclosed the following items not previously
considered:

| | | | Date | |
Cost	Sales Price	Shipped	Billed	Credited to Inventory Control
$284 . . .	$369	12/14	12/16	12/16
391 . . .	502	12/10	12/19	12/10
189 . . .	213	1/2	12/31	12/31

Required:

What adjusting journal entries, if any,
would you make for each of these items?
Explain why each adjustment is necessary.

17.35. **Inventory Cutoff**

In an annual audit for the year ended December 31, you find the following transactions near the closing date:

1. Merchandise costing $182,200 was re-
    ceived on January 3, and the related
    purchase invoice recorded January 5.
    The invoice showed the shipment was
    made on December 29, FOB destina-
    tion.

2. Merchandise costing $625,000 was re-
    ceived on December 28 and the invoice
    was not recorded. You located it in the
    hands of the purchasing agent; it was
    marked "on consignment."

3. A packing case containing merchan-
    dise costing $816,000 was standing in
    the shipping room when the physical
    inventory was taken. It was not in-
    cluded in the inventory because it was
    marked "Hold for shipping instruc-
    tions." Your investigation revealed
    that the customer's order was dated
    December 18, but that the case was
    shipped and the customer billed on
    January 10. The product was a stock
    item of your client.

4. Merchandise received on January 6
    costing $72,000 was entered in the pur-
    chase register on January 7. The in-

voice showed equipment was made FOB supplier's warehouse on December 31. Since it was not on hand December 31, it was not included in inventory.

5. A special machine, fabricated to order for a customer, was finished and in the shipping room on December 31. The customer was billed on that date and the machine excluded from inventory, although it was shipped on January 4.

Required:

Assume that each of the amounts is material:

a. State whether the merchandise should be included in the client's inventory.

b. Give your reason for your decision on each item in (*a*) above.

(*AICPA* adapted)

17.36. **Statistical Sampling Used to Estimate Inventory**

Ace Corporation does not conduct a complete annual physical count of purchased parts and supplies in its principal warehouse, but instead uses statistical sampling to estimate the year-end inventory. Ace maintains a perpetual inventory record of parts and supplies and believes that statistical sampling is highly effective in determining inventory values and is sufficiently reliable to make a physical count of each item of inventory unnecessary.

Required:

a. List at least 10 normal audit procedures that should be performed to verify physical quantities whenever a client conducts a periodic physical count of all or part of its inventory.

b. Identify the audit procedures you should use that change or are in addition to normal required audit procedures when a client utilizes statistical sampling to determine inventory value and does not conduct a 100 percent annual physical count of inventory items.

(*AICPA* adapted)

17.37. **Long-term Purchase Contracts**

Part A: During the audit of Mason Co., Inc., for the calendar year 1985, you noticed that the company produces aluminum cans at the rate of about 40 million units annually. Also, on the plant tour you noticed a large stockpile of raw aluminum in storage. Your inventory observation and pricing procedures showed this stockpile to be the raw materials inventory of 400 tons valued at $240,000 (LIFO cost). The production chief said 400 tons was about a four-month supply of raw materials.

Required:

What additional information about the purchase of inventory might you expect to find, and how would you proceed in gathering more information?

Part B: Suppose you learn that Mason had executed a firm long-term purchase contract with All-Purpose Aluminum Company to purchase raw materials on the following schedule:

Delivery Date	Quantity	Total Price
Jan. 30, 1986	500 tons	$300,000
June 30, 1986	700 tons	420,000
Dec. 30, 1986	1,000 tons	500,000

Because of recent economic conditions, principally a decline in the demand for raw aluminum and a consequent oversupply, the price stood at 20 cents per pound as of January 15, 1986. Commodities experts predict that this low price will prevail for 12–15 months or until there is a general economic recovery.

Required:

a. Describe the procedures you would employ to gather evidence about this contract (including its initial discovery).

b. In Part B above, what facts are cited which you would have to discover for yourself?

c. What effect does this contract have on the financial statements?

17.38. **Inventory Procedures Using Generalized Audit Software**

You are conducting an examination of the financial statements of a wholesale cosmetics distributor with an inventory consisting of thousands of individual items. The distributor keeps its inventory in its own distribution center and in two public warehouses. An inventory computer file is maintained on a computer disk, and at the end of each business day the file is updated. Each record of the inventory file contains the following data:

Item number.
Location of item.
Description of item.
Quantity on hand.
Cost per item.
Date of last purchase.
Date of last sale.
Quantity sold during year.

You are planning to observe the distributor's physical count of inventories as of a given date. You will have available a computer tape of the inventory file data on the date of the physical count and a general-purpose computer software package.

Required:

You are planning to perform basic inventory auditing procedures. Identify the basic inventory auditing procedures and describe how the use of the general-purpose software package and the tape of the inventory file data might be helpful to the auditor in performing such auditing procedures.

Organize your answer as follows:

Liabilities

17.39. **Unrecorded Liabilities Procedures**

You were in the final stages of your examination of the financial statements of Ozine Corporation for the year ended December 31, 1985, when you were consulted by the corporation's president who believes there is no point to your examining the 1986 voucher register and testing data in support of 1986 entries. He stated that: (1) bills pertaining to 1985 which were received too late to be included in the December voucher register were recorded as of the year-end by the corporation by journal entry, (2) the internal auditor made tests after the year-end, and (3) he would furnish you with a letter certifying that there were no unrecorded liabilities.

Required:

a. Should your procedures for unrecorded liabilities be affected by the fact that the client made a journal entry to record 1985 bills which were received late? Explain.

b. Should your audit for unrecorded liabilities be affected by the fact that a letter is obtained in which a responsible management official certifies that to the best of his knowledge all liabilities have been recorded? Explain.

c. Should your audit for unrecorded liabilities be eliminated or reduced because of the internal audit work? Explain.

d. What sources in addition to the 1986 voucher register should you consider to locate possible unrecorded liabilities?

(*AICPA* adapted)

Basic Inventory Auditing Procedures	How General Purpose Computer Software Package and Tape of the Inventory File Data Might be Helpful
Observe the physical count, making and recording test counts where applicable.	Determining which items are to be test counted by selecting a random sample of a representative number of items from the inventory file as of the physical count date.

(*AICPA* adapted)

17.40. **Accounts Payable Confirmations**

Clark and his partner, Kent, both CPAs, are planning their audit program for the audit of accounts payable on the Marlboro Corporation's annual audit. Saturday afternoon, they reviewed the thick file of last year's working papers, and both of them remembered all too well the six days they spent last year on accounts payable.

Last year, Clark had suggested that they mail confirmations to 100 of Marlboro's suppliers. The company regularly purchases from about 1,000 suppliers, and these account payable balances fluctuate widely, depending on the volume of purchases and the terms Marlboro's purchasing agent is able to negotiate. Clark's sample of 100 was designed to include accounts with large balances. In fact, the 100 accounts confirmed last year covered 80 percent of the total accounts payable.

Both Clark and Kent spent many hours tracking down minor differences reported in confirmation responses. Nonresponding accounts were investigated by comparing Marlboro's balance with monthly statements received from suppliers.

Required:

a. Identify the accounts payable audit objectives that the auditors must consider in determining the audit procedures to be performed.

b. Identify situations when the auditors should use accounts payable confirmations and discuss whether they are required to use them.

c. Discuss why the use of large dollar balances as the basis for selecting accounts payable for confirmation might not be the most efficient approach and indicate what more efficient sample selection procedures could be followed when choosing accounts payable for confirmation.

Prepaid Items

17.41. **Travel Advances**

XYZ Corporation has several hundred employee travel advances outstanding at all times. Subsidiary ledger cards for individual employees are controlled by a general ledger account. Certain advances are specifically designated "permanent"; all others are intended to be cleared at the end of each field trip. All cash transactions for advances, reimbursements or returns, and all expenses reported are posted to the subsidiary ledger cards.

Required:

Assuming no restrictions have been placed on the scope of your audit, prepare an audit program for the examination of the outstanding travel advances and the general ledger control account.

(*AICPA* adapted)

17.42. **Prepaid Expenses**

You are examining the financial statements of the ABY Company, a retail enterprise, for the year ended December 31, 1985. The client's accounting department presented you with an analysis of the prepaid expenses account balance of $31,400 at December 31, 1985, as shown below:

ABY COMPANY
Analysis of Prepaid Expenses Account
December 31, 1985

Description	Balance December 31, 1985
Unexpired insurance:	
Fire	$ 750
Liability	4,900
Utility deposits	2,000
Loan to officer	500
Purchase of postage meter machine, one half of invoice price	400
Bond discount	3,000
Advertising of store opening	9,600
Amount due for overpayment on purchase of furniture and fixtures	675
Unsalable inventory—entered June 30, 1985	8,300
Contributions from employees to employee welfare fund	(275)
Book value of obsolete machinery held for resale	550
Funds delivered to Skyhigh with purchase offer	1,000
Total	$31,400

Additional informaion includes the following:

1. Insurance policy data:

Type	Period Covered	Premium
Fire	12/31/84 to 12/31/86	$1,000
Liability	6/30/85 to 6/30/86	9,500

2. The postage meter machine was delivered in November, and the balance due was paid in January. Unused postage of $700 in the machine at December 31, 1985, was recorded as expense at time of purchase.

3. Bond discount represents the unamortized portion applicable to bonds maturing in 1986.

4. The $9,600 paid and recorded for advertising was for the cost of an advertisement to be run in a monthly magazine for six months, beginning in December 1985. You examined an invoice received from the advertising agency and extracted the following description:

"Advertising services rendered for store opened in November 1985 . . . $6,900."

5. ABY has contracted to purchase Skyhigh Stores and has been required to accompany its offer with a check for $1,000 to be held in escrow as an indication of good faith. An examination of canceled checks revealed the check had not been returned from the bank through January 1986.

Required:

a. What is the correct balance of prepaid expenses?

b. For each item in the account analysis, give:

  (1) The evidence that should be gathered.

  (2) The adjusting entry, if any.

                              (*AICPA* adapted)

DISCUSSION CASES

17.43. **Grover Manufacturing—Purchasing Defalcation**

On January 11 at the beginning of your annual audit of the Grover Manufacturing Company's financial statements for the year just ended December 31, the company president confides to you that an employee is living on a scale in excess of that which his salary would support.

The employee has been a buyer in the purchasing department for six years and has charge of purchasing all general materials and supplies. He is authorized to sign purchase orders for amounts up to $200. Purchase orders in excess of $200 require the countersignature of the general purchasing agent.

The president understands that the usual examination of financial statements is not designed to disclose immaterial fraud or conflicts of interest, although their discovery may result. The president authorizes you, however, to expand your regular audit procedures and to apply additional audit procedures to determine whether there is any evidence that the buyer has been misappropriating company funds or has been engaged in activities that were in a conflict of interests.

Required:

a. List the audit procedures that you would apply to the company records and documents in an attempt to:

  (1) Discover evidence within the purchasing department of defalcations being committed by the buyer. Give the purpose of each audit procedure.

  (2) Provide leads as to possible collu-

sion between the buyer and suppliers. Give the purpose of each audit procedure.

b. Assume your investigation disclosed that some suppliers have been charging the Grover Manufacturing Company in excess of their usual prices and apparently have been making "kickbacks" to the buyer. The excess charges are material in amount.

What effect, if any, would the defalcation have upon: (1) the financial statements that were prepared before the defalcation was uncovered and (2) your auditor's report? Discuss.

(*AICPA* adapted)

17.44. **Trinity Company—Defalcations***

Assume you are participating in the audit of the Trinity Company's financial statements. The situations described below came to your attention when you performed certain substantive audit procedures on account balance details.

1. The July sales journal indicated that customers were billed $140,000 during that month. This amount was posted as a debit to Accounts Receivable and a credit to Sales. However, you tested the footing of the July sales journal and determined that the correct sum of the customer billings was $144,500.

2. You noted that an $8,500 debit posting had been entered in a general ledger expense account, but you could not vouch this posting to any "preceding" record (such as a purchases journal, payroll journal, general journal, etc.).

3. When you examined a voucher for the purchase of office supplies, you noted that the check signer had initialed the vendor's invoice to indicate her approval, but the purchase order and receiving report had not been initialed or otherwise cancelled.

4. When you tested the reconciliation of the company's checking account at year-end, you noted that a $6,000 check had been omitted from the list of outstanding checks. The check had been issued and recorded as a disbursement during the previous month, but had not yet cleared the bank.

Required:

1. Describe how each situation *may* indicate an attempted concealment of a defalcation.

2. Answer the following general questions:

   a. Are certain types of concealment "temporary" in the sense that further actions will be required to prevent detection?

   b. How might the direction of audit testing (testing for overstatement or understatement) be influenced by the auditor's responsibility to search for material defalcations?

   c. Can auditors rely exclusively on a good internal accounting control system to fulfill their responsibility to search for material defalcations?

   d. Can auditors rely exclusively on analytical review procedures to fulfill their responsibility to search for material defalcations?

---

* Adapted from case contributed by Deloitte Haskins & Sells to *The Auditor's Report*, Summer 1982.

CHAPTER 18

PROFESSIONAL STANDARDS SOURCES		
Compendium Section	Document Reference	Topic
AU 318	SAS 23	Analytical Review Procedures
AU 326	SAS 31	Evidential Matter
AU 327	SAS 16	The Independent Auditor's Responsibility for the Detection of Errors or Irregularities
AU 328	SAS 17	Illegal Acts by Clients
AU 332	SAS 1	Evidential Matter for Long-Term Investments
AU 9332		Interpretation: Evidential Matter for Investments
AU 333	SAS 19	Client Representations
AU 337	SAS 12	Inquiry of a Client's Lawyer Concerning Litigation
AU 9337		Interpretations: Inquiry of a Client's Lawyer
AU 339	SAS 41	Working Papers
AU 1020	SAS 45	Related Parties

Long-Term Assets and Equities, Related Revenue and Expense

LEARNING OBJECTIVES

This chapter covers the substantive audit procedures for the noncurrent accounts and related revenue and expense accounts. After completing this chapter, in relation to the investments, fixed assets, long-term liabilities, owners' equity and related accounts, you should be able to:

☐ Identify specific audit procedures used to gather evidence to ascertain whether assertions are materially correct, given the financial statement assertions.

☐ Identify the major working paper for each major noncurrent account and list common procedures documented on that working paper.

☐ Describe the procedures and documentation of a controlled count of securities.

☐ Explain for fixed assets, long-term liabilities and owners' equity, why the entire account balance is usually not audited, but only current period additions and disposals or retirements are audited.

☐ Describe the types of fraud or misstatement that might occur in the noncurrent accounts.

INVESTMENTS AND RELATED INTANGIBLES

In this chapter, the discussion of audit procedures for examining the balances of investments, fixed assets, long-term liabilities and owners' equity is organized around the five audit objectives of existence or occurrence, completeness, valuation, rights and obligations, and presentation and disclosure. The preparation of an audit program should begin with the audit supervisor's recognition that these broad objectives represent assertions by management embodied in the financial statements. The assertions point directly to hypothesis questions that can be tested by gathering sufficient, competent evidential matter.

The broad assertions are usually divided into more detailed assertions about each account balance. For example, some of the assertions typical of investments and intangibles (and related accounts) are:

- ☐ Investment securities are on hand or are properly held by a trustee.
- ☐ Investment cost does not exceed market value.
- ☐ Investments pledged as collateral are properly disclosed.
- ☐ Controlling investments are accounted for by the equity method.
- ☐ Purchased goodwill is properly recorded.
- ☐ Capitalized intangibles costs relate to intangibles acquired in an exchange transaction.
- ☐ Amortization is properly calculated.
- ☐ Investment income has been received and recorded.
- ☐ Research and development costs are properly classified.

The assertions above are not a complete list of all matters of audit interest, but they are illustrative of the types of problems that should be recognized. The next task is to consider the evidence that might support or refute these assertions so that auditors can select the most efficient procedures for gathering that evidence.

Substantive Audit Procedures Related to Objectives

The internal accounting controls over acquisition and expenditure discussed in Chapter 14 are most relevant to the noncurrent accounts discussed in this chapter. Weaknesses in controls in the acquisition and expenditure cycle must be carefully evaluated to determine the likelihood of material errors appearing in the financial statements. Standards require auditors to plan the audit to search for errors or irregularities that would have a material effect on financial statements.[1]

Unlike the current assets and liabilities which are characterized by numerous small transactions, the noncurrent accounts usually consist of very few large transactions. This difference has internal control and substantive audit procedures implications. The impact on auditors' consideration of controls is that since each individual transaction affecting noncurrent accounts is likely to be material in itself, the most essential control is authorization of the transaction (commonly by the board of directors). Further, the controls are usually not reviewed, audited and evaluated at an interim date, but are incorporated into the year-end procedures.

---

[1] "The Independent Auditor's Responsibility for the Detection of Errors or Irregularities," SAS 16, AU 327.

The implication on substantive procedures is that, except for the initial year of an audit, the entire balance is not verified. Only the changes in the account that occurred in the current period need to be audited. Therefore, many of the working papers will be in the form of account analyses (similar to the working paper for prepaid insurance, Exhibit 17–13). Many of the accounts will have "carry-forward" schedules which are maintained in the permanent working paper file, showing the changes that have occurred each year since the initial audit. The changes are cross-referenced to the appropriate period's working papers, in case a question arises regarding a specific change.

These differences in control and substantive procedures will be reflected in the discussion of the procedures for each major noncurrent account area. The discussion of the first of these account areas, investments and intangibles, follows.

Existence, Completeness and Rights. The first three major audit objectives must begin with the audit procedure of *verbal inquiry*. Auditors need to know what changes occurred during the year and where investment securities are held. If the investment securities are in the client's custody, a physical inspection and count can be performed. If the investment securities are held by a trustee or broker, they can be confirmed. The fact that securities are not held by the client may mean they are pledged as collateral.

The practice of obtaining independent written *confirmation* from outside parties is fairly limited in the area of investments, intangibles, and related income and expense accounts. Securities held by trustees or brokers should be confirmed, and the confirmation request should seek the same descriptive information as obtained in a physical count by the auditor (described below).

Company counsel can be queried about knowledge of any lawsuits or defects relating to patents, copyrights, trademarks or trade names. This confirmation can be sought by a specific request in the attorney's letter.

Cash surrender values of life insurance policies may be determined by inspecting the policies and by confirming the in-force status of the policy with the insurance company. Inspection of the policy itself will produce information of cash surrender values, but possession of the policy document does not guarantee that the policy has not lapsed or that premiums have not been "paid" with policy loans. For participating life insurance policies, auditors may wish to confirm the amount of accumulated dividends if they have not been used to reduce current cash premiums. In connection with the audit of liabilities, the life insurance confirmation may produce evidence of an unrecorded policy loan.

Royalty income from patent licenses received from a single licensee may be confirmed. However, such income amounts are usually audited by vouching the licensee's reports and related cash payment.

Physical inspection and observation is a procedure having only limited application in the investment and intangible assets group. Most of these assets have no physical form to observe, but some of them may be evidenced by formal documents that can be inspected and counted.

A controlled count of securities is a necessary procedural application. Generally, the count consists of an audit team gaining access to the securities in the presence of a responsible client officer. The count is first controlled by simultaneously counting or sealing off other negotiable funds (such as securities held as collateral) and second by an auditor personally conducting the count. The count working papers should contain the name of the issuer and a description of the security, the number of shares, certificate numbers, maturity value, interest and preferred dividend rates and the date of issue. When the count is completed, the auditor should obtain a written statement from the client's representative that the securities were returned intact to their safekeeping place.

Investment property may be observed and inspected in a manner similar to the inspection of fixed assets. The principal goal is simply to determine actual existence and condition of the property. Official documents of patents, copyrights and trademark rights can be inspected to see that they are, in fact, in the name of the client.

Valuation.   Investment cost should be *vouched* to brokers' advices (invoices), monthly statements or other documentary evidence of cost. At the same time it is usually convenient to trace the amounts of sales to gain or loss accounts and to vouch the amounts to the brokers' statements of sales price and proceeds. The auditor should determine what method of cost-out assignment was used (i.e., FIFO, specific certificate or average cost) and whether it is consistent with prior years' transactions. The cost of real and personal property likewise can be vouched to invoices or other documents of purchase, and title documents (such as on land, buildings) may be inspected.

Vouching may be extensive in the area of research and development efforts. The principal evidential problem is to ascertain whether costs classified as assets or as R&D expense indeed belong in that classification. Amounts recorded are generally selected on a sample basis and the purchase orders, receiving reports, payroll records, authorization notices and management reports are compared to them. Some R&D costs may closely resemble non-R&D costs (such as supplies, payroll costs), so the auditor must be very careful in the vouching to perceive costs that appear to relate to other operations.

Basic *calculations* such as footings and crossfooting of investment schedules with reconciliation to ledger accounts should be made to check for inadvertent error. Other basic recalculations important for the investment asset and investment income audit involve related data from other sources. By consulting quoted market values of securities, auditors can calculate values and determine whether investments should be written down. If quoted market values are not available, financial statements related to investments must be obtained and analyzed for evidence of basic value. If such financial statements are unaudited, evidence indicated by them is considered extremely weak.

Income amounts can be calculated and audited by consulting published dividend records for quotations of dividends actually declared and paid during a period. Since auditors know the holding period of securities, dividend income can be calculated and compared to the amount in the account. Any difference could indicate a cutoff error, misclassification, defalcation or failure to record a dividend receivable. In a similar manner, application of interest rates to bond investments produces a calculated-audited interest income figure (making allowance also for amortization of premium or discount if applicable).

When investments are accounted for by the equity method, auditors will have to obtain financial statements of the investee company. These should be audited statements. (Inability to obtain audited statements may indicate that the investor actually does not have a significant control influence.) These statements would be used as the basis for recalculating the amount of the investor's share of income to recognize in the accounts. In addition, these statements may be used to audit the disclosure of investees' assets, liabilities and income presented in footnotes to the investor's financial statements (a disclosure recommended when investments accounted for by the equity method are material).[2]

Recalculations can be combined with limited vouching procedures to audit rental income and expense, royalty income and expense, and gains and losses on sales of investments. Generally, the application involves multiplying rent and royalty rates by time periods and production units. Amounts of accrued income receivable can be recalculated in a similar manner. Gain and loss on investment disposal involves the recalculation of asset cost by the appropriate cost method (such as FIFO).

Amortization of goodwill and other intangibles should be recalculated. Like depreciation, amortization expense owes its existence to a calculation; and recalculation based on audited costs and rates is sufficient audit evidence.

Presentation and Disclosure. *Inquiries* should deal with the nature of investments and the reasons for holding them. Management's expressed intention that a marketable security investment be considered a long-term investment may be the only available evidence for classifying it as long-term and not as a current asset. Control relations with near-20 percent owned affiliates should be probed with regard to applications of the equity method of accounting for such investments. The status of real estate and

---

[2] See "Evidential Matter for Long-Term Investments" (SAS 1, AU 332).

EXHIBIT 18–1
Investments

E-1   River Publishing Company   RB
                              Investments   1-22-86
                              12-31-85

	Balance 12-31-84	Transactions Dr. (Cr.)	Balance 12-31-85
Investments -- General			
Mooney Airlines common 2,000 shares ① @ 25.85	51,700 ◇		51,700 7
K & K common 400 shares ① @ 50 1/8	20,050 ◇		20,050 7
Ⓧ { Land, lot 4, block 12, River City (held for future plant site)	95,630 ◇	(95,630) Ⓧ	-0-
(New Building -- construction costs -- sale of building		235,000 Ⓧ ✓ (235,000) Ⓧ	-0-
	167,380	(95,630)	71,750 T/B,
Investments -- Savings			
Deposit in United Bank of Berlin (423,360 marks 3/1/85)	-0-	210,000 ②	210,000 T/B,
Investment Income			
Land rental		800 ①	
Dividends: Mooney 2000 shares @ 2.80 ②		5,600	
K & K 400 shares @ 3.60 ②		1,440	
Balance per books 12-31-85		7,840 T/B₅	

T/B Traced to working trial balance.
✓ Vouched to contractor's invoice. Approved by Board $210,000 (PF 25); $46,000 (PF 21)
◇ Per prior audit.
① Stock certificates inspected Ⓔ/2
Ⓧ Sale and leaseback. See Ⓔ/5 and Ⓔ/6.
② Confirmation Ⓔ/4. Also see Ⓔ/4 for conversion from West German marks
    and computation of income.
7 See Ⓔ/3 for analysis of noncurrent marketable equity securities.
① Land rental same as prior year $800 per month. Rented only one
    month this year because construction of new building began
    in February 1985.
② Per Standard & Poor's Annual Dividend Record.

personal property held as investments (not in the fixed, productive-property classification) should be reviewed, particularly with regard to any rental or lease operations.

Merger and acquisition transactions should be *reviewed* in terms of the appraisals, judgments and allocations used to assign portions of the purchase price to tangible assets, intangible assets, liabilities and goodwill. In the final analysis, nothing really substitutes for the audit of transaction documentation, but the verbal inquiries may help auditors fully understand the circumstances of a merger.

Questions about lawsuits challenging patents, copyrights or trade names may produce early knowledge of problem areas for further investigation. Likewise, discussions and questions about research and development successes and failures may alert the audit team to problems of valuation of assets and related expenses. Responses to questions about licensing of patents can be used in the audit of related royalty revenue accounts.

Major Working Paper

The major working paper for investments is an analysis of the activity in the account for the year, such as the illustration in Exhibit 18–1. Many of the audit procedures described are indicated as performed by the tick marks and the accompanying explanation. References are made to detailed working papers that support this lead working paper.

FIXED ASSETS AND RELATED ACCOUNTS

The fixed assets acquired during the year were subject to the controls reviewed, tested and evaluated in the acquisition and expenditure cycle. Weaknesses noted during this earlier work should be evaluated by the audit supervisor to determine if more extensive substantive procedures are required. Unless numerous fixed asset addition and disposal transactions occur, each transaction for the period is verified (as illustrated in Exhibit 18–3). Note that where appropriate, the use of generalized audit software is described in the discussion of the audit procedures of fixed assets and related accounts.

Substantive Audit Procedures Related to Objectives

The construction of an audit program utilizing substantive procedures should begin with explicit recognition of the specific assertions contained in fixed asset and related expense account records. The assertions can be audited by gathering sufficient, competent evidential matter. Some of the explicit and implicit assertions in fixed assets accounts are:

☐ All recorded fixed assets are in productive use.
☐ All asset disposals have been recorded.
☐ All asset additions have been recorded.

□   Repair and maintenance expenses have not been capitalized.

□   Asset additions have not been improperly charged to repair and maintenance expense.

□   All costs of freight and installation on additions have been capitalized.

□   Leases have been capitalized in conformity with FASB statements.

□   Depreciation has been calculated accurately.

EXHIBIT 18–2
Audit Program—Selected
Substantive Procedures

A.   Investments and Related Income.
1.   Prepare, or have client prepare, a schedule of all investments. Reconcile with investment accounts per general ledger.
2.   Vouch recorded investments to broker's advices, contracts, canceled checks and other supporting documentation.
3.   Inspect or confirm with a trustee or broker the name, number, identification, interest rate and face amount (if applicable) of securities held as investments.
4.   Recalculate interest income and/or look up dividend income in a dividend reporting service (such as Moody's or Standard & Poor's Annual Dividend Record).
5.   Vouch recorded sales to bank deposit slips and recalculate gain or loss on disposition.
6.   Obtain market values of investments and determine whether any write-down or write-off is necessary. Scan transactions soon after the client's year-end to see if any investments were sold at a loss.
7.   Inspect title documents, if any, of property held for investment.
8.   Review rental agreements on property and trace indicated amounts to income accounts. Vouch a sample of recorded rent income entries to bank deposit slips.
9.   Obtain written representations from the client concerning any pledging of investment assets as collateral.
10.   Obtain audited financial statements of joint ventures, investee companies (equity method of accounting), subsidiary companies and other independent entities in which an investment interest is held.

B.   Intangibles and Related Expenses.
1.   Review merger documents for proper calculation of purchased goodwill.
2.   Inquire of management about legal status of patents, leases, copyrights and other intangibles.
3.   Review documentation of new patents, copyrights, leaseholds and franchise agreements.
4.   Vouch recorded costs of intangibles to supporting documentation and canceled check(s).
5.   Select a sample of recorded R&D expenses. Vouch to supporting documents for evidence of proper classification.
6.   Recalculate amortization of goodwill, patents and other intangibles.

EXHIBIT 18-3
Fixed Assets

F-1

Larson's Hot Cakes Company
Fixed Assets
December 31, 1985

Prepared by TNGR
Date 1-31-86

	Asset Cost				Depreciation Rate/Method	Accumulated Depreciation			
	Beginning Balance	Additions	Disposals	Ending Balance		Beginning Balance	Expense Additions	Disposals	Ending Balance
Land - plant site	65800 α			65800 Ⓣ			-0-		-0-
Land - warehouse site	12800 α		16800 Ⓣ	-0-			-0-		-0-
Buildings - plant	1609400 α			1609400 Ⓣ	30 years	391,107 α √	36,417 ℒ		447,524 Ⓣ
Buildings - warehouse	252200 α		252200 Ⓣ	-0-		63000 α	4200 ℒ	67200 Ⓣ	-0-
Machinery and equipment	4286400 α			4286400 Ⓣ	5%	1,107,160 α √	214,432 ℒ		1,385,92 Ⓣ
Automobiles	721,00 α	84200 Τ		805,20 Ⓣ	25%	232,284 α √	190,782 ℒ		423,62 Ⓣ
Furniture and fixtures	198,200 α	8420	42,000 ✗	178,200 Ⓣ	5%	259,470 α √	39,91 ℒ		299,31 Ⓣ
	8517760	8420	82,180	828,180		201,791	505,68	67200 ✗	2,45639

Ⓣ Traced to subsidiary ledger accounts.

ℒ Traced disposed asset amounts to Asset Disposition account.

√ Reviewed assignment of useful lives, zero salvage, no straight-line method. No exceptions taken. (TB)

r Vouched new auto acquisition to purchase invoice and title, agreed to approval to purchase, no liability. Purchase approved by board in capital budget for 1985.

ℒ Recalculated depreciation for the year. ½ year depreciation taken on new assets and on asset disposed. No exceptions.

α Per prior year audit workpaper.

☐ Taxes have been paid or accrued on all taxable asset property.

☐ Casualty insurance is carried.

☐ Assets pledged as collateral have not been improperly removed.

The above assertions are not a complete list of all matters of audit interest, but they are illustrative of the types of problems that should be recognized. The next task is to consider the evidence that might support or refute these assertions, and then the auditor can select the most effi-

EXHIBIT 18–4
Audit Program—Selected
Substantive Procedures

A. Fixed Assets.
   1. Foot and summarize detail fixed asset subsidiary records and reconcile to general ledger control account(s).
   2. Select a sample of detail fixed asset subsidiary records:
     a. Perform a physical observation (inspection) of the assets recorded.
     b. Inspect title documents, if any.
   3. Prepare, or have client prepare, a schedule of fixed asset additions and disposals for the period:
     a. Vouch to documents indicating proper approval.
     b. Vouch costs to invoices, contracts or other supporting documents.
     c. Determine whether all costs of shipment, installation, testing and the like have been properly capitalized.
     d. Vouch proceeds (on dispositions) to cash receipts or other asset records.
     e. Recalculate gain or loss on dispositions.
     f. Trace amounts to detail fixed asset records and general ledger control account(s).
   4. Prepare an analysis of fixed assets subject to investment tax credit for correlation with tax liability audit work.
   5. Observe a physical inventory-taking of the fixed assets and compare with detail fixed assets records.
   6. Obtain written representations from management regarding:
     a. Pledging of assets as security for loans.
     b. Leasing of assets.

B. Depreciation.
   1. Analyze depreciation expense for overall reasonableness with reference to costs of assets and average depreciation rates.
   2. Prepare, or have client prepare, a schedule of accumulated depreciation showing beginning balance, current depreciation, disposals and ending balance. Trace to depreciation expense and asset disposition analyses. Trace amounts to general ledger account(s).
   3. Recalculate depreciation expense and trace to general ledger account(s).

C. Other Accounts.
   1. Analyze insurance for adequacy of coverage.
   2. Analyze property taxes to determine whether taxes due on assets have been paid or accrued.
   3. Recalculate prepaid and/or accrued insurance and tax expenses.
   4. Select a sample of rental expense entries. Vouch to rent/lease contracts to determine whether any leases qualify for capitalization.

cient procedures for gathering that evidence. A selection of substantive audit procedures is given in Exhibit 18–4.

Existence, Completeness and Rights.   Like goods held for sale, tangible assets can be *observed* and *counted* (that is "inventoried"), although extensive inventory procedures for fixed assets are generally considered "extended procedures" to be used only when the internal control system exhibits deficiencies. The assets are inspected and traced to the detail records to ascertain that existing assets are recorded. (For leased assets, the tracing may be to lease documents and rental expense records.) The recorded assets are inspected in order to determine that they actually exist. In both procedures, auditors can make observations on the quantity, quality, condition and apparent extent of utilization. Assets not in production may have to be classified separately from fixed assets. Obsolete assets may be subject to write-down or write-off.

The *tracing* procedure involves finding source records and following the transaction through the data processing system to entries in the accounts. In connection with the audit of fixed asset accounts, the major tracing begins with the directors' authorizations for expenditures and the identification in the capital budget of planned expenditures. This tracing may be carried out during the internal control evaluation or when auditing the asset additions to ascertain whether all authorized additions indeed were acquired. (The findings, however, may be of more interest to an internal auditor than to an independent auditor who does not report on the correspondence of plans to actual events.)

If repair and maintenance work order documents are maintained in a separate file, they may be sampled and traced to the expense account. Misclassifications might then be detected.

Confirmation with independent parties to a fixed asset-related transaction is generally considered an "extended procedure," because most documentary evidence is of the external-internal or formal documents quality. Invoices, contracts, lease agreements, insurance policies, tax notices, canceled checks and inspection of assets can provide persuasive evidence for audit purposes, and this evidence may be relatively easy to obtain. However, confirmation may be utilized in these situations:

To confirm the terms and status of important leases.

To confirm the in-force status of an insurance policy.

To confirm that title is clear and taxes are paid.

Confirmations may reveal that tangible property has been pledged as collateral for liabilities. Letters addressed to lessors, insurance companies, government officials and creditors may be used if the audit team needs evidential information of higher persuasive quality than the evidence available in the client's records.

Valuation.   The *vouching* (examination) of documents generally produces a large portion of the evidence related to fixed asset accounts. Remember that the vouching procedure has been defined as the process of selecting an item in the account records and searching "backward" to find supporting source documents.

In connection with fixed assets, auditors may select fixed asset additions or disposals and high dollar value repair and maintenance items for vouching. The random sampling, mathematical-limit functions and report-selection functions of a generalized audit software system may be employed. Recorded tax and insurance expense items likewise may be selected. However, the purpose for selection of these items is not to test proper internal control and data processing, but to audit for evidence of existence, rights, valuation, accounting principles and completeness.

Selected asset records may be vouched to invoices, contracts, cancelled checks and other supporting documentation. One important point is to notice any capitalized item that should have been expensed. The vouching of repair and maintenance items to invoices, work orders and cost records may reveal items expensed that should have been capitalized.

Mathematical checks are made throughout the internal control examination procedures as a guard against inadvertent error in the accounts. The subsidiary records should be reconciled with the asset control accounts. Expense accounts should be footed. Allocations of insurance premiums and tax assessments and related accruals should be *recalculated*.

The major set of recalculations involves depreciation provisions and estimates related to disposals and write-offs. Accounting depreciation exists only as a calculated amount, so the audit of it is a recalculation. However, auditors must first determine by vouching and analysis procedures that the bases for the calculation are accurate (that is, cost, prior depreciation, useful life, rate and salvage value). If book and tax methods of depreciation are different, then both will have to be recalculated and the difference considered in connection with amounts of deferred income taxes.

The computer may be used to perform many recalculation procedures. Consider the depreciation calculations. They can be audited 100 percent with the computer in less time than with a manual sampling application. Before recalculation, the auditors must be satisfied that all the bases for the calculation are accurate. These can be audited by vouching a random sample of records selected by the random selection function of a generalized audit software (GAS) system. The depreciation formulas may be programmed by the auditor using generalized audit software. Then processing a work file of the client's fixed asset records against the GAS program will yield audited numbers that are, in effect, a parallel simulation of the recorded depreciation calculations. Differences between the

GAS-calculated depreciation and the client's records can be printed and investigated manually on an item-by-item basis.

Presentation and Disclosure. Questioning of client officers may lead to performance of other procedures. Responses may constitute the only available evidence, particularly when the issues concern future commitments, tentative plans to sell assets or to remove them from production, or other actions that are in the planning stage or in early stages of negotiation.

Complete working paper documentation should be kept of *inquiries* relating to fixed assets and related accounts. These inquiries should cover: replacement or other disposition of assets, the pledging of assets as collateral, the accounting treatment of fully depreciated assets, the in-production status of assets, the maintenance of insurance policies in force, the timely payment of any special tax assessments or the fact of any reappraisal of properties for tax purposes, and the maintenance and repair program. Many of these items may not be evidenced anywhere in ordinary accounting records and therefore would be included in the client's representation letter.

Another class of inquiries is directed toward obtaining preliminary information about accounting policies and other matters for disclosure. In these cases, responses are usually amenable to corroboration in the records for such things as depreciation methods, the basis of accounting for assets transferred in nonmonetary transactions, methods of accounting for leases, and changes in accounting policies respecting capitalization and depreciation methods. Extensive inquiries about leases may be required because several necessary disclosures relate to future amounts cited in lease agreements but not yet recorded in the rental expense account. These include such items as minimum rental commitments for future years, revenue from existing subleases for future years and the present value of noncapitalized lease commitments. Other related items include the existence and terms of renewal or purchase options, escalation clauses, guarantees, restrictions on paying dividends and restrictions on incurring additional debt or further leasing. All leases should be reviewed to determine whether the requirements of accounting principles for capitalization have been met by the facts stated in the lease contract documents.

Major Working Paper The primary working paper for fixed assets is the account analysis illustrated in Exhibit 18–3. Account analysis schedules, also called input/output schedules, show the beginning balance, transactions increasing and decreasing the account, and the year-end balance. Notice that only additions and disposals are vouched to supporting documentation because the beginning balance has already been verified in past audits.

LONG-TERM LIABILITIES, CONTINGENCIES AND COMMITMENTS

The primary audit concern with the verification of long-term liabilities is that all liabilities are recorded, therefore the audit objective of completeness is paramount. Alertness of auditors to the possibility of unrecorded liabilities during the performance of procedures in other areas will frequently uncover liabilities that have not been recorded. For example, when fixed assets are acquired during the year under audit, auditors should inquire about the source of funds for financing the new asset. (Other examples discussed previously are the questions regarding liabilities in the bank and insurance confirmations.) Cross-referencing all related working paper items will ensure these related audit disclosures are not overlooked.

Substantive Audit Procedures Related to Objectives

The preparation of an audit program of substantive procedures should begin with the audit supervisor's recognition that the audit report applies to financial statements. Therefore, the management representations embodied in the financial statement components are most important. The assertions regarding management's representations of existence, completeness, obligations, valuation, and presentation and disclosure must be the broad objectives of the audit of each account. These broad assertions should then be expressed in more specific terms for the area under consideration. For example, for long-term liabilities a few typical specific assertions are:

- [ ] All material long-term liabilities are recorded.
- [ ] Liabilities are properly classified as to their current or long-term nature.
- [ ] New long-term liabilities and debt extinguishment are properly authorized.
- [ ] Terms, conditions and restrictions relating to noncurrent debt are adequately disclosed.
- [ ] All important contingencies are either accrued in the accounts or disclosed in footnotes.

These assertions are not a complete list of all matters, but examples of audit interest that should be recognized. The next task is to consider the evidence that might support or refute the assertions.

Existence and Obligations. Independent written *confirmations* are usually obtained for notes and bonds payable. In the case of notes payable to banks, the standard bank confirmation may be used. The amount and terms of bonds payable, mortgages payable and other formal debt instruments can be confirmed by letter to the holder or trustee. The confirmation request should include questions not only of amount, interest rate and due date, but also questions about collateral, restrictive covenants and other matters of agreement entered into between lender and borrower. Confirmation requests should be sent to lenders and lessors with whom the company has done business in the recent past, even if no liability balance is shown at the confirmation date. Such extra confirmation coverage is a part of the *search for unrecorded liabilities.*

Confirmation and *inquiry* procedures may be used to obtain responses on a class of items that can be loosely termed "off-balance sheet information." Within this category are such things as: terms of loan agreements, leases, endorsements, guarantees and insurance policies (whether issued by a client insurance company or owned by the client). Among these items are the difficult-to-define contingencies and commitments that oftentimes pose evidence-gathering problems. Frequently encountered types of contingencies and commitments are listed below:

Type of Contingency or Commitment	Typical Procedures and Sources of Evidence
1. Endorsements on discounted notes.	1. Standard bank confirmation.
2. Debt guarantees (such as obligations of subsidiaries).	2. Inquiry of client management, confirmation by direct debtor.
3. Repurchase or remarketing agreements.	3. Vouching of contracts, confirmation by customer, inquiry of client management.
4. Commitments to purchase at fixed prices.	4. Vouching of open purchase orders, inquiry of purchasing personnel, confirmation by supplier.
5. Commitments to sell at fixed prices.	5. Vouching of sales contracts, inquiry of sales personnel, confirmation by customer.
6. Loan commitments (as in a savings and loan association).	6. Vouching of open commitment file, inquiry of loan officers.
7. Lease commitments.	7. Vouching of lease agreement, confirmation with lessor or lessee.
8. Legal judgments, litigation, pending litigation, claims, assessments.	8. Confirmation with client counsel (i.e., attorney's representation letter).

All of the items listed above may become subjects for footnote disclosures. Some of them may be amenable to estimation and valuation and thus may be recorded in the accounts and shown in the financial statements themselves (such as obligations for endorsements on defaulted debts of others, losses on fixed-price purchase commitments, probable tax deficiency settlements).

One of the most important confirmations is the response known as the attorney's representation letter. Prior to 1976, some difficulties had arisen over lawyers' willingness to respond to auditors' requests for information about contingencies, litigation, claims and assessments. Lawyers themselves were facing legal liability for failure to respond properly. At about the same time, the FASB issued *Statement of Financial Accounting Standards No. 5,* "Accounting for Contingencies," which defined pending litigation, claims, assessments and the "probable," "reasonably possible" and "remote" likelihoods that future events (such as court judgment) would confirm a loss from an existing contingency. SFAS 5 sets forth standards for accrual and disclosure of litigation, claims and assessments in financial statements.

Statement on Auditing Standards No. 12 (AU 337), "Inquiry of a Client's Lawyer Concerning Litigation, Claims and Assessments," is the auditors' counterpart of FASB 5. This SAS requires auditors to make certain inquiries designed to elicit the information upon which accounting in conformity with SFAS 5 can be determined.

Opportunities to use the *physical observation* technique in connection with liabilities and owners' equity accounts are limited. With regard to liabilities, the auditors may wish to inspect assets pledged as collateral in order to ascertain whether they are kept in the location and/or condition required by the collateral agreement. This inspection may involve looking at fixed assets or inventory pledged, observing their condition and safekeeping; or it may involve inspection of securities pledged but in the custody of the client. Bonds, notes, other formal debt instruments, and shares of common or preferred stock that have been redeemed, retired, converted, or acquired as treasury bonds or stock may be inspected in much the same manner as security investment assets are inspected.

Completeness.   The concern is not with the recorded long-term liabilities, but for those *not recorded* and those considered candidates for disclosure as *off-balance sheet financing arrangements*. The procedures described in Chapter 17 in the search for unrecorded current liabilities will usually not bring to light long-term liabilities that are unrecorded. Procedures related to other audit areas are more likely to uncover the long-term liabilities.

New issues of debt are *vouched* to the authorization in the director's minutes or stockholders' approval and may be vouched to security registration documents as well as to cash receipts and loan agreements. Liabilities for and disclosures about pension and profit-sharing plans should be vouched to the plan or contract as to terms, conditions and amounts. In most cases, the audit will also involve important *recalculations* of amounts (sometimes performed by a consulting actuary in the case of complex pension plans).

A *tracing* procedure particularly relevant to long-term liabilities involves the examination of IRS audit reports and correspondence and the audit reports of state and local tax authorities. Errors and deficiencies revealed and assessed in such reports should be traced to the accounts to ascertain whether proper provisions for probable liabilities have been recorded. Tax audits typically lag, and the period of the last completed audit may be disclosed in footnotes to the financial statements. Oftentimes, this review of tax agents' reports reveals some deductions or assessments in dispute. Information on such matters is important for disclosure of contingent liabilities if probable assessments have not already been recorded.

Valuation.   *Analytical review,* especially interrelationships between interest expense and interest-bearing liabilities, is useful in the search of unrecorded liabilities as well as being related to valuation of the interest expense. Interest expense is generally related item-by-item to interest bearing liabilities. At the same time that the liabilities are audited (including those that have been retired during the year), the related interest expense amounts can be *recalculated* based on the amount of debt, the interest rate and the time period. By comparing the results to the interest expense account, auditors may be able to detect: (1) greater expense than their calculations show, indicating some interest paid on debt unknown to them, possibly an unrecorded liability, (2) lesser expense than their calculations show, indicating misclassification, failure to accrue interest, or an interest payment default, or (3) interest expense equal to their calculations. The first two possibilities raise questions for further study, and the third shows a correct correlation between debt and debt-related expense.

An example of a working paper showing this interrelationship and recalculation of interest expense and other payables procedures is presented in Exhibit 18–5.

Lease obligations and the liabilities related to capitalized lease-purchase agreements should be *recalculated.* When such a liability is based on the discounted present value of future contractual payments, auditors should use the mathematics of present value calculations in their audit procedures. Similarly, in connection with debt discount or premium amortization, present-value or straight-line amortization method applications should be recalculated to check their accuracy.

Several types of deferred credits also depend upon calculations for their existence and valuation. Examples include: (1) deferred profit on installment sales involving the gross margin and the sale amount, (2) deferred income taxes and investment credits involving tax-book timing differences, tax rates, and amortization methods and (3) deferred contract revenue involving contract provisions for prepayment, percentage-of-completion revenue recognition methods or other terms unique to a contract. All of these features are incorporated in calculations which auditors can check for accuracy.

Obligations, Presentation and Disclosure.   The attorney's letter serves as a major means to learn of material contingencies. Even so, a devious or forgetful management or a careless attorney may fail to tell the auditor of some important factor or development. Auditors have to be alert and sensitive to all possible contingencies so they can ask the right questions at the right time. Such questions should be directed not only to attorneys but also to management, because an auditor has the right to

EXHIBIT 18–5
Notes Payable and Interest Expense

I-1

Harrell & Son Productions
Notes Payable and Interest Expense
December 31, 1985

Prepared by SH
Date 1-5-86

	Big City National Bank	Mutual Insurance Co.		Recalculated Interest Expense
	1	2	3	4
Balance 12-31-84				
10% Long-Term note due 1989		300,000 ✕		30,000 ≉ ✓
Additions				
11% note dated 6-30-85 unsecured, due 6-30-86	100,000 Cta			5,500 ≉ ✓
Repayments – None				
Balance 12-31-85	100,000 T/B₃	300,000 T/B₃		35,500 T/B₃

✕ Agrees with prior year audit working papers.
c Obtained confirmation from creditor (see A-2) *
≉ Recalculated interest expense
✓ Vouched to canceled check ($30,000) and accrued interest payable ($5,500).
t Traced to cash deposit and bank statement.
T/B Traced to working trial balance.
a Traced to Director's authorization (P/F)

expect to be informed by management about all material contingent liabilities. Audit procedures useful in this regard include:

Inquire and discuss with management the policies and procedures for identifying, evaluating and accounting for litigation, claims and assessments.

Obtain from management a description and evaluation of litigation, claims and assessments.

Examine documents in the client's possession concerning litigation, claims and assessments, including correspondence and invoices from lawyers.

Obtain assurance from management that it has disclosed all unasserted claims that the lawyer has advised them are probable of litigation.

Read minutes of meetings of stockholders, directors and appropriate committees.

Read contracts, loan agreements, leases and correspondence from tax-ing or other governmental agencies.

Obtain information concerning guarantees from bank confirmation forms.

Auditors have a natural conservative tendency to look for adverse contingencies. However, potentially favorable events also should be investigated and disclosed (such as the contingency of litigation for damages wherein the client is the plaintiff). In an effort to assist management in observing the law and to provide adequate disclosure of information in financial statements, the auditor should be alert to all types of contingencies.

Major Working Paper   The major working paper for long-term liabilities is the schedule of all activity for each liability for the year. An example of this working paper listing the outstanding notes payable and related interest expense is provided in Exhibit 18–5. Note that only the note issued during the year was confirmed (as part of the bank confirmation) and the proceeds vouched to a cash deposit. The existing note was validated by prior year's audit work.

EXHIBIT 18–6
Audit Program—Selected Substantive Procedures—Notes Payable

> 1. Prepare, or have client prepare, a schedule of notes payable showing beginning balances, new notes, repayment and ending balances. Trace to general ledger accounts.
> 2. Confirm new notes payable—amount, interest rate, due date, collateral, other terms—with creditors.
> 3. Review the standard bank confirmation for evidence of unrecorded obligations.
> 4. Obtain written representations from management concerning notes payable, collateral agreements and restrictive covenants.

OWNERS' EQUITY   Major financing transactions generally receive formal review and exhaustive analysis by officers, directors and analysts in the organization. Such reviews are usually described in formal proposals, board minutes, and finally in prospectuses and correspondence accompanying the offer and sale of securities. Some transactions in these categories may require stockholders' approval, and in some cases they may require amendment of the corporate charter (such as authorization of new classes of stock or of increase in number of authorized shares). Stock dividends, stock splits, option plans and treasury stock transactions fall into this category of major financing transactions subject to high-level review and regulation.

The circumstances and constraints surrounding major financing transactions are generally sufficient for control. The documentation usually is voluminous, though nonstandardized, and ample review and approval is common. Accounting for such transactions—large in amount but few in number—usually does not involve extensive double-checking and review for errors in the same systematic sense that would be appropriate for large-volume transaction events. An auditor (independent auditor or internal auditor) can recheck completely for accounting error in a very short time.

Substantive Audit Procedures Related to Objectives

The assertions of existence, completeness, rights and obligations, valuation, and presentation and disclosure, which have been emphasized as audit objectives in these past two chapters, apply to owners' equity as well. The broad assertions would be tailored to fit particular audit concerns in this area. Typical specific assertions relating to owners' equity include:

☐ Capital stock terms and other stock issue plans are properly accounted for and disclosed.

☐ Options, warrants and other stock issue plans are properly accounted for and disclosed.

☐ All owners' equity transactions have been authorized by the board of directors.

The audit objective of valuation is usually not an audit concern for the owners' equity area in most audit engagements. In the case of complex changing of capitalization such as stock splits, conversion of preferred or other forms of equity to common stock, or pooling of interests, the major concern is with interpreting and following generally accepted accounting principles, not with valuation in some market value sense.

Existence, Completeness, Rights, and Presentation and Disclosure.   In connection with the capital accounts, there may be changes in the number of authorized shares, issues of warrants, grants of stock options, dividends, treasury stock transactions, appropriations or restrictions of retained earnings, or other events of major significance. In many cases, auditors will *vouch* the transactions to directors' minutes, stockholders' approvals, stock option and warrant plan documents, or other authorizations. When cash receipts or cash disbursements are involved, the appropriate cash receipt and canceled check documents may be examined. New issues of debt or capital stock may be vouched to securities registration documents as well as to cash receipts records and loan agreements.

Retained earnings are interrelated with income and dividends. In fact, retained earnings balances are little more than the accumulated results of such transactions. The retained earnings balance is essentially audited by relating charges and credits to income and dividend amounts, which themselves may be audited by retracing, vouching and recalculation. (If other entries are in retained earnings such as prior period adjustments or error correction entries, the audit would also involve vouching the transaction documentation.)

Capital stock may be subject to *confirmation* when independent registrars and transfer agents are employed. Such agents are responsible for knowing the number of shares authorized and issued and for keeping lists of stockholders' names. The basic information about capital stock such as number of shares, classes of stock, preferred dividend rates, conversion terms, dividend payments, shares held in the company name, expiration dates, terms of warrants, and stock dividends and splits can be confirmed with the independent agents. Many of these items can be corroborated by the auditor's own *inspection and reading* of stock certificates, charter authorizations, directors' minutes and offering prospectuses. When there are no independent agents, however, most audit evidence is gathered by vouching stock record documents (such as certificate book stubs). When circumstances call for extended procedures, information on outstanding stock may be confirmed directly with the holders.

Major Working Paper   The major working paper for owners' equity is the carry-forward schedule of all transactions relating to this area since the initial audit. If a significant transaction occurred during the period under audit, a schedule or memorandum will be prepared on that one transaction to document all of the evidence gathered.

Planning the procedures around objectives (as illustrated in this chapter) is a sound method to ensure that all objectives are covered. However, once the substantive year-end procedures are determined, the audit program is usually finalized into a list of procedures by audit areas as has been illustrated. Selected procedures for owners' equity accounts are presented in Exhibit 18–7.

EXHIBIT 18–7
Audit Program—Selected
Substantive
Procedures—Owners'
Equity

1. Confirm outstanding common and preferred stock with stock registrar agent.
2. Vouch stock option and profit-sharing plan disclosures to contracts and plan documents.
3. Vouch treasury stock transactions to cash receipts and cash disbursement records and to director's authorization. Inspect treasury stock certificates.

MAJOR TYPES OF FRAUD AND MISSTATEMENT   The simple theft of assets by employees should be addressed by internal control procedures and is not considered to be a major type of fraud or misstatement. The types of fraud and misstatement that must be considered are the material items that could affect fairness of financial statements. These practices are more frequently committed by supervisors and managers than lower-level employees. Management personnel are usually either not subject to the same degree of control as employees or can override the controls.

Investments and Intangibles

Major losses or manipulations in the area of investments and intangibles can be classified in three categories: (1) theft or diversion of funds—securities, sales proceeds, income receipts; (2) manipulation of accounting values through purchase or lease transactions at inflated prices or by fallacious judgment in valuation of intangibles; and (3) business espionage—the unauthorized use or transmittal of secret processes or methods. The first two of these categories are within the auditors' sphere of interest. However, the third area—business espionage—is generally outside the scope of the independent auditors' concern, although they should be alert to obvious indications. Internal auditors may be much more involved in investigations of business security.

Theft, diversion or unauthorized use of investment securities can occur in several ways. If safekeeping controls are weak, securities simply may be stolen, becoming then a police problem rather than an auditing problem. Somewhat more frequent, however, are diversions such as use of securities as collateral during the year, having them returned for a count and then given back to the creditor without disclosure to the auditor. If safekeeping methods require entry signatures (as at a safe-deposit vault), then auditors may be able to detect the in-and-out movement. The best chance of discovery is that the creditor will confirm the collateral arrangement. In a similar manner, securities might be removed by an officer and sold, then repurchased before the auditor's count. The auditor's record of the certificate numbers should reveal this change since the returned certificates (and their numbers) will not be the same as the ones removed.

Cash receipts from interest, royalties on patent licenses, dividends and sales proceeds might be stolen. The accounting records may or may not be manipulated to cover the theft. In general, this kind of defalcation is in the area of cash receipts control, but since these receipts are usually irregular and infrequent, the cash control system may not be as effective as it is for regular receipts on account. If the income accounts are not manipulated to hide stolen receipts, auditors should find less income in the account than the amount indicated by their audit calculations based on other records such as license agreements or published dividend records. If sales of securities are not recorded, auditors should be able to notice that securities are missing when they try to inspect or confirm them. If the income accounts have been manipulated to hide stolen receipts, vouching of cash receipts should detect the theft or vouching may reveal some offsetting debit buried in some other account.

Cash received as a return premium on an insurance policy cancellation may be stolen. The auditor's review of policies and recalculation of prepaid insurance may not catch this irregularity unless the policy in-force status is confirmed. Generally, however, such amounts are not material to the financial statements as a whole and such policy confirmation is considered an "extended procedure."

Accounting values can be manipulated in a number of ways involving purchases at inflated prices, leases with affiliates, acquisitions of patents for stock given to inventor/promoters, sales to affiliates and fallacious decisions about amortization. Business history has recorded several cases of nonarm's-length transactions with promoters, officers, directors and controlled companies (even "dummy" companies) designed to drain the company's resources and/or fool the auditors. In one case, a company sold assets to a dummy purchaser set up by a director in order to bolster sagging income with a gain. The auditors did not know that the purchaser was a shell. All the documents of sale looked in order, and cash sales proceeds had been deposited. The auditors were not informed of a secret agreement by the seller to repurchase the assets at a later time. This situation illustrates a very devious manipulation. All transactions with persons closely associated with the company (related parties) should be audited carefully with reference to market values, particularly when a nonmonetary transaction is involved (such as stock exchanged for patent rights). Sales and leaseback and straight lease transactions with insiders likewise should be audited carefully.

Business espionage is an area that tends to be highly technological and oftentimes outside the scope of an auditor's expertise. Often involved is the transfer of some trade or technological secret that aids a competitor. The computer industry is particularly sensitive to the problem of keeping new computer product developments secret.

Espionage tends to exist in the eye of the beholder, and if it is really a serious matter, litigation will probably begin. At this point, the auditors are most likely to learn of the event, and disclosure of the litigation will be appropriate. However, the independent auditor is most interested in timely disclosure of events that could result in material adverse effects on financial position and results of operations. The auditor's duty is to insist on disclosure of information about such events as it becomes known and not to speculate on the future effect of present leaky security. Security problems, as matters of internal control, may be brought to the attention of the client.

Fixed Assets Outright theft of material fixed assets or abstraction of the proceeds of sales of these assets is easy to detect. Adequate procedures to inspect and observe assets would reveal material thefts.

More difficult to detect are practices of purchasing supervisors accepting kickbacks from contractors, suppliers and lessors in consideration of business directed their way. Such practices are undesirable, but since they may not enter the client's accounting records, they are difficult to detect. Auditors should watch for asset costs in excess of market prices because of the seller's need to recover the kickback. Such assets may be overvalued in the accounts.

Even more subtle variants are the purchase or lease of assets or purchase of insurance from companies controlled by insiders (officers, directors, purchasing agents), or from the insider individually. Such transactions may involve prices that are not the same as market determined prices, and disclosure should be made in footnotes to financial statements. At worst, such events as the sham sale of an asset to create a gain in order to bolster income or the siphoning of cash through overcharges can cause material misstatements in financial statements and reports. (The inherent accounting assumption is that transaction data reflect market prices determined in "arm's-length" bargaining transactions.) Internal auditors would be very interested in these types of fraud because they are contrary to managerial policies and criteria of efficiency and effectiveness.

Long-Term Liabilities and Owners' Equity

The kinds of fraud and misstatement connected with liability and owners' equity accounts differ significantly from those associated with asset and revenue accounts. Few employees are tempted to steal a liability, although fictitious liabilities may be created in the records as a means of misdirecting cash payments into the hands of an employee. Auditors should be alert for such fictions in the same sense that they are alert to the possibility of having fictitious accounts receivable.

Although there are opportunities for employee fraud against the company, the area of liabilities and owners' equity also opens up possibilities for company fraud against outsiders. This class of fraud is most often accomplished through material misrepresentations or omissions in financial statements and related disclosures.

In addition to various means of misappropriating cash by manipulation of liability records, officers and employees might use stock or bond instruments improperly. Unissued stock or bonds and treasury stock or bonds might be used as collateral for personal loans. Even though the company may not be damaged or suffer loss by this action (unless the employee defaults and the securities are seized), the practice is unauthorized and contrary to company interests. Similarly, employees might gain access to stockholder lists and unissued or treasury bond coupons and cause improper payments of dividends and interest on securities not outstanding. Proper custodial control of securities (either by physical means such as limited-access vaults or by control of an independent disbursing agent) would prevent most such occurrences. An auditing procedure of reconciling authorized dividend and interest payments (calculated using declared dividend rates, coupon interest rates and known quantities of outstanding securities) to actual payments would detect unauthorized payments. If the company does not perform this checking procedure, auditors may include it among their own overall recalculation procedures.

Many liability, equity and "off-balance sheet" transactions are above the reach of normal internal control systems which can operate effectively over ordinary small-value transactions (such as purchases and sales) processed by clerks and machines. The size, impact and infrequency of many liability and equity transactions, however, cause them to be handled by high corporate officers, and these persons have power to override normal procedural control systems. Thus, the auditors are generally justified in extensive auditing of liability, equity and high-level-managed transactions and agreements since control depends in large part on the integrity of management.

Income tax evasion and fraud result from actions taken by managers and experts. Evasion and fraud may be accomplished by simple omission of income, by taking unlawful deductions (such as contributions to political campaigns, depreciation on nonexistent assets, or depreciation in excess of cost) or by contriving sham transactions for the sole purpose of avoiding taxation. Auditors should be able to detect errors of the first two categories if the actual income and expense data has been sufficiently audited in the financial statements. The last category—contrived sham transactions—are hard to detect because a dishonest management generally disguises them skillfully.

Financial statements can be materially misstated by reason of omission or understatement of liabilities and by failure to disclose technical defaults on loan agreement restrictions. The several means of auditing to discover unrecorded liabilities through a "search for unrecorded liabilities" may be used to attempt to discover such omissions and understatements. If auditors discover that loan agreement terms have been violated, they should bring the information to the client's attention and insist upon proper disclosure in footnotes to the financial statements. In both situations (liability understatement and loan default disclosure), management's actions, reactions and willingness to adjust the financial figures and make adverse disclosures will be important inputs to an auditor's subjective evaluation of managerial integrity. An accumulation of inputs relevant to managerial integrity can have an important bearing on the auditors' perceptions of risk for the audit engagement taken as a whole.

A company, individual managers and the auditors can run afoul of securities regulations if they are not careful. The general framework of regulation by the SEC was reviewed briefly in Chapter 4. Auditors must be cognizant of the general provisions of the securities laws to the extent that they can identify situations that constitute obvious fraud and to the extent that they can identify transactions that might be subject to the law. Having once recognized or raised questions about a securities transaction, the auditor should under no circumstances proceed to act as his or her own attorney. The facts should be submitted to competent legal counsel for an opinion. Even though auditors are not expected to be legal experts, they have the duty to recognize obvious instances of impropriety and pursue investigations with the aid of legal experts.

Similarly, auditors should assist clients in observing SEC rules and regulations on matters of timely disclosure. In general, the timely disclosure rules are phrased in terms of management's duties and do not require auditors to do any specific procedures or make any specific disclosures. Their purpose and spirit are to require management to disseminate to the public any material information, whether favorable or unfavorable, so the market can incorporate it in investment decisions. Various rule provisions require announcements and disclosures very soon after information becomes known. Oftentimes, relevant situations arise during the year when the independent auditors are not present, so of course they cannot be held responsible or liable. In other situations, however, auditors may learn of the information inadvertently, or auditors' advice may be sought by the client. In such cases, the accountant should act in the public interest as an auditor, consistent with the requirements of law and regulation.

Presently, pressures are on the auditors to discover more information about "off-balance sheet" contingencies and commitments and to discover the facts of management involvement with other parties to transactions. As explained earlier in this chapter, auditors' knowledge of contingencies and commitments that are not evidenced in accounting records depends almost entirely on what management and its attorneys will reveal. Management's control of buyers and sellers and the existence of side guarantees in purchase and sale transactions may be concealed with relative ease. The current pressures on auditors to discover more information is a part of the public pressure on auditors to take more responsibility for fraud detection.

SOURCES AND ADDITIONAL READING REFERENCES

Andrews, Wesley T. "Obtaining the Representations of Legal Counsel." *CPA Journal,* August 1977, pp. 37–40.

Benis, M., and R. T. Johnson. "A Case of Premature Income Recognition." *CPA Journal,* October 1973, pp. 863–67.

Benson, Benjamin. "Lawyers' Responses to Audit Inquiries—A Continuing Controversy." *Journal of Accountancy,* July 1977, pp. 72–78.

Cohen, G. D., and D. B. Pearson. "Auditing The Clients' Judgments." *Journal of Accountancy,* May 1981, pp. 58–64.

Clay, R. J., Jr., and W. W. Holder. "Unasserted Claims: Accounting Measurement and Disclosure." *CPA Journal,* October 1977, pp. 83–85.

Gallups, W. C., and W. A. Hillison. "Using ARPs to Increase Audit Efficiency." *The Internal Auditor,* June 1983, pp. 35–39.

Kask, A. W. "Regression and Correlation Analysis." *CPA Journal,* pp. 35–41.

Kinney, William R., Jr. "Predicting Auditor-Initiated Adjustments Using Paired Balance Sheet Methods." *The Journal of Accounting, Auditing and Finance,* Fall 1981, pp. 5–17.

Leininger, W. E., and M. J. Conley. "Regression Analysis in Auditing." *CPA Journal,* October 1980, pp. 43–47.

Pomeroy, Harlan. "Restrictive Covenants: What the CPA Should Know." *Journal of Accountancy,* February 1981, pp. 61–68.

Wallace, Wanda A. "Analytical Review: Misconceptions, Applications and Experience." *The CPA Journal,* Part I, January 1983, pp. 24–37; Part II, February 1983, pp. 18–27.

Whittington, R., M. Zulinsky, and J. W. Ledwith. "Completeness—The Elusive Assertation." *The Journal of Accountancy,* August 1983, pp. 82–92.

REVIEW QUESTIONS

Investments and Intangibles

18.1. What procedures do auditors employ in the audit of investment securities to obtain the names of the issuers, the number of shares held, certificate numbers, maturity value, and interest and dividend rates?

18.2. Describe the procedures and documentation of a controlled count of client's investment securities.

18.3. If the dividends accrued on life insurance policies are not used to reduce premiums, how can the auditor obtain evidence of the amount of accumulated dividends?

18.4. What procedures does the auditor employ to obtain evidence of the cost of investments, investment gains and losses and investment income?

18.5. Why is the auditor interested in substantial investment losses occurring early in the period following year-end?

Fixed Assets and Related Accounts

18.6. Auditors organize the audit work using managements' assertions in the financial statements. In addition to the broad assertions, such as existence and completeness, specific assertions are made in each major account area. List 10 such specific assertions related to the fixed assets and related accounts.

18.7. In determining the existence of fixed assets, how might the auditor obtain preliminary evidence? What procedures are used to gather corroborating evidence?

18.8. Explain why a fixed asset account may not properly reflect fixed assets "in productive use."

18.9. When might auditors utilize confirmations in their audit of fixed assets? When might they conduct an extensive inventory of fixed assets?

18.10. Why is the repairs and maintenance account audited at the same time as the fixed asset accounts?

18.11. Why is verbal inquiry important in an audit of fixed assets? What verbal evidence should be documented?

18.12. What unusual transactions would the auditor be looking for in the scanning of fixed asset transactions?

Long-term Liabilities, Contingencies and Commitments

18.13. Explain why for long-term liabilities (and fixed assets and owners' equity) only the current period additions and disposals are audited, and not the entire account balance.

18.14. How are confirmations used in auditing notes and bonds payable?

18.15. In regard to contingencies and commitments, why would an auditor vouch open purchase orders?

18.16. Define and give five examples of "off-balance sheet information." Why should auditors be concerned with such items?

18.17. In addition to the attorney's letter, what other procedures are used to gather evidence regarding contingencies?

18.18. How might the auditor's report be affected by the following reply to a confirmation request by client's counsel regarding a pending lawsuit against a client? "Several agreements and contracts to which the company is a party are not covered by this response since we have not advised or been consulted in their regard." Explain.

Owners' Equity

18.19. What features of capital stock are of importance to the audit?

18.20. What information about capital stock could be confirmed with outside parties? How could this information be corroborated by the auditors?

18.21. Generally, how much emphasis is placed upon adequate internal control in the audit of long-term debt, capital stock, warrants, options, paid-in capital and retained earnings? Explain.

Fraud and Misstatement

18.22. What are the three categories of major losses or manipulations in the area of investments? Are all three within the auditor's sphere of interest?

18.23. Identify some major types of fraud and material misstatement related to fixed asset accounts.

EXERCISES AND PROBLEMS

Investments and Intangibles

18.24. **Noncurrent Investment Securities**
You are engaged in the audit of the financial statements of Bass Corporation for the year ended December 31, 1985, and are about to begin the work on the noncurrent investment securities. Bass' records indicate that the company owns various bearer bonds, as well as 25 percent of the outstanding common stock of Commercial Industrial, Inc. You are satisfied with evidence that supports the presumption of significant influence over Commercial Industrial, Inc. The various securities are at two locations as follows:

Recently acquired securities are in the company's safe in the treasurer's custody.

All other securities are in the company's bank safe-deposit box.

All securities in Bass' portfolio are actively traded in a broad market.

Required:
a.   Assuming that the system of internal control over securities is satisfactory and may be relied upon, what are the objectives (specific assertions) for the audit of the noncurrent securities?

b.   What audit procedures should you undertake with respect to the audit of Bass' investment securities?
                                            (*AICPA* adapted)

18.25. **Securities Examination and Count**
You are in charge of the audit of the financial statements of the Demot Corporation for the year ended December 31. The corporation has had the policy of investing its surplus funds in marketable securities. Its stock and bond certificates are kept in a safe-deposit box in a local bank. Only the president and the treasurer of the corporation have access to the box.

You were unable to obtain access to the safe-deposit box on December 31 because neither the president nor the treasurer were available. Arrangements were made for your assistant to accompany the treasurer to the bank on January 11 to examine the securities. Your assistant has never examined securities kept in a safe-deposit box and requires instructions. Your assistant should be able to inspect all securities on hand in an hour.

Required:

a. List the instructions you would give to your assistant regarding the examination of the stock and bond certificates kept in the safe-deposit box. Include in your instructions the details of the securities to be included in the working papers and the reasons for examining these details.

b. After returning from the bank, your assistant reports that the treasurer had entered the box on January 4 to remove an old photograph of the corporation's original building. The photograph was loaned to the local chamber of commerce for display purposes. List the additional audit procedures that are required because of the treasurer's action.

(*AICPA* adapted)

18.26. **Securities Procedures**

You were engaged to examine the financial statements of Ronlyn Corporation for the year ended June 30. On May 1, the corporation borrowed $500,000 from the Second National Bank to finance plant expansion. However, due to unexpected difficulties in acquiring the building site, the plant expansion had not begun as planned. To make use of the borrowed funds, management decided to invest in stocks and bonds; and on May 16, the $500,000 was invested in securities.

Required:

In your audit of investments, how would you:

a. Verify the dividend or interest income recorded?

b. Determine market value?

c. Establish the authority for security purchases?

(*AICPA* adapted)

18.27. **Research and Development**

The Hertle Engineering Company depends upon innovation and new product development to maintain its position in the market for drilling tool equipment. The company conducts an extensive research and development program for this purpose and it consistently charges research and development costs to current operations in accordance with Statement on Financial Accounting Standards 2.

The company began a project called "Project Able" in January 1984, with the goal of patenting a revolutionary drilling bit design. Work continued until October 1985 when the company applied for a patent. Costs were charged to the research and development expense account in both years, except for the cost of a computer program which engineers plan to use in "Project Baker," scheduled to start in December. The computer program was purchased from Computeering, Inc., in January 1985 for $45,000.

Required:

a. Give an audit program for the audit of research and development costs on "Project Able." Assume you are auditing the company for the first time at December 31, 1985.

b. What evidence would you require for the audit of the computer program which has been capitalized as an intangible asset? As of December 31, 1985, this account has a balance of $40,000 (cost less $5,000 amortized as a part of "Project Able").

18.28. **Intangibles**

Sorenson Manufacturing Corporation was incorporated on January 3, 1984. The corporation's financial statements for its first year's operations were not examined by a CPA. You have been engaged to examine the financial statements for the year ended December 31, 1985, and your examination is substantially completed.

A partial trial balance of the company's accounts is given below:

SORENSON MANUFACTURING CORPORATION
Trial Balance
At December 31, 1985

	Debit	Credit
Cash	$11,000	
Accounts receivable	42,500	
Allowance for doubtful accounts. .		$ 500
Inventories	38,500	
Machinery.	75,000	
Equipment	29,000	
Accumulated depreciation		10,000
Patents	85,000	
Leasehold improvements	26,000	
Prepaid expenses	10,500	
Organization expenses.	29,000	
Goodwill	24,000	
Licensing agreement no. 1	50,000	
Licensing agreement no. 2	49,000	

The following information relates to accounts which may yet require adjustment:

1. Patents for Sorenson's manufacturing process were purchased January 2, 1985, at a cost of $68,000. An additional $17,000 was spent in December 1985 to improve machinery covered by the patents and charged to the Patents account. The patents had a remaining legal term of 17 years.

2. On January 3, 1984, Sorenson purchased two licensing agreements which at that time were believed to have unlimited useful lives. The balance in the Licensing Agreement No. 1 account included its purchase price of $48,000 and $2,000 in acquisition expenses. Licensing Agreement No. 2 was also purchased on January 3, 1984, for $50,000 but has been reduced by a credit of $1,000 for the advance collection of 1986 revenue from the agreement.

    In December 1984, an explosion caused a permanent 60 percent reduction in the expected revenue-producing value of Licensing Agreement No. 1, and in January 1986, a flood caused additional damage which rendered the agreement worthless.

    A study of Licensing Agreement

No. 2 made by Sorenson in January 1985 revealed that its estimated remaining life expectancy was only 10 years as of January 1, 1985.

3. The balance in the Goodwill account includes $24,000 paid December 30, 1984, for an advertising program which is estimated will assist in increasing Sorenson's sales over a period of four years following the disbursement.

4. The Leasehold Improvement account includes: (*a*) the $15,000 cost of improvements with a total estimated useful life of 12 years which Sorenson, as tenant, made to leased premises in January 1984, (*b*) movable assembly-line equipment costing $8,500 which was installed in the leased premises in December 1985 and (*c*) real estate taxes of $2,500 paid by Sorenson which, under the terms of the lease, should have been paid by the landlord. Sorenson paid its rent in full during 1985. A 10-year, nonrenewable lease was signed January 3, 1984, for the leased building which Sorenson used in manufacturing operations.

5. The balance in the Organization Expenses account includes preoperating costs incurred during the organizational period.

Required:
Prepare adjusting entries as necessary.
(*AICPA* adapted)

Fixed Assets

18.29. **Audit Procedures Related to Assertions**
Audit procedures may be classified as:

Physical observation.

Recalculation.

Confirmation.

Representations (oral and written) by client personnel.

Examination of documents (vouching and tracing).

Scanning.

Analytical review.

Describe how each of these procedures might be used to gather evidence on fixed assets and which broad financial statement assertion(s) (existence, completeness, rights, valuation or allocation, and presentation and disclosure) is being addressed by the use of the procedure.

18.30. Donated Land and Buildings

You have been engaged to make an audit of the financial statements of a new client, the ABC Manufacturing Corporation, for its fiscal year ended December 31. Among the fixed assets are accounts for "Land and Buildings," with a balance of $1,007,000 and "Reserve for Depreciation—Land and Building," with a balance of $301,000.

The president informs you that "The land and factory were donated by Grand City to the ABC Manufacturing Corporation three years ago. This property had been purchased by Grand City a few months earlier for $1,000,000. ABC Manufacturing Corporation will get title to the donated property seven years from now, provided the average weekly payroll numbers a minimum of 200 each calendar year. The corporation intends to meet these provisions."

Required:

List the procedures you would follow in auditing these accounts. Organize your procedures by financial statement assertions.

(*AICPA* adapted)

18.31. Replacement of Fixed Asset Components

While auditing an urban bus company in a city of 500,000 population, you encounter the following situation:

1. You have seen an authorization for the purchase of five engines to replace the engines in five buses.

2. The cost of the old engines was removed from the Equipment account, and the purchase prices of the new en-

gines properly capitalized. The work was done in the company garage.

3. You find no credits for salvage nor for the sale of any scrap metal at any time during the year. You have been in the garage and did not see the old engines.

4. The accountant is also treasurer and office manager. She is an authorized check signer and has access to all cash receipts. Upon inquiry, she says she does not recall the sale of the old engines nor of any scrap metal.

Required:

Assuming that the engines were sold as scrap, outline all procedures which this fact would cause you to take in connection with your audit. Give consideration to the five financial statement assertions in planning your procedures.

(*AICPA* adapted)

18.32. Manufacturing Equipment and Accumulated Depreciation

In connection with a recurring audit of the financial statements of the Louis Manufacturing Company for the year ended December 31, you have been assigned the audit of the Manufacturing Equipment, Manufacturing Equipment—Accumulated Depreciation, and Repairs to Manufacturing Equipment accounts. Your review of Louis' policies and procedures has disclosed the following pertinent information:

1. The Manufacturing Equipment account includes the net invoice price plus related freight and installation costs for all of the equipment in Louis's manufacturing plant.

2. The Manufacturing Equipment and Accumulated Depreciation accounts are supported by a subsidiary ledger which shows the cost and accumulated depreciation for each piece of equipment.

3. An annual budget for capital expenditures of $1,000 or more is prepared by the budget committee and approved by

the board of directors. Capital expenditures over $1,000 which are not included in this budget must be approved by the board of directors, and variations of 20 percent or more must be explained to the board. Approval by the supervisor of production is required for capital expenditures under $1,000.

4. Company employees handle installation, removal, repair and rebuilding of the machinery. Work orders are prepared for these activities and are subject to the same budgetary control as other expenditures. Work orders are not required for external expenditures.

Required:

a. Cite the major *objectives* (assertions) for your audit of the Manufacturing Equipment, Manufacturing Equipment—Accumulated Depreciation, and Repairs of Manufacturing Equipment accounts. Do not include in this listing the auditing *procedures* designed to accomplish these objectives.

b. Prepare the portion of your audit program applicable to the review of current-year additions to the Manufacturing Equipment account.

(*AICPA* adapted)

18.33. **Exchange of Fixed Assets**
Part A: During the course of your audit of Presto Gadgets, Inc., you found the following transaction recorded in the general journal:

Investment in Electro Enterprises
common stock 65,000
Accumulated depreciation—Gear
machine, model Y 25,000
   Gear machine, model Y. . . . 90,000
Explanation: To record exchange of fixed assets for 10,000 shares of Electro common stock.

In a conversation with the treasurer, you are told that the gear machine, model Y, was a fixed asset, and that depreciation was recorded to the date of the exchange. The treasurer said that this exchange was a

"better deal" than selling the machine outright in the used equipment market where it probably would have brought about $70,000, because Electro's common shares were worth $7.25 each.

Required:

a. What corroborating evidence should you seek by: (1) other inquiries, (2) vouching, (3) recalculation, (4) observation, (5) confirmation and (6) analytical review. Explain the purpose of each item of evidence so gathered.

b. Assume that $7.25 per share is a verifiable price for the Electro common stock. Is the Presto journal entry correct? What adjustment, if any, should be made?

Part B: Assume that instead of exchanging its asset for Electro common stock, Presto received from Electro a similar asset (gear machine, model X) and $20,000 in cash in exchange for the gear machine, model Y. The exchange was recorded in Presto's accounts as follows:

Gear machine, model X 45,000
Cash 20,000
Accumulated depreciation—
Gear machine, model Y 25,000
   Gear machine, model Y 90,000

The treasurer has told you that this was a "good deal" because the model X machine would cost $60,000 in the used-equipment market.

Required:

a. What evidence should you obtain about the model X machine?

b. Assume that the $60,000 is a verified market value for the model X machine. Is the Presto journal entry correct? What adjustment, if any, should be made?

18.34. **Property, Plant and Equipment—Adjustments**
Rivers, CPA, is the auditor for a manufacturing company with a balance sheet that includes the caption, "Property, Plant and

Equipment.'' Rivers has been asked by the company's management if audit adjustments or reclassifications are required for the following material items that have been included (excluded) from ''Property, Plant and Equipment.''

1. A tract of land was acquired during the year. The land is the future site of the client's new headquarters which will be constructed in the following year. Commissions were paid to the real estate agent to acquire the land, and expenditures were made to relocate the previous owner's equipment. These commissions and expenditures were expensed and are excluded from Property, Plant and Equipment.

2. Clearing costs were incurred to make the land ready for construction. These costs were included in Property, Plant and Equipment.

3. During the land clearing process, timber and gravel were recovered and sold. The proceeds from the sale were recorded as other income and are excluded from Property, Plant and Equipment.

4. A group of machines was purchased under a royalty agreement which provides royalty payments based on units of production from the machines. The cost of the machines, freight costs, unloading charges and royalty payments were capitalized and are included in Property, Plant and Equipment.

Required:

a. Describe the general characteristics of assets, such as land, buildings, improvements, machinery, equipment, fixtures and so on that should normally be classified as Property, Plant and Equipment, and identify audit objectives in connection with the examination of ''Property, Plant and Equipment.'' Do not discuss specific audit procedures.

b. Indicate whether each of the above items numbered 1 to 4 requires one or more audit adjustments or reclassifications and explain why such adjustments or reclassifications are required or not required.

(*AICPA* adapted)

Organize your answer as follows:

Item Number	Is Audit Adjustment or Reclassification Required?	Reasons Why Audit Adjustment or Reclassification Is Required or Not Required
	Yes or No	

Long-term Liabilities, Contingencies and Commitments

18.35. Long-term Note

You were engaged to examine the financial statements of Ronlyn Corporation for the year ended June 30. On May 1, the corporation borrowed $500,000 from the Second National Bank to finance plant expansion. The long-term note agreement provided for the annual payment of principal and interest over five years. The existing plant was pledged as security for the loan.

Due to unexpected difficulties in acquiring the building site, the plant expansion had not begun as planned. To make use of the borrowed funds, management decided to invest in stocks and bonds, and on May 16, the $500,000 was invested in securities.

Required:

a. What are the audit objectives in the examination of long-term debt?

b. Prepare an audit program for the examination of the long-term note agreement between Ronlyn and Second National Bank.

(*AICPA* adapted)

18.36. Long-term Financing Agreement

You have been engaged to audit the financial statements of Broadwall Corporation for the year ended December 31, 1985. During the year, Broadwall obtained a long-term loan from a local bank pursuant to a financing agreement which provided that the:

1. Loan was to be secured by the company's inventory and accounts receivable.
2. Company was to maintain a debt-to-equity ratio not to exceed two to one.
3. Company was not to pay dividends without permission from the bank.
4. Monthly installment payments were to commence July 1, 1985.

In addition, during the year the company also borrowed, on a short-term basis, from the president of the company. A substantial amount was borrowed just prior to the year-end.

Required:

a. For purposes of your audit of the financial statements of Broadwall Corporation, what procedures should you employ in examining the described loans? Do not discuss internal control.

b. What are the financial statement disclosures that you should expect to find with respect to the loan from the president?

18.37. Bond Indenture Covenants

The following covenants are extracted from the indenture of a bond issue. The indenture provides that failure to comply with its terms in any respect automatically advances the due date of the loan to the date of noncompliance (the regular date is 20 years hence). Give any audit steps or reporting requirements you believe should be taken or recognized in connection with each one of the following:

1. "The debtor company shall endeavor to maintain a working capital ratio of 2 to 1 at all times and in any fiscal year following a failure to maintain said ratio, the company shall restrict compensation of officers to a total of $100,000. Officers for this purpose shall include chairman of the board of directors, president, all vice presidents, secretary and treasurer."

2. "The debtor company shall keep all property which is security for this debt insured against loss by fire to the extent of 100 percent of its actual value. Policies of insurance comprising this protection shall be filed with the trustee."

3. "The debtor company shall pay all taxes legally assessed against property which is security for this debt within the time provided by law for payment without penalty and shall deposit receipted tax bills or equally acceptable evidence of payment of same with the trustee."

4. "A sinking fund shall be deposited with the trustee by semiannual payments of $300,000, from which the trustee shall, in his discretion, purchase bonds of this issue."

(*AICPA* adapted)

18.38. Pension Plan

You have been assigned to the audit of Southampton Shipping Company. The company has adopted a funded pension plan in the past year which allows management to add a discretionary amount each year to the pension fund, recognizing concurrently a liability equal to the amount in the fund.

Required:

a. One of your objectives as an auditor is to determine whether all liabilities are reflected in the financial statement in the proper amounts. In view of this objective, why might you dispute Southampton's pension plan accounting?

b. Assume the amounts associated with the pension plan are material to the company's financial position and results of operations. If the plan is accounted for as proposed by management, what effect would this have on the audit report?

c. What procedures might you use to audit the pension fund liability account?

18.39. **Contingent Liabilities and Commitments**

Prepare an audit program which would bring to light various types of contingent liabilities and commitments. (The program should be in general terms for each area covered and should briefly describe the type of contingent item which might be found under each step. Ignore the fact that several of the steps in the program might normally be included in programs for other parts of your examination.) In order to consider a wide variety of contingencies, organize the program around the following persons and documents:

a. Bank confirmation.

b. Client counsel.

c. Board minutes.

d. Purchasing agent.

e. Personnel director.

f. President.

(*AICPA* adapted)

Owners' Equity

18.40. **Stockholders' Equity**

You are a CPA engaged in an examination of the financial statements of Pate Corporation for the year ended December 31. The financial statements and records of Pate Corporation have not been audited by a CPA in prior years.

The stockholders' equity section of Pate Corporation's balance sheet at December 31, follows:

Stockholders' equity:
Capital stock—10,000 shares of $10
  par value authorized; 5,000
  shares issued and outstanding . . . . . $ 50,000
Capital contributed in excess of
  par value of capital stock   32,580
Retained earnings   47,320
Total stockholders' equity $129,900

Pate Corporation was founded in 1980. The corporation has 10 stockholders and

serves as its own registrar and transfer agent. There are no capital stock subscription contracts in effect.

Required:

a. Prepare the detailed audit program for the examination of the three accounts comprising the stockholder's equity section of Pate Corporation's balance sheet. Organize the audit program under broad financial statement assertions. (Do not include in the audit program the audit of the results of the current year's operations.)

b. After every other figure on the balance sheet has been audited by the CPA, it might appear that the retained earnings figure is a balancing figure and requires no further audit work. Why does the CPA not audit retained earnings as he does the other figures on the balance sheet? Discuss.

(*AICPA* adapted)

18.41. **Oil Leases Exchanged For Capital Stock**

A and B form a corporation and transfer to it oil leases owned equally by them for which they had paid $30 in capitalized fees. They had also paid $1,280 for delay lease rentals which they had charged to expense in the year paid by them as individuals. A and B had no other costs or expenses applicable to these leases.

At the time of the transfer, geological and geophysical reports on the property were favorable, but no production had begun in the area. The board of directors of the new corporation issued $300,000 par value common stock for the leases, one half the stock going to A and one half to B. A and B donated concurrently one half of their respective shares to the corporate treasury to be sold at par for working capital.

Required:

a. Discuss the proper balance sheet presentation of the leases and of the capital and donated stock.

b. What audit procedures would you apply to the leases? (Consider the audit objectives in planning the proper audit procedures.)

c. Must this stock issue be reported or registered with the SEC? Explain.

(*AICPA* adapted)

DISCUSSION CASE

18.42. **Intercompany and Interpersonal Investment Relations**

You have been engaged to audit the financial statements of Hardy Hardware Distributors, Inc., as of December 31. In your review of the corporate nonfinancial records, you have found that Hardy Hardware owns 15 percent of the outstanding voting common stock of Hardy Products Corporation. Upon further investigation, you learn that Hardy Products Corporation manufactures a line of hardware goods, 90 percent of which is sold to Hardy Hardware.

Mr. James L. Hardy, president of Hardy Hardware, has supplied you with objective evidence that he personally owns 30 percent of the Hardy Products voting stock and the remaining 70 percent is owned by Mr. John L. Hardy, his brother and president of Hardy Products. James L. Hardy also owns 20 percent of the voting common stock of Hardy Hardware Distributors, another 20 percent is held by an estate of which James and John are beneficiaries, and the remaining 60 percent is publicly held. The stock is listed on the American Stock Exchange.

Hardy Hardware has consistently reported operating profits greater than the industry average. Hardy Products Corporation, however, has a net return on sales of only 1 percent. The Hardy Products investment has always been reported at cost, and no dividends have ever been paid by the company. During the course of your conversations with the Hardy brothers, you learn that you were appointed as auditor because they had had a heated disagreement with the former auditor over the issues of accounting for the Hardy Products investment and the prices at which goods had been sold to Hardy Hardware.

For Discussion:

a. Identify the issues in this situation as they relate to: (1) conflicts of interest and (2) controlling influences among individuals and corporations.

b. Should the investment in Hardy Products Corporation be accounted for on the equity method?

c. What evidence should the auditor seek with regard to the prices paid by Hardy Hardware for products purchased from Hardy Products Corporation?

d. What information would you consider necessary for adequate disclosure in the financial statements of Hardy Hardware Distributors?

CHAPTER 19

PROFESSIONAL STANDARDS SOURCES		
Compendium Section	**Document Reference**	**Topic**
AU 318	SAS 23	Analytical Review Procedures
AU 9318		Interpretation: Analytical Review Procedures
AU 333	SAS 19	Client Representations
AU 9333		Interpretation: Client Representations
AU 390	SAS 46	Consideration of Omitted Procedures After the Report Date
AU 560	SAS 1	Subsequent Events
AU 9509		Interpretation: Disclosures of Subsequent Events
AU 561	SAS 1	Subsequent Discovery of Facts Existing at the Date of the Auditor's Report

Completion of the Field Work

LEARNING OBJECTIVES This chapter covers the process of completing the field work and gathering up the loose ends of the audit. The following principal items are covered: completing the audit of revenue and expense, obtaining written client representations, events subsequent to the balance sheet date and events subsequent to the audit report date, and final wrap-up to the audit (audit review). Your learning objectives relative to these topics are to be able to:

☐ Describe the related balance sheet account group where the audit of the major revenue and expense accounts is normally associated.

☐ Describe how analytical review procedures can be used to evaluate the appropriateness of revenue and expense accounts.

☐ Describe the reasons written client representations are obtained and list the four items that must appear.

☐ Given a set of facts and circumstances, classify a subsequent event by type, and describe the proper disclosure in the financial statements.

☐ Specify the sequence of decisions and actions auditors must consider upon discovery (after the issuance of the report) of information about facts that may have existed at the date of the auditors' report.

☐ Specify the considerations and procedures applied by auditors upon conclusion, after the audit report date, that one or more auditing procedures were omitted.

AUDIT OF REVENUE AND EXPENSE

The major revenue and expense accounts have been audited in connection with related balance sheet accounts. As the field work nears an end, auditors need to consider other revenue and expense accounts that have not yet been examined.

Revenue

The following types of revenue and related topics will already have been audited, either in whole or in part, at this stage of the engagement.

Revenue and Related Topics	Related Account Groups
Sales and sales returns	Receivables
Lease revenue	Fixed assets and receivables
Franchise revenue	Receivables, intangibles
Dividends and interest	Receivables, investments
Gain, loss on asset disposals	Fixed assets, receivables and investments
Rental revenue	Receivables and investments
Royalty and license revenue	Receivables and investments
Long-term sales commitments	Revenue and receivables
Product-line reporting	Revenue and receivables
Accounting policy disclosure	Revenue and receivables

To the extent that these revenue items have been audited completely, the audit working papers should show cross-reference indexing to the revenue account in the trial balance. The accounts that have not been audited completely will be evident. Auditors should ascertain by reference to the trial balance (or other source if the trial balance does not contain sufficient detail) that they have a list of all the revenue and gain or loss accounts and amounts.

Audit Procedures. *Analytical review procedures* can be used to compare the revenue accounts and amounts to prior year data and to multiple-year trends to ascertain whether any unusual fluctuations are present. Comparisons should also be made to budgets, monthly internal reports and forecasts to ascertain whether events have occurred that require explanation or management analysis. These explanations themselves would then be subjected to audit. For example, a sales dollar increase may be explained as a consequence of a price increase—which can be corroborated by reference to vouching of price lists performed during the compliance audit of sales transaction control.

Auditors should also ascertain whether account classifications, aggregations, and summarizations are consistent with those of the prior year. This information will have a bearing on the consistency portion of the auditors' opinion.

All "miscellaneous" or "other" revenue accounts and all "clearing" accounts with credit balances should be analyzed. *Account analysis* in this context refers to the identification of each important item and amount in the account, followed by *vouching and inquiry* to determine whether amounts should be classified elsewhere. All clearing accounts should be eliminated and the amounts classified as revenue, deferred revenue, liabilities, deposits or contra-assets, as the case may be.

Miscellaneous revenue and other suspense accounts can harbor many accounting errors. Proceeds from sale of assets, insurance premium refunds, insurance proceeds and other receipts may simply be credited to such an account. Oftentimes, such items reveal unrecorded asset disposals, expiration of insurance recorded as prepaid, or other asset losses covered by insurance.

Unusual transactions. Significant audit evidence and reporting problems can arise with transactions designed by management to manufacture earnings. Oftentimes, such transactions are complicated through a structure of subsidiaries, affiliates and related parties. Generally, the amounts of revenue are large. The transactions themselves may not be concealed, but certain guarantees may have been made by management and not revealed to the auditors. The timing of the transactions may be carefully arranged to provide the most favorable income result.

These unusual types of transactions take a wide variety of characteristics and are difficult to classify for useful generalization. Controversies have arisen in the past over revenue recognized on the construction percentage-of-completion method, over sales of assets at inflated prices to management-controlled dummy corporations, over sales of real estate to independent parties with whom the seller later associates for development of the property (making guarantees as to indemnification for losses), and over disclosure of revenues by source. These revenue issues pose a combination of: evidence-gathering problems, auditor responsibility for detecting errors and irregularities, and reporting disclosure problems. Three illustrations of such problems are given below.

Illustration. National Fried Chicken, Inc., a large fast-food franchiser, began negotiations in August to purchase State Hot Dog Company, a smaller convenience food chain. At August 1, 19X1, State's net worth was $7 million and National proposed to pay $8 million cash for all the outstanding stock. On June 1, 19X2, the merger was consummated, and National paid $8 million even though State's net worth had dropped to $6 million. Consistent with prior years, State lost $1 million in the 10 months ended June 1; and as in the past, the company showed a net profit of $1.5 million for June and July. At June 1, 19X2, the fair value of State's net assets was $6 million, and National accounted for the acquisition as a purchase, recording $2 million goodwill. National proposed to show in consolidated financial statements the $1.5 million of postacquisition income and $50,000 amortization of goodwill.

Audit resolution. The auditors discovered that the purchase price was basically set at 16 times expected earnings and that management had carefully chosen the consummation date in order to maximize goodwill (and reportable net income after amortization in fiscal 19X2). The auditors required that $1 million of "goodwill" be treated as prepaid expenses which expired in the year ended July 31, 19X2, so that bottom-line income would be $500,000.

Illustration. In August, the company sold three real estate properties to BMC for $5,399,000 and recognized profit of $550,000. The letter agreement that covered the sale committed the company to use its best efforts to obtain permanent financing and to pay underwriting costs for BMC, and it provided BMC with an absolute guarantee against loss from ownership and a commitment by the company to complete construction of the properties.

SEC Resolution (ARS 153; February 24, 1974). The terms of this agreement made the recognition of profit improper because the company had not shifted the risk of loss to BMC.

Illustration. In December 19X1, White Company sold one half of a tract of undeveloped land to Black Company in an arm's-length transaction. The portion sold had a book value of $1.5 million, and Black Company paid $2.5 million in cash. Black Company planned to build and sell apartment houses on the acquired land. In January 19X2, White and Black announced a new joint venture to develop the entire tract. The two companies formed a partnership, each contributing its one half of the total tract of land. They agreed to share equally in future capital requirements and profits or losses.

Audit resolution. The $1 million profit from the sale was not recognized as income in White's 19X1 financial statements, but instead was classified as a deferred credit. White's investment in the joint venture was valued at $1.5 million. White's continued involvement in development of the property and the uncertainty of future costs and losses were cited as reasons.

Expenses   Although many major expense items will have been audited in connection with other account groupings, numerous minor expenses may still remain unaudited. As a brief review, the following major expenses and related topics have been audited in whole or in part at this late stage of the engagement.

Expenses and Related Topics	Related Account Groups
Purchases, cost of goods sold	Inventories
Inventory valuation losses	Inventories
Warranty and guarantee expense	Inventories and liabilities
Royalty and license expense	Inventories
Marketing and product R&D	Investments and intangibles
Investment value losses	Investments and intangibles
Rental property expenses	Investments and intangibles
Amortization of intangibles	Investments and intangibles
Bad debt expense	Receivables
Depreciation expense	Fixed assets
Property taxes, insurance	Fixed assets and liabilities
Lease and rental expense	Fixed assets
Repairs and maintenance	Fixed assets and liabilities
Legal and professional fees	Liabilities and equity
Interest expense	Liabilities
Pension and retirement benefits	Liabilities, equity, and payroll
Payroll and compensation costs	Payroll
Sales commissions	Payroll
Contingencies	Liabilities and equity

Like the revenue accounts mentioned in the previous section, if expense account audit work is complete, the working papers should show cross-reference indexing from the evidential papers to the trial balance. Some of the expenses may not have been audited completely (such as property tax expense), and some finishing-touch vouching of supporting documents may be required.

Audit Procedures.   Several minor expenses, such as office supplies, telephone, utilities and similar accounts are not audited until late in the engagement. Generally, the dollar amounts in these accounts are not material (taken singly), and the relative risk is small that they might be misstated in such a way to create misleading financial statements. Auditors usually audit these kinds of accounts with *analytical review procedures*. With these procedures, a list of the expenses is made with comparative balances from one or more prior periods, and the dollar amounts are reviewed for unusual changes (or lack of unusual changes if reasons therefor are known).

Such a comparison may be enough to enable the auditor to decide that the amounts are fairly presented. On the other hand, questions might be raised, and additional evidence might be sought. In the latter case, auditors may *vouch* some expenses to supporting documents (i.e., invoices and canceled checks). In many cases, expense entries in the accounts will have been audited during the audit of cash disbursement and accounts payable transactions, and the evidence thus produced in other phases of the audit should not be overlooked. Comparisons to budgets, internal reports and forecasts may also be made. Variations from budget may already have been subject to management explanation, or the audit manager may need to investigate variations.

All "miscellaneous" or "other" expense accounts and "clearing" accounts with debit balances should be analyzed by listing each important item on a working paper and *vouching* it to supporting documents. Miscellaneous and other expenses may include abandonments of property, items not deductible for tax purposes, or payments that should be classified in other expense accounts. Clearing accounts should likewise be analyzed and items therein classified according to their nature or source so that all clearing account balances are removed and accounted for properly.

Advertising expense, travel and entertainment expense and contributions are accounts that are typically analyzed in detail. These accounts are particularly sensitive to management policy violations and income tax consequences. Travel, entertainment and contributions must be documented carefully in order to stand the IRS auditor's examination. Questionable items may have an impact on the income tax expense and liability.

Travel and entertainment sometimes harbor abuses of company policy respecting expense allowances and minor embezzlements or cheating which can be detected by careful auditors. However, a detailed audit of expense account payments may be of greater interest to the efficiency-minded internal auditor than to the independent auditor. As far as independent auditors are concerned, even if employees did overstate their reimbursable expenses, the actual paid-out amount is still fairly presented as a financial fact. If there is evidence of expense account cheating, independent auditors may present the data to management.

A SEQUENCE OF AUDIT EVENTS

One finds it easy to visualize the auditor performing some audit work at an interim period sometime before a balance sheet date and then completing the work *on* the magic balance sheet date. True, much audit work is done months before the balance sheet date with auditors working for a time, leaving the client's offices, and then returning for the year-end work. Actually, auditors may not even do any work on the balance sheet date itself, but they *always* perform evidence-gathering *after* that date—sometimes as much as six months afterwards.

Interim and Final Audit Work in Independent Auditing

In the "interim" audit work period, the auditor is generally involved in a preliminary study and evaluation of internal accounting control—completing the questionnaires, constructing flowcharts, writing narratives, evaluating strengths and weaknesses, and planning the compliance audit. Some compliance audit procedures are usually performed at interim, and tentative judgments about internal accounting control reliability are made early. Also, auditors can apply audit procedures for substantive auditing of balances as of an interim date, and in this way a significant amount of recalculating, vouching, observing and confirming can be performed early.

When the audit team returns around year-end and receives the final unaudited financial statements (or trial balance) prepared by the client personnel, the auditors can start where they left off at interim and complete the work on internal accounting control evaluation and audit of balances. As a capstone to the procedures, auditors always obtain written client representations.

Client Representations

Management makes many responses to auditors' inquiries during the course of an audit. Many of these responses are very important. To the extent that additional evidence is obtainable through other procedures, the auditor should corroborate client representations.

In addition, *Statement on Auditing Standards, No. 19* (AU 333), "Client Representations," requires that auditors obtain *written* client representations on matters of audit importance. These written representations, however, are not substitutes for corroborating evidence obtainable through applying other auditing procedures. The written representations take the form of a letter on the client's letterhead, addressed to the auditor, signed by a responsible officer (normally the chief executive officer and/or chief financial officer), and dated as of the date of the auditor's report. Thus, the letter covers events and representations running beyond the balance sheet date up to the end of all important field work.

In suggesting audit procedures in previous chapters for the various account areas, oral inquiry of management was frequently cited as applicable. Written representations are normally obtained to formalize responses to oral inquiries, to reduce the possibility of misunderstanding and to document the auditors' investigation of the item. (Auditors frequently draft the management representations to be prepared on company letterhead paper for signature by company representatives.) One purpose of the representations is to remind management of their responsibilities for the financial statements and disclosures.

The following items must appear in management's representations with no limitation due to the materiality:

1. Management's acknowledgement of primary responsibility for fair presentation of financial statements in conformity with generally accepted accounting principles.
2. Availability of all financial records and related data.
3. Completeness of the minutes of stockholders, directors and important committee meetings.
4. Irregularities involving management or employees.

SAS 19 (AU 333) contains a list of 16 other items and discussions of several other points that may be included. The SAS also contains a sample letter. Matters discussed in this and previous chapters that may be included in such a letter are:

☐   Noncompliance with contractual agreements.
☐   Information concerning related party transactions.
☐   Information concerning events occurring subsequent to the balance sheet date.
☐   Disclosure of compensating balances or other restrictions on cash balances.

The written client representations are evidence of the extent of management's cooperation with the auditors. If information is withheld or erroneous information is given by management, the letter serves as a record. Should a lawsuit or other controversy arise, management may be called to account for misinformation given in written client representations.

Client representations are considered an essential part of evidential matter (although not a substitute for other procedures). Management's refusal to furnish a representation the auditor considers essential constitutes a scope limitation which requires a qualification of the auditor's opinion. (See example report in Exhibit 20–12–B in Chapter 20).

However, prior to preparing the representation letter, the auditor will have performed procedures during a time after the balance sheet date on: (1) balances and events that existed at the balance sheet date and (2) events that occurred *after* the balance sheet date.

EVENTS SUBSEQUENT TO THE BALANCE SHEET DATE

Certain material events that occur *subsequent to the balance sheet date but before the end of field work* (thus before issuance of the audit report) require disclosure in the financial statements and related notes. Auditors (and management) are responsible for gathering evidence on these subsequent events and evaluating the proposed disclosure. Material subsequent events have been classified into two types which are disclosed differently. The first type (Type I) requires adjustment of the dollar amounts in the financial statements, while the second (Type II) requires footnote (or pro forma statement) disclosure.

Type I, Adjustment of Dollar Amounts Required

This type of subsequent event provides new information regarding a financial condition that *existed at the date of the balance sheet*. The condition would have been disclosed in the financial statements (or notes thereto) without the subsequent event; however, the subsequent event will affect the estimates and require adjustments in the financial statements.

The following examples of Type I subsequent events are provided in SAS 1 (AU 560.04):

☐ A loss on uncollectible trade accounts receivable as a result of a major customer's bankruptcy. (The customer's deteriorating financial condition is reasoned to have existed prior to the balance sheet date.)

☐ The settlement of litigation for an amount different than estimated (assuming the litigation was initiated prior to the balance sheet date).

Type II, No Adjustment of Financial Statements, but Disclosure Required

The second type of subsequent event involves occurrences that had both their cause and manifestation arising *after the balance sheet date*. Recall that the auditor's responsibility for adequate disclosure runs to the date marking the end of the field work.[1] Consequently, even for those events that occurred after the balance sheet date and are not of the first type requiring financial statement adjustment, auditors must consider their impact on the financial statements and footnotes taken as a whole and may insist that disclosure be made.

Some events that did not exist prior to the balance sheet date may be of such magnitude that disclosure is necessary to keep the financial state-

---

[1] In connection with a registration statement filed under the Securities Act of 1933, responsibility runs to the effective date of the registration statement.

ments from being misleading. Disclosure is normally by footnote; however, occasionally an event may be so significant that the best disclosure would be pro forma financial data. ***Pro forma financial data*** presents supplemental financial statements as if the event had occurred on the date of the balance sheet. For example, in addition to historical financial statements, pro forma financial data may be required if a business is purchased or a major portion of the assets are sold. However, a Type II subsequent event involving stock dividends requires retroactive restatement of the earnings per share computations on the income statement.[2]

Examples of Type II subsequent events provided in SAS 1 (AU 560.04–.06) are:

- ☐ Loss on an uncollectible trade receivable resulting from a fire or flood subsequent to the balance sheet date (as opposed to bankruptcy cited as a Type I event above).

- ☐ Sale of bonds or capital stock.

- ☐ Settlement of litigation when the event giving rise to the claim took place subsequent to the balance sheet date.

- ☐ Loss of plant or inventories as a result of fire or flood.

The aspect of retroactive recognition of the effect of stock dividends and splits is an exception that may be explained briefly with an example. The problem is one of timing and one of informative communication to financial statement users. When the financial statements reach the users, the stock dividend or split may have been effected, and to report financial data as if it had not occurred might be considered misleading.

Illustration.   The company approved a 2-for-1 stock split to be effective February 1. The fiscal year-end was December 31, and the financial statements as of December 31 showed 50 million shares authorized, 10 million shares issued and outstanding and earnings per share of $3.

Audit Resolution. Footnote disclosure was made of the split and of the relevant dates. The equity section of the balance sheet showed 50 million shares authorized, and 20 million shares issued and outstanding. The income statements indicated earnings per share of $1.50. Earnings per share of prior years were adjusted accordingly. The footnote disclosed comparative earnings per share on the predividend shares. The audit report was dated February 25.

Dual Dating in the Audit Report

Dual dating refers to dating the report as of the end of field work along with an additional later date attached to disclosure of a significant subsequent event. Sometimes it happens that *after completion of field work*, but before issuance of the report, a significant event comes to the audit manager's attention. For example, imagine in the illustration given above that

---

[2] *APB Opinion 15,* "Earnings Per Share," (AC 2011A.04).

field work had been completed on January 20 and the audit report was to be so dated, but not yet typed and delivered. Then the auditor learned of the 2-for-1 stock dividend while in the process of preparing the report (or perhaps during the post-field work review described subsequently). In this case, the report would be dated "January 20, except as to footnote X which is dated February 1," (where footnote X is the disclosure of the stock dividend). The audit resolution described above would be the same as before.

The purpose of dual dating is twofold: (1) to provide a means of inserting in the financial statements important information learned after field work is complete and (2) to inform users that the auditor takes full responsibility for all subsequent events only up to the end of field work (January 20, in the example) and for the specifically identified later event (the stock split disclosed in footnote in the example). However, responsibility is not taken for other events not referred to which may have occurred after the end of field work.

Audit Program for the Subsequent Period

Some audit procedures performed in the period subsequent to the balance sheet date may be part of the audit program for determining cutoff and proper valuation of balances as of the balance sheet date. For example:

Using a cutoff bank statement to:

Examine checks paid after year-end that are, or should have been, listed on the bank reconciliation.

Examine bank posting of deposits in transit listed on the bank reconciliation.

Vouch collections on accounts receivable in the month following year-end for evidence of existence and collectibility of the year-end balance.

Trace cash disbursements of the month after year-end to accounts payable for evidence of any liabilities unrecorded at year-end.

Vouch write-downs of fixed assets after year-end for evidence that such valuation problems existed at the year-end date.

Vouch sales of investment securities, write-downs or write-offs in the months after the audit date for evidence of valuation at the year-end date.

Vouch and trace sales transactions in the month after year-end for evidence of proper sales and cost of sales cutoff.

However, the procedures specifically designed for gathering evidence about the two types of subsequent events is different and apart from the rest of the audit program. The procedures shown in Exhibit 19–1 should be performed at or near the completion of field work (or near the effective date, in the case of an SEC registration engagement).

EXHIBIT 19-1
Auditing Procedures for
Subsequent Events

1. Read the latest available interim financial statements, compare them with the financial statements being reported upon, and make any other comparisons considered appropriate in the circumstances. In order to make these procedures as meaningful as possible for the purpose expressed above, the auditor should inquire of officers and other executives having responsibility for financial and accounting matters as to whether the interim statements have been prepared on the same basis as that used for the statements under examination.

2. Inquire of and discuss with officers and other executives having responsibility for financial and accounting matters (limited where appropriate to major locations) as to:
   a. Whether any substantial contingent liabilities or commitments existed at the date of the balance sheet being reported on or at the date of inquiry.
   b. Whether there was any significant change in the capital stock, long-term debt, or working capital to the date of inquiry.
   c. The current status of items, in the financial statements being reported on, that were accounted for on the basis of tentative, preliminary, or inconclusive data.
   d. Whether any unusual adjustments have been made during the period from the balance sheet date to the date of inquiry.

3. Read the available minutes of meetings of stockholders, directors, and appropriate committees; as to meetings for which minutes are not available, inquire about matters dealt with at such meetings.

4. Inquire of client's legal counsel concerning litigation, claims, and assessments. (See SAS 12, AU 337, covered in Chapter 16 of this textbook.)

5. Obtain a letter of representations, dated as of the date of the auditor's report, from appropriate officials, generally the chief executive officer and chief financial officer, as to whether any events occurred subsequent to the date of the financial statements being reported on by the independent auditor that in the officer's opinion would require adjustment or disclosure in these statements. The auditor may elect to have the client include representations as to significant matters disclosed to the auditor in his performance of the procedures in subparagraphs 1–4 above and 6 below.

6. Make such additional inquiries or perform such procedures as he considers necessary and appropriate to dispose of questions that arise in carrying out the foregoing procedures, inquiries, and discussions.

Source: *Statement on Auditing Standards No. 1* (AU 560.12), "Subsequent Events."

The auditing procedures for subsequent events constitute a large part of the *S-1 review,* which is the audit for subsequent events contemplated by the Securities Act of 1933, respecting the auditor's responsibility running to the effective date of a registration statement. In addition to the procedures listed above, the auditor should read the entire prospectus and other pertinent portions of the registration statement and make inquires and obtain written representations (as in item 5 in Exhibit 19–1) up to the effective date. (Refer to SAS 37 (AU 711), "Filings under Federal Securities Statutes.")

However, recall that in the *Escott v. BarChris* lawsuit (Appendix 4–B), the S-1 review was found to be deficient. The audit program for the review was in accordance with generally accepted auditing standards, but the court found that its execution was faulty. Notwithstanding the fact that the several procedures are set out by the AICPA in an authoritative pronouncement, auditors must be careful to see that the execution of them will stand the test of a reasonable critical review. In addition, auditors must be careful to apply procedures that are not on the list if circumstances indicate matters that should be investigated further. Reliance on the *form* of an audit program *may not* serve as a complete defense in some future controversy.

RESPONSIBILITIES AFTER THE AUDIT REPORT HAS BEEN ISSUED

The next two topics do not deal with responsibilities or concerns during the audit, but with responsibilities after the audit is completed and the report has been issued. They are covered here because it is easy to confuse these issues with audit responsibilities; therefore, by presenting them in the same chapter, perhaps you will understand the difference. The topics are: (1) subsequent discovery of facts existing at the date of the audit report and (2) consideration of omitted procedures after the report date. The most important concept to remember is that auditors are responsible to discover subsequent events and for their proper disclosure, but are not responsible to *search for* subsequent facts or omitted procedures. There is no requirement to carry out any retrospective review once the report on financial statements has been issued. However, auditors do have responsibilities once they become aware of the subsequent facts or omitted procedures.

Subsequent Discovery of Facts Existing at the Date of the Auditor's Report

Auditing standards actually deal with two subsequent things: (1) *events* that occur after the balance sheet date and (2) *knowledge* gained after the balance sheet date of events that occurred or conditions that existed on or before the balance sheet date. The subsequent event or subsequently acquired knowledge may arise: (1) before the end of audit field work, (2) after the end of field work, but before issuance of the report or (3) after the audit report is issued. Exhibit 19–2 show a time continuum of these combinations with a key to the auditing standards sections that deal with them.

**EXHIBIT 19–2
Subsequent Events and
Subsequent Discovery**

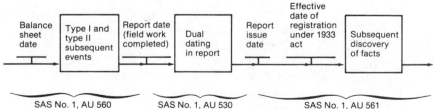

Audit standards relating to discovery of facts subsequent to report issuance may be traced to the *Yale Express* case (*Fischer v. Kletz,* see Appendix 4–B). The situation is one in which the auditors had already issued a report and later become aware of facts that existed at the report date. Auditors are under no obligation to continue performance of any auditing procedures past the report date (except when engaged on an SEC registration statement). However, when they happen to learn of facts that are apparently important, they have the obligation to determine whether the information is reliable and whether the facts existed at the date of the report.[3]

When both of these conditions are affirmed and the auditors believe persons are relying on the report, steps should be taken to withdraw the first report, issue a new report, and inform persons currently relying on the financial statements. These measures are facilitated by cooperation on the part of the client. However, the auditors' duties to notify the public that an earlier report should not be relied upon are not relieved by client objections.

The sequence of decisions is explained in Exhibit 19–3. Basically, these decisions relate to the importance and impact of the information, the cooperation of the client in taking necessary action, and the actions to be taken.

Consideration of Omitted Procedures after the Report Date

Although auditors have no responsibility to continue to review their work once the audit report has been issued, their reports and working papers may be subjected to postissuance review by an outside peer review or the firm's internal inspection program.[4] A *peer review* is a quality assurance review by another auditing firm of an audit firm's quality control policies and procedures and the compliance thereto. As discussed in Chapter 1, firms belonging to the AICPA Division for Firms are required to have a peer review every three years. Such postissuance review may reveal a situation in which the audit was *not* performed in accordance with Generally Accepted Auditing Standards.

Statement on Auditing Standards No. 46, (AU 390) "Consideration of Omitted Procedures After the Report Date," provides guidance for such situations. The sequence of decisions embodied in the SAS is presented in Exhibit 19–4. Because of legal implications of some of the actions proposed, consultation with the firm's attorney is advised. The relevance of the omitted procedure should be measured against the auditors' present ability to support the previously expressed opinion. It may be that after a review of the working papers and discussion with involved audit staff

---

[3] *Statement of Auditing Standards No. 1,* (AU 561.04).

[4] See SAS 25, "The Relationship of Generally Accepted Auditing Standards to Quality Control Standards" (AU 161.02), and related Quality Control Standards regarding the quality control function of inspection.

EXHIBIT 19–3
Subsequent Discovery of
Facts Existing at the Date
of the Auditor's Report

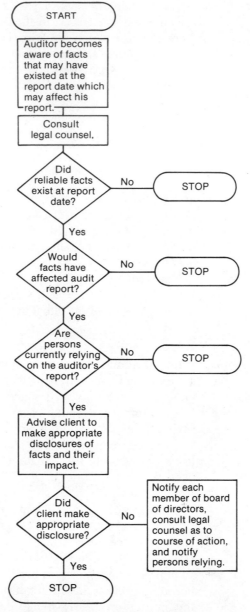

Source: *The CPA Journal*, March 1984, p. 38.
Copyright © 1984 by The New York Society of
Certified Public Accountants.

**EXHIBIT 19–4
Consideration of Omitted
Procedures after the
Report Date**

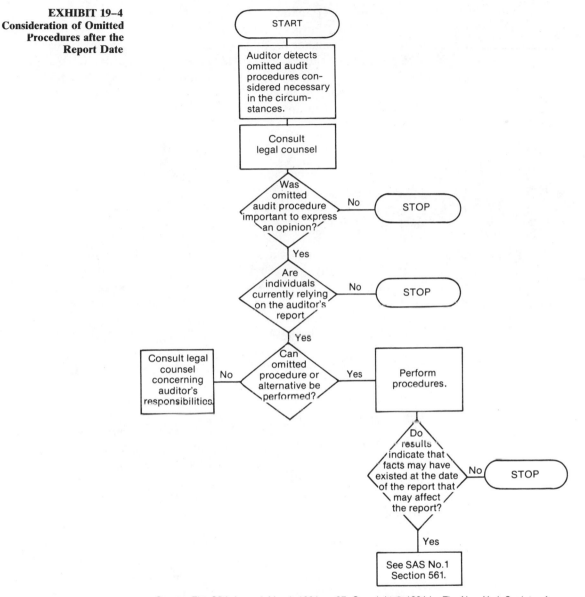

Source: *The CPA Journal,* March 1984, p. 37. Copyright © 1984 by The New York Society of Certified Public Accountants.

personnel, the results of other procedures tend to compensate for the one omitted. In such circumstances, the omitted procedure is not considered to impair the report.

However, if the other procedures are not adequate to compensate for the omitted procedure and the previously expressed opinion cannot be supported, further action is necessary. As with subsequent discovery of facts, the next step is to determine if the auditors' report is still being relied upon. If reliance is still possible, the omitted procedure (or alternative procedures) should be undertaken promptly to provide a basis for the opinion. If in subsequently applying omitted or alternative procedures, facts become known that existed at the date of the original report, then the discussion of the previous section on subsequent discovery of facts applies.

FINAL WRAP-UP

Several items must be completed after all of the evidence is presented before an engagement can be considered finished. The client must approve the proposed adjusting entries and the financial statement footnotes, and the audit work must be reviewed.

Client Approval of Adjusting Entries and Financial Statement Disclosure

The financial statements are the responsibility of management, although auditors frequently draft them. The adjusting entries shown on the sample working papers in this text have been labeled "proposed" to indicate this responsibility of management. Many of the adjusting entries will be approved by management as they are prepared during the work on that area; others will await the final wrap-up to be approved. A formal list of all approved adjusting entries should be given to the client so that formal entries can be made in the accounting records to bring them into balance with the financial statements.

In a like manner, approval of all disclosure by footnotes must be obtained from the client. The footnotes considered necessary are usually drafted as a *proposed* footnote by auditors performing the audit procedures on that item and considered carefully by the audit manager and partner before being presented to the client management for approval. For some items, such as loss contingencies or related party transactions, approval may not be automatic and several rewrites may be necessary before everyone is satisfied that the disclosure is adequate.

Working Paper and Report Review

The audit supervisor must close up the working trial balance by crossfooting each line. The adjusted account balances may be summarized or reclassified (such as moving the current portion of long-term debt to the current liabilities) before financial statements are prepared.

The audit supervisor would also make a final review to ensure all accounts on the trial balance have a working paper reference key number (an indication the audit work has been finished for that account) and that all procedures in the audit program are "signed off" with a date and initials.

The working papers of the audit staff are reviewed soon after being completed by the audit supervisor and sometimes by the audit manager. This review is to ensure that all tick-mark notations are clear, all procedures performed are adequately documented, and all necessary procedures were performed with due care.

The review by the audit manager and engagement partner will focus more on the overall scope of the audit. The audit manager and engagement partner are very involved with the planning of an audit, and they perform some of the field work on special difficult areas. However, they are usually not involved in preparing the detail working papers, such as those illustrated in previous chapters. Even though the working papers were reviewed by the onsite audit supervisor, the review by the partner who is going to sign the audit report is essential.

The working papers and financial statements, including footnotes, are sometimes given a final review on a large engagement by a partner not responsible for the client. This **cold review** is to ensure that the quality of audit work and reporting is in keeping with the quality standards of the audit firm.

The final administrative details (auditors' reports of time on the job, etc.) must be prepared and the working papers prepared for storage. Usually, at the completion of the field work, performance evaluation reports are prepared on the staff auditors by the audit supervisor. During the audit work, especially the study and evaluation of internal control, items are noted which can be made as recommendations to the client. When field work is completed, these items are gathered and written in a letter (commonly referred to as the **management letter**) to be sent to the client. This management letter, which is not required by professional standards, should not be confused with the communication of *material* control weaknesses which is required by the standards (SAS 20, AU 323, discussed in Chapter 7).

To the Reporting Obligation

No matter where the study of auditing is begun, all roads lead to one end product—the auditor's report. The next three chapters deal with the attestation rendered by independent auditors. All the decisions based on sufficient competent evidential matter finally become a part of the reporting decision. It is here that accounting, auditing and your professional sense of fairness in communication join in the art of report construction. The auditor's reporting obligation is the obligation to serve the public interest.

SOURCES AND ADDITIONAL READING REFERENCES

Bacski, J. M., and S. R. M. Rizzo. "Review of Audit Workpapers." *The CPA Journal,* November 1983, pp. 12–20.

Benis, Martin. "The Small Client and Representation Letters." *Journal of Accountancy,* September 1978, pp. 78–85.

Blocher, Edward. "CPA Firms' Staff Evaluation Process." *CPA Journal,* July 1980, pp. 41–47.

Leight, Lester A. "Review of Statement on Auditing Procedure No. 47—'Subsequent Events'." *CPA Journal,* February 1972, pp. 123–26.

Serlin, Jerry. "When an Audit Isn't an Audit." *Journal of Accounting, Auditing and Finance,* Fall 1983, pp. 77–83.

Weirich, T. R., and E. J. Ringelberg. "Omitted Audit Procedures." *The CPA Journal,* March 1984, pp. 34–39.

Zell, B., and D. R. Carmichael. "Management Representation Letters—Adapting Them to the Circumstances." *Journal of Accountancy,* March 1979, pp. 87–90.

REVIEW QUESTIONS

19.1. Certain revenue and expense accounts tend to be audited in conjunction with related balance sheet accounts. For the following revenue and expense accounts, list the most likely related balance sheet accounts:

   Lease revenue.

   Franchise revenue.

   Royalty and license revenue.

   Depreciation expense.

   Repairs and maintenance expense.

   Interest expense.

19.2. Why are many of the revenue and expense accounts only audited by analytical review procedures and not by other procedures?

19.3. Why can "unusual revenue transactions" cause significant audit evidence and reporting problems?

19.4. What is the purpose of a client representation letter? What representations would you expect management to make in a client representation letter with respect to receivables? Inventories? Minutes of meetings? Subsequent events?

19.5. What are the two types of "subsequent events"? In what way(s) are they disclosed differently in the financial statements?

19.6. What treatment is given stock dividends and splits which occur after the balance sheet date, but before the audit report is issued? Explain.

19.7. What is the purpose of "dual dating" an audit report?

19.8. Generally, what additional actions should auditors take in the period between the audit report date and the effective date of a registration statement?

19.9. Distinguish between a "subsequent event" and a "subsequent discovery of fact existing at the report date." Describe the auditors' responsibility for each.

19.10. If subsequent to issuance of a report the audit partner discovers information which existed at the report date and materially impacts the financial statements, what actions should the partner take if the client consents to disclose the information? What an audit of financial statements, are the engagement (arrangements) letter and the client's representation letter.

19.11. If after the report is issued and it is discovered that an auditing procedure was omitted, what are the proper steps the auditors should take?

19.12. Describe a "cold review." What is its purpose?

EXERCISES AND PROBLEMS

19.13. Client Representation Letter

In connection with your audit, you request that management furnish you with a letter containing certain representations. For example: (1) the client has satisfactory title to all assets; (2) no contingent or unrecorded liabilities exist except as disclosed in the letter; (3) no shares of the company's stock are reserved for options, warrants or other rights; and (4) the company is not obligated to repurchase any of its outstanding shares under any circumstances.

Required:

a. Explain why you believe a letter of representation should be furnished you.

b. In what way, if any, do client representations affect your audit procedures and responsibilities?

(*AICPA* adapted)

19.14. Engagement and Client Representation Letters

The two major written understandings between a CPA and client, in connection with an audit of financial statements, are the engagement (arrangements) letter and the client's representation letter.

Required:

a. (1) What are the objectives of the engagement (arrangements) letter?

(2) Who should prepare and sign the engagement letter?

(3) When should the engagement letter be sent?

(4) Why should the engagement letter be renewed periodically?

b. (1) What are the objectives of the client's representation letter?

(2) Who should prepare and sign the client's representation letter?

(3) When should the client's representation letter be obtained?

(4) Why should the client's representation letter be prepared for each examination?

c. A CPA's responsibilities for providing accounting services sometimes involve the association with unaudited financial statements. Discuss the need in this circumstance for:

(1) An engagement letter.

(2) Client's representation letter.

(*AICPA* adapted)

19.15. Client Representation Letter Omissions

During the audit of the annual financial statements of Amis Manufacturing, Inc., the company's president, R. Alderman, and Duddy, the engagement partner, reviewed matters that were supposed to be included in a written representation letter. Upon receipt of the following representation letter, Duddy contacted Alderman to state that it was incomplete.

To Fuddy and Duddy, CPAs:

In connection with your audit of the balance sheet of Amis Manufacturing, Inc., as of December 31, 1985, and the related statements of income, retained earnings and changes in financial position for the year then ended, for purpose of expressing an opinion as to whether the financial statements present fairly the financial position, results of operations and changes in financial position of Amis Manufacturing, Inc., in conformity with generally accepted accounting principles, we confirm, to the best of our knowledge and belief, the following representations made to you during your audit. There were no:

☐ Plans or intentions that may materially affect the carrying value or classification of assets or liabilities.

☐ Communications from regulatory agencies concerning noncompliance with, or deficiencies in, financial reporting practices.

☐ Agreements to repurchase assets previously sold.

☐ Violations or possible violations of laws or regulations whose effects should be considered for disclosure in the financial statements or as a basis for recording a loss contingency.

☐ Unasserted claims or assessments that our lawyer has advised are probable of assertion that must be disclosed in accordance with Statement of Financial Accounting Standards 5.

☐ Capital stock repurchase options or agreements or capital stock reserved for options, warrants, conversions or other requirements.

☐ Compensating balance or other arrangements involving restrictions on cash balances.

R. Alderman, President
Amis Manufacturing, Inc.
March 14, 1986

Required:

Identify the other matters that Alderman's representation letter should specifically confirm.

(*AICPA* adapted)

19.16. **Subsequent Events**

You are nearing the completion of an examination of the financial statements of Jubilee, Inc., for the year ended December 31, 1985. You are concerned with ascertaining the occurrence of subsequent events that may require adjustment or disclosure essential for a fair presentation in conformity with generally accepted accounting principles.

Required:

a. Briefly explain what is meant by the phrase "subsequent event."

b. How do those subsequent events which require financial statement adjustment differ from those that require financial statement disclosure?

c. What are the procedures which would be performed to ascertain the occurrence of subsequent events?

(*AICPA* adapted)

19.17. **Subsequent Events and Contingent Liabilities**

Dudwin, Inc. is preparing its annual financial statements and annual report to shareholders. Management wants to be sure that all of the necessary and proper disclosures are incorporated into the financial statements and the annual report. Two classes of items which have an important bearing on the financial statements are subsequent events and contingent liabilities. The financial statements could be materially inaccurate or misleading if proper disclosure of these items is not made.

Required:

a. With respect to subsequent events:

(1) Define what is meant by a "subsequent event."

(2) Identify the two types of subsequent events and explain the appropriate presentation of each type.

b. With respect to contingent liabilities:

(1) Identify the essential elements of a contingent liability.

(2) Explain how a contingent liability should be disclosed in the financial statements.

c. Explain how a subsequent event may relate to a contingent liability. Give an example to support your answer.

(*CMA* Adapted)

19.18. **Subsequent Events Procedures**

You are in the process of "winding up" the field work on Top Stove Corporation, a company engaged in the manufacture and sale of kerosene space heating stoves. To date, there has been every indication that the financial statements of the client present fairly the position of the company at December 31 and the results of its operations for the year then ended. Top Stove had total assets at December 31 of $4 million and a net profit for the year (after deducting federal and state income tax provisions) of $285,000. The principal records of the company are a general ledger, cash receipts record, voucher register, sales register, check register and general journal. Financial statements are prepared monthly. Your field work will be completed on February 20, and you plan to deliver the report to the client by March 12.

Required:

a. Prepare a brief statement about the purpose and period to be covered in a review of subsequent events.

b. Outline the postaudit review program which you would follow to determine what transactions involving material amounts, if any, have occurred since the balance sheet date.

(*AICPA* adapted)

19.19.   Subsequent Events—Cases

The following events occurred in independent cases, but in each instance the event happened after the close of the fiscal year under audit, but before all members of the audit team had left the office of the client. State in each case what disclosure, if any, you would expect in the financial statements (and notes thereto). The balance sheet date in each instance is December 31.

1. Merchandise handled by the company had been traded in the open market in which it procures its supplies at $1.40 on December 31. This price had prevailed for two weeks, following an official market report that predicted vastly enlarged supplies; however, no purchases were made at $1.40. The price throughout the preceding year had been about $2 which is the level experienced over several years. On January 18, the price returned to $2 following public disclosure of an error in the official calculations of the prior December, correction of which destroyed the expectations of excessive supplies. In-

ventory at December 31 was valued on a lower-of-cost-or-market basis.

2. On February 1, the board of directors adopted a resolution accepting the offer of an investment banker to guarantee the marketing of $100 million of preferred stock.

3. On January 22, one of the three major plants of the client burned with a loss of $50 million which was covered to the extent of $40 million by insurance.

4. The client in this case is an investment company of the open-end type. In January, a wholly new management came into control. By February 20, the new management had sold 90 percent of the investments carried at December 31 and had purchased others of a substantially more speculative character.

5. This company has a wholly owned but not consolidated subsidiary producing oil in a foreign country. A serious rebellion began in that country on January 18 and continued beyond the completion of your audit work. The press in this country has carried extensive coverage of the progress of the fighting.

(*AICPA* adapted)

19.20.   Subsequent Events—Cases

In connection with your examination of the financial statements of Olars Manufacturing Corporation for the year ended December 31, your postbalance sheet data audit procedures disclosed the following items:

1. January 3: The state government approved a plan for the construction of an express highway. The plan will result in the appropriation of a portion of the land area owned by Olars Manufacturing Corporation. Construction will begin late next year. No estimate of the condemnation award is available.

2. January 4: The funds for a $25,000 loan to the corporation made by Mr. Olars on July 15 were obtained by him with a

loan on his personal life insurance policy. The loan was recorded in the account entitled Loan from Officers. Mr. Olars's source of the funds was not disclosed in the company records. The corporation pays the premiums on the life insurance policy, and Mrs. Olars, wife of the president, is the owner and beneficiary of the policy.

3. January 7: The mineral content of a shipment of ore en route on December 31 was determined to be 72 percent. The shipment was recorded at year-end at an estimated content of 50 percent by a debit to raw material inventory and a credit to accounts payable in the amount of $20,600. The final liability to the vendor is based on the actual mineral content of the shipment.

4. January 15: A series of personal disagreements have arisen between Mr. Olars, the president, and Mr. Tweedy, his brother-in-law, the treasurer. Mr. Tweedy resigned, effective immediately, under an agreement whereby the corporation would purchase his 10 percent stock ownership at book value as of December 31. Payment is to be made in two equal amounts in cash on April 1 and October 1. In December, the treasurer had obtained a divorce from his wife who was Mr. Olars's sister.

5. January 31: As a result of reduced sales, production was curtailed in mid-January and some workers were laid off. On February 5, all the remaining workers went on strike. To date the strike is unsettled.

6. February 10: A contract was signed whereby Mammoth Enterprises purchased from Olars Manufacturing Corporation all of the latter's fixed assets (including rights to receive the proceeds of any property condemnation), inventories, and the right to conduct business under the name "Olars Manufacturing Division." The effective

date of the transfer will be March 1. The sale price was $500,000, subject to adjustment following the taking of a physical inventory. Important factors contributing to the decision to enter into the contract were the policy of the board of directors of Mammoth Industries to diversify the firm's activities and the report of a survey conducted by an independent market appraisal firm which revealed a declining market for Olars' products.

Required:

Assume that the above items came to your attention prior to completion of your audit field work on February 15. For each of the above items:

a. Give the audit procedures, if any, that would have brought the item to your attention. Indicate other sources of information that may have revealed the item.

b. Discuss the disclosure that you would recommend for the item, listing all details that should be disclosed. Indicate those items or details, if any, that should not be disclosed. Give your reasons for recommending or not recommending disclosure of the items or details.

(*AICPA* adapted)

19.21. **Subsequent Discovery of Fact**
On June 1, Albert Faultless of A. J. Faultless & Co., CPAs noticed some disturbing information about his client, Hopkirk Company. A story in the local paper mentioned the indictment of Tony Baker whom A. J. knew as the assistant controller at Hopkirk. The charge was mail fraud. A. J. made discreet inquiries with the controller at Hopkirk's headquarters and learned that Baker had been speculating in foreign currency futures. In fact, part of Baker's work at Hopkirk involved managing the company's foreign currency. Unfortunately, Baker had violated company policy, lost a small amount of money, decided to specu-

late some more, lost some more, and eventually lost $7 million in company funds. The mail fraud was involved in his attempt to cover his activity until he recovered the original losses. Most of the events were in process on March 1, when A. J. had signed and dated the unqualified report on Hopkirk's financial statements for the year ended on the previous December 31.

A. J. determined that the information would probably affect the decisions of external users and advised Hopkirk's chief executive to make the disclosure. She flatly refused to make any disclosure, arguing that the information was immaterial. On June 17, A. J. provided the subsequent information in question to a news reporter and it was printed in *The Wall Street Journal* along with a statement that the financial statements and accompanying audit report could not be relied upon.

Required:

Evaluate the actions of Faultless & Co., CPAs with respect to the subsequent information discovered. What other action might Faultless & Co. have taken? What are the possible legal effects of the firm's actions, if any?

19.22. **Omitted Audit Procedures**
The following are independent situations that have occurred in your audit firm, Arthur Hurdman (AH):[5]

1. During the internal inspection review by the regional office of AH, one of your clients, Wildcat Oil Suppliers, was selected for review. The reviewers questioned the thoroughness of inventory obsolescence procedures, especially in light of the depressed state of the oil exploration industry at the time. They felt that specific procedures, which they considered appropriate, were not performed by your audit team.

2. Top Stove, one of your clients, installed a microcomputer in July of 1984 to process part of their accounting transactions. You completed the audit of Top Stove's December 31, 1985 statements on February 15, 1985. During the April 1985 review work on Top Stove's first quarter financial information, you discovered that during the audit of the 1985 statements only the manual records were investigated in the search for unrecorded liabilities.

3. AH belongs to the Private Companies Practice Section (PCPS) of the AICPA Division of Firms. In keeping with membership requirements of the PCPS, AH contracted with Haskin and Anderson (HA) to conduct a peer review of AH's audit quality control procedures. In HA's report to AH, the audit of Al's Hardware Store Organization (AHSO) was criticized with references to the letterhead on AHSO's representation letter. Although the representation letter complied with the requirements of SAS 19, it was prepared on the letterhead of the Palo Alto Garden Club. (Al's wife, Alice, had been president of the club during the period of the audit.)

Required:
a. Without regard to the specific situations given, answer the following questions:
   (1) What are the proper steps auditors should take when they discover, after the report date, an important auditing procedure was omitted?
   (2) How are auditors' decisions affected if, after review of the workpapers, compensating procedures were found to have been performed in place of the omitted procedure?
   (3) If in subsequently applying the omitted procedure the auditors become aware of mate-

---

[5] Situation derived from examples given in Thomas R. Weirich and Elizabeth J. Ringelberg, "Omitted Audit Procedures," *The CPA Journal,* March 1984, p. 36.

rial new information that should have been disclosed in the financial statements, how should they proceed?

b. Describe the proper action to take in each situation given the additional information provided below:

Case 1: A thorough consideration was made by you of the scope of the audit of Wildcat Oil Suppliers, and you made a detailed review of the working papers. You have concluded that compensating procedures were conducted sufficiently to support the valuation of inventory.

Case 2: Your subsequent investigation of the microcomputer records of Top Stove revealed that material liabilities were not recorded as of December 31.

Case 3: You were requested to investigate the AHSO alleged audit procedure deficiency. Your investigation revealed that AHSO had a significant loan from the local bank that had received the AH report on AHSO's financial statements. The loan is still outstanding, and indeed the representation letter was written on the garden club letterhead.

19.23.   **Cold Review and Dual Dating**
You have been assigned to perform a cold review of a correspondent CPA firm's audit of Oxford Millwork Company for the calendar year ending December 31. In the audited financial statements of Oxford Millwork Company, you find the following representations:

Common stock, par $10, authorized
  400,000 shares, outstanding
  100,000 shares (note 1) $1,000,000

Note 1: Subsequent event (dated January 20). The board of directors approved a 3-for-1 stock dividend effective January 20. At the effective date, the par value of outstanding common stock is $3,000,000.

You have reviewed the correspondent CPA firm's audit report and found the opinion dated "January 15, 19xx, except as to note 1 which is dated January 20, 19xx."

Required:
a. What is the purpose of a cold review?
b. What is the purpose of dual dating?
c. What recommendations would you make to the CPA firm concerning presentation of the subsequent event?

DISCUSSION CASE

19.24.   **Recognizing Income of a Purchased Subsidiary**
The following brief dialogue occurred in a controversy wherein a plaintiff claimed that management backdated the effective date of an acquisition in order to pump up earnings improperly. The independent auditors, Eastford and Redwood, are involved because they signed an unqualified report on the consolidated financial statements in question.

Plaintiff's Attorney: Plaintiff alleges that COSIF Company's purchase of 100 percent of the stock of Prosper, Inc., was effective on April 28, almost four months after the beginning of COSIF's fiscal year on January 1. COSIF included in consolidated income the results of Prosper's operations for the full 12 months ended December 31. This was improper accounting which failed to reflect the substance of the transaction.

Eastford and Redwood knew, or should have known, that the effective date was April 28. The evidence shown today proves that the first written agreement concerning the acquisition was a memorandum agreement dated March 5 which set forth the general terms of the transaction. The final written agreement was signed and dated on April 28. Their unqualified opinion was improperly rendered.

Eastford and Redwood. The issue is whether January 1 or some later date should have been used as the acquisition date for accounting purposes. We stipulate that the first written memorandum was dated March 5 and the final agreement April 28. However, we have also introduced into evidence written representations from the president of COSIF and COSIF's outside counsel that an oral agreement substantially equivalent to the March 5 memorandum agreement was reached on or about January 1. COSIF's outside counsel is one of the most highly regarded law firms on the East coast.

These representations were meaningful to us because we were not engaged as COSIF's auditors until November 14 and were not present when the actual negotiations took place.

Plaintiff alleges that applicable accounting principles were misapplied (APB Opinion No. 16, paragraph 93, Section 1091.93), because no written agreement existed on January 1.

We insist that elements of the April 28 agreement, which made the acquisition effective *as of* January 1, show that the *substance* of the transaction supports our conclusion that January 1 was the proper accounting date. We cite the following:

1. COSIF and Prosper clearly intended an effective date of January 1.
2. The fixed portion of the purchase price depended upon a minimum amount of Prosper's income through December 31 of the year preceding. (At March 5 the audit of Prosper's prior fiscal year had not yet been completed.)
3. The contingent portion of the purchase price depended upon an agreed minimum amount of Prosper's income for the year beginning January 1 and two years thereafter.
4. Warranties made by Prosper as to assets and liabilities were as of December 31 (just prior to the January 1 effective date).
5. Interest on COSIF's notes issued as a part of the payment package ran from January 1.
6. The full amount of Prosper's earnings from January 1 inured to the benefit of COSIF.

Question:

What is the proper accounting date for COSIF's acquisition of Prosper?

P A R T 4

Reporting Responsibilities

CHAPTER 20

PROFESSIONAL STANDARDS SOURCES

Compendium Section	Document Reference	Topic
AU 340	SAS 34	Auditor's Considerations When a Question Arises About an Entity's Continued Existence
AU 410	SAS 1	Adherence to Generally Accepted Accounting Principles
AU 9410		Interpretations: Adherence to GAAP
AU 411	SAS 5	Meaning of "Present Fairly in Conformity with Generally Accepted Accounting Principles" in the Independent Auditor's Report
AU 9411		Interpretations: The Meaning of "Present Fairly . . ."
AU 420	SAS 1	Consistency of Application of Generally Accepted Accounting Principles
AU 9420		Interpretations: Consistency of Application of GAAP
AU 431	SAS 32	Adequacy of Disclosure in Financial Statements
AU 504	SAS 26	Association with Financial Statements
AU 9504		Interpretations: Association with Financial Statements
AU 509	SAS 2	Reports on Audited Financial Statements
AU 9509		Interpretations: Reports on Audited Financial Statements
AU 530	SAS 1	Dating of the Independent Auditor's Report
AU 542	SAS 1	Other Conditions Which Preclude the Application of Necessary Auditing Procedures

PROFESSIONAL STANDARDS SOURCES		
Compendium Section	Document Reference	Topic
AU 544	SAS 1	Lack of Conformity with Generally Accepted Accounting Principles (Regulated Companies)
AU 545	SAS 1	Inadequate Disclosure
AU 546	SAS 1	Reporting on Inconsistency
AU 621	SAS 14	Special Reports (Comprehensive Basis Other than GAAP)
AU 9621		Interpretations: Special Reports

Reports by Independent Auditors

LEARNING OBJECTIVES

Auditors maintain that company management has the primary responsibility for the fair presentation of financial statements in conformity with generally accepted accounting principles. Nevertheless, auditors have primary responsibility for their own audit reports on the financial statements. The fourth reporting standard requires auditors to report: (1) the character of an audit in the scope paragraph and (2) their conclusion (opinion) on the financial statements in the opinion paragraph.

You must know the standard unqualified report as a starting place since this chapter explains various reasons for changing the standard language when auditors cannot give this so-called "clean" opinion. Your objectives with respect to variations in audit reports are to be able to:

□ Determine whether an accountant is *associated with* financial statements in given factual circumstances.

□ Describe the extent of evidence auditors need to give the unqualified and adverse opinions and the opinions qualified for departures from GAAP and inconsistent application of GAAP.

673

□ Identify and describe at least seven departures from the standard unqualified report language, and explain the circumstances involved. (Given such circumstances, be able to write the reports.)

□ Name and describe one or more *comprehensive bases of accounting other than GAAP,* and tell how auditors report on such financial statements.

□ Identify and describe at least six circumstances that cause auditors to qualify the consistency phrase in audit opinions.

□ Discuss the problems of reporting on *uncertainties,* particularly the options for reporting when the going concern assumption is in doubt.

□ Write an audit report conforming to GAAS for a given description of accounting facts and audit circumstances.

□ Identify errors of form and substance in an audit report and rewrite the report in accordance with applicable GAAS.

Auditing standards require a report to be rendered in *all* cases where an accountant's name is *associated with* financial statements. As a public accountant, you are associated with financial statements when (1) you have consented to the use of your name in connection with the statements or (2) you have prepared, or assisted in preparing, the statements, even if your name is not used in any written report.[1]

The concept of association is far-reaching. Public accountants and auditors are associated with financial statements and must render reports even in cases such as these: (1) Financial statements are merely reproduced on an accountant's letterhead; (2) Financial statements are produced by the accountant's computer as part of a bookkeeping service and (3) A document containing financial statements merely identifies an accountant as the public accountant or auditor for the company. The reason a report is required is that most users of financial statements assume an audit has been conducted and "everything is OK" whenever an independent accountant is known to be involved with financial statements. Consequently, an obligation exists to inform the users about the nature of the work performed, if any, and conclusions the accountant has made about the financial statements.

In practice, accountants and auditors can render a variety of conclusions about financial statements, and the range of this variety is known as *levels of assurance.* You were introduced to several such levels in Exhibit 1–1 in this book. The highest level of assurance is considered to be the

---

[1] SAS 26, *Association with Financial Statements* (AU 504.03).

standard unqualified report (sometimes known as the "clean opinion"). Various changes in the language of the standard unqualified report are the signs of lower levels of assurance. In auditing standards, these language changes are called *qualifications, modifications* and *expansions.* This chapter explains many forms of these changes, and they are summarized at the end of the chapter. More changes are explained in Chapters 21 and 22.

The lowest level of assurance is the *disclaimer of opinion.* With the disclaimer, you assert that you have no opinion or conclusions about the financial statements.

The decisions required in formulating a report have characteristics of ethical decisions. Accountants must evaluate objectively the impact of the report on users' decisions. Reporting decisions also have characteristics of technical decisions requiring knowledge of generally accepted accounting principles and generally accepted auditing standards.

AN ETHICAL-TECHNICAL ENVIRONMENT

The rule of ethics most closely related to reporting decisions is Rule 301: "A member shall not disclose any confidential information obtained in the course of a professional engagement except with the consent of the client." However, Rule 301 also states: "This rule shall not be construed (*a*) to relieve a member of his obligation under Rules 202 and 203. . . ." The latter two rules require auditors to comply with generally accepted auditing standards and to report on compliance with generally accepted accounting principles. Both the auditing standards of reporting and the accounting principles require adequate disclosure of materially important financial information.

Thus, the confidential information rule is not relevant with regard to information necessary for adequate financial communication. In a social context, the user's needs are superior to management's desire to consider information confidential. However, the distinction between materially important information and unimportant information is often difficult to make in practice. In questionable situations, auditors find themselves involved in a process of ethical reflective choice, particularly in terms of projecting thoughts about information forward to users' information needs.

Subordination of Time-Cost Constraints

Throughout this textbook, an underlying presumption has been that an audit must be completed in a timely manner at a cost acceptable to management. However applicable these time and cost constraints may be in the performance of field work, they are ultimately subordinate when writing the report. Consistent with a scientific decision-making approach and consistent with the third AICPA field work standard (requiring sufficient competent evidential matter as a basis for an opinion), the quality and quantity of evidential matter is ultimately evaluated independently of the time and cost taken to obtain it.

If the evidence is insufficient at the time the report is written, an unqualified opinion cannot be rendered. Attestation report decisions are governed by what auditors know through evidence, without any "discount" for the ease or difficulty experienced in gathering the evidence.

As a general rule, auditors cannot resort to the device known as *negative assurance* when writing an attestation opinion on financial statements purporting to show financial position and results of operations. A *negative assurance* is a statement to the effect that, "Nothing came to our attention which would indicate that these statements are not presented properly." The negative assurance of this type does not adequately indicate whether appropriate attention was given to enable the accountants to know whether statements were or were not presented properly.[2]

Basic Content of the Standard Report

The standard unqualified report was introduced in Chapter 1 of this text and an actual example is in Exhibit 20–2. The technical explanation of the contents of the report is not repeated here but should be reviewed at this time. (Refer to Chapter 1.)

Scope Paragraph. The standard report consists of two segments. The *scope paragraph* is the auditor's report of the character of his or her own work in the audit examination. This portion of the report is vitally important for disclosure of the quality and extent of the audit itself. Auditors must render a fair presentation of their own work, as well as an opinion on the financial statements.

All of the meaning of the general and field work standards is implicit in the scope paragraph, including: (1) The auditors were trained and proficient; (2) The auditors were independent; (3) Due professional care was exercised; (4) The work was planned and supervised; (5) Internal control was properly studied and evaluated and (6) Sufficient competent evidential matter was obtained. To the extent that one or more of these general and field work standards is *not* actually satisfied during an audit, the scope paragraph must be *qualified.* A qualification in this paragraph means the addition of words explaining exactly *which* standard was not satisfied and *why* it was not satisfied. Such qualifications may be caused by lack of independence, lack of sufficient competent evidence, or restrictions on procedures imposed by the client. In practice, auditors always change the standard opinion paragraph language when the scope paragraph is qualified.

---

[2] SAS 26 (AU 504.18). However, negative assurances are permitted in letters to underwriters (SAS 38, AU 631) and in certain financial statements that do not purport to present financial position and results of operations (SAS 26, AU 504.20), in certain kinds of special reports (SAS 14, AU 621.18–.19 and SAS 35, AU 622.05–.06), and in certain reports on a review of interim financial information (SAS 36, AU 722.16–.22).

Opinion Paragraph.   The other basic segment of the report is the **opinion paragraph**. Users of audited financial statements are generally most interested in the opinion. The opinion paragraph contains the accountant's conclusions about the financial statements. It is a public manifestation of the private audit decision process.

The reporting standards are incorporated in the opinion paragraph:

1. The report shall state whether the financial statements are presented in accordance with generally accepted accounting principles.
2. The report shall state whether such principles have been consistently observed in the current period in relation to the preceding period.
3. Informative disclosures in the financial statements are to be regarded as reasonably adequate unless otherwise stated in the report.
4. The report shall either contain an expression of opinion regarding the financial statements, taken as a whole, or an assertion to the effect that an opinion cannot be expressed. When an overall opinion cannot be expressed, the reasons should be stated. In all cases wherein an auditor's name is associated with financial statements, the report should contain a clear-cut indication of the character of the auditor's examination, if any, and the degree of responsibility he is taking.

When reading the reporting standards, you should understand the term *financial statements* to include not only the traditional balance sheet, income statement, and statement of changes in financial position, but also all the footnote disclosures and additional information (e.g., earnings per share calculations) that are integral elements of the basic financial presentation required by FASB pronouncements. The first, second and fourth standards are explicit in the standard report. The third standard is effective on an exception-reporting basis; that is, the report comments on disclosures only when they are considered inadequate. The adequacy of disclosures may be judged by GAAP requirements, but auditors must also be sensitive to the information needs of investors, creditors and other users when considering the need to disclose information that is not explicitly required by GAAP. Disgruntled investors often use the ''lack of informative disclosure'' criterion as a basis for lawsuits.

The objective of the fourth reporting standard is to enable shareholders, credit grantors and others who use financial statements to determine the extent to which financial statements reported by CPAs may be relied upon. This standard requires that when an auditor's name is associated with financial statements, the auditor should (1) express an opinion on the financial statements taken as a whole or (2) assert that an opinion cannot be expressed.

A **disclaimer of opinion** is an assertion that an opinion cannot be expressed. When a disclaimer is given, the auditor takes no responsibility whatsoever for reporting on the financial statements. This assertion is a "no opinion." The auditor does not know whether the statements are fairly presented or materially misleading.

Both the unqualified opinion and the adverse opinion are opinions regarding the financial statements "taken as a whole." The *unqualified opinion* states that financial statements *are* presented in conformity with GAAP, and the *adverse opinion* states that they *are not*. Even though the adverse opinion is an "overall opinion," reasons are always given to explain why the opinion is adverse. You should be aware that an auditor needs at least as much evidence to support an adverse opinion as an unqualified opinion. Both opinions assert that the auditor *knows,* and knowing requires a sufficient competent evidential basis. With both types of opinion, auditors take full responsibility for their reports on financial statements.

However, the degree of responsibility taken may be less than full when some kinds of *qualified opinions* are rendered. Qualified opinions are opinions on financial statements "taken as a whole" but with an exception taken to one or more specific discrepancies or uncertainties. Auditing standards also provide for the use of "subject to" qualification language when uncertainties exist in the client's business. Examples of such uncertainties include questions about the realizable value of major plant and equipment assets held for sale and the future outcome of significant lawsuits. Evidence about the future outcome of such uncertainties is not obtainable, so auditors *flag* them by writing that the opinion is "subject to" the outcome of the specific matter. Theoretically, the "subject to" qualification means the auditor expresses no opinion on the conformity with GAAP of the item affected by uncertainty. Usually, the GAAP problem at issue is the proper valuation of an asset or liability.

Some opinion qualifications are matters of auditor knowledge and auditor responsibility. Qualifications based on a departure from generally accepted accounting principles or an inconsistency in the application of accounting principles become qualifications because the auditor has full knowledge of them. Flagging matters such as these as the reasons for a qualified opinion means that the auditor takes responsibility for the accuracy of his or her statement about the item in question.

REPORTS AND THE MATERIALITY DIMENSION

When an auditor makes decisions about the audit report, immaterial or unimportant information can be ignored and treated as if it did not exist. However, when information passes a materiality threshold, the audit report decision is affected. In connection with reporting decisions, there is also a theory of *lesser* and *greater* materiality. *Lesser materiality* means that the item in question is important and needs to be disclosed or the opinion needs to be qualified for it. The information cannot simply be ignored. *Greater materiality* means that the item in question is very important and has an extreme impact on the reporting decision.

Quantitative measures of materiality, however, are only part of the problem. Information may be considered *material* or *important* in light of these considerations:

Magnitude. The quantitative size of an amount in question is one feature of its importance. Size—materiality—may be analyzed in terms of an absolute amount or in relation to other financial statement amounts.

Uncertainty of outcome. An event whose occurrence is probable is more important than one whose occurrence is merely possible or remote.

Likelihood of error. A financial statement item in a high-risk area (for example, receivables on land sales contracts) deserves more attention than one in a low-risk or routine area.

Expertise of the auditor. Whether an auditor can reach a decision or needs to call upon the skills of another expert has an impact on the reporting decision. For example, valuations of diamond inventories or mineral reserves are usually beyond the expertise of auditors. Also, auditors' ability to predict the future is usually no better than other persons' abilities (for example, predicting the outcome of litigation in progress).

Pervasive impact on financial statements. Financial statement items may affect a few accounts or many. Errors in inventory valuation, for example, affect cost of goods sold, gross margin, net income, income tax expense, inventory balances, and tax liabilities. Items with such pervasive effects are handled differently from items that have limited or isolated effects.

Auditing standards refer to eight basic circumstances that cause departures from the standard, unqualified audit report. These circumstances are shown in Exhibit 20–1 in relation to a materiality dimension. Each report that is qualified when the item is of *lesser materiality* becomes a disclaimer or an adverse report when the item is one of *greater materiality*.

REPORTING WITH FULLY SUFFICIENT COMPETENT EVIDENCE

Decisions about the content of an audit report may also be organized along an evidence dimension. The remainder of this chapter adopts the evidence dimension because it pervades all choices of report form and content and because it is related directly to the technical-procedural elements of an audit. The remaining coverage in this chapter is limited to ''financial statements taken as a whole which purport to present financial position and results of operations.''

EXHIBIT 20–1
The Effect of Materiality
on Audit Reports

Circumstances for Departure from Standard Audit Report	Required Type of Report	
Materiality Dimension	**←Lesser**	**Greater→**
	Materiality	
Limitation on scope (AU 509.10–.13).	*Qualified* "Except For" Opinion paragraph refers to possible effects on financial statements.	*Disclaimer* Separate paragraph discloses limitation—no reference to procedures performed.
Opinion based partially on report of another auditor (AU 509.14, 543).	*Unqualified* Scope paragraph discloses reliance and opinion paragraph refers to report of other auditors. (See Chapter 21 for details.)	
Departure from GAAP (AU 509.15–.17).	*Qualified* "Except For" Separate paragraph discloses substantive reasons and principal effects.	*Adverse* Separate paragraph discloses substantive reasons and principal effects.
Departure from an official pronouncement (AU 509.18–.19).	*Qualified** "Except For" Separate paragraph discloses substantive reasons and principal effects.	*Adverse** Separate paragraph discloses substantive reasons and principal effects.
Lack of consistency (AU 509.20, 546).	See Exhibit 20–7.	
Auditor is not independent (AU 504).	*Disclaimer* Scope paragraph states explicitly that the auditor is not independent.	
Uncertainty (AU 509.21–.26).	*Qualified* "Subject To" Separate paragraph discloses substantive reasons.	*Disclaimer* Separate paragraph discloses substantive reasons.
Emphasis of a matter (AU 509.27).	*Unqualified* Separate paragraph discusses the matter.	

* Where the departure is *necessary* to make the financials not misleading, an unqualified opinion is issued with an explanation of the circumstances (Ethics Rule 203).

Source: Adapted from D. Causey, "Newly Emerging Standards of Auditor Responsibility," *Accounting Review*, January 1976, p. 25.

Auditors are in the most comfortable position when they have all the evidence needed to make a report decision. The standard form of the report can be used without modification if the unqualified opinion is to be given. Likewise, auditors must have sufficient competent evidence in order to decide to use the adverse form of the opinion.

Unqualified Opinion   Auditing standards explain the unqualified opinion as follows:

> An unqualified opinion states that the financial statements present fairly financial position, results of operations, and changes in financial position in conformity with generally accepted accounting principles (which include adequate disclosure) consistently applied. . . . This conclusion may be expressed only when the auditor has formed such an opinion on the basis of an examination made in accordance with generally accepted auditing standards.[3]

This explanation ties the quality of "present fairly" closely to conformity with generally accepted accounting principles, but the parenthetical phrase—"(which include adequate disclosure)"—opens the possibility that matters on which official accounting pronouncements are silent might be necessary for a fair presentation. In fact, Ethics Rule 203 provides for the possibility that *adherence* to pronouncements of accounting standards *might* create misleading financial statements.

> **Rule 203.**   A member shall not express an opinion that financial statements are presented in conformity with generally accepted accounting principles if such statements contain any departure from an accounting principle promulgated by the body designated by Council to establish such principles which has a material effect on the statements taken as a whole, *unless* the member can demonstrate that due to unusual circumstances the financial statements would otherwise have been misleading. In such cases his report must describe the departure, the approximate effect thereof, if practicable, and the reasons why compliance with the principle would result in a misleading statement. (Emphasis added.)

Auditing standards place some emphasis on Rule 203 by providing that when such unusual circumstances exist, the auditor's report should explain them in a middle paragraph(s). In such cases, the opinion paragraph can be unqualified with respect to conformity with generally accepted accounting principles.[4] Public opinion and court cases have tended to assert dominance of the idea of "present fairly" over "conformity with generally accepted accounting principles." Ethics Rule 203 and the audit-

---

[3] SAS 2 (AU 509.28).

[4] SAS 2 (AU 509.19). This provision has the effect of allowing financial statements to contain a departure from an official pronouncement, permitting the auditor to explain why the departure was necessary in order that financial statements *not* be misleading, and then allowing the departure to be "in conformity with generally accepted accounting principles" as indicated by the unqualified opinion paragraph.

ing standards tend to confirm this dominance. However, "Rule 203 opinions" are very rare in practice.

A typical unqualified report is shown in Exhibit 20–2. The report covers comparative financial statements. The report in Exhibit 20–3 is an example of an unqualified report that conforms to Ethics Rule 203, noting a departure from promulgated accounting principles. Generally, however, departures from accounting principles cause the auditor to render an adverse or qualified opinion.

EXHIBIT 20–2
Unqualified Report

Board of Directors
Texas Commerce Bancshares, Inc.:

We have examined the consolidated balance sheets of Texas Commerce Bancshares, Inc., and subsidiaries and the balance sheets of Texas Commerce Bancshares, Inc. (parent company only) as of December 31, 1982 and 1981, and the related statements of income, changes in stockholders' equity, and changes in financial position for each of the three years in the period ended December 31, 1982. Our examinations were made in accordance with generally accepted auditing standards and, accordingly, included such tests of the accounting records and such other auditing procedures as we considered necessary in the circumstances.

In our opinion, the financial statements referred to above present fairly the consolidated financial position of Texas Commerce Bancshares, Inc. and subsidiaries and Texas Commerce Bankshares, Inc. (parent company only) at December 31, 1982 and 1981, and the results of their operations and changes in their financial position for each of the three years in the period ended December 31, 1982, in conformity with generally accepted accounting principles applied on a consistent basis.

/s/Ernst & Whinney
January 21, 1983

Comprehensive Basis Other than GAAP

Companies sometimes choose to present financial information in accordance with a comprehensive basis of accounting other than GAAP. A *comprehensive basis* in this context refers to a coherent accounting treatment in which substantially all the important financial measurements are governed by criteria other than GAAP. Some examples include: (1) insurance company statements conforming to state regulatory agency accounting rules, (2) tax basis accounting, (3) cash basis accounting and (4) other fairly well-defined methods such as constant-dollar price-level-adjusted financial statements.

When a non-GAAP accounting method is used, the first reporting standard does not apply. It is satisfied by a sentence saying the statements are not intended to conform to GAAP. The reporting responsibility is governed by the *Special Reports* rules (AU 621.02–.08). For all practical purposes, the GAAP criteria are replaced by criteria applicable to the other comprehensive basis of accounting. However, all the other audit

EXHIBIT 20–3
Report Conforming to
Ethics Rule 203

Board of Directors
Health Industries, Inc.:

We have examined the consolidated balance sheet of Health Industries, Inc., and subsidiaries as of December 31, 1975 and 1974, and the related statements of operations and deficit and changes in financial position for the years then ended. Our examination was made in accordance with generally accepted auditing standards and, accordingly, included such tests of the accounting records and such other auditing procedures as we considered necessary in the circumstances.

As explained in Note B, the company has changed its method of recording revenues from recognition at the time of sale to recognition over the membership term and has applied this change retroactively in the accompanying financial statements. Accounting Principles Board (APB) *Opinion Number 20,* "Accounting Changes," provides that such a change be made by including, as an element of net earnings during the year of change, the cumulative effect of the change on prior years. Had APB *Opinion Number 20* been followed literally, the cumulative effect of the accounting change would have been included as a charge in the 1975 statements of operations. Because of the magnitude and pervasiveness of this change, we believe a literal application of APB *Opinion Number 20* would result in a misleading presentation, and that this change should therefore be made on a retroactive basis.

In our opinion, the aforementioned consolidated financial statements present fairly the financial position of Health Industries, Inc., and subsidiaries at December 31, 1975 and 1974, and the results of their operations and the changes in their financial position for the years then ended, in conformity with generally accepted accounting principles applied on a consistent basis after restatement for the change described in the preceding paragraph . . . with . . . which we concur.

Touche Ross & Co.
Certified Public Accountants
March 20, 1976

report obligations remain essentially the same. An auditor's special report on non-GAAP financial statements must contain the following:

☐ A scope paragraph that identifies the audited financial statements.

☐ A description of the comprehensive basis other than GAAP.

☐ A description of how the non-GAAP accounting differs from GAAP accounting.

☐ A statement that the financial statements are *not intended* to be presented in conformity with GAAP.

☐ An opinion paragraph expressing the audit opinion on conformity with the non-GAAP comprehensive basis (including any exceptions, qualifications, or adverse conclusions related to the non-GAAP basis.)

An example of such a report is shown in Exhibit 20–4. The Rouse Company report shown in Chapter 22, Exhibit 22–4, is also a special report, referring to a current value basis of accounting.

To the Certificate Holders and Trustees of
North European Oil Royalty Trust:

We have examined the statements of assets, liabilities and trust corpus of North European Oil Royalty Trust as of October 31, 1983 and 1982, the related statements of income and expenses on a cash basis, undistributed earnings (excess distributions), trust corpus, and changes in cash for each of the three years in the period ended October 31, 1983. Our examinations were made in accordance with generally accepted auditing standards and, accordingly, included such tests of the accounting records and such other auditing procedures as we considered necessary in the circumstances.

Since, as discussed in Note 1, the accounts of the Trust are maintained on the cash basis rather than on the accrual basis of accounting, the accompanying financial statements do not purport to present and, in our opinion, do not present financial position and results of operations in conformity with generally accepted accounting principles. On the cash basis, income is recorded only when collected instead of when earned, and expenses are recorded when paid instead of when incurred.

In our opinion, the financial statements referred to above present fairly the assets, liabilities and trust corpus of North European Oil Royalty Trust as of October 31, 1983 and 1982, and the income and expenses, undistributed earnings (excess distributions), trust corpus and changes in cash for each of the three years in the period ended October 31, 1983, all on the cash basis applied on a consistent basis.

Arthur Andersen & Co.
November 10, 1983

Adverse and GAAP-Exception Opinions

An adverse opinion is exactly the opposite of the unqualified opinion. In this type of opinion, auditors say that the financial statements *do not* present financial position, results of operations, and changes in financial position in conformity with generally accepted accounting principles. The scope paragraph should not be qualified because, in order to decide to use the adverse opinion, the audit team must possess all evidence necessary to reach the decision. When this opinion is given, *all* the substantive reasons must be disclosed in the report in explanatory paragraphs. (See the hypothetical example in Exhibit 20–5.)

As a practical matter, however, auditors generally require *more* evidence to support an adverse opinion than to support an unqualified opinion.[5] Perhaps this phenomenon can be attributed to auditors' reluctance to be bearers of bad news. In addition, client relations considerations typically are intermingled in the decision process. However, auditing standards are quite clear on the point that, if an auditor has a basis for an

_____

[5] Carmichael, *The Auditor's Reporting Obligation: The Meaning and Implementation of the Fourth Standard of Reporting,* Auditing Research Monograph No. 1 (New York: AICPA, 1972) pp. 123, 126.

EXHIBIT 20–5
Adverse Opinion

To the Board of Directors and Shareholders of
the Brooklyn Life Insurance Company:

We have examined the balance sheet (statutory basis) of the Brooklyn Life Insurance Company as of December 31, 1985, and the related statements (statutory basis) of income and changes in financial position for the year then ended. Our examination was made in accordance with generally accepted auditing standards and, accordingly, included such tests of the accounting records and such other auditing procedures as we considered necessary in the circumstances.

The company presents its financial statements in conformity with accounting practices prescribed or permitted by the Insurance Department of the State of New York. The effects on the accompanying financial statements of the variances between such practices and generally accepted accounting principles are described in Note 10.

In our opinion, because of the materiality of the effects of the differences between generally accepted accounting principles and the accounting practices referred to in the preceding paragraph, the aforementioned financial statements do not present fairly the financial position of the Brooklyn Life Insurance Company at December 31, 1985, or the results of its operations or changes in its financial position for the years then ended, in conformity with generally accepted accounting principles.

Clark, Kent & Co.
March 8, 1986

adverse opinion, he cannot extricate himself from an uncomfortable position by giving a disclaimer of opinion.[6]

The materiality dimension is important when making decisions on whether to use the adverse opinion. If the financial statements contain a departure from accounting principles, and if sufficient evidence shows the effect to be immaterial, an unqualified opinion may be rendered (as if the departure had not existed). If the effect of the departure is material (but not extremely material) and isolated to a single event, a qualified opinion may be given. (Examples of qualifications using "except for" language with reference to departures from GAAP are shown in Exhibit 20–6.)

Adverse opinions may arise from situations other than events of departure from officially promulgated accounting principles. In *Auditing Research Monograph No. 1,* the adverse opinion is described as an auditor's means of expressing strong disapproval of the financial representations of management, especially where the intent of management appears to be to mislead readers of the financial statements.[7] In some other situations, evidence may clearly indicate that the going-concern assumption is not valid and that the company faces bankruptcy or liquidation. Hence, financial statements prepared on the cost basis of accounting are not appropri-

---

[6] SAS 2 (AU 509.45).

[7] Carmichael, *The Auditor's Reporting Obligation,* p. 126.

A. Qualification Based on Generally Accepted Accounting Principles without Reference to an Official Pronouncement

To the Board of Directors, Wisconsin Natural Gas Company:

We have examined the balance sheet of Wisconsin Natural Gas Company as of December 31, 1975 and 1974, and the related statements of income, retained earnings and changes in financial position for the years then ended. Our examinations were made in accordance with generally accepted auditing standards and accordingly included such tests of the accounting records and such other auditing procedures as we considered necessary in the circumstances.

As more fully set forth in Note A of Notes to Financial Statements, the company has unbilled revenues which would increase net income and shareholder's equity if recorded in the accounts.

In our opinion, except that unbilled revenues have not been recorded as described in the preceding paragraph, the financial statements examined by us present fairly the financial position of Wisconsin Natural Gas Company at December 31, 1975 and 1974, the results of its operations and changes in financial position for the years then ended, in conformity with generally accepted accounting principles consistently applied.

/s/Price Waterhouse & Co.
February 15, 1976

B. Exception Based on Generally Accepted Accounting Principles with Reference to Financial Accounting Standards Board Statement No. 14

To the Stockholders and Board of Directors of Sony Corporation
(Sony Kabushiki Kaisha):

We have examined the consolidated balance sheets of Sony Corporation (Sony Kabushiki Kaisha) and its consolidated subsidiaries as of October 31, 1982 and 1983, and the related consolidated statements of income and retained earnings and of changes in financial position for each of the three years in the period ended October 31, 1983, expressed in yen. Our examinations were made in accordance with generally accepted auditing standards and accordingly included such tests of the accounting records and such other auditing procedures as we considered necessary in the circumstances.

The company has not presented segment information for each of the three years in the period ended October 31, 1983. In our opinion, the presentation of segment information concerning the company's foreign operations and export sales is required by accounting principles generally accepted in the United States of America for a complete presentation of the consolidated financial statements.

In our opinion, except for the omission of segment information as discussed in the preceding paragraph, the consolidated financial statements examined by us present fairly the financial position of Sony Corporation (Sony Kabushiki Kaisha) and its consolidated subsidiaries at October 31, 1982 and 1983, and the results of their operations and the changes in their financial position for each of the three years in the period ended October 31, 1983, in conformity with accounting principles generally accepted in the United States of America consistently applied.

/s/Price Waterhouse
December 19, 1983

ate. In such cases, when evidence is fully persuasive, an adverse opinion may be given.

Consistency
Qualifications in the
Opinion

The second standard of reporting (the "consistency standard") requires that the report shall state whether accounting principles have been observed consistently in the current period in relation to the preceding period. The materiality dimension is explicit in the objective of this reporting standard:

> The objective of the consistency standard is (*a*) to give assurance that the comparability of financial statements between periods has not been *materially* affected by changes in accounting principles, which include not only accounting principles and practices but also the methods of applying them or (*b*) if comparability has been *materially* affected by such changes, to require appropriate reporting by the independent auditor regarding such changes. It is implicit in the objective that such principles have been consistently observed *within* each period. (Emphasis added.)[8]

Consistency qualifications arise from knowledge based on sufficient competent evidence. In order to state an explicit qualification, auditors must know about it and must have evidence of the materiality of the effect. However, in some first-time audits, an engagement may not be extended sufficiently to prior periods to attest to consistency. In such cases, a form of "disclaimer of consistency" may be given by omitting the consistency phrase, with adequate disclosure of the reasons for the omission. The consistency phrase may simply be omitted in a report on a business's first year of operations.

Statements on Auditing Standards No. 1 explains circumstances that do and do not require consistency exceptions in the auditor's report (AU 420 and 546). The circumstances requiring exceptions are condensed and described in Exhibit 20–7. These circumstances parallel very closely the accounting prescribed in *APB Opinion No. 20* ("Accounting Changes"). Certain changes do *not* require consistency qualifications, namely: (1) changes in accounting estimates; (2) error corrections that do not involve a change in accounting principles; (3) changes in the classification or aggregation of financial statement amounts; (4) changes in the format or basis of the statement of changes in financial position (for example, from a balancing format to a net change format and from a working capital basis to a cash basis) and (5) changes in the subsidiaries included in consolidated financial statements as a result of forming a new subsidiary, buying another company, spinning off or liquidating a subsidiary or selling a subsidiary. However, failure to disclose any of these changes would amount to a GAAP departure and could be a reason for qualifying the opinion. (APB Opinion 20 contains disclosure requirements related to these and other accounting changes.)

---

[8] SAS 1 (AU 420.02).

EXHIBIT 20–7
Reporting on Inconsistency

Nature of Possible Inconsistency Requiring Departure from Standard Report	Required Type of Report		Middle Paragraph Required	Restatement of Prior Years' Financials When Presented for Comparison
	Material Inconsistency	Greatly Material Inconsistency		
1. Change from GAAP to GAAP reported by restating prior financials (AU 546.02).	*Modified Opinion Paragraph* State consistent after giving retroactive effect to change (1 yr), or . . . consistent after restatement (2 yrs).		No.	Yes.
2. Change from principle not conforming to GAAP (AU 420.10).	*Modified Opinion Paragraph* State consistent after giving retroactive effect to change.		No.	Yes.
3. Change from GAAP to GAAP reported by means other than restating prior financials (AU 546.03), including change in principle inseparable from change in estimate (AU 420.11).	*Modified Opinion Paragraph* State "except for the change . . . have been applied on a basis consistent with that of the preceding year."		No.	No.
4. Change from GAAP to GAAP without reasonable justification (AU 546.06).	*Qualified* "Except For." Relates to both GAAP and consistency.	*Adverse*	Yes. Explains why change is not justified.	Yes/No. (APB 20)
5. Change to principle not conforming to GAAP (AU 546.05).	*Qualified* "Except For."	*Adverse* No reference to consistency since not in conformance with GAAP.	Yes. Explains change to a "non-GAAP."	No.
6. Change in reporting entity (AU 420.07–.08) including a pooling of interest combination (AU 546.12–.13), but not when the consolidated entity changes as a result of creation, cessation, purchase, or disposition of a subsidiary or other business unit (AU 420.09).	*Modified Opinion Paragraph* State . . . consistent after giving retroactive effect to the change (1 year) or . . . consistent after restatement (2 years).		No.	Yes. (See APB 20.)

Source: Adapted from D. Causey, "Newly Emerging Standards of Auditor Responsibility: A Reply," *Accounting Review*, January 1977, p. 260.

When evaluating a change in accounting principle, auditors must be satisfied that management's justification for the change is reasonable. *APB Opinion No. 20,* "Accounting Changes," states: "The presumption that an entity should not change an accounting principle may be overcome only if the enterprise justifies the use of an alternative acceptable accounting principle on the basis that it is preferable." A change solely "to increase profits" may be preferable from management's viewpoint, but such a reason is not reasonable justification for most auditors. When

EXHIBIT 20–8
Consistency and
Accounting Changes

A.   Accounting Change Not Related to Official Pronouncements

To the Shareholders and Board of Directors of Masonite Corporation:

We have examined the consolidated balance sheets of Masonite Corporation (a Delaware Corporation) and subsidiaries as of August 31, 1983 and 1982, and the consolidated statements of income, retained earnings and changes in financial position for each of the three years in the period ended August 31, 1983. Our examinations were made in accordance with generally accepted auditing standards and, accordingly, included such tests of the accounting records and such other auditing procedures as we considered necessary in the circumstances.

In our opinion, the financial statements referred to above present fairly the financial position of Masonite Corporation and subsidiary as of August 31, 1983 and 1982, and the results of their operations and the changes in their financial position for each of the three years in the period ended August 31, 1983, in conformity with generally accepted accounting principles applied on a consistent basis, except for the change (with which we concur) in actuarial cost method as described in Note 7 to the financial statements.

Arthur Anderson & Co
October 11, 1983

*   *   *   *   *

Footnote 7, Retirement Plans: The company has retirement plans covering substantially all domestic and certain foreign employees, as well as a deferred compensation plan available to certain officers and key employees funded primarily through life insurance.

The total expenses of these plans for 1983, 1982 and 1981 were approximately $3,093,000, $3,040,000 and $4,952,000, respectively. During 1982, the company changed the actuarial cost method for its Salaried Employees' Pension Plan from the "aggregate cost" method to the "entry age normal cost" method. Also during 1982, the company reduced the "salary increase" actuarial assumption to 6 percent from 8 percent, to reflect a lower inflation element for expected salary increases. Management believes, based on discussions with the company's actuaries, these changes more closely match funding with accrued benefits. Under the "aggregate cost" method, the company has funded $6,885,000 more to the Salaried Employees' Pension Plan through September 1, 1981 than what would have been funded under the "entry age normal cost" method. This amount is being treated as an actuarial gain. Accordingly, the company reduced the funding contribution and recognized a reduction of retirement plans expenses by approximately $805,000 in 1983 and 1982, and will amortize the remaining excess funding through 1990.

Exhibit 20–8
(*concluded*)

B.   Accounting Change Related to an Official Pronouncement (FASB Statement No. 43)

To the Shareholders and Board of Directors of Grand Central, Inc.

We have examined the balance sheet of Grand Central, Inc. as of July 31, 1983, and August 1, 1982, and the related statements of income (loss) and retained earnings and changes in financial position for the years ended July 31, 1983, August 1, 1982, and August 2, 1981. Our examinations were made in accordance with generally accepted auditing standards and, accordingly, included such tests of the accounting records and such other auditing procedures as we considered necessary in the circumstances.

In our opinion, the financial statements referred to above present fairly the financial position of Grand Central, Inc. at July 31, 1983, and August 1, 1982, and the results of its operations and changes in financial position for the years ended July 31, 1983, August 1, 1982, and August 2, 1981, in conformity with generally accepted accounting principles consistently applied during the periods, except for the changes, with which we concur, in the methods of accounting for vacation pay and inventories as described in Note 9 to the financial statements.

> /s/Coopers & Lybrand
> September 21, 1983, except for Note 11
> as to which the date is October 28, 1983

*   *   *   *   *

Footnote 9, Accounting Changes: Statement of Financial Accounting Standards No. 43 requires accrual of vacation time as earned, instead of when used as previously reported. The effect of the change for the year ended August 1, 1982, was an increase in the loss before cumulative effect of change in accounting method of $44,500 or $.02 per share. Net income for the year ended August 2, 1981, has been restated. The effect of the restatement was to increase income before the cumulative effect of changes in accounting methods by $14,621. The adjustment to retroactively apply the new method is $323,683 after reduction for income taxes of $327,591. Proforma amounts have not been presented since the information necessary to calculate the effect of the change on the prior year is not available. . . .

During 1982, the Company changed its method of determining cost of retail inventories. Cost of retail inventory was calculated using cost information for a three-month period rather than a twelve-month period. This change was made to more accurately reflect inventory cost and to better match cost with related revenue. The effect of this change was to decrease the loss by $489,580 or $.23 per share. The adjustment to retroactively apply the new method is $341,694 after reduction for income taxes of $316,675. Proforma amounts have not been presented since the information necessary to calculate the effect of the change on the prior year is not available.

change is made, auditors must state concurrence by stating in the audit report: ". . . in conformity with generally accepted accounting principles applied on a consistent basis except for the change, *with which we concur,* in the method of determining pension costs (for example)." If the auditors cannot concur, then an opinion qualification based on a departure from

GAAP is appropriate.[9] In audit reports on subsequent years' financial statements, an appropriate consistency exception should be stated as long as the financial statements for the year of the change are included in the years presented.

Examples of audit reports recognizing accounting changes are shown in Exhibit 20–8.

Summary: Reporting with Fully Sufficient Competent Evidence

Fully sufficient competent evidential matter is required for several reporting alternatives. This level of evidence is clearly required for the unqualified opinion and for the adverse opinion because they are factual and definite statements. Equally factual and definite are the auditor's statements concerning departures from generally accepted accounting principles and consistency (or lack thereof) in the application of accounting principles. In all these types of opinions and their variations, auditors must possess the knowledge that supports the message in the opinion paragraph.

REPORTING UNDER PERVASIVE EVIDENTIAL DEFICIENCIES

At the other end of the evidence continuum is the situation where auditors are unable to obtain sufficient competent evidence for an opinion on financial statements taken as a whole. Such situations involve uncertainties about continuation of the entity (the going-concern assumption) and engagements in which a complete audit is not performed. A disclaimer of opinion—a statement that *no opinion* is given—results from pervasive evidential deficiencies.

General Disclaimer of Opinion

When lack of evidence is a consequence of a client's imposed restriction on the scope of audit field work, or when important audit evidence could not be obtained for other reasons, the scope paragraph of the report should be modified to explain the circumstances. A scope qualification should only be used when the restriction on procedures or the inability to perform procedures has resulted in lack of sufficient competent evidential matter, further resulting in a qualified opinion or disclaimer of opinion. If the audit scope has been restricted in some specific respect (for example, a client's refusal to let the auditor confirm receivables), but sufficient competent evidence is gathered by other procedures, the standard scope paragraph need not be qualified. The general guide is that scope paragraph qualification is necessary only when an associated opinion qualification or disclaimer results. Whenever an opinion is disclaimed, all substantive reasons for the expression of no opinion must be explained. The audit report shown in Exhibit 20–12B contains such a qualified scope and a

---

[9] SEC *Accounting Series Release No. 177* (Financial Reporting Release No. 1, section 304.02) required independent accountants to submit a letter stating whether a change is to a preferable principle—one that provides a better measure of business operations.

disclaimer of opinion regarding the statements of income and changes in financial position.

"Going-Concern" Problems

Generally accepted accounting principles are based on the ***going-concern assumption,*** which means that the entity is expected to continue in business with the ability to meet its obligations when they come due without substantial disposal of assets, restructuring of debt, externally forced revision of operations, or similar actions.[10] Hence, an opinion that financial statements are in conformity with GAAP means that continued existence may be presumed.

No formal accounting principles exist for "quitting concerns." Presumably, the appropriate accounting is a comprehensive basis of liquidation accounting which would value assets at net realizable value and list liabilities in their order of preference as claims to the remaining assets. Such statements may be prepared in bankruptcy proceedings, but independent auditors generally do not render opinions on them.

Dealing with questions of going-concern, or lack thereof, is very difficult because auditors are forced to evaluate matters of financial analysis, business strategy and financial forecasting. Most managements are unwilling to give up and close their businesses without strong attempts to survive. Sometimes, survival optimism prevails until the creditors force bankruptcy proceedings and liquidation. Auditors are generally reluctant to puncture any balloons of optimism. Managers and auditors view news of financial troubles in an audit report (a qualification or disclaimer based on going-concern doubt) as a "self-fulfilling prophecy" which *causes* bankruptcy. However fallacious this view might be, it still prevails and inhibits auditors' consideration of going-concern questions.

According to auditing standards, auditors do not routinely search for evidence related to the going-concern assumption (AU 340.03). However, no careful auditor would ignore signs and operate entirely on the *assumption* that the client is a going concern. Financial difficulties, labor problems, loss of key personnel, litigation, and other such things may be important signals. Likewise, elements of financial flexibility (salability of assets, lines of credit, debt extension, dividend elimination) may be available as survival strategies.

Accounting and finance research efforts have produced several bankruptcy prediction models. These models use publicly available financial information to classify companies in "fail" and "nonfail" categories. At least one auditing firm uses such a model as an analytical review procedure tool. Auditing standards, however, make no mention of research models, specifying instead many company-specific considerations and elements of internal information for analysis (SAS 34, AU 340).

Three options exist for opinions when the going-concern assumption is in doubt. SAS 34 (AU 340.12) illustrates a middle paragraph disclosing

---

[10] SAS 34 (AU 340), *The Auditor's Considerations When a Question Arises about an Entity's Continued Existence.*

fully a going-concern uncertainty accompanied by a "subject to" opinion using the standard language illustrated in SAS 2, AU 509.39. In addition, this same standard suggests auditors may disclaim an opinion on the grounds that the uncertainty of going concern is so great that no determination of overall conformity to GAAP can be made. Such a disclaimer is illustrated in Exhibit 20-9. The third option is to give an adverse opinion in the extreme case when the business is definitely failing and financial statements conforming to going-concern-based GAAP accounting are definitely *not* appropriate. Financial statements presented on the going-concern basis may not be appropriate when substantial doubts exist about the recoverability and classification of reported asset amounts and the amounts and classifications of reported liabilities.

EXHIBIT 20–9
Disclaimer of Opinion

To the Shareholders and Board of Directors of General Recreation, Inc.:

We have examined the consolidated balance sheets of General Recreation, Inc. (a Delaware corporation) and subsidiaries as of December 31, 1982 and 1981, and the related consolidated statements of operations, shareholders' investment and changes in financial position for each of the three years in the period ended December 31, 1982. Our examinations were made in accordance with generally accepted auditing standards and, accordingly, included such tests of the accounting records and other auditing procedures as we considered necessary in the circumstances.

As reflected in the accompanying financial statements, the Company incurred net losses of $861,074 in 1982 and $161,235 in 1981. As discussed in Note 3, the Company did not make all required principal and interest payments under two loan agreements during 1982 and is not in compliance with financial and performance covenant requirements of the agreements. The debt under these agreements ($6,344,685) has been classified as a current liability at December 31, 1982, as the lenders may, at their option, demand payment. Realization of the amount at which assets included in the accompanying balance sheet are carried is dependent upon the restructuring of debt repayment terms and the success of future operations. Management has indicated that there is serious question concerning the ability of the Company to continue operations unless substantial relief can be obtained through a restructuring of debt repayment terms.

In view of the significance of the possible losses in realization of the investment in the assets noted in the preceding paragraph, we are unable to express, and we do not express, an opinion on the financial statements referred to above.

Arthur Andersen & Co.
March 4, 1983

Disclaimers on Unaudited Financial Statements

Clients often want a CPA to be associated with the preparation or delivery of financial statements without doing a complete audit. Sometimes such work may involve the CPA only in writing up the financial statements in proper form from the client's books and records. Such financial statements are **unaudited** if the CPA has not applied any auditing procedures or has not applied procedures which produced sufficient evidence for an opinion on the statements taken as a whole.

Clients generally desire the association of the CPA's name in order to lend some credibility to the statements—which is the essence of the attest function. But CPAs cannot afford to lend credibility in this manner and accept exposure to liability without performing an audit in accordance with generally accepted auditing standards.

Consequently, in all cases where a CPA is associated by name or participation with unaudited financial statements of public companies, he or she must submit a disclaimer.[11] Exhibit 20–10 contains an example of a disclaimer within a report that also gives an unqualified opinion. The disclaimer applies to Stauffer Chemical Company's presentation of a 12-month earnings statement for the period ended September 30, 1983, which represents a different fiscal year end than the prior year (December 31). Such statements are often issued when a company is in the process of changing its fiscal year.

EXHIBIT 20–10
Report Including a
Disclaimer on Statements
of a New Accounting Year

To the Stockholders of Stauffer Chemical Company:

We have examined the consolidated balance sheets of Stauffer Chemical Company and subsidiaries as of September 30, 1983, and December 31, 1982, and the related statements of consolidated earnings, consolidated stockholders' equity and changes in consolidated financial position for the nine-month period ended September 30, 1983, and the twelve-month periods ended December 31, 1982 and 1981. Our examinations were made in accordance with generally accepted auditing standards and, accordingly, included such tests of the accounting records and such other auditing procedures as we considered necessary in the circumstances.

In our opinion, such consolidated financial statements present fairly the financial position of Stauffer Chemical Company and subsidiaries at September 30, 1983, and December 31, 1982, and the results of their operations and the changes in their financial position for the nine-month period ended September 30, 1983, and the twelve-month periods ended December 31, 1982 and 1981, in conformity with generally accepted accounting principles consistently applied during the period except for the change, with which we concur, in 1982 in the method of accounting for inventories as described in the notes to the financial statements.

The accompanying statements of consolidated earnings and changes in consolidated financial position for the twelve month period ended September 30, 1983, were not audited by us, and accordingly, we do not express an opinion on them.

Deloitte Haskins & Sells
November 21, 1983

---

[11] Standards for reporting on the compiled or reviewed unaudited statements of *nonpublic companies* are contained in the *Statements on Standards for Accounting and Review Services* (Chapter 22).

In addition to the standard disclaimer language, these other guides should be followed:

1.   If the CPA should learn that the statements are not in conformity with generally accepted accounting principles (including adequate disclosures), the departures should be explained in the disclaimer.
2.   If prior years' unaudited statements are presented, the disclaimer should cover them as well as the current year statement.
3.   Each page of the statements should be labeled clearly as unaudited.

Disclaimer When CPA Is Not Independent   Independence is the foundation of the attest function. _When indepen-dence is lacking, an audit in accordance with generally accepted auditing standards is impossible._ An audit is not just the applications of tools, techniques, and procedures of auditing, but also the independence in mental attitude of the auditors. Nowhere in auditing standards is this idea set forth more clearly than in the following excerpt:

> When an accountant is not independent, any procedures he might perform would not be in accordance with generally accepted auditing standards, and he would be precluded from expressing an opinion on such statements.[12]

In keeping with this standard, evidence gathered by an auditor who is not independent is not considered sufficient competent evidence. The pervasive deficiency lies in the lack of independence. In such cases, the disclaimer shown in Exhibit 20–11 is appropriate.[13] In addition, these guides should be followed:

1.   The report should not mention any reasons for not being independent because the readers might erroneously interpret them as unimportant.
2.   The report should make no mention whatsoever of any audit procedures applied because readers might erroneously conclude that they were sufficient.
3.   If the CPA should learn that the statements are not in conformity with generally accepted accounting principles (including adequate disclosures), the departures should be explained in the disclaimer.
4.   Each page of the financial statements should be labeled clearly as unaudited.

---

[12] SAS 26 (AU 504.09).

[13] In the case of nonpublic company unaudited statements, an accountant who is not independent may disclose the fact and give the compilation report (AR 100.22) but may not give the review report (AR 100.38). The report in Exhibit 20–11 was issued before the compilation standard permitting a report by a non-independent accountant became effective. Since the Austin Symphony Orchestra Society, Inc., is not a public company, a compilation report (which includes a disclaimer, see Exhibit 1–1 in Chapter 1) could be issued. A sentence saying the accountant is not independent would be added, as shown in the example in Chapter 22, Exhibit 22–6.

EXHIBIT 20–11
Disclaimer When a CPA
Is Not Independent

The Board of Directors
The Austin Symphony Orchestra Society, Inc.:

   We are not independent with respect to the Austin Symphony Orchestra Society, Inc., and the accompanying balance sheet as of June 30, 1977, and the related statements of revenues and expenditures and changes in fund balances for the year then ended were not audited by us. Accordingly, we do not express an opinion on them.

                                                     Peat, Marwick, Mitchell & Co.
                                                     November 8, 1977

Summary: Pervasive Evidential Deficiencies

When evidence is insufficient, for whatever reason, auditors should issue a disclaimer of opinion. A general lack of evidence can result from inability to perform some important procedures or from the existence of a massive uncertainty about the validity of the going-concern assumption. Unaudited statements of public companies and statements with respect to which the CPA is not independent should carry a clear expression of "no opinion."

   Sometimes, however, distinguishing a *pervasive* evidence deficiency from an *isolated* evidence deficiency, or a *massive* uncertainty from an *ordinary* uncertainty is difficult. In the next section, opinion qualifications based on these finer distinctions are discussed.

ISOLATED EVIDENCE DEFICIENCIES AND UNCERTAINTIES

Difficult decision problems arise when auditors have too little evidence to support a clear-cut unqualified opinion or adverse opinion and too much evidence to justify an outright disclaimer. Such problems usually result from a lack of evidence about some specific event, amount or account. The lack of evidence many times is attributable to restrictions on the scope of the audit, to the fact that important procedures were impracticable, or to the existence of an uncertainty about which evidence is simply not available at the time the report decision must be made.

   Once the uncertainty is identified, auditors must attempt to assess the potential importance and materiality of the amount involved. Materiality in this context is multidimensional, referring not only to the absolute or relative dollar amount of an item but also to the (1) nature, (2) probability and (3) time horizon of the event in question. As a general rule of thumb, such problems are resolved with mild qualification language (sometimes even with an unqualified opinion) when: (1) The potential monetary impact is small, (2) The item itself is not especially dramatic, (3) The probability of serious adversity is small and (4) The time of likely occurrence is distant. When each of these four facets have the opposite characteristics, a report decision would lean toward a disclaimer (or even an adverse opinion where the going-concern assumption is persuasively in doubt).

The report decision is more complex when the four facets are not all at one extreme.

Scope Paragraph Qualifications

The auditor's report of his own work should describe any deficiency of evidence that resulted from failure to perform auditing procedures necessary in the circumstances. Evidence deficiencies may arise in a variety of situations. Common ones involve inability to confirm receivables, inability to observe the physical count of inventories, and inability to obtain evidence about investments accounted for on the equity method (for example, evidence on the value of such investments and on the transactions between investor and investee that should be eliminated under the equity method).[14] For example: The client may refuse to permit confirmation of important receivables; the audit firm might be engaged after the physical count of inventory has been conducted; management may be unable to obtain audited financial statements of investees and detailed information about investor-investee transactions.

If these types of deficiencies can be overcome by obtaining sufficient, competent evidence through alternative procedures, no scope qualification is required, and an unqualified opinion may be given. For example, receivables may be audited through the alternative procedure of vouching payments received after the balance sheet date to the receivables balances. However, observation of inventories must be performed (even if at a date subsequent to the balance sheet date). Likewise, reliable information on material investor-investee transactions must be obtained in order to audit the intercompany eliminations. In addition, auditors must obtain satisfactory written client representations (AU 333.11–.12).

When evidence deficiencies persist, auditors usually add language to the scope paragraph calling attention to an exception. For example: "Our examination was made in accordance with generally accepted auditing standards . . . , except as stated in the following paragraph." The middle paragraph then explains the circumstances and nature of the evidence deficiency. If the auditors were unable to observe beginning inventory because they were not engaged until later, but were able to observe the ending inventory, the paragraph should say so. In this case, the opinion could be both (1) a disclaimer on the results of operations and changes in financial position (because beginning inventory enters into income determination) and (2) an unqualified opinion on financial position (because the ending inventory was audited).

Reporting When Uncertainties Exist

A different type of evidence deficiency arises when uncertainties exist. An auditing "uncertainty" is similar to an accounting "contingency," which is defined in FASB Statement No. 5:

> A contingency is . . . an existing condition, situation, or set of circumstances involving uncertainty as to possible gain ("gain contingency") or

---

[14] See *Statement on Auditing Standards No. 1* (AU 542).

loss ("loss contingency") to an enterprise that will ultimately be resolved when one or more future events occur or fail to occur. Resolution of the uncertainty may confirm the acquisition of an asset or the reduction of a liability or the loss or impairment of an asset or the incurrence of a liability. . . .

FASB Statement No. 5 (SFAS 5) sets forth accounting and disclosure standards for handling contingencies. One of the most common contingencies involves the uncertain outcome of litigation pending against the company. Audit uncertainties include such things as the value of fixed assets held for sale (for example, a whole plant or warehouse facility) and the status of assets involved in foreign expropriations.

Auditors may perform procedures in accordance with generally accepted auditing standards, yet the uncertainty and lack of evidence may persist. The problem is that it is impossible to obtain audit "evidence" about the future. The concept of audit evidence includes information knowable at the time a reporting decision is made and does not include predictions about future resolution of uncertainties.

Consequently, auditors usually do not qualify the scope paragraph when contingencies and uncertainties exist. The audit usually has been performed in accordance with generally accepted auditing standards, and the auditor has done all the things possible in the circumstances. Auditors cannot predict the future better than anyone else. Of course, auditors have extrapolated the future in ordinary accounting ways (for example, estimating collectibility of trade receivables based on collection history and assessing useful lives of fixed assets based on the client's pattern of use), and thus have reduced the *information risk* to users of the financial statements. ***Information risk*** refers to the probability that erroneous accounting measurements or disclosures are published in financial statements.

However, the auditor can do nothing to reduce the *business risk* faced by the client company. ***Business risk*** refers to such environmental forces as the ups and downs of demand in markets, fluctuation of prices, exposures in foreign economies and the unusual uncertainties arising from litigation and from holding major assets for sale.

In 1978, the Commission on Auditors' Responsibilities concluded that auditors have an obligation to mitigate information risk. This obligation is fulfilled in the auditor's report by using "except for" language in connection with scope limitations and clients' nonconformity with accounting principles. The disclaimer of opinion is another way to put users on guard against information risk.

The commission also concluded that assessment of business risk was the responsibility of the users of financial statements. The client's accountants are responsible for full disclosure and proper accounting for contingencies (using SFAS 5 standards). The *auditor's responsibility* is to determine whether the client's accounting and disclosure is in conformity with generally accepted accounting principles. If so, according to the commission, an unqualified opinion should be given.

This commission recommendation would effectively eliminate the opinion known as the *subject to opinion,* which has been used by auditors for many years. The ***subject to opinion*** directs attention to material uncertainties and is considered a useful "red flag" for financial statement users. Canadian auditors no longer use the *subject to* opinion language, but it is still used by American auditors.

"Subject to"
Language

Significant uncertainties about future events may exist with regard to such matters as tax deficiency assessments, contract disputes, recoverability of asset costs, lawsuits and other important contingencies. Important uncertainties should be explained clearly and completely in a paragraph following the scope paragraph. The opinion then contains a statement that the overall opinion on financial statements taken as a whole is *subject to the effects of any adjustments that might have been required had the outcome of the uncertainty been known.* Two examples of such situations and qualifications are given in Exhibit 20–12.

EXHIBIT 20–12
Reporting When
Uncertainties Exist

A.   Isolated Uncertainty Subject of Opinion Paragraph Qualification

To the Shareholders and Board of Directors, Pauley Petroleum Inc.:

We have examined the consolidated balance sheets of Pauley Petroleum Inc. and subsidiaries as of August 31, 1983 and 1982, and the related consolidated statements of operations, shareholders' equity and changes in financial position for each of the three years in the period ended August 31, 1983. Our examinations were made in accordance with generally accepted auditing standards and, accordingly, included such tests of the accounting records and such other auditing procedures as we considered necessary in the circumstances.

As commented upon in Note 6 to the consolidated financial statements, the Company has significant uncertainties relating to contingent liabilities in its petroleum operations. The ultimate outcome of these uncertainties cannot be presently determined, and no provision for any liability that may result has been made in the financial statements.

In our opinion, subject to the effects of such adjustments, if any, as might have been required had the outcome of the uncertainties referred to in the preceding paragraph been known, the financial statements referred to above present fairly the consolidated financial position of Pauley Petroleum Inc. and subsidiaries, as of August 31, 1983 and 1982, and the consolidated results of their operations and changes in their financial position for each of the three years in the period ended August 31, 1983, in conformity with generally accepted accounting principles applied on a consistent basis.

Coopers & Lybrand
November 23, 1983

Exhibit 20–12
(continued)

B.   Going-Concern Opinion on Company in Bankruptcy Proceedings; and Illustrations of Several Audit Scope Restrictions Leading to a Disclaimer and Other Qualifications

The Board of Directors, Saxon Industries, Inc.:

We have examined the consolidated balance sheet of Saxon Industries, Inc. (Debtor-in-Possession) and subsidiaries as of September 30, 1982. Our examination was made in accordance with generally accepted auditing standards and, accordingly, included such tests of the accounting records and such other auditing procedures as we considered necessary in the circumstances.

As set forth in Note 1 to the consolidated financial statements, the parent company, on April 15, 1982, filed a petition for reorganization under Chapter 11 of the United States Bankruptcy Code. The process of determining the amount of allowable pre-petition claims just began, and the ultimate settlement of these claims will be determined when a plan of reorganization has been agreed to with creditors and confirmed by the Bankruptcy Court.

As described in Note 14, the Company is subject to a number of lawsuits and contingencies. Although some provision has been made for these matters, the final outcome and its effect, if any, on the Company's consolidated balance sheet is not presently determinable.

As described in Note 6, the Company has available net operating loss and investment tax credit carryforwards. Determination of the amounts of these carryforwards involve complex State and Federal tax issues, and the operating loss carryforward may be contingent upon the resolution of which year for tax purposes such losses were incurred and upon the terms of the plan of reorganization settling the bankruptcy proceedings.

The accompanying consolidated balance sheet has been prepared in conformity with principles of accounting applicable to a going-concern. Continuation of the Company as a going-concern and realization of its assets and liquidation of its liabilities are dependent upon, among other things: (1) confirmation of a plan of reorganization (which will, among other things, result in significant adjustments and reclassifications in the amounts reflected as liabilities and shareholders' equity (deficit) in the accompanying consolidated balance sheet) and (2) the ability of the Company to maintain adequate financing, combined with the achievement of profitable continuing operations. The eventual outcome of these matters is not presently determinable. The consolidated balance sheet does not include any adjustment relating to the recoverability and classification of recorded asset amounts or the amount and classification of liabilities that might be necessary should the Company be unable to continue its existence.

In our opinion, subject to the effect on the consolidated balance sheet of such adjustments, if any, as might have been required had the outcome of the matters discussed in the preceding four paragraphs been known, the aforementioned consolidated balance sheet presents fairly the financial position of Saxon Industries, Inc. (Debtor-in-Possession) and subsidiaries, as of September 30, 1982, in conformity with generally accepted accounting principles applied on a basis consistent with that of the preceding year.

We have examined the consolidated statement of operations and accumulated deficit and the consolidated statement of changes in financial position of Saxon Industries, Inc. (Debtor-in-Possession) and subsidiaries for the nine months ended September 30, 1982. However, as described below, we were not able to perform certain procedures required under generally accepted auditing standards:

Exhibit 20–12
(concluded)

(1)   The balance sheet of the Company as of December 31, 1981, was examined by other certified public accountants who were unable to express an opinion thereon, and the company did not consider it practical for us to extend our audit procedures to examine the January 1, 1982, balance sheet.

(2)   The scope of our examination was limited in that we were instructed to exclude the operations of the Business Products Group and the Chukerman Division, both of which have been sold.

(3)   We did not extend our procedures to investigate alleged irregularities in the Company's books and records as described in the Court-appointed Examiner's reports.

(4)   Company management was not in a position to make certain representations to us as required by generally accepted auditing standards.

Accordingly, we express no opinion on the consolidated statement of operations and accumulated deficit and the consolidated statement of changes in financial position of Saxon Industries, Inc. (Debtor-in-Possession) and subsidiaries for the nine months ended September 30, 1982.

For reasons set forth in Note 19, with which we concur, supplementary information on the effects of inflation in accordance with Financial Accounting Standards Board Opinion No. 33 is not presented.

Peat, Marwick, Mitchell & Co.

REPORTING OBLIGATIONS—A SUMMARY

In the final analysis, the auditors' reporting decisions rest upon how much is known about the financial statements—the evidence dimension. The standard unqualified report is the basic starting point for a reporting decision, but several circumstances may exist that require departure from the standard language. The circumstances covered in this chapter include:

Departure from GAAP—an accounting deficiency.

Departure from an official pronouncement—an accounting deficiency (modified by Ethics Rule 203).

Use of a comprehensive basis of accounting other than GAAP—an accounting principles matter.

Lack of consistency—an accounting deficiency.

Limitation on scope—an evidence deficiency related to restrictions of audit procedures.

Uncertainty—an evidence deficiency related to future events.

Unaudited financial statements—pervasive absence of audit evidence.

Auditor is not independent—related to auditing standards.

Another modification of the standard report language is used when one auditor relies on the work and reports of other independent auditors. This topic and others related to reporting are covered in Chapter 21.

Some confusion over terminology may become a problem when learning about changes to the standard report wording. Three terms are used widely:

☐ **Qualification.** A *scope paragraph* is qualified when explanation is offered about how an audit did not conform to GAAS. An *opinion* is qualified when the "except for" and "subject to" wording is used.

☐ **Modification.** A report is modified when additional explanation is offered (for example, an emphasis paragraph or reference to reliance on other auditors), but neither the scope or opinion paragraphs are qualified.

☐ **Expansion.** A report is expanded when, in addition to the standard language, it contains exception-basis commentary on information not considered part of the basic GAAP financial statements. (*Expanded* reports are clarified in Chapter 22 with regard to supplementary information topics.)

All of these changes plus the adverse and disclaimed opinions are often described as *departures* from the language of the standard unqualified report.

SOURCES AND ADDITIONAL READING REFERENCES

Alderman, C. W., D. M. Guy, and D. R. Meals. "Other Comprehensive Bases of Accounting: Alternatives to GAAP?" *Journal of Accountancy,* August 1982, pp. 52–63.

Altman, E. I., and T. P. McGough. "Evaluation of a Company as a Going Concern." *Journal of Accountancy,* December 1974, pp. 50–57.

Bailey, William T. "The Effect of Audit Reports on Chartered Financial Analysts' Perceptions of the Sources of Financial-Statement and Audit-Report Messages." *Accounting Review,* October 1981, pp. 882–96.

Banks, D. W., and W. R. Kinney, Jr. "Loss Contingency Reports and Stock Prices: An Empirical Study." *Journal of Accounting Research,* Spring 1982, pp. 240–54.

Carmichael, D. R. "Auditor's Reports—A Search for Criteria." *Journal of Accountancy,* September 1972, pp. 67–74.

————. *The Auditor's Reporting Obligation: The Meaning and Implementation of the Fourth Standard of Reporting, Auditing Research Monograph No. 1,* New York: AICPA, 1972.

Casey, Cornelius J., Jr. "The Usefulness of Accounting Ratios for Subjects' Predictions of Corporate Failure: Replication and Extensions." *Journal of Accounting Research,* Autumn 1980, pp. 603–13.

Commission on Auditors' Responsibilities. "Reporting on Significant Uncertainties," sec. 3 in *Report, Conclusions, and Recommendations.* New York: CAR, 1978, pp. 23–30.

Dominiak, G. F., and J. G. Louderback, III. " 'Present Fairly' and Generally Accepted Accounting Principles." *The CPA Journal,* January 1972, pp. 45–49.

Hill, Henry. "Reporting on Uncertainties by Independent Auditors." *Journal of Accountancy,* January 1973, pp. 55–60.

Isbell, David B., and D. R. Carmichael. "Disclaimers and Liabilities—The Rhode Island Trust Case." *Journal of Accountancy,* April 1973, pp. 37–42.

Kida, Thomas. "An Investigation into Auditors' Continuity and Related Qualification Judgments." *Journal of Accounting Research,* Autumn 1980, pp. 506–23.

Libby, Robert. "Bankers' and Auditors' Perceptions of the Message Communicated by the Audit Report." *Journal of Accounting Research,* Spring 1979, pp. 99–122.

Mautz, R. K., and H. A. Sharaf. *The Philosophy of Auditing,* especially chap. 7, "Fair Presentation." American Accounting Association, 1961.

Ohlson, James A. "Financial Ratios and the Probabilistic Prediction of Bankruptcy." *Journal of Accounting Research,* Spring 1980, pp. 109–31.

Revsine, Lawrence. "The Preferability Dilemma." *Journal of Accountancy,* September 1977, pp. 80–89.

Shank, J. K., and R. J. Murdock. "Comparability in the Application of Reporting Standards: Some Further Evidence." *Accounting Review,* October 1978, pp. 824–35.

Warren, Carl S. "Uniformity of Auditing Standards: A Replication." *Journal of Accounting Research,* Spring 1980, pp. 312–24.

REVIEW QUESTIONS

20.1. Why should public accountants issue a report whenever they are *associated with* financial statements?

20.2. What is the most important distinction between an auditor's *opinion* on financial statements and an auditor's *disclaimer of opinion?*

20.3. What is the relationship of the time-cost constraint to the type of report issued by an independent auditor?

20.4. Think about the standard unqualified scope paragraph. (*a*) What does it identify as the objects of the audit? (*b*) What is *meant* by the second sentence: "Our examination was made in accordance with generally accepted auditing standards and, accord-ingly, included such tests of the accounting records and such other auditing procedures as we considered necessary in the circumstances?"

20.5. What is a "negative assurance?" Why is it generally prohibited? When is a negative assurance permitted?

20.6. Explain the effect of the *materiality dimension* on an auditor's report when the client uses an accounting method that departs from generally accepted accounting principles.

20.7. With reference to an *evidence dimension,* what extent of evidence is required as a basis for the unqualified opinion? Adverse opinion? Opinion qualified for a GAAP departure? Opinion qualified with respect to consistent application of GAAP? Opinion qualified with respect to an uncertainty? Disclaimer of opinion?

20.8. What are eight major reasons for changing the standard unqualified report language?

20.9. Which of the AICPA Rules of Conduct enforce the GAAS reporting standards? (Hint: Several rules are applicable.)

20.10. In what kind(s) of reporting situations is the first standard of reporting considered inapplicable? How is the inapplicability handled in an audit report?

20.11. What circumstances cause auditors to recognize inconsistent applications of GAAP in their reports on financial statements? What circumstances are *not* considered inconsistencies?

20.12. When might omission of the standard consistency phrase be appropriate?

20.13. What kinds of opinions can be expressed when the "going-concern assumption" is in doubt?

20.14. What are unaudited statements? In connection with unaudited statements, what general guides should the auditor follow for public companies?

20.15. If an auditor is not independent with respect to a client, what type of opinion must be issued? Why?

20.16. In connection with *uncertainties*, what aspects of the materiality of an event in question are important in addition to the absolute or relative dollar amount?

20.17. Why might an unqualified opinion be appropriate when a material uncertainty exists?

20.18. Explain the difference between *qualified*, *modified*, and *expanded* audit reports. What feature do they have in common?

EXERCISES AND PROBLEMS

20.19. **Association with Financial Statements**
This series of questions is a drill on the subjects of "association with" financial statements, unaudited financial statements and the disclaimer of opinion. Refer to SAS 2 (AU 509) and SAS 26 (AU 504), and in each case below, respond to the question: What kind of report can you give?

a. Able Corporation engaged you to prepare financial statements from its books and records without performing any audit or review procedures. Able is a public company.

b. Baker Corporation, a public company, uses your computerized bookkeeping service. You deliver monthly financial statements to Baker's controller. Another CPA performs the annual audit for Baker Corp.

c. Charlie Corporation engaged you to audit its financial statements. Charlie

is not a public company. You serve as the corporation's part-time financial vice president.

d. Dagmar Partnership engaged you on January 30 to audit its financial statements for the year just ended on the previous December 31. Dagmar has never been audited and has never conducted a physical inventory. Sale of manufactured goods is the major business and inventories amount to about 75 percent of total assets.

20.20. **Association with Financial Statements**
For each of the situations described below, state whether the CPA is or is not *associated with* the financial statements. What is the consequence of being associated with financial statements?

a. CPA audits financial statements, and his name is in the corporate annual report containing them.

b. CPA prepares the financial statements in the partnership tax return.

c. CPA uses his computer to process client-submitted data and delivers financial statement output.

d. CPA uses his computer to process client-submitted data and delivers a general ledger print-out.

e. CPA lets client copy client-prepared financial statements on the CPA's letterhead.

f. Client issues quarterly financial statements and mentions CPA's review procedures but does not list CPA's name in the document.

g. CPA renders consulting advice about the system to prepare interim financial statements but does not review the statements prior to their release.

20.21. **Reports and the Evidence Dimension**
Nancy Miller, CPA, has completed the field work for her examination of the financial statements of Nickles Manufacturers, Inc., for the year ended March 31, 1985, and is now preparing her auditor's report.

She was engaged on April 15, 1985, to examine the financial statements for the year ended March 31, 1985, and was not present to observe the taking of the physical inventory on March 31, 1985. Her alternative procedure included: (1) examination of shipping and receiving documents with regard to transactions since the year-end, (2) extensive review of the inventory-count sheets and (3) discussion of the physical inventory procedures with responsible company personnel. She has also satisfied herself as to inventory valuation and consistency in valuation method. Inventory quantities are determined solely by means of physical count. (Note: Assume that she is properly relying upon the examination of another auditor with respect to the beginning inventory.)

Required:

a. Discuss the appropriate disclosures, if any, in the financial statements and accompanying footnotes.

b. Discuss the effect, if any, on the auditor's standard report.

(*AICPA* adapted)

20.22. **Comprehensive Basis Other than GAAP**
The Brooklyn Life Insurance Company prepares its financial statements on a statutory basis in conformity with the accounting practices prescribed and permitted by the Insurance Department of the State of New York. This statutory basis produces financial statements that differ materially from statements prepared in conformity with generally accepted accounting principles. On the statutory basis, for example, agents' first-year commissions are expensed instead of being partially deferred, and equity securities are reported at market value lower than cost, even if a "permanent impairment" of value is not evident.

The company engaged its auditors, Major-Major Associates, to audit the statutory basis financial statements and report on them. Footnote 10 in the statements contains a narrative description and a numerical table explaining the differences between the statutory basis and GAAP accounting. Footnote 10 also reconciles the statutory basis assets, liabilities, income, expense and net income (statutory basis) to the measurements that would be obtained using GAAP.

Required:

Write the special report appropriate in the circumstances on a comprehensive basis of accounting other than GAAP. The year-end date is December 31, 1985, and the audit field work was completed on February 20, 1986.

20.23. **Reporting on a Company in Financial Difficulty**
Client Corporation (a public company whose fiscal year will end December 31, 1985) informs you on December 18, 1985, that it has a serious shortage of working capital because of heavy operating losses incurred since October 1, 1985. Applica-

tion has been made to a bank for a loan, and the bank's loan officer has requested financial statements.

Required:

Indicate the type of opinion you would render under each of the following independent sets of circumstances. Give the reasons for your decision.

a. Client Corporation asks that you save time by auditing the financial statements prepared by Client's chief accountant as of September 30, 1985. The scope of your audit would not be limited by Client in any way.

b. Client Corporation asks that you conduct an audit as of December 15, 1985. The scope of your audit would not be limited by Client in any way.

c. Client Corporation asks that you conduct an audit as of December 31, 1985, and render a report by January 16. To save time and reduce the cost of the audit, Client's president requests that your examination not include confirmation of accounts receivable or observation of inventory taking.

d. Client Corporation asks that you prepare financial statements as of December 15, 1985, from the books and records of the company without audit. The statements are to be submitted on plain paper without your name being associated with them in any way. The reason for your preparing the statements is your familiarity with proper form for financial statements.

(*AICPA* adapted)

20.24. **Reports and the Materiality Dimension**

The concept of materiality is important to CPAs in audits of financial statements and expressions of opinion on these statements.

How will materiality influence an auditor's reporting decision in the following circumstances?

a. The client prohibits confirmation of accounts receivable, and sufficient competent evidence cannot be obtained using alternative procedures.

b. The client is a gas and electric utility company that follows the practice of recognizing revenue when it is billed to customers. At the end of the year, amounts earned but not yet billed are not recorded in the accounts or reported in the financial statements.

c. The client leases buildings for its chain of transmission repair shops under terms that qualify as capital leases under SFAS 13. These leases are not capitalized as leased property assets and lease obligations.

d. The client company has lost a lawsuit in federal district court. The case is on appeal in an attempt to reduce the amount of damages awarded to the plaintiffs.

20.25. **Reporting on Consistency**

CPAs must comply with the generally accepted auditing standards of reporting when they prepare opinions on clients' financial statements. One of the reporting standards relates to consistency.

Required:

a. Discuss the statement regarding consistency the CPA is required to include in the opinion. What is the objective of requiring this statement about consistency?

b. Discuss what mention of consistency, if any, a CPA must make in the opinion relating to a first audit of the financial statements of the following companies:

(1) A newly organized company ending its first accounting period.

(2) A company established for a number of years.

c. Discuss whether the changes described in each of the cases below would require recognition in the CPA's opinion as to consistency. (Assume the amounts are material.)

(1) The company disposed of one of its three subsidiaries that had been included in its consolidated statements for prior years.

(2) After two years of computing depreciation under the declining-balance method for income tax purposes and under the straight-line method for reporting purposes, the declining-balance method was adopted for reporting purposes.

(3) The estimated remaining useful life of plant property was reduced because of obsolescence.

(AICPA adapted)

20.26. **Reporting on Consistency**

Various types of "accounting changes" can affect the second reporting standard of the generally accepted auditing standards. This standard reads: "The report shall state whether such principles have been consistently observed in the current period in relation to the preceding period."

Assume that the following list describes changes which have a material effect on a client's financial statements for the current year:

1. A change from the completed-contract method to the percentage-of-completion method of accounting for long-term, construction-type contracts.

2. A change in the estimated useful life of previously recorded fixed assets based on newly acquired information.

3. Correction of a mathematical error in inventory pricing made in a prior period.

4. A change from prime costing to full absorption costing for inventory valuation.

5. A change from presentation of statements of individual companies to presentation of consolidated statements.

6. A change from deferring and amortizing preproduction costs to recording such costs as an expense when incurred because future benefits of the costs have become doubtful. The new accounting method was adopted in recognition of the change in estimated future benefits.

7. A change to including the employer share of FICA taxes in "retirement benefits" on the income statement from including it in "other taxes."

8. A change from the FIFO method of inventory pricing to the LIFO method of inventory pricing.

Required:

Identify the type of change described in each item above. State whether any modification is required in the auditor's report *as it relates to the second standard of reporting,* and state whether the prior year's financial statements should be restated when presented in comparative form with the current year's statements. Organize your answer sheet as shown in Exhibit 20.26–1.

For example, a change from the LIFO method of inventory pricing to the FIFO method of inventory pricing would appear as shown in Exhibit 20.26–1.

(AICPA adapted)

EXHIBIT 20.26–1

Item No.	Type of Change	Should Auditor's Report Be Modified?	Should Prior Year's Statements Be Restated?
Example	An accounting change from one generally accepted accounting principle to another generally accepted accounting principle.	Yes.	Yes.

20.27. **Qualified Opinions in Audit Reports**
The following cases and questions illustrate selected circumstances which require departures from the standard audit report. *Statements on Auditing Standards No. 2—* "Reports on Audited Financial Statements" (AU 509) and textbook Chapters 1 and 2 provide the necessary background.

For each case: (1) identify the nature of the circumstance that causes a departure from the standard audit report, (2) state whether the scope paragraph should be qualified and (3) state how the opinion would be qualified with "except for" or "subject to" language.

Case A:

San Fran Company engaged its auditors for the first time on August 10, 1985. The company's fourth fiscal year had ended on July 30, 1985, and a physical count of inventory was taken then. No perpetual records are kept, and the audit team was unable to observe any subsequent inventory taking or devise any other procedures to obtain evidence. San Fran's inventories are a significant asset, and sales of it are the source of 78 percent of total revenue.

Case B:

Seattle Ship Fitters, Inc., leased some lifting equipment which the auditors determined should be capitalized according to the requirements of SFAS 13. All necessary auditing procedures were performed, and the financial amounts affected were determined. Management did not adjust the financial statements.

Case C:

Vancouver Construction Company this year changed from the completed-contract method of accounting to the percentage-of-completion method. The change was made because the stage of completion costs and revenues for recent construction jobs could be reasonably estimated, whereas this had not been the case in the past. Under these conditions, the change to percentage of completion is justifiable as a change to a preferable method under APB 20.

Case D:

Portland Cement Company has been sued by a quarry company alleging underpayment of royalties on sand and gravel. The amounts involved are not small, but Portland could pay any ultimate judgment without suffering irreparable financial harm. Counterclaims have been filed, and the company's outside counsel believes Portland has a good chance of avoiding additional payments. However, the ultimate outcome cannot be determined as of the audit report date.

Case E:

Salt Lake Cement Company is also being sued by the same quarry company that sued Portland Cement Company. However, in this case the quarry company has already won a $50 million judgment in district court. Salt Lake's current assets amount to $10 million and net worth is $35 million, before taking the judgment into account. Salt Lake and its lawyers have filed an appeal, but the situation is in considerable doubt as of the audit report date.

20.28. **Opinion Reflecting Departure from GAAP**
The board of directors of Jersey Lee Company has engaged you to audit the financial statements for the year ended June 30, 1985. The company stock is traded over the counter. You previously audited the fiscal 1984 financial statements and are well aware that the company values its inventories at the cost of labor and materials, without any allocation of manufacturing overhead.

Jersey Lee management has not restricted your audit in any way. After proposing several relatively minor adjustments, which were accepted and entered, you prepared an analysis of the effect of the inventory-valuation method. (See Exhibit 20.28–1.)

Required:

Prepare the audit report on the 1985 statements for the board of directors. As-

EXHIBIT 20.28-1

Index _____

JERSEY LEE COMPANY
Summary of Effect
of Inventory Valuation
June 30, 1985

By _____

Date _____

	Reported	Corrected	Understatement (Overstatement)
Balance sheet:			
Inventories.	$3,567,000	$4,257,000	$690,000
Income taxes payable.	23,000	373,000	350,000
Retained earnings	1,242,000	1,582,000	340,000
Statement of operations:			
Cost of products sold	9,348,000	9,187,000	(161,000)
Loss before income taxes	(316,000)	(155,000)	(161,000)
Federal income taxes	122,000	199,000	77,000
Net loss	(438,000)	(354,000)	(84,000)
Statement of retained earnings:			
Balance at beginning of year . . .	1,762,000	2,018,000	256,000
Net loss	(438,000)	(354,000)	(84,000)
Balance at end of year	1,324,000	1,664,000	340,000
Statement of changes in financial position:			
Net loss	(438,000)	(354,000)	(84,000)
Funds used in operations	628,000	544,000	(84,000)
Increase in inventory	773,000	612,000	(161,000)

sume that all financial statements and required footnotes are presented, but Jersey Lee has not adjusted the accounts for your findings about the inventory valuation method.

20.29. Rewrite an Audit Report

Roscoe, CPA, has completed the audit of the financial statements of Excelsior Corporation as of, and for, the year ended December 31, 1985. Roscoe also examined and reported on the Excelsior financial statements for the prior year. Roscoe drafted the following report for 1985.

We have examined the balance sheet and statements of income and retained earnings of Excelsior Corporation as of December 31, 1985. Our examination was made in accordance with generally accepted accounting standards and, accordingly, included such tests of the accounting records as we considered necessary in the circumstances.

In our opinion, the above-mentioned financial statements are accurately prepared and fairly presented in accordance with generally accepted accounting principles in effect at December 31, 1985.

/s/Roscoe, CPA
March 15, 1986

Other information:

a. Excelsior is presenting comparative financial statements.

b. Excelsior does not wish to present a statement of changes in financial position for either year.

c. During 1985, Excelsior changed its method of accounting for long-term construction contracts and properly reflected the effect of the change in the current year's financial statements and restated the prior year's statements. Roscoe is satisfied with Excelsior's justification for making the change. The change is discussed in footnote 12.

d. Roscoe was unable to perform normal accounts receivable confirmation procedures, but alternate procedures were used to obtain evidence about the receivables.

e. Excelsior Corporation is the defendant in a lawsuit, the outcome of which is highly uncertain. If the case is settled in favor of the plaintiff, Excelsior will be required to pay a substantial amount of cash which might require the sale of certain fixed assets. The litigation and the possible effects have been properly disclosed in footnote 11.

f. Excelsior issued debentures on January 31, 1986, in the amount of $10,000,000. The funds were used to finance the expansion of plant facilities. The debenture agreement restricts the payment of future cash dividends to earnings after December 31, 1990. Excelsior declined to disclose this essential data in the footnotes to the financial statements.

Required:

Consider all facts given and rewrite the auditor's report in acceptable and complete format incorporating any necessary departure from the standard report.

(*AICPA* adapted)

20.30. **Explain Deficiencies in an Audit Report**

The following audit report was written by your partner yesterday. You need to describe the reporting deficiencies, explain the reasons for them, and discuss with him how the report should be corrected. This may be a hard job because he has always felt somewhat threatened because you were the first woman partner in the firm. You have decided to write up a three-column worksheet showing the deficiencies, reasons and correction needed. This was his report:

I made my examination in accordance with generally accepted auditing standards. However, I am not independent with respect to Mavis Corporation because my wife owns 5 percent of the outstanding common stock of the company. The accompanying balance sheet as of December 31, 1985, and the related statements of income and retained earnings and changes in financial position for the year then ended were not audited by me. Accordingly, I do not express an opinion on them.

Required:

Prepare the worksheet described above.

DISCUSSION CASES

20.31. **Information Disclosure—Fallhard Manufacturing Company**

In 1985, Fallhard Manufacturing Company was experiencing financial difficulty. After reporting a small profit in 1983, the loss for 1984 was $3.8 million. Total assets were $89 million, shareholder's equity was $38 million, and outstanding long-term and short-term debt to financial institutions was $31.6 million as of December 31, 1984. The company obtained shareholder approval to sell $10 million of 9 percent cumulative preferred stock to Gofast, Inc., and closed the sale in December, 1985. The proceeds were used to pay off $5 million of the long-term debt.

After purchasing the preferred stock, Gofast, Inc., became a "related party" as defined in SAS 45 (AU 1020).

However, in December 1984, prior to the stock transaction, Gofast had purchased a manufacturing facility from Fallhard for $3 million, which was Fallhard's book value of the plant. Repayment terms were: (1) immediate down payment of $500,000; (2) $.50 for each unit of product produced at the plant, payable semiannually and (3) five sixths of the proceeds from the sale of any equipment or real estate transferred with the plant property. Fallhard took a nonrecourse note for $2.5 million, and at December 31, 1984, this amount was classified as a non-current asset.

After Fallhard reported a $1 million loss in 1985, some stockholders began to complain. One spoke up at the annual meeting, held on March 1, 1986, saying: "The comparative financial statements in the annual report for 1984 and 1985 are materially misleading. In particular, they fail to disclose the nature and terms of the related party transaction with Gofast, Inc. We might have grounds for a lawsuit."

For Discussion:

a. Gofast, Inc., was not a related party in 1984 when the plant was purchased. Should the nature and terms of the transaction and the note have been disclosed anyway?

b. As of December 31, 1985, however, Gofast, Inc., had become a related party. Should the auditor qualify the opinion on the 1985 statements because Fallhard did not retroactively apply the related party transaction disclosure rules to the plant sale transaction?

20.32. **Preferability of Accounting Methods**
Hughes-Hyland Freight Company (HH) operates a large overland trucking business. HH has a fleet of 100 trucks based in 10 depots scattered throughout 12 western states. Freight customers contract for pickup and delivery and pay rates regulated by the Interstate Commerce Commission.

Customers who use HH are frequently billed monthly on the basis of shipments delivered. Other customers pay the freight charges at the time of pickup. HH is obligated to deliver the shipment in good condition to the destination. If goods are damaged in transit (a rare occurrence), HH must refund the freight charges. However, HH is not liable for the damage, and customers usually purchase their own insurance.

Several years ago, Arch Conserve, the corporate controller, chose to use the "de-

livered method" of recognizing freight revenue. However, an alternative method ("picked up") is now used by about two thirds of the companies in the industry. These two methods are described as follows:

Delivered Method. Upon reaching the destination, the truck driver records the time and date on a copy of the shipping papers. This copy is returned to the accounting office and (1) serves as the basis for billing customers who receive monthly statements or (2) serves as the basis for transferring amounts from the Deposit Revenue account to the Revenue account for customers who paid at the time of pickup. At the fiscal year-end, an entry is made to defer to the next year some operating costs related to shipments in transit. This deferral is never very large because the time between pickup and delivery seldom exceeds 10 days.

Picked-Up Method. Under this method, revenue is recognized at the time of pickup without regard to when the shipment is actually delivered. At the fiscal year-end, estimated operating expenses related to shipments in transit (delivered in the next accounting period) are accrued. This method is simpler than the "delivered method" because drivers' reports of delivery time and date do not have to be processed directly through the revenue recognition and account system.

For Discussion:

a. As an auditor, would you be able to evaluate management's original choice of the "delivered method?" Is it an appropriate accounting method that properly reflects the substance of HH's revenue recognition transactions?

b. Assume a new controller took over and changed to the "picked-up method." As a successor auditor (newly engaged by HH), would you be able to evaluate management's new choice of method? Is it an appropriate accounting method that properly reflects the substance of HH's revenue recognition transactions?

c. Assume you were the auditor both before and after HH's change of method and must prepare a report stating whether the change was to a "preferable accounting method that provides a better measure of business operations." Would you be able to decide whether the "picked-up method" was or was not preferable in this sense?

d. Independent of your response in (c) above, would your decision be harder or easier if GG Truck Lines, another client, used the "delivered method" and did not plan to change?

20.33. **Going-Concern Problems—Tenfour Company**[15]

On December 10, 1976, you are trying to complete the audit for the year ended September 30 of Tenfour Company, a manufacturer of CB (citizen's band) radios. Tenfour is a major company in the industry and has enjoyed the boom times of heavy demand for CB radio units. Earlier in 1976, investors snatched up a public stock offering at $25 per share, a price that amounted to 15 times 1975 earnings per share.

Late in the day, you are studying—for the 10th time—the following footnote disclosures that have been prepared by Tenfour management. They are very accurate.

Note E—Government Regulation. Because of serious overcrowding of citizen's radio bands, the Federal Communications Commission has banned the sale of 23-channel CB radios. Forty channels are now authorized, but the FCC has ruled that manufacturers can accept no orders prior to January 1, 1977. Consumers apparently do not want to buy the old 23-channel units, and the result has been a dramatic

downturn in sales as the company approaches the traditionally busy Christmas season.

Note F—Bank Debt. The company's $40 million bank debt, bearing 11 percent interest, is in default as a result of lack of sales and sales revenue. Temporary waivers of default action have been obtained, and the company is renegotiating the terms of the debt.

Note G—Quarterly Results Unaudited.

Sales in Millions	Fiscal Year 1975		Fiscal Year 1976	
	Sales	EPS	Sales	EPS
Quarter ended:				
December 31 . . .	$15	$ .53	$18	$ .60
March 31.	10	.36	12	.38
June 30	12	.43	7	(.15)
September 30 . .	10	.35	2	(.58)
Year ended				
September 30 . .	$47	$1.67	$39	$0.25

Note H—Pending Litigation. Certain shareholders who purchased stock in the January 1976 public offering have filed suit in federal district court claiming unspecified damages and alleging the company's violation of the Securities Act of 1933. The company's outside legal counsel has not had an opportunity to study the complaint, and proceedings are still in the discovery phase. Company management believes this lawsuit has no merit and that its ultimate resolution will have no material effect on the company's financial position.

After re-reading these notes, you also review certain other information.

The company has a huge inventory of 23-channel CB units. When consumer demand was heavy, distributors would book multiple orders to ensure a supply. Now that demand has dried up, they are canceling orders and refusing to accept shipments.

Sixteen other manufacturing companies compete in the domestic market. Four

---

[15] The 1976 and 1977 dates in this case are used because FCC actions occurred at that time.

of them have already declared bankruptcy and sought protection under Chapter XI of the Bankruptcy Act.

The company has not switched to 40-channel production, counting instead on marketing a $25 converter that will be sold with a 23-channel unit. Right now, there is extremely sharp price-cutting among manufacturers of 40-channel sets.

An analysis by a respected investment research organization has predicted a serious shakeout among companies in the industry. The analyst's report guesses that half the companies will fold, but no predictions were made about which ones.

Industry lobbyists in Washington, D.C., are pushing hard for a substantial increase in import duties on cheaper Japanese units. However, the government's inflation fighting and counterpressures in favor of free trade may blunt this effort.

The industry is in a mess, but Tenfour has a recent history of great success. If 1977 demand picks up, if consumers want the 23-channel set plus converter package, if cash holds out until the demand develops, and if foreign competition does not drive prices down too much, the company might have a decent chance to return to profitability.

The company is anxious to see the audit report. Tenfour's president has already told you that he must hand-carry a copy to the lending banks, and he thinks anything less than an unqualified opinion will make the renegotiations very tough.

For Discussion:

a. Is Tenfour Company going or gone?

b. Will a disclaimer of opinion on the grounds of a massive going-concern uncertainty *cause* Tenfour to declare bankruptcy?

c. Would the auditor be in a better professional position if he or she did not

have to try to predict the outcome of future events?

d. What kind of opinion would you give on the Tenfour Company financial statements?

20.34. **Issuing the Audit Report**

About two years ago, you were engaged to conduct an annual audit of Flymire Company. This was shortly after the majority stockholders assumed control of the company and discharged the president and several other corporate officers. A new president canceled a wholesaler's contract to distribute Flymire Company products. The wholesaler is a Flymire Company minority stockholder and was one of the discharged officers. Shortly after you commenced your initial audit, several lawsuits were filed against Flymire Company by the wholesaler. Flymire Company filed countersuits.

None of the suits has been decided. The principal litigation is over the canceled contract. The other suits are claims against the company for salary, bonus, and pension fund contributions. Flymire Company is the plaintiff in suits totaling approximately $300,000 and defendant in suits totaling approximately $2 million. Both amounts are material in relation to net income and total assets. Flymire's legal counsel believes the outcome of the suits is uncertain and will be in court proceedings for a long time.

You were instructed by the board of directors each year to issue an audit report only if it contained an unqualified opinion. Flymire Company refuses to provide for an unfavorable settlement in the financial statements because legal counsel advised the board of directors that such a provision in the financial statements could be used against Flymire by the opposition. The pending litigation was fully disclosed in a footnote to the financial statements, however.

You did not write a report on the completion of your audit one year ago, and you have now completed your second annual audit. The scope of your audits was not restricted in any way, and you would render unqualified opinions if there were no pending litigation. You have attended all meetings of the stockholders and the directors and answered all questions directed to you at these meetings. You have been paid promptly for all work completed to the current date. The board of directors of Flymire Company has invited you to deliver to them an audit report containing an unqualified opinion or to attend the annual meeting of the stockholders one week hence to answer questions concerning the results of your audit if you are unwilling to render an unqualified opinion.

Required:

a. Discuss the issues raised for the CPA by the fact that he attended the stockholders' and directors' meetings and answered all questions addressed to him. Do not consider the propriety of his failure to issue a written audit report.

b. Should a CPA issue his audit report promptly after he has completed his examination? Why?

c. What kind of auditor's opinion would you render on Flymire Company's financial statements for the year just ended? Why?

(*AICPA* adapted)

20.35. **Harper Hoe Co.—Report Writing**
The Harper Hoe Company report writing case is presented in Chapter 1, problem 1.21. It requires reports for certain accounting facts and auditing circumstances. You may find it very beneficial for practicing the reporting topics covered in Chapter 20.

20.36. **Complex Report with Scope Limitation**
Ross, Sandler & Co., CPAs, completed an examination of the 1985 financial statements of Fairfax Corporation on March 17, 1986, and concluded that an unqualified opinion was warranted. Because of a scope limitation arising from the inability to observe the January 1, 1984 inventory, the predecessor auditors, Smith, Ellis & Co., issued a report which contained an unqualified opinion on the December 31, 1984 balance sheet and a qualified opinion with respect to the statements of income, retained earnings, and changes in financial position for the year then ended.

The management of Fairfax Corporation has decided to present a complete set of comparative (1985 and 1984) financial statements in their annual report.

Required:

Prepare an auditor's report assuming the March 1, 1985, auditors report of Smith, Ellis & Co. is not presented.

20.37. **Uncertainty and Accounting Issues**
Peaco Corp. builds pollution control equipment. In the year just ended December 31, 19X4, the company had sales of $600 million and net income of $26 million. In the fourth quarter of the year, however, reported net income was $7 million or $.84 per share, exactly the same as in the fourth quarter of 19X3. Company management takes pride in the fact that earnings have increased about 10 percent each quarter of the corresponding year-earlier period for the last four years.

These fourth quarter data were released January 20. It is now February 20, and you are about to complete your audit covering the comparative 19X4 and 19X3 financial statements. Only one matter remains for resolution.

During the fourth quarter of 19X4, Peaco experienced difficulty with a subcontractor on a medium-size project. The result was that the subcontractor was released, and Peaco filed lawsuits totaling $4 million for breach of contract, claiming that the company had incurred additional costs of $2.5 million as a result of the subcontractor's actions. The subcontractor has filed counterclaims for $6 million in damages. Peaco attorneys say that all this litigation will take a long time to settle in court unless it is negotiated in out-of-court agreements.

In the meantime, Peaco accounted for the $4 million damage claims as cost offsets against the $2.5 million actual additional cost (an amount you have found to be materially accurate). Your problem now concerns the accounting validity of recognizing the $4 million claim. The effect of alternative accounting is that net income would be $5 million in the fourth quarter (and EPS would be 60 cents), and net income for the year would be $24 million (and EPS would be $2.88 for 19X4 compared to $2.40 for 19X3).

Required:

Decide what to do about the audit report and write the opinion paragraph and any explanatory or emphasis paragraphs you consider necessary. You may assume that all matters of litigation were fully described in footnote L to the financial statements.

CHAPTER 21

PROFESSIONAL STANDARDS SOURCES		
Compendium Section	**Document Reference**	**Topic**
AU 435	SAS 21	Segment Information
AU 505	SAS 15	Reports on Comparative Financial Statements
AU 9505		Interpretations: Reports on Comparative Statements
AU 543	SAS 1	Part of Examination Made by Other Independent Auditors
AU 9543		Interpretations: Other Auditors
AU 545	SAS 1	Inadequate Disclosure (Omission of Statement of Changes in Financial Position)
AU 621	SAS 14	Special Reports (Specified Elements, Accounts or Items, and Compliance with Contractual or Regulatory Requirements)
AU 9621		Interpretations: Special Reports
AU 622	SAS 35	Special Reports—Applying Agreed-Upon Procedures to Specified Elements, Accounts or Items of a Financial Statement
AU 631	SAS 38	Letters for Underwriters
AU 9631		Interpretations: Letters for Underwriters

Reports by Independent Auditors (concluded)

LEARNING OBJECTIVES

This chapter covers seven additional topics involving audit reports. In addition to the variations covered in Chapter 20, auditors can be requested to render other reports or may be required to follow additional procedures. The seven topics in this chapter are discussed separately to enable you to see them as specific considerations in audits. After studying this chapter, you should be able to:

☐ Write an audit report on comparative financial statements when the opinion on the current-year financial statements is different from the opinion on the prior-year financial statements.

☐ Identify circumstances with relation to segment information in which the audit opinion should be qualified.

☐ Write an audit report in which a principal auditor refers to the work and report of another independent auditor.

☐ Write a report qualified because the statement of changes in financial position was omitted.

☐ Explain auditors' responsibilities in special engagements to report on elements, accounts or items of financial statements, and compliance with contractual agreements or regulatory requirements.

☐ Explain underwriters' reasons for requesting a "comfort letter" from an auditor in connection with a Securities Act (1933) registration.

☐ Discuss the general features of accounting, auditing and reporting related to personal financial statements.

REPORTING ON COMPARATIVE STATEMENTS

Public companies usually present comparative balance sheets for two years and comparative income statements for three years. Financial statement footnotes also usually contain disclosures in comparative form for two or three years. Auditors' reports relate to "financial statements taken as a whole," referring to the financial schedules and footnotes taken together. SAS No. 15 (AU 505), *Reports on Comparative Financial Statements,* expanded the concept of "financial statements taken as a whole" to include the statements of one or more comparative prior periods as well as the current-year statements.

When auditors previously have issued a report on prior-year statements presented in current-year comparative form, they should *update* the report previously issued. An **updated report** is one based not only on the prior year audit but also on information that has come to light since then (particularly in the course of the current-year audit work). An updated report may be the same as previously issued, or it may be different depending on whether current information causes a retroactive change in the auditor's reporting decision. An updated report carries the date of the end of the most recent field work.[1]

The language of a report on comparative financial statements cites two (or more) balance sheet dates and two (or more) accounting periods and expresses the opinion on all of the statements. The date of the report is the date on which all important field work was completed on the current-year audit. Thus, the standard report on comparative financial statements contains an updated report on the prior-year financial statements, as well as a report on the current-year statements, when there is no change in auditors.

Complications arise, and care must be taken with report language when the two (or more) comparative statements carry differing opinions and when a successor auditor is reporting on the current-year statements. Differing opinions cases involve the following:

Qualified opinion on current-year financial statements with prior-year unqualified.

Qualified opinion on prior-year financial statements with the current-year qualified for the same and an additional reason.

Unqualified opinion on the current-year financial statements with disclaimer of opinion on the prior-year statement of income.

Unqualified opinion on current-year balance sheet with disclaimer of opinion on prior-year unaudited financial statements.

---

[1] An *updated report* differs from the **reissuance** of a previously expressed report. A reissuance amounts to providing more copies of the report or giving permission to use it in another document sometime after its original delivery date. The report date of a reissued report is the original date of the end of field work on that year's audit, indicating a cutoff date for the auditor's responsibility to report on subsequent events. (See SAS 1, AU 530.06–.08.)

Disclaimer of opinion on current-year unaudited financial statements with opinion on prior-year audited financial statements.

An example of a differing opinion is shown in Exhibit 21–1. The auditor's report on fiscal 1982, when issued in 1982, contained qualifying language related to an uncertainty about the outcome of an IRS investigation of a tax controversy. In 1983, the uncertainty was resolved, and the updated opinion on the 1982 financial statements, when issued in 1983 in comparative form, was changed to an unqualified opinion.

EXHIBIT 21–1
Comparative Statement
Opinion Changed from
Qualified to Unqualified

To the Stockholders and Board of Directors, Zapata Corporation:

We have examined the consolidated balance sheet of Zapata Corporation (a Delaware corporation) and subsidiary companies as of September 30, 1983 and 1982, and the related consolidated statements of income, reinvested earnings and capital in excess of par value and changes in financial position for each of the three years in the period ended September 30, 1983. Our examinations were made in accordance with generally accepted auditing standards and accordingly, included such tests of the accounting records and such other auditing procedures as we considered necessary in the circumstances.

In our auditors' report dated November 17, 1982, our opinion on the consolidated financial statements was qualified as being subject to the effect of such adjustments, if any, as might have been required had the outcome been known of the controversy with the Internal Revenue Service with respect to the taxation of unremitted earnings of Zapata's foreign drilling subsidiaries. As explained in Note 4 to the Financial Statements, a settlement for the years 1971 through 1979 was reached with the Internal Revenue Service in November 1983, with no material impact on Zapata's results of operations or financial position, and management is of the opinion that this issue will be settled for the years 1980 through 1983 in a similar manner. Accordingly, our present opinion on the consolidated financial statements, as presented herein, is different from that expressed in our previous report.

In our opinion, the financial statements referred to above present fairly the financial position of Zapata Corporation and subsidiary companies as of September 30, 1983 and 1982, and the results of their operations and changes in their financial position for each of the three years in the period ended September 30, 1983, in conformity with generally accepted accounting principles applied on a consistent basis.

Arthur Andersen & Co.
November 11, 1983

AUDITED
SEGMENT
INFORMATION

Segment information is part of the "financial statements taken as a whole" for public companies. Therefore, the standard unqualified report covers the segment information as well as the other financial statements. The financial accounting standards in SFAS 14, *Financial Reporting for Segments of a Business Enterprise,* requires disclosure of segment information in financial statements presented in conformity with generally accepted accounting principles. The information is a disaggregation of elements of a business's financial statements—revenue, operating profit or loss, identifiable assets, depreciation, capital expenditures—on the basis of industries, foreign operations, export sales, and major customers. Segment information on segments representing 10 percent or more of total revenue is required in the financial statements of public companies but not in statements of nonpublic companies.

According to SAS 21 (AU435.03), *Segment Information,* the objective of auditing procedures applied to segment information is to provide evidence for deciding whether the information is presented in conformity with SFAS 14. The procedures do not necessarily enable auditors to express an opinion on the segment information taken by itself. The spirit of SAS 21 is to guide auditors with respect to the segment information when expressing an opinion on the financial statements taken as a whole.

A client may represent that there are no segments of the business requiring disaggregated presentation in conformity with SFAS 14. In such cases, auditors must be able to use knowledge of the business and the industry to determine whether the client's representation is correct. If so, an unqualified opinion may be rendered. However, if auditors cannot determine whether segments exist, and the client will not develop further information, the audit team faces a *limitation on the scope of the audit.* In such a case, the scope paragraph of the report would be qualified to explain the lack of evidence, and the opinion paragraph would be qualified with the language: "In our opinion, except for the possible omission of segment information, the financial statements present. . . ." (See SAS 21, AU 435.15–.16, for other examples of illustrative qualification language.)

When segment information is presented, the following procedures should be applied:

☐ *Review, evaluate* and *become acquainted with:*
Internal accounting control in operating segments.
Nature, number, and size of industry segments, subsidiaries and divisions, and geographic areas.
Accounting principles used in industry segments and geographic areas.

☐ *Inquire* of management concerning methods of determining segment information and *evaluate* the reasonableness of those methods.

☐ *Inquire* about the basis of accounting for sales or transfers among segments and areas, and *audit* a sample of such transactions.

☐ *Audit* the disaggregation of financial statement information into segment information, utilizing *analytical review* procedures.

> ☐ *Inquire* about allocation methods, *evaluate* reasonableness of the methods, and *audit a sample* of the allocations.
>
> ☐ *Determine* whether segment accounting methods and segment information are presented consistently from period to period.

These compliance and substantive procedures essentially outline the audit work applicable to segment information. They call for no less than sufficient competent evidence regarding the disaggregated segment information.

The audit report on financial statements containing segment information is *implicit*. That is, the report is unqualified as long as the auditor takes no exception. The standard unqualified report on the financial statements is qualified only when auditors find: (1) material error in the segment information, (2) technical misapplication of SFAS 14, (3) omission of segment information or (4) inconsistency in the presentation of the segment information. The *materiality* in each of these cases is evaluated with reference to the "financial statements taken as a whole." However, auditors must be careful to consider not only the relative dollar amount of errors, misapplications or omissions, but also the *qualitative* characteristics of the information. For example, a material error (say, 30 percent) in the revenue attributed to a small segment may amount to only three percent of total company revenue, but if the segment is represented by management as a key segment for business development and future profitability, the error should be considered material. Other qualitative features would include errors that distort segment trends or errors involved in segments representing business in politically sensitive foreign countries.

When a material error, misapplication, omission or inconsistency exists, the audit report is qualified with language indicating either a departure from generally accepted accounting principles (SFAS 14) or a consistency exception that affects the financial statements taken as a whole. Consistency matters related strictly to the segment information (not affecting the aggregated financial statements) are covered in the accounting principles. So, any change not accounted for and disclosed in conformity with SFAS 14 would cause an opinion to be qualified for nonconformity with accounting principles rather than a consistency exception.

Audit reports usually contain no special mention of segment information, thus letting readers assume it is covered by the opinion. However, many actual reports contain identification of the segment information; for example, with the notice: "We have also audited the accompanying segment information. . . ." The segment information is often covered explicitly in the opinion paragraph: "Also, in our opinion, the segment information referred to above is presented fairly in conformity with generally accepted accounting principles applied on a consistent basis." Of course, opinion qualifications must refer to errors or omissions in the segment information. If a company simply declines to present segment information, the audit report will contain a qualification based on SFAS 14, but auditors are not required to produce and present the omitted information in the report.

Auditors can report separately on segment information. In this case, the context is a special report on elements of financial statements. Guiding standards are in SAS 14 on *Special Reports* (AU 621.09–.13).

USING THE WORK AND REPORTS OF OTHER INDEPENDENT AUDITORS

Often a *principal auditor* audits a material portion of a reporting entity's assets, liabilities, revenues and expenses. At the same time, other independent auditors may be engaged to audit subsidiaries, divisions, branches, components or investments that are included in the reporting entity's financial statements. However, the ***principal auditor*** is the one whose signature appears on the report of the financial statements of a consolidated or parent entity. The auditor of the reporting entity must first determine who is the principal auditor and then must make other decisions regarding use of the work and reports of the other independent auditor(s).

The principal auditor must first obtain information about the independence and professional responsibility of the other auditor(s). If the principal auditor is satisfied with these qualities, he or she must next communicate with the other auditor and decide whether to make reference in the audit report to the other auditor. The principal auditor may decide to make no reference, and the audit report will follow the form and wording of the standard unqualified report.

On the other hand, the principal auditor may decide to refer to the work and reports of other auditors in his or her own audit report. Such a reference is not in itself a scope or an opinion qualification, and the report is not inferior to a report that does not contain a reference. The decision to refer to the other auditor(s) shows *divided responsibility* for the audit work, and the explanation should show very clearly the extent of the divided responsibility by disclosing the percent or amount of assets, revenues and expenses covered by other auditors' work. However, the opinion paragraph must be consistent with the sufficiency and competency of evidence gathered by all the auditors. If other auditors have rendered opinions qualified in some way, the circumstances must be considered by the principal auditor in writing his or her own opinion.

When the principal auditor refers to the other auditors' work, the other auditor is ordinarily not identified by name. (See the example in Exhibit 21–2.) In fact, the other auditor can be named in the principal auditor's report only by express permission *and* provided his audit report on his part of the entity is published along with the report of the principal auditor.

An example of an opinion with references to work and reports of other auditors is shown in Exhibit 21–2.

Exhibit 21–3 contains a detailed explanation of the several elements of

EXHIBIT 21–2
Reference to Work and
Report of Other Auditors

To the Board of Directors, Eaton Vance Corp.:

We have examined the consolidated balance sheets of Eaton Vance Corp. as of October 31, 1983 and 1982, and the related consolidated statements of income, changes in shareholders' equity, and changes in financial position for each of the three years in the period ended October 31, 1983. Our examinations were made in accordance with generally accepted auditing standards, and accordingly included such tests of the accounting records and such other auditing procedures as we considered necessary in the circumstances. We did not examine the financial statements of Serio Exploration Company or Investors Bank & Trust Company, unconsolidated subsidiaries. The Company's investments in Serio Exploration Company and Investors Bank & Trust Company aggregated $3,253,588 and $3,246,044 at October 31, 1983 and 1982, respectively, and its equity in the earnings of such companies amounted to $176,126, $202,770, and $393,273 for the years ended October 31, 1983, 1982, and 1981, respectively. The financial statements of such companies were examined by other auditors whose reports thereon have been furnished to us, and our opinion expressed herein, insofar as it relates to the amounts included for such companies, is based solely upon such reports.

In our opinion, based upon our examinations and the reports of the other auditors referred to above, the aforementioned financial statements present fairly the consolidated financial position of Eaton Vance Corp. at October 31, 1983 and 1982, and the consolidated results of its operations and the changes in its consolidated financial position for each of the three years in the period ended October 31, 1983, in conformity with generally accepted accounting principles applied on a consistent basis.

Meahl, McNamara & Co.,
Certified Public Accountants
December 16, 1983

a principal auditor's decision on whether to use, rely on, and/or refer to the work of other auditors. These decisions involve the materiality of financial operations audited by others and the extent of familiarity with the other auditors' professional qualifications.

OMISSION OF
BASIC FINANCIAL
STATEMENT(S)

APB Opinion No. 19, *Reporting on Changes in Financial Position,* requires a statement of changes in financial position to be presented with financial statements of a for-profit entity which purport to show both financial position and results of operations. If such a statement of changes is omitted, the audit report must be qualified because of a departure from generally accepted accounting principles.

A failure to disclose required information normally results in auditors including the information in the report. However, auditing standards make an exception in this case. It is not appropriate for an auditor to prepare and present a whole financial schedule—the statement of changes in financial position—in the audit report.[2] Consequently, the recom-

---

[2] *Statement on Auditing Standards No. 1* (AU 545.05), as amended by SAS 21 (AU 435).

EXHIBIT 21–3
Using the Work and Reports of Other Auditors (interpretation of *SAS 1*, AU 543)

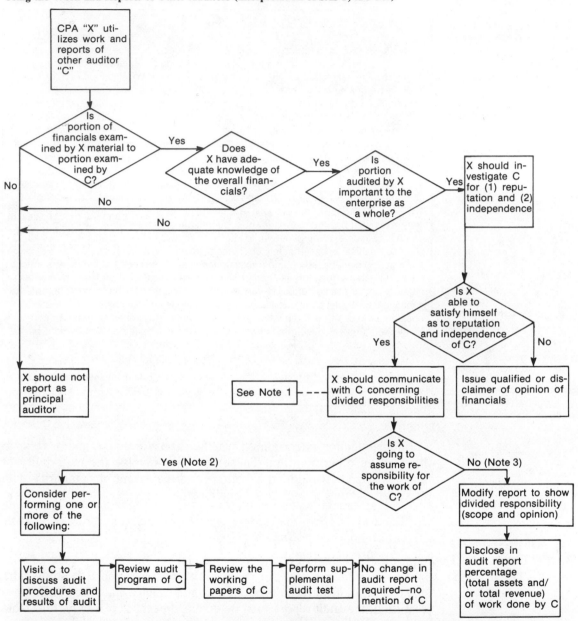

Note 1: X should ensure that C understands (1) the financials examined by him will be included in financials reported on by X, (2) United States GAAP and auditing standards, (3) the relevant reporting requirements of the SEC (if appropriate), and (4) a review will be made of (a) matters affecting intercompany eliminations and, if appropriate, (b) uniformity of accounting practices employed in component statements.

Note 2: Ordinarily this alternative is adopted when C (other auditor) is a correspondent firm, an agent of X, or the portion of financials examined by C is not material.

Note 3: This alternative is usually adopted when (1) it is impracticable for X to review C's work or apply other procedures to gain satisfaction and (2) financials examined by C are material in relation to overall financials.

Source: *Journal of Accountancy*, March 1974, p. 84. Copyright © 1974 by the American Institute of Certified Public Accountants, Inc. (adapted).

mended report form is as follows: (Notice that there is no mention of the statement of changes in financial position in the scope paragraph.)

> We have examined the balance sheet of X Company as of December 31, 19—, and the related statements of income and retained earnings for the year then ended. Our examination was made in accordance with generally accepted auditing standards and, accordingly, included such tests of the accounting records and such other auditing procedures as we considered necessary in the circumstances.
>
> The company declined to present a statement of changes in financial position for the year ended December 31, 19—. Presentation of such statement summarizing the company's financing and investing activities and other changes in its financial position is required by *Opinion No. 19* of the Accounting Principles Board.
>
> In our opinion, except that the omission of a statement of changes in financial position results in an incomplete presentation as explained in the preceding paragraph, the aforementioned financial statements present fairly the financial position of X Company at December 31, 19—, and the results of its operations for the year then ended in conformity with generally accepted accounting principles applied on a basis consistent with that of the preceding year.

The sequence of decisions involved in reporting on the omission of the statement of changes is shown in Exhibit 21–4.

In some engagements, auditors may be requested to report on only one aspect of financial affairs; for example, only on financial position and not on results of operations, or only on results of operations and not on financial position. Auditing standards interpret such constraints as limited reporting objectives and not as limitations on the scope of an engagement.[3] However, this kind of situation creates a problem because APB Opinion No. 19 requires *three* financial schedules (balance sheet, income statement, and statement of changes in financial position) in order to present *two* financial aspects (financial position and results of operations).

Auditing standards permit auditors to associate the income statement schedule with a report on results of operations and the balance sheet with a report on financial position. The statement of changes in financial position seems to be associated with neither when they are presented separately, but it is a required and integral statement when they are presented together.

Consequently, an opinion only on the fair presentation of financial position may be on the balance sheet alone, and an opinion only on results of operations may be on the income statement alone. In either case, it is not considered necessary to supply the missing financial statements in the audit report itself nor is it necessary to modify the audit report in any way other than to omit any mention in the scope and opinion paragraphs of the omitted financial statements. Thus, auditors do not insist that each and

---

[3] *Statement on Auditing Standards No. 1* (AU 509.13).

EXHIBIT 21-4
Reporting on the Statement of Changes in Financial Position (interpretation of SAS 1, AU 420.15–.16, 504.12 and 545.04–.05)

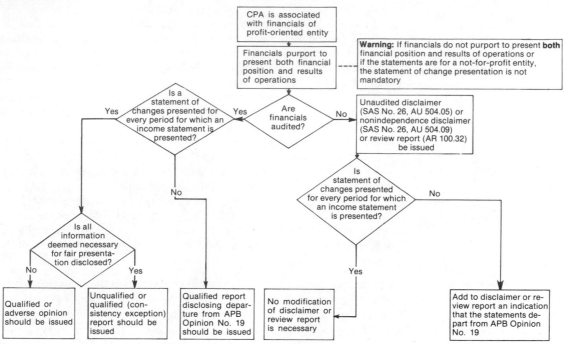

Source: *Journal of Accountancy,* March 1974, p. 86. Copyright © 1974 by the American Institute of Certified Public Accountants, Inc. (adapted).

every financial presentation be complete with all three financial statements.

SPECIAL ENGAGEMENTS AND REPORTS

Auditors may perform a variety of services *acting in the capacity of auditor* (not as tax advisor or management consultant) that require a report other than the standard unqualified audit report. Such services involve special reports issued in connection with:

Engagements to report on specified elements, accounts, or items of a financial statement (SAS 14, AU 621.09–14, and SAS 35, AU 622).

Engagements to report on compliance with contractual agreements or regulatory requirements (SAS 14, AU 621.18–.19).

Limited-scope engagements to perform procedures agreed upon by the client (SAS 35, AU 622).

Specified Elements, Accounts, or Items

Auditors may be requested to render special reports on such things as rentals, royalties, profit participations, or a provision for income taxes. The first AICPA reporting standard does not apply because the specified element, account or item does not purport to be a financial statement of financial position or results of operations. The second AICPA reporting standard (consistency) applies only if the element, account or item is measured according to some provision of generally accepted accounting principles.

Special engagements with limited objectives enable auditors to provide needed services to clients. SAS 14 (AU 621.14) gives examples of reports relating to amount of sales used in computing rental, reports relating to royalties, reports on a profit participation, and a report on the adequacy of a tax provision in financial statements. Exhibit 21–5 contains a hypothetical report on prize payments made by a magazine.

EXHIBIT 21–5
Report on a Financial
Element (Unrestricted
Scope)

To American Handy Magazine:

We have examined the schedule of cash prize payments as defined by *American Handy Magazine* for the period January 1, 1983, through January 31, 1985. Our examination was made in accordance with generally accepted auditing standards and, accordingly, included such tests of the accounting records relating to prize payments and such other auditing procedures as we considered necessary in the circumstances.

In our opinion, the schedule of cash prize payments showing a total amount of $117,655 presents fairly the cash prizes paid by *American Handy Magazine* for the period January 1, 1983, through January 31, 1985, according to the definition of cash prizes set forth in official contest disclosure circulars distributed with entry blanks.

Lamb & Company
Certified Public Accountants
February 4, 1985

Compliance with
Contractual
Agreements or
Regulatory
Requirements

Clients may have restrictive covenants in loan agreements. Lenders may require a periodic report on whether the client has complied with such contractual agreements. Following a scope paragraph, the auditor may give a *negative assurance* of the following type:

> In connection with our examination, nothing came to our attention that caused us to believe that the company was not in compliance with any of the terms, covenants, provisions, or conditions of sections 32 through 46 of the indenture dated January 1, 1984, with First National Bank. However, it should be understood that our examination was not directed primarily toward obtaining knowledge of such noncompliance.

A similar negative assurance may be given with regard to federal and state regulatory requirements. Examples would include limitation on investments according to section 993(*d*)(2) and (3) of the 1954 Internal Revenue Code, or state insurance department regulations about the nature of insurance company investments.

Regulatory agencies may seek to have auditors sign assertions in prescribed report language that goes beyond acceptable professional reporting responsibilities and involve auditors in areas outside their function and responsibility. In such cases, auditors should insert additional wording in the prescribed report language or write a completely revised report which reflects adequately their position and responsibility.

Applying Agreed-Upon Procedures

In some cases, clients may ask auditors to perform a specified set of procedures—the *agreed-upon procedures*—to examine a particular element, account or item in a financial statement. Such work should not be considered an audit because the specified set of agreed-upon procedures is usually *not* sufficient to be considered *in accordance with generally accepted auditing standards*. These special-purpose engagements have a *limited scope,* so the third and fourth field work standards and the reporting standards do not apply.

For example, a client may request an examination of the cash and accounts receivable of a company it plans to acquire—not an audit of the company's complete financial statements. SAS 35 (AU 622, *Special Reports—Applying Agreed-Upon Procedures to Specified Elements, Accounts or Items of a Financial Statement*) gives an example report on such an engagement. The scope paragraph, quoted below, is clearly *not* a standard scope explanation describing an examination in accordance with generally accepted auditing standards:

> To the Board of Directors of X Company:
>
> We have applied certain agreed-upon procedures . . . to accounting records of Y Company, Inc., as of December 31, 1985, solely to assist you in connection with the proposed acquisition of Y Company, Inc. It is understood that this report is solely for your information and is not to be referred to or distributed for any purpose to anyone who is not a member of management of X Company. Our procedures and findings are as follows:
>
> (procedures paragraphs omitted)
>
> Because the above procedures do not constitute an examination made in accordance with generally accepted auditing standards, we do not express an opinion on any of the accounts or items referred to above. In connection with the procedures referred to above, no matters come to our attention that caused us to believe that the specified accounts or items should be adjusted. Had we performed additional procedures or had we made an examination of the financial statements in accordance with generally accepted auditing standards, matters might have come to our attention that would have been reported to you. This report relates only to the accounts and items specified above and does not extend to any financial statements of Y Company, Inc., taken as a whole.
>
> Signed by Accountants

The conclusions paragraph quoted above follows the guide in SAS 35 (AU 622.04) by: (1) disclaiming an audit opinion on the accounts and items, (2) giving a *negative assurance* that "no matters came to our attention that caused us to believe the specified accounts and items should be adjusted,'' (3) giving the warning that adjustments might have been proposed if other audit procedures had been performed and (4) stating that the report does not relate to Company Y's complete financial statements. You can see how the objectives of this kind of service are very limited and how the report conclusions are also very limited.

LETTERS FOR UNDERWRITERS

In connection with public offerings of securities, auditors become involved with serving the needs of underwriters as well as serving the public need with an opinion on financial statements. *Underwriters* are persons who take securities of an issuer for the purpose of making a public distribution. They have a duty for diligence regarding misleading statements or omissions as defined in Section 11(*b*) of the Securities Act of 1933. Underwriters have sought the assistance of independent auditors in meeting this diligence requirement, and the assistance comes in the form of *letters for underwriters* (sometimes called "comfort letters").

The letter to an underwriter is not required by the Securities Act (1933), and it is not a report filed with the SEC. The letter, in the opinion of underwriters, is supposed to be evidence of their discharge of the duty to conduct a reasonable investigation of financial matters that are not otherwise covered by the expert opinion of the independent auditor. Thus, independent auditors often act as agents and report on their findings to the underwriter.

You should bear in mind that the "reasonable investigation" required of the underwriter is relevant only to unaudited financial information in a registration statement. The audited statements are covered by the expert auditor's opinion, and the underwriter is justified in relying upon that expert opinion. The procedures contemplated by the underwriter's diligence duty do not constitute a complete audit, and the letter is not a true audit report. At best, the limited procedures for an underwriter's letter can produce negative assurances made by the auditor to the underwriter.

In keeping with the context of letters for underwriters, auditing standards prescribe that it is the underwriter's responsibility to specify the investigatory procedures considered necessary and sufficient in the circumstances.[4] The auditor may make suggestions in order to assist the underwriters. Nevertheless, the ultimate responsibility rests with the underwriter because it is the underwriter's diligence duty that is being discharged.

Matters covered in a typical letter include:

a. A statement about the independence of the accountants.
b. An opinion on whether the audited financial statements and schedules included in the registration statement comply as to form in all mate-

---

[4] *Statement on Auditing Standards No. 38* (AU 631.05–.07).

rial respects with the applicable accounting requirements of the act and the published rules and regulations thereunder.

c. Negative assurances on whether the unaudited financial statements and schedules included in the registration statement:

(i) Comply as to form with the applicable accounting requirements of the act and the published rules and regulations thereunder.

(ii) Are fairly presented in conformity with generally accepted accounting principles on a basis substantially consistent with that of the audited financial statements and schedules included therein.

d. Negative assurances on whether, during a specified period following the date of the latest financial statements in the registration statement and prospectus, there has been any change in capital stock or long-term debt or any decrease in other specified financial-statement items.

Upon performing procedures for the underwriter, auditors may learn of matters such as material decreases in a financial balance or misstatement in the unaudited financial statements that should be disclosed in the registration statement. If disclosure is appropriate but management decides not to disclose the matter in the registration statement, mention of it should be made in the letter to the underwriter. In this manner, the underwriter may be considered to have learned of a material misstatement or omission. The accounting firm must then decide what impact such a discovery will have on its own report on the audited financial statements.

PERSONAL FINANCIAL STATEMENTS

Personal financial statements may be prepared for an individual, a husband and wife, or a larger family group, as the circumstances may require. The AICPA *Personal Financial Statements Guide* (AICPA, 1983), makes *current value accounting* the generally accepted accounting principle basis for such statements. Auditors' reports basically follow the framework outlined in Chapter 20, but now the legend *in conformity with generally accepted accounting principles* implicitly refers to current value accounting and not to historical cost-basis accounting. In fact, if an individual presents personal financial statements on an historical cost basis, an audit report would be qualified (or adverse) because of the departure from generally accepted accounting principles.

Audit reporting on these current value statements also puts an interesting twist on the subject of *uncertainties:* The AICPA guide does not emphasize "subject to" opinion language. The assumption is this: Situations in which the current values are not auditable arise from the inability to obtain sufficient competent evidence about the methods used by an individual to value assets. Therefore, doubts about the proper measure of current values are expressed as *departures from GAAP* with "except for" or adverse opinion language, rather than with the "subject to" language, which is reserved for other kinds of uncertainties.

SUMMARY   Several situations may arise in practice which do not fit the system of reporting responsibilities explained in Chapter 20. This chapter has examined seven additional topics involving reporting standards:

☐ Reporting on comparative financial statements of two or more years (SAS 15, AU 505).

☐ Segment information audits and reports (SAS 21, AU 435).

☐ Reliance on the work and reports of other independent auditors (SAS 1, AU 543).

☐ Reporting on the omission of the statement of changes in financial position (SAS 1, AU 545).

☐ Special reports and engagements (SAS 14, AU 621 and SAS 35, AU 622).

☐ Letters for underwriters (SAS 38, AU 631).

☐ Personal financial statement accounting, auditing and reporting.

SOURCES AND ADDITIONAL READING REFERENCES

Burton, John C., ed. *Corporate Financial Reporting: Conflicts and Challenges.* New York: American Institute of Certified Public Accountants, 1969.

New York Stock Exchange, Inc. "Recommendations and Comments on Financial Reporting to Shareholders and Related Matters." A White Paper, 1973.

Reiss, Harry F., Jr. "Letters for Underwriters." *CPA Journal,* December 1971, pp. 935–37.

Sommer, A. A., Jr. "Financial Reporting: Who is Liable? (1) Legal Liability of Accountants, (2) Reporting Obligations of Financial Executives." *Financial Executive,* March 1974, pp. 18–29.

Werner, R. H., and L. J. Greenberg. "Audits of CETA Programs." *CPA Journal,* April 1978, pp. 13–20.

REVIEW QUESTIONS

21.1.   What is an *updated* audit report?

21.2.   What is a *reissued* audit report?

21.3.   Why is the standard unqualified report considered an *implicit* audit report on segment information?

21.4.   What criteria define a "principal auditor?"

21.5.   What actions are taken by the principal auditor *only* if he or she assumes full responsibility for the work of another auditor?

21.6.   Is the reference in an audit report to work performed by another auditor a scope qualification? Explain.

21.7.   What type of report is required if all financial statements are fairly presented, but the statement of changes in financial position is omitted? Explain.

21.8. What general conditions indicate that a *special report* format should be used?

21.9. What is an underwriter? In letters to underwriters, what representations does the au-

ditor make with respect to audited financial statements? Unaudited financial statements and schedules?

21.10. What kind of audit report should be issued on personal financial statements prepared and presented on the traditional historical cost basis of accounting?

EXERCISES AND PROBLEMS

21.11. **Comparative Statements: Change   of Opinion**

G. Alexander, CPA, completed the annual audit of Casino, Inc. for the fiscal year ended July 31, 1986, on October 17, 1986. Alexander has audited Casino for the past five years. The audit scope was not limited.

However, Casino, Inc. has been in trouble with the SEC since 1984. In its report dated October 1, 1985, on the statements for the year ended July 31, 1985, G. Alexander qualified its audit opinion with reference to uncertainties related to the SEC investigation into the adequacy of certain disclosures. An adverse outcome might have resulted in recision of a stock offering sold by Casino in August, 1984.

In Note 17 to the 1986 financial statements, Casino disclosed the following:

> Since December, 1984, the Securities and Exchange Commission has been investigating the adequacy of disclosures in the Company's registration statement of $40 million common stock, which was sold in a public offering in August, 1984. The board of directors received a report from special counsel in January, 1986, expressing the opinion that the disclosures in question were adequate and that the outcome of the SEC investigation would not have a material adverse effect upon the Company's financial condition or results of operations.

Required:

Assume G. Alexander concludes, based on the report of special counsel, that no further information has come to the auditor's attention to suggest that the SEC investigation will have a material adverse effect on the financial statements. Consequently, G. Alexander decides to change the prior qualified opinion and render an unqualified opinion on the comparative financial statements for the years ended July 31, 1985 and 1986. Write the report, assuming no other reasons exist for modifying or qualifying the report language.

21.12. **Segment Information and Opinion Qualification**

Albacore Fish Food Fabrication produces specialty fish food products for two markets. The domestic U.S. market for pet store products is supplied by the output of the Richmond plant. The foreign market for commercial fish farm products is served from the Norfolk plant. Overseas shipments are put on freighters for shipment to Europe and Africa. Corporate headquarters is in Richmond.

Albacore proposes to make the following segment information disclosure in a footnote:

> *Segment Information.* Albacore operates in two markets—domestic and foreign. The domestic market is principally pet store products, and the foreign market is principally commercial fish farm products. Information related to these two segments of the business is given below. There were no significant intersegment sales or transfers. Identifiable

Year Ended 19XX ($000)	Domestic	Foreign	Headquarters	Combined
Sales and revenue	$135,000	$117,494	—	$252,494
Operating profit before depreciation and taxes	18,377	16,574	—	34,951
General corporate expense . . .			$ 4,265	(4,265)
Depreciation			14,000	(14,000)
Interest expense			3,121	(3,121)
Income taxes			5,420	(5,420)
Net income				8,145
Identifiable assets	113,193	126,869	42,931	282,993
Capital expenditures	16,701	12,932	1,121	30,754

assets by segment consist of inventories, land and plant directly identified with each segment. General corporate assets (net) consist of all cash, receivables, investments, headquarters property and liabilities. Albacore has no major customers as defined in *FASB Statement on Financial Accounting Standards No. 14.*

Required:

a. Do you detect any omissions of segment information as presented above?

b. Albacore management has made representations that there were no significant intersegment sales and no "major customers" as defined by SFAS 14. What should the auditor do with respect to these representations?

c. Give four specific procedures to be applied in the audit of the segment information.

d. Should the audit opinion be qualified in any way that you can see?

21.13. **Using the Work and Report of Another Auditor**

Lando Corporation is a domestic company with two wholly-owned domestic subsidiaries. Michaels, CPA, has been engaged to examine the financial statements of the parent company and one of the subsidiaries and to act as the principal auditor. Thomas, CPA, has examined the financial statements of the other subsidiary whose

operations are material in relation to the consolidated financial statements.

The work performed by Michaels is sufficient for Michaels to serve as the principal auditor and to report as such on the financial statements. Michaels has not yet decided whether to make reference to the examination made by Thomas.

Required:

a. There are certain required audit *procedures* Michaels should perform with respect to the examination made by Thomas, whether or not Michaels decides to make reference to Thomas in Michaels' auditor's report. What are these audit procedures?

b. What are the reporting requirements with which Michaels must comply if Michaels decides to name Thomas and make reference to the examination of Thomas?

c. What report should be issued if Michaels can neither assume responsibility for Thomas' work nor divide responsibility by referring to his work?

(*AICPA* adapted)

21.14. **Reference to Another Auditor in Principal Auditor's Report**

Presented below is an independent auditor's report that contains deficiencies. The corporation being reported on is profit oriented and publishes general-purpose financial statements for distribution to owners, creditors, potential investors, and the general public:

We have examined the consolidated balance sheet of Bonair Corporation and subsidiaries as of December 31, 1985, and the related consolidated statements of income and retained earnings and changes in financial position for the year then ended. Our examination was made in accordance with generally accepted auditing standards and, accordingly, included such tests of the accounting records and such other auditing procedures as we considered necessary in the circumstances.

We did not examine the financial statements of Caet Company, a major consolidated subsidiary. These statements were examined by other auditors whose report thereon has been furnished to us, and our opinion expressed herein, insofar as it relates to Caet Company, is based solely upon the report of the other auditors.

In our opinion, except for the report of the other auditors, the accompanying consolidated balance sheet and consolidated statements of income and retained earnings and changes in financial position present fairly the financial position of Bonair Corporation and subsidiaries at December 31, 1985, and the results of its operations and the changes in its financial position for the year then ended, in conformity with generally accepted accounting principles applied on a basis consistent with that of the preceding year.

Required:

Describe the reporting deficiencies, explain why they are considered deficiencies, and briefly discuss how the report should be corrected. (Exclude the addressee, signatures, and date.) Organize your answer sheet as follows:

Deficiencies	Reason	Correction

(*AICPA* adapted)

21.15. **Principal Auditor's Reference to Another Auditor**

M. Jackson, CPA, is the principal auditor on the December 31 consolidated financial statements of Bleeker Company and subsidiaries. However, other auditors do the work on certain subsidiaries for the year under audit amounting to:

	1986	1985
Total assets	29%	31%
Total revenues	36%	41%

M. Jackson investigated the other auditors, as required by auditing standards, and they furnished him with their audit reports. Jackson has decided to rely on their work and to refer to the other auditors in his own audit report. None of the audit work showed any reason to qualify any of the audit opinions.

Required:

Write M. Jackson's report referring to the work and reports of the other auditors.

21.16. **Incomplete Presentations and Omission of the Statement of Changes in Financial Position**

You are presently serving as the auditing standards advisor in the national executive office of your public accounting firm. Auditors in local offices often ask questions about the applicability of auditing standards, and your job is to provide authoritative answers. These questions are on your desk this morning. You need to answer them by noon.

a. We are auditing Alcindor Hoop Mfg. Company. The board engaged us to audit and report only on the balance sheet as of December 31, 1985. What kind of qualified opinion must we give because of the omission of the statements of income and changes in financial position?

b. We are auditing the Central City Hospital, owned and operated by the City of Centralia. The directors want to publish balance sheets for three years, income statements for two years, and a statement of changes in financial position for only the most recent year. How do we word the qualification for omission of the prior year statement of changes in financial position?

c. We are preparing unaudited financial statements (balance sheet and income statement) for the EZ Retail Co. store chain. Management will not present a statement of changes in financial position. Are we correct in assuming we can just write the standard unaudited statement disclaimer of opinion?

d. We are auditing the Muse Music Company, which makes and sells band instruments. Management plans to publish balance sheets for the current and prior years, income statements for the latest three years, and a statement of changes in financial position only for the current year. Do we need to qualify the audit opinion which will cover all of these statements?

e. This year, Southwest Metal, Inc. changed the basis of its statement of changes in financial position from working capital to cash. The prior year's statement has been changed to the cash basis for comparative purposes. Do we need to mention the inconsistent application of accounting principles in the audit report?

21.17. **Omission of Statement of Changes in Financial Position**
You have finished field work in connection with the annual audit of Western Associates Corporation for the year ended December 31 and are preparing to render your opinion. Western's management has not prepared a statement of changes in financial position. All audit work performed with respect to the other basic financial statements has been completed to your satisfaction, and you have the *audited* information available to prepare the statement of changes.

Required:
a. Generally, what is the auditor's obligation with respect to information the client refuses to disclose but which is necessary for adequate disclosure?

b. Should the auditor prepare the statement of changes in financial position? Explain.

c. Prepare the middle paragraph (if applicable) and the opinion paragraph of your audit report for Western Associates Corporation.

d. Assume that all financial statements are *unaudited*. (Western Association is a public company.) Prepare the audit report if the statement of changes is omitted.

21.18. **Special Reports: Non-GAAP Accounting and Compliance with Loan Agreement**
You will need to refer to SAS 14 (AU 621) "Special Reports" for a good response to the requirements of this problem.

All Saints' Church this year borrowed $425,000 from the National Bank on a 40-year, 12 percent first mortgage to finance additions to its physical plant. The church prepares its financial statements on a modified cash basis—accounting for physical assets and long-term liabilities, for cash receipts and disbursements, and for changes in the operating fund balance. The church financial statements also include similar accountings for memorial and endowment funds. Able Associates has audited and reported on these financial statements for several years.

The loan agreement with National Bank specifies certain restrictions on church finances, namely: (1) salaries and benefits to clergy shall not exceed 25 percent of cash receipts, (2) cash gifts to agencies outside the parish shall not exceed 10 percent of cash receipts and (3) total contractual debt service (principal and interest) shall not exceed 20 percent of cash receipts. The bank also requires the church to engage its auditors to submit a compliance report.

For the year 1985, Able found that cash receipts were $250,000 (excluding $50,000 received from a member as a noninterest-bearing loan with no repayment terms), clergy salaries and benefits were $60,000, cash gifts were $24,000, and total contractual debt service (all paid to National Bank) was $51,500. The church has no debt other than the two loans mentioned in this scenario.

Required:

a. Write an unqualified audit report (special report) on the All Saints' Church financial statement.

b. Write a separate compliance report for the National Bank.

21.19. **Reporting on Engagement to Apply Agreed-Upon Procedures**

You will need to read and analyze SAS 35 (AU 622), *Special Reports—Applying Agreed-Upon Procedures to Specified Elements, Accounts, or Items of a Financial Statement* in order to respond to the requirements of this problem. The textbook does not contain enough detail to serve as a good basis for a response.

To obtain information necessary to make informed decisions, management often calls upon independent auditors for assistance. This may involve a request that independent auditors apply certain audit procedures to specific accounts of a company that is a candidate for acquisition and report upon the results.

At the completion of an engagement performed at the request of Aurand Corporation, which was limited in scope as explained above, the following report was prepared by an audit assistant and was submitted for review:

To the Board of Directors of Wareing Corporation:

We have applied certain agreed-upon procedures, as discussed below, to accounting records of Wareing Corporation, as of December 31, 1985, soley to assist Aurand Corporation in connection with the proposed acquisition of Wareing Corporation.

We have examined the cash in banks and accounts receivable of Wareing Corporation as of December 31, 1985, in accordance with generally accepted auditing standards and, accordingly, included such tests of the accounting records and such other auditing procedures as we considered necessary in the circumstances.

In our opinion, the cash and receivables referred to above are fairly presented as of December 31, 1985, in conformity with generally accepted accounting principles applied on a basis consistent with that of the preceding year. We, therefore, recommend that Aurand Corporation acquire Wareing Corporation pursuant to the proposed agreement.

Signature

Required:

Comment on the proposed report describing those assertions that are:

a. Incorrect or should otherwise be deleted.

b. Missing and should be inserted.

(*AICPA* adapted)

21.20. **Letter to an Underwriter**

Albert and Hannibal, CPAs, have been contacted by Kelly Underwriters to prepare an underwriter's letter in connection with a public offering of stock by Norris Needle Corporation. Norris has made several contracts which required cash in the near future, and they are pressing the underwriters and auditors to expedite registration and issue of the securities. To speed up the registration process, Albert and Hannibal sent the underwriters a list of procedures they would perform, unless otherwise notified by either Norris or Kelly. During application of these procedures, Norris notified the CPAs of a long-term secured note recently made with Everett Bank, payable in five years. The proceeds from the note increased long-term liabilities by 10 percent. An opinion included in the letter from the CPAs to Kelly Underwriters read as follows:

> In our opinion, the financial statements and schedules, the summary of earnings, and the interim unaudited financial statements (dated March 31) examined by us are presented in conformity with accounting principles and comply as to form in all material respects with the applicable accounting requirements of the act and the published rules and regulations thereunder.

Required:

a. What problems do you see with the agreement between the CPAs and the underwriters concerning which audit procedures will be performed?

b. In accordance with current auditing practice, what action, if any, would the auditor take to disclose the increase in long-term debt?

c. Is the opinion prepared by Albert and Hannibal satisfactory? Explain.

DISCUSSION CASES

21.21. Changing the Opinion—Fallhard Manufacturing Company

Refer to the fact situation concerning purchase of a plant by Gofast, Inc., from Fallhard Manufacturing Company as given in Discussion Case 20.31.

The 1985 annual report will contain 1984 and 1985 financial statements in comparative form. Assume that Fallhard failed to disclose the nature of the repayment terms of the note, and the auditors wanted to qualify the opinion on the 1985 financial statements for this reason. The previously issued audit report on the 1984 financial statements was unqualified, and Gofast, Inc., did not become a related party until after the 1984 report was delivered.

Required:

Assume the auditor decides to change the unqualified opinion on the 1984 statements and issue a qualified opinion covering both years. Write the report. The audit field work was completed on February 20, 1986.

21.22. Special Report on Nonfinancial Information

Aggieland, Inc., is a farm management company. Aggieland sells parcels of land to investors who seek a tax shelter. Tenant farmers work the land in corn, paying all expenses of production. The crop is harvested by independent contractors using mechanized equipment. When the crop is sold, tenants' costs are paid plus a salary based on production, and the contractors are paid a fee for the harvesting. Any remaining net cash flow is paid to the investors.

Usually, there is no remaining cash flow for investors. Their expectation of investment return is based mainly on appreciation in value of the land, which is located near a large urban area.

The harvest season is approaching. Aggieland's president wants you to provide an audit report on the reasonable measurement of the harvest in terms of bushels of corn. The report will be sent to the investors. He does not want you to audit the Aggieland, Inc., financial statements.

If you accept this engagement, you can review the grain harvest procedures, observe the harvest in process, trace observed harvest truckloads to harvest records, confirm acreage with independent surveyors, review reports from storage elevators, recalculate the accuracy of the harvest records, and confirm yields per acre with the tenants.

For Discussion:

Does *Statement on Auditing Standards No. 14* (AU 621) provide for issuance of a report like the one requested by Aggieland? If so, what kind of report would be issued?

CHAPTER 22

PROFESSIONAL STANDARDS SOURCES

Compendium Section	Document Reference	Topic
AU 504	SAS 26	Association with Financial Statements
AU 9504		Interpretations: Association with Financial Statements
AU 550	SAS 8	Other Information in Documents Containing Audited Financial Statements
AU 9550		Interpretations: Other Information
AU 551	SAS 29	Reporting on Information Accompanying the Basic Financial Statements in Auditor-Submitted Documents
AU 553	SAS 27	Supplementary Information Required by the Financial Accounting Standards Board
AU 554	SAS 28	Supplementary Information on the Effects of Changing Prices
AU 555	SAS 33	Supplementary Oil and Gas Reserve Information
AU 556	SAS 40	Supplementary Mineral Reserve Information
AU 722	SAS 36	Review of Interim Financial Information
AU 9722		Interpretations: Review of Interim Financial Information
AR 100	SSARS 1	Compilation and Review of Financial Statements
AR 9100		Interpretations of SSARS 1
AR 200	SSARS 2	Reporting on Comparative Financial Statements
AR 9200		Interpretations of SSARS 2

Reporting on Supplementary and Unaudited Information

LEARNING OBJECTIVES

This chapter covers two areas of accounting and auditing practice that are outside the mainstream of reporting topics discussed in Chapters 20 and 21. Part I—Supplementary Information—deals with several types and forms of financial information not strictly required for statements to conform to generally accepted accounting principles. Part II—Unaudited Information—deals with accounting services most typically performed for small business clients who do not wish to have a full-scale audit.

Your learning objectives relate to each of the separate topics in both parts of the chapter. You should be able to:

☐ Explain auditors' responsibilities with regard to information other than the audited financial statements in client-prepared and auditor-submitted documents.

☐ Specify the circumstances in which exception-basis reports characterize auditors' reporting obligation.

☐ Distinguish matters of inconsistency with audited financial statements from material misstatement of facts in relation to "other information."

□ Define the various financial presentations and levels of
service involved in accountants' association with
prospective financial information.

□ Write appropriate reports for compilation and review
engagements, given specific fact circumstances.

**I.
SUPPLEMENTARY
INFORMATION**

A great deal of financial information is distributed publicly in annual
reports and other documents containing audited financial statements. The
company president's letter to shareholders, management's discussion and
analysis of results of operations, interim financial statements and supplementary schedules all contain financial information that is not mentioned
explicitly in auditors' reports. Yet, auditors have professional responsibilities with regard to much of this information.

The FASB has issued standards *requiring* disclosure of supplementary
information on changing prices (SFAS 33) and oil and gas and other
mineral reserves (SFAS 19, SFAS 25, SFAS 39 and SFAS 69). The SEC
requires a comprehensive Management Discussion and Analysis of operations (MD & A). Also, the SEC requires public companies to publish
interim (quarterly) financial statements. Before the FASB and SEC entered the picture, all such information was issued voluntarily by management. However, FASB has now made a distinction between (1) financial
accounting information required in basic financial statements for them to
be in conformity with GAAP and (2) other required supplementary information which is presented outside the basic financial statements. The
SEC has made a similar distinction between accounting requirements in
Regulation S-X and other disclosure requirements in Regulation S-K.

The AICPA has recognized the distinction in its rules of ethics. The
FASB has been designated as the body to establish generally accepted
accounting principles enforceable under Rule 203. However, disclosure
requirements for information supplementary to the basic financial statements are not considered necessary for GAAP statements and hence are
not covered by Rule 203. The supplementary information requirements
(SFAS 33, SFAS 19, SFAS 25, SFAS 39 and SFAS 69) are enforced under
Rule 204.

The AICPA also designated the Auditing Standards Board under Rule
204 as the body authorized to promulgate standards for auditors' responsibilities regarding such supplementary information. The auditor's responsibility is a *review* responsibility with *exception reporting,* not a full
audit responsibility with explicit reporting. An ***explicit reporting responsibility*** is the responsibility to give the recommended standard report (for

example, the standard audit report on audited financials or the standard negative assurance report on reviewed financials) whenever a service is performed. An *exception reporting responsibility* is the responsibility to add language to a recommended standard report only when specified problem conditions exist.

Supplementary information appears in *client-prepared documents*. This label is self-explanatory: A *client-prepared document* is an annual report, prospectus or other information package containing required supplementary information, and other information not explicitly required by rules, as well as the audited financial statements. The client might also include *condensed financial statements*, which present less detail than complete statements. Auditors have specific reporting responsibilities for such condensed statements.

Management and owners of small businesses sometimes request auditors to produce a very detailed report with information and analyses that go beyond the basic financial statements. Prior to 1980, such reports were known as "long-form reports" (to distinguish them from the "short-form" standard report on basic financial statements). With the issuance of SAS 29 (AU 551), such reports became known as "Information Accompanying the Basic Financial Statements in Auditor-Submitted Documents." The key distinction between other kinds of information mentioned earlier and this information is the feature of its being in *auditor-submitted* documents.

The general area of supplementary information has been organized in three categories for further explanation:

A. Supplementary Information in Client-Prepared Documents.

    1. Supplementary information required by FASB (SAS 27, AU 553).

        a. Changing prices information (SAS 28, AU 554).

        b. Oil and gas reserve information (SAS 33, AU 555).

        c. Mineral reserve information (SAS 40, AU 556).

    2. Interim financial information (SAS 36, AU 722).

    3. Supplementary information not required.

        a. Other information (SAS 8, AU 550).

        b. Financial forecast information.

        c. Current value accounting information.

B. Additional Information in Auditor-Submitted Documents (SAS 29, AU 551).

C. Summarized Information in Condensed Financial Statements (SAS 42, AU 552).

SUPPLEMENTARY INFORMATION: CLIENT-PREPARED DOCUMENTS

Clients can publish whatever they wish in an information package such as the annual report to shareholders, as long as the information is not false or misleading. Such an information package often contains the audited financial statements accompanied by the audit report. Auditors are *not associated with* such information within the meaning of the fourth AICPA reporting standard, and an explicit audit report is not required. However, in the same context as you have heard of "guilt by association," auditors can be "connected by nearness." Supplementary information often contains financial statistics: It looks financial, and the audit report is only a few pages away. Thus, some users connect the auditors with everything disclosed in the information package. Auditing standards provide guidance for auditors' responsibilities when other financial information is "connected by nearness."

Supplementary Information Required by FASB

SAS 27 (AU 553) *Supplementary Information Required by the FASB,* sets the general framework for responsibility regarding supplementary information required by FASB. This SAS was written without any specific kinds of supplementary information in mind. Subsequent SASs (explained later) deal with specific requirements.

The professional responsibility is not an audit responsibility. It is less than that: It is a *review* responsibility for applying limited procedures. In general, the limited procedures are: (1) Inquire of management whether the information conforms to FASB guidelines, whether measurement or presentation methods have been changed (a matter of consistency) and whether significant assumptions or interpretations are reasonable; (2) Compare the supplementary information itself to responses to these inquiries; (3) Decide whether to obtain written management representations about the supplementary information; (4) Apply procedures specified in other SASs (SAS 28, SAS 33 and SAS 40) dealing with particular types of information and (5) Investigate further any apparent evidence that FASB guidelines are not being followed.

The reporting obligation is known as **exception** reporting. Its basic premise is that the supplementary information is not a required part of the basic financial statements and is not audited, hence the standard report ordinarily need not mention it.[1] No kind of departure from standard report language is necessary, *except* when the events listed below occur. Then, the report should be *expanded*.

☐   The information required by the FASB is omitted.

☐   The information departs materially from FASB guidelines.

---

[1] At one time, the SEC hoped the Auditing Standards Board would adopt requirements for explicit reports instead of exception reports on supplementary information required by FASB. To reduce the risk of explicit reporting, the SEC proposed to exclude such reports from liability under Section 11(*a*) of the Securities Act of 1933. After ASB decided on exception reporting, the SEC withdrew its proposal to limit the liability exposure (Financial Reporting Release No. 5, 1982).

☐ The prescribed review procedures cannot be completed.

☐ Management's presentation of the information indicates the auditor performed procedures without also saying the auditor does not express an opinion on it.

☐ Management places the information close to, or within, the basic financial statements (in a financial statement footnote) and does not label it unaudited.

The *expanded report* in the first three cases calls attention to omission, departure from FASB guides or failure to review. In the latter two cases, a disclaimer of opinion on the supplementary information is added to the standard report. Examples of appropriate wording are given in SAS 27, AU 553.08.

The applicability of SAS 27 (AU 553) and its satellite SASs (SAS 28, SAS 33 and SAS 40) can be a little complicated. SAS 27 is *not applicable* when an auditor is engaged to *audit* the supplementary information. In such a case, the procedural responsibility is an audit responsibility, and the report would take the form of a special report (SAS 14, AU 621). The FASB applies a size test or a public-nonpublic distinction to require supplementary information from some, but not all, companies. When a company not otherwise required to disclose the information does so voluntarily, then SAS 27 is applicable, unless: (1) the company discloses along with its presentation the fact that its auditor has not performed any procedures or (2) the audit report is expanded to include a disclaimer on the information. In all cases of voluntary disclosure, auditors have the responsibility for *other information* (SAS 8, AU 550) described later in this chapter.

Changing Prices Information.   SAS 28 (AU 554), *Supplementary Information on the Effects of Changing Prices,* is a companion to SAS 27 (AU 553), *Supplementary Information Required by the Financial Accounting Standards Board.* Measurement and disclosure of constant dollar and current cost financial information is required by *FASB Statement No. 33.* Large public companies come under the requirement, and other companies are encouraged to submit the information voluntarily. The FASB is prompting experimentation with new financial accounting measurements.

Auditors' procedural responsibilities include inquiries and determinations specifically related to the SFAS 33 information. Inquiries should be about: (1) sources of information used to develop constant dollar/current cost measurements; (2) assumptions and judgments made when calculating amounts and (3) needs to reduce calculated amounts to lower recoverable amounts and how such recoverable amounts were determined.

Companies are also encouraged to write narrative explanations about the effects of changing prices on the business to help investors and creditors understand the information. Auditors are obligated to read such narratives to determine: (1) whether their message is consistent with the audited financial statements and the SFAS 33 information and (2) whether they contain any material misstatement of fact. If an inconsistency or a misstatement exists, the audit report should be expanded to describe its nature and amount. (This reporting obligation is the same as that for *other information,* described later.) Otherwise, the exception-basis reporting obligation of SAS 27 is to be followed. The Saxon Industries audit report in Exhibit 20–12B contains an exception-based paragraph about the omission of SFAS 33 information.

Oil and Gas Reserve Information.   Requirements to disclose oil and gas reserve information were created by SFAS 19, SFAS 25, SFAS 69 and SEC Regulation S-X, which once required value estimates as well as quantity measurements. This information is perceived as very complex and technical, requiring the knowledge and experience of a reservoir engineer. One important review procedure specified by SAS 33 (AU 555), *Supplementary Oil and Gas Reserve Information,* is to inquire about the qualifications of the engineer who estimated the reserve quantity information. (See also SAS 11, AU 336, *Using the Work of a Specialist.*)

SAS 33 specifies a number of technical inquiries too detailed to mention in this textbook. Suffice it to observe that the nature of the inquiries matches the nature of the oil and gas reserve information. If these inquiries raise questions about conformity with applicable FASB or SEC guidelines, further inquiries might not contribute much information if the audit team finds the task too complex. SAS 33 provides an escape route with illustrative report expansion language that expresses doubts about the information but admits inability to resolve them. This special reporting provision is the SAS 27 exception-basis report for oil and gas reserve information.

Mineral Reserve Information.   Mineral reserve information other than oil and gas is required by SFAS 39. The auditing standards in SAS 40 (AU 556), *Supplementary Mineral Reserve Information,* essentially extend the technical procedures related to oil and gas reserves (SAS 33, AU 555) to other kinds of mineral reserves. The specialist in this case is a mining engineer or geologist, and the standards on using the work of a specialist are applicable.

SAS 40 provides an example of a report to use when the auditors have doubts about the information (AU 556.05). It is essentially the same modification as the one specified for oil and gas reserves in SAS 33 (AU 555.06). This special reporting provision is the SAS 27 exception-basis report applied to mineral reserve information.

Interim Financial Information   Accounting principles do not require interim financial information as a basic and necessary element of financial statements conforming to GAAP. When interim information is presented, however, they should conform to the principles expressed in *APB Opinion No. 28*. The SEC, on the other hand, requires the presentation of interim information as supplementary information outside the basic financial statements. Thus, interim information is voluntary insofar as FASB is concerned but required insofar as the SEC is concerned. Likewise, auditing standards do not require auditors' reviews of interim information presented voluntarily by nonpublic companies, but the SEC requires reviews (but ordinarily without an explicit report) of interim information presented pursuant to its rules.

A *review* of interim financial information differs considerably from an audit. According to SAS 36 (AU 722.03), *Review of Interim Financial Information,* the objective of a review of interim financial information is to give the accountant a basis for reporting whether material modifications should be made for such information to conform to APB 28. This review does not require a complete study and evaluation of internal accounting control each quarter nor the gathering of sufficient competent evidential matter on which to base an opinion on interim financial information. At best, the accountant may be able to recommend improvements in the system for producing interim statements and adjustments for accounting errors that may have been discovered. However, the nature, timing and extent of review procedures explained below presume that the reviewer has a knowledge base of the company from the audit of the most recent annual financial statements.

Nature of Review Procedures. The nature of review procedures consists mainly of inquiry and analytical review. SAS 36 (AU 722.06) suggests the following:

Inquire about the accounting system.
> Obtain an understanding of the system.
> Determine whether there have been any significant changes in the system used to produce interim information.

Perform analytical review procedures to identify relationships and individual items that appear to be unusual.

Read the minutes of stockholder, board of director and board committee meetings to identify actions or events that may affect interim financial information.

Read (study) the interim financial information and determine whether it conforms with generally accepted accounting principles.

Obtain reports from other accountants who perform limited reviews of significant components, subsidiaries, or other investees.

Inquire of officers and executives about:
> Conformity with generally accepted accounting principles.
> Consistent application of accounting principles.
> Changes in the client's business or accounting practices.

Matters about which questions have arisen as a result of applying
other procedures (listed above).

Events subsequent to the date of the interim information.

Obtain written representations from management about interim information matters.

Timing of Review Procedures.   Review procedures should be performed at or near the date of the interim information. Starting the engagement prior to the cutoff date will give auditors a chance to deal with
problems and questions without undue deadline pressures.

Extent of Review Procedures.   The accountant needs to acquire a
sufficient knowledge of the client's business, just as if the engagement
were a regular audit. Knowledge of strengths and weaknesses in the internal control system and of problem accounting areas obtained during the
most recent audit is very useful in judging the extent of review procedures. Basically, the extent of review procedures depends upon the accountant's professional judgment of what problem areas may continue to
exist in the system of internal accounting control, the severity of unique
accounting principles problems and the errors that have occurred in the
past. With knowledge of these areas, the accountant can direct and fine
tune the review procedures in the interest of improving the quality of the
interim information.

Reporting on a Review of Interim Information.   An accountant may
report on interim information presented separately from audited financial
statements, provided that a review has been satisfactorily completed. The
basic content of the report is (SAS 36, AU 722.17):

A statement that a review was made in accordance with standards for
reviews of interim information.

An identification of the interim information reviewed.

A description of the review procedures.

A statement that a review is substantially less in scope than an audit in
accordance with GAAS.

A disclaimer of opinion on the interim information.

Negative assurance about the need for any material modifications.

Each page should be marked "unaudited."

An illustrative standard report on reviewed interim information is
shown in Exhibit 1–1 (Chapter 1).

When the interim information is presented to the SEC as required
supplemental information and when it is presented voluntarily under
GAAP and the client has requested a review, reporting obligations similar

to those in SAS 27 (AU 553) are effective. Under this exception basis of reporting, interim information is mentioned in an expanded standard report only in case the information is omitted (SEC registrants only), it departs from APB 28 principles, the review cannot be completed, management indicates the auditor performed procedures without also saying the auditor expresses no opinion, or management fails to label information in a footnote as "unaudited."

Supplementary Information Not Required

Three categories of voluntary supplementary information prepared by management are explained below:

☐   "Other" information.

☐   "Prospective" financial information.

☐   "Current value" financial statements.

None of these presentations are required by FASB rules, although some "other information" is required by the SEC's Regulation S-K. Auditors have responsibilities regarding these disclosures and presentations when management elects to present them.

Other Information.   SAS 8 (AU 550), *Other Information in Documents Containing Audited Financial Statements,* established the general framework for auditor involvement with information outside the basic financial statements. The involvement is limited to review procedures and exception-based reporting. All annual reports to shareholders and SEC filings contain sections such as a president's letter and management's discussion and analysis of operations. These sections are separate from the audited financial statements and are not covered by the audit opinion. Nevertheless, auditors have an obligation to read (study) the other information and determine whether it is inconsistent with the audited financial statements.

This obligation exists only with regard to (*a*) other information in documents that contain audited financial statements (such as annual reports and 10-K reports filed with the SEC)[2] and (*b*) other information in other kinds of documents reviewed at the request of the client. Auditors are not obligated to review press releases, analysts' interviews, or other forms of irregular financial news releases unless specifically engaged to do so.

If you decide a ***material inconsistency*** exists in other information, such as the president's selective use of audited financial statement numbers, action is required. The appropriate actions are diagrammed in Exhibit 22–1.

---

[2] SAS 38 (AU 631) and SAS 37 (AU 711) specify the kinds of "other information" that should be reviewed in connection with letters for underwriters and documents filed under the Securities Act of 1933 (see AU 631.38–.43 and 711.08). These types of other information are defined more narrowly than the other information discussed in this portion of the textbook.

EXHIBIT 22–1
Action When Other Information Is Materially Inconsistent (*SAS No. 8*, AU 550.04)

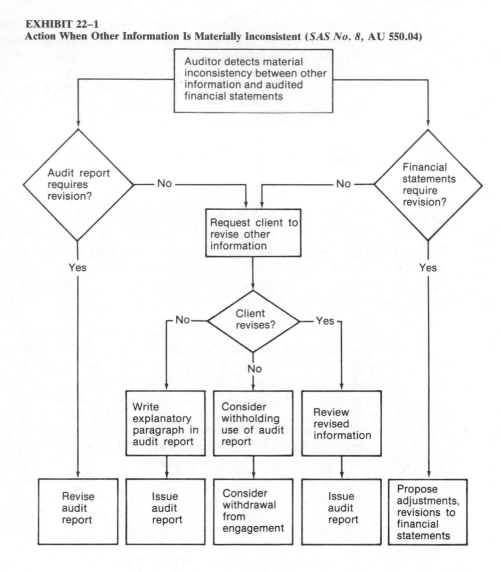

An example of "other information" is a president's letter remark: "Earnings increased from $1 million to $2 million, an increase of 50 cents per share." This statement can be corroborated by comparison to the audited financial statements. The president's comment would be considered inconsistent if the $1 million was income before an extraordinary loss and the $2 million was income after an extraordinary gain, or if the 50-cent change in EPS was the difference between last year's fully diluted EPS and this year's primary EPS. The president may have selected numbers without due regard to their meaningful comparison. Other kinds of "other information," however, might not be so directly related to audited figures. For example, the marketing vice president might write: "This year's sales represent a 20 percent share of the total market for our product."

If you detect a *material misstatement of fact* (not necessarily a direct inconsistency with audited financial statement numbers), the information should be discussed with the client. One example would be the marketing vice president's comment about market share. You must decide whether you have the expertise to evaluate the information in question, whether management has experts who developed the information, and whether consultation with some other expert is needed. This last step would be taken only if you have a valid basis for pursuing the matter and if it concerns information that is particularly important.

If a misstatement of material fact exists, auditing standards provide the following: (1) Notify the client in writing of the auditor's views; (2) Consult with legal counsel about appropriate action to take and (3) Take the action indicated by professional judgment in the particular circumstances. These three points are vague, mainly because there is no catalog of "other information" that is *not* under the auditor's opinion. Likewise, little or no guidance can be offered about what is a "material misstatement of fact in other information" that is *not* presented in financial statements prepared in conformity with generally accepted accounting principles. This portion of auditing standards provides auditors some latitude to decide what to do about material misstatement of other information, providing an analogy to the third AICPA reporting standard. (Informative disclosures in the financial statements are to be regarded as reasonably adequate unless otherwise stated in the report.)

The reporting obligation is exception reporting. The standard report is silent about other information unless an inconsistency or a material misstatement of fact exists.

Association with Prospective Financial Information.   Prospective financial information is useful in all business planning and investment decisions.[3] Clients may wish to make financial estimates of future events for such purposes as: estimating corporate or personal income tax payments; deciding whether to lease or purchase equipment; developing an operating budget; and promoting a real estate venture for sale as limited partnership interests. Accountants are most clearly associated with prospective financial information when a client requests that they compile or review it. When accountants have *compiled or reviewed **prospective financial***

---

[3] The SEC encourages publication of forecasts and has made a "safe harbor" liability rule in connection with them. In essence, a safe harbor rule provides that no one connected with a company's forecast will be liable for damages so long as the forecast was disclosed in good faith with a reasonable basis for belief. Also, plaintiffs bear the burden of showing lack of good faith and lack of a reasonable basis for belief. The rule is intended to discourage nuisance lawsuits in an area of developing practice.

statements, they should render a report on them.[4] The characteristics of compilation and review of prospective financial statements are explored later in this section.

Prospective Financial Statements. The first link leading to an accountant's report is the content and nature of the prospective information. *Prospective financial statements* can be complete in the same format as historical statements or less than complete, but in any event, they must contain the following items (if applicable in the circumstances):

a. Sales or gross revenue.
b. Gross profit.
c. Unusual or infrequently occurring items.
d. Provision for income taxes.
e. Discontinued operations or extraordinary items.
f. Net income.
g. Primary and fully diluted earnings per share.
h. Summary of significant changes in financial position.
i. Summary of significant assumptions.
j. Summary of significant accounting policies.

Any presentation omitting one or more of the items *a* through *h* in this list is considered a *partial presentation—not* a prospective financial statement. Accountants are not ordinarily requested by clients to report on partial presentations.

Given the inclusion of the minimum items listed, the nature of prospective financial statements can be one of these:

1. *Financial forecast.* A forecast presents, to the best of the preparer's knowledge and belief, an entity's expected financial position, results of operations and changes in financial position. A forecast is based on assumptions about expected conditions and expected courses of action.

2. *Financial projection.* A projection is similar to a forecast, with the important exception that a projection depends upon one or more *hypothetical assumption(s).* A hypothetical assumption expresses a condition or course of action that the preparer, exercising his knowledge and belief, does not necessarily *expect* to occur but which is consistent with the purpose of the projection. A projection answers the question: "What might happen if . . .?" For example, a promoter trying to sell limited partnership interests in a new hotel project might

---

[4] Professional literature giving guidance to public accountants with regard to prospective information include: (*a*) *Guidelines for Systems for the Preparation of Financial Forecasts* (AICPA, MAS Division, Guidelines Series No. 3, 1975); (*b*) *Presentation and Disclosure of Financial Forecasts* (AICPA, Accounting Standards Division, Statement of Position 75–4, 1975); and (*c*) *Guide for a Review of a Financial Forecast* (AICPA, 1980). A new accounting and auditing guide tentatively entitled *Guide for Prospective Financial Statements* was under consideration in 1984. When it is issued, it will supersede the three earlier documents and include guidance on projections as well as forecasts.

present a cash flow projection based on the hypothetical assumption: "What will be the cash flow if annual hotel room occupancy averages 75 percent?"

3. ***Multiple projections.*** Multiple projections consist of two or more projections based on a range of hypothetical assumptions (for example, hotel room occupancy of 50 percent, 75 percent and 90 percent). A preparer should reasonably expect the future results to fall within the range, however.

Association with Prospective Financial Statements.   Accountants can be associated with prospective financial information in a number of ways. However, work on partial presentations is generally excluded from any obligation to render a report. Likewise, most services in the nature of assembly, supplying computer software or other kinds of assistance are excluded from a reporting obligation so long as the accountant's name is not identified with the client's prospective financial statements. Reporting obligations arise when accountants compile or review forecasts or projections at the request of a client.

The primary objective of association with forecasts and projections is to lend credibility to them—similar to the attestation objective related to historical financial statements. In this regard, two levels of service are recognized—compilation and review.

1. ***Review of Prospective Financial Statements.*** A review of a forecast or projection is a substantial task. It is based on standards that resemble auditing standards, namely:

   Reviewers should be trained and proficient.
   Independence in mental attitude is to be maintained.
   Due professional care is to be exercised.
   The work should be planned and assistants supervised.
   An understanding of the system to produce the prospective statements should be obtained as a basis for determining the scope of the review.
   Appropriate supporting evidence should be obtained as a basis for the report.
   The report shall state whether the statements conform to AICPA presentation guidelines and have been prepared using reasonable assumptions.

Reviews include numerous procedures for gathering supporting evidence about assumptions, relationships and calculations. These procedures are more extensive than the ones specified for a review of unaudited historical financial statements—discussed in Part II of this chapter.

2. ***Compilation of Prospective Financial Statements.*** A compilation of a forecast or projection involves considerably less work than a review. Compilation procedures mainly facilitate the mechanical preparation

of the forecast or projection presentation. The accountants are not expected to gather a significant amount of supporting evidence. However, they are expected to notice assumptions that are obviously inappropriate in the circumstances. (Except for the need to obtain written client representations, these compilation procedures are very similar to the ones specified for a compilation of unaudited historical financial statements—discussed in Part II of this chapter.)

Reports on Prospective Financial Statements. Standard unofficial compilation and review reports on forecasts are reproduced in Exhibits 22–2 and 22–3. The reports identify the financial statements and describe the accountant's work. The compilation report contains a disclaimer: It offers no conclusions or any other form of assurance. The review report, in contrast, gives the accountant's conclusions about proper presentation and about the reasonableness of the assumptions.

EXHIBIT 22–2
Compilation Report on a
Financial Forecast

To the Board of Directors of XYZ Company:

The accompanying forecasted balance sheet, statements of income, retained earnings, and changes in financial position and summaries of significant assumptions and accounting policies of XYZ Company as of December 31, 1985, and for the year then ending, present, to the best of management's knowledge and belief, the Company's expected financial position, results of operations, and changes in financial position for the forecast period. Accordingly, the financial forecast reflects its judgment, based on present circumstances, of the expected conditions and its expected course of action. However, some assumptions inevitably will not materialize and unanticipated events and circumstances may occur. Therefore, the actual results achieved during the forecast period will vary from the forecast, and the variations may be material.

We have compiled the forecast in accordance with applicable standards established by the American Institute of Certified Public Accountants. A compilation of a forecast does not include evaluation of the support for the assumptions underlying the forecast. Because a compilation of a forecast is limited as described above, we do not express a conclusion or any other form of assurance on the accompanying statements or assumptions. We have no responsibility to update this report for events and circumstances occurring after the date of this report.

Accountant's signature
December 15, 1984

In general, accountants do not give qualified review reports on forecasts or projections. The reports are either unqualified (see Exhibit 22–3), adverse or disclaimers resulting from scope limitations. The reasoning is that such things as the effects of unreasonable assumptions are usually too difficult to explain in a qualified report, and they should be modified before the prospective statements are issued. Inconsistent or incomplete

EXHIBIT 22-3
Review Report on a
Financial Forecast

To the Board of Directors of XYZ Company:

The accompanying forecasted balance sheet, statements of income, retained earnings and changes in financial position and summaries of significant assumptions and accounting policies of XYZ Company as of December 31, 1985, and for the year then ending, present, to the best of management's knowledge and belief, the Company's expected financial position, results of operations, and changes in financial position for the forecast period. Accordingly, the financial forecast reflects its judgment, based on present circumstances, of the expected conditions and its expected course of action.

We have reviewed the forecast in accordance with applicable standards for a review of a financial forecast established by the American Institute of Certified Public Accountants. Our review included those procedures we considered necessary to evaluate both the assumptions used by management and the preparation and presentation of a forecast. We have no responsibility to update this report for events and circumstances occurring after the date of this report.

Based on our review, we believe that the accompanying forecast is presented in conformity with applicable guidelines for presentation of a financial forecast established by the American Institute of Certified Public Accountants. We believe that the underlying assumptions provide a reasonable basis for management's forecast. However, some assumptions inevitably will not materialize and unanticipated events and circumstances may occur. Therefore, the actual results achieved during the forecast period will vary from the forecast, and the variations may be material.

Accountant's signature
December 15, 1984

information (for example, omission of interest expense on proposed debt) should be incorporated before the statements are issued. Also, accountants ordinarily do not report on presentations that omit the summary of significant assumptions or the explanation of hypothetical assumptions. These disclosures are essential for understanding the basis for forecasts and projections.

AICPA Rules of Conduct 201(*e*) prohibits association of an accountant's name with a forecast or projection in a manner which may lead readers to believe the accountant attests to the *achievability* of the prospective results. This prohibition is limited strictly to the matter of *achievability*. You can see in Exhibit 22-3 that the accountant's review report lends credibility and assurance to the forecast, but it does *not* attest to achievability.

Current Value Financial Statements. Accounting theorists have long favored various measurements in current value accounting, including discounted present value of cash flows, entry values (replacement cost, current cost) and exit values (disposal value, current cash equivalent). Measurement by anything other than historical cost received little notice from the practicing profession until the mid-1970s when five things happened: (1) Inflation accelerated in the United States and worldwide; (2) Critics voiced loud discontent with historical cost measurement; (3) British, Australian, Dutch, and other accountants started promoting accounting measurement alternatives; (4) The SEC issued *Accounting Series Release No. 190* requiring disclosure of certain replacement cost information and (5) The FASB Conceptual Framework for Financial Accounting and Reporting project moved into the phase of considering measurement bases, including some kinds of current value accounting, finally culminating in *FASB Statement No. 33*.

Before SFAS 33 became fully effective, the Rouse Company began issuing a current value balance sheet. Excerpts from the balance sheet and the audit report are reproduced in Exhibit 22–4. The audit opinion is a

EXHIBIT 22–4

THE ROUSE COMPANY AND SUBSIDIARIES
Consolidated Cost Basis and Current Value Basis Balance Sheets
December 31, 1983 and 1982 (in thousands of dollars)

	1983		1982	
Assets	**Current Value Basis (note 1)**	**Cost Basis**	**Current Value Basis (note 1)**	**Cost Basis**
Property and receivables under finance leases (notes 3, 4, 5, 8, and 14):				
Operating properties:				
Current value	$1,018,528		$ 816,320	
Property and deferred costs of projects		$613,445		$518,992
Less accumulated depreciation and amortization.		96,887		87,731
		516,558		431,261
Receivables under finance leases.		5,436		5,562
Current value of interests in retail centers managed under contract	24,120	—	15,949	—
	1,042,648	521,994	832,269	436,823
Development operations:				
Construction and development in progress.	25,774	25,774	29,887	29,887
Preconstruction costs	8,627	8,627	5,424	5,424
	34,401	34,401	35,311	35,311
Less development reserve	3,229	3,229	3,142	3,142
	31,172	31,172	32,169	32,169
Real estate finance receivables (notes 6 and 8)	60,759	60,081	63,003	62,050
Current value of mortgage loan administration and insurance agency	31,423	—	16,726	—
Other property, net (note 14)	23,813	16,206	28,344	21,027
Other assets and deferred charges	25,292	25,292	23,622	23,622
Accounts and notes receivable (note 7)	40,844	40,844	29,720	29,720
Cash and temporary investments	20,583	20,583	26,451	26,451
Total.	$1,276,534	$716,172	$1,052,304	$631,862

EXHIBIT 22–4
(*concluded*)

The Board of Directors and Shareholders
The Rouse Company:

We have examined the consolidated cost basis balance sheets of The Rouse Company and subsidiaries as of December 31, 1983 and 1982, and the related consolidated cost basis statements of earnings, common stock and other shareholders' equity and changes in financial position for each of the years in the three year period ended December 31, 1983. Our examinations were made in accordance with generally accepted auditing standards and, accordingly, included such tests of the accounting records and such other auditing procedures as we considered necessary in the circumstances.

In our opinion, the aforementioned consolidated cost basis financial statements present fairly the financial position of The Rouse Company and subsidiaries at December 31, 1983 and 1982, and the results of their operations and the changes in their financial position for each of the years in the three year period ended December 31, 1983, in conformity with generally accepted accounting principles applied on a consistent basis.

We have also examined the consolidated current value basis balance sheets of The Rouse Company and subsidiaries as of December 31, 1983 and 1982, and the related current value basis statements of changes in revaluation equity for each of the years in the three year period ended December 31, 1983. As more fully described in note 1 to the consolidated financial statements, the current value basis financial statements supplement the financial statements prepared on a cost basis. They are not intended to present financial position and changes in shareholders' equity in conformity with generally accepted accounting principles but to provide relevant financial information about The Rouse Company and its subsidiaries which is not provided by the cost basis financial statements. In our opinion, the aforementioned consolidated current value basis financial statements present fairly the information set forth therein at December 31, 1983 and 1982, and for each of the years in the three year period ended December 31, 1983, on the basis of accounting described in note 1 applied on a consistent basis.

Peat, Marwick, Mitchell & Co.
February 24, 1984

combination of a standard report on the cost basis measurements and a special report (see Chapter 20) on the current value measurements.

ADDITIONAL INFORMATION IN AUDITOR-PREPARED DOCUMENTS

Many small business clients ask auditors to prepare additional financial information beyond the basic financial statements. Detailed reports prepared by auditors are often submitted to owners and managers of small businesses that do not have the accounting staff to produce regular analytical reports. Banks and other lenders often request the detailed reports on small business for similar reasons—in order to analyze the business and assess the lending risk more fully.

When auditors prepare and submit a detailed report, they are obligated to report on all information in it. The report should consist of: (1) a standard report on the basic financial statements and footnotes, (2) additional wording that extends an unqualified opinion to identified detail information with language like, "Such (additional detail) information has been subjected to the auditing procedures applied in the examination of the basic financial statements and, in our opinion, is fairly stated in all material respects in relation to the basic financial statements taken as a whole" and/or (3) a disclaimer of opinion on all or part of the detail information.

In addition to the basic financial statements and disclosures (which would be covered by a standard report), the more detailed report may contain one or more of the following:

Additional details or explanations of items in the basic financial statements.

Consolidation accounting details.

Historical summaries of financial statement items.

Statistical data.

Nonaccounting company information.

Industry and economy information.

Explanations of auditing procedures applied.

This information is considered to be presented outside the basic financial statements. It is not considered necessary for a presentation in conformity with GAAP.

Whatever the specific content of the more detailed report, auditors must still observe the reporting standards. Generally, the fourth standard is observed by including a "short-form opinion" (standard report) on the basic financial statements. Along with the additional information, supplementary expressions of opinion may be added. When presenting the additional information, you should be careful to maintain a clear distinction between management's representations (detail schedules, statistical data, and explanatory comments, for example) and your own representations (explanations of the audit scope and opinion). You should clearly establish your position regarding the additional information. Furthermore, auditors should be extremely careful that none of the additional information contradicts the overall opinion on the financial statements taken as a whole.

SAS 29 (AU 551), *Reporting on Information Accompanying the Basic Financial Statements in Auditor-Submitted Documents,* makes one alteration in connection with reporting on supplementary information required by the FASB when it is presented in an auditor-submitted document. Auditors must explicitly disclaim an opinion on it instead of following entirely the exception-reporting obligation of SAS 27 (AU 553). However, if the engagement specifies an *audit* of such information, the disclaimer would *not* be made, and a special report (SAS 14, AU 621) would be issued on the supplementary information.

SUMMARIZED INFORMATION IN CONDENSED FINANCIAL STATEMENTS

While all the preceding topics in this chapter dealt with *more* information, the matter of condensed financial statements deals with *less* information. *Condensed financial statements* and *selected financial data* are: (*a*) financial statements presented in considerably less detail than financial statements that conform with GAAP and (*b*) selected parts of detail financial statements presented separately in other schedules.

A company may ask its auditors to report on condensed statements of unconsolidated subsidiaries presented in a footnote or on condensed historical statements presented as a column next to a forecast. *Condensed financial statements do not constitute a fair presentation of financial position, results of operations and changes in financial position in conformity with GAAP*. Therefore, auditors should not give standard unqualified reports on them.

Ordinarily, the auditors have audited and reported on the full financial statements. Their reports on condensed versions of these statements should indicate that the condensation is derived from the full statements, as shown in the following suggested report (SAS 42, AU 552.06):

> We have examined, in accordance with generally accepted auditing standards, the consolidated balance sheet of X Company and subsidiaries as of December 31, 19X0, and the related consolidated statements of income, retained earnings, and changes in financial position for the year then ended (not presented herein); and in our report dated February 15, 19X1, we expressed an unqualified opinion on those consolidated financial statements. In our opinion, the information set forth in the accompanying condensed consolidated financial statements is fairly stated in all material respects in relation to the consolidated financial statements from which it has been derived.

If the full financial statements are not readily available, either by being in the same document or by being incorporated by reference (refer to the "integrated disclosure system" discussed in Chapter 4), the audit opinion should be adverse, stating ". . . because of the omission of financial details and disclosures, the condensed financial statements do not present fairly the financial position, results of operations or changes in financial position in conformity with GAAP" (AU 552.06). This strong conclusion is derived from the need to present adequate disclosures (AU 431, AU 509.17) and from the reporting judgment concerning the summarization of information in a manner that is neither too detailed nor too condensed (AU 411.04(*d*)).

Clients may also engage their auditors to report on selected parts of the financial statements presented separately. For example, a company president may want an audit report to cover a separate schedule of five years' history of sales, income, earnings per share, dividends per share, working capital and long-term debt/total equity ratios. The report is accomplished by adding a paragraph to the standard report, illustrated as follows (AU 552.10):

(Standard Scope Paragraph)
(Standard Opinion Paragraph)

We have also previously examined, in accordance with generally accepted auditing standards, the consolidated balance sheets as of December 31, 19X3, 19X2, and 19X1, and the related consolidated statements of income, retained earnings, and changes in financial position for the years ended December 31, 19X2 and 19X1 (none of which are presented herein); and we expressed unqualified opinions on those consolidated financial statements. In our opinion, the information set forth in the selected financial data for each of the five years in the period ended December 31, 19X5, appearing on page XX, is fairly stated in all material respects in relation to the consolidated financial statements from which it has been derived.

As long as the separate presentation contains only financial data selected or derived from financial statements, the paragraph illustrated above will suffice. However, if the presentation includes other data (for example, number of employees or order backlogs), the added paragraph should identify specifically the financial items the auditor intends to cover with his reporting responsibility.

SUMMARY OF REPORTING OBLIGATIONS: SUPPLEMENTARY INFORMATION

Accountants and auditors are associated with many types of financial and nonfinancial information other than the basic financial statements and footnotes. Users of the information expect auditors to take some responsibility in connection with this association. The broad category of "other information" sets the general stage for *exception reporting*—a standard report mentions other kinds of information only if something is wrong. This exception basis of reporting applies to supplementary information required by FASB and SEC, interim financial information presented alongside but outside basic financial statements, and all other information in a document containing audited financial statements.

Explicit reporting is expected in connection with other kinds of supplementary or additional information supplied voluntarily. Report forms are specified for reporting on compilations and reviews of financial forecasts and projections and on detailed information in auditor-submitted documents. Other kinds of information, such as current value financial statements, can be reported using the "special report" rules. In addition, other kinds of reports are required for condensed financial statements and financial data selected from full financial statements.

Auditors need not feel constrained by rules and regulations about reporting. Whatever the subject matter, a legitimate avenue for some type of report is available.

II. UNAUDITED FINANCIAL STATEMENTS

Many CPA firms conduct practice in *accounting and review services* for small business clients. These engagements include bookkeeping, financial statement preparation, and financial statement review to help small businesses prepare financial communications. Until the late 1970s, auditing standards concentrated on one level of assurance based on a full audit and appeared to deny small clients the full benefit of CPAs' services.

The Moss and Metcalf investigations in 1977–78 highlighted the problem by centering attention on the idea that auditing standards handicapped the business of small CPA firms and their services to small business clients. The argument has become known as the "Big GAAS—Little GAAS" question. "Big GAAS" was portrayed as the villain in the play with the proposition that existing standards were enacted under the influence of large CPA firms whose practice is centered on big business. Even though this proposition is not true, the fact is that small CPA firms *want* to give, and small businesses *want* to receive, some level of assurance as a result of accountants' work even though an audit in accordance with GAAS is not performed.

Recognizing the tenacity of the issue and the heat of congressional criticism, the AICPA formed a new senior technical committee in 1977—the Accounting and Review Services Committee. The committee has continuing responsibility to develop and issue pronouncements of standards concerning the services and reports an accountant may render in connection with unaudited financial statements. This committee issues *Statements on Standards for Accounting and Review Services* (SSARS). SSARS apply to work on unaudited financial statements of nonpublic companies. Auditing standards (SAS), in comparison, apply to work on all audited financial statements (both public and nonpublic companies) and to work on unaudited financial statements of public companies. According to SSARS, a public company is one: (1) whose securities trade in a public market—stock exchange, over-the-counter, and locally quoted markets, (2) which files with a regulatory agency in preparation for sale of securities in a public market or (3) a subsidiary, joint venture or other entity controlled by a company meeting either criterion (1) or (2). All other companies are considered nonpublic ones (AR 100.04).

The new committee issued its first standard in December 1978, entitled "Compilation and Review of Financial Statements." *Compilation* services and *review* services represent two different kinds of engagements, both of which are less than a full audit.

REVIEW SERVICES

The concept of *review services* is both broad and loose. Not only do auditors audit financial statements, but they can also *review* interim financial information, supplementary information, and forecasts and projections. While these kinds of work are all *reviews,* they differ from one another in terms of specific procedures prescribed by standards and other guides. The *review service* explained in this section, however, applies specifically to accountants' work on the *unaudited* financial statements of nonpublic companies.

In a *review services engagement,* an accountant performs some procedures to achieve a level of assurance. This level is not the same that could be attained by performing an audit in accordance with GAAS. The objective of a review of financial statements, according to SSARS 1 is:

> To achieve, through the performance of inquiry and analytical procedures, a reasonable basis for expressing limited assurance that there are no material modifications that should be made to the statements in order for them to be in conformity with generally accepted accounting principles or, if applicable, with another comprehensive basis of accounting.

Review work on unaudited financial statements consists primarily of inquiry and analytical review procedures. The information gained thereby is similar to audit evidence, but the recommended limitation on procedures (listed below) does not suggest performance of typical auditing procedures of evaluating internal control, conducting physical observation of tangible assets, sending confirmations or examining documentary details of transactions.

Obtain knowledge of the client's business.

> Know the accounting principles of the client's industry.
>
> Understand the client's organization and operations.

Inquire about the accounting system and bookkeeping procedures.

Perform analytical review procedures to identify relationships and individual items that appear to be unusual.

Inquire about actions taken at meetings of stockholders, directors and other important executive committees.

Read (study) the financial statements for indications that they conform with generally accepted accounting principles.

Obtain reports from other accountants who audit or review significant components, subsidiaries or other investees.

Inquire of officers and directors about:

> Conformity with generally accepted accounting principles.
>
> Consistent application of accounting principles.
>
> Changes in the client's business or accounting practices.
>
> Matters about which questions have arisen as a result of applying other procedures (listed above).
>
> Events subsequent to the date of the financial statements.

Perform any other procedures considered necessary if the financial statements appear to be incorrect, incomplete or otherwise unsatisfactory.

Prepare working papers showing the matters covered by the inquiry and analytical review procedures, especially the resolution of unusual problems and questions.

Obtain a written representation letter from the owner, manager or chief executive officer and from the chief financial officer. (This step is optional.)

A review service does not provide a basis for expressing an opinion on financial statements. Each page of the financial statements should be marked "See Accountant's Review Report." The report on a completed review services engagement should include the following:

Statement that a review service was performed in accordance with standards established by the AICPA.

Statement that all information included in the financial statements is the representation of the management or owners of the business.

Statement that a review consists primarily of inquiries of company personnel and analytical procedures applied to financial data.

Statement that a review service is substantially less in scope than an audit, and an opinion of financial statements is not expressed.

Statement that the accountant is not aware of any material modifications that should be made or, if aware, a disclosure of departure(s) from generally accepted accounting principles.

When other independent accountants are involved in audit or review of parts of the business, a principal reviewer can divide responsibility by referring to the other accountants in the review report. You can follow the spirit of the auditing standards (SAS 1, AU 543) to write the form and content of the reference to the work and reports of other auditors. However, an accountant who is not independent may not issue a review services report

The recommended standard language of the review report is shown in Exhibit 1–1 (Chapter 1). An example of an actual review report is in Exhibit 22–5. (It contains minor variations in wording, compared to the SSARS wording, showing how practice can follow SSARS guidance without copying recommended reports word-for-word.)

COMPILATION SERVICES

Compilation is a synonym for an older term—"write-up work." Both terms refer to an accountant helping a client "write up" the financial information in the form of financial statements. A *compilation service* is accounting work in which an accountant performs few, if any, procedures, and it is substantially less than a review service. The objective of a compilation of financial statements, according to SSARS 1 is:

> To present in the form of financial statements information that is the representation of the management or owners without undertaking to express any assurance as to whether there are material modifications that should be made to the statements in order for them to be in conformity with generally accepted accounting principles, or if applicable, with another comprehensive basis of accounting.

EXHIBIT 22–5
Review Report with
Review of a Supplemental
Analysis

Board of Directors
Children's Shoe World, Inc.:

We have performed a review of the statements of financial position of Children's Shoe World, Inc. as of January 31, 1983 and 1982, and of the related statements of operations and retained earnings and of changes in financial position for the years then ended in accordance with standards established by the American Institute of Certified Public Accountants. All information included in these financial statements is the representation of the management of Children's Shoe World, Inc.

A review consists principally of inquiries of company personnel and analytical procedures applied to financial data. It is substantially less in scope than an audit in accordance with generally accepted auditing standards, the objective of which is the expression of an opinion regarding the financial statements taken as a whole. Accordingly, we express no such opinion.

Based upon our review, we are aware of no material modifications that should be made to the accompanying financial statements in order for them to be in conformity with generally accepted accounting principles.

The supplemental analysis of operations is presented as supplemental information for analytical purposes. Such information has been subjected to the inquiry and analytical procedures applied in the review of the basic financial statements. We are aware of no material modifications that should be made to the supplemental information.

McIntosh and Associates
February 25, 1983

In a compilation service, an accountant should read (study) the financial statements, looking for obvious clerical or accounting principle errors, but no other procedures need be performed. Each page of the financial statements should be marked "See Accountant's Compilation Report." The report can be issued by an accountant who is not independent, provided the lack of independence is disclosed. The report should contain the following:

Statement that a compilation service has been performed in accordance with standards established by the AICPA.

Statement that financial statement information is the representation of the management or owner(s) of the business.

Statement that the financial statements have not been audited or reviewed and the accountant does not express an opinion or any other form of assurance on them.

Three other report items may be included in a compilation report when applicable: (1) A statement that management or owners have elected to omit substantially all footnote disclosures, and if they were included, they might influence the users' conclusions about the business, (2) a statement that the accountant is not independent if such is the case and (3) disclosure of the basis of accounting if it is something other than GAAP.

EXHIBIT 22–6
Compilation Report,
Accountant is Not
Independent

President and Sole Stockholder
Petro-Chem Products Corporation:

We have performed a compilation of the accompanying statements of financial position of Petro-Chem Products Corporation as of August 31, 1983 and 1982, and the related statements of operations and retained earnings, changes in financial position, and supplemental schedules of manufacturing costs and operating expenses for the six month periods then ended in accordance with standards established by the American Institute of Certified Public Accountants.

A compilation is limited to presenting in the form of financial statements information that is the representation of management. We have not performed an audit examination or a review of the accompanying financial statements and supplemental information, and accordingly, we express no opinion or any other form of assurance thereon.

We are not independent with respect to Petro-Chem Products Corporation.

McIntosh and Associates
October 20, 1983

The recommended standard language of the compilation report is shown in Exhibit 1–1 (Chapter 1). An example of an actual compilation report is in Exhibit 22–6. A compilation report must also disclose significant departures from GAAP, as illustrated in Exhibit 22–7.

COMPARATIVE FINANCIAL STATEMENTS

SSARS 2 (AR 200), *Reporting on Comparative Financial Statements,* deals with reporting variations that turn out to be rather complex. The complexity arises from the several possible combinations of prior and current services. The sections below contribute some organization to the technical details found in SSARS 2.

Same or Higher Level of Service

These combinations are (in prior-year/current-year order): (1) compilation followed by compilation; (2) compilation followed by review and (3) review followed by review. The essence of comparative reporting is to report on the current service and *update* the report on the statements of the prior period. Examples of report language are given in SSARS 2 (AR 200.09–.10). The higher level of service when the current-year work is an audit is governed by auditing standards, not by SSARS. (See AU 504, 505.02 and 505.12.)

When the current-year service is being performed by a successor accountant, he or she cannot update the predecessor's report. In this case, the successor can request the predecessor to reissue the prior report and distribute it along with the current report (in which case the predecessor must decide whether to reissue, as guided by AR 200.20–.24). Alternatively, the successor can simply write in the current report a paragraph describing the predecessor's report on the prior period. The paragraph:

EXHIBIT 22–7
Compilation Report with
GAAP Departure
Disclosed

To the Partners
Delta Investments and Subsidiaries:

We have performed a compilation of the accompanying consolidated statement of assets, liabilities and partnership equity—income tax basis, of Delta Investments and Subsidiaries as of March 31, 1983, and of the related consolidated statements of operations, partnership equity, and changes in financial position—income tax basis and the supplemental schedules of cost and market values, and of income from operations for the three month period then ended in accordance with standards established by the American Institute of Certified Public Accountants.

A compilation is limited to presenting in the form of financial statements information that is the representation of management. We have not performed an audit examination or a review of these financial statements and supplemental information and, accordingly, do not express an opinion or any other form of assurance thereon.

As described in Note 1 to the financial statements, it is the partnership's policy to prepare financial statements utilizing the accounting principles employed for federal income tax reporting purposes. Since these principles may differ significantly from generally accepted accounting principles, particularly for the partnership's oil and gas operations and sales of real estate, the accompanying financial statements do not purport to present financial position, results of operations or changes in financial position in conformity with generally accepted accounting principles.

The effects upon financial position, results of operations and changes in financial position, had generally accepted accounting principles been utilized instead of the accounting principles utilized in the accompanying financial statements, are not practically determinable. However, as more fully described in Note 1, the application of generally accepted accounting principles may result in valuations of assets and partnership equity at March 31, 1983, at amounts materially in excess of those reflected in the accompanying statements. Accordingly, financial statements prepared in conformity with generally accepted accounting principles may reflect results of operations and changes in financial position significantly different than those reflected in the accompanying statements.

McIntosh and Associates
July 1, 1983

(1) states that prior period financials were compiled or reviewed by other accountants, (2) gives the date of the previous report, (3) describes the compilation disclaimer or review report negative assurance rendered last year and (4) describes any modifications written in the prior year report. (See AR 200.17–19, for examples.)

Lower Level of Service

These combinations are (in prior-year/current-year order): (1) review followed by compilation; (2) audit followed by compilation and (3) audit followed by review. The essence of comparative reporting is to report on the current service and *reissue* (not *update*) the report on the statements of the prior period. The underlying theory calling for reissuance in such cases is that an accountant cannot update a previous report when currently performing a lesser level of work.

The alternative to reissuing and reprinting a prior report is to write into the current report a paragraph describing the report on the prior-year financial statements. The paragraph: (1) states that prior-period financials were reviewed or audited by the same or other (predecessor) accountants, (2) gives the date of the previous report, (3) describes the type of service previously rendered (review or audit), (4) describes the review report negative assurance or the type of audit opinion previously rendered, (5) explains any modifications or opinion qualifications expressed last year and (6) in the case of a prior-year audit, states that no auditing procedures were performed after the date of the previous audit report, and in the case of a prior-year review, states that no review procedures were subsequently performed. Example reports are given in SSARS 2 (AR 200.12, .28).

When the current-year service is being performed by a successor accountant, the predecessor can be asked to reissue the prior report (subject to decisions to do so, AR 200.20–.24). When the predecessor's report is not presented, the descriptive paragraph about the report can be added to the current-year report.

PRESCRIBED FORMS

Industry trade associations, banks, government agencies and regulatory agencies often use *prescribed forms* (standard, pre-printed documents) to specify the content and measurement of accounting information required for special purposes. Such forms may not request disclosures required by GAAP or may specify measurements that do not conform to GAAP.

When such forms are *compiled* (not when reviewed) by an accountant, the compilation report does not need to call attention to GAAP departures or GAAP disclosure deficiencies. The presumption is that the organization that prescribed the form knew what it was doing and does not need to be informed of the ways the form calls for GAAP departures. The reporting obligation is satisfied by adding the following paragraph (SSARS 3, AR 300.03) to the standard compilation disclaimer:

> The financial statements are presented in accordance with the requirements of (name of trade association, bank, agency or other body), which differ from generally accepted accounting principles. Accordingly, these financial statements are not designed for those who are not informed about such differences.

However, departures from the information specified in a prescribed form should be treated in the report as the accountant otherwise would treat GAAP departures—by disclosing them. Likewise, GAAP departures that are not specified in the prescribed form should still be treated as GAAP departures.

COMMUNICATIONS BETWEEN PREDECESSORS AND SUCCESSORS

You may recall in the case of audits, successor auditors are required to make certain inquiries of predecessor auditors when a new client is obtained (SAS 7, AU 315; Chapter 6 in this textbook.) However, in compilation and review work, successor accountants are *not required* to communicate with predecessor accountants.

Nevertheless, SSARS 4 (AR 400) gives advice to accountants who decide to talk to the predecessor. The standard suggests that inquiries may be a good idea if the successor does not know much about the new client, if the change in accountants occurred long after the end of the client's fiscal year (hinting at problems between the client and the predecessor), and if the client is one who changes accountants frequently. When inquiries are to be made, the successor must obtain the client's permission for the predecessor to disclose confidential information. Otherwise, SSARS 4 gives advice about inquiries that will give the successor a chance to learn about problem areas.

FUTURE SSARS

In 1983, the Accounting and Review Services Committee was reduced from 15 members to nine. You may expect to see a few, well-chosen SSARS pronouncements in the future. However, AICPA members are presently being careful not to issue standards simply for the sake of issuing standards. The concern with "standards overload" has caused a reduction in the committee's activities.

SOURCES AND ADDITIONAL READING REFERENCES

Accounting Standards Division. *Presentation and Disclosure of Financial Forecasts,* SOP 75–4. New York: AICPA, August 1975.

Asebrook, R. J., and D. R. Carmichael. "Reporting on Forecasts: A Survey of Attitudes." *Journal of Accountancy,* August 1973.

Burton, John C. "Management Auditing." *Journal of Accountancy,* May 1968, pp. 41–46.

Carmichael, D. R. "Reporting on Forecasts: A U.K. Perspective." *Journal of Accountancy,* January 1973, pp. 36–47.

————. "The Attest Function—Auditing at the Crossroads." *Journal of Accountancy,* September 1974, pp. 64–72.

————. "Standards for Financial Reporting." *Journal of Accountancy,* May 1979, pp. 76–84.

Clay, J. R., D. M. Guy, and D. R. Meals. "Solving Compilation and Review Practice Problems." *Journal of Accountancy,* September 1980, pp. 74–83.

Clay, J. R., and S. D. Holton. "Prescribed Form Engagements: Some Practical Guidance." *Journal of Accountancy,* May 1982, pp. 66–79.

Feder, Melvin. "SAS No. 29—Reporting on Information Accompanying Basic Financial Statements in Auditor-Submitted Documents." *CPA Journal,* January 1981, pp. 75–76.

Goldwasser, Dan L. "Liability Exposure in Compilation and Review." *CPA Journal,* September 1980, pp. 27–32.

Guide for a Review of a Financial Forecast. New York: AICPA, 1980, 99 pages.

Guy, D. M., and R. J. Clay, Jr. "SAS 8 (Other Information) Flowchart." *Journal of Accountancy,* July 1978, pp. 52–53.

Ijiri, Yuji. "On Budgeting Principles and Budget-Auditing Standards." *Accounting Review,* October 1968, pp. 662–67.

Institute of Chartered Accountants in England and Wales. *Accountant's Reports on Profit Forecasts,* July 1969.

Israeloff, Robert L. "Practitioners' Answers to Compilation and Review." *CPA Journal,* November 1979, pp. 25–30.

Lambert, J. C., and S. J. Lambert. "Review of Interim Financial Information." *CPA Journal,* September 1979, pp. 25–32.

————. "Association, Supplementary Information and Accompanying Information." (SAS 26, 27, 28, and 29) *CPA Journal,* February 1981, pp. 70–77.

Langenderfer, H. Q., and J. C. Robertson. "A Theoretical Structure for Independent Audits of Management." *Accounting Review,* October 1969, pp. 777–87.

Management Advisory Services Executive Committee. *Guidelines for Systems for the Preparation of Financial Forecasts.* Guideline Series No. 3. AICPA, 1975.

Miller, Robert D. "Compilation and Review: Standards' Impact on Risk." *Journal of Accountancy,* July 1983, pp. 60–75.

Munter, P., and T. A. Ratcliffe. "A Synthesis of Compilation and Review Standards." Part I *CPA Journal,* July 1982, pp. 37–47, Part II *CPA Journal,* August 1982, pp. 22–29.

New York Stock Exchange, Inc. "Recommendations and Comments on Financial Reporting to Shareholders and Related Matters." A White Paper, 1973.

Norgaard, C. T. "Extending the Boundaries of the Attest Function." *Accounting Review,* July 1972, pp. 433–42.

Ratcliffe, T. A., and P. Munter. "Reporting on Comparative Financial Statements: SSARS No. 2." *CPA Journal,* March 1980, pp. 69–73.

————. "Auditors' Responsibility Regarding Supplementary Information." *CPA Journal,* March 1981, pp. 36–41.

Robertson, J. C., and R. W. Clarke. "Verification of Management Representations: A First Step Toward Independent Audits of Management." *Accounting Review,* July 1971, pp. 562–71.

Rosenblatt, M. J., and D. M. Guy. "A Flowchart Analysis of SAS No. 27 (Supplementary Information Required by FASB)." *Journal of Accountancy,* March 1980, pp. 88–89.

————. "A Flowchart Analysis of SAS No. 29" (Reporting on Information Accompanying the Basic Financial Statements in Auditor-Submitted Documents). *Journal of Accountancy,* January 1981, pp. 44–46.

Securities and Exchange Commission. "Notice of Adoption of Amendments to *Regulation S-X* Requiring Disclosure of Certain Replacement Cost Data." *Accounting Series Release No. 190,* March 23, 1976.

Shank, J. K., and J. B. Calfee, Jr. "Case of the Fuqua Forecast." *Harvard Business Review,* November-December 1973.

Skekel, T. D., and O. R. Whittington. "Management Reports on Financial Statements." *CPA Journal,* July 1979, pp. 32–37.

Solomon, K. I., C. Chazen, and R. L. Miller, Jr. "Compilation and Review: The Safety Factor." *Journal of Accountancy,* July 1983, pp. 50–59.

Weirich, T. R., and G. M. Pintar. "Interpretation and Flowchart of SSARS No. 1." *Journal of Accountancy,* November 1979, pp. 60–66.

REVIEW QUESTIONS

22.1.   Can an auditor comply with Rule 203 of the AICPA Rules of Conduct by issuing an unqualified opinion on financial statements that omit changing prices supplementary information? Should an audit report in these circumstances be expanded?

22.2.   Do audit responsibilities differ for supplementary information required by FASB and information required by FASB for financial statements to be in conformity with generally accepted accounting principles? Explain.

22.3.   What are the five reasons for *expanding* the standard audit report with regard to supplementary changing prices information required by FASB?

22.4.   Explain the similarity between auditors' responsibilities for "other information in documents containing audited financial statements" (SAS 8, Section 550), responsibilities for unaudited interim financial information and responsibilities for SFAS 33 changing prices information.

22.5.   What auditing standards, other than the specific ones on supplementary information (AU 550–AU 556), are important when financial reports include oil and gas and other mineral reserve information?

22.6.   What are six of the procedures an auditor should perform in a review of interim financial information?

22.7.   Is a disclaimer of opinion required in an auditor's report on a review of interim financial information?

22.8.   What two kinds of disclosure problems must an auditor be alert to detect when reading "other information" in an annual report? Explain them.

22.9.   How are *prospective financial statements* defined?

22.10.   What three kinds of prospective financial statements might a client produce?

22.11.   How would you describe the standards that guide accountants when they perform reviews of prospective financial statements?

22.12.   What are the similarities and differences between review reports on forecasts and review reports on historical financial statements? Compilation reports on forecasts and compilation reports on historical financial statements?

22.13.   What restrictions are placed upon auditors' association with forecasts by Ethics Rule 201(*e*)?

22.14.   What is an SEC "safe harbor" rule? Explain.

22.15.   What auditing standards govern the form and content of an audit report of price-level-adjusted financial statements? Current value financial statements?

22.16. In auditor-submitted detailed (long form) reports, to what special problems should auditors be alert?

22.17. What types of additional information not given in the auditor's standard report are typically included in auditor-submitted (long form) reports?

22.18. Should auditors give standard unqualified audit reports on condensed financial statements that are based on complete audited financial statements? Explain.

22.19. Explain the influences and pressures that led to creation of the Accounting and Review Services Committee.

22.20. In what area(s) of practice are Accounting and Review Service Committee pronouncements applicable?

22.21. What is the difference between *unaudited financial statements* and *unaudited information in a document containing audited financial statements?*

22.22. How is a public company defined in SSARS ?

22.23. What is the difference between a *review services engagement* and a *compilation service engagement* regarding historical financial statements? Compare both of these to an *audit engagement.*

22.24. Compare the review services specified in SSARS 1 (AR 100, *Compilation and Review of Financial Statements*) with the review services specified in SAS 36 (AU 722, *Review of Interim Financial Information*).

EXERCISES AND PROBLEMS

22.25. **Review of Current Costs**

Ajax Pipefitting Company fabricates pipe joints and flow systems for customers. The joints are welded electrically, and Ajax uses a ZB40 X-ray machine to inspect the strength of the welds. Ajax bought its ZB40 three years ago for $60,000. Most such X-ray machines last 10 years, so Ajax has recorded $6,000 depreciation expense for the current year—the third year the machine has been used.

A new ZB40 now costs $75,000. Ajax is planning to purchase a second one because no technologically improved machine is on the market.

When Ajax's accountants prepared the required supplementary current cost information, the ZB40 was reflected as follows:

Machinery and equipment	$75,000
Accumulated depreciation	22,500
Current year depreciation expense	7,500

Required:

a. Auditing standards specify some review procedures that an auditor should perform with regard to required sup-

plementary current cost information. With reference to the ZB40 machine, explain the procedures.

b. How do these procedures differ from those specified in auditing standards for a review of unaudited interim financial information?

22.26. **Reporting on Voluntary SFAS 33 Information**

Atkinson Electric Company is not large enough to be subject to SFAS 33 requirements for changing prices information. However, the controller has voluntarily prepared constant dollar and current cost information following the SFAS 33 guidelines. The information has been placed in a section at the front of the corporate annual report, apart from the audited financial statements. The section declares that its auditors have not performed any review procedures on the information and do not express any opinion on it.

Required:

a. Should the audit report contain a disclaimer on the changing prices information voluntarily disclosed? Explain.

b.   Are SAS 27 and 28 applicable? Explain.

c.   Does the audit firm have *any* responsibility regarding the voluntarily disclosed changing prices information?

22.27.   **Review of Interim Financial Information**
Loman, CPA, who has audited the financial statements of the Broadwall Corporation, a publicly held company, for the year ended December 31, 1985, was asked to perform a review of the interim financial statements of Broadwall Corporation for the period ending March 31, 1986. The engagement letter stated that such a review does not provide a basis for the expression of an opinion.

Required:

a.   Explain why Loman's review will not provide a basis for the expression of an opinion.

b.   What are the review procedures which Loman should perform, and what is the purpose of each procedure? Structure your response as follows:

Procedure	Purpose of Procedure

(*AICPA* adapted)

22.28.   **Reporting on Interim Financial Information**
The Candy Stripe Company published a comprehensive interim financial report covering the first two quarters of the fiscal year which ends December 31. Management even engaged its auditors to perform a review, and the review report reproduced below was published along with the interim financial statements.

To the Board of Directors of The Candy Stripe Company:

We have made a review of the interim balance sheet of The Candy Stripe Company as of June 30, 1985, and of the interim statements of operations and changes in financial position for the three-month and six-month periods then ended, in accordance with generally accepted auditing standards.

Based on our review, we are not aware of any material modifications that should be made to the accompanying interim financial information for it to be in conformity with generally accepted accounting principles.

/s/Able and Associates
July 10, 1985

Required:
Identify the deficiencies in the report and tell how to correct them. Do not rewrite the report.

22.29.   **Reporting on Supplementary and Other Information**
For the separate fact situations given below, specify the appropriate form and content of the audit report on the related financial statements.

a.   Mona Corporation is required by SFAS 33 to present constant-dollar and current cost supplementary information. This year, however, time ran short, and the controller's staff was unable to assemble the information before the deadline for the annual report to shareholders.

b.   The financial statements Lisa Corporation managed to file this year included the comparative statements of the prior year. When the controller prepared the constant-dollar information last year, he used the GNP implicit price deflator instead of the consumer price index, as specified in SFAS 33.

c.   When Kinky Korp Co. presented its interim financial figures in a footnote to the financial statements, the footnote was labeled "Interim Financial Results," and the closing sentence of the narrative introduction was: "Grey & Fox, CPAs, reviewed the interim financial results in accordance with standards established by the American Institute of Certified Public Accountants."

d.   Kaviar, Inc.'s president, Sharon Kaviar, wrote a management discussion and analysis section in the annual report to shareholders, in which she said: "Research and development expenses increased this year by 20 percent." Consulting the R & D expense disclosure in the financial statements, you see that the expense for last year is reported to be $3 million and for this year $3.75 million.

22.30. **Reporting on Multiple Projections**

The Newt Restaurant Corporation proposed to sell to investors limited partnership interests in 40 new restaurant buildings. Newt Corp. would be the general partner. The deal was structured to raise funds for business expansion by offering a real estate tax shelter investment. As part of the offering material, Newt management produced multiple projections based on assumptions of $1 million, $1.5 million and $2.0 million gross annual revenue for each new location. The lease income to the partnership is to be a base rental fee plus 10 percent of gross revenue in excess of $1.5 million. Newt's existing restaurants have gross revenues ranging from $800,000 to $1.75 million.

Newt engaged its auditors to review the projections and submit a review report. The first paragraph of the auditor's report was the following:

> To the Limited Partners, Newt Ltd.:
>
> The accompanying financial forecasts and related summaries of significant assumptions and accounting policies of Newt, Ltd. as of December 31, 1986, and for the year then ended, is the General Partner's estimate of the most probable results under three levels of gross revenues. Accordingly, the financial forecast reflects the General Partner's judgment, based on present circumstances, of the most likely conditions and its most likely course of action.

Required:

What is fundamentally wrong with this part of the auditor's review report?

22.31. **Review of Forecast Assumptions**

You have been engaged by the Dodd Manufacturing Corporation to attest to the reasonableness of the assumptions underlying its forecast of revenues, costs and net income for the calendar year 1986. Four of the assumptions are shown below. For each assumption, state the evidence sources and procedures you would use to determine the reasonableness.

a. The company intends to sell certain real estate and other facilities held by Division B at an aftertax profit of $600,000; the proceeds of this sale will be used to retire outstanding debt, as described below.

b. The company will call and retire all outstanding 9 percent subordinated debentures (callable at 108). The debentures are expected to require the full call premium given present market interest rates of 11 percent on similar debt. A rise in market interest rates to 12 percent would reduce the loss on bond retirement from the projected $200,000 to $190,000.

c. Current labor contracts expire on September 1, 1986, and the new contract is expected to result in a wage increase of 5½ percent. Given the forecasted levels of production and sales, aftertax operating earnings would be reduced approximately $50,000 for each percentage-point wage increase in excess of the expected contract settlement.

d. The sales forecast for Division A assumes that the new Portsmouth facility will be completed and operating at 40 percent of capacity on February 1, 1986. It is highly improbable that the facility will be operational before January of 1986. Each month's delay would reduce sales of Division A approximately $80,000 and operating earnings by $30,000.

22.32. **Auditing a Current-Value Balance Sheet**

Your client, the Neighborhood Paper Company, has a fiscal year-end of December

31. NPC needs to borrow money from a local bank and believes current value financial statements that reported the appreciated value of its assets would be helpful. A loan is needed for working capital purposes.

NPC owns two paper recycling processors. Old paper is chemically processed, reduced to a wet mass, and then pressed out into thick, semifinished paper mats. The mats are sold to customers who use them for packing material. Recycling processors are fairly complex pieces of integrated machinery and are built on a customized basis by a few specialized engineering firms.

NPC has owned one of the processors for five years. It was appraised last year at $135,000 by a qualified engineering appraiser. The second processor was purchased last month for $125,000—its appraised value—and $10,000 was spent in bringing certain maintenance up to date. Both processors have identical throughput production capabilities.

The other major asset is a nine-acre plot of land NPC bought four years ago when management thought the plant would be moved. The land was purchased for $195,000 and was appraised by a qualified appraiser at $250,000 only 20 months after the purchase date. The nine acres is located near a rapidly expanding industrial area.

Management has prepared the balance sheet summary shown below:

	Cost	Current Value
Cash	$ 5,000	$ 5,000
Accounts receivable	7,000	7,000
Recycling processors	215,000	270,000
Land	195,000	250,000
	$422,000	$532,000
Accounts payable	$ 6,000	$ 6,000
Long-term debts	100,000	100,000
Stockholders' equity	316,000	316,000
Revaluation equity		110,000
	$422,000	$532,000

Since the recycling processors were appraised/purchased so recently, management does not want to bear the expense of new appraisals this year. No plans have been made to obtain a new appraisal on the land. NPC, however, is a profitable operation. The unaudited income statement for the current year (historical cost basis) shows net income of $46,000.

For Discussion:

a. What auditing standards are applicable to the engagement to review and report on the current value balance sheet?

b. What primary auditing procedures should you apply in addition to those necessary for the audit of the historical cost financial statements?

c. Will any additional disclosures in footnotes be necessary?

d. Are there any evidential problems in the NPC situation that might prevent your rendering a report on the current value balance sheet?

22.33. **Reporting on Information in Auditor-Submitted Documents**

Independent certified public accountants may issue two types of auditor's reports in connection with an examination of financial statements: a so-called short-form (standard) report in connection with financial statements intended for publication and a so-called auditor-submitted detail (long-form) report for the purposes of management and other parties.

Required:

a. Outline in *general terms* the kinds of materials which are commonly included in an auditor-submitted detail (long-form) report other than those commonly included in a short-form report.

b. Does the auditor assume the same degree of responsibility for other data in the auditor-submitted detail (long-form) report that is assumed for individual items in the customary basic financial statements (balance sheet and statements of income, retained income and capital)? State the reasons for your answer.

(*AICPA* adapted)

22.34. Prepare a Compilation Report

You have been engaged by the Coffin Brothers to compile their financial schedules from books and records maintained by James Coffin. The brothers own and operate three auto parts stores in Central City, and even though their business is growing, they have not wanted to employ a full-time bookkeeper. James specifies that all he wants is a balance sheet, a statement of operations, and a statement of changes in financial position. He does not have time to write up footnotes to accompany the statement.

James directed the physical count of inventory on June 30 and adjusted and closed the books on that date. You find that he actually is a good accountant, having taken some night courses at the community college. The accounts appear to have been maintained in conformity with generally accepted accounting principles. At least, you have noticed no obvious errors.

Required:

You are independent with respect to the Coffin brothers and their Coffin Auto Speed Shop business. Prepare a report on your compilation services engagement.

22.35. Negative Assurance in Review Reports

One portion of the report on a review services engagement may read as follows:

Based on my (our) review, I am (we are) not aware of any material modifications that should be made to the accompanying financial statements in order for them to be in conformity with generally accepted accounting principles.

Required:

a. Is this paragraph a "negative assurance" given by the CPA?

b. Why is "negative assurance" generally prohibited in *audit* reports?

c. What justification is there for permitting "negative assurance" in a review services report?

22.36. Compilation Presentation Alternatives

Jimmy C. operates a large service station, garage, and truck stop on Interstate 95 near Plainview. His brother, Bill, has recently joined as a partner, even though he still keeps a small CPA practice. One slow afternoon, they were discussing financial statements with Bert, the local CPA who operates the largest public practice in Plainview.

Jimmy: The business is growing, and sometimes I need to show financial statements to parts suppliers and to the loan officers at the bank.

Bert: That so.

Jimmy: Yea-boy, and they don't like the way I put 'em together.

Bert: That so.

Bill: Heck, Jimmy, I know all about that. I can compile a jim-dandy set of financial statements for us.

Jimmy: What does Jim Dan over at the cafe have to do with it?

Bert: Never mind, Jimmy. Bill can't do compiled financial statements for you. He's not independent.

Jimmy: I know. Momma didn't let him outa the house 'til he was 24. The neighbors complained.

Bert: That so.

Bill: Shucks.

Jimmy: But Bert, those fellas are always asking me about accounting policies, contingencies and stuff like that. Said something about "footnotes." I don't want to fool with all that small print.

Required:

Think about the financial disclosure problems of Jimmy's and Bill's small business. What three kinds of compiled financial statements can be prepared for them and by whom? (Refer to SSARS 1.)

22.37. Reporting on Comparative Unaudited Financial Statements

Anson Jones, CPA, performed a review service for the Independence Company in 19X2. He wants to present comparative financial statements. However, the 19X1 statements were compiled by Able and Associates, CPAs, and Able does not want to cooperate with Jones by reissuing the prior-year compilation report. Jones has no indications that any adjustments should be made to either the 19X2 or 19X1 statements, which are to be presented with all necessary disclosures. However, he does

not have time to perform a review of the 19X1 statements. He completed his work on January 15 for the statements dated December 31, 19X2.

Required:

Write Jones' review report and include the paragraph describing the report on the 19X1 statements. (Refer to SSARS 2.)

DISCUSSION CASES

22.38. **Problem Areas in an Unaudited Statement Engagement**

Brown, CPA, received a telephone call from Calhoun, the sole owner and manager of a small corporation. Calhoun asked Brown to prepare the financial statements for the corporation and told Brown the statements were needed in two weeks for external financing purposes. Calhoun was vague when Brown inquired about the intended use of the statements. Brown was convinced that Calhoun thought Brown's work would constitute an audit. To avoid confusion, Brown decided not to explain to Calhoun that the engagement would only be to compile the financial statements. Brown, with the understanding that a substantial fee would be paid if the work were completed in two weeks, accepted the engagement and started the work at once.

During the course of the work, Brown discovered an accrued expense account labeled "professional fees" and learned that the balance in the account represented an accrual for the cost of Brown's services. Brown suggested to Calhoun's bookkeeper that the account name be changed to "fees for limited audit engagement." Brown also reviewed several invoices to determine whether accounts were being classified properly. Some of the invoices were missing. Brown listed the missing invoice numbers in the working papers with a note indicating that there should be a follow-up on the next engagement. Brown also discovered that the available records included the fixed asset values at estimated current re-

placement costs. Based on the records available, Brown prepared a balance sheet, income statement and statement of stockholder's equity. In addition, Brown drafted the footnotes but decided that any mention of the replacement costs would only mislead the readers. Brown suggested to Calhoun that readers of the financial statements would be better informed if they received a separate letter from Calhoun explaining the meaning and effect of the estimated replacement costs of the fixed assets. Brown mailed the financial statements and footnotes to Calhoun with the following note included on each page: "The accompanying financial statements are submitted to you without complete audit verification."

Required:

Identify the inappropriate actions of Brown and indicate what Brown should have done to avoid each inappropriate action.

Organize your answer sheet as follows:

Inappropriate Action	What Brown Should Have Done to Avoid Inappropriate Action

22.39. **Compilation Service and Legal Liability**

Pelham & James, CPAs, were retained by Tom Stone, sole proprietor of Stone Housebuilders, to compile Stone's financial statements. Stone advised Pelham & James that the financial statements would be used in connection with a possible incorporation of the business and sale of stock to friends. Prior to undertaking the engagement, Pelham & James were also advised to pay particular attention to the trade accounts payable. They agreed to use every reasonable means to determine the correct amount.

At the time Pelham & James were engaged, the books and records were in total disarray. Pelham & James proceeded with the engagement applying all applicable procedures for compiling financial statements. They failed, however, to detect and disclose in the financial statements Stone's liability for certain unpaid bills. Documentation concerning those bills were available for Pelham & James's inspection had they looked. This omission led to a material understatement ($60,000) of the trade accounts payable.

Pelham & James delivered the compiled financial statements to Tom Stone with their compilation report which indicated that they did not express an opinion or any other assurance regarding the financial statements. Tom Stone met with two prospective investors, Dickerson and Nichols. At the meeting, Pelham & James stated they were confident the trade accounts payable balance was accurate to within $8,000.

Stone Housebuilders was incorporated. Dickerson and Nichols, relying on the financial statements, became stockholders along with Tom Stone. Shortly thereafter, the understatement of trade accounts payable was detected. As a result, Dickerson and Nichols discovered that they had paid substantially more for the stock than it was worth at the time of purchase.

Required:

Will Pelham & James be found liable to Dickerson and Nichols in a common law action for their damages? Explain.

(AICPA adapted)

Index

This book has been set Linotron 202 in 10 and 9 point Times Roman, leaded 2 points. Part numbers are 36 point Helvetica Medium Outline and chapter numbers are 24 point Helvetica Medium Outline. Part and chapter titles are 24 point Trooper Roman Bold. The size of the type page is 36 by 47 picas.